The California Winter League

ALSO BY WILLIAM F. MCNEIL
AND FROM MCFARLAND

*All-Stars for All Time: A Sabermetric Ranking
of the Major League Best, 1876–2007* (2008)

*Miracle in Chavez Ravine:
The Los Angeles Dodgers in 1988* (2008)

*Black Baseball Out of Season:
Pay for Play Outside of the Negro Leagues* (2007)

*Backstop: A History of the Catcher and a
Sabermetric Ranking of 50 All-Time Greats* (2006)

The Evolution of Pitching in Major League Baseball (2006)

Gabby Hartnett: The Life and Times of the Cubs' Greatest Catcher (2004)

*The Single-Season Home Run Kings:
Ruth, Maris, McGwire, Sosa, and Bonds*, 2d ed. (2003)

*Cool Papas and Double Duties:
The All-Time Greats of the Negro Leagues* (2001; paperback 2005)

*Baseball's Other All-Stars: The Greatest Players from
the Negro Leagues, the Japanese Leagues, the Mexican League,
and the Pre–1960 Winter Leagues in Cuba,
Puerto Rico and the Dominican Republic* (2000)

*The King of Swat: An Analysis of Baseball's Home Run
Hitters from the Major, Minor, Negro and Japanese Leagues* (1997)

The California Winter League

America's First Integrated Professional Baseball League

by WILLIAM F. McNEIL

McFarland & Company, Inc., Publishers
Jefferson, North Carolina, and London

The present work is a reprint of the illustrated case bound edition of The California Winter League: America's First Integrated Professional Baseball League, *first published in 2002 by McFarland.*

LIBRARY OF CONGRESS CATALOGUING-IN-PUBLICATION DATA

McNeil, William.
The California Winter League : America's first integrated professional baseball league / by William F. McNeil.
p.   cm.
Includes bibliographical references (p.) and index.

ISBN 978-0-7864-3881-5
softcover : 50# alkaline paper ∞

1. California Winter League (Baseball league)—History.
2. Baseball—California—History—20th century.   I. Title.
GV875.C35 M36   2008   796.357′64′09794—dc21   2002006093

British Library cataloguing data are available

©2002 William F. McNeil. All rights reserved

No part of this book may be reproduced or transmitted in any form or by any means, electronic or mechanical, including photocopying or recording, or by any information storage and retrieval system, without permission in writing from the publisher.

Cover photographs: Pitcher Buck "Bobo" Newsom and Mule Suttles

Manufactured in the United States of America

*McFarland & Company, Inc., Publishers
Box 611, Jefferson, North Carolina 28640
www.mcfarlandpub.com*

To my children,
Michael, Danny, Jeanne, and Eileen,
and to their partners,
Carol (Vernine) McNeil, Marnie (Schermerhorn) McNeil,
Phil Kurcon, and Chuck Simonelli,
all of whom have enriched my life.
They have met and overcome many obstacles,
and have always been loving husbands, wives, and parents.

Contents

Acknowledgments	ix
Introduction	1
1. California—From Wasteland to Fantasyland	5
2. The California Winter League—An Overview	9
3. The Early Years 1900–1919	24
4. Season Summaries 1920–1924	66
5. Season Summaries 1925–1929	104
6. Season Summaries 1930–1934	143
7. Season Summaries 1935–1939	173
8. Season Summaries 1940–1944	201
9. Season Summaries 1945–1947	223
10. A Final Look Back	236
Appendix A. League Champions, Season by Season	243
Appendix B. Individual Career Leaders	245
Appendix C. Individual Season Leaders	247
Appendix D. Who's Who in the California Winter League	249
Appendix E. Batters vs. Pitchers	298
Appendix F. Batting Statistics, League to League	305
Appendix G. Satchel Paige's Spectacular 1933-34 Winter League Record	308
Appendix H. Satchel Paige vs. Bob Feller	309
Bibliography	311
Index	313

Acknowledgments

Walt Wilson is a member of SABR and one of this country's foremost baseball researchers. He spent countless hours at the Chicago Public Library, Northwestern University Library, and the Center For Research, poring over five decades of old microfilm copies of the *Chicago Defender, Pittsburgh Courier, California Eagle, Los Angeles Times,* and *Los Angeles Examiner* newspapers to help reconstruct the California Winter League, season by season.

Larry Zuckerman provided me with his notes on the California Winter League and some of the ballparks that were used by the league over the years, including White Sox Parks I and II. He was always available to answer my sometimes foolish questions via email, and provided me with many valuable suggestions and leads.

Lyle K. Wilson provided me with dozens of photocopies of California Winter League games from California newspapers, covering a timespan of more than forty years. He also sent me his voluminous research notes on the subject.

Larry Lester provided me with photocopies of California Winter League games taken from issues of various California newspapers. He also supplied me with several photos of Negro league players who participated in the league.

Bob Bluthardt sent me information on California ballparks including Wrigley Field, Washington Park, and Gilmore Field.

John E. Spalding loaned me many interesting player photographs for publication. He also supplied me with valuable information about baseball in early California, and allowed me to quote from his fine book on the subject, *Always on Sunday*.

John W. Outland loaned me many photographs of major league and minor league players who were active in the California Winter League, as well as two unique and scarce photos of Turkey Stearnes and Bullet Joe Rogan in their California Winter League uniforms. The photos were taken during the 1920s by John's father, George E. Outland, an avid baseball fan, and an early chronicler of home runs.

Additional photographs, or authorization to publish existing photographs, were generously provided by Ray Medeiros, Judith P. Dobbins (for her deceased husband Dick), L. Robert Davids, Jay Sanford, James A. Riley, Robert W. Peterson, John Holway, and NoirTech Research.

Introduction

Blacks began playing baseball soon after the first game was played on Elysian Field in Hoboken, New Jersey, in 1845. According to John Holway in his book, *The Complete Book of Baseball's Negro Leagues*, "The first known baseball game by African-Americans was played July 4 (1859), reports researcher Bruce Sullivan. It was an integrated game as 64-year-old Congressman Joshua Giddings, a leading Abolitionist, took his swings." During the Civil War, the sounds of integrated baseball games could be heard coming from Union Army camps up and down the east coast. Even in Confederate prison camps, Union soldiers, both black and white, helped pass the time by playing the good old "American game."

The National League of Professional Baseball Players, a segregated league, first saw the light of day in 1876. A conglomeration of minor leagues flourished around the eastern half of the United States during the same period, but they were not so restrictive, so it was only a matter of time before they became integrated. In 1878, the first black player became a member of a minor league baseball team. John "Bud" Fowler was a pitcher for the Lynn Live Oaks of the International Association. In 1884, two black players, Moses Fleetwood Walker and his brother Welday, played major league baseball for the Toledo club of the Union Association.

That situation, however, changed dramatically in 1888 when segregation became the law of the land in baseball. Major league club owners, to their unending shame, entered into an unwritten "gentlemen's agreement" to systematically eliminate blacks from organized baseball. The last black players in the minor leagues graced the rosters of teams in the Iron & Oil League and the Kansas State League in 1898. It would be 47 years before another black man would play organized baseball.

In the ensuing decades, blacks formed their own leagues, playing a set schedule from April to October each year. They even had their own World Series. During the fall and winter, Negro league players traveled the western hemisphere in search of employment. During October and November, many black teams toured the U.S. playing exhibition games against white major league opponents. According to research done by John Holway, Dick Clark, and other dedicated baseball historians, box scores of more than 400 exhibition games have been uncovered—and the Negro leaguers were victorious in over 60 percent of those games. In the winter, the players migrated to such warmer climes as Florida or Cuba.

The Cuban Winter League was active from 1878 until 1960, when Fidel Castro eliminated all professional sports in Cuba. The league showcased the talents of the many great and near great Cuban players, such as Jose Mendez, Martin Dihigo, and Valentin Dreke. From about 1908 on, Negro league players began wintering in the island nation and participating in the league. Their ranks included the legendary John Henry Lloyd, Jud Wilson, Oscar Charleston, and Dobie Moore. Occasionally a few major leaguers made the trek south and joined the league, but it didn't occur often enough to be able to compare the relative talents of the various players. The 1923-24 Cuban Winter League season had probably the best mixture of Cuban, black, and major league players, with Charlie Dressen, "Glass Arm" Eddie Brown, and Jimmy Cooney from the big leagues, Moore, Lloyd, and Charleston, from the Negro leagues, and Cuba's own Torriente, Oms, and Bernardo Baro.

The Cuban league experience did prove one thing. It proved without a doubt that blacks and whites could play together in the same league, and on the same team, in perfect harmony. Someone once said that all men are the same under the skin, and nowhere was that shown to be more true than in the Cuban Winter League.

People have been asking the same questions for more than 50 years. "How good were the old Negro league players?" "Could they have played in the major leagues?" I believe these questions were answered forcefully enough during the 1950s with the emergence of many black superstars, and Negro league graduates, like Willie Mays, Hank Aaron, Ernie Banks, Jackie Robinson, and Roy Campanella. As every baseball fan knows, Hank Aaron broke Babe Ruth's "unbreakable" career home run record. And Willie Mays is generally considered to be the greatest all-around player of the twentieth century, or at least the last half of the twentieth century. Joe DiMaggio has strong support as the greatest all-around player of the first half of the twentieth century.

The questions posed above can be answered by reviewing the performances of the 65 Negro league graduates who entered the major leagues between 1947 and 1960. From 1949 through 1960, Negro league veterans won nine of 22 Most Valuable Player awards. They also won six of twelve Rookie-of-the-Year awards, and the first Cy Young award. To date, sixteen major league players have accumulated 500 or more career home runs. Seven of them are black, and three of them were veterans of the Negro leagues. Two of the three players with more than 600 home runs are Negro league veterans, as is one of the two with more than 700. Eight of the players are now enshrined in the National Baseball Hall of Fame in Cooperstown, New York. "Could the old Negro league players have played in the major leagues?" The answer is a resounding "yes." Not only could they have played in the major leagues, but many of them would have been Hall of Fame inductees based on their major league performances.

The first four decades of the twentieth century in the United States, were a time of isolation for the black ballplayer—with one exception. There was one arena where Negro league baseball players could measure their skills against their major league counterparts, in hand-to-hand competition. That arena was called The California Winter League, an integrated, professional baseball league that operated in Southern California from 1910 until 1945. It was the most important professional league in the country outside the Negro leagues and the major leagues.

There were many integrated baseball leagues in the western hemisphere during the twentieth century, as noted above, but none of them provided the unique opportunity the California experience did. It was only on the west coast that Negro leaguers could compare their baseball skills with their major league and minor league counterparts. The 1910-11 winter league season marked the first time that a Negro league team wintered in California, and joined the league. The Leland Giants, led by the great Rube Foster, fielded a team of black all-stars, including Cyclone Joe Williams, Frank

Introduction

Wickware, Chappie Johnson, and Bill Pettus. They competed against such major leaguers as Cleveland Indian second baseman Neal Ball, Cincinnati Reds shortstop Tom Downey, and St. Louis Cardinal outfielder Rube Ellis, plus many Pacific Coast League players like Kid Mohler, Rosy Carlisle, and Tom Seaton.

Over the years a parade of major league stars invaded the popular west coast league, with Bob Meusel, Irish Meusel, Babe Herman, Fred Haney, Smead Jolley, Ping Bodie, Jigger Statz, Ferdie Schupp, Larry French, Buck Newsom, and Bob Feller leading the way. The black brigade included at least ten Hall Of Famers: Turkey Stearnes, John Henry Lloyd, Cyclone Joe Williams, Oscar Charleston, Satchel Paige, Bullet Joe Rogan, Willie Foster, Willie Wells, Cool Papa Bell, and Rube Foster.

This book is the first complete history of the California Winter League from its murky beginnings in the decade after 1910, to its golden years, from 1924 to 1935, through its final demise in the mid–1940s. The great teams are all reviewed here, the exciting pennant races between the Negro league entries and the white professional teams are covered in detail. Reexamined are the historic individual performances of such legendary players as Jimmie Foxx, Al Simmons, Tony Lazzeri, Earl Averill, Satchel Paige, Turkey Stearnes, Mule Suttles, and Bullet Joe Rogan.

In the following pages, you will read about Bob Meusel playing long ball with the legendary Cuban hurler, Jose Mendez, Hall of Famer Earl Averill ripping three base hits off Negro league ace Chet Brewer, and Pug Cavet tossing a shutout at Rogan, Mackey, Carr and company. You will also read about Turkey Stearnes blasting two homers off former Chicago White Sox 20-game-winner Sloppy Thurston, John Beckwith punishing Herm Pillette with three home runs in just 12 at-bats, and Satchel Paige tossing a 17 strikeout one-hitter at the White Kings, beating Sloppy Thurston, 4–0.

The year by year pennant winners are listed, as are the career leaders in many batting and pitching categories such as batting average, home runs, complete games, victories, and shutouts. Batting and pitching statistics are provided for each season, as are the California Winter League career records for dozens of the more active players. In addition, there are tables showing how the top Negro league hitters fared against the top major league pitchers, and how the top major league batters fared against the best of the Negro league pitchers.

1

California—From Wasteland to Fantasyland

California is a modern day miracle, a twentieth century fairy tale of an ugly duckling that was transformed into a magnificent swan. In the beginning, tribes of Native Americans lived an idyllic life along the balmy Pacific Coast of North America. The valleys were green and lush. The mountains were majestic. And the animals and fish, necessary for sustenance, were plentiful.

The first inhabitants of this land probably made their way over the Bering Strait land bridge 20,000 to 40,000 years ago. Other migrations may have come via ship over the Pacific Ocean or across the Atlantic Ocean to Central America, then northward. Over the millennia many different tribes learned to share the land in harmony, respecting each other's territory, inter-marrying occasionally, and carrying on a lively commerce. In fact, trading expeditions traveled as far north as Canada, as far south as Mexico, and as far east as Missouri.

Unfortunately, all things must come to an end. And this heavenly way of life came to an abrupt halt for the Native Americans in the 16th century. One day in the spring of 1519, an Aztec Indian, looking out over the Atlantic Ocean, spied a large sail on the horizon. It was a Spanish exploration party under the command of Hernando Cortes, en route from Cuba to Mexico with 600 men and 17 horses. Within two years, Cortes had crushed the Aztec Empire, and looked around for other worlds to conquer. In 1536, after many other adventures and misadventures, the Spanish soldier of fortune had made his way to the coast of southern California.

The Spanish Empire spread like an unrelenting carnivore, slowly devouring much of Central and South America, as well as large chunks of the continental United States, in addition to Mexico. In 1539, Fransisco de Ulloa explored the lower west coast, naming the territory California after a mythical country that was described in a romantic Spanish novel published about 1510.

At the time of the Spanish discovery, there were between 100,000 and 350,000 Native Americans living in what is now California. More than 200 Indian tribes, each speaking a different dialect, inhabited the territory. Tragically, after the Spanish colonization, their numbers were soon decimated through disease and hostility, so that very few of them survived to see the twentieth century.

Occupation of the vast wasteland by Spanish explorers did not begin until the 17th century, although periodic visitations were recorded in the journals. Juan Rodriguez Cabrillo explored the California coast in 1542, Sebastian Vizcaino explored the San Francisco area in 1602, and San Francisco Bay was visited in 1769. That same year, a Mission was established at San

Diego by Captain Fernando Rivera y Moncado, who along with Father Junipero Crespi, continued north, until they encountered a beautiful river in a lush green valley. The explorers established communications with the inhabitants, the Yang-Na Indians, while they were there and they named the river, the El Rio de Nuestra Senora de Reina de Los Angeles de Porciuncula (The river of Our Lady the Queen of the Angels Parciuncula), in honor of St. Mary of the Angels, whose holy day it was.

In 1776, as the Continental Congress adopted the Declaration of Independence in Philadelphia, the Presidio (or military garrison) of San Francisco was established. Five years later, the Pueblo (town) of Los Angeles was founded per order of the Spanish Governor of California. The Pueblo was created to prevent Russia and England from claiming the territory, and also to provide the Spanish military garrisons with food and supplies. Governor Felipe de Neve recruited eleven settlers for the new town, along with their wives and 22 children. They were accompanied by a detachment of soldiers, and some mission priests, to the site alongside the Los Angeles River. The settlers were a potpourri of races, including Spaniards, Mulattos, Mestizos, Blacks, and Indians. El Pueblo de la Reina de Los Angeles (The Town of the Queen of Angels) was officially settled on September 4, 1781.

According to the University of Southern California Historic Archives, "The new Pueblo grew slowly, and amenities were few. The houses were very small, usually of adobe with flat roofs—glassless windows, and rawhide doors. The narrow streets were almost impassable when it rained. There were, of course, no sidewalks or lawns, and the trees along the river rapidly disappeared."

"By 1790 Los Angeles had 28 households and a population of 139. By 1800 the population was 70 households and a population of 315. There were also a town hall, guardhouse, army barracks, and granaries."

In 1821 Mexico declared its independence from Spain, and the California territories fell under Mexican rule. The first "American" visited the Los Angeles area, when John Chapman arrived by ship. In 1826 the first "American" reached California by an overland route. He was trapper Jedediah Smith. The same year, a wagon train from the east reached California.

Los Angeles became a city in 1835, with a population of 1,250. San Francisco was incorporated as a city in 1850. And, on September 9 of that year, California was admitted into the Union as a free non-slavery state.

Four years earlier, the United States had declared war on Mexico, and in the ensuing conflict, won sizeable land areas, including California. At the time of the treaty of Guadalupe Hidalgo, on February 2, 1848, the population of Los Angeles was still just 1,500, excluding Indians, while San Francisco had a mere 850 inhabitants. The total population of California was 8,000, consisting primarily of soldiers and convicts who were sent to the state against their will. But things were about to change. The first organized group of settlers made their way down into California over the Oregon Trail in 1846, starting a migration that would continue unabated up to the present time. Then, in 1848, James Marshall discovered gold in the American River at the site of John Sutter's sawmill, near Sacramento. And all hell broke loose.

Almost immediately humanity of all kinds poured into northern California by the thousands. Most of them came by ship, but some hardy souls fought their way over the mountains, braving flooded rivers, blizzards, and Indian attacks. The San Francisco area was transformed overnight from a tiny village of 850 inhabitants into a lawless city of 21,000 people; many of them con men, hucksters, thieves, gamblers, prostitutes, gunfighters, and ne'er-do-wells. Murders became an almost daily occurrence until outraged citizens took the law into their own hands. Vigilante rule lasting two decades sent criminals to their creator at the end of a rope, until a structured police force and judicial system finally assumed control of the situation.

By 1860, the population of San Francisco had grown to an unwieldy 149,000. The heavy influx of people even affected the Los Angeles area 400 miles away, as the inhabitants of the north quickly exhausted their supply of foodstuffs. Beef, particularly, was in great demand, so Southern California responded to the crisis, and soon became a major supplier of meat, vegetables, and other provisions to the populous north. Cattle ranches sprang up all over the valley around the Los Angeles River, and cattle drives soon became a common sight, as they wound their way north to the gold fields.

It was a time of rapid growth all up and down the west coast, although the growth was much slower in the south than in the north. In 1850, the census showed a scant 1,650 people in Los Angeles. That number grew to 4,385 in 1860, 5,728 in 1870, and 11,183 in 1880. All in all, it took the better part of five decades for the City of Angels to reach San Francisco's 1860 population.

The first public building in L.A. was a jail, built in 1853. The same year, a farmer named Don Mateo Keller planted the first orange trees in California. Four years later, the first overland stage coach service from the east was established. And in 1859, the first library opened.

The gold rush was the event that changed San Francisco from a sleepy little colonial hamlet into a bustling metropolis. The extension of the railroad from the east coast to the west coast was the event that put little Los Angeles on the map. The first railroad in California, an interstate line constructed in 1856, linked Sacramento with Folsom. Thirteen years later, the country's first transcontinental railroad was completed when the golden spike was driven into the last railroad tie at Promontory, Utah, connecting the Union Pacific Railroad Line that originated in Omaha, Nebraska, with the Central Pacific Railroad Line that originated in San Francisco. Finally, in 1885, the Santa Fe Railroad completed a run from Chicago to Los Angeles, bringing the two coasts even closer together. The population of the City of Angels jumped from 11,183 in 1880 to 50,395 in 1890, as a new wave of pioneers and businessmen flooded the territory. The population doubled between 1890 and 1900, and increased six-fold during the next two decades. By 1970, California was the most populous state in the country.

Baseball arrived in the west with the new pioneers. It came to San Francisco with the businessmen, bankers, and shop owners from the east, at the time of the gold rush. And it made its first appearance in Los Angeles with the introduction of the transcontinental railroad in the mid to late 80s. Prior to the 80s, the inhabitants of Los Angeles were too busy trying to scratch a living out of the dusty soil to even think about recreation. Leisure time was something that was unknown in colonial America. The work day lasted from sunup to sundown, and it was a grueling 12 to 14 hour struggle, six or seven days a week.

As the population exploded, Los Angeles began feeling the strain on its natural resources, particularly its water supply. The L.A. area drew all its water from the Los Angeles River, and the river was unable to handle the demands of modern civilization. The need to provide drinking water for all its inhabitants was an absolute necessity. But water was also needed for cooking, for feeding the livestock, for fighting fires, and for irrigation. It became paramount to transform southern California from a vast wasteland of scrub grass into farm country with abundant pasture land, and fertile soil suitable for growing fruits and vegetables.

In 1904, after much study, a viable source of fresh water was located in the foothills of the Sierra Nevada Mountains, some 233 miles distant, and construction of an aqueduct was begun, to carry the vital fluid to its users. On November 5, 1913, the Owens River Aqueduct was opened and a plentiful supply of water poured southward. The city also completed a major harbor project that year, opening Los Angeles up to a large shipping industry.

That was the beginning of modern-day Southern California. The oil discoveries of 1892 around Los Angeles had made the state the second largest petroleum producer in the country, after Texas. In 1906, the first motion picture studio was established in Hollywood, and the industry expanded over the years to include television and other entertainment related businesses. Now, with a plentiful water supply, a new wave of settlers and business people flooded the area. The railroads, anxious to capitalize on its balmy year-round temperatures, promoted Southern California as an exotic land of year-round sunshine. Entrepreneurs developed a number of popular resort areas, including Santa Catalina Island, San Luis Obispo, and San Juan Capsitrano. Palm Springs, which is located in beautiful Coachella Valley, an oasis in the desert, became a fashionable residential area and winter resort.

During the last half of the twentieth century, two events completed the transformation of California from a rag-tag wasteland into a veritable Utopia. In 1955, Walt Disney, a cartoonist-turned-movie mogul, created an amusement park featuring his famous cartoon characters, Mickey Mouse and Donald Duck. The huge theme park, named Disneyland, soon became a multi-million dollar business. It not only brought huge revenues to Disney, it also spilled over into related businesses, such as food, lodging, transportation, and clothing. Over the next several decades, with the explosion of electronic and computer technologies, defense industries and high-tech companies created the largest manufacturing region in the United States, in Southern California. In the north, Silicon Valley, a 20 mile strip between Palo Alto and San Jose, grew into a major producer of semiconductors and became the birthplace of computer software.

As the 20th century came to a close, California led the country in the production of fruits and vegetables, and was a major manufacturer of dairy products and domestic wine. And Los Angeles had grown into the second largest city in the United States, with a population of three and a half million people. Only New York City was larger.

2

The California Winter League — An Overview

Los Angeles was declared a city by the Mexican Congress in 1835. In 1850, now part of the United States, it was incorporated as one of California's original counties. The first African American to settle in the city was Thomas Fisher, who arrived in 1818. By 1850, the city census showed 1,650 inhabitants of which 8 were Jewish and 15 were black.

Baseball, like most things, was a late arrival in California. Little boys were throwing baseballs on Boston Common two hundred years before the first pitch was thrown on the west coast. When the modern game of baseball was first played on the Elysian Field in Hoboken New Jersey, the 1,600 inhabitants of Los Angeles were too busy trying to carve out an existence for themselves in the hostile patch of land between the Pacific Ocean and the mountains to the east and north, to concern themselves with such trivial pursuits. The game of baseball, as played in America in the 17th and 18th centuries, was a game for children. When adults first became involved with the game in New York in the 1840s, the players were middle and upper class businessmen, whose work allowed them time for recreational activities.

The game made its first appearance on the west coast in the San Francisco area, when the well to do bankers, and other businessmen, familiar with the game from their days in the northeast, formed teams all over the Bay area. According to John E. Spalding in his book, *Always on Sunday*, "Among the early residents was a group of cricket players who organized the city's first base ball team — late in 1859. Called the San Franciscos, the members issued a challenge in January, 1860, to "any nine base ball players to a match game" on February 22 at Centre's Bridge. A group playing as the Red Rovers accepted."

"Using a ball made of woolen yarn from a sock and rubber from a pair of overshoes, the teams battled to a 33–33 tie over nine innings in the Washington's birthday holiday contest."

From there, the game took off. In 1866, as reported by Spalding, representatives of seven of the city's teams met to standardize the rules used to determine a champion. The next year, officials of 25 teams attended the meeting. Then, in 1868, the game received a significant boost when California's first enclosed baseball field was constructed in San Francisco, near Folsom and 26th Street. Spalding wrote "Although it was some distance from the heart of the city, between 3,000 and 4,000 fans showed up for the inaugural game on Thanksgiving Day at the ballpark, called Recreation Grounds. They were treated to a three hour and seventeen minute game in which the Eagles defeated the cross-bay rival Wide Awakes of Oakland, 37–22."

The Pacifics were one of the early amateur teams in San Francisco. The country's first professional baseball team, the Cincinnati Red Stockings, beat them 66–4 and 54–5. (John E. Spalding)

The next year, San Francisco baseball hit the big time. The powerful Cincinnati Red Stockings, America's first professional baseball team visited the Bay Area, to do battle with the local clubs. The Red Stockings, boasting such legendary talents as George and Harry Wright, and pitcher Asa Brainard, were in the midst of an 80 game undefeated streak, covering two years, and they showed no mercy to the Californians. They whipped the Eagles easily in the first game, 35–4, before 2,000 mesmerized spectators. The next day, they took the measure of the San Francisco team by an even greater margin, 58–4. They went on to clobber the Pacifics by a score of 54–5, and the Atlantics by a whopping 76–5, in a game called after only five innings.

It was an education for the California sporting public, as well as for its baseball players. But it demonstrated how the game could be played by professionals. It was difficult for the amateur players of the bay area to achieve that level of proficiency, since they had jobs that took up most of their time, and the California "blue laws" prevented them from playing baseball on Sunday.

The 1870s were an important period in the growth of baseball on the coast. The first league, the Pacific Base Ball League, was formed in 1878 and, after the blue laws were changed, games were permitted on Sunday. Following the practice in the east, admission was charged to the games, and the players split the gate receipts, making them semi-professionals. The lure of money changed the game forever. It attracted working men from the lower classes, who needed the extra income, and who were willing to work hard to improve their ballplaying skills.

Once again, John E. Spalding reported on the events of the day. "As professionalism grew, so did the level of play and the crowds. On Nov. 10, 1878, the Californias and Athletics met in what was billed as the Pacific League Championship....

"The game was played at the Trotting

Park Race Track in Oakland. More than 5,000 spectators paid the 25 cent admission, although the facility was small and the field badly maintained....

"There were not enough seats in the small grandstand so many fans crowded onto the field, interfering with play several times. The Athletics won 9 to 7, over the protests of the Californias, who claimed the umpire blew a call that permitted the Athletics to score four runs."

A rival league, the California League, was organized in 1879, and over the next few years, it replaced the Pacific League in the northern part of the state. By 1882, according to Spalding, "Baseball no longer was a 'gentlemen's game,' played for the love of the sport. In fact, the middle and upper class men who had built the potent amateur teams in the early days, looked down upon the modern game as played by commoners who moved from team to team looking for the best monetary arrangement, drank heavily, and gambled, sometimes on their own games."

But the game thrived. By 1886, the California League had expanded to five teams, three in San Francisco, one in Oakland, and one in Sacramento, 60 miles away. The league continued, with minor interruptions, until 1915, when it finally succumbed to the competition from the Class AA Pacific Coast League.

In 1892, the Los Angeles Angels joined the California League, marking the first time a professional baseball team represented the Southern California area. And the Angels rewarded their fans with a pennant in their first year of operation. After capturing the second half title, they defeated San Jose, the first half winners, in a playoff series, winning five games and tying one.

Another milestone was reached in the mid 1890s, thanks to the hospitable year round climate in California. Major league baseball teams began visiting the state in the fall, after the close of the major league season, playing exhibition games up and down the coast. By 1895, during a four year interruption in the California League, a winter league began operation. According to Spalding, the league rosters consisted of major league players and minor league players. The four teams included San Francisco, San Jose, Oakland, and Los Angeles. Although the league folded within a month, it was the beginning of winter league baseball in Northern California. In 1897, a new Northern California Winter League was formed, with teams in Oakland, Sacramento, Stockton, and San Francisco. The season opened on October 3 at San Francisco's new Recreation Park. Crowds of 4,000 to 5,000 were not uncommon as fans were thrilled to have baseball during the winter months. The Sacramento Gilt Edge won the league championship with a 7–2 record, becoming the first official Northern California Winter League champion.

In the south, baseball was growing at a rapid pace also as the 19th century drew to a close. Many local clubs were organized in and around Los Angeles during the late 1880s and early 1890s. According to Larry Zuckerman, "Athletic Park (1891–1896) was the first L.A. park to be used in organized baseball." It also hosted numerous "town ball" games involving not only two white teams, but white teams vs. black teams, as well. Zuckerman noted, "Local black clubs and winter black all-star teams regularly played at Fiesta Park (1897–1900), and the three Pacific Coast League Parks in Southern California: Chutes Park/Washington Gardens (1901–1910), and its successor Washington Park (1911–1925), and Vernon Park/Southside Park (1909–1915)."

One history of California stated that "Historically blacks have suffered least from racial discrimination in California because of their small numbers." That may have been true, but discrimination was still alive and well in the state. It arrived in California along with the pioneers from the eastern seaboard. In fact, there was a strong popular movement in the late 1840s to have California enter the Union as a slave state, but fortunately it was defeated. And, one week after the election of 1850, Governor Peter H. Burnett recommended that blacks be barred from California. That didn't happen either, and the Governor resigned one week later.

The racial situation was better in the western part of the country than in the eastern part, but many opportunities were still unavailable to blacks because of their color. And baseball was no exception. Although black baseball teams routinely played white teams, blacks and whites did not play on the same team. The teams themselves were segregated—the games and the leagues were integrated. In 1899, as reported by John E. Spalding, ."..the California League's Santa Cruz team had a young black mascot, Edward Purse. As he grew older, Purse became a good baseball player, and one observer reported years later that 'it broke his heart that he couldn't play for the team.'"

As the twentieth century got underway, winter league baseball was flourishing up and down the west coast, with the bulk of the activity centered around San Francisco in the north and Los Angeles in the south. Professional leagues in both sections of the state had a number of major league players on their rosters, as well as players from the Pacific Coast League, and other minor leagues. The Southern California Winter League (later referred to as just the California Winter League) soon became the most popular winter league in the state, because of the areas balmy climate, and because of the league's ability to attract the best baseball talent from around the country, including the legendary Walter Johnson. But what really set the league apart from other leagues was the inclusion of strong Negro league teams. The addition of talented black players like "Cyclone Joe" Williams, "Bullet Joe" Rogan, Satchel Paige, Turkey Stearnes, and Mule Suttles, gave the southern league a level of skill unmatched by any other league. It also represented the first modern, integrated professional baseball league in the United States, making it a valuable historical and social record.

The second decade of the new century was a period of growth for the west coast venture. The level of play in the league improved year by year. From a semi-pro level in 1900, the quality of the California Winter League probably reached a class A level by 1910, then a class AA to AAA level by 1920. As early as 1909 talented black players made the trek west to play ball. One of the greatest Negro pitchers of all time, Hall of Famer "Cyclone Joe" Williams played for the local Trilby Baseball Club in 1909. The talented white players in the league included a number of major leaguers, such as Johnson, Ted Easterly, who batted .324 for the Cleveland Indians in 1911 and .335 for the Kansas City Packers of the Federal League in 1915, George Stovall, a hot-tempered first baseman, who played in the Big Time for 12 years, Elmer Flick, a career .313 hitter in the majors, Bert Whaling, and Drummond Brown.

In 1910, Rube Foster's Leland Giants went west to participate in the league, a practice that soon became an annual event for Negro league teams. The Giants roster included Joe Williams, as well as other notable black players like Chappie Johnson, Frank Wickware, and Pete Booker. Among the white players in the league were Tom Seaton, who would lead the National League in victories in 1913 with 27, Rube Ellis of the St. Louis Cardinals, second baseman Neal Ball of the Cleveland Indians, and Gavvy Cravath, a future National League home run king, who had played for three American League clubs in 1908-09, but who spent the 1909-1911 seasons with Minneapolis of the American Association. The Giants came home in second place in the league, finishing behind the pennant winning San Diego club.

Rube Foster, called the "Father of Negro League Baseball," brought the first Negro league team to California, to compete in the 1910-11 winter league.

After missing a year, Rube Foster was back in 1912-13, this time with his new club, the Chicago American Giants, boasting such baseball talents as Pete Hill, Bruce Petway, Bill Monroe, Frank Duncan, and Bill Lindsay, "The Kansas Cyclone." Foster's team walked off with the Winter League Championship, according to the *Chicago Defender*, but that claim was not substantiated by the playing records. In any case, they did prove their ability to play on an equal basis against big league stars like Harry Hooper, Ivy Olson, Dave Bancroft, Chief Meyers and Fred Snodgrass.

The California experience was an important part of baseball's integration process because it gave Negro league players a stage on which to showcase their skills in direct competition against major league players and top minor league players. And the Negro leaguers didn't disappoint. They won more than their share of Winter League pennants over the years.

One of the more discriminatory actions on the west coast during the early part of the century, was the banning of blacks from playing in Pacific Coast League parks. In April 1914, Pacific Coast League President Allen T. Baum insisted that the color line be drawn, and that blacks be barred from playing in the league's parks. That edict apparently stood until 1930 when the Philadelphia Royal Giants utilized Wrigley Field, home of the PCL's Los Angeles Angels.

The 1915 edition of the mighty American Giants captured the first clear-cut California Winter League pennant by a black team, beating out a strong San Diego Pantages club. The Giants not only had Hill, Duncan, and Petway back, they also had Hall of Famers John Henry Lloyd and "Cyclone Joe" Williams. The Pantages were no pushovers, however. They had some decent talent of their own, with former major leaguers Pug Bennett (.248 in 240 ML games, and .285 in 1,976 minor league games), Joe Berger (.282 in 2,608 minor league games), and Chick Autry, in the field, and pitchers Roy Hitt (201–147 in the PCL), Pete Schneider (a 20 game winner for the Cincinnati Reds in 1917), and Charlie Chech (33–31 in the majors, 239–186 in the minors, including seasons of 24–9, 27–8, 25–11, 25–14, and 20–16 in AAA).

The period from 1917 through 1919 might be called the "Dark Ages" of the California Winter League. The ban on blacks playing in Pacific Coast League parks, put a damper on the integrated league experiment, and discouraged Negro league teams from traveling to the west coast during the winter. The only baseball facilities that were available to black players were humiliatingly small, with limited seating capacity that made the enterprise economically unfeasible. A few players—Bullet Joe Rogan, John Donaldson, and Tank Carr for instance—struggled through the 1917-18 season, playing for the Los Angeles White Sox, by this time a semi-pro outfit, but over the last two years of the decade there were apparently no Negro leaguers playing on the coast. Many players, like "Cyclone Joe" Williams, John Henry Lloyd, Spot Poles, Frank Wickware, Frank Duncan, and Oscar Charleston opted for the peace and quiet of the Florida Hotel League in Palm Beach, while some took "honest" jobs in their midwestern and eastern habitats.

By 1920, the California Winter League was facing extinction, until two men, Doc Anderson and Joe Pirrone, entered the scene. Doc Anderson, a local black entrepreneur, came to the rescue of the league in the late teens, after blacks were barred from playing in Pacific Coast League parks. He built Anderson Park, a.k.a. White Sox Park, at East Anderson and Fourth Streets, making it the home of the winter league's black team, from 1920 to 1923.

In 1924, Joe Pirrone, a southern California native, a former professional baseball player, and a strong supporter of the integrated winter league concept, built White Sox Park II to house the black team, replacing the more primitive White Sox Park I. Pirrone was the guiding force behind the winter league during the '20s and '30s, and even made trips to the east coast to recruit Negro professional teams for the league. In 1931 Joe and his brother John, who was his partner, installed lights in their park to permit the teams to play mid-week night games. Prior to that time, all winter league games were played on Saturday and Sunday afternoons, and on holidays. As a result of his dedicated efforts to provide the fans of Southern California with the best winter baseball possible, Joe Pirrone was known as "The Father of Winter League Baseball," a title he richly deserved.

The 1920s were an exciting time for winter league baseball fans in California. With the segregated major leagues isolated in the northeast quadrant of the country, the west coasters got to see the greatest players in the world, both black and white. The league, which approached a Triple A level by 1925, had a good mix of major league and high minor league talent, and the cream of the crop from the Negro leagues.

The strength of the Negro league representative in the winter league reached a dominant level in 1925, when the powerful Philadelphia Royal Giants, with "Bullet Joe" Rogan, Biz Mackey, Rap Dixon, Crush Holloway, and Newt Allen, defeated the White Kings in a playoff to win the league championship. Negro league entries captured 13 of the next 16 California Winter League titles.

Baseball Commissioner Kenesaw Mountain Landis disrupted the California Winter League briefly in 1927, when he issued an edict that prohibited major league players from participating in the league under pain of expulsion. The league partially circumvented the edict, which took effect on October 31, by starting the league schedule two weeks early, thereby giving the major leaguers the opportunity to play five or six games. When the season opened, major league stars like Bob Meusel and Babe Herman were in the starting lineup for Pirrone's All-Stars. After October 31, the white teams counted on former major league players and AAA minor leaguers, to stop the powerful Negro league teams. A few major leaguers defied Landis' ruling by playing under assumed names.

The quality of play in the California Winter League continued at a high level into the 1930s. It might even have gotten better from the Negro league side. The black entries reached their peak during the 1934-35 season when Tom Wilson's Nashville Elite Giants ran rampant through the league, winning 34 of 39 games played.

As the fourth decade of the twentieth century wound down, the California Winter League began to wind down with it. The 1940s brought several severe disruptions to the league, effectively ending one of America's most important professional baseball leagues, and the first integrated professional baseball league in the country. With the Japanese attack on Pearl Harbor on December 7, 1941, the winter league that year came to a screeching halt. President Franklin Delano Roosevelt subsequently encouraged the various professional baseball leagues around the country to continue playing ball during the conflict, in order to maintain a high level of citizen morale during one of the most difficult periods in the country's history. The league did struggle on during the four war years, but the talent was seriously depleted, as thousands of players answered the call to arms. The professional ranks were limited to older men, married men, and men with physical limitations.

In 1943, Baseball Commissioner Kenesaw Mountain Landis put another nail in the California Winter League coffin, with his directive that all major leaguers must "desist further from pastiming in the Southern California Winter League." Landis' action came after it was discovered that 19 major leaguers were playing in the league as late as November 14, violating the rule that permitted them to play exhibition games for just ten days after the close of the major league season, on October 13.

Shortly after the war ended, Branch Rickey of the Brooklyn Dodgers signed Jackie Robinson to an organized baseball contract, accelerating the Negro league's demise. During the last three years of the 1940s, defections from the Negro leagues to the major leagues essentially reduced the Negro leagues to a lower minor league level. The defectors included future Hall of Famers Monte Irvin, Roy Campanella, Larry Doby, Willie Mays, Ernie Banks, and of course, the old war horse Satchel Paige whose heroics with the Cleveland Indians brought the Tribe their first American League pennant in 28 years.

Not only did the integration of organized baseball lead to the demise of the Negro leagues, it also spelled doom for the California Winter League. The league was seriously weakened by World War II, and integration finished it off, although limited league play and exhibition games continued at least into the late 1940s. The Negro leagues struggled on until 1960.

The players who participated in the California Winter League over a period of nearly forty years, represented some of the most outstanding players in professional baseball history, not only from the major leagues, but also from the Pacific Coast League and the Negro leagues. Big leaguers included Irish Meusel of the New York Giants, his brother Bob Meusel of the New York Yankees, Ping Bodie, Smead Jolley, Ferdie Schupp, Charlie Root (who threw the famous Babe Ruth "Called Shot" home run ball), Buck Newsome, Bob Feller, Babe Herman, and Larry French. Other Hall of Famers like Kiki Cuyler, Al Simmons, Stan Musial, Dizzy Dean, Ted Williams, and Jimmie Foxx appeared less frequently.

Emil "Irish" Meusel was a hustling left fielder on John McGraw's great New York Giant teams, winners of four straight National League pennants from 1921 to 1924. The right-handed hitter drove in 87, 132, 125 and 102 runs during those years. In his 11 year major league career, he tattooed the ball at a .310 clip in 4,900 at-bats. Bob Meusel, the other half of the slugging Meusel brothers, played right field for the New York Yankees, alongside Babe Ruth, from 1920 to 1930. He hit a solid .309 for 11 years in the Big Show, and even led the

American League in home runs in 1925, with 33. Between them, the Meusel brothers appeared in ten World Series, six for Bob and four for Irish. The California natives faced each other in three consecutive World Series, from 1921 to 1923. Emil's Giants won two of the Series.

Ping Bodie was a colorful right-handed hitting outfielder whose major league career lasted nine years, primarily with the Chicago White Sox and New York Yankees, where he compiled a .275 batting average. The stocky Californian was Babe Ruth's roommate on the Yankees, but he insisted he didn't really room with the carousing Bambino. He only roomed with his suitcase. Bodie also spent nine years in the PCL, batting .295 with 1,356 base hits in 4,590 at-bats. He was the first Coast League player to hit 30 home runs in a season, and he did that in the dead ball year of 1910.

Smead Jolley was a professional hitter. He could hit .300 in a darkened closet. His four year major league career resulted in a .305 batting average with Chicago and Boston in the American League, but his fielding deficiencies got him a return ticket to the minors. He starred in the minor leagues for 20 years, hitting a sizzling .366 (#3 all-time). His offensive output included 3,037 base hits in 8,298 at-bats, with 612 doubles, 75 triples, and 334 home runs. The 6'3", 210 pound left-handed slugger tortured Pacific Coast League pitchers to the tune of .372 over a nine year period.

Ferdie Schupp pitched for John McGraw on the New York Giants from 1913 to 1919, helping the team win two National League flags. He went 21–7 as a starting pitcher for the Giants in 1917, on his way to a career mark of 61–39, but most of his major league career was spent as a closer, which explains his modest victory totals. He was a starting pitcher one other time, in addition to 1917. He won 16 games against 13 losses for the St. Louis Cardinals in 1920.

Charlie Root, more famous for his pitch to Babe Ruth, was an outstanding major league pitcher, who won 201 games against 160 losses over a 17 year career. Root went 26–15 for the Chicago Cubs in 1927, and won 15 or more games in seven other seasons. He also won 25 and 26 games for Los Angeles in the PCL. Root was a veritable workhorse for the Cubs, pitching more than 200 innings in a season, eight times.

Louis "Buck" Newsom, also known as "Bobo," was a long time major leaguer, putting together a 211–222 won-loss mark over a busy 20 year career. Buck was the original traveling man, changing teams in both the major leagues and minor leagues, an unbelievable 26 times in 25 years. In spite of his many moves, the 6'3", 200 pound workhorse won 20 games three times, and pitched more than 200 innings fifteen times, with a high of 330 innings in 1938. He also pitched in two World Series, splitting four decisions.

Bob Feller is unquestionably one of the four or five greatest pitchers in the history of professional baseball. He won 266 games over a glorious 18 year major league career, and he probably lost another 100 victories due to four years of military service during World War II. If it hadn't been for that interruption, Feller might well have finished with the third highest victory total in major league history, trailing only Cy Young and Walter Johnson. The big strong Iowan farmboy led the American League in strikeouts seven times and in victories six times, even though he missed those four years during his prime (ages 24–27). His dominance is reflected in his three no-hitters and twelve one-hitters. Rapid Robert pitched against the great Satchel Paige more than 20 times over the course of their careers, both in exhibition games and in the California Winter League, and although the record of their meetings is incomplete, it is obvious that there was little difference between the two great pitchers. They both belonged in a higher league.

Ping Bodie, New York Yankee outfielder, shown with George E. Outland, played in the California Winter League for five years. (George E. Outland)

Babe Herman, the pride of Brooklyn, hit .325 during a 13 year major league career, with 40 doubles, 11 triples, 18 home runs, and 100 RBIs a year. In 1930, he batted .393 for the Dodgers, but lost the batting title to Bill Terry who hit .401, the last .400 hitter in National League history. Herman played seven years in the Pacific Coast League, with an identical .325 batting average.

Larry French enjoyed a successful 15 year major league career from 1929 to 1941, during which time he won 197 games against 171 losses. The California native won 15 or more games eight times, with a high of 18–9 in 1936.

Those major league stars were backed up by the legends of the Pacific Coast League: Buzz Arlett, Jigger Statz, Fuzzy Hufft, Frank Brazill, George Payne, Doc Crandall, Wheezer Dell, and Herm Pillette.

Buzz Arlett compiled a batting average of .342 in thirteen years in the PCL. He also went 108–93 on the mound, with three twenty-win seasons, before his arm went dead. Jigger Statz piled up 3,356 base hits over an 18 year Pacific Coast League career, good for a .315 career batting average. Fuzzy Hufft played on the coast for seven years, during which time he pummeled AAA pitchers for a .346 average. Brazill also spent seven years in the PCL, and left a .342 batting average behind when he moved on.

George Payne compiled a 1–-1 record for the Chicago White Sox in 1920, his only major league appearance. The rest of his long, 28 year career was spent bouncing around the minors, where he won 348 games against 262 losses. Payne's total of 900 games pitched and his 348 victories are both #3 all-time in minor league history. George Payne won more than 20 games in a season five times, including 21–13 with Los Angeles in the Pacific Coast League in 1924, and 28–12 in the tough Texas League in 1929.

Doc Crandall was a big winner in both the major leagues and the Pacific Coast League, winning 102 games in the big show and 230 games in the PCL. Wheezer Dell had a short major league career where he won 19 games and lost 23, but he starred in the Coast League, going 138–94. He was a twenty game winner four consecutive years. Herm "Old Folks" Pillette was a legend in the Pacific Coast League where he toiled for a record 23 years. He was a twenty game winner twice, finishing with a career minor league mark of 264–264. He also went 34–32 for the Detroit Tigers in the American League during a four year stopover there.

The Negro league players who enjoyed the balmy weather in Southern California during the first half of the twentieth century included some of the more romantic figures from the distant past, such as "Bullet Joe" Rogan, Chet Brewer, Newt Allen, Dobie Moore, Biz Mackey, Satchel Paige, Mule Suttles, Turkey Stearnes, and Burnis "Wild Bill" Wright.

Bullet Joe Rogan, a veteran of the U.S. Army's famous 25th Infantry Division, and one of the Negro league's representatives in Cooperstown, played in the Negro leagues for more than a decade after leaving the Army and joining the Kansas City Monarchs of the Negro National League, as a 30-year-old rookie in 1920. Rogan was one of the greatest all-around players in black baseball. In addition to his career pitching record of 151–65, the stocky right-hander was also considered to be the best fielding pitcher in Negro league history. And he was the team's cleanup hitter, on the basis of his .348 batting average and 16 home runs a year. When not pitching, Rogan was equally at home in center field or at second base. Bullet Joe Rogan could do it all.

Chet Brewer was another of the legendary black pitchers who wintered on the coast. The tall, slim finesse pitcher compiled a 87–63 record in the Negro leagues between 1923 and 1946, when not spending his summers in Mexico or the Dominican

The famous 1920 Kansas City Monarchs sent at least nine players to the California Winter League including: Top row John Donaldson (left), Rube Currie (third from left), Zack Foreman (5th from left), Tank Carr (2nd from right), Joe Rogan (right), Bottom row, Jose Mendez (left), Dobie Moore (4th from left), Otto Ray (2nd from right), Hurley McNair (right). (National Baseball Hall of Fame Library, Cooperstown, N.Y.)

Republic. He also pitched winter ball in Cuba and Puerto Rico, in addition to his 14 years in the California Winter League.

Newt Allen, known as "Colt," was one of the greatest second basemen in Negro league history. He could do it all, both offensively and defensively. A master of the double play, Allen hit a respectable .302 during a 19 year career. He also played winter league baseball in Cuba, hitting .278 over two seasons, and spent six years in California.

Dobie Moore was the greatest shortstop of the 1920s, maybe the best of all time, but his glorious career was cut short by a gunshot wound, delivered by an angry girlfriend. According to John Holway's research, Moore's .355 career batting average was the highest in Negro league history, for batters with more than 1,700 at-bats. He also demonstrated outstanding power, as evidenced by his 35 doubles, 15 triples, and 16 home runs a year. Standing 5'11" tall and weighing in at a rugged 230 pounds, the big right-hander attacked the ball at a .356 clip in Cuba during the winter of 1923-24. He also led the league in triples.

Biz Mackey was probably the greatest all-around catcher in Negro league history. Over a long 28 year career, the rugged backstop ripped the ball at a .322 average, with good power. More important, he was by far the best defensive catcher of the 20s and 30s, and he taught Roy Campanella all the tricks of the trade. Baseball was Mackey's life. He played in the California Winter League for a record 26 years from 1920 to 1945. Showing his versatility, the tall 6', 200 pounder often played shortstop, third base, or first base, with the same skills he exhibited behind the plate.

First and foremost among the great players of the 1930's was the mythical figure of Leroy "Satchel" Paige, a tall, skinny, right-handed flamethrower, who was by far the most dominant pitcher in Negro league history. Over a storied 21 year career, the gangly 6'4" Paige drew crowds in record numbers wherever he pitched—and he pitched wherever there was a baseball diamond and fans who loved the game. He traveled the United States north and south, east and west, pitching in just about every state in the Union. He also pitched in Canada, Mexico, Cuba, the Dominican Republic, and Puerto Rico, and he was the best pitcher in the league, wherever he pitched. He still holds the Puerto Rican Winter League record for most wins (19) and most strikeouts (208) in one season. He led General Rafael Trujillo's team to the Dominican Republic championship in 1937 under very adverse conditions. And he helped the Cleveland Indians win the 1948 American League pennant when, as a 42-year-old rookie, he went 6–1 down the stretch, including two complete game shutouts over the Chicago White Sox in an eight day period.

Another renowned figure in black baseball annals was George "Mule" Suttles. The big, 6'3", 215 pound black bomber popped eyeballs when he sent the little white sphere into orbit, which was often. He played in the Negro leagues for 22 years, averaging 40 home runs for every 550 times at bat. He also hit for a .341 career average, proving he was not just a one dimensional player. He was a member of the Negro league entry in the California Winter League for eight years, and he became the darling of the newspapermen with his prodigious home runs.

Norman "Turkey" Stearnes, who was elected to the National Baseball Hall of Fame in Cooperstown, N.Y., in 2000, was another superstar, a genuine five tool player. The 6' tall, 170 pound greyhound was a sensational center fielder, a speedy baserunner, a deadly hitter, and a serious long ball threat. He starred in the Negro leagues for 20 years, batting .352 with 30 home runs a year. And he gave California natives many thrills during his nine year winter league career.

The two great sluggers, Suttles and Stearnes were complete opposites. The Mule was big and brawny, built for power. His home runs were majestic shots that ascended high into the California sky and seemed to disappear from view before coming back to earth somewhere beyond the outfield fence. His swing was a mighty all-or-nothing stroke like Babe Ruth's, that often left the big man whiffing the air. But even though he struck out frequently, he still hit for a high average. Norman "Turkey" Stearnes was slender, and built for speed. Where Suttles was slow afoot and slow on the bases, Stearnes was a gazelle. He was an outstanding base runner, and the best center fielder in the game. Even though his frame was small, the 170 pound left-handed swinger generated tremendous power from his shoulders and wrists. His hits, unlike Suttles, were line drives that sent infielders diving for cover. Many of them caromed off the outfield fence for extra bases. Since right field at White Sox Park II was protected by an 80 foot high screen, Stearnes' line shots often hit the screen while Suttles' skyscrapers would clear the fence with room to spare. The two men were as different as night and day—but they were both great sluggers. One is in the Hall of Fame. The other should be.

Burnis "Wild Bill" Wright was called the most dangerous hitter in the California Winter League by baseball experts on the west coast. He was a big, powerful line drive hitter who struck out only 33 times for every 550 at-bats, and who was particularly deadly in the clutch. When the chips were down, Wild Bill would, more often than not, win the game with a timely base hit. The 6'4", 220 pound outfielder was also a terror in the field and on the bases. He had blazing speed, outstanding range, and a strong throwing arm.

Four of the above players now reside in Cooperstown, and both Suttles and Mackey should join them shortly. Brewer and

Mule Suttles, Willie Foster, Turkey Stearnes, and Alex Radcliffe (L to R) all played in California during the early 1930s. Suttles, Radcliffe, and Stearnes won four batting titles between them from 1930 to 1932, and Foster was the top pitcher twice. (Robert W. Peterson)

Moore also deserve a niche but probably won't get one. Other potential Hall of Fame players who wintered in California included Sammy T. Hughes, as well as the top two career hitters in Negro league history, Jud Wilson (.354) and John Beckwith (.352).

Throughout its almost forty year run, the California Winter League experienced its share of growing pains, as well as a variety of business problems. Some years, there were just two teams in the league, the Negro league entry and Pirrone's All-Stars. Occasionally there were as many as six, eight, or even ten teams in the league. But for the most part, the league consisted of four teams, one Negro league team and three white teams, with league games being scheduled on a week to week basis. To make matters more confusing, non-league games were intermixed with league games, and were included in the league standings. And in 1924-25 and 1930-31, there were two winter leagues competing with each other for fan support.

The California Winter League was apparently intended as a showcase for Negro league baseball. White Sox Park, which was strategically located in or near black sections of the city, hosted the majority of league games. And the Negro league team was involved in most of the games. Usually they squared off against a different white team each weekend, playing a three-game series—one game on Saturday and a doubleheader on Sunday. That meant the other two white teams didn't play unless they could schedule a weekend series with each other, or with another team, at a different location. Some of the white players solved the inactivity problem by playing for more than one team. And near end of season, if the Negro league team was in first place, Joe Pirrone would combine the rosters of the three white teams in an effort to derail the Negro league express. Somehow the strategy never succeeded.

Since the league schedule was designed to attract the black fans to White Sox Park, the final standings often showed a large discrepancy in games played, with the Negro league team playing two or three times as many games as the white teams. However, the strategy apparently worked because the large crowds, which were approximately 70 percent black, made the league a financial success.

The talent pool in the California Winter League over a 40 year period was extraordinary. Unfortunately, there were no published statistics for the many great players. The California Winter League did not have an official scorer, or a centralized authority for compiling and preserving batting and pitching statistics. Each team maintained its own records. And newspapermen who followed the games for the *Los Angeles Examiner*, *Los Angeles Times*, *California Eagle*, etc., kept their own records. As a result, there were many statistical discrepancies from one source to another.

The box score for a 1929 game between the Cleveland Giants and the Shell Oilers is presented below as a graphic example of the problems associated with attempting to assemble accurate statistics for the league. The first box score is from the *Chicago Defender*. The second box score is from the *California Eagle*.

Shell Oil

Name	Pos.	AB	R	H
Rhyne	SS	5	2	2
Kerr	2B	5	1	0
Averill	CF	3	1	2
Jolley	RF	5	0	2
Emmer	3B	4	0	1
BruckerB	1B	4	0	1
Christensen	LF	4	0	3
Jenkins	C	4	0	0
Pillette	P	3	1	1
Hulvey	P	0	0	0
Brazill	3B	0	0	0
Totals		37	5	12

Cleveland Giants

Name	Pos.	AB	R	H
Allen	SS	5	1	3
Day	2B	5	0	1
Mackey	C	4	2	2
Beckwith	3B	5	2	3
Rogan	RF-P	5	2	3
Dixon	LF	2	0	1
Stearnes	CF	4	1	1
Mothell	1B	3	1	2
Brewer	P	1	0	0
Green	P	3	1	2
		37	10	18

Shell Oil

Name	Pos.	AB	R	H
Rhyne	SS	5		3
Kerr	2B	5		0
Averill	CF	4		3
Jolley	RF	5		4
Emmer	3B	4		1
Brucker	1B	5		2
Christensen	LF	5		3
Jenkins	C	4		0
Pillette	P	2		1
Brazill		1		0

Cleveland Giants

Name	Pos.	AB	R	H
Allen	SS	5		3
Day	2B	5		0
Mackey	C	4		2
Beckwith	3B	4		3
Rogan	RF	4		3
Dixon	LF	2		0
Stearnes	CF	4		2
Mothell	1B	3		2
Brewer	P	1		0
Green		3		2

	Shell Oil					Cleveland Giants		
Name	Pos.	AB	R	H	Name	Pos.	AB	R	H
Hulvey	P	0		0				
Totals		40		18			35		17

As can be seen, there are many differences from one box score to the other. The total at-bats are different for both teams. In the *Chicago Defender*, Shell Oil and Cleveland both had 37 at-bats. In the *California Eagle*, Shell Oil had 40 at-bats, while Cleveland had only 35 at-bats. Individually, Earl Averill was 2 for 3 in the *Defender*, and 3 for 4 in the *Eagle*. John Beckwith was 3 for 5 in the *Defender*, but 3 for 4 in the *Eagle*. Joe Rogan was 3 for 4 or 3 for 5 depending on which paper you believed. And Smead Jolley was 4 for 5 in one paper, but only 2 for 5 in the other. The same situation existed with most of the batting and pitching statistics, including doubles, triples, home runs, innings pitched, strikeouts, and bases on balls. And games reported by the *Los Angeles Examiner* and the *Los Angeles Times* suffered from the same statistical inaccuracies.

There will never be complete statistics for the California Winter League for the same reason John Holway said there will never be complete statistics for the Negro leagues—"some box scores were never published in the press." Some days, newspapers carried only game accounts, with no box scores. Other days, there was just a line score, with the batteries. Some box scores did not include at-bats, so those had to be estimated. For this study, at-bats were estimated at 11 ABs for every three games, or 3.67 ABs per game. And then there is the age and condition of the newspaper itself. Microfilm of the newspapers of the period often have box scores that are nearly illegible, requiring educated guesses to be made for players' names, at-bats, base hits, etc.

The black newspapers of the day, the *California Eagle*, the *Chicago Defender*, and the *Pittsburgh Courier*, reported only games involving the Negro league teams. There were very few box scores or written accounts of games between two white teams. Other problems included typos, players names being misspelled, and two or more players with the same last name not being properly identified with a first initial, like Bob and Irish Meusel, or Steve, Joe and Pete Coscarart. And some players, particularly major league players, often played under assumed names to hide their identities from the probing eyes of the Commissioner.

In spite of all the problems, it was still possible to reconstruct the California Winter League batting and pitching statistics reasonably well, by conducting original research into the box scores and game accounts that were published in the leading newspapers of the day, both black and white. Many hundreds of box scores and game accounts were reviewed and cross checked, and the data compiled. Occasionally, educated guesses had to be made when there was conflicting information. And estimates had to be made when there was incomplete information. The season batting statistics for the Negro league team were published in the black newspapers several years, but even those tended to be unreliable. Still, a careful review of the available data made it possible to develop reliable statistics, which permit a realistic evaluation of the players in the league, Negro leaguers and major leaguers alike. Surprisingly, the Negro league players fared quite well against their major league adversaries over a period of more than forty years.

3

The Early Years 1900–1919

The California Winter League first saw the light of day around the turn of the 20th century.

The league began as a conglomeration of local amateur clubs, gradually evolving into a strong semi-professional league. According to Larry Zuckerman, black teams and white teams competed against each other in Fiesta Park between 1897 and 1900, then at three Pacific Coast League parks— Chutes Park (1901–1910), Washington Park (1911–1925), and Vernon Park (1909–1915). The first black winter baseball teams of note were the Los Angeles Giants, Pioneers, Trilbys, and the Occidentals.

The 1906-07 Season

California was a year-round baseball haven in 1906, with winter and summer leagues showcasing some of the finest players in the country. There were numerous organized leagues, plus many independent clubs that played a full schedule, against league teams as well as other independent teams. At this time, no black teams were playing in an organized league. The all-white California Winter League opened on November 25, with eleven teams: Hoegee Flags, Anaheim, Santa Barbara, L.A. Pacifics, L. A. Morans, San Diego, Tufts-Lyons, Hamburgers, Pasadena, Olindas of Fullerton, and San Bernardino. The *Los Angeles Times* documented the opening game. "The Hoegees will go to Santa Barbara today to meet the crack professional team representing that town. ... There will be an automobile parade with a brass band before the game. The Mayor of the town will pitch the first ball. Rube Vickers and Charlie Hall predict the most successful ball season Santa Barbara has ever had. The Channel City team is composed mostly of Coast League players."

Players of note in the league included Fred Snodgrass, Roy Hitt, Hal Chase, and Rube Vickers. The left fielder for the Hoegees was a man named Johnson. Whether or not it was Walter Johnson is not known. What is known is that "The Big Train" lived in the area and participated in the league between 1907 and 1910, occasionally as an outfielder.

There was very little coverage of the winter league in the local newspapers, and no box scores were published, but the few game accounts that were reported indicated the league was very competitive. In one early season encounter, Pasadena and the Hoegees battled to a 7–7 tie, in a game called on account of darkness at the end of the eighth inning. The Olindas beat Morans 3–2 in 15 innings. Pasadena edged the Hoegees 5–4. Hamburgers shut out Olindas 2–0 behind a two-hit, 17 strikeout performance by Charlie Hartman of the Boston Red Sox. And Morans outlasted Pasadena 4–3 in ten innings.

There were not enough games documented to determine a league champion, and no standings were published, but the *Times* reported that Tufts-Lyons and San Bernardino were battling for the league lead late in the season. "The Tufts-Lyons and the San Bernardino teams are playing the best ball just at present and the fans are wondering why the San Bernardino team is not far in the lead. It has a number of cracking good players in its lineup, among them being pitcher (Roy) Hitt, (Walter) Carlisle and (Rube) Ellis of the Los Angeles Team, McClelland, Weed, and Le Brandt."

A few statistics were gleaned from independent box scores.

Name	Team	G	AB	H	D	T	HR	BA
Hal Chase	San Jose	7	28	9	2	0	0	.321
Frank Chance	Stockton	4	13	1	1	0	0	.077
Gavvy Cravath	San Jose	3	12	2	2	0	0	.167

Pitching

Name	Team	G	CG	W	L	IP	SO	BB	SH
Leifield, A. "Lefty"	San Jose	3	3	2	1	27	13	10	1

The 1907-08 Season

The 1907-08 winter league consisted of eleven all-white teams, including Santa Ana, the Los Angeles Hoegees, Meeks, McCormicks, Christopher-Levy, Edisons, Santa Monica, Pasadena, Santa Barbara, San Pedro, Dolgeville, and Morans. A young 20-year-old Californian was the star of the league. He was a pitcher who was practically unhittable, and who had just completed his rookie season with the Washington Senators of the American League, winning five games while losing nine. His name was Walter Johnson, and he pitched for Santa Ana.

Henry W. Thomas reported on Johnson's season in his excellent biography, *Walter Johnson, The Big Train*. "...the season kicked off with an exhibition doubleheader against Huntington Beach on October 27. Johnson played center field in the opener, hitting his first home run ever and unleashing a throw that was still clear in the mind of Santa Ana left fielder Lester Slaback 50 years later.... "that's the only time I have ever seen a man thrown out at home (from third) on a clean base hit. Walter's throwing ability was unbelievable." ... (Johnson) celebrated (his 20th birthday) by outdueling future Washington teammate Sleepy Bill Burns (of the Los Angeles Angels, champions of the Pacific Coast League), 1–0. Sixteen Angels went down on strikes, three hits and a walk the sum of their meager offensive output." Captain Dillon of the Angels was tormented all afternoon by L.A. fans who reminded the skipper that he once had an opportunity to sign Johnson to a PCL contract, and declined.

The local newspapers once again failed to publish box scores of the league games, but at least they published weekly rosters, game accounts, and league standings. Many major leaguers and Pacific Coast Leaguers graced the team rosters, including Elmer Flick of the Cleveland Indians, Fred Snodgrass of the New York Giants, Oscar Jones and Harry McIntyre of the Brooklyn Superbas, Jake Beckley of the St. Louis Cardinals, and Chick Autry and Roy Hitt of the Cincinnati Reds.

But it was Walter Johnson, pitching for the Santa Ana Yellow Sox, whose appearance thrust the California Winter League into national prominence for the first time. During his three year tour of duty in the league, his celebrity made the league an important venue for wintering major leaguers and Pacific Coast League players. Johnson, who was born in Humboldt, Kansas, on November 6, 1887, moved to Olinda, California, 23 miles southeast of Los Angeles, with his family in 1901, so his father could work in the oil fields. The man who would later be known as "The Big Train," was an overpowering pitcher, even as a youth. He starred on his local high school team, as well as on several amateur and semi-pro teams in the area. He became a professional baseball player in 1906, at the age of 18, when he joined Tacoma of the Northwestern League. The following year, he jumped all the way to the major leagues with the Washington Senators. He also participated in the California Winter League in the fall of 1907.

In his first start of the winter season, he got no better than a 4–4 tie with the Hoegees, but he had better luck in his second start, tossing a two-hitter, and fanning 13 batters, in a 4–3 win over Meeks. Then came two weeks of frustration, as he dropped a 1–0 contest to Santa Barbara, followed by a 2–1 loss to McCormicks.

The Santa Barbara Eagles played an exhibition game against the Los Angeles Giants, called the champion colored team, the day before their league contest. They blanked the Giants 3–0 behind Elmer Rieger. Buddy Clark took the loss for the black team.

On December 22, Johnson whipped Meeks 12–1 in a complete game effort, to pull his team into a 4th place tie with a 4–3 record. Morans held the league lead with 5 wins against a single loss. From that point on, the Yellow Sox stepped up the pressure. Johnson blanked Christopher-Levys 2–0, while Pasadena beat Morans 9–6 in what the *Times* called "a rather loose game." The big game of the week was the game between the Hoegees and Dolgeville, won by the Hoegees 1–0 on the strength of a no-hitter by Fred Snodgrass. The 19-year-old Californian went on to enjoy a successful nine year major league career with the New York Giants, playing many positions, including catcher, but he never pitched in the big time.

The California Winter League turned into a dogfight over the last three months of the season. Santa Barbara jumped into the lead on December 30. They were knocked off the top rung by San Pedro two weeks later. And San Pedro was passed by the streaking Santa Ana Yellow Sox on February 17.

After Johnson's shutout win over Christopher-Levy, he was sorely tested by San Pedro on January 6. The game pitted "The Big Train" against Russ Ford, a future 20 game winner with the New York Highlanders. Although the Washington side-wheeler sent 22 men back to the bench dragging their bats behind them, the game ended in a 0–0 tie after 12 innings. Apparently the long scoreless game didn't affect Johnson's concentration because he came back the following week to no-hit the Hoegees, 1–0.

Unfortunately, that was the end of the season for Johnson. He fell deathly ill, as reported in the *Los Angeles Times*. "Walter Johnson ... was operated upon in a hospital at Fullerton for acute mastoiditis Thursday.... A piece of bone was removed from an abscess back of Johnson's right ear and to perform the operation it was necessary to put him under the influence of anesthetics, from which he did not awaken until near noon Friday.... He is a little better today ... and recognizes members of his family.... Johnson kept to his bed for nearly two weeks before the operation and his condition grew steadily worse until the surgeons decided that the abscess had to be removed.... The injury is practically the same from which Thomas A. Edison, the inventor, is suffering, and Johnson came very near to a fatal illness as a result ... the attending physicians say that they believe the sick man will pull through all right."

Walter Johnson of Olinda, California, dominated the winter league from 1907 through 1909.

The Santa Ana Yellow Sox suffered a devastating blow with the loss of their ace pitcher, but they gamely hung on, and captured the league championship.

Final Standings

Team	Wins	Losses	Ties
Santa Ana Yellow Sox	13	3	2
Pasadena	16	6	0
San Pedro	13	6	3
Santa Barbara	13	5	0
Santa Monica	9	7	2
Hoegees	9	7	2
Edisons	9	10	1
McCormicks	8	11	0
Meeks	4	16	1
Christopher-Levy	3	15	0
Dolgeville	1	1	0

Overall, Walter Johnson's season was a spectacular success, as shown below.

G	AB	H	D	T	HR	BA
(11)	(43)	(16)	5	0	2	.372

G	CG	W	L	IP	SO	BB	SH
(11)	(11)	(7)	(2)	102	152	5	(5)

The basic statistics were reported by Henry W. Thomas. The figures in parentheses are estimates based on the best available information. Johnson was obviously a good hitter. He compiled a career .235 batting average in the major leagues, and occasionally played the outfield.

The 1908-09 Season

The Santa Ana Yellow Sox were happy to have Walter Johnson pitching for them again in the winter league, since he was rapidly becoming a major league star. He finished the 1908 American League season with a highly respectable 14–14 mark, after recovering from his surgery. His team, the lowly Washington Senators, won only 67 games against 85 losses, finishing a distant 22.5 games behind the pennant winning Detroit Tigers. As strange as it seems, Johnson may have been one of the more influential factors behind the formation of the country's first integrated, professional baseball league, as well as the focal point for the increased respect paid to black players for their expertise on the diamond. His contribution was inadvertent, yet significant, and resulted from an exhibition game he pitched in the early fall.

At the time, the California Winter League was still a segregated league. Although black independent teams were active in Southern California, they were generally held in low esteem by the baseball establishment, probably with good reason. The black teams in the area in the late 1890s and early 1900s were amateur teams drawn from the local labor market, while the white semi-pro and professional teams in the organized leagues had many major league and Pacific Coast League players. That situation changed abruptly on October 18, 1908, when the black Los Angeles Giants shocked the baseball world by defeating Walter Johnson, 6–5 in 11 innings. Henry Thomas reported on the game. "...he (Johnson) went to Los Angeles to pitch for the Olive club against the Los Angeles Giants, called 'the champion colored team', by the Los Angeles Herald. Despite striking out 20, Johnson lost in 11 innings, the defeat of Walter Johnson elevating the Giants to brief prominence in Southern California baseball, bringing challenges from the winter league champion San Diego Pickwicks and the PCL champion Los Angeles Angels."

Olives

Name	Pos.	AB	H
Meats	1B	5	2
Collins	C	4	0

Los Angeles Giants

Name	Pos.	AB	H
Boggs	2B	5	0
Brock	LF	5	2

	Olives					Los Angeles Giants		
Name	Pos.	AB	H		Name	Pos.	AB	H
Carpenter	SS	5	0		Lane	SS	5	3
Johnson	P	4	0		Clark	3B-P	4	1
Echonda	LF	5	0		Slater	C	5	1
H. Hendricks	RF	3	1		Hubert	RF	5	0
Bush	CF	5	1		McLain	1B-3B	5	1
W. Hendricks	3B	3	1		Bartletts	CF	4	0
Valencia	2B	4	0		Hunt	P	2	0
					Bronson	1B	4	1
Totals		38	4				44	9

Los Angeles Olives   0 1 0   3 0 0   0 1 0   0 0—5—4—6
Los Angeles Giants   1 0 0   1 3 0   0 0 0   0 1—6—9—7

Two base hit: Lane

	IP	H	SO	BB
W. Johnson (LP)	11	9	20	1
Hunt			4	4
Clark (WP)			10	1

The success of the L.A. Giants against one of the top pitchers in the major leagues marked the first time that a black team was recognized by their white counterparts as being a respectable opponent. Over the next two years the Giants continued to impress the fans, as well as baseball officials, with their continually improving skills. And the gate appeal of white vs black confrontations, that packed the ballparks with fans of both races, did not go unnoticed either. The *Los Angeles Herald*, in reporting the game between the PCL champion Los Angeles Angels and the Giants, noted, "A crowd of 5000, ½ colored and ½ white, watched the Angels beat the here-to-fore invincible (34–1 record) L.A. Giants, the pride of darktown." The score was 14–2.

The popularity of integrated contests reached its climax in the fall of 1910 when Negro league baseball impresario Rube Foster brought a highly talented professional black team to Los Angeles to compete in the winter league.

The 1908-09 California Winter League received little media attention in the local newspapers, but apparently the San Diego Pickwicks captured the league championship. Only four of Walter Johnson's games were located. He lost to the Hoegees 1–0 on November 1, endured a 10 inning 0–0 tie with Salt Lake, then blanked both the Pickwicks and the Hoegees, by scores of 1–0 and 2–0 respectively.

The Salt Lake team had the best record in the games that were recovered, but published reports in the local newspapers named San Diego as the league champion.

1908-09 California Winter League

	Wins	Losses	Ties	
San Diego	3	1	0	League champion
Salt Lake	9	2	1	
Pasadena	3	1	0	
Maiers	7	4	0	
Hoegees	3	3	1	
Santa Ana	3	4	1	
San Pedro	4	6	1	

1908-09 California Winter League

	Wins	Losses	Ties
McCormicks	3	5	0
Azusa	2	7	0
Edisons	1	5	0

Selected Statistics

Batting — 1908-09 Season

Name	Team	Pos	G	AB	H	D	T	HR	BA
Whaling, Bert	San Pedro	C	7	23	6	2	0	0	.273
Stovall, George	Edison	1B	1	1	5	0	0	0	.000
Flick, Elmer	Hoegees	2B	4	18	4	0	0	0	.222
Ellis, Rube	San Pedro	LF	4	15	5	1	1	0	.333
Snodgrass, Fred	Hoegees	LF	3	11	3	0	0	0	.273
Rieger, Elmer	Salt Lake	1B-P	6	17	1	0	0	0	.059

Pitching — 1908-09 Season

Name	Team	G	CG	W	L	IP	SO	BB	SH
Rieger, Elmer	Salt Lake	3	3	3	0	27	29	1	2
Harkness, Fred	Hoegees	1	1	1	0	9	10	2	1
Johnson, Walter	Santa Ana	4	4	2	1	36	52	4	3
Hall, Charlie	S.L., S.P.	6	6	5	0	56	54	20	1
Gray, Dolly	Hoegees	1	1	0	0	10	2	3	0
Ford, Russ	San Pedro	3	3	1	2	28	21	2	1

The *Los Angeles Times* chose to allot most of its coverage to the upstart Los Angeles Giants. The local black team played a heavy independent schedule, including games with most of the California Winter League teams, and finished with a respectable 9–8 record. They faced many major leaguers along the way, including Walter Johnson, Fred Snodgrass, Elmer Rieger, Chick Autry, Bert Whaling, George Stovall, Ted Easterly, Happy Hogan, and Doc Newton.

Los Angeles Giants — Batting Statistics 1908-09

Name	Pos	G	AB	H	D	T	HR	BA
Boggs	2B	9	34	0	0	0	0	.000
Brock	RF	10	41	6	0	0	0	.146
Lane	SS	12	55	11	1	0	0	.200
Clark, Buddy	P-3B	14	52	13	7	0	0	.250
Bronson	1B	10	35	7	0	0	0	.200
Battles	CF	13	51	9	3	0	0	.176
Slater	C-2B	15	55	12	3	0	0	.218
McClain	3B-P	8	26	4	0	0	0	.154
Hawkins, Lem	SS	11	41	12	1	0	0	.293
Hunt, J.	LF-P	8	25	1	0	0	0	.040
Hubert	RF	7	24	10	1	0	0	.417
Bartlett	2B	3	10	0	0	0	0	.000
Carroll	C	3	12	0	0	0	0	.000
Pryor, Wes	LF	4	12	1	0	0	0	.084

Pitching 1908-09

Name	G	CG	W	L	IP	SO	BB	SH
Clark, Buddy	11	9	6	5	94	95	12	2
McClain	2	1	0	1	14	4	2	0
Hunt	2	1	0	1	13	9	6	0
Locker	1	1	1	0	9	6	0	0
Hinkle	1	1	0	1	9	7	3	0
Lane	2	2	2	0	18	10	4	0

The 1909-10 Season

The winter league was still not integrated in 1909-10, but the continued success of black independent teams against strong, white competition, opened the door for them to become full fledged members of the league the following season. The California Winter League was an eight team all-white league, composed of San Diego, Santa Barbara, San Bernardino, McCormicks, Maiers, Pasadena, Salt Lake, and Orange. The only box score uncovered pitted Salt Lake against San Bernardino, with Elmer Rieger of Salt Lake, who had appeared in 13 games with the Cincinnati Reds of the National League in the season just completed, tossing a four hit shutout at the Monks, winning 1–0. Rieger's teammates included major leaguers Chief Meyers, Bert Whaling, and Peaches Graham. George Stovall and Elmer Flick also participated in the league. The majority of players, however, were local semi-professional players who had regular jobs during the week and played baseball on the weekends.

Walter Johnson was the most famous player active on the coast over the winter, after having suffered through a devastating 13–25 season with the cellar dwelling Senators. The Big Train began the winter season as a member of a traveling major league all-star team, playing exhibition games up and down the coast between Los Angeles and San Francisco. His All-National team made their first appearance in San Francisco, splitting a doubleheader with the Coast League champion San Francisco Seals. After dropping the opener by a score of 12–8, the All-Nationals rebounded in the nightcap 7–0 behind the spectacular pitching of Johnson. The 6'1" 200 pound fireballer blanked the Seals on four hits, while his mates pounded Weldon Henley and Frank Browning for 14 safeties.

The next week, in Los Angeles, "The Big Train" handcuffed the Angels 9–1, scattering seven hits, and issuing just two bases on balls. He fanned three. He also chipped in with one hit in three times at-bats. Ed Konetchy of the St. Louis Cardinals led the All-Star attack with two hits. Fred Snodgrass had a double. The last reported exhibition game involving Walter Johnson took place in San Francisco on November 25. The raw-boned side-arming right-hander defeated Connie Mack's powerful Philadelphia Athletics by a score of 7–2. The losing pitcher was Jack Coombs, who would lead all American League pitchers with 31 victories in 1910.

After the exhibition season ended, "The Big Train" joined the Santa Ana Yellow Sox of the California Winter League once again, and made his presence felt almost immediately. December 26 was designated as "Walter Johnson Day" in Santa Ana in honor of their major league hero, and he rewarded his fans by distributing over 2,000 photos. Then the man from Olinda took the mound and shackled Salt Lake with a no-hitter, the second of his winter league career. He went on from there to blaze a sensational path through the coast league competition, running up nine consecutive victories, with four shutouts, and 117 strikeouts in 81 innings.

G	CG	W	L	IP	SO	BB	SH
9	9	9	0	81	117	3	4

That was Walter Johnson's last year in the California Winter League. His three year totals showed:

G	CG	W	L	T	PCT.	IP	SO	BB	SH
24	24	18	3	3	.857	219	321	12	12

His strikeout average of 13 strikeouts for every nine innings was the best in California Winter League history, edging out Satchel Paige, who averaged 12 K's for every nine innings.

The Imperial Valley League was also active in Southern California over the winter of 1909-10, celebrating its third year of operation. The league was composed of El Centro, Imperial, Holtville, Yuma, and Brawley. Some of the more notable players were Kitty Brashear, Oscar Jones, Ted Easterly, Jim Wiggs, Heine Berger, Dazzy Vance, and "Death Valley" Jim Scott. This league, which was probably a mid level professional league, was also an all-white league. Easterly was the league's top slugger, banging two home runs in one game.

In addition to the two Southern California winter leagues, there were also many independent teams playing a full schedule of games. Three black teams competed around the L.A. area over the winter of 1909-10. They were the Occidentals, the Los Angeles Giants, and Trilbys. Newspaper coverage of the teams was almost nonexistent. The first game that was reported during the 1909 season matched the Occidentals, which the *Los Angeles Times* identified as "the champion baseball team of Utah," and the Los Angeles Giants, at Macy Park on October 31. The Occidentals raked L.A. pitching for 13 base hits, on their way to a 9–2 drubbing of the local team. Although the black players were semi-pros, several future or past Negro leaguers were in the line-ups, including Lem Hawkins, Ad Langford, Wes Pryor, and Sol White.

Lem Hawkins batted just .059 for Occidental in 1909, but went on to a successful career with the Kansas City Monarchs from 1921 to 1929. (Noir Tech Research)

Occidentals				Los Angeles Giants			
Name	Pos.	AB	H	Name	Pos.	AB	H
Black,	2B	4	1	Hubert,	2B	4	1
Hawkins, Lem	3B	5	1	Pryor, Wes	CF	4	1
Lanley,	C	5	1	Clark, Buddy	SS-P	4	0
Burns,	LF	5	3	Branson,	1B	4	0
Langford, Ad	CF	5	2	Slater,	C-2B	4	0
Middleton,	1B	4	1	Banks,	C-2B	3	1
Robinson,	SS	4	1	Wilson,	RF	3	1
Harrison,	P	4	1	Hunt,	LF	3	0
Campbell,	RF	4	1	Hinkle,	P	1	0
				McLain,	P	1	1
				White, Sol	3B	1	1
Totals		40	13			32	6

Occidentals	1 0 2	3 0 2	1 0 0—9—13—0
L.A. Giants	0 0 0	0 1 0	1 0 0—2—6—3

Two base hits: Hawkins, Burns, Harrison, Langford

Name	IP	SO	BB
Harrison (WP)	9	12	1
Clark, Buddy (LP)	6	3	0
Hinkle	2	1	1
McLain	1	1	2

Three weeks later, the Occidentals played a white team from Los Angeles, stacked with Pacific Coast League and future major league players like Gavvy Cravath, Bill Tozer, Curt Bernard, Pop Dillon, Kid Mohler, and Jud Smith. Although Los Angeles escaped with a victory, the play of the black players continued to impress the fans and baseball officials on the west coast.

On the 28th, the Occidentals whipped the All-Stars at Chutes Park, home of the PCL Los Angeles Angels, by the score of 3-1. George Stovall of the Cleveland Indians hit the first pitch of the game over the left field fence, but was given only a double when the ball struck the roof of a building outside the fence and bounced back into the field of play. The *L.A. Times* covered the game. "About 1,000 persons, principally colored, saw the game, and it was a good one after the second inning when the Stars made enough bungles and boots to allow the blacks to make two of the three runs they got in that inning, the other one resulting from hits. The black boys covered themselves with glory in their fielding, for they grabbed everything that went their way, and put up a much better game than when they were against the Los Angeles team.... The Stars made their only run in the seventh on Moore's single to right, a passed ball, and Tonneson's drive to right field."

On January 9, the Occidentals battled McCormicks Shamrocks to a 1-1, twelve inning draw. A pitcher named Smith hurled for the Occidentals. The McCormicks roster included former Cincinnati Reds pitcher Bill Tozer. Bill Pettus was the leading hitter for Occidentals with two hits in five at-bats.

The next day, the Occidentals played another twelve inning 0-0 tie, this time against the All-Stars, a professional aggregation that included major leaguers Truck Eagan, Eli Cates, Ed McDonough, and Tom Seaton. Elmer Rieger of the Stars tossed a five-hitter, with five strikeouts, while his opponent, named Harrison, threw a six-hitter, and fanned nine.

On January 30, the Occidentals had the misfortune of meeting the great Walter Johnson in Santa Ana, and "The Big Train" exacted a measure of revenge for his earlier defeat at the hands of the L.A. Giants two years previous. Johnson blanked the Occidentals 3–0 with a two-hitter. He fanned 15 batters and walked two.

Over the years, Walter Johnson pitched at least five games against black teams, winning two and losing three, but one of his losses was a 2–0 shutout at the hands of "Gunboat" Thompson of the Lincoln Stars, while pitching for the New York Fire Department team, and probably shouldn't be counted. Still, he always had a battle on his hands when he faced the Negro leaguers.

He lost to Frank "The Red Ant" Wickware and the Schenectady Mohawk Giants 1–0 in a much publicized battle, and beat Dan McClellan of the New York Lincoln Giants 5–3.

Late in the 1909-10 season, a newly organized black team called Trilbys entered the fray. They were greatly overmatched. In fact, they were shut out in all three games reported. Cyclone Joe Williams was a member of the team, playing first base and pitching. He was the victim of one of the shutouts, going down to defeat before (Bill?) Clark of the McCormicks, 2–0. Cyclone Joe actually outpitched his opponent, striking out five, walking two, and allowing only four hits, but poor defensive support saddled him with the loss. As a batter, Cyclone Joe was less impressive, going 0 for 8.

1909-10 Independent Team Records

	Wins	Losses	Ties
Occidental	4	1	2
Trilbys	0	3	0
L.A. Giants	0	1	0
McCormicks	2	0	1
All-Stars	0	1	1
Japanese A-S	0	1	0

Miscellaneous Batting Statistics 1909-1910 Season

Name	Team	Pos	G	AB	H	D	T	HR	BA
Hawkins, Lem	Occidental	3B	4	17	1	1	0	0	.059
Langford, Ad	Occid, Trilbys	LF	4	17	4	1	0	0	.235
Pettus, Bill	Occidental	1B	3	14	5	0	0	0	.357
Pryor, Wes	L.A. Giants	CF	1	4	1	0	0	0	.250
White, Sol	L.A. Giants	3B	1	1	1	0	0	0	1.000
Williams, Joe	Trilbys	1B	3	8	0	0	0	0	.000
Eagan, Truck	A.S., Holtville	2B	1	4	1	0	0	0	.250

Miscellaneous Pitching Statistics 1909-1910

Name	Team	G	CG	W	L	IP	SO	BB	SH
Williams, Joe	Trilbys	1	1	0	1	9	5	4	0
Langford, Ad	Trilbys	1	1	0	1	8	12	2	0
Mooney,	Trilbys	1	1	0	1	12	9	3	0
Harrison,	Occidental	2	2	1	0	21	21	1	0
Rieger, Elmer	A.S., Salt Lk	4	4	2	1	39	—	—	2
Tozer, Bill	McCormicks	1	1	1	0	9	4	0	1

1909-10 Imperial Valley League
Standings—Incomplete

	Wins	Losses	Ties
El Centro	11	5	0
Imperial	9	6	1
Holtville	8	7	1
Yuma	6	7	0
Brawley	3	11	0

Miscellaneous Batting Statistics 1909-10 Season

Name	Team	Pos	G	AB	H	D	T	HR	BA
McCoy, Bernie	Santa Barbara		1	3	1	0	1	0	.333
Whaling, Bert	Salt Lake	C	1	4	1	0	0	0	.250
Flick, Elmer	San Ber'dino	SS	1	4	1	0	0	0	.250
Stovall, George	All-Stars	1B	1	3	1	0	1	0	.333
Brashear, Kitty	El Centro		1	3	1	0	0	1	.333
Easterly, Ted	El Centro	CF	1	4	2	0	0	2	.500

Led league with an estimated 4-5 home runs during 24 game schedule

| McKune, Terry | El Centro | SS | Batted about .400 with 4-5 home runs |
| Brown, Drummond | El Centro | C | Batted over .400 |

Miscellaneous Pitching Statistics 1909-10 Season

Name	Team	G	CG	W	L	IP	SO	BB	SH
Wiggs, Jim	Holtville	3	3	1	2	27	—	—	0
Vance, Dazzy	El Centro	1	1	1	0	9	—	—	0
Jones, Oscar	Imperial	1	1	1	0	9	—	—	0
Scott, Death Valley	Imperial	2	2	4 (est.)	2	17	—	—	0

The 1910-11 Season

The time was ripe for a black team to integrate the California Winter League, and the legendary Rube Foster was the man who did it. He brought an entire eastern black team to the west coast, to play in the league. Foster was a devoted baseball man, an outstanding pitcher in his own right, an astute field manager, a successful club owner, and eventually the founder and President of the Negro National League, the first organized black professional baseball league in the United States. He was also a consummate promoter, entrepreneur, and businessman. In 1910, he was part owner of the Chicago Leland Giants, and he was always on the lookout for opportunities to keep his team active during the winter months.

Prior to 1910, the California Winter League was essentially a low level minor league of little interest outside the local area. But all that changed when Foster made the trek across the country with his Leland Giants team. Rube had what he considered to be the greatest team ever assembled, with future Hall of Famer "Cyclone Joe" Williams, Chappie Johnson, Frank Wickware, Pete Booker, Zack Pettus, Mike Moore, Ad Langford, Walter Ball, and Bill Gatewood. Unfortunately, three of the Giants' stars, John Henry Lloyd, Bruce Petway, and Pete Hill, decided to play winter ball in Cuba, leaving the California contingent less than unbeatable.

The league consisted of four teams; the Giants, the San Diego Griefers, Doyles, and McCormicks Shamrocks. Many Pacific Coast League players participated in the league, as well as a few major leaguers. Some of the better known names were Neal Ball, an infielder with the Cleveland Indians and

New York Yankees from 1907 through 1913, Bill Tozer, who pitched for Cincinnati in 1908, Elmer Rieger, who pitched for the St. Louis Cardinals in 1910, and Tom Downey, a six year major leaguer (1909–1915). PCL players included Flame Delhi, who went 27–23 in 446 innings for Los Angeles in 1911, Bill Tozer (31–12 for Los Angeles in 1909), Tom Seaton (24–16 for Portland in 1911), Harry Stewart (19–12 for Vernon in 1911), Kid Mohler, an 11 year veteran of the PCL, and slugger Walt "Rosy" Carlisle, an eight year veteran of the PCL who led the league in home runs (14) in 1907, in doubles (49) and triples (10) in 1911, and in triples in 1912 and 1915 (17 and 14 respectively).

The fans were treated to an exciting pennant race, with the Lelands, McCormicks, and San Diego battling for the title. Only the Doyles were not competitive. Although the Doyles had some outstanding players, their pitching rotation was not as stable as the other teams. And, in the California Winter League, with games played only on weekends, it was imperative to have two reliable starting pitchers. The Lelands had four—Joe Williams, Bill Gatewood, Mooney, and Frank Wickware. San Diego had Harry Stewart, Alex Carson (29–20 for Portland in 1909), and Jack Killilay (15–4 for Oakland in 1912). The McCormicks had Bill Tozer, Tom Seaton, and Lafferty. San Diego used at least seven starting pitchers and, in the field, only Mohler, Warrender, Tennant, and McClelland played regularly.

The highlight of the season was the January 7 game between the Leland Giants and the Doyles. Cyclone Joe Williams, perhaps the greatest pitcher in the annals of

Cyclone Joe Williams, who was part Indian, may have been the greatest pitcher in Negro league history. (John B. Holway)

Negro league baseball, was magnificent, according to the *Los Angeles Times*. "Big, long-legged Williams, pitcher for the colored Giants team, broke all Coast records, and certainly all out of big league ball, when he fanned nineteen batsmen in the game played with the Doyle club at the Vernon grounds yesterday afternoon.... In the second and third innings, Williams struck the side out and, in the fifth, he fanned the first man to bat, walked the next one, and then struck out the next two."

According to the *Times*, Cyclone Joe kept the batters off balance all day with a blazing fast ball and an effective "floater." He also teased the hitters with pitches just out of the strike zone. When the dust had settled, Williams had tossed a three-hit shutout, and won going away, 7–0. The Giants scored their first run off Miller in the sixth inning when Mike Moore blasted a triple to center field and scored on a sacrifice fly by Chappie Johnson. They pushed over three more runs in the seventh on a walk, two doubles and a single, and added a run in the eighth and another in the ninth.

Williams' opponent, Frank Miller, had compiled a record of 20–15 with San Francisco in the Pacific Coast League in 1910, but he couldn't keep the Giants under control. He matched the big Leland right-hander pitch for pitch for five innings, but Foster's boys tattoed him for seven runs, eleven base hits and four bases on balls over the last four innings.

Giants

Name	Pos	AB	H
Pettus, Bill	1B	5	2
Winston, Bobby	LF	4	1
Moore, Mike	CF	4	2
Johnson, Chappie	C	3	1
Ball, Walter	RF	4	0
Wright, George	SS	4	2
Lane, Isaac	3B	4	0
Harris, Nate	2B	4	1
Williams, Joe	P	4	2
Totals		36	11

Doyles

Name	Pos	AB	H
Warrender,	LF	4	0
Graham, Peaches	3B	3	0
Burrell,	2B	3	0
Tennant, Tom	1B	3	2
Pitman,	CF	4	1
McClelland,	SS	3	0
Rieger, Elmer	RF	3	0
Hasty,	C	3	0
Miller, Frank	P	3	0
		29	3

Leland Giants   0 0 0   0 0 1   3 1 2–7–11–0
Doyles   0 0 0   0 0 0   0 0 0–0–3–0

Three base hits: Moore
Two base hits: Pettus, Winston, Wright

	IP	SO	BB
Williams, Joe	9	19	5
Miller, Frank	9	5	4

The games uncovered in this study indicated that the McCormicks had the best record. However, an independent day-by-day study of the 1910-11 CWL season by other SABR researchers determined that San Diego won the pennant. They also noted that the Leland Giants handled themselves admirably on the west coast, in what was probably equivalent to a lower level minor league. Playing out of Maier Park, the home of the PCL Vernon Tigers, the Lelands fought the San Diego team to a virtual standstill in the pennant race, eventually finishing in second place. In a postseason series against the McCormicks, the Giants won the opener, then dropped the last four games in the best of seven series.

Incomplete statistics of the 1910-11 winter league season credit Walt "Rosy" Carlisle of the McCormicks with the highest batting average, .412. He was also high in doubles with five. Tom Seaton, also of the McCormicks, was the league's top pitcher, with a record of 5–0. Cyclone Joe Williams finished with a record of 4–1, and led the league in games pitched (7), complete games (6), innings pitched (60), strikeouts (78), bases on balls (16), and shutouts (2).

After the season ended, Foster supplemented his revenues by playing exhibition games with Pacific Coast League teams and local amateur and semi-pro teams throughout Northern California, Washington, Oregon, and into Canada at Vancouver and Victoria, before heading back to Chicago for the summer season. John Holway noted, "They (the Giants) traveled in style in private Pullman cars hooked onto the regular trains."

1910-11 California Winter League Standings—Incomplete

	Wins	Losses	Ties
San Diego	7	4	0
Leland Giants	10	7	2
McCormicks	12	5	1
Doyles	2	14	1

Leland Giants Batting Statistics 1910-11 Season

Name	Pos	G	AB	H	D	T	HR	BA
Winston, Bobby	LF	15*	55*	19*	5*	0	0	.345
Wright, George	SS	14	47	10	2	1	1*	.213
Pettus, Bill	1B	14	54	13	4	2*	1*	.241
Moore, Mike	CF	13	37	11	5*	2*	1*	.297
Ball, Walter	RF	12	43	10	1	1	1*	.233
Lane, Isaac	3B	14	51	5	0	0	0	.098
Harris, Nathan	2B	10	35	7	1	0	0	.200
Johnson, Chappie	C	11	32	4	0	0	0	.125
Williams, Joe	P	6	21	8	2	0	0	.381

Leland Giants Pitching statistics 1910-11 Season

Name	G	CG	W	L	IP	SO	BB	SH
Williams, Joe	7*	6*	4	1	60*	78*	16*	2*
Gatewood, Bill	5	5	2	3	44	20	5	1
Mooney,	4	4	2	1	29	12	6	1
Wickware, Frank	4	3	2	2	30	27	7	1

McCormicks Batting Statistics 1910-11 Season

Name	Pos	G	AB	H	D	T	HR	BA
Carlisle, Walt	CF	10	34	14	5*	1	0	.412*
Breen, R.	3B	7	27	7	1	0	0	.259
Bernard, Curt	RF	10	37	14	2	0	0	.378
Daley, Tom	LF	4	15	3	0	0	0	.200
Howard, Ivan	2B	4	17	5	1	0	0	.294
Lindsay, Bill	SS	14	51	16	2	0	1*	.214
Manes,	1B	16	50	6	2	0	0	.120
La Longe, Mick	C	12	37	4	0	1	0	.108
McKay, Bernie	2B	9	30	9	0	0	0	.300
Seaton, Tom	P-RF	11	36	12	2	0	0	.333

McCormicks Pitching Statistics 1910-11 Season

Name	G	CG	W	L	IP	SO	BB	SH
Seaton, Tom	5	5	5*	0	43	39	8	0
Tozer, Bill	5	5	3	2	35	18	8	0
Lafferty,	5	5	3	2	45	31	10	0

Doyles Batting Statistics 1910-11 Season

Name	Pos	G	AB	H	D	T	HR	BA
Ellis, Rube	CF	5	21	3	0	0	0	.143
Mohler, Kid	2B	5	17	4	0	0	0	.235
Warrender,	LF	11	44	6	1	1	0	.136
Tennant, Tom	1B	11	41	15	1	1	0	.366
Burrell, L.	3B	8	26	5	1	1	0	.192
McClelland,	SS	11	29	1	0	1	0	.034
Hasty,	C	12	32	7	1	0	0	.067
Pfirrman,	C	5	15	1	0	0	0	.067

Doyles Pitching Statistics 1910-11 Season

Name	G	CG	W	L	IP	SO	BB	SH
Tonneson, T.	2	2	0	2	13	5	4	0
Rieger, Elmer	4	2	0	2	19	14	2	0
Thorsen, E.	4	2	1	3	27	15	3	0
Delhi, Flame	2	2	0	2	20	15	5	0
Jones, Oscar	2	2	1	1	17	16	3	0

San Diego Batting Statistics 1910-11 Season

Name	Pos	G	AB	H	D	T	HR	BA
Ball, Neal	2B	3	9	3	1	0	1*	.333
Downey, Tom	3B	1	5	2	1	0	0	.400
Autry, Chick	1B	1	4	1	0	0	0	.250
McArdle, H.	SS	1	3	1	0	0	0	.333
Hosp, Franz	CF	1	4	1	0	0	0	.250
Myers,	RF	1	4	0	0	0	0	.000
Clynes,	LF	1	3	0	0	0	0	.000
Grindle,	C	1	4	1	0	0	0	.250

San Diego Pitching Statistics 1910-11 Season

Name	G	CG	W	L	IP	SO	BB	SH
Stewart, Harry	4	4	4	0	36	—	—	1
Carson, Alex	2	2	0	2	18	—	—	0
Killilay, Jack	3	2	1	2	26	—	—	0

The 1911-12 Season

The inclusion of a strong Negro league team in the CWL in 1910 had a profound effect on the fortunes of the league. Attendance increased significantly. Revenues followed suit. And the reputation of the league spread up and down the west coast. Unfortunately, Rube Foster grasped other opportunities the following year, and did not return to Los Angeles. He was busy organizing his own professional team, the Chicago American Giants. Some of his players, like Pettus, Lloyd, Hill, and Petway, spent the winter in Cuba, while Wickware, Spec Webster, and Wes Pryor, sunned themselves in Palm Beach, Florida, working at the prestigious Breakers and Royal Poinciana Hotels, and playing baseball for the hotel teams. Foster spent at least part of the winter in Cuba.

With the departure of the Negro leaguers, the 1911-12 California Winter League reverted back to a semi-pro league. Not only was there no strong black representation, but the white teams were mostly semi-pro players and lower minor league players. Some of the more recognizable names in the league included Boston Brave shortstop Al Bridwell, Cleveland Indian second baseman George Stovall, Bert Whaling, and Kitty Brashear.

The winter league included the following teams:

> Harris & Frank
> San Bernardino
> Henry & Cornett
> Oxnard
> Fillmore
> Ventura
> Jeffries
> Pomona

The only box score located was a 2–0 shutout by Jeffries over Pomona. Sam Ferraris tossed a four hitter for Jeffries, with one strikeout and one base on balls. The Pomona pitcher, Pitts, was victimized by two errors that permitted both runs to score.

In addition to the recognized California Winter League, there were several other leagues in operation in Southern California, including one in the Los Angeles area with the following teams:

> Los Angeles Colored Giants
> McCormicks Shamrocks
> Santa Monica Beach Combers
> Maier Joy Riders

No team rosters were published except for the McCormick team which consisted of both semi-pro players and lower level minor leaguers. The Colored Giants were semi-pros from Los Angeles Santa. Monica had at least one solid pitcher, a 19-year-old local boy named Pete Schneider. The 6'1" 173 pound right-handed pitcher was two years away from pitching for the Cincinnati Reds. Schneider's major league career lasted six years, during which time he accumulated a 59–86 record, including a 20–19 slate in 1917. In the only game reported in the newspapers, Schneider pitched a five-hitter against Maier, fanning eight men, en route to a 6–1 victory at Maier Park.

The 1912-13 Season

After spending the 1911-12 season in Cuba, Rube Foster returned to California with another competitive Negro league lineup. This time the Chicago American Giants had Pete Hill and Bruce Petway in tow, as well as second base sensation Bill Monroe, Candy Jim Taylor, Mike Moore, Frank Duncan, and Bill Lindsay. The major leagues were also well represented with such players as Rube Ellis of the St. Louis Cardinals, Ivy Olson of the Cleveland Indians, Chief Meyers, Fred Snodgrass, Fred Merkle, and Tillie Shafer of the New York Giants, Tilly Walker of the Washington Senators, Charles "Sea Lion" Hall of the Boston Red Sox, future Hall of Fame shortstop Dave "Beauty" Bancroft, and Earl Hamilton of the St. Louis Browns. It was the strongest white professional group yet to play in the winter league. Hamilton won 116 major league games over an 14 year career, while Tilly Walker batted .281 with 118 home runs in 13 years, Ivy Olson enjoyed a 14 year career in the majors, Dave Bancroft played in the Big Show for 16 years with 2,004 base hits, and Chief Meyers was an outstanding major league catcher for nine years. Fred Snodgrass also played in the major leagues for nine years, with a batting average of .275, while Fred Merkle batted .273 with 1,580 base hits over a memorable 16 year career.

According to Lyle K. Wilson, in his article in *The National Pastime*, "Starting in November 1912, CAG (Chicago American Giants) played in the California Winter League. The other three teams were white teams made up of Pacific Coast League and major league players. On opening day, there was a parade complete with an African American band, and speeches by several local mayors. Foster's opening day lineup was:

Jess Barbour	RF
Pete Hill	CF
Frank Duncan	LF
Candy Jim Taylor	3B
Bill Pierce	1B
Bill Monroe	2B
Bruce Petway	C
Pat Dougherty	P
Fred Hutchinson	SS

One of the highlights of the opener was a throw by Petway, picking off a runner who had taken a lead at second. For a long time, the runner refused to believe that he was out, maintaining that no catcher could throw him out with only a four foot lead.

In the third game that winter, Pierce had two unassisted double plays and a two-run home run. Bill Lindsay, known as the "Kansas Cyclone," tossed a four hitter, striking out ten and walking none, en route to a 3–1 victory over the McCormick Shamrocks.

On November 8, the Giants faced off against the tough Tufts-Lyons squad in a crucial early season series. Prior to the start of the opener, Tufts-Lyons manager Walter Nagle was quoted in the *Los Angeles Times* as saying, "The addition of (Johnny) Kane gives us the strongest club in the league, according to my way of thinking.... Mr. Nagles remarks were reported to Rube Foster. Foster's only reply was a scornful grunt."

On Sunday, November 11, Bill Lindsay faced Tufts-Lyons in the rubber match of the three game series. Pitching against Roy Hitt, former Cincinnati Reds pitcher, the hard throwing right-hander of the Giants blanked the Tufts-Lyons team, 6–0 on a four-hitter. In the process, he issued just one base on balls and sent eight batters back to the bench dragging their bats behind them. Ivy Olson was the only batter to solve Lindsay's deliveries, pounding out a single and a double in four trips to the plate. One dejected Tufts-Lyons fan noted, "If these brunnette babies had been on (John) McGraw's staff, the world's championship would be reposing in Gotham instead of in Boston." The *L.A. Times* commented, "While I am neither ready to agree or disagree with the gentleman from New York, I am willing to doff my dicer to Messrs. Lindsay and Petway as one of the best batteries ever seen in this strip of sunshine.... Wow! How this black boy can pitch."

Bill Lindsay was one of the tragic figures in Negro league history. The Kansas City native broke in with the American Giants in 1910, and quickly became one of the top pitchers in the Negro leagues. According to Jim Riley, Lindsay was the ace of Rube Foster's staff in 1912. Two years later, as the Giants were preparing to play the Brooklyn Royal Giants for the World Championship, "The Kansas Cyclone" suddenly fell ill, and died within days. The date was September 1, 1914.

Rube Foster, months removed from pitching under game conditions, attempted to take some of the load off his embattled pitching staff, by taking the mound against the McCormick Shamrocks on November 24, but he was routed in two innings. According to the *Times*, "Rube Foster, regarded in his prime as the greatest colored pitcher that ever lived, 'got his' yesterday. Rube started in to pitch for the Giants in the final game of the series. At the end of the second inning he retired, fully convinced that a pitcher must work more than once a month in order to deliver.... The McCormicks won, 9 to 6, and two-thirds of their runs were accumulated during Rube's stormy sojourn."

In one of the more exciting games of the season, played on November 30, the Giants trailed the Tufts-Lyons team 3–2 as they came to bat for the last time. In a dramatic bottom-of-the-ninth climax, Frank Duncan slammed a game winning, two run home run. The *Chicago Defender* was ecstatic. "Never before in the history of baseball, have a colored team accomplished what the American Giants under the leadership and management of Andrew (Rube) Foster, have accomplished on their present trip on the Pacific coast. They have won the highest praise from the fans and citizens everywhere they have played; not only for their high-class baseball playing, but also for their gentlemanly conduct on the ball field...."

The Giants indeed were tough to beat on their home grounds, but a review of the *San Diego Union* game coverage indicates they were not a good road team. The San Diego Bears posted a strong 5–1 home record to go with their 2–3 road mark, to give them an overall 7–4 record in games recovered. And according to the *Union* on December 9, "Bullfrog Foster they called him. After seven and a half innings, with the score 3–1 for the Gold Dust team, Rube Foster weakened for a moment, lost the game to the Bears, lost the series, and the place at the top of the Winter League column."

The 1912-13 winter league season provided Southern California fans with the strongest professional baseball league ever seen in those parts. The Giants had a team that could hold its own with any AAA contingent in the country. The three white teams were also of AAA caliber, with many major leaguers on every team.

During the teens, the league schedule generally ran from early November until early January, a period of about eight to ten weeks, giving each team about 20 playing dates. Over the years, the schedule was lengthened until it stretched from mid-October into mid-February, with a total of about 42 games played per team. The average attendance was between 1,000 and 2,000 people. Some games attracted as few as a two or three hundred fans, especially if the weather was threatening, while key games might draw up to 3,500 fans. The 1912-13 season was hotly contested from start to finish, with the Bears winning the championship by the narrowest of margins. The *Chicago Defender* claimed the American Giants won the 1912-13 California Winter League championship, but the recovered box scores do not substantiate that claim.

1912-13 California Winter League
Standings — incomplete

	Wins	Losses
San Diego Bears	7	4
Tufts-Lyons	6	6
Chicago American Giants	6	7
McCormicks	2	4

Chicago American Giants Batting Statistics 1912-13

Name	Pos	G	AB	H	D	T	HR	BA
Petway, Bruce	C	8	27	8	1	0	0	.296
Duncan, Frank	LF	10	39*	8	2	1*	1	.205
Pierce, Bill	1B	11*	35	10	2	0	2*	.286
Barbour, Jess	RF	8	30	9	1	0	0	.300
Hill, Pete	CF	10	34	8	5*	0	0	.235

Taylor, C.J.	3B	8	27	11*	2	1*	0	.407
Monroe, Bill	2B	10	35	11*	1	0	2*	.314
Hutchinson, Fred	SS	7	22	5	1	0	0	.227

Chicago American Giants Pitching Statistics 1912-13

Name	G	CG	W	L	IP	SO	BB	SH
Lindsay, Bill	6*	5*	3*	2	50*	45*	15	1*
Johnson, Dicta	4	3	3*	0	29	16	5	0
Gatewood, Bill	3	0	0	1	9	5	5	0
Dougherty, Pat	2	0	0	0	9	8	3	0
Foster, Rube	2	0	0	2	10	2	7	0

Miscellaneous Teams Batting Statistics 1912-13

Name	Team	Pos	G	AB	H	D	T	HR	BA
Chadbourne, Chet	McCormicks	LF	2	9	3	1	0	0	.333
Thomas, Pinch	McCormicks	C	6	21	4	0	0	0	.190
Killefer, Red	McCormicks	SS	4	13	1	0	0	0	.077
Whaling, Bert	McCormicks	RF	2	7	0	0	0	0	.000
Meyers, Chief	San Diego	C	6	23	9	2	0	1	.391
Downey, Tom	San Diego	SS	7	23	10	4	0	1	.435*
Bennett, Pug	San Diego	2B	7	22	4	0	1*	0	.182
Roche, Jack	San Diego	C	4	11	4	2	0	0	.364
Olson, Ivy	Tufts-Lyons	2B	5	20	6	0	0	0	.300
Bancroft, Dave	Tufts-Lyons	SS	5	18	8	4	0	0	.444
Ellis, Rube	Tufts-Lyons	RF	2	8	2	0	0	0	.250
Berger, Joe	Tufts-Lyons	1B	3	11	5	0	0	2	.455

Miscellaneous Teams Pitching Statistics 1912-13

Name	Team	G	CG	W	L	IP	SO	BB	SH
Hamilton, Earl	San Diego	5	3	3*	2	36	—	—	1
Higginbotham, Irv	San Diego	4	2	2	0	27	20	5	0
Driscoll,	San Diego	4	4	2	2	35	20	6	0
Rieger, Elmer	McCormicks	1	1	0	1	9	4	1	0
Chech, Charlie	McCormicks	2	2	0	2	17	2	5	0
Slagle, Walt	McCormicks	1	1	1	0	9	3	0	0
Castleman, Roy	McCormicks	1	1	0	1	9	4	0	0
Leverenz, Walter	Tufts-Lyons	1	1	1	0	9	8	3	0
Hitt, Roy	Tufts-Lyons	1	1	0	1	8	4	3	0

The 1913-14 Season

The details of the 1913-14 winter league season are sketchy. The newspapers provided no box scores of the games, making it difficult to determine who participated in the league. The Chicago American Giants may have played in the league because Lyle K. Wilson noted that they played exhibition games on the coast in the spring, but the Giants were never mentioned in the local newspapers. One game did mention the Los Angeles Colored Giants, but the names of the battery were not familiar.

The *Los Angeles Times* reported on games involving at least fifteen teams during the winter, but it didn't identify a specific winter league. Since there were no box scores, nor any detailed game descriptions, it was not possible to determine complete batting or pitching statistics, or even a league champion.

The *Los Angeles Times* reported on two interesting league games. "The winter

league season of baseball opened here (Long Beach) today with a flattering crowd for the initial game, and the fans were given a good exhibition of major league ball. The opposing teams were Long Beach and Stockton, composed of players from the Coast, Pacific, and American Leagues. Schneider and Chech for Long Beach and Klipper, Tozer, and Hoffman for Stockton, were the opposing batteries." Pete Schneider tossed a six-hitter as Long Beach prevailed 5–1. McMillan pounded out three hits for the winners.

The December 8 issue of the *Times* included an article headlined "Meusel Goes Wild With The Willow." It went on to say, "Long Beach met its first defeat in the winter league today, falling victims to the speedy Hoegee team with Concannon pitching.... The hitting features of the day were those of Meusel (Irish), who secured two doubles, a home run and a single in five times at bat."

Team records from the available line scores follow.

1913-14 California Winter League
Standings—Incomplete

	Wins	Losses	Ties
Phoenix	2	0	0
Urbita Stars (San Bernardino)	4	1	0
Oxnard	3	1	0
Santa Barbara	4	3	2
Tufts-Lyons	2	2	2
Long Beach	1	1	0
Los Angeles Hoegees	2	3	0
Los Angeles Colored Giants	0	1	0
Boynton Beavers	0	1	0
Santa Maria	0	1	0
Stockton	0	1	0
Whittier	0	1	0
Newton All-Stars	0	1	0
L.A. Brewery	0	1	0
Perris	0	1	0

Miscellaneous Batting Statistics 1913-14

Name	Team	Pos	G	AB	H	D	T	HR	BA
Meusel, Irish	Los Angeles	LF	1	5	4	2	0	1	.800
McMillan,	Long Beach		1	4	3	0	0	0	.750
Litschi, Louis	Oxnard	RF	1	3	1	0	0	1	.333
Cook,	Phoenix	C	1	3	1	0	0	1	.333

Miscellaneous Pitching Statistics 1913-14

Name	Team	G	CG	W	L	IP	SO	BB	SH
Schneider, Pete	Long Beach	1	1	1	0	9	—	—	0
Concannon,	Los Angeles	2	2	1	1	18	—	—	0
Chech, Charlie	L.A., Oxnard	3	3	2	1	27	—	—	0
Brown, Curly	Santa Barbara	8	8	4	2	80	—	—	2

Opposite: Chet Chadbourne played in his first winter league game in 1912, and in his last in 1924, when he was 40 years old. (George E. Outland)

1913-14 Imperial Valley League
Standings—Incomplete

	Wins	Losses
Holtville	1	0
Imperial	1	1
Calexico	0	1

Miscellaneous Batting Statistics 1913-14

Name	Team	G	AB	H	D	T	HR	BA
Ryan, Jack	Imperial	2	6	2	0	0	2	.333
Edmonds,	Imperial	1	3	1	0	0	1	.333

Miscellaneous Pitching Statistics 1913-14

Name	Team	G	CG	W	L	IP	SO	BB	SH
Ryan, Jack	Imperial	2	2	1	1	18	—	—	0

In March 1914, the Giants made their usual barnstorming tour through the northwest, prior to returning east for their hectic summer schedule. On their way north, they stopped in the bay area to play exhibition games against both San Francisco and Oakland. They were disappointed. On April 11, 1914, the *Defender*'s headlines blared the disturbing news that Allen T. Baum, President of the Pacific Coast League insisted that the color line be drawn, and that PCL teams should not play games against black teams, or allow black teams to use their parks. According to the *Chicago Defender*, "Oakland and San Francisco heartily agreed and refused to play. Mgr. Walter McCredie of the champion Portland team thought otherwise and spoke so. Not only did he do this but he played the Giants." Rube Foster took his crew to Portland, Oregon, where they played a series against the PCL Beavers. Rube Foster's boys won four of the five games played that year, including a nifty no-hitter by "Cyclone Joe" Williams. Over a four year period however, from 1913 to 1916, McCredie's Beavers got even. They won ten of the 19 games played, losing eight, and tying one.

The following year, McCredie ran into an racial buzzsaw when he tried to sign a Hawaiian player to a Portland contract. He was finally forced to withdraw his offer because, as he said, "His skin's too dark.... I don't think the color of the skin ought to be a barrier in baseball. They have Jim Thorpe, an Indian, in the big leagues; there are Cubans on the rosters of the various clubs. Here in the Pacific Coast league we have a Mexican and a Hawaiian, and yet the laws of baseball bar Afro-Americans from organized diamonds. If I had my say, the Afro-Americans would be welcomed inside the fold. I would like to have two such ballplayers as Petway and Lloyd of the Chicago Colored Giants, who play out here every spring. I think Lloyd is another 'Hans' Wagner around shortstop, and Petway is one of the greatest catchers in the world."

Unfortunately, people like McCredie were in the minority in organized baseball. It appears that, by 1917, the ban against blacks playing in PCL parks had reached the Los Angeles area. In 1916-17, the L.A. White Sox, the black entry in the California Winter League, played its games on "the Vernon diamond," probably Maier Park, home of the PCL Vernon team. But by 1917, there is no record of black teams playing in Maier Park, or any other PCL park. In fact, it is questionable whether or not any black teams even participated in the winter league between 1917 and 1919. By 1920 however, the California Winter League was once again integrated, as a local businessman name Doc Anderson made his park available for league play. Winter League games were not played in a PCL park again until 1930, when the Philadelphia Royal Giants played in Wrigley Field, home of the PCL's Los Angeles Angels.

Another humiliating situation encountered by the Giants during their 1914 tour of the northwest, emphasized the delicate nature of the racial situation during this period. The *Chicago Defender* reported "On Wednesday, the first of April, they (Chicago American Giants) arrived in Medford, Ore., and were turned down by every hotel and restaurant in town. They threatened to strike. Through a misunderstanding no arrangements were made for feeding the men.... (Finally) the proprietor (of a Japanese restaurant) secured cheese and crackers and these comprised the Giants breakfast."

The 1914-15 Season

The 1914-15 winter season in Southern California was a hodgepodge of baseball. Games were played all over the Los Angeles area, but there was apparently no organized winter league. The season seemed to consist of dozens of independent games involving numerous semi-professional baseball teams. Not all the players were semi-pros however. There were many high level minor league players gracing the rosters of many teams, including several future major leaguers such as Howard Ehmke, Jack Ryan, Charlie Chech, and Clarence Smith but, for the most part, the players were less talented.

The most interesting league on the west coast was the Imperial Valley League, a four team league centered around El Centro, 114 miles east of San Diego, on the Mexican border. The member teams were El Centro, Brawley, Calexico, and Imperial. It was not an integrated league, but it did attract some very talented white players.

El Centro, the eventual pennant winner, had a powerful pitching staff headed by Erv Kantlehner of the Pittsburgh Pirates, Charlie Chech formerly of the Cincinnati Reds, and Slim Love of the Washington Senators and New York Yankees. Since games were played only on weekends, a team only needed to have two or three starting pitchers to survive. Other members of the team included major leaguers Dave Bancroft, Fred McMullin, Johnny Bassler, Irish Meusel, and Walt Alexander.

The Calexico team had "Death Valley" Jim Scott who won 20 games for the Chicago White Sox in 1913, Claude "Lefty" Williams, a 23 game winner for the infamous Chicago Black Sox, and Roy Hitt, who won 32 games for San Francisco in the Pacific Coast League in 1906, on the mound. Other familiar names were Walter Schmidt of the Pittsburgh Pirates, Joe Wilhoit of the Boston Braves, Tom Downey of the Chicago Cubs and Buffalo Buffeds, and Eddie Foster of the Washington Senators.

Imperial was represented on the mound by two workhorses, Jack Ryan, formerly of the Brooklyn Dodgers who won 24 games with a league leading 1.84 ERA for Los Angeles in the PCL in 1914, and Skeeter Fanning, a 24 game with San Francisco. Ryan would go on to win 26 games for L.A. in 1915 and 29 games in 1916. Roy Corhan, who played for the White Sox and Cardinals, held down shortstop, Red Downs of the Cubs was on second, Gus Hetling, formerly of the Detroit Tigers was on third, and Harl Maggert of the Boston Braves, and Roxy Middleton and Tom Kaylor both of the Oakland Oaks, patrolled the outfield.

Brawley had a mound staff composed of R. Willis of the PCL, Jeff Pfeffer of the Brooklyn Dodgers, "King" Cole of the New York Yankees, and a pitcher named Baeder or Bader. George Cutshaw of the Brooklyn Dodgers was at second base, Dolly Stark,

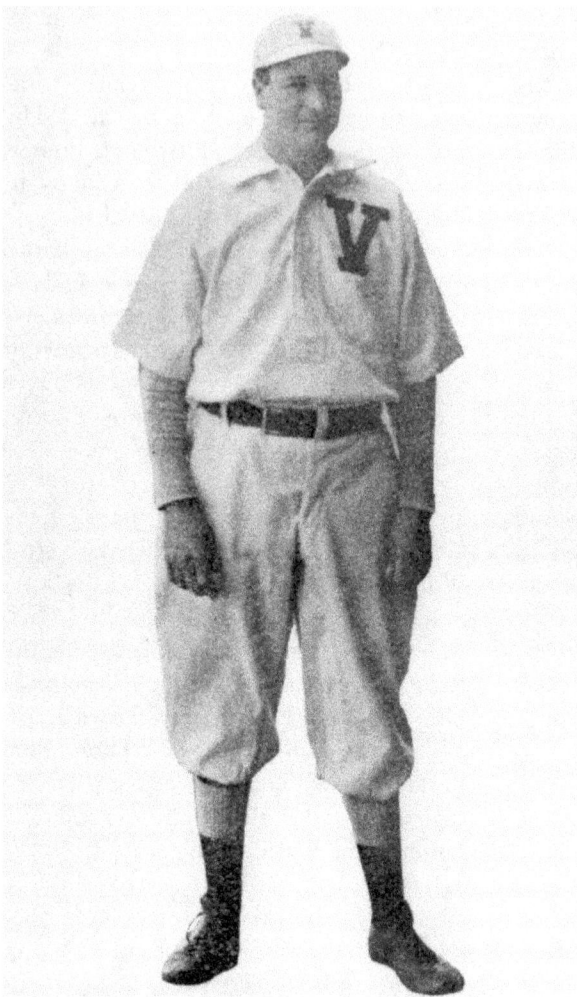

Roy Hitt, who went 25–18 for Venice in the PCL, posted a 3–0 record for Calexico in the 1914–15 Valley League. (Dick Dobbins)

formerly of Brooklyn held down the shortstop position, Gus Getz of Brooklyn was at third, and Gus Gleichman of Vernon's PCL team, was on first. Bert Daniels of the Cincinnati Reds, Beals Becker of the Philadelphia Phillies, and Charlie Graham formerly of the PCL, were in the outfield, and McCarthy was the catcher.

The league was a strong high level minor league overall, probably close to a AA or AAA league, by today's classifications. The season, which ran from the first of November to the end of February, saw a close race between three of the teams, with Brawley out of the running from day one. In the first reported game, Calexico defeated Imperial 5–4. Roy Hitt, who relieved Gregg on the mound in the seventh, drove in the winning run in the ninth.

Imperial took it on the nose again two days later, when the strong El Centro team walloped them 7–2. Erv Kantlehner outpitched Skeeter Fanning, and Irish Meusel homered to lead El Centro's eight hit attack. Imperial got revenge the following week. The *L.A. Times* reported, "Imperial defeated El Centro this afternoon in a game replete with sensational fielding and hitting. Hetling made a beautiful stop of Alexander's grounder in the fifth.... Jerry Downs put the ball over the right field fence in both the sixth and seventh innings." Fanning outdueled Slim Love to even his record at 1–1.

On November 26, the *Times* noted, "El Centro and Imperial crossed bats on the El Centro diamond today in what resulted in one of the best games of baseball ever witnessed in the Imperial Valley. Imperial won 1–0. Kantlehner and Ryan were both in splendid condition, allowing but three hits each.... Ryan scored the only run made in the game on a pass and Corhan's three-bagger to center."

As the season reached the halfway point, El Centro jumped into first place with a Christmas Day 4–1 victory over Brawley. El Centro scored their first run in the third on singles by Meusel, Baerwald, and Gardner. They added another run in the seventh and two in the eighth, to support Alvah Gipe's five-hitter.

El Centro continued to lengthen their lead week after week. On January 17, they claimed a 3–2 win over Brawley with an electrifying comeback. King Cole led Erv Kantlehner 2–0 after eight innings, on the strength of a brilliant four-hitter. But, in the ninth he faltered. Fred McMullin opened the fateful inning by grounding a single past third base. Dave Bancroft then slashed another single over the head of first baseman Gus Gleichman, putting runners on the corners. The *L.A. Times* reported, "Bassler went out, Cole to Gleichman. Meusel was next man up and caught onto a shoot which he clouted far into deep center. He beat the ball to the plate and (the) whole grandstand swarmed down upon his neck." Kantlehner, who had been married the previous night in San Jose, arrived at the park after an all night ride, and still scattered eleven hits for the win.

In the game that clinched the pennant for them, El Centro crushed Imperial 12–0. The *Times* covered the game. "Erwin Kantlehner, the king hurler of the Valley League, who has won eleven games out of thirteen, held Imperial to four hits and a blank score here today while his teammates piled up a dozen runs.... Dave Bancroft was the willow king, slapping out three doubles and two singles out of five times at bat. He made the circuit on each hit." Johnny Bassler, a true hitting machine, went four for five, while Irish Meusel had a double and a triple in four at-bats.

1914-15 Imperial Valley League Standings—Incomplete

	Wins	Losses
El Centro	14	8
Calexico	12	10
Imperial	10	11
Brawley	7	14

El Centro Batting Statistics 1914-15

Name	Pos.	G	AB	H	D	T	HR	BA
Bancroft, Dave	SS	11	43	14	4	0	1	.326
McMullin, Fred	3B	11	40	7	1	0	0	.175
Gardner, Rube	1B	11	38	10	0	0	0	.263
Meusel, Irish	LF	10	39	13	2	4*	2*	.333
Baerwald,	CF	11	42	10	4	2	0	.238
Flick, Elmer	2B	9	29	5	0	0	0	.172
Bassler, Johnny	RF	10	36	13	1	0	0	.361
Alexander, Walt	C	11	35	7	2	0	1	.200
Butler,	2B	2	6	1	0	0	0	.167

El Centro Pitching Statistics 1914-15

Name	G	CG	W	L	IP	SO	BB	SH
Kantlehner, Erv	14*	12*	11*	3	124*	105*	25	2*
Love, Slim	1	1	0	1	9	4	4	0
Chech, Charlie	1	1	0	1	9	—	—	0
Gipe, Alvah	2	1	1	0	10	—	—	0

Calexico Batting Statistics 1914-15

Name	Pos	G	AB	H	D	T	HR	BA
Wilhoit, Joe	LF	7	30	10	4	0	0	.333
Foster, Eddie	3B	6	21	5	2	0	0	.238
Bayless, Dick	CF	8	27	8	5*	1	1	.296
Williams, Alva	1B	7	23	7	0	0	1	.304
Downey, Tom	2B	7	26	5	0	0	0	.192
Litschi, Louis	RF	7	22	5	2	0	0	.227
Hosp, Franz	SS	7	25	2	1	1	0	.080
Schmidt, Walter	C	6	17	3	0	1	0	.176

Calexico Pitching Statistics 1914-15

Name	G	CG	W	L	IP	SO	BB	SH
Gregg,	5	3	2	2	41	16	16	0
Hitt, Roy	3	2	3	0	24	14	9	1
Williams, Claude	2	2	2	0	18	8	4	0
Scott, Jim	2	1	1	1	14	9	6	0

Imperial Batting Statistics 1914-15

Name	Pos	G	AB	H	D	T	HR	BA
Middleton, Roxy	LF	11	46*	15	0	0	0	.326
Corhan, Roy	SS	11	46*	7	0	2	0	.152
Maggert, Harl	CF	11	39	15*	0	2	0	.385*
Downs, Red	2B	11	43	13	1	0	2*	.302
Hetling, Gus	3B	12	40	6	1	0	0	.150
Kaylor, T.	RF	12	43	13	1	0	1	.302
Arbogast, Charlie	1B	10	36	7	1	0	1	.194
Brooks,	C	11	41	12	1	0	0	.293

Imperial Pitching Statistics 1914-15

Name	G	CG	W	L	IP	SO	BB	SH
Ryan, Jack	9	8	2	6	64	50	27	1
Fanning, Skeeter	5	4	4	1	44	31	10	0

Brawley Batting Statistics 1914-15

Name	Pos	G	AB	H	D	T	HR	BA
Daniels, Bert	CF	10	38	7	0	0	0	.184
Cutshaw, George	2B	2	7	1	0	0	0	.143
Becker,	LF	10	38	7	2	1	0	.181
Getz, Gus	3B	3	12	1	0	0	0	.084
Graham, Charles	RF	10	37	8	0	0	1	.216
Gleichman, Gus	1B	11	42	12	1	0	2*	.286
Stark, Dolly	SS	9	34	6	0	0	0	.176
McCarthy,	C	9	27	5	0	0	0	.185
Page,	2B	8	30	7	1	0	1	.267
LaLonge,	SS	5	11	4	0	1	1	.364
Butler,	SS	7	26	4	0	0	0	.154

Brawley Pitching Statistics 1914-15

Name	G	CG	W	L	IP	SO	BB	SH
Pfeffer, Edward "Jeff"	2	1	0	2	16	—	—	0
Baeder,	6	3	2	2	37	—	—	—

Brawley Pitching Statistics 1914-15

Name	G	CG	W	L	IP	SO	BB	SH
Willis, R.	3	2	0	2	19	7	4	—
Cole, Leonard "King"	3	2	0	3	25	14	21	—

Baseball was not restricted to the Imperial Valley League in 1914-15. There was also a Southern California League, that was a semi-professional league, although some of the players were high level minor leaguers or major leaguers. A few statistics follow.

Southern California Winter League
Standings—Incomplete

	Wins	Losses	
San Pedro	4	3	Champions
Oxnard	3	2	
Santa Barbara	2	3	
Coast League A.S.	1	0	

Miscellaneous Teams Batting Statistics 1914-15

Name	Team	G	AB	H	D	T	HR	BA
Maggert, Harl	Coast League A.S.	1	3	1	0	0	1	.333
Mitchell, Johnny	Santa Barbara	1	3	1	0	0	1	.333
Ferraris,	Santa Barbara	1	3	1	0	1	0	.333
Schultz, Mickey	San Pedro	2	7	3	0	0	0	.429
DeMaggio, Nick	San Pedro	3	12	3	0	0	0	.250
Fitzgerald,	San Pedro	1	4	2	0	0	0	.500
Whaling, Bert	Maier	2	8	2	0	0	0	.250
Martin, Eddie	San Pedro	1	4	2	2	0	0	.500
Schneider, Pete	Los Angeles	1	3	1	0	0	1	.333

Miscellaneous Teams Pitching Statistics 1914-15

Name	Team	G	CG	W	L	IP	SO	BB	SH
Emhke, Howard	Coast League A.S.	1	1	1	0	9	—	—	—
Killeen, Jack	San Diego	1	0	0	1	6	—	—	--
Hitt, Roy	San Pedro	1	1	1	0	9	11	—	—
Chech, Charlie	Oxnard	1	1	1	0	9	15	—	—
Smith, Clarence	San Pedro	6	6	3	3	56	—	—	2

The 1915-16 Season

In 1915, the Chicago American Giants were back on the west coast for the winter season, this time playing out of Athletic Park in San Diego. They had their strongest team yet with not only Pete Hill, Joe Williams, and Bruce Petway, but with all-time great John Henry Lloyd, Frank Duncan, Frank Wickware, and Dizzy Dismukes, as well.

The league was a four team league, with the Giants, the San Diego Pantages, San Bernardino, and Cline-Cline of Los Angeles, and all the teams were loaded with big league talent. San Diego had at least seven former major league players including pitchers Roy Hitt (6–10 in the majors) and Pete Schneider (59–86), plus Pug Bennett (St. Louis Cardinals), Joe Berger (Chicago White Sox), Dick Bayless (Cincinnati Reds), Chick Autry (Cincinnati Reds), and Tom Downey (Buffalo Feds). San Bernardino had two starting pitchers who could cross swords with anybody; Pol Perritt (92–78 in majors) and Charlie Chech (33–30), as well as Joe Wagner (Cincinnati Reds), Charlie Hanford (Buffalo Feds), and Art Griggs (Buffalo Feds). And Cline-Cline had 'Honolulu Johnnie' Williams (Detroit Tigers) and Hi West (Cleveland Indians) on the mound, with Bert Whaling (Boston Braves), Charlie French (Boston Red Sox), Carter Elliott (Chicago Cubs), Ed Mensor (Pittsburgh Pirates), and Ted Easterly (Kansas City Feds), covering the diamond. The *Los Angeles Times* noted that several Federal League players, like Art Griggs and Johnny Rawlings, played under assumed names.

The Giants opened their season with an exhibition game against the Los Angeles White Sox, a local black club that was slowly evolving from a semi-pro team into a full fledged professional organization. The Sox were composed primarily of local boys trying to climb the ladder of athletic success. One of their players was a big, strapping 6'2", 20-year-old first baseman with excellent power. His name was George "Tank" Carr, and he was on the verge of becoming an outstanding professional baseball player. Tank Carr played with the White Sox in the winter, and with local teams during the summer, until he joined the Kansas City Monarchs of the Negro National League in 1920. He went on to enjoy a 15 year career in the Negro leagues, compiling a .310 batting average with 10 home runs for every 550 at-bats. He also played 13 years in the California Winter League, batting .336 with 21 home runs a year, and one year in Cuba where he pummeled Cuban pitchers to the tune of .416.

The semi-pro L.A. White Sox gave the powerful Chicago American Giants all they could handle, before succumbing 10–6. In the process, they drove "Cyclone Joe" Williams from the mound after just three innings of work. Carr contributed two base hits in five at-bats to the Sox attack. Standouts for the Giants were Duncan and McAdoo with two hits each. But Bruce Petway was the biggest thorn in L.A.'s side. The game's greatest defensive catcher threw out three baserunners trying to steal second. There were no survivors.

When the league season opened on November 6, the Giants got off to a slow start. They were roughed up by the San Diego Pantages 7–4 in the opener, with "Cyclone Joe" Williams being pounded for 14 hits including five for extra bases. After two more losses, the Foster-men finally righted the ship with a 4–0 decision over Cline-Cline of Los Angeles. Frank "The Red Ant" Wickware, conqueror of the great Walter Johnson in 1913, stifled the big city boys with a three hit shutout. Wickware was wild but effective in the clutch, fanning six men to go along with six walks. The winning run scored in the bottom of the fourth inning when Pete Hill drove a Fitchner fastball over the right field fence. Tully McAdoo added a triple and Frank Duncan a double, to the Giant barrage.

From there, the Chicago contingent began to exert their superiority. They beat San Bernardino 6–3 on a Dismukes six hitter, then edged the Pantages 3–2 behind a courageous 12 hitter by Williams, who helped his own cause with a fluke line-drive home run that carried over Hosp's head in left field, then bounced over the fence. Jess Barbour also hit for the circuit. On Thanksgiving Day, Frank Wickware came within a whisker of tossing a no-hitter against San Diego. He carried a no-no into the ninth, but Dick Bayless, formerly of the Cincinnati Reds, dropped a Texas leaguer into center field, as Bauchman, Lloyd and Hill failed to communicate with each other, and let the ball drop between them for the Pantages' only hit of the game. Barber, Hill, and Lloyd all contributed two hits to the 4–0 shutout.

The new year found Rube Foster's boys safely ensconced in first place, just ahead of the tough San Diego team. The Giants clinched the pennant by sweeping the Pantages in two successive weekend doubleheaders, on December 17–18 and 25–26. On the 17th, Dizzy Dismukes started for the Chicago nine, but was relieved by Wickware in the seventh after being pounded for two runs, for a 6–5 San Diego lead. Pete Hill took matters into his own hands in the top of the eighth, when he smashed a two-run single to right, giving the Giants their final margin of victory, 7–6. Three innings earlier, Hill had driven in another run with a booming triple to the center field fence.

The Chicago team which, under Rube Foster, had earned a reputation for playing aggressive baseball, drew first blood in the second inning with some daring baserunning. Harry Bauchman cracked a single to right with Jude Gans on first base, and Gans raced around to third at full throttle, as if he were going to try to score on the play. A hurried throw from right fielder Litschi went wild, and Gans trotted home with the first run of the game.

In the Sunday game, Frank Wickware, with help from Joe Williams, stopped the Pantages 7–3, behind a 12 hit Giant attack. Wickware allowed only three hits in six innings, but six free passes kept him in constant trouble, and when Tom Downey, formerly of the Cincinnati Reds, touched him up for a two-run home run in the bottom of the sixth, narrowing the Chicago lead to 3–2, manager Foster went to the bullpen for "Cyclone Joe." A three run outburst by the Giants in the top of the seventh iced the games for Foster's crew.

The game had many batting heroes. Harry Bauchman was the big gun, with a single, triple, and home run to his credit. John Henry Lloyd had a single and a double, Pete Hill and Tully McAdoo had two hits apiece, and Jess Barbour rapped a home run.

The following weekend, the San Diego Pantages and Chicago American Giants met again to close out the season, the Giants needing two wins to clinch the pennant. In the Saturday game, manager Rube Foster sent his ace, Frank Wickware, to the mound, and "The Red Ant" didn't let him down. He pitched a gutty game, yielding 11 safe hits and walking three batters, but bearing down in the clutch, to gain the victory. The Pantages drew first blood in the second inning when Chick Autry opened with a single, went to second on a sacrifice, stole third, and scored on a well executed squeeze bunt by Litschi. Bill Palmer's men pushed across two more runs in the bottom of the fifth. Pug Bennett, former St. Louis Cardinal outfielder, stepped to the plate with two men on, and promptly rapped a two-run double off the right field wall. That was the Pantages' last gasp, as Wickware settled down and blanked them the rest of the way.

In the meantime, the boys from the Windy City clawed their way back into contention. In the top of the sixth, Pete Hill lined a long single down the left field line. Frank Duncan beat out an infield roller, putting men on first and second, and bringing the Giants' cleanup hitter, John Henry Lloyd, to the plate. Lloyd took two vicious cuts at Roy Hitt's deliveries, without making contact. His third attempt was much better. He caught hold of a Hitt curveball and sent it on a line over the center field fence for a three run homer. It was the longest hit in Athletic Park that winter. Two innings later, with the game deadlocked at three-all, the Giants struck again. This time, Lloyd led off the rally. With Roy Hitt trying to give him nothing to hit, Lloyd reached out and punched an outside pitch down the left field line for two bases. He moved to third on a sacrifice by McAdoo, and scored the eventual winning run on a two-out single to center by Harry Bauchman.

The Sunday game was even tighter. The starting pitchers were "Cyclone Joe" Williams for Rube Foster's club and former

Cincinnati Reds hurler Charlie Chech for Bill Palmer's warriors. The Pantages jumped out on top, as the Chicago pitcher had trouble finding the plate. After the Giants were retired 1-2-3 in the top of the first, San Diego broke through. With two men out and a runner on second, "Cyclone Joe" walked four men in succession, forcing in two runs. Warmup activity was already underway in the Giant bullpen when Roche forced Litschi at second, ending the torment.

Once again, the Giants had to fight an uphill battle, And once again, they came through. In the second, "Old Reliable" John Henry Lloyd, who always seemed to be in the middle of the action, whistled a triple to right center field, and came home on an infield grounder by McAdoo. Four innings later, they tied the score when Pete Hill hit a two-out double to right, and came around to score on a single by Frank Duncan.

Tha game remained 2–2 into the ninth. Then Duncan lined a double down the left field foul line, and went to third on a sacrifice by Lloyd. Left fielder Hosp backed up a little deeper to defend against the long-ball hitting Tully McAdoo, but Rube Foster saw the move and ordered McAdoo to hit short. The big first baseman did as he was told, and dropped a Texas leaguer into short left field, sending Duncan across the plate with the tie-breaking run. But the game was not over yet. San Diego fought back. In the bottom of the ninth, Hosp singled over second, and Bennett reached when Pete Hill dropped his fly ball for an error. As the *Chicago Defender* reported it, "With men on first and second and the heavy hitters coming up, the fans rose up from their seats. Bieloper tried to bunt and fouled out to Petway. Bayless grounded out to McAdoo unassisted, Hosp going to third and Bennett to second. Autry fanned and it was all over."

Chicago American Giants				
Name	Pos	AB	H	E
Barbour, J.	3B	4	0	1
Hill, P.	RF	4	1	1
Duncan, F.	LF	4	3	0
Lloyd, J.	SS	3	1	0
McAdoo, D.	1B	4	0	0
Gans, J.	CF	3	0	0
Bauchman, H.	2B	4	0	0
Petway, B.	C	3	0	0
Williams, J.	P	2	0	0
Totals		31	5	2

San Diego Pantages				
Name	Pos	AB	H	E
Hosp,	LF	3	1	1
Bennett, J.	2B	5	2	0
Bieloper,	3B	5	0	0
Bayless, R.	LF	3	1	0
Autry, W.	1B	3	0	0
Downey, T.	SS	3	0	0
Litschi,	RF	3	1	0
Roche, J.	C	4	1	0
Chech, C.	P	4	1	0
		33	7	1

Chicago American Giants 0 1 0   0 0 1   0 0 1–3–5–2
San Diego Pantages   2 0 0   0 0 0   0 0 0–2–7–1

Two base hits: Hill, Duncan
Three base hit: Lloyd

	IP	SO	BB
J. Williams (WP)	9	4	7
C. Chech (LP)	9	4	2

The Chicago American Giants were the California Winter League champions for the season of 1915-16. The title was a milestone in black baseball because it marked the first winter league championship for a Negro league team.

The Early Years 1900-1919

1915-16 California Winter League
Standings—Incomplete

	Wins	Losses
Chicago American Giants	9	5
San Diego Pantages	5	8
San Bernardino	4	3
Cline-Cline	2	4

Chicago American Giants Batting Statistics 1915-16

Name	Pos.	G	AB	H	D	T	HR	BA
Barbour, Jess	3B	12	51*	12	0	0	2*	.235
Hill, Pete	CF	13	51*	19*	1	3*	1	.373
Duncan, Frank	RF	13	50	14	3*	3	0	.280
Lloyd, John Henry	SS	13	44	18	3*	2	1	.409*
McAdoo, Dudley "Tully"	1B	13	50	13	0	2	0	.260
Gans, Jude	LF	13	38	6	0	2	0	.158
Bauchman, Harry	2B	13	46	15	1	2	2*	.326
Petway, Bruce	C	9	33	3	0	0	0	.111
Jenkins, Horace	OF	1	2	0	0	0	0	.000
Brazleton, Clarkson	C	2	4	0	0	0	0	.000
Clonson,	C	1	2	1	0	0	0	.500
Dismukes, Dizzy	P	3	8	1	0	0	0	.125
Williams, Joe	P	6	12	3	0	0	1	.250
Wickware, Frank	P	6	14	0	0	0	0	.000

Chicago American Giants Pitching Statistics 1915-16

Name	G	CG	W	L	IP	SO	BB	SH
Williams, Joe	7*	3	2	3	42	27	20	0
Dismukes, Dizzy	5	2	1	1	34	—	—	0
Wickware, Frank	7*	4*	6*	1	46*	28*	24	2*
Jenkins, Horace	1	0	0	0	6	—	—	0
Whitworth, Richard	1	0	0	0	1	—	—	0

San Diego Pantages Batting Statistics 1915-16

Name	Pos	G	AB	H	D	T	HR	BA
Hosp, Franz	LF	8	32	9	0	0	0	.281
Bennett, Pug	2B	8	33	9	1	0	0	.273
Berger, Joe	SS	3	13	4	2	0	0	.308
Bayless, Dick	CF	8	27	8	0	1	0	.296
Autry, Chick	1B	7	30	5	1	0	0	.167
Downey, Tom	3B	8	34	13	1	0	2*	.382
Litschi, Louis	RF	7	26	8	3*	1	0	.308
Roche, Jack	C	4	13	2	0	0	0	.154
Bieloper,	C	6	23	4	0	2	0	.174
Bliss,	C	2	6	2	0	0	0	.333
Pike,	C	2	6	2	0	0	0	.333
Hitt, Roy	P	3	8	3	0	1	0	.375
Killeeen, Jack	P	2	8	1	0	0	0	.125
Schneider, Pete	P	1	3	0	0	0	0	.000
Chech, Charlie	P	1	4	1	0	0	0	.250

San Diego Pantages Pitching Statistics 1915-16

Name	G	CG	W	L	IP	SO	BB	SH
Hitt, Roy	4	4	1	3	362	8	8	0
Killeen, Jack	3	3	0	3	27	9	21	0
Schneider, Pete	1	1	0	1	9	3	3	0
Chech, Charlie	1	1	0	1	9	4	2	0

The recovered statistics for Cline-Cline and San Bernardino were minimal. Pol Perritt, who pitched for the St. Louis Cardinals and New York Giants from 1912 to 1921, compiling a record of 92–78, was charged with one loss in one game pitched for San Bernardino. Charlie Chech pitched for San Bernardino as well as for San Diego. He went 2–1 in three games for San Bernardino, and 0–1 with San Diego.

The Imperial Valley League was also in operation during the 1915-16 season, with such talented major leaguers, such as Dazzy Vance, Irish Meusel, Dutch Ruether, Fred McMullin, Claude "Lefty" Williams, Charlie Pick (Washington Senators), Sam Bohne (Cincinnati Reds), Walt Alexander (New York Yankees), Joe Wilhoit (Boston Braves), and Bill Piercy (Boston Red Sox).

The names of McMullin and Williams should be familiar to most readers. They were members of the infamous Chicago Black Sox team, that threw the 1919 World Series to the Cincinnati Reds. Lefty Williams, a 23 game winner during the season, went 0–3 in the World Series, with a 6.61 ERA. McMullin, a utility infielder and .294 hitter during the season, played in only two Series games, going one for two.

Nineteen box scores were recovered for the Imperial Valley League season. The records show El Centro, with Vance, Meusel, Piercy, Alexander, McMullen, and Pick, to be the league champion.

1915-16 Imperial Valley League Standings—Incomplete

	Wins	Losses
El Centro	8	2
Imperial	6	3
Calexico	5	4
Brawley	0	10

Miscellaneous Teams Batting Statistics 1915-16

Name	Team	Pos	G	AB	H	D	T	HR	BA
Meusel, Irish	El Centro	CF	5	20	6	2	0	0	.300
Ruether, Dutch	Calexico	1B	5	19	6	2	1	0	.316
McMullen Fred	El Centro	3B	5	21	3	0	0	0	.143
Pick, Charlie	El Centro	2B	5	19	7	1	1	0	.368
Wilhoit, Joe	Calexico	CF	5	18	4	1	0	1	.222
Alexander, Walt	El Centro	C	5	16	6	2	0	1	.375

Miscellaneous Teams Batting Statistics 1915-16

Name	Team	Pos	G	AB	H	D	T	HR	BA
Bohne, Sam	Calexico	2B	5	20	6	4	0	0	.300
Rader, Don	El Centro	SS	5	22	7	1	1	0	.318

Miscellaneous Teams Pitching Statistics 1915-16

Name	Team	G	CG	W	L	IP	SO	BB	SH
Ryan, Jack	Calexico	3	2	1	2	23	21	9	0
Piercy, Bill	El Centro	2	1	1	1	14	11	4	0
Vance, Dazzy	El Centro	3	1	2	0	19	22	9	1
Williams, Lefty	Calexico	2	1	1	1	16	17	4	0
Ruether, Dutch	Calexico	2	0	0	0	6	6	4	0
Kantlehner, Erv	El Centro	2	1	1	0	12	12	7	0

Southern California was a hotbed of winter baseball over the years. But Northern California was also entertaining the fans with some high level professional baseball games. The *Los Angeles Times* reported on one game between San Francisco and Ossie Vitt's All-Stars. The game was won by San Francisco 10–1, behind Cleveland Indians pitcher Bill Steen. Vitt's team included Joe Oeschger of the Philadelphia Phillies (who was knocked out of the box in the third inning) and Jimmy Johnston of the Brooklyn Dodgers.

The 1916-17 Season

The 1916-17 winter league season saw a return to the semi-pro status of the early years. The five-team league consisted of the Los Angeles White Sox, Anheuser-Busch, San Pedro, Pacific Electric, and San Diego. The White Sox were essentially a local club again, and not in the same class with Rube Foster's Chicago American Giants. They did surprisingly well in the league considering they had only two genuine professional players, George "Tank" Carr, and John Donaldson, but they probably came in no better than second place. Donaldson, who is generally recognized as one of the top two or three southpaw pitchers in Negro league history, played with the famous All Nations team during the summer, from 1913 through 1917, before joining the Kansas City Monarchs for their inaugural season in the Negro National League in 1920. Washington, Perry, and Woods may also have seen some service in the Negro leagues, but the other members of the team probably spent their careers on the west coast.

The Anheuser-Busch team included Cleveland Indian pitcher Hi West, Pittsburgh Pirate infielder Tony Boeckel, and Bert Whaling of the Boston Braves. None of the other players have been located in organized baseball.

The San Diego Hulls had minor league pitcher Jack Killeen, and Jack Roche of the

John Donaldson, one of the great southpaw pitchers in Negro league history, played in the winter league in 1916–17 and 1917–18. (James A. Riley)

St. Louis Cardinals. San Pedro had Carl Sawyer of the Washington Senators, Kid Butler of the St. Louis Browns, and former major league pitchers Harry Ables and Walt Slagle. No players on the Pacific Electric entry are easily recognizable. All in all, the league appeared to be a lower level minor league in 1916.

On November 18, the *Chicago Defender* noted that the White Sox broke the winning streak of the San Diego Hulls, "the fastest white semi-pro team in this section of the country," but it didn't record how many games the Hulls had won. The Sox ace was a pitcher named Mooney, but not much is known about him. The newspaper said he was an underhand southpaw pitcher, who would be trying out with the Chicago Giants in 1917, but no record of him has been found in the Negro league journals.

Nonetheless, in the game of November 17, Mooney was in complete control. In the bottom of the sixth, with L.A. up 3–0, San Diego loaded the bases against the White Sox ace with nobody out, but Mooney was equal to the task. As the *Defender* noted, "(He) just took another notch in his belt, caused the next batter to pop out, and fanned the two following." The Hulls did push across two runs in the bottom of the eighth, narrowing the gap to 3–2, but the White Sox iced the game in the top of the ninth. Washington, the hard hitting shortstop of the Sox crashed a double, and scored on another two bagger by King, who scored himself moments later on an infield out.

Los Angeles hosted Anheuser-Busch on February 21, to open the second half of the winter league season, at Maier Park in Vernon. The *Defender* reported the event. "After a parade through the principal streets in automobiles by both teams in uniform, headed by a brass band of 25 pieces, the fast Anheuser-Bush team (white) crossed bats with that famous team better known as the Los Angeles White Sox in one of the fastest games ever played on the Vernon diamond." The opposing pitchers were Mooney for the Sox and major league pitcher Hi West for Anheuser-Busch. The game turned out to be an exciting pitchers' duel, with Mooney gaining the decision, 4–2. L.A.'s southpaw ace shackled the visitors with just five hits, while the White Sox were raking West for eleven. Perry, Carr, and Washington all collected two hits for the home club. Smith and West rapped out triples for Anheuser-Busch.

A February 23 news release by the *Chicago Defender* News Service stated that John Donaldson had turned down a $10,000 offer to play organized baseball for a team in the New York State League. According to the report, Donaldson would have had to travel to Cuba, assume another name, then come back to America claiming he was Cuban.

On the weekend of March 3 and 4, the White Sox played a two game series against the San Pedro team on the Vernon diamond. The Saturday game was won by San Pedro 4–2, when William Woods, who pitched a masterful game, was betrayed by his defense. George Kelly was touched up for ten hits by White Sox batters, but bore down in the clutch, blanking the L.A. team over the last seven innings.

The *Chicago Defender* described the second game of the series. "The field was so crowded that ground rules were in force. Mooney was on the mound for the Sox while (Harry) Ables and (Walt) Slagle were pitted against him. This was the first time that the crack San Pedro team had been defeated in three months, they having won eighteen straight games…. The remarkable thing about this game was that no one on the San Pedro team struck out." They forgot to note the score of the game, which was 2–1. Baker slammed a double for the White Sox, while Tank Carr had two singles.

Two weeks later, the season came to

an end with the Los Angeles White Sox defeating the Pacific Electric team 9–8. John Donaldson started for the Sox, but couldn't hold a 6–2 lead, and was relieved by the eventual winning pitcher, Mooney, in the eighth inning. Donaldson was the batting star of the game however, pounding out a single, two doubles, and a triple in four trips to the plate. An estimated 5,000 fans were in attendance, and the band saluted Mooney with a rendition of "The Conquering Hero Comes."

Very few box scores were located for the season, and no final standings were uncovered, so the eventual pennant winner is unknown. Most probably it was San Pedro. The newspapers did note that San Pedro had enjoyed an 18 game winning streak during the season. One note of future interest was that a young pitcher by the name of Joe Pirrone, pitching for the Western Pool Hall, was on the losing end of a 4–0 shutout tossed by L.A.'s Mr. Mooney.

From 1916 through the remainder of the decade, the league declined in stature. One of the major reasons may have been the edict issued by Pacific Coast League president Allen T. Baum in April 1914. The bigoted baseball executive banned all PCL teams from playing exhibition games against black teams. He also banned black teams from playing games in PCL parks. It appears to have taken several years for all Pacific Coast League teams to comply with these edicts because it is known that the Portland club, owned by Walter McCredie, continued to play exhibition games against Rube Foster's team until at least 1917. It is also known that games involving black teams were being played in Maier Park in Vernon in 1915 and 1916.

Without a suitable ballpark to play in, it became financially impossible for a black team to survive in the California Winter League. Rube Foster, for one, may have found the situation to be untenable, because he never returned to the west coast for league play after his championship season, although he did barnstorm through California, Oregon, and Washington, during the spring. He took his team to Cuba in 1916, then to Florida for the 1917 and 1918 winter seasons. By this time, the old baseball pioneer was exploring other horizons, particularly the formation of an organized professional Negro baseball league. The need for a structured Negro league became obvious during the teens when player raids between teams caused player salaries to skyrocket and team profits to plummet.

1916-17 California Winter League
Standings—Incomplete

	Wins	Losses	Ties
San Pedro	1	1	0
Los Angeles White Sox	5	3	0
San Diego Hulls	1	1	0
Pacific-Electric	1	2	1
Anheuser-Busch	0	1	0
Pasadena	0	1	0
Santa Barbara	0	0	1

Los Angeles White Sox Batting Statistics 1916-17

Name	Pos.	G	AB	H	D	T	HR	BA
Glenn,	CF	5	17	4	0	0	0	.235
Paschel,	RF	4	15	5	0	0	0	.333
Carr, George	1B	6	21	10	2	1	0	.476*
Donaldson, John	LF	4	8	6	2	1	0	.750

Los Angeles White Sox Batting Statistics 1916-17

Name	Pos.	G	AB	H	D	T	HR	BA
Washington, Namon (?)	SS	5	16	7	1	0	0	.438
Kyle,	3B	5	19	5	0	1	0	.263
Baker,	C	6	20	4	2	0	0	.200
Perry, Carl (?)	2B	5	17	7	0	0	0	.412
Goodwin,		1	1	0	0	0	0	.000
Cooper,	RF	2	6	2	0	0	0	.333
Hamock,	LF	1	3	1	0	0	0	.333
King,	CF	1	4	2	1	0	0	.500
Woods, William	P	1	3	0	0	0	0	.000
Mooney,	P	4	12	3	0	0	0	.250

Los Angeles White Sox Pitching Statistics 1916-17

Name	G	CG	W	L	IP	SO	BB	SH
Mooney,	6*	3*	4*	1	39*	23*	5	0
Woods,	1	1	0	1	9	7	2	0
Donaldson, John	4	1	1	1	22	—	—	0

The 1917-18 Season

The Los Angeles White Sox were again entered in the winter league for the 1917-18 season, but very few details on the season, or the teams that participated in the league, are available. Bullet Rogan may have been a member of the White Sox team. As John Holway noted in *Blackball Stars*, "Rogan left the service briefly in the fall of 1917 to pitch for the Los Angeles White Sox, a black team, in the California Winter League, then returned to the army, to the old Indian-fighting outpost of Fort Huachuca on the sun parched Mexican border. Tank Carr batted third in the White Sox lineup."

The L.A. team may also have had the services of Jose Mendez, and Dave Malarcher, but without a "home," they could not earn enough money to keep bread on the table. The newspaper coverage was mediocre with very few box scores reported, and almost no game accounts published. The fragmentary information in the press indicated that as many as 15 teams participated in the league, which would not have been unusual since there were numerous teams operating in and around Los Angeles. There were also many leagues, such as The Major Circuit, the All-Professional League, the County League, and the Valley League, plus the usual number of independent teams. One year the AAA league's published standings showed 12 members.

The only Los Angeles White Sox game reported in the newspapers was the December 9 game against the San Pedro Merchants. The *Times* noted, "The Los Angeles White Sox defeated the San Pedro Merchants here (San Pedro) today by a score of 5–3. Inability to hit Donaldson in the pinches, and errors at critical moments, were responsible for the results."

1917-18 California Winter League Standings—Incomplete

	Wins	Losses
Los Angeles White Sox	1	0
Los Angeles	1	0
Pasadena	1	0

	Wins	Losses
Submarine Base	2	1
Standard-Murphy	2	1
San Pedro	3	3
Vernon	2	2
Pacific Electric	1	1
Army	1	1
Navy	1	2
Tufts-Lyons	0	1
Camp Kearny	0	1
Fullerton-Anaheim	0	1
Rathskellers	0	0

Miscellaneous Teams Batting Statistics 1917-18

Name	Team	G	AB	H	D	T	HR	BA
Sawyer, Carl	San Pedro	3	12	6	0	0	0	.500
Cutshaw, George	San Pedro	2	8	2	0	0	0	.250
Meusel, Irish	San Pedro	4	16	7	1	0	0	.438*
Chadbourne, Chet	Vernon	4	16	2	0	0	0	.125
Flick, Elmer	San Pedro	3	11	2	0	0	0	.182
Elliott, Carter	Tufts-Lyons	1	3	0	0	0	0	.000
Crawford, Sam	Vernon	2	7	2	0	1	0	.287
Hannah, Truck	Std-Murphy	1	4	1	0	0	0	.250
Boeckel, Tony	Std-M'phy, Navy	5	19	5	1	0	0	.263
DeMaggio, Nick	Submarine Base	3	12	5	1	0	0	.417
Meusel, Bob	Submarine Base	2	8	2	1	1	0	.250
Fournier, Jack	Submarine Base	1	5	1	0	0	0	.250
Leathers, Hal	Los Angeles	4	13	1	0	0	0	.077

Miscellaneous Teams Pitching Statistics 1917-18

Name	Team	G	CG	W	L	IP	SO	BB	SH
Brown, Curly	San Pedro	4*	4*	3*	0	36	31*	4	1*
Schneider, Pete	Vernon	5	4	2	3	40*	16	9*	0
Chech, Charlie	Vernon	1	1	0	1	9	5	3	0
Ehmke, Howard	San Pedro S.B.	3	3	2	1	26	17	6	1*
Donaldson, John	L.A. White Sox	1	1	1	0	9	—	—	0
Pertica, Bill	Los Angeles	1	0	1	0	7	5	3	0
Shellenback, Frank	All Majors	1	0	0	0	5	2	0	0
Salazar, Lazaro	Pacific-Electric	1	1	1	0	9	11	3	0

The 1918-19 Season

The 1918-19 winter league season seemed to be composed of seven teams, but with no black team represented. Coincidentally or not, the white teams enjoyed the use of both Pacific Coast League parks in the area, Washington Park and Maier Park. There was still a good blend of major league players and high level minor league players in the loop, including the Meusel brothers, Fred McMullin, George Cutshaw, Tony Boeckel, Howard Ehmke, Doc Crandall, and Wheezer Dell, but without a black team, the attendance continued to drop.

There were also other factors that contributed to the league's problems. World War I decimated the player base and restricted travel, while an outbreak of influenza drove fans away from the ballparks by the hundreds. In Europe, a war that had raged since 1914 finally reached the United

States in 1917. America declared war on Germany on April 6 of that year after repeated acts of aggression against American shipping by German U-Boats. The sinking of the British liner *Lusitania*, with the loss of 1,200 lives, including 128 Americans, was the first step in the deterioration of U.S.–German relations.

A military draft took thousands of baseball players away from their jobs, leaving professional baseball leagues around the U.S. lacking qualified players. Negro league players left their teams in record numbers to enlist in the army. Players like Spot Poles, Jude Gans, Lem Hawkins, and Frank Wickware traded their fancy baseball uniforms for U.S. Army olive drab. Others, like John Henry Lloyd, became heavily involved in the defense industry at home.

At the same time the war was heating up, a deadly influenza epidemic was creating havoc all across the United States. The flu bug first struck in May 1918, but the effect was mild with few complications. The second wave, occurring in the fall of 1918, was deadly. Thousands of people succumbed to the disease. The *Los Angeles Times* described a baseball game that was played on January 26, 1919. "With players and spectators alike wearing influenza masks, a baseball game was played here (Pasadena) this afternoon.... Several policemen were on hand to see that the masks were kept in place.... Even when sliding for their bases, the runners managed to keep the cheesecloth over their noses and mouths."

Chet Chadbourne had the highest batting average for the few games that were recorded in the newspapers, a strong .429, with three doubles in 28 at-bats. A pitcher named Tally had a perfect 4–0 slate.

The highlight of the season was an 18 inning double no-hitter between the Dyas All-Stars and Pasadena at Maier Park on February 23, 1919. The lack of hitting can be attributed to the weather. As the *Los Angeles Times* noted, "For eighteen long innings the Pasadenas and the Dyas fought it out in the mud without a score. Owing to the steady drizzle that fell during the game, the ball was partly wet at all times, and therefore automatically served itself as a spitter. Ote Crandall heaved them over for Pasadena and Pete Schneider for the Dyas. Not a semblance of a single was made off either moundsman and the game was called on account of darkness.... Inning after inning the pitchers were monarchs of all they surveyed. After Irish Meusel had struck out for the seventh time, he turned to a friend and confided, 'I'm almost ashamed to sign a Phillie contract.'"

Several baseball games were reported from Northern California, around the San Francisco and Sacramento areas, but many of the games pitted a professional team against a college team. In one game, Dazzy Vance and Bill Piercy pitched against Santa Clara University, with Piercy finally winning 6–5 in 14 innings. In another game Erv Kantlehner of the Pittsburgh Pirates defeated Santa Clara 10–2.

1918-19 California Winter League
Standings—Incomplete

	Wins	Losses	Ties
Hollywood	4	0	0
Vernon Tigers	2	1	0
Dyas All-Stars	3	3	1
Pasadena	1	2	1
Los Angeles	0	1	0
Athletics	0	1	0
Rall's All-Stars	0	2	0

Miscellaneous Teams Batting Statistics 1918-19

Name	Team	G	AB	H	D	T	HR	BA
Chadbourne, Chet	Hollywood, Dyas	7	28	12	3	0	0	.429*
Alcock, Scotty	Hollywood, Dyas	7	31	5	0	0	0	.161
Kingdon, Wes	Hollywood	3	4	0	0	0	0	.000
Hosp, Franz	Vernon, Dyas	3	11	2	1	0	0	.182
Kruger, Art	Hollywood, Dyas	6	23	3	1	1	0	.130
Leathers, Hal	Hollywood	3	13	6	0	1	0	.462
Meusel, Bob	Dyas, Rall's A.S.	2	10	5	1	0	0	.500
Thomas, Pinch	Dyas All-Stars	4	14	3	1	0	0	.214
Leake,	Hollywood	4	14	4	0	1	0	.287
Meusel, Irish	Pasadena	4	20	3	0	1	0	.150
Sawyer, Carl	Pasadena	4	19	6	0	0	0	.316
McMullin, Fred	Rall's All-Stars	4	16	4	1	0	0	.250
Cutshaw, George	Pasadena	3	12	2	0	0	0	.167
Haas, Mule	Pasadena	3	11	3	0	0	0	.273
Haney, Fred	Pasadena	2	5	1	0	0	1*	.200
Boeckel, Tony	Dyas All-Stars	2	8	5	0	1	0	.625
Rader, Don	Dyas All-Stars	1	4	2	0	1	0	.500
DeMaggio, Nick	Rall's A.S., L.A.	2	10	3	0	0	0	.300

Miscellaneous Teams Pitching Statistics 1918-19

Name	Team	G	CG	W	L	IP	SO	BB	SH
Tally,	Hollywood, Pasadena	5*	4*	4*	0	40*	21*	4	0
Penner, Ken	Dyas	3	0	1	0	10	6	5	0
Crandall, Doc	Pasadena	1	1	0	0	18	—	—	1
Miller,	Dyas All-Stars	3	2	0	2	21	15	6	0
Dell, Wheezer	Vernon	2	0	1	0	9	—	2	0
Piercy, Bill	Pasadena	1	0	0	0	2	2	4	0
Schneider, P.	Dyas, Pasadena	4	1	2	0	39	14	20	1
Ehmke, H.	Pasadena	2	1	1	0	16	12	2	0
Pertica, Bill	Pasadena, L.A.	3	0	0	2	6	7	—	0

The 1919-20 Season

By 1919, the country was recovering from the Great War. The influenza epidemic was just a bad memory. And baseball fans around the country were flocking out to their local ballparks to see their favorite players in action. Everywhere that is except on the west coast. The California Winter League did not recover from the doldrums as hoped. For the fourth year in a row, no professional level Negro league team made the trip to the west coast to participate in a winter league. There seemed to be a dearth of amateur and semi-pro teams around the Los Angeles area, based on the lack of coverage in the local newspapers.

A team called the Los Angeles White Sox was active in L.A. in November, but it appeared to be a local semi-pro team, not a professional team from the east. The *California Eagle* reported on their first game of the season. "The L.A. White Sox played their first regular game last Sunday afternoon with the Hazard nine at the Hazard playgrounds since reorganizing. What the Sox didn't have isn't worth speaking of. Their fielding was near perfect; at bat they hit the horsehide until they felt sorry for the Hazard pitchers and to save the fielders the worry of trying to catch the long flys. The Sox resorted to home runs or no count.... There was a long, hungry looking gent by the name of Jack Mendenhall who played right field for seven innings, then he relieved Wood in the box.... With a little more coaching Jack will be a world beater. For a sticker he can't be beat. In Sundays game, out of four trips, he got two triples, a double, and a single.... The team is made up of all hard hitters that spell trouble for any pitcher that faces them. Hawkins, who is holding down the third base berth, is a wonder; at bat he is a sure sticker, on the bases he is a greyhound; in his position at third he is perfect. Manager (George) Carr has a well-balanced team which should give all the semi-pros all the baseball they are looking for this winter."

The article failed to give the score of the game, but did note that the White Sox had a game scheduled the following week against the Downey team at the Downey playgrounds. Whether or not the game was ever played is unknown. The Los Angeles White Sox were not mentioned again in the *Los Angeles Times* or any of the black newspapers the rest of the season.

Professional baseball was played in Los Angeles during November and December, between major and minor league all-star teams. The two most impressive teams were Killefer's All-Stars and Weaver's All-Stars. Killefer's All-Stars had such major league luminaries as Sam Crawford, Jimmy Austin, Fred McMullin, Bill Piercy, Gavvy Cravath, and Johnny Rawlings. Weaver's All-Stars included Buck Weaver, Babe Ruth, Jack Fournier, Bob Meusel, and Irish Meusel.

It is interesting to note that Buck Weaver's team played their first game on November 1, just 23 days after the 1919 World Series ended. That Series, between the Chicago White Sox and the Cincinnati Reds came to be known as the Black Sox scandal. Seven members of the Chicago White Sox team were accused of conspiring with gamblers to throw the World Series. At least five of the Black Sox were actively involved in the conspiracy. Two others, "Shoeless Joe" Jackson and Buck Weaver, if not actively involved, were at least aware of the plot and did not report it. Although all seven men were exonerated in court, the new Baseball Commissioner, Kenesaw Mountain Landis, barred all of them for life, in November 1920.

For the record, Joe Jackson led all World Series hitters with a .375 average, drove in six runs in eight games, and played errorless ball in the outfield. Buck Weaver also excelled, batting .324 with 11 base hits (second most behind Jackson's 12), and playing errorless ball at third base. The real conspirators were easy to identify. Swede Risberg batted .080 with four errors at shortstop, Chick Gandil hit .233, and Happy Felsch hit .192. Lefty Williams, who went 23–11 during the season, was 0–3 in the Series, with a 6.61 ERA. Eddie Cicotte was 1–2 with a 2.92 ERA.

In addition to Weaver, another conspirator, Fred McMullin was active in California that year. Two others, Claude "Lefty" Williams and Swede Risberg had played in the California Winter League during the 1915-16 season.

The *Los Angeles Times* covered three games played between the various all-star teams. In the opener, Killefer's All-Stars defeated Weaver's All-Stars 4–3, but Babe Ruth got all the raves. In the sixth inning the Sultan of Swat crushed a pitch from Piercy, and drove it into the 14th row of the right field bleachers. Harry A. Williams, covering the game, noted "Babe's home run will live in the baseball lore of Los Angeles.... It was as hard as any drive ever made, and by far the hardest in the recollection of the writer. The ball literally spurted from Ruth's bat, and traveled on a rising line at about the trajectory of a shell fired from a field piece until stopped by the bleachers.... The smash, had it not been intercepted by the bleachers would have been good for a clean 500 feet."

That blast was the high point of Babe Ruth's visit. He batted only .222 with two hits in nine at-bats. The big left-handed slugger was more successful on the golf course. According to the *Times*, "He sure got the surprise of his life on the Griffith Park Municipal links, when he holed the 453 yard seventh hole in 2, the first time it was ever done.... Babe hooked his shot up into the 'tullies' on the hill, but the ball was going so swift it tore through everything, curved down the hill onto the green, went between the feet of Mr. Freidlander and quietly dropped into the cup."

The big hitters in the series were Bob Meusel who slugged the ball at a .545 clip, and Gavvy Cravath and Irish Meusel who hit .500.

1919-20 California Winter League
Standings—Incomplete

	Wins	Losses
Killefer's All-Stars	1	1
Weaver's All-Stars	1	1
Ruth's All-Stars	1	0
Dyas' All-Stars	0	1

Miscellaneous Teams Batting Statistics 1919-20

Name	Team	G	AB	H	D	T	HR	BA
Killefer, Bill	Killefer, Ruth A.S.	3	8	2	0	0	0	.250
Austin, Jimmy	Killefer's All-Stars	2	6	1	0	1*	0	.167
Johnson,	Killefer's All-Stars	2	8	3	0	0	0	.375
Crawford, Sam	Killefer's All-Stars	2	8	0	0	0	0	.000
Cravath, Gavvy	Killefer's All-Stars	2	8	4	2*	0	0	.500
McMullin, Fred	Killefer's All-Stars	1	4	2	0	0	0	.500
Griggs, Art	Killefer's All-Stars	1	4	2	0	0	0	.500
Hannah, Truck	Killefer's All-Stars	1	4	0	0	0	0	.000
Rawlings, Johnny	Killefer, Ruth A.S.	2	8	2	0	0	0	.250
Mitchell, Johnny	Weaver's All-Stars	2	8	3	1	1*	0	.375
Chadbourne, Chet	Weaver's All-Stars	2	9	2	0	0	0	.222
Weaver, Buck	Weaver's All-Stars	2	7	2	0	1*	0	.287
Ruth, Babe	Weaver, Ruth A.S.	3	9	2	1	0	1*	.222
Fournier, Jack	Weaver's All-Stars	2	8	2	1	0	0	.250
Meusel, Bob	Weaver's All-Stars	3	11	6	1	1*	0	.545*
Fisher,	Weaver's All-Stars	2	6	1	0	0	0	.167
Thomas, Pinch	Weaver, Ruth A.S.	3	8	2	0	0	0	.250
Meusel, Irish	Weaver, Ruth A.S.	2	5	2	1	0	0	.400

Miscellaneous Teams Pitching Statistics 1919-20

Name	Team	G	CG	W	L	IP	SO	BB	SH
Piercy, Bill	Killefer's All-Stars	1	1	1	0	9	1	3	0
Fittery,	Killefer's All-Stars	1	1	0	1	8	2	2	0
Love, Slim	Killefer, Ruth A.S.	1	0	1	0	8	2	1	0
Schultz	Killefer, Ruth A.S.	1	0	0	0	1	0	0	0
Ross,	Weaver's All-Stars	1	1	0	1	9	1	1	0
Scott,	Weaver's All-Stars	1	0	1	0	7	0	1	0
Ruth, Babe	Weaver's All-Stars	1	0	0	0	2	0	0	0
Maples,	Weaver's All-Stars	1	0	0	1	6	0	1	0

The outlook for the future of the California Winter League looked bleak in the spring of 1920, but things were about to change in a big way. Doc Anderson and Joe Pirrone saw to that.

4

Season Summaries 1920–1924

The 1920-21 Season

The 1920-21 season was a breakthrough season for the California Winter League. It could even be considered to be the first year of the "real" California Winter League. During the previous decade the league had suffered through a series of ups and downs. It became apparent to interested observers that when Negro league teams participated in the California Winter League, attendance soared and the level of professional competition approached that of a AA league, even occasionally a AAA league, by today's standards. But when there was no Negro league team in the league, games were played to near-empty grandstands, and the level of play declined to a semi-pro level, since there was no money to pay professionals. One survey conducted by the *California Eagle* during a period when the league was integrated, found that 75 percent of the fans who attended the games were from the black community. This large bloc of fan support was lost when the league became lily white. The lack of an adequate baseball field for black teams to use was also a contributing factor.

In the fall of 1920 the California Winter League teetered on the brink of extinction. The lack of professional baseball talent, the lack of fan interest over the previous two years, and the lack of a suitable baseball field for a black team to use, did not bode well for the future of the winter game on the west coast. But, just when things looked bleakest, two saviors stepped out of the shadows to save the game.

Doc Anderson, a local businessman, and Joe Pirrone, a professional baseball player and local nightclub owner, may have realized that a truly professional winter baseball league, in order to survive, had to have significant fan support. And in order to achieve that, it had to take advantage of the large black population in Southern California. To accomplish its objectives, the league would have to have at least one black team and, since blacks were banned from Pacific Coast League parks, the black team would have to have a park of its own. And, almost as important, the black team would have to have strong white competition to maintain fan interest.

Anderson saw to it that the black team had a field, and that a Negro league team participated in the league. Pirrone, for his part, recruited talented white major league and high minor league players for his team, the Pirrone All-Stars, and also encouraged other white teams to join the league. Beginning in 1920, black professional baseball teams played in the California Winter League every year for more than twenty years. As the years passed, Joe Pirrone also recruited Negro league teams for the league, often traveling to the east coast to negotiate a deal.

There were many leagues operating up and down the west coast in the twentieth century, but the league commonly referred to as "The California Winter League" had three defining characteristics:

- It included at least one Negro league team.
- The Negro league team played most of its games in its own ballpark, commonly known as White Sox Park, which was located in or close to the city's black neighborhoods.
- One of the white competing teams was Joe Pirrone's All-Stars.

The league catered to the black community. In addition to drawing most of its fan base from that section of the city, the park employed a large number of blacks year-round. The league was not like other leagues. It was primarily a showcase for its black players, and was designed to attract black fans. Therefore, most games pitted the Negro league "home team" against one of the white teams. As a result, there was frequently a large discrepancy in the number of games played, with the Negro league team playing two or three times as many games as the league's white members.

Once the "real" winter league began operations in 1920, the quality of play got better each year, culminating in what could be called "The Golden Age" of the California Winter League, from 1924 to 1935. The league began to decline in the late 1930s caused, in part, by opportunies for black players, in other countries, such as Puerto Rico, the Dominican Republic, Mexico, and a number of Central and South American countries. Negro league players, still chafing under the yoke of social segregation in the United States, were first class citizens in other western hemisphere countries. As Willie Wells once said about playing in Mexico, "Here they treat me like a man." The integration of organized baseball in 1945 spelled finis to a significant historical and social chapter in the growth of our nation.

Little is known of Doc Anderson, except that he was there when the California Winter League needed him. When the league was floundering in the late teens, due to the despicable action of Pacific Coast League President Allan T. Baum, Anderson came forward with the perfect solution. He provided the California Winter League's black team with a baseball park of its own. It is unknown if Anderson built the park in 1920 expressly for the black team, or if he leased the team an existing park but, whatever the situation, he gave the Negro leaguers a home.

Anderson Park, which was located at East Fourth and Anderson Streets "just over the bridge," was an enclosed park, completely surrounded by a ten foot high board fence. It had box seats, and grandstands down both foul lines, with a reported seating capacity of 2,800 people, although one game account noted there was a capacity crowd of 4,000 fans on hand. The pitchers enjoyed a decided advantage in the league—at least between 1920 and 1923. Anderson Park, also known as White Sox Park, was a pitcher's paradise, with plenty of wide open spaces for the outfielders to roam. The left field fence measured 348 feet from home plate. Right field was a distant 394 feet away, the power alleys, left to right, were 455 and 430 feet respectively, and center field was a barely visible 546 feet from home. Singles, doubles, and triples were plentiful in Anderson Park, but home runs were almost nonexistent. In fact, of the more than 150 box scores, line scores, and game descriptions recovered, only 41 home runs were recorded, 34 of them by the Negro league teams. Bullet Joe Rogan led the league with five home runs in 1920. Hurley McNair hit two. No one else had more than one. And the entire Pirrone All-Star team, with Max Carey, Bob Meusel, and Irish Meusel, went homerless!

The pitching advantage disappeared in 1924 when Pirrone Park, a.k.a. White Sox Park II, opened. Pirrone's new ballpark was a slugger's dream, a tiny bandbox like Ebbets Field and Baker Bowl.

Doc Anderson, in addition to providing the winter league with its own ballpark, also took advantage of an untapped source of fan support, the ever growing black community in Southern California, by bringing a Negro league team back to the west coast, to compete against white professional teams. The Negro league entry in the 1920-21 league, called the Los Angeles White Sox, was an outstanding team, with such stalwarts as future Hall of Famer "Bullet Joe" Rogan, Dobie Moore, arguably the greatest shortstop in Negro league history, Rube Currie, Hurley McNair, and Los Angeles natives Lem Hawkins and George "Tank" Carr. McNair had a career batting average of .322 in the Negro leagues, and Tank Carr checked in with a .310 average. Currie compiled a 70–44 slate in nine years.

Joe Pirrone supplemented Doc Anderson's efforts by providing strong, white, professional talent to compete against the Negro league entry. Pirrone was a native of Southern California, and one of its outstanding amateur and semi-professional baseball players. He even had playing experience in the California Winter League, having pitched for Western Pool Hall in the 1916-17 season. According

Hurley McNair was an important cog in the 1920-21 L.A. White Sox pennant drive. He led the league in doubles (11) and triples (6) while hitting .313. (John B. Holway)

to the *California Eagle*, "Joe Pirrone, one of the best all around ball tossers in Southern California, and who goes to the Yakima club of the (Pacific Coast) International League this year, has rounded up a powerful squad of minor and major leaguers to face the White Sox." It is not known if Joe Pirrone did pitch for Yakima, or if he ever played organized baseball, but he did contribute significantly to the long lasting success of the CWL. His efforts to recruit the best white professional baseball players for the league made the CWL an artistic as well as a financial success over a period of more than two decades. As the league's primary promoter, Pirrone, along with his brother John, also made trips to the east coast to recruit Negro league teams for the league. His continuing efforts for the benefit of the winter league earned him the presidency of the league in the 1930s, and the title "Father of the California Winter League."

In 1920, Joe Pirrone assembled a team of major league and high minor league players, that would be the envy of many big league owners. Seven of his position players and four of his pitchers had played in the big time in 1920. Three more would be full time major leaguers in 1921. His roster included Tony Boeckel (batted .282 during six year major league career), Lu Blue (.287 in 13 years in majors), Eddie Ainsmith (Walter Johnson's favorite catcher from 1910 to 1918), Max Carey (.285 in 20 years), Bob Meusel (.309 in 11 years), Irish Meusel (.310 in 11 years), as well as a bevy of pitchers.

Pitching dominated the rosters of both the White Sox and the All-Stars. Since games were played only on Saturday and Sunday afternoons, and on holidays, a team could survive with just two or three topnotch starting pitchers. The White Sox, in fact, relied on just two men to carry the load—but what men they were. Hall of Famer "Bullet Joe" Rogan was the ace of the staff, ably supported by Rube Currie, a lanky 6'4", 195 pound curveball artist. Rogan was one of the two or three greatest pitchers in Negro league history—many baseball experts say #1—while Currie was rated as one of the best pitchers of the 1920s. John Holway's research credits Currie with a 70-44 slate in the Negro leagues, an excellent .614 winning percentage. Newspa-

Joe Pirrone was the "Father of the Winter League." He brought a Negro league team west in 1920, beginning the first continuous integrated professional baseball league.

pers of the time, both black and white, spelled his name "Curry" but since modern day historians such as Holway, Clark, Lester, and Riley, spell it Currie, that's the way it is spelled here.

On the All-Star side, Joe Pirrone paraded a long line of major league hurlers to the mound to face Doc Anderson's cohorts, including Red Oldham (39-48 in the majors), Frank Shellenback (10-15), Specs Meadows (188-180), Duster Mails (32-25), Bill Piercy (27-43), Wheezer Dell (19-23), Ray Keating (30-51), Bill Pertica (22-18), Sloppy Thurston (89-86), Doc Crandall (102-62), Speed Martin (29-42), Byron Houck (26-24), and Slim Love (28-21).

According to newspaper accounts, there were a total of ten teams that participated in the California Winter League during the 1920-21 season, although several of

Wheezer Dell pitched in the California Winter League for four years, compiling a record of 5–13. (Dick Dobbins)

the major-minor all-star teams reported in the press were, in all probability, the same team. It was not unusual for the different newspapers, in reporting league games, to call the same team by different names. Teams called Casey Stengel's All-Stars, Edington's All-Stars, and Blue's All-Stars were, in all probability, Pirrone's All-Stars, and have been identified as such in this study. Like many CWL seasons, all teams did not play the same number of games in the league. In fact, the league was primarily a two team league, with Pirrone's All-Stars and the L.A. White Sox meeting on the field of battle a total of 23 times. Anderson's warriors and Pirrone's sluggers ended in a dead heat in head to head competition, with each team winning 11 games, with one tie. Other teams that played anywhere from one to seven games in the league included Fisher's All-Stars, Rall's All-Stars, Alexander's Giants, R.H. Dyas, and San Pedro.

In addition to the California Winter League, there was a lot of other baseball being played in Southern California. In fact, two other black teams were active over the winter months, the Lincoln Giants and Alexander's Giants. Their exploits will be discussed later in the chapter.

The class of the coast, however, was concentrated in the California Winter League, with the White Sox and the aforementioned white all-star teams. The season opened in White Sox Park on October 24, with Anderson's "Bear Cats" matched against Blue's (or Pirrone's) All-Stars. In what the *L.A. Times* called "a riotous game," Detroit Tiger right-hander Red Oldham bested "Bullet Joe" Rogan 5–4. With the White Sox leading 2–1 in the top of the third, the All-Stars pounced on Rogan for four runs after two were out. Joe Pirrone, "The Gumshoe Kid," started the rally with a single to center, then proceeded to steal second base. Lu Blue sent Pirrone to third with another single. After Blue raced to second on a passed ball, Stump Edington brought both runners home with yet another single to center, giving the All-Stars the lead 4–3. But the All-Stars were not done. Hale walked, both runners advanced on a wild pitch, and Rose scored them with a single. Truck Hannah then grounded out to end the misery. Rogan shut the Stars down with just two hits over the final five innings, but the damage had been done.

The Los Angeles bats were quiet until the ninth inning. Then they made an abortive attempt to steal the game from Pirrone's boys. Tank Carr led off the ninth by drawing a base on balls. McNair singled and Rogan rescued Carr with a ringing double to left center. McNair cut the margin to 5–4 moments later when he scored on an outfield error that put the tying and winning runs in scoring position, with no outs. The home crowd was on its feet anticipating a glorious White Sox comeback. But it was not to be. Frank Shellenback, who had relieved Oldham in the seventh, took a deep breath, bore down, and retired Hawkins, Kyle, and Baker in order, leaving Dobie Moore and Joe Rogan stranded on second and third.

All-Stars

Name	Pos.	AB	H
Elliot, Carter	SS	3	1
Westhall,	3B	4	0
Pirrone, Joe	CF	3	1
Blue, Lu	1B	3	1
Edington, Jacob	RF	4	1
Hale, Sammy	2B	3	0
Rose,	LF	3	1
Hannah, J. "Truck"	C	3	0
Oldham, Red	P	1	0
Shellenback, Frank	P	1	1
Samis,	CF	1	0
Totals		29	6

L.A. White Sox

Name	Pos.	AB	H
Woods, William	CF	4	0
Fagan, Bob	2B	4	0
Carr, George	3B	3	1
McNair, Hurley	LF	4	2
Rogan, Joe	P	4	2
Moore, Dobie	SS	4	2
Hawkins, Lem	1B	4	0
Kyle, A.	RF	4	0
Shorrs,	C	0	0
Kyle, W.	PH	0	0
Baker,	C	2	0
		33	7

All-Stars   0 1 4   0 0 0   0 0 0—5—6—2
White Sox   0 2 0   0 0 0   0 0 2—4—7—2

Two base hits—McNair, Shellenback, Rogan

	IP	SO	BB
Oldham, Red (WP)	6	7	2
Shellenback, Frank	3	2	0
Rogan, Joe (LP)	9	10	9

After the opening day loss, Doc Anderson's troops regrouped, and proceeded to rake the All-Stars over the coals for the next two months, winning eight games, losing one, and tying one. On October 30, they nosed out Pirrone's team 5–4 in 12 innings, behind Rube Currie. Dobie Moore singled in the winning run off Joe Pirrone. Truck Hannah and Irish Meusel smashed three-baggers in a losing cause. Two weeks later, Bullet Joe Rogan got a measure of revenge for his opening day loss by whipping the Philadelphia Phillies right-hander, Specs Meadows, and Casey Stengel's All-Stars, 6–4. Rogan shut down the Meusel boys, Irish and Bob, four times each, and helped his own cause with two hits. Catcher Otto Ray pounded out a triple and two singles, Dobie Moore had a double and a single, and William Woods had two singles.

On November 21, the first "high profile" game of the California Winter League was played, with Walter "Duster" Mails toeing the rubber for Pirrone's All-Stars, against White Sox ace, Rube Currie. Mails had played for the Cleveland Indians in 1920, and the 24-year-old rookie was unbeatable. He went 7–0 for the American League champion Cleveland Indians during the regular season, then climaxed his storybook year by tossing a three-hit, 1–0 shutout at the Brooklyn Dodgers in Game Six of the World Series, as Tris Speaker's team claimed the World Championship. Mail's All-Star teammates enjoyed banner seasons in 1920 as well. Irish Meusel, in his prime at 27 years old, had batted .309 for the Philadelphia Phillies, while younger brother Bob, in his rookie season, hit a resounding .328, with 40 doubles, 7 triples, and 11 home runs, for the New York Yankees.

The *L.A. Times* heralded the news. "Walter Mails, the pitching sensation of the big leagues last year will be seen in action this afternoon at the L.A. White Sox grounds, Anderson and Fourth Streets. Walter will be in the points for the All-Stars, a team made up of big league stars and numbering among them the famous Meusel brothers, Bobby and Irish.... The L.A. White Sox defeated the All-Stars yesterday afternoon at the formers park, 6–2 in a very fast game. The contest was featured by the hard hitting of the colored lads, Rogan and McNair getting homers. Irish Meusel featured for the All-Stars with a triple, double, and single, in four times up."

Doc Anderson's Bear Cats showed no respect for the great Mails during the game, according to the *Times*. "These Los Angeles White Sox black birds seem to have a happy faculty of mussing up any old kind of a white team that has the courage to fling a challenge at them.

"Joe Pirrone's All-Stars, flaunting the invincible Walter Mails as their heavesman, fell again before the prowess of the colored experts, losing to them yesterday afternoon at the latter's grounds, 4–2.

"As the Sox had trounced the All-Stars the day before with the redoubtable Speed Martin doling out the cards for Pirrone's pets, it begins to look as if the colored lads will be a mighty tough aggregation to beat from now on."

The White Sox drew first blood by scoring a run in the first inning on an error and a ringing double by Tank Carr. They added three more in the sixth on another error, a double by Lem Hawkins, and hits by Dobie Moore, and Andy Kyle. The All-Stars rallied in the top of the seventh, scoring two runs on a single by Stumpy Edington, a two-bagger to left by Carter Elliot, and a single by Chet Thomas, but Rube Currie took a deep breath and retired the last two batters in order, ending the All-Stars' hopes of a comeback.

The seriousness with which both teams approached these games was demonstrated by a published incident. "Umpire Beans Reardon put down a slight demonstration of Bolshevism in the first of the sixth inning, when he called Boeckel out at the plate on Moore's throw to Ray. Irish Meusel dissented, whereupon Beans pulled off his mask and chest protector and did a Jack Dempsey that made Irish wince with envy. About twenty-five cops intervened and pressed all the bellicose disposition out of both Meusel and Reardon and the game went merrily on."

During the L.A. White Sox streak, Rogan went 5–1 against Joe Pirrone's troops, while Rube Currie ran up a 4–1–1 slate. Mails was a victim of the White Sox bats a second time on December 12, before a packed house of 2,800 at White Sox Park. Bullet Joe Rogan bested him, 4–1, on a two-hitter, liberally sprinkled with ten strikeouts. Hurley McNair was the batting star of the game, raking Mails for a single and a triple, good for three RBIs. He also made the defensive play of the game, chasing down a long drive to left field.

Then, just as suddenly as the streak began, the momentum shifted. The All-Stars could do no wrong and the Sox could do nothing right. Sloppy Thurston got the ball rolling by whipping Los Angeles 8–5 as, once again, Joe Pirrone started a rally against Bullet Joe Rogan, that led to five big runs, and the ball game. Rube Currie took a tough 6–5, 10 inning loss on February 6, with Bob Meusel, Tony Boeckel, and Carter Elliot rapping three hits apiece. Rogan was defeated by Ray Keating 7–4 in his next start. A combination of timely hitting, seven bases on balls, and two disastrous errors by the Sox spelled Bullet Joe's downfall. And the beatings continued. Rogan lost 6–2. Rube Currie was pounded 13–3 on February 23, when his wildness yielded eight walks and, coupled with ten base hits, did him in. After Rogan was routed again 10–8, Rube Currie finally righted the ship. He tossed a three-hitter to beat Sloppy Thurston 4–1. The only All-Star run crossed the plate in the third inning on an error by Tank Carr at second. As usual, Dobie Moore paced the offense with two booming triples. Currie won the next game 14–7, but Rogan went down to defeat in the finale 5–2, before Bill Pertica. Six White Sox errors, three by Bob Fagan at second, were more than Bullet Joe could overcome.

The final statistics show how evenly matched these two teams were. In addition to the record of 10–10–1, the pitching records were just as well balanced. For the Los Angeles White Sox, Rube Currie went 5–4–1 against Joe Pirrone's boys, while Joe Rogan had a mediocre 5–6 slate. On the All-Star side, Ray Keating was 4–2, Sloppy Thurston was 2–1, Red Oldham was 1–2, Bill Pertica was 1–0, and Duster Mails lost both of his decisions.

The overall records of Rogan and Currie showed Bullet Joe with a modest season record of 8–8, while Rube Currie would have been the Cy Young award winner, if such an award were given. His 12–4 record left Rogan and the other league pitchers far in arrears. Currie led the league in victories (12), winning percentage (.750), complete games (17), and innings pitched (154). In fairness to Joe Rogan, he may simply have run out of gas after pitching for ten consecutive months. His season began almost one year earlier when he pitched for the U.S. Army's 25th Infantry Division baseball team in Fort Huachuca, Arizona. In midseason he left the army and joined the Kansas City Monarchs for the summer. Then it was on to California.

He pitched brilliantly during the first half of the winter season, going 5–1, then struggled to a 3–7 record over the last six weeks. His tank was dry. But his tank never went dry again. Over his last four years in California, he compiled a record of 34–6.

Rogan did capture two accolades for the 1920–21 season however. He was both the league's home run champion, with five circuit blows in 106 at-bats, and its batting champion, with an average of .368.

Dobie Moore was the top gun of the L.A. White Sox during the season, produc-

Dobie Moore, in addition to being an outstanding defensive shortstop, was one of the most devastating hitters everywhere he played — Negro leagues (.355), Cuba (.356), and California (.385). (Robert W. Peterson Collection, National Baseball Hall of Fame Library)

ing numerous game-winning base hits. The 5'11", 230 pound right-handed slugger, rapped the ball at a .331 clip, while leading the league in games played (34), at-bats (139), base hits (46), and triples (6). He also recorded 7 doubles, while playing a dazzling defensive game at shortstop.

For the white professionals, only Bunny Fabrique (.357) and Art Griggs (.350) were able to crack the magic .300 barrier. Bob Meusel hit .286, while his brother Irish was held to a meager .235 average. Tony Boeckel and Max Carey both hit .273, Lu Blue hit .242, and Fred Haney hit .231.

There was no official California Winter League champion proclaimed for the 1920-21 season, although the Los Angeles White Sox would qualify as the champions, based on their 25-14-1 record, which was tops in the league. Based on the head-to-head battles between the White Sox and Pirrone's All-Stars, which ended in a 10-10-1 deadlock, the two teams might well have been co-champions. However, since no box scores were recovered of games between Pirrone's All-Stars and other teams in the league, the Sox would win the title by default.

1920-21 California Winter League
Final Standings (Incomplete)

	Wins	Losses	Ties
Los Angeles White Sox	22	15	2
Pirrone's All-Stars	10	10	1
(Includes record of Stengel's, Edington's, and Blue's All-Stars)			
Fisher's All-Stars	4	4	
Blue's All-Stars	1	0	
Alexander's Giants	0	2	
Rall's All-Stars	0	2	1
San Pedro	0	4	

Los Angeles White Sox Batting Statistics 1920-21

Name	Pos	G	AB	H	D	T	HR	BA
Woods, William	CF	14	47	7	0	0	0	.149
Carr, George "Tank"	3B	31	123	34	7	2	1	.276
McNair, Hurley	LF	32	131	41	11*	6*	2	.313
Rogan, "Bullet Joe"	P-CF	30	106	39	3	4	5*	.368*
Moore, Dobie	SS	34*	139*	46*	7	6*	1	.331
Hawkins, Lem	1B	29	107	27	1	0	0	.252
Kyle, Andy	RF	8	26	8	0	0	1	.308
Baker,	C	9	18	8	0	0	0	.444
Foote,	3B	10	36	6	0	0	0	.167
Ward,	RF	13	49	10	0	0	0	.204
Ray, Otto	C	18	64	13	3	2	0	.203
Currie, Rube	P	12	37	8	0	1	0	.216
Riddle,	2B	8	22	6	0	1	0	.273
Fagan, Bob	2B	27	96	29	4	0	0	.302
Washington,	RF	2	6	0	0	0	0	.000
Perry, Carl	SS	2	9	3	0	0	0	.333

Season Summaries 1920-1924

Los Angeles White Sox Pitching Statistics 1920-21

Name	G	CG	W	L	IP	SO	BB	SH
Rogan, "Bullet Joe"	16	16	8	8	144	110*	74*	1*
Currie, Rube	18*	17*	12*	4	154*	43	20	1*
McNair, Hurley	1	1	1	0	9	3	0	0
Foote,	1	0	0	0	3	1	3	0

Pirrone's All-Stars Batting Statistics 1920-21

Name	Pos	G	AB	H	D	T	HR	BA
Pirrone, Joe	CF	17	69	12	3	0	0	.174
Boeckel, Tony	3B	13	55	15	1	0	0	.273
Carey, Max	LF	12	44	12	0	0	0	.273
Griggs, Art	1B	6	20	7	1	2	0	.350
Bassler, Johnny	C	5	17	2	0	0	0	.118
Elliott, Carter	SS	18	63	17	2	0	0	.270
Niehoff, Bert	2B	14	57	14	4	2	0	.246
Billings, Josh	RF	7	24	2	0	0	0	.083
Meusel, Bob	LF	12	45	14	1	2	0	.286
Blue, Lu	1B	10	33	8	0	0	0	.242
Thomas, Chet	C	5	17	3	0	0	0	.176
Ainsmith, Eddie	C	2	7	4	1	0	0	.571
Meusel, Irish	RF	9	34	8	1	4	0	.235

Pirrone's All-Stars Pitching Statistics 1920-21

Name	G	CG	W	L	IP	SO	BB	SH
Mails, Duster	2	2	0	2	17	10	1	0
Keating, Ray	8	8	4	2	68	20	18	0
Oldham, Red	4	2	1	2	25	22	4	0
Thurston, Sloppy	4	3	2	1	34	12	6	0
Pertica, Bill	2	2	1	0	17	6	2	0
Pirrone, Joe	1	0	0	1	5	—	—	0
Martin, Speed	1	1	0	1	8	—	—	0
Meadows, Spec	1	1	0	1	8	—	—	0

Fisher's All-Stars Batting Statistics 1920-21

Name	Pos.	G	AB	H	D	T	HR	BA
Mitchell, Johnny	SS	14	51	10	0	1	0	.196
Smith, Red	3B	14	50	10	0	1	0	.200
Chadbourne, Chet	CF	14	54	10	1	0	0	.185
Fisher, Bobby	2B	14	51	6	0	1	0	.118
Schneider, Pete	RF	12	44	12	1	1	1	.273
Alcock, Scotty	1B	14	53	14	0	0	0	.264
Morse,	LF	14	45	10	2	0	0	.222
Hannah, Truck	C	17	60	16	1	1	0	.267
Bogart,	LF	4	0	0	0	0	0	.000

Fisher's All-Stars Pitching Statistics 1920-21

Name	G	CG	W	L	IP	SO	BB	SH
Houck, Byron	9	6	3	6	70	57	14	1*
Dell, Wheezer	6	3	0	5	39	29	9	0
Piercy, Bill	2	0	0	0	5	—	—	0
Shellenback, Frank	4	2	0	2	27	7	2	0

Fisher's All-Stars Pitching Statistics 1920-21

Name	G	CG	W	L	IP	SO	BB	SH
Love, Slim	1	1	0	0	9	10	2	0
Schneider, Pete	1	0	0	0	2	3	1	0

Miscellaneous Teams Batting Statistics 1920-21

Name	Team	Pos	G	AB	H	D	T	HR	BA
Sawyer, Carl	Ralls, San Pedro	2B	5	17	2	0	0	0	.118
Altrock, Nick	San Pedro	1B	5	16	1	0	0	0	.063
Haney, Fred	Love's A.S.	3B	5	13	3	1	0	0	.231
Fabrique, Bunny	San Pedro	SS	4	14	5	0	0	0	.357
Lapan, Pete	San Pedro	C	3	9	1	0	0	0	.111
Kingdon, Wes	Dyas A.S.	SS	3	10	1	0	0	0	.100
Cutshaw, George	Ralls A.S.	2B	1	4	0	0	0	0	.000
Haas, G. "Mule"	Pasadena	LF	1	4	2	0	0	0	.500
Cuyler, Kiki	Pacific Redi-Cuts	CF	1	4	1	0	0	0	.250

Miscellaneous Teams Pitching Statistics 1920-21

Name	Team	G	CG	W	L	IP	SO	BB	SH
Thomas, Lefty	San Pedro	3	3	0	3	25	13	5	0
Crandall, Doc	S.P., Ralls, Dyas	6	5	0	5	46	15	8	0

While the Los Angeles White Sox were entertaining fans in the California Winter League, two other black baseball teams were also enjoying the sunny climes of the coast. One of these, the Lincoln Giants, were members of the Eastern Colored League during the summer months. The winter contingent was managed by William Carroll, and played their games in Carroll Park, located at 32nd and Long Beach Ave. The Giants took on, and defeated, all comers around the Los Angeles area. Their main competition came from Fisher's All-Stars and Dyas' All-Stars, although they also played the tough San Pedro team with Fred Haney, Nick Altrock, Carl Sawyer, Doc Crandall, and Lefty Thomas. Fisher's team included Truck Hannah, Chet Chadbourne, Wheezer Dell, and Bill Piercy, while Dyas' All-Stars had such diamond talents as Lu Blue, Joe Jenkins, Wes Kingdon, and Art Kruger, as well as pitchers Crandall and Dell.

Still, as talented as these teams were, they were no match for the powerful Lincoln Giants. The New Yorkers were blessed with a wealth of talent, such as "The black Ty Cobb," Spot Poles, potential Hall of Famer Biz Mackey, sluggers Henry Blackman, Bill Pettus, and Jules "Home Run" Thomas, and pitchers Jess "Mountain" Hubbard and Ping Gardner. Poles was one of the best hitters of his generation, as well as an outstanding outfielder and a dangerous base stealer. Blackman was a stellar defensive Negro league third baseman for five years. His untimely death in 1924 cut short an all-star career. Bill Pettus was a big, strong, left-handed power hitter, who had hit for a .434 average with the Giants in the 1920 Eastern Colored League. As Jim Riley noted, he was a smart player, whose all-around game included extra base hits, a high batting average, good defensive skills, and strategic base stealing capabilities. Jules Thomas was a giant of a man, who could hit for average as well as distance. A lifetime .300 hitter, he was also a spectacular defensive outfielder, and a base stealing threat. Hubbard was a light complexioned pitcher who almost made it to the major leagues. One year he played for the New York Giants' farm team in Massena, New York, according to Riley, but no major league team would chance signing him to a major league contract. Ping Gardner was a submarine right-hander, who had a successful 15 year career in the Negro leagues.

The Lincoln Giants took Fisher's All-Stars to task six times in seven meetings. They also beat Dyas' All-Stars four out of five. There were no losses recorded against any other Lincoln opponent that winter. When the season ended, the Lincoln Giants had compiled an enviable record of 20-2. They were led by Mackey who posted a vicious .494 average, with 8 doubles and 5 triples in just 81 at-bats. Spot Poles hit .353, and Neal Pullen chipped in with a .333 batting average. On the mound, Hubbard (9-1), Ping Gardner (8-1), and 19-year-old Johnny "Wizard" Baugh (5-2), kept the opposition at bay.

Spot Poles, shown with his wife, Bertha, was called the "Black Ty Cobb." He was the fastest player in the Negro leagues in the early 1900s. (John B. Holway)

1920-21 California Winter Season
Independent Play

	Wins	Losses
Lincoln Giants	20	2
Dyas' All-Stars	1	4
Fisher's All-Stars	1	6
San Diego	0	1
Western Stars	0	1
Love's All-Stars	0	1
San Pedro	0	2
Alexander's Giants	0	2

Lincoln Giants Batting Statistics 1920-21

Name	Pos	G	AB	H	D	T	HR	BA
Poles, Spot	LF	19	74	27	3	5	1	.365
Scott, Robert	RF	16	57	18	1	1	0	.316
Thomas, Jules	CF	19	74	19	1	1	1*	.257
Pettus, Bill	1B	20	72	29	4	6	1*	.403
Mackey, Biz	C	25*	81	40*	8*	5*	0	.494*
Hill, John	3B	25*	92*	28	6	4	0	.304
Downs, Bunny	SS	19	72	23	6	4	0	.319
Perry, Carl	2B	16	52	12	2	2	0	.231
Blackman, Henry	2B	19	49	15	1	3	0	.306
Pullen, Neal	C	17	51	17	1	2	0	.333

Lincoln Giants Pitching Statistics 1920-21

Name	G	CG	W	L	IP	SO	BB	SH
Gardner, Ping	9	7	8	1	73	39	23	1
Baugh, Wizard	10*	5	5	2	65	48	21	1
Hubbard, Jess	10*	9*	9*	1	87*	60*	33*	3*

Baugh's record includes a 2–2 record with Alexander's Giants, and Gardner's record includes a 1–0 record with Alexander's Giants.

In addition to the two Negro league teams that competed in California, another black team, Alexander's Giants, were also active. Based on the published statistics for Alexander's, they had a very busy schedule, with Davis playing 82 games, Butcher playing 79, Williams playing 72, and Curtis playing 75. Although the player's first names were not given, it would appear as if several of the Lincoln Giants also played for Alexander's, including Carl Perry and John Hill. Other players who played a few games with the Giants, but whose statistics are included with their primary team were Biz Mackey, Ping Gardner, Jess Hubbard, Wizard Baugh, Bill Pettus, Neal Pullen, and Henry Blackman, of the Lincoln Giants, and Foote and Tank Carr of the L.A. White Sox.

Alexander's Giants Batting Statistics 1920-21

Name	Pos	G	AB	H	Total Bases	BA
Perry, Carl (?)	2B	64	359	119	152	.331
Woods, William (?)	CF	51	241	86	109	.357
Davis,	CF	82	336	87	97	.259
Ross,	P-RF	43	100	28	42	.280
Curtis,	1B	75	264	89	100	.337
Foote,	P-3B	63	240	71	89	.296
Hill, John (?)	3B	42	235	74	86	.315
Butcher, Spencer	CF-C	79	314	87	116	.277
Bradshaw,	C	39	98	28	32	.286
Williams, Gerard (?)	SS	72	224	67	85	.299
Washington, Namon (?)	RF	17	41	10	14	.244

Pitching statistics—1920-21 (pitching statistics were not published. The only pitching statistics available are those that were reported in the few box scores that were recovered).

Name	G	CG	W	L	IP	SO	BB	SH
Ross,	1	0	0	0	5	2	2	0
Foote,	2	1	1	1	0	15	8	6
Mooney,	3	2	1	2	22	8	8	0
Mackey, Biz	2	2	1	1	18	8	5	0
Cooper,	1	1	1	0	9	4	3	0

The 1921-22 Season

The 1921-22 winter league was composed of the Colored All-Stars, Pirrone's All-Stars as well as other major-minor league all-star teams managed by Fisher, Sawyer, and Meusel, plus Calpaco, Public Service, Public National, and Dyas' All-Stars.

A major change occurred in the ownership of the winter league's black baseball franchise prior to the opening of the season, as announced in the *California Eagle*. "That the base ball plant across the little stream is to be put on a concrete foundation financially as well in the matter of business intelligence is evidenced by the fact that last week four hard headed business men incorporated into what is to be known as the White Base Ball And Amusement Association with the following stockholders; Frank Howard, pres.; J.E. Walton, secy.; J.H. Graham, treas.; and James P. White, general manager.

"During the next five months the new concern will devote its energy toward promoting a top notch brand of big league baseball ably managed by Alonzo Alfred Goodwin (an officer with the Negro league Lincoln Giants) who will have absolute charge of the maneuvers of the ball club which winters here this season A three year lease has been taken on the park by the new corporation so it looks like the old lot is going to produce nuggets after all."

Oscar Charleston is considered by many baseball experts to be the greatest all-around player in Negro league history.

The new Negro league entry was called the Colored All-Stars, although the manpower was essentially the same a the previous seasons L.A. White Sox team, with Carr, Moore, Fagan, McNair, Mackey, and Hawkins. Rogan and Currie were gone, but Oscar Charleston brought his big bat to the coast, and Jose Mendez gave the team great defensive support as well as pitching excellence. Jim Jeffries, an outstanding southpaw pitcher with the Indianapolis ABCs of the NNL, and John Taylor, another of the famous Taylor clan that also included Ben and Candy Jim, shared the mound duties. And the team was still called the "Bear Cats."

Surprisingly, midway through the season, the Colored All-Stars manager, Lonnie Goodwin, retired from the game. He was replaced by James P. White as manager, with Oscar Charleston his field captain. The change did not prove to be a distraction to the Bear Cats, who played sensational baseball from start to finish.

Meusel's All-Stars provided the major opposition to the Bear Cats, with Norm Boeckel, Irish Meusel, Bob Meusel, Johnny Rawlings, and Lu Blue. Other teams in the league fielded such talents as George Cutshaw, Red Oldham, Slim Love, Lefty Thomas, Bill McKechnie, and Fred Haney. Rawlings was a smooth fielding shortstop, who enjoyed a 12 year major league career, batting .250. Blue stayed in the majors for 13 years, playing a graceful first base, batting .287 and walking an average of 103 times a year.

Winter baseball was also being played in Northern California. The fast paced professional league there, had teams in Vernon, Los Angeles, San Francisco, and Mission. George Sisler, Harry Heilmann, Hack Miller, and other talented major leaguers made the league extremely popular with fans around the San Francisco and Sacramento areas. Many players, including Wheezer Dell, Truck Hannah, Dutch Ruether, and Pete Schneider, alternated their efforts between the all-white northern league and the integrated southern league.

The California Winter League season opened with a two game series between the Colored All-Stars and Pirrone's major-minor leaguers at Anderson Park. The Saturday game featured the slugging exploits of Lu Blue and Biz Mackey, as reported in the *Chicago Defender*. "Big leaguer Lu Blue, on his first arrival at the plate in the second session, rode one of (Mackey's) curves out to the right field fence for four cushions, and again in the sixth scene, with Bob Fisher and (Bill) McKechnie on base, his Blue ship carried a circuiter to center, so in both the sixth and seventh frames, Mr. Mackey retaliated in like measure, which left the count Pirrone's 4, Mackeyites 7." The White Sox won the game by the final score of 9–6. In the Sunday game, with John Taylor pitching for Lonnie Goodwin's team, just four hours after stepping off the train from Chicago, the All-Stars won going away, 12–9. Taylor lasted only seven minutes, leaving after being tattooed for three singles, a double, and a triple.

Crowds were large and boisterous at Anderson's White Sox Park during the season. The *Los Angeles Times* reported on the game of January 15th. "The big crowd of 2000 spectators almost raised the roof with its cheering." Six days later, the *California Eagle* described the action. "Two huge crowd records were splintered at White Sox Park last Saturday and Sunday when Irish Meusel's All-Stars bumped into field manager Oscar Charleston's trained animals.... By far the mightiest throng that ever witnessed a Saturday game was present and was also the biggest gathering in the park this season. The Sabbath mob was the greatest ever crammed in the enclosure in its history, not excepting the famous Walter Mails multitude of 1920." Many fans had to stand around the outfield fence, indicating that the crowd exceeded 3,000, since the park reportedly had seating capacity for at least 2,800 people. The fans were treated to two exciting games, with the Colored All-Stars capturing the Saturday contest 3–2, and Meusel's hired hands prevailing on Sunday, 7–6. Dobie Moore was the defensive star of the Sunday game, making a one handed grab of a hot liner off the bat of "Long Bob" Meusel. Meusel got even by hitting a three-run homer off John Taylor.

The Meusel brothers, in particular, were big drawing cards in Southern California in the fall of 1921. They were local heroes, after having just competed in the recent World Series, won by Irish Meusel's New York Giants over "Long Bob" Meusel's New York Yankees, five games to three. Irish Meusel, after batting .343 during the regular season, hit .345 in the fall classic, and led both teams with 7 RBIs. Bob Meusel had a sensational regular season, batting .318 with 40 doubles, 16 triples, 24 home runs, and 135 RBIs. The aggressive Yankee outfielder stole home in Game Two of the Series, to spark Miller Huggin's team to a 3–0 win.

The most exciting game of the winter season was played on January 28, when Meusel's All-Stars crossed bats with Charleston's Bear Cats in the little park on East 4th Street. The Meusel brothers, Bob and Irish, dominated the proceedings, whacking out six hits between them, five for extra bases. The *California Eagle* described the action. "Bob Meusel was the brightest of the stars by reason of his double in the third and homer in the fifth; the latter sailed over the left garden wall, marking the first fair ball ever raised out of the lot." The left field fence was a good shot in those days. The foul pole was 345 feet from home plate, but the fence opened up sharply until it measured 455 feet in left center field.

Big brother Irish was not to be outdone however. The 6', 180 pound right-handed slugger hit for the cycle, with a single in the third, a double in the fifth, a homer in the sixth, and a triple in the eighth, good for ten total bases. Jim Jeffries was the victim of the onslaught, yielding all six blows except Irish's eighth inning triple.

Meusel's All-Stars					Colored All-Stars			
Name	Pos	AB	H		Name	Pos	AB	H
Blue, Lu	1B	5	1		McNair, Hurley	LF	5	2
Rawlings, Johnny	SS	5	3		Hawkins, Lem	1B	6	0
Boeckel, Norm	3B	6	2		Charleston, Oscar	CF-P	5	3
Meusel, Bob	RF	5	2		Mackey, Biz	3B	4	1
Meusel, Irish	CF	5	4		Carr, Tank	RF-CF	4	2
Sawyer, Carl	2B	5	4		Fagan, Bob	2B	5	2
Byler, C.	C	5	1		Moore, Dobie	SS	5	2
Lewis, Sam	P	5	1		Pullen, Neal	C	5	2
Pirrone, Joe	LF	4	0		Jeffries, Jim	P-RF	5	3
Totals		45	18				44	17

Meusel's All-Stars   4 0 1   0 3 4   2 1 0—15—18—1
Los Angeles White Sox   1 5 0   0 0 0   0 2 2—10—17—3

Two Base Hits: B. Meusel, I. Meusel, Byler, Sawyer (3), Boeckel
Three Base Hits: Sawyer, I. Meusel, Charleston (2)
Home Runs: B. Meusel, I. Meusel

	IP	SO	BB
Lewis, Sam	9	11	2
Jeffries, Jim	6	6	2
Charleston, Oscar	3	0	1

WP—Lewis
LP—Jeffries

When the season ended, the Colored All-Stars stood atop the pack, with a record of 25–15–1. In a not-unusual season, most of the games featured a white team against the Colored All-Stars in Anderson Park. As a result, the recovered records show the Colored All-Stars with 41 games played, the combined major/minor all-star teams (Pirrone, Meusel, Sawyer, Edington, and Fisher), with 25 games played (12 wins and 13 losses), Calpaco with seven games played, and four other teams with a combined total of eight games played.

Irish Meusel captured the batting championship with an average of .425, after having hit a sizzling .343 in the National League, and Biz Mackey took home run honors with four circuit clouts to his credit. Charleston and McNair banged out six triples, and Lem Hawkins hit ten doubles. Jim Jeffries led the league in pitching victories with 9, and Hurley McNair led in winning percentage with a perfect 4–0 record.

Other big bombers for the Colored All-Stars were Henry Blackman with an average of .403, Biz Mackey at .392, and Oscar Charleston at .375. Midget Rose of Pirrone's All-Stars had a stratospheric .462 batting average, but showed only 26 at-bats. Norm Boeckel hit .342 for Meusel's, Johnny Rawlings hit .314, and Bob Meusel came in at .308. Sam Lewis led all All-Star pitchers with a record of 5–2.

Bob Meusel, New York Yankee outfielder, hit Negro league pitching for averages of .286 and .308 in 1920-21 and 1921-22.

1921-22 California Winter League
Final Standings—Incomplete

	Wins	Losses	Ties
Colored All-Stars	25	15	1
Pirrone's All-Stars	4	2	0
Sawyer's All-Stars	2	0	0

Meusel's All-Stars	4	7	0
Fisher's All-Stars	2	3	0
Edington's All-Stars	0	1	0
Kruger's All-Stars	0	1	0
Dyas' All-Stars	0	3	0
Calpaco	1	6	1
Pacific National	1	2	0
Public Service	0	1	0

Colored All-Stars Batting Statistics 1921-22

Name	Pos	G	AB	H	D	T	HR	BA
Charleston, Oscar	CF	21	79	32	7	6*	0	.405
Blackman, Henry	3B	21	74	30	4	2	3*	.405
Mackey, Biz	3B	31	123	47*	8	5	3*	.382
Carr, Tank	RF	33*	134*	45	8	5	3*	.336
Hawkins, Lem	1B	30	116	39	10	3	0	.336
Pullen Neal	C	12	46	15	1	1	1	.326
McNair, Hurley	CF	32	124	36	6	6*	2	.290
Foote,	RF	2	7	2	2	0	0	.287
Fagan, Bob	2B	32	121	33	3	1	2	.280
Moore, Dobie	SS	22	80	22	4	3	0	.275
Jeffries, Jim	P	22	63	16	0	2	0	.254
Mendez, Jose	SS	24	82	20	3	3	2	.244
Ward, Tom	RF	10	37	8	1	0	1	.244
Taylor, John	P	13	32	5	0	2	0	.216

Colored All-Stars Pitching Statistics 1921-22

Name	G	CG	W	L	IP	SO	BB	SH
Mackey, Biz	5	2	3	1	41	30	9	0
McNair, Hurley	7	5	4	1	48	18	16	1
Taylor, John	13	10	7	6	100*	54	22	1
Jeffries, Jim	14*	11*	9*	5	98	46	28	1
Charleston, Oscar	2	0	0	0	5	2	3	0
Mendez, Jose	2	0	0	0	7	2	3	0

Miscellaneous Teams Batting Statistics 1921-22

Name	Team	G	AB	H	D	T	HR	BA
Smith, Red	Pac. Natl., Sawyer, Pirrone	9	37	9	1	0	1	.243
Pirrone, Joe	Pirrone, Meusel	14	54	10	1	1	1	.185
Rose, Midget	Pirrone's All-Stars	6	26	12	2	0	0	.462
Blue, Lu	Pirrone, Sawyer, Meusel	17	58	16	3	2	2	.276
Sawyer, Carl	Pirrone, Meusel	13	51	15	5	2	0	.294
Kingdon, Wes	Pirrone's All-Stars	2	8	0	0	0	0	.000
Boeckel, Tony	Pirrone, Meusel	17	64	22	3	3	0	.344
Herman, Babe	Pirrone, Meusel A.S.	2	8	3	1	0	0	.375
DeMaggio, N.	Pirrone, Calpaco	7	27	8	1	0	0	.296
Rawlings, J.	Meusel's All-Stars	9	35	11	1	2	0	.314
Meusel, Irish	Meusel's All-Stars	10	40	17	1	1	1	.425*
Meusel, Bob	Meusel's All-Stars	9	39	12	2	2	2	.308
Cutshaw, Geo.	Pacific National	2	7	4	0	0	0	.571
Hannah, Truck	Sawyer's All-Stars	2	6	2	1	0	0	.333

Miscellaneous Teams Pitching Statistics 1921-22

Name	Team	G	CG	W	L	IP	SO	BB	SH
Lewis, Sam	Meusel, Sawyer	7	6	5	2	56	41	18	0
Thomas, Lefty	Meusel, Fisher A.S.	9	8	2	6	71	35	19	0
Oldham, Red	Pirrone, Calpaco	2	2	2	0	18	—	—	0
Love, Slim	Kruger, Edington A.S.	4	1	0	3	20	—	—	0
Pertica, Bill	Pirrone, Meusel A.S.	3	3	2	1	27	12	10	0

The 1922-23 Season

The black entry in the 1922-23 California Winter League was once again the Los Angeles White Sox. And their manager was once again Doc Anderson. The team looked exceptionally strong with Rube Currie and Jose Mendez anchoring the pitching staff, and sluggers Dobie Moore, Tank Carr, Oscar "Heavy" Johnson, and Biz Mackey providing the offense. Heavy Johnson was another member of the famed 25th infantry division baseball team, along with Moore, Rogan, Hawkins, and McNair. The husky 250 pound outfielder was one of the Negro league's top power hitters during the 1920s, compiling a career batting average of .350, with 16 home runs a year.

The league was essentially a two team league with Pirrone's All-Stars the opposition. There were a few games with other teams, but most of these appeared to be independent games, outside the league format. Joe Pirrone had his team well stocked for the season. Sloppy Thurston, Tony Faeth, and Pirrone himself handled most of the pitching duties, although Bill Piercy and Elmer Rieger were in the wings. Red Smith, Truck Hannah, Wes Kingdon, Heinie Manush, Ping Bodie, and Babe Herman gave the team strong offense and good defense. Red Smith played third base for the Brooklyn Dodgers and Boston Braves for nine years and, according to Mike Shatzkin in The Ballplayers, he was "consistently among the best third basemen in the league." Red Smith had a career batting average of .278.

The league was called the "Major Circuit" in the Los Angeles Times. Other leagues around the area included the Triple A League, the City League, and the County League. There were also many other teams playing an independent schedule.

The White Sox got off to a fast start when the season opened on November 5, dumping Pirrone's All-Stars two straight. The following week, the two teams were at it again. In the opener of the series, they fought to a 3-3 tie, with the game called on account of darkness after nine innings. There was very little offense on either side, with Rube Currie and Nick Dumovich in complete control. Oscar Johnson, called "Chubby" in the Times, and Jose Mendez, were the exceptions. Johnson cracked a triple and two singles, while Mendez chalked up a double and a single. The Pirrone gang got their revenge on the Sox for the two beatings the first week, winning the last two games by scores of 7-4 and 7-2. Bill Piercy, with help from Dumovich, tossed a one hitter at Anderson's hired guns in the Sunday game, with Bob Fagan's single the only hit. The All-Stars pummeled Currie for 16 base hits, including three each by DeMaggio, Smith, Oldham, and Lapan.

The White Sox put forth their best all-around effort on December 3, as noted in the Times. "With Jose Mendez, the colored Walter Johnson, on the mound for them, Doc Anderson's Los Angeles White Sox won their first Sunday game of the present winter season from Pirrone's All-Stars, 6-0, yesterday at the Sox Park. Mendez was in his old-time form and was practically unhittable by the All-Star sluggers and allowed but two scattered hits, one coming in the

Left: Oscar "Heavy" Johnson was a powerful, 250 pound slugger who starred in the Negro leagues for 12 years. *Above:* Jose Mendez was the greatest pitcher in Cuban baseball history. He also played in the Negro leagues. (*Both photographs,* Robert W. Peterson Collection, National Baseball Hall of Fame Library)

second and the other in the sixth." The game was a tight pitchers' duel between the Cuban fireballer and Tony Faeth for seven innings, with the Sox clinging to a slim 2–0 lead. But in the eighth, they fell on Faeth for four big runs, sparked by Johnson's homer and triples by Carr and Mackey.

Pirrone's All-Stars				Los Angeles White Sox			
Name	Pos	AB	H	Name	Pos	AB	H
DeMaggio, Nick	LF	4	0	Hawkins, Lem	SS	4	1
Pirrone, Joe	CF	4	1	Fagan, Bob	2B	3	1
Oldham, Red	RF	4	0	Mackey, Biz	3B	4	1
Smith, Red	3B	3	0	Johnson, Osacr	C	4	3
Thurston, Sloppy	2B	3	0	Carr, Tank	1B	4	2
Peckham,	1B	3	0	Williams,	LF	4	0
Kingdon, Wes	SS	3	1	Ward, Tom	CF	4	2
Tobin, Frank	C	3	0	Currie, Rube	LF-P	3	0
Faeth, Tony	P	3	0	Mendez, Jose	P-RF	3	0
Totals		30	2			33	10

Pirrone's All-Stars   0 0 0   0 0 0   0 0 0—0— 2—2
Los Angeles White Sox   0 0 0   2 0 0   0 4 x—6—10—1

Two base hits: Pirrone, Ward, Hawkins
Three base hits: Carr, Mackey
Home run: Johnson

	IP	SO	BB
Faeth, Tony	8	6	1
Mendez, Jose	8	5	1
Currie, Rube	1	1	0

WP—Mendez
LP—Faeth

The battle between the two teams continued through late November and into December. Pirrone's troops took three games in a row by scores of 9–4, 3–2, and 5–2. The 3–2 game in particular was exciting, with Sloppy Thurston outdueling Mendez. According to the *Los Angeles Times*, "The game was one of the best ever played on the local diamond. Throughout the game the spectators were brought to their feet by spectacular plays or a snappy piece of base stealing. Joe Pirrone, All-Star leader, made a beautiful running catch which saved the game for the winners."

Currie, called King Currie in the L.A. newspapers, finally stopped the White Sox slide on Christmas Day, by blanking the All-Stars 6–0 on a tight two-hitter. A crowd of 2,500 that packed the grandstand and box seats were treated to a masterful exhibition by Currie, who set four batters down on strikes while walking three. Tom Ward with a triple and a single, and Heavy Johnson with a double and a single, led the Sox attack. Heinie Manush and Babe Herman had the only two hits for Pirrone's boys.

The lead see-sawed back and forth into February, with the White Sox clinging to first place by a thread. Finally, the two teams met in a three game series over the weekend of February 17–18, to determine the league champion. The Sox unleashed a 17 hit attack on Saturday, to eke out a 14–12 victory, giving them a one game lead with just two games to play. The All-Stars pounded out 19 hits off Lem Hawkins, but fell two runs short. A six run sixth inning gave Anderson's troops a commanding 14–8 lead, and they held on for the victory. Mendez, Fagan, Blue, and Currie rapped three hits apiece for L.A., while Wes Kingdon had a single, double, and triple for the All-Stars, and Nick DeMaggio had three singles.

The Sunday doubleheader was a fitting climax to the season. With their backs to the wall, the All-Stars, needing a sweep to claim the pennant, battered Rube Currie for 15 hits and 14 runs, en route to a 14–0 rout of the proud L.A. team. Joe Pirrone, the Gumshoe Kid, threw the shutout. Wes Kingdon continued his torrid hitting with a single and a double, Babe Herman ripped two doubles, and Truck Hannah punched out a double and two singles.

In game two, for all the marbles, Doc Anderson unveiled his secret weapon. He sent Jose Mendez to the mound to oppose Elmer Rieger. Mendez was a money pitcher, who had pitched in big games in both Cuba and the American Negro league for almost two decades, and he rose to the occasion one more time, blanking Pirrone's sluggers 4–0 on five hits. The White Sox got only four hits but made them count. Wes Kingdon with a single and a double, and Wally Hood with two singles, were the only All-Star hitters to give Mendez any trouble. Herman and Hannah both drew the collar.

The final won-loss records uncovered in this study unfortunately do not reflect the White Sox victory totals, but according to the *Los Angeles Times*, they were the official 1922-23 California Winter League champions.

Heavy Johnson led all hitters at the plate with an average of .340. Mackey also hit .340 but lost the title by .0004. Wes Kingdon hit .328. Truck Hannah hit .409, Babe Herman hit .375, and Ping Bodie hit .368, but none of them played in the required ten games to qualify for the batting title. Wes Kingdon was the home run king with two. Four players tied for pitching honors with identical 3–1 records.

In addition to the Los Angeles White Sox, the St. Louis All-Stars were also active in California, apparently playing an independent schedule. Jay Bell, a 19-year-old rookie, who would later come to be known

Truck Hannah played in the minor leagues for 32 years. He played winter league ball for nine years. (Dick Dobbins)

as "Cool Papa," was a pitcher for the All-Stars. He talked about his California sojourn to John Holway. "I went to California that winter on the pitching staff to play in the winter league. We got rooms in a little hotel down by the station—a big room, had two beds. My brother Fred Bell and I slept in one. Turkey Stearnes slept in the other.... (Stearnes) went to Cuba and they needed an outfielder, so they put me out there. One Saturday we were playing in Pasadena and a lot of balls were hit over the center fielder's head. I'd run over behind him and catch them. So from then on I played center field. I wasn't a pitcher anymore."

The St. Louis All-Stars' record was not published, but their batting averages were. Turkey Stearnes hit .324, Henry Blackman hit .297, and Crush Holloway hit .270, for the nine games published. Jay Bell hit .667 with four hits in six at-bats.

1922-23 California Winter League
Final Standings—Incomplete

	Wins	Losses	Ties
Los Angeles White Sox	9	11	2
Pirrone's All-Stars	11	9	2
San Diego	4	2	0
Vernon Tigers	0	2	0

Los Angeles White Sox Batting Statistics 1922-23

Name	Pos	G	AB	H	D	T	HR	BA
Hawkins, Lem	1B	16	63*	14	2	0	0	.222
Mendez, Jose	SS	14	50	12	1	0	0	.240
Carr, Tank	3B	16	56	12	0	2*	0	.214
Mackey, Biz	3B	13	50	17	3	1	0	.340
Johnson, Oscar	C	11	47	16	2	1	0	.340*
Fagan, Bob	2B	16	55	14	1	0	0	.255
Ward, Pinky	CF	16	55	14	3	1	0	.255
Williams	LF	13	48	11	3	1	0	.229

Los Angeles White Sox Pitching Statistics 1922-23

Name	G	CG	W	L	IP	SO	BB	SH
Currie, Rube	6*	6*	2	3	52*	26*	18	1*
Linder,	3	3	0	3	27	—	—	0
Mendez, Jose	4	4	3*	1	34	17	7	2*
Mackey, Biz	1	0	0	1	7	6	3	0
Hawkins, Lem	3	2	3*	1	20	5	7	0

Pirrone's All-Stars Batting Statistics 1922-23

Name	Pos	G	AB	H	D	T	HR	BA
DeMaggio, Nick	LF	16	61	13	1	0	0	.213
Pirrone, Joe	CF	13	48	8	1	0	0	.167
Oldham, Red	RF	9	30	8	0	0	0	.267
Smith, Red	3B	16	58	15	3	0	0	.259
Peckham, Frank	1B	7	24	6	0	0	0	.250
Manush, Heinie	RF	6	23	7	3	0	0	.304
Herman, Babe	1B	6	24	9	4	1	0	.375
Kingdon, Wes	SS	16	58	19*	3	2*	2*	.328
Niehoff, Bert	2B	7	27	8	4*	0	0	.296

Pirrone's All-Stars Batting Statistics 1922-23

Name	Pos	G	AB	H	D	T	HR	BA
Hannah, Truck	C	7	22	9	1	0	0	.409
Bodie, Ping	RF	5	19	7	2	1	0	.368

Pirrone's All-Stars Pitching Statistics 1922-23

Name	G	CG	W	L	IP	SO	BB	SH
Faeth, Tony	4	2	3*	1	31	—	—	0
Thurston, Sloppy	4	4	2	2	35	9	4	0
Pirrone, Joe	4	3	3*	1	31	15	6	0

St. Louis All-Stars Batting Statistics 1922-23

Name	Pos	G	AB	H	D	T	HR	BA
Bell, Jay "Cool Papa"	P	3	6	4	0	0	1	.667
Stearnes, Turkey	CF	9	37	12	2	1	3	.324
Burnett, Tex	C	7	28	9	2	1	0	.321
Miller, Percy	LF	7	23	7	0	0	2	.304
Blackman, Henry	3B	9	37	11	1	1	0	.297
Fagan, Bob	1B	4	11	3	0	0	0	.272
Holloway, Crush	RF	8	37	10	0	2	0	.270
Pullen, Neal	C	1	4	1	0	0	0	.250
Riggins, Bill	SS	9	39	9	1	0	0	.236
Day, Connie	2B	9	38	4	0	0	0	.105

St. Louis All-Stars Pitching Statistics 1922-23

Name	G	CG	W	L	IP	SO	BB
Bell, Jay "Cool Papa"	1	1	1	0	9	6	2

The 1923-24 Season

For some reason, Doc Anderson and his Los Angeles White Sox did not return to the California Winter League for the 1923-24 season. They were replaced by Lorenzo S.N. Cobb's St. Louis Stars. Cobb brought an all-star group of players to the coast, headed by a 22-year-old outfielder who had just completed a sensational rookie season with the Detroit Stars of the Negro National League. Turkey Stearnes had hit .353 with a league leading 17 home runs in 57 games for Detroit, on his way to a Hall of Fame career. He was supported by such baseball talents as Henry Blackman, Crush Holloway, Connie Day, Bill Riggins, Andy Cooper, Bob McClure, and the Bell brothers, Fred and Jay.

The Stars main opposition consisted of Pirrone's All-Stars and Universal Studio. Joe Pirrone had assembled his usual "cast of characters," Nick DeMaggio, Chet Chadbourne, Pete Lapan, Babe Herman, and Jess Doyle. One exciting member of the cast was Pete Schneider, who had pitched in the major leagues from 1914 to 1919, compiling a record of 59–86. After being converted to an outfielder, Schneider went on to have a successful career in the Pacific Coast League, batting .333 with 22 home runs a year, over a seven year period. Playing for the Vernon Tigers on May 11, 1923, the 6'1", 194 pound slugger had a career day, blasting five home runs and a double in eight at-bats, and driving in 14 runs in Vernon's 35–11 rout of Salt Lake City.

The Universal Studio team was anchored by major and high minor league veterans Red Smith (.327 with Vernon of the PCL), Bert Adams (8 year major league veteran), Chicken Hawks (hit .322 with

Andy Cooper was one of the top pitchers in both the Negro leagues (121–54) and the California Winter League (22–6) during the 1920s and '30s. (Luis Munoz)

Philadelphia Phillies in 1925), Bert Niehoff (6 year major league veteran), Tex Vache (hit .313 with Boston Red Sox in 1925), Art Griggs (.329 with L.A.), Jess Doyle (20–15 for Vernon in 1922), and Bill Bailey (23–15 with Omaha, Western League in 1924).

Unfortunately, the coverage of the league by the local newspapers, as well as by the black papers across the country, was almost nonexistent. The press did not name a league champion, and since there were less than two dozen box scores uncovered, it was impossible to project a winner. However, there were several newsworthy items to report.

The St. Louis Stars met Pirrone's All-Stars on Armistice Day, November 11, in a game covered by the *Los Angeles Times*. "A home run swat to left field by right fielder (Percy) Miller with one man on in the fifth inning gave the St. Louis colored All-Stars a 6–3 victory over Joe Pirrone's Major and Minor League Stars yesterday at White Sox Park before a crowd of about 4000 fans. Up until Miller's wallop, it was anybody's game. Cooper was on the mound for the St. Louis club and had the better of the hurling argument with "Pinches" Kunz, Pittsburgh moundsman. ... After the fifth, Cooper had the situation well in hand, not allowing a hit until Lapan slapped out a Texas-Leaguer with two away in the ninth.... Riggins, Holloway, and Miller hit the ball hard for the colored club, while Chadbourne drew two doubles for the Pirrone Stars. Day's fielding at second featured for the winners, while Pirrone pulled off a star catch in deep right of a liner that looked labeled for three bases."

The St. Louis Stars who had moved into the California Winter League after playing independent baseball on the west coast during the 1922-23 season, held their own against tough competition, particularly from the Universal Studio team. In the only four games reported between the two teams, Universal won two games, lost one and tied one. Connie Mack once said that pitching was 80 percent of the game, and that concept is as valid now as it was seventy years ago. The St. Louis squad learned that bitter lesson the hard way. They had the best offense in the league with seven players batting over .300, led by Neal Pullen at .400 and Henry Blackman at .341. Their .285 team batting average was a full 40 points higher than Universal's, but their pitching did not match up well with the Studio team's pitching.

In the battles between the two teams, Universal outscored St. Louis by a combined total of 28–12. In the first game, Jess Doyle, who had won 20 games for Vernon in 1922, shackled the big bombers from the east while the Studio team took advantage of 11 bases on balls issued by the Bell brothers

(6 by Fred and 5 by Jay), to coast to an easy 12–2 victory. Chicken Hawks and Henry Blackman homered in the game.

Bob Fagan's boys, far from discouraged, bounced back in game two behind Andy Cooper, with a save from Bob McClure, to edge the movietown crew, 4–3. Blackman had three singles to lead the attack. Cooper had a comfortable 4–1 lead after seven innings, but weakened in the eighth and ninth. Universal scored one run in the eighth, and had the tying run on base with one out in the ninth, when manager Riggins yanked Cooper in favor of Bob McClure, who recorded the final two outs.

McClure wasn't so fortunate the next day, however. Universal's hired guns, led by Red Smith with a homer and a single, and Bert Adams and Chicken Hawks with two singles apiece, pounded the Stars' righthander freely, on their way to a 9–2 win. They scored five runs in the second inning to ice the game early, then tacked on three more runs in the sixth and one in the seventh for good measure. Bill Whitaker, who pitched for the New Orleans team in the Southern Association during the summer, scattered seven hits for the win.

The fourth and final game recorded between the two teams was a hard fought battle that ended in a 4–4 ten inning tie. Bill Bailey started on the mound for the Universal team once again, opposing hard throwing southpaw Fred Bell. Neither pitcher finished the game. Bailey was relieved by Whitaker in the eighth, and Bell handed the reigns over to Andy Cooper in the ninth. Actually Bell had the Studio nine under control most of the game, and entered the ninth inning with a commanding 4–0 lead, before he suddenly collapsed. By the time Cooper stopped the bleeding, the movie gang had tied the game at four apiece, thanks to timely base hits by Tex Vache and Bert Niehoff. Connie Day's two-run home run was the big blow for the St. Louis Stars.

A tragedy put a damper on the winter baseball season as it was winding down. Tony Boeckel, a 31-year-old third baseman, who had just finished his seventh year in the National League, batting .298 for the Boston Braves, was killed in an auto crash in Torrey Pines, just north of San Diego on February 16th. Boeckel was a Los Angeles native and a local favorite, who had played for Stockton in the defunct California Baseball League in 1913 and 1914, batting around .316. He also spent six years in the California Winter League between 1916 and 1922, hitting .301.

1923-24 California Winter League
Final Standings—Incomplete

	Wins	Losses	Ties
St. Louis Stars	5	4	2
Universal Studio	2	1	1
Pirrone's All-Stars	1	6	0
San Diego	3	2	1

St. Louis Stars Batting Statistics 1923-24

Name	Pos	G	AB	H	D	T	HR	BA
Riggins, Bill	CF	11	43	14	1	0	0	.326
Day, Connie	2B	11	43	8	1	0	1	.186
Stearnes, Turkey	SS	9	36	11	0	1	2	.306
Holloway, Crush	LF	11	45	11	2	1	0	.244
Miller, Percy	RF	8	29	11	1	0	2	.379
Ray, Otto	C	9	32	5	0	0	0	.156
Blackman, Henry	3B	11	41	14	1	1	2	.341

Name	Pos	G	AB	H	D	T	HR	BA
Burnett, Tex	C	7	22	10	1	1	0	.455
Pullen, Neal	C	6	25	10	2	1	2	.400
Fagan, Bob	1B	8	21	7	0	1	0	.333
Bell, Cool Papa	P	5	11	2	0	0	1	.181

St. Louis Stars Pitching Statistics 1923-24

Name	G	CG	W	L	IP	SO	BB	SH
Cooper, Andy	4	1	2*	0	22	7	9	0
McClure, Bob	5	2*	2*	1	29	25	14	0
Bell, Fred	8	1	1	4	40*	28*	20	0
Bell, Cool Papa	3	0	0	0	16	11	10	0

Pirrone's All-Stars Batting Statistics 1923-24

Name	Pos	G	AB	H	D	T	HR	BA
DeMaggio, Nick	LF	8	30	5	0	0	0	.167
Pirrone, Joe	RF	10	25	7	0	0	0	.280
Chadbourne, Chet	CF	6	20	6	3	0	0	.300
McDowell,	3B	6	24	9	0	1	1	.375
Doyle, Larry	2B	6	16	5	2	0	0	.313
Lapan, Pete	C	9	36	9	0	1	0	.250
Schneider, Pete	LF	4	14	4	0	0	1	.287
Gay,	3B	5	21	6	1	0	0	.287
Herman, Babe	RF	4	16	4	2	0	0	.250

Pirrone's All-Stars Pitching Statistics 1923-24

Name	G	CG	W	L	IP	SO	BB	SH
Kunz, Earl	4	1	1	2	18	19	11	0
Doyle, Jess	6	1	3	1	39	26	9	0
Shanklin,	2	2	0	2	16	5	4	0

Miscellaneous Teams Batting Statistics 1923-24

Name	Team	G	AB	H	D	T	HR	BA
Kingdon, Wes	White Kings, Buick	6	21	3	1	0	0	.143
Hawks, Chicken	Universal Studio	5	15	5	0	0	2	.333
Griggs, Art	Universal Studio	4	7	5	1	0	0	.716
Niehoff, Bert	Universal Studio	5	19	6	1	0	0	.316
Falk, Bib	Hammond	2	8	2	0	1	0	.250
Cox, Dick	Pasadena	2	8	5	1	2	1	.625
Goslin, Goose	Asuza	1	3	1	0	0	0	.333
Bodie, Ping	Harlow A.S.	1	4	1	0	0	0	.250

Miscellaneous Teams Pitching Statistics 1923-24

Name	Team	G	CG	W	L	IP	SO	BB	SH
Killeen, Jack	San Diego	3	2	2	1	26	5	5	0
Schneider, P.	Union Pacific	1	1	0	1	9	7	2	0
Shellenback, F.	Hammond	1	1	1	0	9	—	—	0
Vance, Dazzy	Montebello	1	1	0	1	9	4	5	0
Campbell,	Buick Auto	1	1	0	1	8	4	1	0

The 1924-25 Season

The 1924-25 winter season was the beginning of "The Golden Age" of the California Winter League. That year there were two black teams playing in two different leagues. The Los Angeles White Sox were members of the All-Professional Winter League, the "official" California Winter League, while another Negro league team, the St. Louis Giants, participated in the Southern California Winter League.

The All-Professional League consisted of four teams, the White Sox, Pirrone's All-Stars, the White King Soapsters, and the Vernon Tigers. They played their games in the newly constructed Pirrone Park, also known as White Sox Park II, located at Thirty-Eighth and Compton Avenue. Some league games, involving two white teams, were occasionally played at Washington Park. As noted earlier, the new White Sox Park was a hitter's paradise for men who could hit to right field. The left field fence was a long 356 foot wallop from home plate, but the right field barrier hovered over the first baseman, just 235 feet from home, reminiscent of Nashville's infamous Sulphur Dell Stadium. The legitimacy of the game was protected however by an 80 foot high screen that extended from the right field foul line to dead center field.

Joe Pirrone and his brother John built the park to replace the older, obsolete Anderson Park that had served as the official winter league park for four years. The *California Eagle* reported on the construction. "From an authentic source comes the information that a new baseball park, that will be the home of Negro league players, will be built and completed in time for an opening game on Sunday, October nineteenth.... Lonnie Goodwin, one of the pioneer managers and developers of baseball talent hereabouts will manage the team of players that are to be recruited from the pennant winning teams of the Negro National and Eastern Leagues.... Altho the time is short and work is just starting on the stands today (Thursday), the plant is expected to be in readiness a week from Sunday."

The timing of the completion of the park was a bit optimistic, but the project was still completed in record time. Unfortunately, the Negro league players could not get to the coast in time for the opening game on October 25, so the park was officially dedicated in a game between two white teams, Pirrone's All-Stars and Sawyer's Stars, as covered by the *Times*. "Joe Pirrone's All-Stars celebrated the opening of the new Pirrone Park ... by handing Carl Sawyer's team a 9–5 licking while a large crowd of fans looked on.... Mayor George Cryor officially started things by pitching the first ball to President Weinreich of the Greater Southern California Baseball Association after Dan Tobey had introduced all the players to the assembled multitude.... The heavy hitting of Ken Williams, St. Louis Brown's slugger, who played center field for the victors, featured the game. Williams, who led Babe Ruth and the American League in home runs two years ago, hit one nine miles over the right field fence for the circuit. Williams' clout was one of the longest ever hit in Los Angeles, the ball clearing Ascot Avenue while still rising. Dod Murphy and Johnny Bassler also (s)lammed out circuit clouts.... Hollis Thurston was on the mound for the Pirrone club and succeeded in holding the Sawyer sluggers fairly well in check." Jigger Statz had a double in four at-bats for Sawyer's team, while Babe Herman had a triple and a single for the Pirrone All-Stars.

The following day, the two teams met again, with the same result. Pirrone's All-Stars outlasted Sawyer's Stars 12–9, as 33 base hits rattled around White Sox Park, 17 by the victors. Ping Bodie led the onslaught with four hits in five at-bats.

Lonnie Goodwin's troops arrived in town a few days later, ready to go. Goodwin

brought a top flight team with him, led by Moore, Hawkins, Day, Pullen, McNair, and Fagan, with Currie, Cherry Bell, and William "Plunk" Drake, handling the pitching chores. Drake was a big, strong, talented pitcher whose meanness on the mound kept batters from getting too comfortable in the batter's box. His nickname, "Plunk," came from his penchant for hitting batters who crowded the plate. According to John Holway's research, Drake compiled a 99–61 record during his 16 year Negro league career, good for a .619 winning percentage.

The official California Winter League opening game between Pirrone's All-Stars and the Los Angeles White Sox took place on Sunday, November 2, 1924. The All-Stars fielded a worthy opponent for Lonnie Goodwin's team, with players like Babe Herman (.318 with Little Rock, Southern Association), Ping Bodie (.295 with Vernon), Red Smith (.327 with Vernon/L.A.), "Glass Arm" Eddie Brown (.308 with Brooklyn), and Carl Sawyer. The pitching duties were handled by Pug Cavet (19–14 with New Orleans, S.A.). Brown was a consistent .300 hitter with a weak throwing arm. In 1924, he was a major contributor to the Dodgers' fantastic pennant chase, that had the team in first place until the final week of the season, only to lose out to the hated Giants by 1½ games. Brown's clutch base hits almost brought Wilbert Robinson's team from sixth place to first in just a year.

The *Los Angeles Times* previewed the opener. "With a pair of classy games scheduled, the All-Professional Winter League gets underway this afternoon. At Pirrone Park, the Eastern Colored Giants (L.A. White Sox) will make their debut against Pirrone's Major-Minor All Stars, while the strong White King Soap nine will open against Chet Chadbourne's Vernon Tigers at Washington Park. Both tilts should be exciting ones, not only because of the number of stars on all of the clubs, but because of the fact that the teams are playing on a 60–40 basis. Ball players, like most mortals, are extremely fond of the coin of the realm, and will do anything short of breaking a leg to get the winners end."

The *Times* also reported on the game. "Although outhit, Joe Pirrone's Major-Minor Stars edged out a 6–5 victory over the L.A. White Sox after an exciting game played yesterday at Pirrone Park. A crowd of 2000 fans witnessed the game.

"A home run over the right field fence with two on in the third by Babe Herman gave Pirrone's club a lead which the colored club was unable to overcome, although it did come dangerously close in the eighth by smacking Pug Cavet, Minneapolis southpaw, for a brace of markers. Herman and Pullen, colored catcher, divided hitting honors with three safeties each."

All-Stars				L.A. White Sox			
Name	Pos	AB	H	Name	Pos	AB	H
Smith, M.H. Red	SS	4	2	Hawkins, Lem	SS	5	2
Pirrone, Joe	CF	4	0	Fagan, Bob	2B	5	1
Brown, Eddie	3B	4	1	Evans, Bill (?)	3B	5	1
Herman, Babe	1B	5	2	McNair, Hurley	CF	5	1
Bodie, Ping	LF	5	2	Pullen, Neal	C	4	3
Sawyer, Carl	2B	4	1	Butcher, Spencer	LF	4	1
Lapan, Pete	RF	0	0	Savage,	RF	4	2

Opposite: The Kansas City Monarchs continued to send players to California throughout the 1920s, including Lem Hawkins (left), Frank Duncan (2nd from left), Cherry Bell (3rd from left), Dink Mothell (4th from left), and William "Plunk" Drake (right). (Robert W. Peterson)

Bachant,	C	4	0		Foote,	3B	4	1
Cavet, Pug	P	4	1		Munion,	P	1	0
McGraw, Bob	RF	4	0		Bell, Cherry	P	2	0
Totals		38	9				39	12

Pirrone's All-Stars   0 0 3   0 2 1   0 0 0—6—9—3
Los Angeles White Sox   0 0 0   2 1 0   0 2 0—5—12—3

Two base hits: Bodie (2), Hawkins
Three base hits: Foote
Home runs: Herman

	IP	SO	BB
Cavet, Pug (WP)	9	7	0
Munion, (LP)	4⅓	4	1
Bell, Cherry	4⅔	7	4

The White Sox didn't fare too well in their first few games of the season, but help was on the way. Dobie Moore arrived the second week of November and Tank Carr pulled into town in early December, to lend some powerful offensive support to Goodwin's beleaguered troops. Both Moore and Carr proved to be devastating hitters over the final three months of the season. The stocky shortstop, in particular, was in a zone all year, rapping out extra base hits at a record pace. He slammed 33 extra base hits in just 40 games, while challenging the magic .500 barrier in hitting.

The Moore magic was duly recorded by the *Times* in a November 30 game. "The Los Angeles colored White Sox came from behind and overcame an eight run lead to win, 11–10, and make it three straight victories over Joe Pirrone's All-Stars, yesterday at White Sox Park. 'Home Run' Moore, star White Sox shortstop was responsible for seven of the team's runs, hitting two home runs and a double, all hits coming with men on the sacks. It was Moore's seventh homer in three weeks." Pug Cavet, a former major league pitcher, was the victim of Moore's pyrotechnics, which moved the White Sox from the cellar to second place in the All-Professional League. In addition to Moore, Hawkins and Foreman also had three hits while, on the All-Star side, Pete Lapan had four hits, Babe Herman had three, and Ping Bodie had two including a home run.

The early season slugging barrage was an omen of things to come. Nineteen twenty four was a hitters' year in the California Winter League, as the pitchers struggled to adjust to the physical dimensions of the new ballpark.

George "Tank" Carr made his presence felt immediately after he joined the team. In a game against the Pasadena Eagles shortened to seven inning because of darkness, the 6'2" switch-hitter made the most of his four at-bats. He hit for the cycle, lashing out a single, double, triple, and home run, sparking the White Sox to an easy 11–1 victory. Dobie Moore cracked two doubles as Rube Currie coasted to the victory.

In spite of the White Sox surge, they couldn't seem to put any distance between themselves and the rest of the league. The White Kings, in particular, were tough. They had a seasoned squad that had been through pressure-packed pennant races before, and they weren't about to fall apart. Their pitching staff was headed by George Payne and Doc Crandall, two battle-tested veterans with 597 minor league victories between them, including ten 20-victory seasons. Crandall also won 101 major league games. Both pitchers had just finished pitching for the Los Angeles Angels in the PCL, with the club finishing just 1½ games

George Payne enjoyed a 28 year minor league career. His Winter league career stats read 21 victories against 4 losses. (George E. Outland)

Buzz Arlett began his career as a pitcher. After injuring his arm, he became one of the greatest hitters in minor league history, compiling a .341 average over 20 years. (George E. Outland)

behind the pennant-winning Seattle team. Payne had posted a record of 21–13 with the Angels while Doc Crandall was 19–11. In the field, the Soapsters were an imposing crew, led by all-time minor league great, Buzz Arlett, who compiled a .341 career minor league batting average, with 432 home runs in 8,001 at-bats. Arlett also hit .313 in a one year stint with the Philadelphia Phillies, but was returned to the minor leagues because of his fielding deficiencies and lackadaisical attitude. The infield consisted of Walt Golvin (.216 with Los Angeles), Howard Lindimore (.339 with Salt Lake City), Ike McAuley (.276 with L.A.), and Wes Kingdon (.278 with Buffalo of the International League), with Wally Hood (.338 with L.A.), and Dick Cox (.356 with Portland), joining Arlett in the outfield. Joe Jenkins (.288 with L.A.) was the catcher.

One of the key matchups of the early season was a doubleheader between the White Kings and Pirrone's All-Stars. The *Los Angeles Times* covered the game. "Before an enthusiastic gathering, the strong White King Soaps administered a double defeat to Joe Pirrone's All-Stars yesterday at Washington Park, winning the first game 5–1, and the second 4–2.... With the youthful Doc Crandall pitching great ball, the White Kings won the opener by bunching hits off Bob McGraw in the third inning ... clinching the contest. But for a home run over the left field fence by Ping Bodie, Crandall would have had a shutout. George Payne beat Pug Cavet in the afterpiece.... Pete Thompson and Lyman Smith each

Doc Crandall won 101 games in the major leagues and 249 games in the minor leagues. (Dick Dobbins)

connected for three hits in the second tilt, while Buzz Arlett, with a single and a triple, carried away hitting honors in the opener."

Several weeks later, the White Kings visited Lonnie Goodwin's contingent for a "crucial" weekend series, with the White Sox clinging to first place by a thread. The *Times* reported the event. "The Los Angeles White Sox and the White Kings split their doubleheader at the White Sox Park yesterday, the Soapsters taking the opener 19–5, and dropping the afterpiece 6–2." Buzz Arlett went on a rampage in game one, banging out five hits, two of them home runs. "(Tank) Carr also slammed a couple out of the lot in the twilight tilt." Carr was five for eight all told, while Moore was five for seven with a home run.

Thanks to the split with the Soapsters, the White Sox kept their spot at the top of the league, but they couldn't maintain the momentum. Their pitching suddenly collapsed while, at the same time, the White Kings' pitchers stepped it up a notch. On January 25, the Soapsters gave Pirrone's All-Stars a double dose of goose-eggs, with George Payne blanking Pirrone's club 7–0 in the opener, and Percy Jones zipping them in the nightcap, 8–0. Once again, Buzz Arlett was the big gun, with five hits in the two games. A week later, Payne and Crandall combined on a 1–0 shutout over the Vernon Tigers. Wes Kingdon carried over, what proved to be the game winner, in the third inning.

As the season wound down, the White Kings and the White Sox jockeyed for position, while both Pirrone's All-Stars and the Vernon Tigers dropped out of contention. On February 7 the two adversaries met in White Sox Park, with first place at stake. The White Kings were ready, as the *California Eagle* noted. "After the White Kings had pounded Rube Currie from the box last Saturday ... Munion stopped the White Kings in their tracks, but the game was hopelessly lost. The Kings won 11–6. Incidentally Munion fanned home run king "Buzz" Arlett twice. Arlett got a homer off Currie in the first inning and Lindimore gathered two, along with three other hits that gave him a perfect batting average."

"Dobie Moore was much in the limelight Sunday at the White Sox Park, in a game that was played in a drizzling rain. As advertised, Drake and Payne hooked up in a pitchers battle that was decided in the ninth inning when the White Kings scored three runs. The final score was 3–1. As mentioned above 'Dobie' Moore ... had apparently won the game for Drake when he hit a home run.... Then came the fatal ninth. (With the bases loaded) Faulk hit sharply to Moore who let the ball get between his legs. Before he could retrieve it, two runners crossed the plate. He was so disgusted that he picked up the ball and addressed a few remarks to it. In the meantime, Arlett dashed in from third."

In spite of the Kings' two game sweep, there was some confusion over the outcome of the pennant race, as reported by the *Eagle*. "Because of one or two games being cancelled or thrown out of the league schedule, it has been difficult to determine whether the Sox or the Kings are leading the league, so the five game series is being played to determine the rightful owner of the league pennant. The first game ... will be played Saturday with two doubleheaders following, Sunday and Monday (Washington's Birthday)."

"Cherry Bell and Doc Crandall ... started the series off. Doc came away a winner (4–3) but he had to pitch hard all the way. McAuley quelled a rally when he caught Hawkins line drive and doubled a runner off second."

On Sunday, with Jim Gurley pitching, Lonnie Goodwin's bombers wreaked havoc on Ferdie Schupp, coasting to an easy 14–5 decision. Tank Carr had three hits, including two home runs, one a grand slam. Dobie Moore contributed four base hits, while Bob Fagan had a double and a triple, and Connie Day chipped in with a single and a home run. Ike McAuley had a double and a home run for the visitors. In game two, the White Kings prevailed 5–4, with Payne outpitching William "Plunk" Drake. Dobie Moore and Connie Day homered for the Sox, but a five run fourth inning spelled defeat for the L.A. crew. Although outhit 12 to 7, the Soapsters made the most of the opportunities. In the fourth the White Kings bunched three of their hits along with two bases on balls and an error, for all their runs.

The Monday doubleheader was rained out, so a three game series was scheduled for the weekend of February 28. In the Saturday opener, the White Kings jumped on Currie again for nine runs in four innings, en route to a 9–7 victory. Munion stemmed the tide over the final six innings, but it was too little, too late. Bill Whitaker, although yielding 11 base hits and six walks, hung on for the win. Scott, Jenkins, and Golvin paced the Soapster attack with two hits each. Connie Day homered for the losers. Dobie Moore had the misfortune of hitting into three double plays.

The Sunday doubleheader was the end of the line for Lonnie Goodwin's gallant warriors. As the *California Eagle* noted, "The Soaps won the Saturday game and the first game Sunday thereby clinching the Professional Winter championship and the silver loving cup donated by Spaulding." In first first game Sunday, Charlie Barnabe scattered 13 hits, while the White Kings raked Plunk Drake for no less than 20 hits, including two singles and a home run by Ping Bodie, two doubles by Wes Kingdon, two singles and a double by Walt Golvin, and three hits each by Lindimore and Thompson. The final score was 15–4. In the anti-climatic nightcap, the White Sox prevailed 13–8. Dobie Moore climaxed his season with a single and a home run.

The irrepressible Moore was the league's batting champion with an average of .487, one of the highest season averages in league history. The rugged 5'11", 230 pound right-handed slugger was a veritable one man wrecking crew, also showing the way in base hits (77), doubles (17), triples, (4), and home runs (12). The most impressive thing about Moore's performance was that he didn't play any favorites. He pummeled major league pitching just as viciously as he did minor league pitching. He banged out six hits in nine at-bats against Ferdie Schupp, battered Archie Campbell for five hits in eight at-bats, hit .500 against both Willie Ludolph and Bill Pertica, batted .438 against ten game winner George Payne, .400 against Pug Cavett, and .364 against Bill Whitaker. In all, Moore rapped the ball at a .485 clip against the above pitchers, with six doubles and seven home runs in 68 at-bats. For "The Black Cat," as Babe Herman and the other white players called him, the 1924-25 winter season was just a continuation of the previous summers performance. Dobie Moore was the 1924 Negro National League batting and home run champion with an average of .470 and 8 home runs in 234 at-bats. In California he was just doing what came naturally. Plunk Drake led all pitchers with 11 victories, while George Payne had the best winning percentage at .769 with ten wins in 13 decisions.

1924-25 California Winter League
Final Standings—Incomplete

	Wins	Losses	Ties
White Kings	20	9	0
Los Angeles White Sox	28	21	1
Vernon Tigers	14	9	0
Pirrone's All-Stars	9	16	0

Los Angeles White Sox Batting Statistics 1924-25

Name	Pos	G	AB	H	D	T	HR	BA
Hawkins, Lem	1B	44*	175*	58	9	4*	0	.331
Fagan, Bob	2B	41	146	35	8	1	0	.240
Moore, Dobie	SS	40	158	77*	17*	4*	12*	.487*
McNair, Hurley	CF	15	59	24	4	0	1	.407
Pullen, Neal	C	15	59	20	3	1	2	.339
Day, Connie	3B	39	147	47	5	4*	8	.320
Butcher, Spencer	LF	24	96	25	3	1	0	.260
Foreman, Hooks	RF	36	129	39	12	0	1	.302
Kenilworth,	1B	10	33	10	0	0	0	.303
Carr, Tank	1B	32	115	44	12	3	11	.383

Los Angeles White Sox Pitching Statistics 1924-25

Name	G	CG	W	L	IP	SO	BB	SH
Currie, Rube	23*	8	7	8	123	60	39	2*
Drake, Plunk	20	17*	11*	5	155*	70	54*	1
Bell, Cherry	18	8	7	6	111	84*	44	2*
Munion,	8	3	3	1	51	34	17	0

Pirrone's All-Stars Batting Statistics 1924-25

Name	Pos	G	AB	H	D	T	HR	BA
Smith, Red	SS	12	49	15	0	0	1	.306
Pirrone, Joe	RF	19	71	16	0	0	0	.225
Bodie, Ping	CF	22	87	29	7	2	4	.333
Herman, Babe	1B	17	66	26	6	1	2	.394
Lapan, Pete	C	6	24	9	1	0	0	.375
Smith, Lyman	CF	18	69	18	0	0	0	.261
Whaling, Bert	C	8	21	5	0	0	0	.238
Smith, Marvin	SS	8	34	5	1	1	0	.147

Pirrone's All-Stars Pitching Statistics 1924-25

Name	G	CG	W	L	IP	SO	BB	SH
Thurston, Sloppy	1	1	1	0	9	5	0	0
Cavet, Pug	10	7	4	3	71	28	12	0
Pope,	5	2	0	5	35	12	13	0

White Kings Batting Statistics 1924-25

Name	Pos	G	AB	H	D	T	HR	BA
Falk, Bib	CF	12	41	11	0	0	0	.268
Murphy, Rod	3B	9	37	14	2	0	0	.378
Hood, Wally	LF	27	110	28	8	2	0	.255
Arlett, Buzz	RF	25	95	35	6	2	4	.368
Jenkins, Joe	C	22	66	16	2	0	0	.242
Golvin, Walt	1B	27	92	30	1	0	0	.326
McAuley, Ike	SS	27	95	29	2	1	0	.305
Kingdon, Wes	3B	26	75	24	5	0	0	.320
Thompson, Pete	C	17	52	21	2	0	0	.404
Cox, Dick	CF	20	77	28	6	1	1	.364
Lindimore, Howard	2B	18	75	26	2	0	2	.347

White Kings Pitching Statistics 1924-25

Name	G	CG	W	L	IP	SO	BB	SH
Crandall, Doc	10	5	3	2	61	22	11	0
Payne, George	14	10	10	3	113	75	21	1
Jones, Percy	7	2	2	2	34	16	13	1
Pertica, Bill	7	4	3	2	45	24	7	0

Vernon Tigers Batting Statistics 1924-25

Name	Pos	G	AB	H	D	T	HR	BA
Chadbourne, Chet	CF	15	63	21	4	0	0	.333
Deal, Charlie	3B	5	20	3	1	0	0	.150
Murphy, Danny	C	17	62	13	1	0	1	.210
Griffin, Ivy	2B	17	60	15	1	1	0	.250
Slade, Gordon	SS	11	41	14	1	0	0	.341
Hannah, Truck	C	8	23	5	0	0	0	.211
Gorman,	SS	12	41	11	3	0	0	.268
Cook,	C	11	32	4	1	0	0	.125
Whaley, Bill	RF	12	41	10	2	0	1	.244
Scott, Pete	RF	8	33	13	2	1	1	.394

Vernon Tigers Pitching Statistics 1924-25

Name	G	CG	W	L	IP	SO	BB	SH
Ludolph, Willie	4	3	3	1	37	11	8	0
Reiger, Elmer	3	3	1	2	24	—	—	0
Whittaker, Bill	7	6	3	4	58	18	12	0
Hillman,	5	5	3	2	44	10	15	0

Miscellaneous Teams Batting Statistics 1924-25

Name	Team	Pos	G	AB	H	D	T	HR	BA
Carlisle, Cleo	Gilmore Oil	RF	13	49	13	2	1	1	.265
Twombly, Babe	Long Beach	RF	7	25	8	2	0	1	.320
Haas, Mule	Pasadena	RF	8	32	7	1	0	0	.219

Miscellaneous Teams Pitching statistics 1924-25

Name	Team	G	CG	W	L	IP	SO	BB	SH
Schupp, Ferdie	Gilmore, Wh.Kings	11	10	8	3	91	62	21	0
Ross, Sam	Pasadena	3	1	2	0	18	9	5	0

The St. Louis Giants were active in the Southern California Winter League, another strong professional league. The Giants' main competition came from Gilmore Oil, with 34-year-old Ferdie Schupp on the mound. Some other well known players in the league included George "Mule" Haas, who would go on to a successful 12 year career with the Philadelphia Athletics, hitting .292 in 4,303 at-bats, Howard Lindimore, Sam Ross, Bill Pertica, Jigger Statz, Cleo Carlisle, Tex Vache, Ray French, Chicken Hawks, Babe Twombly, Johnny Cooney, and Goose Goslin. Another black team, the Colored All-Stars, were outmatched in the league.

With the natural competition that existed between the two strong black teams, the St. Louis Giants met the Los Angeles White Sox in two series during the season. The first meeting, at White Sox Park in late December resulted in a split of the three game series. In the opener, Rube Currie was in high gear, and blanked Lorenzo Cobb's hired guns 4–0. Sylvester "Hooks" Foreman, the big catcher of the Sox, was the batting star with a double and two singles off the St. Louis ace, William Ross. In game two, the Giants bounced back behind the shutout pitching of Jim Gurley, to win 3–0. Lem Hawkins got the only three hits surrendered by Gurley, while Cool Papa Bell accounted for two of the Giants six safeties. Fittingly, the getaway game was a 7–7 tie as hitting replaced pitching for the day. Neither Fred Bell nor Cherry Bell had their best stuff, and the batters teed off with a renewed zeal. Neal Pullen, the St. Louis backstop, pounded out two home runs and a single, and Foote chipped in with two doubles. For the White Sox, Lem Hawkins was 3 for 3.

The last meeting between the two clubs took place in early March at the end of the regular season. Lonnie Goodwin's warriors took the first game of the doubleheader 9–3 behind Munion. The White Sox pounded out 13 base hits, with Dobie Moore's two doubles, and Tank Carr's double and triple leading the attack. Cool Papa Bell homered and singled for St. Louis, while Dewey Creacy hit Munion for three singles. In the nightcap, Foote shut down the Los Angeles offense completely, while his teammates ripped Rube Currie for a dozen base hits, en route to a 6–1 thrashing. Foote and Creacy had three hits each, while Bell and Willie Wells each had two. Dobie Moore and Willie Bobo hit home runs.

James "Cool Papa" Bell, now a full time outfielder, won the batting championship with an average of .400. Willie Bobo, an outstanding all-around first baseman, was the home run leader with 5, while Dewey Creacy led in triples with 8, and tied with John Reese in doubles with 7. William Ross, Fred Bell, and Ferdie Schupp shared pitching honors. Bell and Schupp tied for games won (8) and winning percentage (8-3, .727). William Ross led the league in games pitched (15), complete games (12), innings pitched (118), and strikeouts (67).

1924-25 Southern California Winter League
Final Standings — Incomplete

	Wins	Losses	Ties
St. Louis Giants	27	13	1
Gilmore Oil	9	5	0

Pasadena Merchants	4	5	1
Colored All-Stars	2	4	0
Glendale White Sox	2	6	0
Hollywood Merchants	2	5	0

St. Louis Giants Batting Statistics 1924-25

Name	Pos	G	AB	H	D	T	HR	BA
Ward, Pinky	LF	32	121	41	2	4	0	.339
Bell, Cool Papa	CF	30	120	48*	2	0	1	.400*
Bobo, Willie	1B	36*	129*	42	6	5	5*	.326
Murray, Mitch	C	22	85	28	3	1	1	.329
Riggins, Bill	SS	16	62	17	3	1	1	.274
Russell, John Henry	2B	22	83	19	1	3	2	.229
Creacy, Dewey	3B	34	127	43	7*	8*	0	.339
Reese, John	RF	32	103	26	7*	1	0	.252
Goodrich, Joe	2B	9	30	8	0	1	0	.267

St. Louis Giants Pitching Statistics 1924-25

Name	G	CG	W	L	IP	SO	BB	SH
Ross, William	15*	12*	7	5	118*	67*	38	1
Bell, Fred	11	7	8*	3	81	34	36	0
Gurley, Jim	14	8	7	3	94	52	48	1

5

Season Summaries 1925–1929

The 1925-26 Season

The growing pains of the early twenties led to a period of prosperity for the California Winter League, beginning in 1924. Under Joe Pirrone's guidance and management, the league realized a decade of organizational and economic stability. The league was essentially a four team league most years, with the Philadelphia Royal Giants (or another Negro league entry) battling three white professional teams, including Pirrone's All-Stars, the White King Soapsters, and the Shell Oilers. Occasionally teams like Kelley Kars or San Diego joined the league, usually replacing one of the other teams. But Pirrone's All-Stars and the Negro league team were fixtures. They were the anchors of the league.

In 1925, Lonnie Goodwin brought another talented group to the west coast. As usual, the pitching staff was the key to the success of the team. The mound staff was led by the legendary "Bullet Joe" Rogan, who returned to the league after a four year absence. He had led the Negro league in victories the preceding two years with records of 15–5 and 14–2. He also pitched in Cuba during the winter of 1924-25, running up a 9–4 slate. Bullet Joe was ably supported by Rube Currie and George Britton (a.k.a. George Britt), a tough right-handed curveball artist. Dobie Moore did not play in California that winter, but the explosive George "Tank" Carr was back, and he was joined by Newt Allen, Biz Mackey, Crush Holloway, Jess Hubbard, and Rap Dixon. Allen, dubbed "Colt" when he joined the Kansas City Monarchs as a 21-year-old infielder, had four years professional experience under his belt by 1925. He is generally regarded as the top second baseman of the 1920s, and a genuine Hall of Fame prospect. Jess Hubbard was a versatile player, who could pitch or play the outfield. He was a winning pitcher in the Negro leagues, and a lifetime .316 hitter.

Joe Pirrone fielded a team with considerable major league experience, led by pitchers Hal Haid, Red Oldham from the Pittsburgh Pirates, Bill Piercy (21–11 with Salt Lake City in the PCL), and Wee Willie Ludolph (13–12 with Vernon). The supporting staff was built around Babe Herman, the colorful slugger from the Brooklyn Dodgers, and included such big time hitters as Jigger Statz, who would have a sensational year in the Pacific Coast League in 1926, rapping out an unheard-of 291 base hits, with 68 doubles, and 18 triples, to go along with a .354 batting average, Dick Cox, who was coming off a .329 year with the Brooklyn Dodgers, and Fred Haney, the third baseman of the Detroit Tigers. The defending champion White Kings had their ace, George Payne (18–19 with Los Angeles

Left: Bullet Joe Rogan led the California Winter League in pitching in 1925-26. He went 14–2 on the mound, and hit .326. *Right:* Dick Cox, former Brooklyn Dodger infielder, batted .326 over a 9 year California Winter League career. (*Both photographs,* George E. Outland)

in the PCL) back, as well as pitchers Clyde Barfoot, who led the Pacific Coast League with 26 victories in 1925, Hi Bell of the St. Louis Cardinals, and Charlie Root, 25–13 with Los Angeles. Returning fielders included Joe Jenkins, a .304 hitter in the Southern Association, Wally Hood, who had just completed a fine .327 season with Los Angeles, Wes Kingdon, the 25-year-old shortstop for the Buffalo Bisons of the International League, and Howard Lindimore, a .332 hitter with Salt Lake City in the PCL. New additions included Babe Twombly, a .329 hitter with Los Angeles, Frank Brazill, a 26-year-old third baseman, who pummeled Pacific Coast League pitching for a .394 average with 280 base hits, including 67 doubles, 11 triples, and 29 home runs, Art Griggs, a .337 hitter with Omaha in the Western Association, and Cedric Durst of the St. Louis Browns. The Shell Oil team had a strong pitching contingent with eight year major league veteran Hi Bell, former New York Giant ace Ferdie Schupp (21–7 with the Giants in 1917), and Pug Cavet (16–10 with Atlanta in the Southern Association). In the field, the Oilers featured "Sunny Jim" Blakesley, who had ripped Western League pitching for a .359 average with 105 extra base hits in 1923, Ivy Griffin, who was coming off a .335 season with 212 base hits for Milwaukee in the American Association, and Billy Orr, an 11 year Pacific Coast League veteran. The fact that the above three teams, with an imposing mixture of major league veterans and high level minor leaguers, could offer the Negro league entry only minimal opposition, speaks volumes about the skills of the black players.

The California Winter League opened officially on Saturday, October 25, 1925 before, what the *California Eagle* called "the largest Saturday crowd that has ever filed through the White Sox Park gates." The visiting Pirrone All-Stars put a damper on the enthusiasm of Royal Giants fans by hammering out a 7–3 victory behind the stingy pitching of Bob McGraw and Bill Piercy. The All-Stars put the game away early, jumping on Rube Currie for five consecutive hits to score four runs before a man had been retired. A single by Dick Cox, a double by Herman, and a home run by Hugh McMullen KO'd Currie in the fifth. Two of the Sox runs came on a homer by Crush Holloway in the ninth, long after the game had been decided. Biz Mackey hit the first home run of the season in the fourth inning, when his high fly ball dropped over the screen just inside the right field foul pole.

Game two went to the Giants, as reported in the *Chicago Defender*. "Red Oldham, hero of the final game of the recent world series, failed to get his sweeping curve ball away from the middle of the plate, and the Philadelphia Royal Giants banged out a 7–3 victory over the Major League All-Stars at White Sox Park.... The Stars outhit their rivals, 11 to 10, Herman leading the attack with three singles ... but failed to make the blows count." The All-Stars took an early lead in the game when they bunched three hits for two runs in the top of the first. A double by Jigger Statz and singles by Herman and McMullen did the damage. Rap Dixon narrowed the gap to 2–1 in the second with a round tripper, and the Philadelphians pushed across two more in the bottom of the third to take the lead for good. In that stanza, Connie Day doubled in one run, and Tank Carr's two bagger to the center field fence brought in the other. The Giants added one run in the fifth, the All-Stars scored their third run in the seventh on a double by Statz and a single by Herman, and the black bombers put the game away with a three-spot in the eighth, sparked by Dixon's double.

The following weekend was another character building experience for the Negro league representatives. Red Oldham took the mound on Saturday, intent on gaining a measure of revenge for the previous week's beating, and he did just that, taking a 9–5 decision from Jess Hubbard. Things looked bleak for the All-Star ace for awhile as he was raked for four runs in the bottom of the fourth, giving the Giants a 4–1 lead, but Pirrone's boys scratched their way back into the game by scoring one run in the sixth, and two more in the seventh. The game was tied at 4–4 as the ninth inning started. Then, with the help of a Giant error, a base on balls, a hit batter, and four base hits, the All-Stars took a commanding 9–4 lead. A single by Mackey and a double by Dixon in the bottom of the ninth made the final score 9–5. The next day, the Giants entered the ninth inning on the short end of a 7–3 score, but they refused to go quietly. Jess Hubbard led off with a single off Bill Piercy, went to second on a hit by Crush Holloway, and scored ahead of a home run by Connie Day. After the homer, the *California Eagle* noted, "The crowd showered the field with cushions." The next batter, Tank Carr, beat out an infield hit and came around to score on a long blast to center field by Biz Mackey. The big slugger tried to make it an inside-the-park home run but was cut down at the plate, leaving the game to end in a 7–7 tie, called on account of darkness after the ninth inning.

A week later, "Home Run" Day came through again. The Giants and the White Kings were tied at 6–6 in the sixth inning, when the lanky infielder stepped to the plate to face Charlie Root, after a hit batter, a single, and a base on balls had loaded the bases. He promptly lined a home run over the left field fence, sparking his team a 10–9 victory. It was Day's third home run in three games.

The first half of the season was nip and tuck, with all the teams flexing their muscles at one time or another. One of the key games of the early going was a pitchers duel between Clyde Barfoot of the White Kings and Ferdie Schupp of Shell Oil. The game was scoreless through seven innings as both pitchers were in midseason form. Schupp had a tight one-hitter into the eighth, but a double by Pete Scott and a single by Babe Twombly scored what proved to be the game winner. Barfoot threw a five-hitter at the Oilers, fanning five and walking only one. Schupp had four strikeouts and three walks.

Bullet Rogan survived a defensive fiasco by his Royal Giant teammates in early December, as reported in the *Defender*. "Seven errors behind Rogan didn't give the Shell Oils a chance to win. The Giants copped, 8–6, in spite of the bad day in the field (the usually reliable Newt Allen had two errors, and Connie Day booted three). The white boys filled the sacks in the ninth with none out (and the Giants leading 8–4). Two hits scored two runs, but the rally was cut short."

Two weeks later the Giants entertained the White Kings in a crucial two game series. In the Saturday opener, Lonnie Goodwin's troops held a 4–3 lead after seven innings, but George Britton couldn't hold it. In the eighth, with two men on and two out, manager Doc Crandall sent Joe Jenkins up to pinch-hit. The slender right-handed hitter put all his muscle into the first pitch from Britton and drove it over the left field fence to win the game. Philadelphia bounced back on Sunday, for an 11–5 victory behind Joe Rogan. The Giant ace was roughed up for five runs in the first three innings, then settled down to blank the Soapsters over the final six frames. Tank Carr's second home run of the game in the fifth gave the Giants a lead they never relinquished.

The first half ended with another two game series between the leaders, the White Kings and the Royal Giants. Unfortunately for the Philadelphians, who needed a two game sweep to hold down the top spot, the Saturday game was cancelled because of wet grounds. In the Sunday finale, Lonnie Goodwin's hired hands edged the Soapsters 4–3 with a three run fourth. Tank Carr's double, another by winning pitcher Bullet Rogan, and a single by Mackey accounted for the three runs.

The first half statistics showed Tank Carr to be the leading slugger with a .413 batting average and five home runs in 18 games. Biz Mackey hit .389 and Bullet Rogan tattoed opposing pitchers to the tune of .375. Rogan was also the leading pitcher with a record of 6–1.

The Giants were undaunted by their first half loss because they were on a roll, having won seven of their last eight games, with one tie. But they were brought back to earth with a resounding crash when the Kings took two out of three over the New Year's holiday. Joe Rogan won his seventh game of the season with a 7–5 victory on New Year's day, to open the three game series, and he went two for three with a home run to help his own cause. But that was it. On Saturday, the White Kings buried Rube Currie under a 19 hit attack, winning easily 12–1. Wally Hood with a double and three singles, led the barrage. Cedric Durst, Pete Scott, and Gus Sanberg had three hits each. In the finale, Clyde Barfoot scattered eleven hits, and his teammates pounded George Britton and Joe Rogan for 12 safeties, en route to an 8–3 win. Britton was knocked out of the box in the fourth after he loaded the bases with one out, but Rogan couldn't stem the tide. Wally Hood, the first batter to face Bullet Joe, sent a screeching line drive to the left center field alley for a bases clearing triple, turning a tight 2–1 game into a 5–1 laugher.

The White King sluggers put some impressive numbers on the board during the weekend series. Tall, lanky Wally Hood ripped Philadelphia pitching for six hits in 15 at-bats, including a double and a triple, Frank Brazill went 5 for 12, Cedric Durst went 6 for 14, Lindimore had a homer and three singles in eight at-bats, and Gus Sanberg had 4 for 9 with 3 doubles.

The Giants bounced back against the Shell Oil team during a wild weekend on January 9–10. On Saturday, behind the shutout pitching of George Britton, they ran roughshod over the Oilers, winning 20–0. Lonnie Goodwin's warriors struck for 21 base hits including six doubles, and stole eight bases during their rampage. In the Sunday game, perhaps relaxing a little, they saw their ace Bullet Joe Rogan driven from the box under a ten run barrage in the fourth inning, as the Oilers ran to a 10–1 lead. But the Giants regrouped, and fought their way back into the game. Hubbard tripled and scored in the fourth. In the sixth, Tank Carr blasted a three run homer over the left field fence. A single by Rogan, a double by Hubbard, and a double by Day brought in two more in the seventh. Then, in the eighth, the Giants came all the way back to knot the count at 10–10 on a single by Allen and a double by Mackey. Rogan, who had been replaced by Mackey for two-thirds of an inning, took over pitching duties again in the fifth and proceeded to blank the Oilers over the last five innings. The game was called on account of darkness at the end of the ninth inning, and although it was officially a tie game, the Philadelphia crew felt like winners after erasing a nine run deficit.

Casey Stengel was in left field when the All-Stars tangled with the Giants on January 17. The game was a see-saw battle for twelve innings with the lead changing hands several times. The All-Stars tied the game at 7–7 in the top of the ninth on two walks and a pair of singles. Philadelphia scored the winning run in the bottom of the twelfth when Newt Allen was hit by a pitch with the bases loaded. Bullet Rogan pitched the entire twelve innings for the win. Stengel had a single and a double in six trips to the plate.

As the season neared an end, the Royal Giants held a small lead over the White Kings but, in a two game series at White Sox Park in early February, the Soapsters battered Lonnie Goodwin's boys in both games, by scores of 9–0 and 8–4. In the first game, Bullet Rogan was the victim, as Clyde Barfoot handed the Giants their first whitewashing of the year. Joe Jenkins punched out three hits including a home run, and Art Griggs chipped in with a single and two doubles. In game two, Charlie Root, who had just won 25 games with the Los Angeles Angels of the PCL, and would win 18 games for the Chicago Cubs in 1926, bested George Britton, in spite of two home runs by Tank Carr and a singleton by Neal Pullen.

The White Sox' sweep set up a three game playoff for the league title the following week. As usual, it was difficult to reconcile the California Winter League records because, as noted earlier, the league often appeared to be a "Negro league against the world" league, with the black team playing two or three times as many games as the white teams. That unique situation went back to the formation of the "new" winter league in 1920, when Anderson gave the black team its own ballpark, and Pirrone provided white, professional competition for the black entry, with most games involving the black team to be played at White Sox Park to take advantage of the sizeable black population in Southern California.

The White Kings won the first half of the league with a record of 6–3, while the Royal Giants captured the second half with a record of 14–7. Overall, the White Kings had a record of 10–8 for a winning percentage of .556. The Royal Giants' slate showed 24 victories against 15 losses for a

Charlie Root, a 201 game winner in the major leagues, was 2–2 for the White Kings in 1925-26.

percentage of .615. In hand to hand competition, the White Kings took the Royal Giants to task seven times in twelve meetings.

The championship series was played on three successive days, from Saturday, February 20 through Monday, February 22. In the opener, Hi Bell of the St. Louis Cardinals faced Giants ace Bullet Joe Rogan. The game was close for 6½ innings, but the Giants broke loose in the seventh and eighth to take a 5–1 decision behind Rogan's six hitter. Jess Hubbard had two hits and scored two runs.

The next day George Britton was the recipient of a 19 hit Giant attack, and he coasted to a 12–7 victory to clinch the league championship. The Kings scored one run in the top of the first on two singles and an error by Mackey at third, but Biz atoned for his miscue in the bottom of the inning by singling in the tying run off Pug Cavet, and scoring another. In the second, the Soapsters scored two more runs on three singles, but once again Lonnie Goodwin's troops came back to take the lead, this time on a daring steal of home by Connie Day and a run scoring single by Mackey. In the third, the Philadelphians choked off a White King rally with what the *Eagle* called

"one of the fastest double plays of the season, Carr to Allen to Carr." Mackey's fifth inning triple and a perfect squeeze bunt by Day extended the Giant lead to 5–3, but the White Kings tied the score in the sixth on a two-run homer by Frank Brazill. Once again, the Giants stormed back. In the bottom of the inning, they scored three runs on doubles by Holloway, Carr, and Hubbard, and a single by Allen. The Kings narrowed the lead to 8–7 in the eighth on another two-run shot by Brazill, but to no avail. The Philadelphia crew jumped on relief pitcher George Payne for four runs in the bottom half to put the game away. The rally was highlighted by a towering three-run home run over the center field fence by Jess "Mountain" Hubbard.

White Kings					Royal Giants			
Name	*Pos*	*AB*	*H*		*Name*	*Pos*	*AB*	*H*
Durst, Cedric	CF	5	2		Holloway, Crush	CF	5	1
Twombly, Babe	RF	5	1		Allen, Newt	SS	5	1
Hood, Wally	LF	4	0		Carr, Tank	1B	5	3
Griggs, Art	1B	4	1		Mackey, Biz	3B	5	4
Lindimore, Howard	2B	4	1		Hubbard, Jess	RF	5	3
Brazill, Frank	3B	4	3		Pullen, Neal	C	4	1
Hannah, Truck	C	4	3		Dixon, Rap	LF	4	2
McAuley, Ike	SS	4	2		Day, Connie	2B	4	2
Cavet, Pug	P	3	1		Britton, George	P	4	2
Payne, George	P	1	0					
Totals		38	14				41	19

White King Soapsters   1 2 0   0 0 2   0 2 0— 7–14–5
Philadelphia Royal Giants 2 2 0   0 1 3   0 4 x—12–19–4

Two base hits: Hannah, McAuley, Holloway, Carr, Hubbard, Britton
Three base hits: Mackey
Home runs: Brazill (2), Hubbard

	IP	H	SO	BB
Cavet (LP)	5	10	2	2
Payne	3	9	2	0
Britton (WP)	9	14	1	0

In the anticlimactic finale, Rube Currie beat Hi Bell 12–5. The score stood at 2–2 after 4½ innings, but the Giants exploded for five big runs in the bottom of the fifth to complete the sweep. Big Jess Hubbard, the 6'2", 200 pound one man army, spearheaded the attack with four hits in five at-bats. Holloway had three hits, and Carr, Dixon, and Day, each contributed two.

The championship was particularly satisfying for manager Lonnie Goodwin, who captured his first pennant after fifteen

Rube Currie pitched in the Negro leagues for 13 years, winning 70 games against just 44 losses. (Kimshi Productions, Inc.)

years in the league. The victory also avenged the previous year's defeat at the hands of the White Kings. Over the course of the season, the Royal Giants seemed to have an advantage over the other teams in the little things that don't show up in the box score. They excelled on defense, and often dazzled the spectators with the lightning-fast double plays pulled off by their keystone combination of Newt Allen and Connie Day. Catchers Pullen and Mackey kept opposing base runners honest with their powerful throwing arms, gunning down many a would-be base stealer. But it was on the bases where the Giants really let it all hang out. Manager Lonnie Goodwin had them running aggressively from day one. They routinely took an extra base on balls hit to the outfield, and they stole bases with a reckless abandon, often stealing two, three, or even four bases in a game. One of the key plays in the pennant winning game on Sunday was a double steal executed by Day and Britton, with Day sliding across the plate on the front end of the steal. Another was Day's well executed squeeze play.

Goodwin's strategy was a continuation of the strategy formulated twenty years earlier by Rube Foster, the father of winning baseball. During the "Golden Age" of the California Winter League from 1924 through 1935, the Negro leaguers enjoyed outguessing their white opponents. As Cool Papa Bell told John Holway, "When I came up we didn't play baseball like they play in the major leagues. We played tricky baseball. When we played the big leaguers after the regular season, our pitchers would curve the ball on 3–2. They'd say, 'What, are you trying to make us look bad?' We'd bunt and run and they'd say, 'Why are you trying to do that in the first inning?' When we were supposed to bunt, they'd come in and we'd hit away.... We'd go into third standing up so the third baseman couldn't see the throw coming and it might go through him.... The major leaguers would play for one big inning.... I think we had a better system than the majors. Whatever it takes to win, we did."

The bunt and the stolen base were two of the biggest weapons in the Negro leaguer's arsenal. Their winter league teams averaged between one and two stolen bases a game, year in and year out. In 1921-22 Carr, Mackey, Hawkins, and Charleston all stole better than a base every three games. In 1925-26, Crush Holloway swiped 10 bases in 40 games. Even the sluggers ran to daylight. In 1926-27 Turkey Stearnes would lead the winter league in both home runs and stolen bases. Later on, black greyhounds like Bell, Willie Wells, and Sam Bankhead would pick up the baton.

Individual honors for the season went to Joe Jenkins and Bullet Joe Rogan. Jenkins, the slender backstop of the White Kings, terrorized opposing pitchers to capture the batting championship with an average of

Joe Jenkins (on right) punished Negro league pitchers to the tune of .544 in 1925-26, after hitting .304 for Atlanta in the Southern Association. (George E. Outland)

.544, a new record. Rogan dominated the pitching statistics, leading the league in games pitched (18), complete games (16), victories (14) innings pitched (153), and strikeouts (82). He also helped himself at the plate, hitting a solid .326. Tank Carr led the league in doubles with 16 and home runs with 8, to go along with a .342 batting average.

The 1925-26 California Winter League
Final Standings—Incomplete

	Wins	Losses	Ties
Philadelphia Royal Giants	24	15	3
White King Soapsters	10	8	0
Pirrone's All-Stars	5	10	2
Shell Oil	2	9	1

Philadelphia Royal Giants—Batting Statistics 1925-26

Name	Pos	G	AB	H	D	T	HR	BA
Holloway, Crush	RF	41	159	59	7	1	4	.371
Carr, Tank	3B	39	146	50	16*	1	8*	.342
Hubbard, Jess	RF	34	101	35	6	3	2	.347
Mackey, Biz	SS	38	146	48	9	2	5	.329
Rogan, Joe	P	30	89	28	8	0	2	.326
Day, Connie	2B	34	132	37	10	0	3	.280
Dixon, Rap	CF	41	140	38	8	2	1	.271
Pullen, Neal	C	36	130	33	9	0	6	.254
Allen, Newt	2B	29	118	31	4	1	0	.254
Hudspeth, Bob	1B	23	73	18	3	0	2	.247

Philadelphia Royal Giants Pitching Statistics 1925-26

Name	G	CG	W	L	IP	SO	BB	SH
Hubbard, Jess	4	1	1	3	16	—	—	0
Currie, Rube	14	4	5	4	73	—	—	0
Britton, George	17	7	6	6	105	—	—	2
Rogan Joe	18*	16*	14*	2	153*	82*	52*	1

Pirrone's All-Stars Batting Statistics 1925-26

Name	Pos	G	AB	H	D	T	HR	BA
Statz, Jigger	CF	9	41	7	5	0	0	.175
Murray, Bobby	SS	20	86	26	3	0	0	.302
Cox, Dick	RF	14	61	20	1	0	2	.328
Herman, Babe	1B	15	61	21	1	0	0	.344
Haney, Fred	3B	5	13	2	1	0	0	.154
McMullen, Hugh	LF	14	53	16	1	0	1	.302
Pirrone, Joe	RF	13	28	5	0	0	1	.211
Rader, Don	3B	15	51	8	0	0	0	.157
Stengel, Casey	LF	7	29	8	1	0	0	.276
Hawks, Chicken	CF	8	24	4	0	0	0	.167
Cook,	C	11	26	5	0	0	0	.182

Pirrone's All-Stars Pitching Statistics 1925-26

Name	G	CG	W	L	IP	SO	BB	SH
McGraw, Bob	3	1	1	1	18	—	—	0
Oldham, Red	3	2	1	1	19	—	—	0
Piercy, Bill	6	2	0	3	37	—	—	0
Haid, Hal	3	0	0	3	19	—	—	0
Dell, Wheezer	8	4	0	4	44	—	—	0
Ludolph, Wee Willie	1	1	1	0	9	3	2	0

White Kings Batting Statistics 1925-26

Name	Pos	G	AB	H	D	T	HR	BA
Scott, Pete	2B	8	27	5	2	0	0	.185
Twombly, Babe	RF	17	77	20	3	0	1	.260
Brazill, Frank	3B	23	93	30	1	0	5	.301
Hood, Wally	LF	17	72	19	2	0	1	.264
Griggs, Art	1B	12	49	16	1	0	0	.327
Durst, Cedric	CF	16	72	20	2	1	0	.278
Lindimore, Howard	SS	16	64	17	2	0	1	.266
Jenkins, Joe	C	16	57	31	0	0	2	.544*
McAuley, Ike	SS	11	41	8	1	0	0	.195

White Kings Pitching Statistics 1925-26

Name	G	CG	W	L	IP	SO	BB	SH
Barfoot, Clyde	10	5	4	3	52	—	—	1
Root, Charlie	6	2	2	2	24	—	—	0
Payne, George	7	3	3	0	37	—	—	0
Cavet, Pug	11	3	1	3	47	—	—	0
Bell, Hi	6	1	0	5	32	—	—	0

Shell Oil Batting Statistics 1925-26

Name	Pos	G	AB	H	D	T	HR	BA
Sweeney, Bill	CF	10	37	8	0	0	0	.216
Crandall, Doc	2B	10	38	9	0	0	0	.237
Orr, Billy	3B	8	30	6	0	0	0	.200
Blakesly, Jim	RF	10	37	13	0	1	0	.351
Metz, Frank	1B	9	40	13	2	0	0	.325
Snyder,	LF	9	30	11	0	0	0	.378
Kenna, Eddie	C	8	30	8	0	0	0	.228
Butler, Johnny	3B	7	24	5	0	0	0	.208
Griffin, Ivy	SS	8	28	9	1	0	0	.321

Shell Oil Pitching Statistics 1925-26

Name	G	CG	W	L	IP	SO	BB	SH
Bell, Hi	See White Kings							
Cavet, Pug	See White Kings							
Schupp, Ferdie	7	3	4	2	52	25	31	0

The 1926-27 Season

The 1926-27 California Winter League consisted of four teams—the Philadelphia Royal Giants, Pirrone's All-Stars, the White King Soapsters, and the Shell Oilers. The schedule was evenly balanced, and the competition was heated, particularly for the first half title, and for the overall championship.

Lonnie Goodwin's Giants were blessed with an all-star squad, headed by Bullet Rogan and his pitching compatriots George Harney, Andy Cooper and, during the second half of the season, southpaw Willie Foster, generally regarded as the greatest left-handed pitcher in the annals of Negro league baseball. The supporting cast included Turkey Stearnes, returning after a two year absence, Biz Mackey, Rap Dixon, and Crush Holloway. Willie Wells took over shortstop and Newt Allen moved over to second base, giving the Giants one of the greatest double play combinations in baseball history, black or white. An indication of how strong this lineup was, is shown by the fact that no fewer than four players are presently enshrined in the National Baseball Hall of Fame—Stearnes, Wells, Rogan, and Foster. A fifth, Biz Mackey, should join them shortly.

Joe Pirrone had another stellar crew to challenge the Royal Giants, with the Meusel brothers, Bob and Irish, Fred Haney, Johnny Rawlings, a 12 year major league veteran, Chicken Hawks, who had hit .322 for the Philadelphia Phillies in 1925, Ping Bodie, a solid hitter in both the major leagues and the minor leagues, shortstop Bobby Murray, and Eddie Pick, coming off a sensational .334 season with Kansas City in the American Association.

The Shell Oilers were led by George Blaeholder, a 25-year-old right-hander, just a year away from beginning a successful 11 year major league career, Ferdie Schupp, Herb Brett, Former Chicago Cub hurler, and Herm "Old Folks" Pillette, a 226 game winner in the Pacific Coast League, and winner of 33 games for the Detroit Tigers in 1922-23. The field featured such standouts as slick fielding shortstop Johnny Kerr, in the midst of an eight year major league career, "Sunny Jim" Blakesley, Wally Hood, a ten year veteran of the PCL with a career .314 average, Fuzzy Hufft, a seven year PCL'er with an outstanding .346 lifetime average, Bob Jones, a nine year major leaguer with the Detroit Tigers, and Guy Sturdy, who hit .322 over a 20 year minor league career.

The White Kings also had a notable

cast, with pitchers Clyde Barfoot, who won 314 games in the minors including 104 in the PCL, with 26 in 1925, Ray Keating, a seven year major league veteran, and Bob Hasty, a six year major leaguer, coming off a 16–20 season with Seattle. Other members of the team included Jigger Statz, .354 with Los Angeles in 1926, Howard Lindimore, .293 with Fort Worth in the Texas League, Brick Eldred, a .332 hitter in thirteen years in the PCL, coming off a .340 season with Seattle, Art Jahn, .337 with Los Angeles, and Frank Brazill, who was midway through a memorable 20 year minor league career, where he would hit .331, with 2873 base hits, 544 doubles, 151 triples, and 254 home runs. It is mystifying why some players like Brazill, who intimidated Pacific Coast League pitchers for years in his mid-twenties, did not receive more than a cup of coffee in the major leagues. Wes Kingdon was another career minor leaguer who fell into the same category. And Howard Lindimore, an 18 year minor leaguer, including six years in the PCL, never even smelled the coffee.

Ferdie Schupp was one of the more successful pitchers against the Negro league teams in California, with a career record of 12–10. (George E. Outland)

The season opened on Saturday, October 23, with the White Kings battling the Shell Oilers at Signal Hill and Pirrone's All-Stars visiting the Philadelphia Royal Giants at White Sox Park. The Soapsters got on the board first by whipping the Shell nine 7–1 behind Bob Hasty, and the Royal Giants followed suit with a win over the All-Stars, although the score was not recorded. Both teams won the following day also, but again no scores were given.

In week two, the Shell Oilers took another hit, dropping a two game series to

Frank Brazill enjoyed a 20 year career in the minor leagues, including seven years in the Pacific Coast League, where he hit a resounding .342. (George E. Outland)

Pirrone's bombers, by scores of 3–2 and 10–6. In the opener, Wee Willie Ludolph tossed a seven hitter at the Oilers, losing his shutout in the ninth on a two-run triple by Fuzzy Hufft. Hugh McMullen homered and Irish Meusel had a double and a single to pace the All-Stars. The Sunday slugfest was highlighted by Babe Herman's three hits—a home run, a triple, and a single—and a double by Irish Meusel.

At White Sox Park, the Kings and Giants split, with the Soapsters taking the Saturday game 6–4 and Lonnie Goodwin's troops capturing the get-away game 4–3. The Kings actually led the second game 3–0 after eight innings, but they couldn't put the nail in the Giants' coffin. The *Pittsburgh Courier* followed the game. "Stearnes, the first man up, singled but was thrown out stealing second, and the crowd groaned. Dixon and Mothel followed and both walked. Pullen, next up, fanned making two out and two on. Joseph, who had felt the fans' ire most of the afternoon, doubled sharply into left center field. Duncan and Mothel scored and Joseph was once more the fair haired boy. Rogan, up next, with the tying run on second, singled to right scoring Joseph, and the fans covered the field with cushions. 'Crush' Holloway then came to the plate and singled across second on the first pitched ball and Rogan, beating Statz's throw from center, slid across the plate with the winning run ... although two thousand seats have been added to the Sox bleachers, it is a surety fans will be turned away next Sunday when the Giants meet the Kings again." According to the *Courier*, a record breaking crowd did attend the game the following Sunday, but no figures were given.

The first half of the race was hotly contested, with no team able to pull away. As a matter of fact, the Shell Oilers, who had dropped their first four games, came on strong during November, to challenge the White Kings and the Royal Giants.

Standings on December 1

White Kings	8–4
Royal Giants	7–5
Shell Oil	6–6
All-Stars	3–9

Over the final two weeks of the first half, the Kings collapsed, losing four of five, the Giants went 2–3, and the Oilers made the most of their opportunity by taking over the top spot by ½ game. The key game was played on December 12, when the Shell nine faced off against Goodwin's Gladiators, with the title at stake. Herm "Old Folks" Pillette was opposed by Giant ace, Bullet Joe Rogan, in the best pitching duel of the year. According to the *Chicago Defender*, "(Bullet Rogan) was hit freely, but sensational support kept the Oilers from scoring until the seventh when three hits put one marker across the plate," tying the game at 1–1. The score remained unchanged until the bottom of the ninth, when the Shell sluggers pushed across the winning run. Guy Sturdy led the Oiler assault on Rogan by banging out four hits, one of them a double, in four trips to the plate. He scored both Oiler runs. Dink Mothel scored for the Giants.

Shell Oil				Royal Giants			
Name	Pos	AB	H	Name	Pos	AB	H
Sweeney, Bill	CF	2	1	Mothel, Dink	1B	4	2
Kerr, John	CF	0	0	Allen, Newt	2B	4	1
Rhyne, Hal	2B	3	1	Stearnes Turkey	CF	4	1
Jones, Bob	3B	4	1	Dixon, Rap	LF	4	1
Blakesley, Jim	RF	4	0	Holloway, Crush	RF	3	0
Sturdy, Guy	1B	4	4	Pullen, Neal	C	3	0
Emmer, Frank	SS	4	1	Mackey, Biz	3B	3	1
Murphy, Danny	C	3	3	Wells, Willie	SS	3	0
Kenna, Eddie	LF	4	1	Rogan Joe	P	3	1
Pillette, Herm	P	3	0				
Totals		31	12			31	7

Shell Oil	0 0 0	0 0 0	1 0 1—2—12—?
Philadelphia Royal Giants	0 0 0	0 0 1	0 0 0—1— 7—?

Two base hit: Sturdy

	IP	H	SO	BB
Pillette (WP)	9	7	5	0
Rogan (LP)	9	11	4	3

The *Pittsburgh Courier* reported some disturbing news over the midseason break. "It was rumored that a law would be passed at the minor League meeting prohibiting the playing of winter baseball. This rule, if passed, would ruin the huge investment in the baseball plant at 38th and Ascot Avenues and would also kill a nice source of money making for baseball players, black and white, each winter." Future events would result in a ban on winter baseball by active major league players beginning in the fall of 1927, but would not significantly affect the operation of the winter league. Minor league players and former major leaguers would continue to participate in the winter competition.

Lonnie Goodwin's cohorts, after losing the first half of the league by ½ game were determined not to let the same thing happen again, and they got off the mark quickly in the second half, winning their first 11 games, and making a shambles out of the race. Tempers flared during a January 8 game between the Giants and the Shell Oil nine, as described by the *California Eagle*. "An additional thrill was added to the game when Sturdy, the big Shell Oil first sacker, disputed a decision by umpire Beck and, getting abusive, was ruled out of the game. Coming back onto the diamond, he took a hard punch at Beck, who dodged receiving a glancing blow. Instantly policemen swarmed on the diamond from nowhere and with the intervention of some Giant players, Beck was saved from further harm."

The Giants won the game 5–4 thanks to their specialty, a four run rally in the bottom of the ninth. With two men out and Dixon on base after a hit, consecutive hits by Allen, Mackey, Pullen and Mothel brought home the victory.

George E. Outland, a rabid baseball and Ping Bodie fan, was a spectator at a game at White Sox Park on January 15, and he subsequently recorded his recollections. "I suddenly saw that Bodie was to play for an all-star team against a Negro outfit out at the old ramshackled park near Jefferson High School.... I ... finally discovered that to get out to Hooper Avenue one took not the 'H' car but the 'B' car. And get there I did.

"The park was old and ramshackle.... The game started with an all-star colored team playing against one managed by Joe Pirrone, famous semi-pro manager and night club owner in Los Angeles. I looked at the extremely distant left field fence and hoped there might be a chance of his (Bodie) pulling one over the short but extremely high right field screen. By God, he did neither, but he hit almost the first pitch out of the lot! He drove a hard, low liner over the right center field fence, just barely clearing the barrier, and yet ticketed from the moment it was hit, for the distance ... he clunked one off an A-1 Negro pitcher, and ... it went over the most distant part of the fence, and a most difficult

Ping Bodie, former New York Yankee outfielder, hit .284 for Pirrone's All-Stars in 1926-27. (Dick Dobbins)

one for a right-handed batter to clear." The victim of Bodie's blast was Andy Cooper. The All-Stars jumped out to a 2–0 lead in the second, aided by the homer, but the Giants came back to win, 4–3 in the ninth, for their eighth straight.

Willie Foster, one of the greatest southpaw pitchers in Negro league history, arrived on the scene midway through the streak, and went 6–0 the rest of the way to put the icing on the cake. In his first winter start, on January 16, he shut out Pirrone's All-Stars 4–0, behind an eleven strikeout masterpiece. A week later, Rube Foster's little brother chalked up another whitewash job, trouncing the White Kings 11–0, and fanning five in the seven inning nightcap. Stearnes with a homer and a single, Mackey with a homer, and Dixon with three singles led the attack. George Harney got into the act by blanking the Kings in game two, 4–0, scattering seven hits. Turkey Stearnes had a single and a home run.

Finally, on February 11, the Shell Oilers stopped the Philadelphian's winning streak, as Ferdie Schupp outpitched George Harney, 8–4. Jim Blakesley had three hits and Ivy Griffin two for the winners. Biz Mackey's home run, a 396 foot blast over the center field fence, was the only bright spot for the losers.

The second half of the season came to a merciful end for the three also-rans on February 7, with the final results:

Philadelphia Royal Giants	13– 1–1
Shell Oil	8– 6
White Kings	3– 9
Pirrone's All-Stars	2–10–1

A five game playoff between the Royal Giants and the Shell Oilers was scheduled for the weekends of February 18 and 25. Without a doubt, the Giants had all the momentum, after their rousing run through the second half of the schedule. And with Willie Foster on hand, to back up Bullet Joe Rogan, it looked like a long road ahead for Jimmy Austin's team. Ferdie Schupp, the left-handed curve ball specialist took the hill for the Oilers in game one, facing George Harney, the Giants' seven game winner at White Sox Park. Neither starter had anything on the ball on this day, with the big sluggers dominating the game, but Harney seemed to have the best of it as he took a 9–5 lead into the ninth, thanks to two home runs and a single by Turkey Stearnes and a homer by Biz Mackey. But it was all a mirage. The fighting Oilers pushed across four runs to tie it in the ninth off Harney and Andy Cooper, then took Cooper to the cleaners with four more runs in the tenth to win the game, 13–10. Dick Cox homered for the winners, and added a couple of singles. John Kerr also had three hits, including two doubles, while Frank Emmer and Eddie Kenna each had a double and a single, and Hal Rhyne had a triple and a single.

In game two, Willie Foster was Lonnie Goodwin's pitching choice, and the crafty southpaw took no prisoners. He shut down the Shell boys with four scattered hits, besting Leo Moon 3–1 in a pitchers' duel. The *Chicago Defender* noted, "Foster had fanned 11 and given but two safe hits up to the eighth. Then Johnny Kerr caught hold of a fast one and rode it out of the park. Rhyne followed with a double to left and things looked bad for Foster, but he tightened up and retired the next two batters." Dink Mothel had two of the Giants' five hits.

The series moved to Signal Hill, Shell Oil's home park in Long Beach, for the final three games of the series starting February 25. In the opener Herm "Old Folks" Pillette matched pitches with "Bullet Joe" Rogan in the best pitched game of the series. The Royal Giants jumped out in front with two runs in the top of the fifth, but the Oilers came back to tie it with a deuce in the seventh. Lonnie Goodwin's boys pushed across the game winner in the eighth. Rogan pitched the complete game victory. Roy Wilkinson, in relief of Pillette, took the loss. Turkey Stearnes with two singles led the Giant attack, while Biz Mackey contributed a double. Frank Emmer with a triple and Hal Rhyne with a double paced the Oilers.

Unfortunately, there was no box score published for the fourth game of the series, won by the Shell team 5–3. The *Pittsburgh Courier* followed the game. "Sunday the Giants ... saw their chance to win a pennant fade when the Oilers built up a 4–0 lead by the sixth inning. The Giants scored three runs in the lucky seventh, but the Oilers got a run back in the same inning."

A fifth game was never played, for whatever reason, and the season ended with the Philadelphia Royal Giants and the Shell Oilers sharing the title as co-champions.

On March 5, the Giants played a doubleheader against Pirrone's All-Stars before disbanding. The Giants took both games, 5–4 and 12–3. The *Chicago Defender* said, "A brass band gave the boys a great send-off in their final game. Lonnie Goodwin, the manager, leaves with his team for Japan, taking the following players; Pullen, Mackey, Dixon, Cooper, Green, Riddle, and Duncan. Rogan and the remainder of the team will barnstorm their way back east to join their respective league clubs. Mackey, Dixon, Cooper, and Duncan, will write 'finis' behind their careers as major league stars."

The statistics tell the story of a great pennant race. Both the Philadelphia Royal Giants and the Shell Oilers combined outstanding hitting and superior pitching with a tight defense. For Jimmy Austin's Shell team, catcher Danny Murphy, who played for Mission in the PCL in the summer, led all winter league batters with an average of .419. Bob Jones tattoed the ball at a .361 clip, Guy Sturdy hit .329 and Bill Sweeney hit .328. Frank Emmer led the league in triples with 5. Herm Pillette led the league in victories with 8, to go along with six losses. George Blaeholder had a 4–2 record, while Ferdie Schupp went 2–0.

For the Royal Giants, Turkey Stearnes hit .376 with a league-leading 6 home runs, Rap Dixon hit .349, Neal Pullen came in at .343, and Biz Mackey batted .316 and tied Stearnes for home run honors with 6. Willie Foster compile a perfect 6–0 record on the mound. Bullet Joe Rogan went 6–2, Andy Cooper was at 5–2, and George Harney finished with 7 wins against 4 losses.

Pirrone's All-Stars were hampered by mediocre hitting throughout the season, wasting good pitching performances by Ludolph, Oldham, Koupal, and Wilkinson. Hugh McMullen at .317 was their only .300 hitter, while at the other end of the spectrum, Irish Meusel was bogged down with a paltry .200 average. The White Kings also suffered with a poor offense. Although they did have three .300 hitters, led by Art Griggs at .375, they also had three batters below the Mendoza line, with averages between .120 and .179, and no team can survive that.

1926-27 California Winter League
Final Standings—Incomplete

	Wins	Losses	Ties
Philadelphia Royal Giants	26	11	1
Shell Oil	19	15	0
White Kings	12	17	0
Pirrone's All-Stars	8	22	1

Philadelphia Royal Giants Batting Statistics 1926-27

Name	Pos	G	AB	H	D	T	HR	BA
Stearnes, Turkey	CF	28	106	41	4	2	8*	.387
Rogan, Joe	P-CF	28	61	20	2	0	0	.328
Wells, Willie	SS	33	105	19	6	1	0	.181
Mackey, Biz	1B-C	27	95	30	4	0	6	.316
Allen, Newt	2B	21	78	22	1	0	1	.282
Mothel, Dink	1B	32	114	30	2	0	0	.263
Joseph, Newt	3B	31	101	24	7	0	1	.238
Dixon, Rap	LF	35	109	38	9	1	0	.349
Holloway, Crush	RF	33	122	30	4	1	1	.246
Duncan, Frank	C	24	58	16	3	0	0	.276
Pullen, Neal	C	15	35	12	4	0	0	.343

Philadelphia Royal Giants Pitching Statistics 1926-27

Name	G	CG	W	L	IP	SO	BB	SH
Harney, George	16	9*	7	5	116*	—	—	2*
Cooper, Andy	10	5	5	2	71	—	—	1
Rogan, Joe	11	6	6	2	68	38	21*	2*
Foster, Willie	7	5	6	0	55	49*	17	2*

Pirrone's All-Stars Batting Statistics 1926-27

Name	Pos	G	AB	H	D	T	HR	BA
Murray, Bobby	SS	27	95	25	3	0	0	.263
Meusel, Bob	LF	10	33	8	1	0	0	.242
Pick, Eddie	CF	28	101	30	7	1	0	.297
Meusel, Irish	RF	9	35	7	4	1	0	.200
Hawks, Chicken	1B	30	108	31	7	0	0	.287
Rawlings, Johnny	2B	20	66	16	2	0	0	.242
McMullen, Hugh	C	27	82	26	2	0	2	.317
Fonseca, Lew	3B	16	51	14	5	0	0	.275
Pirrone, Joe	CF	16	44	10	1	0	0	.227
Sawyer, Carl	2B	15	33	8	1	0	0	.242
Bodie, Ping	LF	28	96	25	3	0	0	.260
Hufft, Fuzzy	3B	26	95	27	1	0	0	.284
Kingdon, Wes	SS	14	56	19	1	0	0	.339

Pirrone's All-Stars Pitching Statistics 1926-27

Name	G	CG	W	L	IP	SO	BB	SH
Ludolph, Wee Willie	8	3	1	2	50	19	21*	0
Oldham, Red	5	0	0	3	19	8	3	0
Koupal, Lou	10	4	2	4	50	20	12	1
Wilkinson, Roy	18*	7	4	7	85	—	—	0
Purdue,	4	0	0	1	12	—	—	0

Shell Oil Batting Statistics 1926-27

Name	Pos	G	AT	H	D	T	HR	BA
Sweeney, Bill	CF	18	64	21	2	0	0	.328
Kerr, John	SS	26	98	27	4	1	2	.276
Jones, Bob	3B	26	97	35	3	0	0	.361
Sturdy, Guy	1B	23	79	26	2	0	0	.329
Blakesley, Jim	LF	29	112	30	2	1	1	.268

Willie Foster, Rube's little brother, went a perfect 6–0 for the Royal Giants in 1926-27. (John B. Holway)

Shell Oil Batting Statistics 1926-27

Name	Pos	G	AT	H	D	T	HR	BA
Murphy, Danny	C	14	43	18	0	0	0	.419*
Hood, Wally	LF	15	60	17	1	2	1	.283
Kenna, Eddie	C	24	73	19	3	0	0	.260
Emmer, Frank	SS	28	88	24	5	5*	0	.273
Rhyne, Hal	2B	12	47	12	2	1	0	.255
Griffin, Ivy	LF	14	46	15	1	0	0	.326

Shell Oil Pitching Statistics 1926-27

Name	G	CG	W	L	IP	SO	BB	SH
Blaeholder, George	8	5	4	2	54	28	7	1
Pillette, Herm	17	8	8*	6	100	—	—	0
Brett, Herb	5	3	1	3	35	—	—	0
Schupp, Ferdie	5	2	2	0	33	—	—	0
Wilkinson, Roy	9	2	0	4	30	—	—	0

White Kings Batting Statistics 1926-27

Name	Pos	G	AB	H	D	T	HR	BA
Statz, Jigger	CF	6	25	7	0	0	0	.280
Lindimore, Howard	2B	13	47	14	2	0	0	.298
Eldred, Brick	RF	20	47	13	3	2	0	.277

White Kings Batting Statistics 1926-27

Name	Pos	G	AB	H	D	T	HR	BA
Griggs, Art	1B	11	32	12	0	0	0	.375
Golvin, Walt	1B	11	25	3	0	0	0	.120
Jahn, Art	LF	16	56	10	1	0	0	.179
Brazill, Frank	3B	16	42	7	0	0	0	.167
Hannah, Truck	C	13	40	8	1	0	0	.200
Jacobs, Ray	SS	26	90	21	1	1	0	.233
French, Ray	3B	17	51	16	3	1	0	.314
Jenkins, Joe	C	18	46	15	1	0	1	.326
Cox, Dick	CF	17	57	17	2	0	0	.298
Cullop, Nick	1B	10	37	11	1	1	0	.297

White Kings Pitching Statistics 1926-27

Name	G	CG	W	L	IP	SO	BB	SH
Hasty, Bob	11	2	2	1	39	—	—	1
Keating, Ray	12	4	4	5	81	—	—	0
Moudy, Dick	10	3	2	4	47	—	—	0
Barfoot, Clyde	7	2	2	3	42	—	—	0

The 1927-28 Season

The news appeared devastating at first. Headlines in the *Pittsburgh Courier*, dated October 13, seemed to jump off the page. "Landis Bans Colored Winter League Baseball On The Coast." The accompanying article detailed the story. "The Southern California winter League Baseball season scheduled to open October 22 at the White Sox baseball park, Thirty-eighth and Ascot Streets, has been called off by the recent ruling of Commissioner K.M. Landis, prohibiting all minor league ballplayers from playing winter ball under penalty of expulsion from organized baseball.... The Landis ruling is a sad blow to local ball fans who were anticipating a hot winter schedule, following the recent announcement that James P. White, former manager of the Colored Giants in 1922, was to succeed Lonnie Goodwin as lessee of the White Sox Park. Also that White had purchased the franchise of the Philadelphia Royal Giants and intended to pilot that organization in the season's race.

"Four clubs were to have competed in the Winter League, the Philadelphia Royal Giants and the Cleveland Giants of the National Colored League, under the management of S.N. Cobb. ... James (s/b Joe) Pirrone's All-Stars and the Anaheim-Fullerton-Santa Ana organization under the name of the Orange County Club, were to have been the two white entrants."

As it turned out, the ban was not as harmful as first thought. The *California Eagle* noted that major leaguers Bob Meusel and Tony Lazzeri were permitted to play winter baseball into early November, in accordance with "the new ruling." Several minor leaguers played the entire winter season, including Pacific Coast Leaguers Ping Bodie, Fuzzy Hufft, and Joe Jenkins. And Fred Haney, who also played the entire season, had played in the majors in 1927 and would play in the majors again in 1929, so there was some flexibility in the ruling. Apparently major leaguers were limited to playing only thirty days after the end of the major league season, while minor leaguers were not affected at all.

The season opened on Saturday, October 15, at White Sox Park, with the Philadelphia Royal Giants hosting Joe Pirrone's All-Stars. The *Eagle* documented the day's festivities. "Never in the history of Winter baseball in California has there been as auspicious an opening as that last Saturday, which opened the track for the pennant race this season. A long line of busses and cars paraded thru the principal streets with both competing teams, the Hillsdale (Philadelphia) Giants and Pirrone's All-Stars in line. Motion pictures on the streets were taken for the famous Pictures Corporation and also for the Kinograms.

"The 'Soaring Eagles' official Press car headed the parade and bore Editor Bass, Advertising Manager Lamar, Sports Editor Levette, and the cameraman. Arrived at the park, both teams paraded on to the grounds to the strains of Stars and Stripes, and as they lined up side by side all were photographed and introduced in turn. Dixon, Carr, and Shaw, all well-known to the fans, got big applause as did Pirrone, Sherlock, Murray, and others of the All-Stars, but Bob Meusel perhaps received the biggest ovation of all.

"...As the cameras ground, came the shout 'Play ball' and the battle was on.... Babe Herman of the All-Stars stole the show Saturday with two home runs, and Bob Meusel starred with four hits." The All-Stars won easily 12–5, with Ted Shaw absorbing the loss.

On Sunday, Dick Moudy stymied James P. White's troops, tossing a five-hitter, and winning 4–2, over right-hander Bill Holland of the Giants. Hugh McMullen cracked two doubles for the winners, while Rap Dixon hit a home run for the home team. The Royal Giants dropped another game to the All-Stars the following week, then bounced back to run off a five game winning streak, defeating the All-Stars twice, the Cleveland Stars twice, and Orange County once.

On December 3 and 4, Philadelphia met Pirrone's All-Stars in a three game series, but by this time, Bob Meusel and Babe Herman had left the team, putting them at a distinct disadvantage. One thing about Joe Pirrone's team however, was that they were all professionals, and they all wanted the winners' share of the purse, which was 75 percent of the gate. The previous week, the All-Stars had overcome a ten run deficit to tie James P. White's troops 10–10. On Saturday, the two teams engaged in another donnybrook. Lou Koupal and Pud Flournoy proved to be no puzzles to the hitters, and 34 hits rattled around the little ballyard on 38th and Ascot Avenues, 22 by the home team. The lead changed hands a half a dozen times before darkness halted play after nine innings, with the score tied at 9–9. The Giants had scored two runs in the bottom of the ninth to gain the deadlock. John Beckwith with 5 for 5, including two home runs and a double, was the big gun for the Royal Giants. Biz Mackey went 4 for 5, with two singles and two doubles, and little Jake Stephens rapped four singles in five at-bats. On the All-Star side, Irish Meusel went 3 for 3, and Monk Sherlock went 3 for 4.

The Sunday doubleheader was just as competitive. Another 29 base hits shot off the bats of the big lumbermen, much to the chagrin of the starting pitchers, the All-Stars Praul and the Royal Giants' fireballer, Bill Holland. The Giants collected at least one hit in every inning, but couldn't make them count, scoring only eight runs on their 17 hits. Doubles by Stephens and Dixon, triples by Dixon and Thomas, and home runs by Hubbard and Carr, were not enough to carry the day. Pirrone's bombers made their 12 hits count for 9 big runs, with Irish Meusel's single, double, and home run leading the way.

Pirrone's All-Stars

Name	Pos	AB	H
Murray, Bobby	2B	3	1
Sawyer, Carl	1B	3	1

Royal Giants

Name	Pos	AB	H
Hubbard, Jess	RF	4	2
Warfield, Frank	2B	6	3

Pirrone's All-Stars					Royal Giants			
Name	Pos	AB	H		Name	Pos	AB	H
Hufft, Fuzzy	RF	5	2		Dixon, Rap	LF	4	3
Meusel, Irish	LF	4	3		Beckwith, John	3B	6	1
Haney, Fred	3B	5	1		Mackey, Biz	C	5	2
Sherlock, Jack	SS	5	0		Carr, Tank	1B	4	3
DeMaggio, Nick	CF	5	2		Thomas, Clint	CF	5	2
Danning, I.	C	4	2		Stevens, Jake	SS	5	0
Praul	P	3	0		Holland, Bill	P	4	1
Wilkinson Roy	P	0	0		Burnette, Tex	PH	0	0
Thomas,	PH	0	0					
Totals		37	12				43	17

Pirrone's All-Stars   1 0 6   0 0 2   0 0 0—9—12—?
Philadelphia Royal Giants   0 3 0   0 2 2   0 1 0—8—17—?

Two base hits: I. Meusel, Dixon, Stevens
Three base hits: DeMaggio, Dixon, Thomas
Home Runs: I. Meusel, Hubbard, Carr
WP—Praul
LP—Holland

In game two, the Philadelphians came back to win the abbreviated encounter 5–3. Big Jess "Mountain" Hubbard was the winning pitcher.

Controversy reared its ugly head as the first half of the winter league season was coming to an end. The Cleveland Stars under manager S.N. Cobb, threatened to withdraw from the league because of scheduling problems. According to the *Pittsburgh Courier*, "...it is presumed that the rift came through the objection of the (Stars) to the number of dates scheduled for them at the White Sox Park in Los Angeles.... When two teams are playing in the Los Angeles park, the other two teams have been playing in the Orange County Park, about 50 miles from Los Angeles and in a community that does not offer within 75% of the attendance enjoyed in Los Angeles." Cobb pointed out the fact that the Royal Giants took two out of three games from Pirrone's All-Stars recently at White Sox Park, on a 75–25 percentage agreement.

The dispute was obviously resolved amicably because the Cleveland Stars were back in action when the second half of the league began, the Royal Giants having won a closely contested first half race on the basis of 9 wins against 5 losses, with two ties. Cleveland finished with a 3–2 record in box scores recovered, although games played in Orange County were seldom reported in the Los Angeles press. Pirrone's team, after starting the season with a 3–0 record, dropped eight of their last ten decisions, feeling the loss of their big guns, Bob Meusel and Babe Herman. And Orange County had only an 0–2 slate to show for their efforts.

The Cleveland Stars got off to a fast start at the beginning of the second half, winning seven of their first nine games, and giving them a comfortable 3 game lead over James P. White's cohorts. Norman "Turkey" Stearnes, the Stars all-world center fielder, had a red-letter day on January 8 when he poled four home runs in a doubleheader, two in each game. In the opener, the lithe, 170 pound slugger led his team to victory over Pirrone's All-Stars by a 7–4 count, and in the nightcap, he went 4 for 4, adding a single and a double to his two home runs, as Andy Cooper took the Royal Giants measure 5–3.

Unfortunately, the Stars were not able to sustain their momentum, nor could they finish off the tenacious Giants. Philadelphia

Norman "Turkey" Stearnes averaged .375 with 20 home runs in 267 at-bats between 1926 and 1928. (George E. Outland)

ners, while Newt Allen rapped a double and a triple for the Clevelanders.

The final standings showed the Philadelphia Royal Giants to be the league champions with an overall record of 19–11, compared to 10–8 for the Cleveland Stars. Their rousing finish gave them the second half title with a 10–6 record to a 7–6 record for the Stars, thereby eliminating the need for a playoff.

Jess "Mountain" Hubbard captured the batting championship with a hefty .442 batting average, and Turkey Stearnes repeated as the home run king with 7 in just 12 games. Bill Holland was the top pitcher with a 7–3 record and a league leading 4 shutouts.

As a final note of interest regarding winter baseball in California, it should be noted that several members of the infamous Chicago Black Sox, particularly Claude "Lefty" Williams and Buck Weaver, occasionally wintered on the coast, playing in one or more of the leagues. In 1927-28 for

walloped Pirrone's All-Stars 11–1, then beat Cleveland 3–2, to set the stage for the big showdown. The climactic series of the year took place in White Sox Park on the weekend of February 18 and 19, with manager S.N. Cobb's Cleveland Stars facing the revitalized Philadelphia Royal Giants. It was a long weekend for the Stars. In the Saturday opener, Giants ace Bill Holland tossed a 6–0 shutout at the Stars, and on Sunday, his teammates completed the carnage with a convincing 8–5 and 7–6 doubleheader sweep. In the nightcap, the Giants staged one of their patented last inning rallies, scoring three runs in the bottom of the seventh inning to capture the abbreviated encounter. Tank Carr and Rap Dixon each had a double and two singles for the win-

Bill Holland led the California Winter League in pitching in 1927-28 with a 7–3 record.

instance, Buck Weaver held down the shortstop position for both the Sherman Athletic Association and the Merchants National Bank, batting .273 in the six games reported, with one double and one triple. During the summer Weaver often toured the midwest with the Duffy Florals out of Chicago.

1927-28 California Winter League
Final Standings—Incomplete

	Wins	Losses	Ties
Philadelphia Royal Giants	19	11	2
Cleveland Stars	10	8	0
Pirrone's All-Stars	6	14	2
Orange County	0	2	0

Philadelphia Royal Giants Batting Statistics 1927-28

Name	Pos	G	AB	H	D	T	HR	BA
Stephens, Jake	SS	14	56	14	2	1	0	.250
Warfield, Frank	2B	22*	88*	25	2	0	1	.284
Dixon, Rap	3B	20	79	30*	6*	3*	5	.380
Thomas, Clint	CF	21	85	18	3	1	1	.212
Burnett, Tex	C	9	31	8	0	0	0	.258
Carr, Tank	1B	19	69	26	4	1	2	.377
Mackey, Biz	C	18	65	25	5	0	3	.385
Beckwith, John	3B	19	71	22	4	1	5	.310
Hubbard, Jess	RF	20	77	34	1	1	2	.442*

Philadelphia Royal Giants Pitching Statistics 1927-28

Name	G	CG	W	L	IP	SO	BB	SH
Holland, Bill	11	10*	7*	3	90	36	10	4*
Cooper, Sam	8	4	2	2	38	—	—	0
Flournoy, Pud	12*	7	6	3	92*	31	8	0

Cleveland Stars Batting Statistics 1927-28

Name	Pos	G	AB	H	D	T	HR	BA
Gardner, Ping	RF	6	27	4	0	0	0	.148
Allen, Newt	2B	13	56	14	1	1	0	.250
Holloway, Crush	LF	14	56	14	0	0	2	.250
Stearnes, Turkey	CF	12	53	20	3	0	7*	.377
Mothel, Dink	1B	14	54	19	3	0	1	.352
Wells, Willie	SS	14	48	15	3	0	0	.313
Day, Connie	3B	12	44	9	2	1	0	.205
Duncan, Frank	C	8	21	8	2	0	0	.381
Pullen, Neal	C	9	34	7	0	0	0	.206

Cleveland Stars Pitching Statistics 1927-28

Name	G	CG	W	L	IP	SO	BB	SH
Harney, George	5	4	1	3	39	—	—	0
Cooper, Andy	6	5	5	1	51	25	17*	1
Morris, H. "Yellowhorse"	5	4	2	3	42	—	—	0
Shaw, Ted	3	3	2	1	25	—	—	0

Pirrone's All-Stars—Batting Statistics 1927-28

Name	Pos	G	AB	H	D	T	HR	BA
Murray, Bobby	2B	13	54	12	0	0	0	.222
Meusel, Bob	LF	5	20	6	1	0	0	.300
Herman, Babe	1B	5	19	7	1	0	2	.368
Hufft, Fuzzy	RF	6	22	6	0	0	0	.273
Sherlock, Jack	SS	11	42	14	2	0	1	.333
McMullen, Hugh	C	4	13	4	2	0	0	.308
Jenkins, Joe	C	6	13	2	0	0	0	.154
Haney, Fred	3B	14	55	20	2	2	0	.364
Bodie, Ping	CF	10	40	11	0	0	1	.275
Pirrone, Joe	RF	6	23	6	0	0	0	.261
Sawyer, Carl	1B	12	44	11	3	0	0	.250
Meusel, Irish	RF	9	37	14	3	0	2	.378
DeMaggio, Nick	CF	8	30	5	0	1	0	.167

Pirrone's All-Stars—Pitching Statistics 1927-28

Name	G	CG	W	L	IP	SO	BB	SH
Koupal, Lou	4	1	0	2	30	14	5	0
Praul,	5	4	1	4	39	—	—	0
Wilkinson, Roy	7	2	1	1	26	—	—	0

Frank Warfield was considered to be the best second baseman in Negro league history by many baseball experts. (Kimshi Productions, Inc.)

The 1928-29 Season

The Negro league entry for the 1928-29 season, called the Cleveland Giants, was a team drawn from the personnel of both the Philadelphia Royal Giants and the Cleveland Stars, plus several new additions. Returning players included Biz Mackey, Rap Dixon, Tank Carr, and John Beckwith, of the Royal Giants, and Newt Allen, Neal Pullen, and Connie Day of the Clevelend Stars, along with pitchers Chet Brewer, "Bullet Joe" Rogan, Ping Gardner, a right-handed submarine pitcher of the Bacharach Giants, and Carl "Lefty" Glass, the ace of the Memphis Red Sox of the Negro National League.

The Giants' opposition in the league consisted of Pirrone's All-Stars, the White Kings, and Shell Oil. The league promised to be another competitive exercise as numerous major league and minor league talents graced the rosters of the white teams. The All-Stars were particularly strong with Irish Meusel, now back in the PCL, Smead Jolley (the PCL batting champion with an average of .404), and Fred Haney, plus

Emil "Irish" Meusel led the Pirrone All-Stars at bat from 1926 through 1929.

pitchers Lou Koupal and Sloppy Thurston (9–7 with San Francisco). The White Kings boasted Earl Averill, on his way to an illustrious 13 year major league career after pummeling Pacific Coast League pitchers for a .354 batting average, Frank Brazill (.330 with Portland), Dick Cox, and Walt Golvin, with Clyde Barfoot (20–19 with L.A.) and Charlie Barnabe on the mound. Averill, known as "The Earl of Snohomish," was a slugging left-handed hitting outfielder for the Cleveland Indians during the 1930s. His career charts show a .318 batting average with 2,019 base hits. He averaged 35 doubles, 11 triples, 21 home runs, and 101 runs batted in a year. Shell Oil had Dud Lee (.273 with Hollywood), Howard Lindimore, John Kerr, on his way to the Chicago White Sox after hitting .301 for Hollywood, and Walt Christensen, plus pitchers Herm Pillette (who would go 23–13 for Mission in the PCL in 1929), and Ferdie Schupp.

The *California Eagle* announced the start of the winter league season. "Working hard all summer to perfect a lineup of teams for the present season that will surpass all preceding winter leagues, Joe Pirrone, the father of winter baseball and joint owner with his brother John of White Sox Park, is all ready for the opening gong, Saturday at 2:15.... Meusel and Lazzeri (are) expected in the lineup."

The *Eagle* also reported the opener. "You've read about those kind of games; seen them in the movies when a team that seems to be hopelessly a loser, grits its collective teeth and with a determined 'I will win,' does so with a vengeance.

"Six thousand yelling, leaping, hat and cushion throwing fans saw one of those unbelieveable wins on Sunday last when the Cleveland Giants, with the score 3–1 in favor of Pirrone's strong All-Stars, and the crowd leaving, tacked up three runs that made it 4–3.

"They kidded Day about not being much of a hitter, but it was his home run that turned the trick.... With one run in the ninth and two men on, Day clubbed the ball over the fence to give the Giants the decision.... Bullet Rogan pitched for the Giants.... Bob Meusel, Yankee flyhawk, collected two hits yesterday. He received a great ovation every time at bat.... Everybody on both teams did great. Stearnes made a beautiful running catch in center field." Tony Lazzeri was a no-show. He did play one game later in the year under the name of Lunetti.

On October 26, the *California Eagle* reported that Babe Ruth and Lou Gehrig would be in the lineup of Pirrone's All-Stars when they faced the Cleveland Giants on Sunday, the 28th. However, it is doubtful the two stars played in the game, since no record of it has been found.

On Thanksgiving Day, a big crowd turned out to root for the Giants against Joe Pirrone's hired guns. It was an exciting game, with first one team, then the other taking the lead. Chet Brewer and Sloppy Thurston, although struggling throughout, both turned in complete games. The Cleveland team carried a 5–2 lead into the bottom of the seventh, but the All-Stars pushed across three runs to gain a tie. The score remained 5–5 into the tenth, then after Brewer had set Moorehart, Murray, and Pick down in order, the Giants sent the fans home happy. Newt Allen led off the bottom of the tenth, and struck out. But Connie Day followed with a shot between first and second for a single, then stole second. Biz Mackey, who always seemed to be the late inning hero for the Negro league entries, did it again, lining a single to center to plate the winning run. Rap Dixon had a single and a home run for the Cleveland contingent, while Smead Jolley got to Brewer for two singles and a home run.

Although the recovered box scores do not reflect it, the *California Eagle* reported that Shell Oil won the first half of the winter league, with the Cleveland Giants second.

Manager Joe Rogan and his troops were determined not to let the pennant get away from them, so they set out to win the second half of the league with room to spare. Over the Christmas holiday, they took on Pirrone's All-Stars in a three game series. In the opener, the All-Stars knocked Ping Gardner out of the box with a five run outburst in the third inning, but Joe Rogan came on to save the day. He proceeded to shut down Joe Pirrone's boys with a single run over the final six innings, while his teammates battled back with two runs in the sixth and a big four-spot in the seventh, to win 9–6. Newt Allen with four hits was the big gun. Smead Jolley homered for the losers.

The All-Stars bounced back to take the second game by the score of 9–3, pounding Chet Brewer for 14 base hits, including home runs by Jolley and Eddie Pick. In the get-away game on Christmas, Rogan selected "Lefty" Glass to oppose Nick Dumovich. The All-Star starter didn't make it out of the second inning, as the Giants unleashed a 22 hit attack to demolish the Stars by a 16–3 count. Rap Dixon, the batting star of the day, clubbed a three run homer over the center field fence, near 36th Street, to give his team a 5–0 lead in the first, and they coasted from there. John Beckwith had a single and a home run, while Rogan, Stearnes, and Allen, chipped in with three hits apiece.

The Giants made a shambles of the second half of the race, winning five of six between December 16 and New Year's Day, then running off seven more victories, with one tie, to coast home a comfortable winner, with a record of 16–7–1. The big Giant bats exploded in the second half as Beckwith, Mackey, Rogan, Stearnes, and Dixon all smashed the ball at a better than .356 clip, to support the strong pitching of Rogan, Brewer, Glass, and Gardner. John Beckwith was the ring leader of the hit brigade, averaging almost two hits a game. A typical game involved the Giants and the White Kings as covered by the *Pittsburgh Courier*. "The Cleveland Giants came from behind to tie the score at five-all in the seventh inning against the White Kings at White Sox Park Wednesday, when Beckwith singled and Stearnes lifted the ball over the right center field fence for a home run. The visitors gained an early lead, but the Giants kept pecking away and won in the ninth on a double by Beckwith and a single by Mothel. Beckwith had a perfect day at bat, getting four hits in four times up, including two doubles. Earl Averill also had a perfect day, getting two home runs and two singles. Rap Dixon connected for a home run for Cleveland. Brewer went to the rescue of Rogan in the eighth with one run in and two on bases, and stopped the King's rally."

On January 12 and 13, the Cleveland Giants took on Pirrone's All-Stars in a two game series. Bullet Rogan's crew took the first game by a score of 13–6, with Stearnes, Beckwith, Rogan, and Dixon all hitting for the circuit. Smead Jolley hit two for the All-Stars. Game two was a real slugfest, with Irish Meusel hitting a grand slam home run in the top of the first, then watching as the Cleveland bombers came roaring back, as reported by the *Chicago Defender*. "The Giants got to Thurston for three runs in the first inning on a base on balls to Allen, a single by Day and a home run over the fence by Turkey Stearnes. A double by Rogan, Allen's single and Day's homer tied the score seven-all in the fourth inning. A home run by third baseman Beckwith in the eighth, over the left field fence, is the longest ball ever hit in any park in Los Angeles. It went over the fence 368 feet from home plate, over one house, on top of another house, where it fell to the ground. After a measurement was made, the ball had travelled 518 feet from the home plate to where it stopped. This was a mighty blow." The Giants won the game 12–10 with Rogan, who relieved Brewer in the fourth with the score 7–4 in favor of the All-Stars, gaining the decision.

The Cleveland Giants' surge set up a playoff with the Shell Oilers, the first half leaders, to determine the league champion. The series opened in White Sox Park on February 15, with Roy Wilkinson, former Chicago White Sox pitcher, facing Carl "Lefty" Glass. The Cleveland southpaw proved to be no puzzle for the Oilers, who combed him for 16 base hits, en route to a convincing 11–5 victory. Stearnes, Allen, and Dixon hit for the circuit for the Giants, but they were unable to match the flurry of extra base hits by the Shell nine, which included two homers by John Kerr, and one each by Dud Lee and Earl Averill, as well as two base hits by Christensen, Wilkinson, and Jolley. Wilkinson scattered 12 Giant hits effectively, and took a comfortable 11–3 lead into the bottom of the eighth, before he eased up and let the Giants score two more.

Bullet Joe Rogan's troops bounced back in game two, spotting the Oilers a 5–3 lead before running up a seven spot in the bottom of the eighth for the win. Chet Brewer started for Cleveland, but left after three innings with Shell up 4–0. Rogan held the Oilers in check the rest of the way, limiting them to a single run over the last six innings. Meanwhile, the Giants fought their way back. Rogan homered off Herm "Old Folks" Pillette in the fifth, and Beckwith and Mackey scored in the sixth, to cut the Oiler lead to 5–3. The score was unchanged as the eighth inning got underway. Then, in quick succession, seven Giant runners circled the bases. John Beckwith, Cleveland's most valuable player, came up with two men on and one out and promptly drove the ball over the left field fence for a three run homer, putting his team on top 6–5. They added four more runs of five base hits, and coasted home 10–5.

The scene shifted to Signal Hill, the Shell Oilers home park in Long Beach, for the final three games of the series. Apparently the Cleveland Giants won game three, defeating Hank Hulvey, but the score was not reported in any of the Los Angeles newspapers, or in the black newspapers. The *Chicago Defender* was on hand for game four. "Swooping down upon the Shell Oils today like an army of well diggers, the Cleveland Giants pecked and gouged and clawed their way into the championship of the California Winter League by defeating the Shell Oils by the score of 10 to 5.

"Seven thousand, the largest crowd in the history of Shell Oil Park, viewed the ferocious attack of the mighty Giants from Los Angeles.

"By their wanton assault, the Giants won undisputed right to the title." The game was not as easy as the final score, or the *Defender*'s account of the game, would indicate. The Oilers jumped out to a 3–0 lead in the bottom of the third inning on a three-run home run by Earl Averill. John Beckwith homered in both the fourth and sixth innings, but Roy Wilkinson still clung to a tenuous 5–3 lead after seven. Then in the top of the eighth, the roof fell in for Wilkinson and the Oilers. Biz Mackey opened the fateful eighth with a line single to right center field. Wilkinson, remembering Beckwith's two home runs earlier in the game, pitched carefully to Big John and walked him on four pitches. The error of that move became immediately obvious when Bullet Rogan rescued Mackey with a base hit to left, and Rap Dixon brought in Beckwith with the tying run on a hit to center. But the Giants weren't through yet. Dixon stole second, and Dink Mothel drove in two with a single to left center. A base hit by Green, a sacrifice fly by Turkey Stearnes, a double by Allen, a sacrifice by Day, a walk to Mackey, up for the second time, and a single by Beckwith ended the scoring. Rogan mercifully fanned for the third out.

Shell Oil				Cleveland Giants			
Name	*Pos*	*AB*	*H*	*Name*	*Pos*	*AB*	*H*
Rhyne, Hal	SS	3	1	Allen, Newt	SS	4	1
Lindimore, Howard	2B	5	1	Day, Connie	2B	5	1
Averill, Earl	CF	5	3	Mackey, Biz	C	4	2
Jolly, Smead	RF	5	0	Beckwith, John	3B	4	3
Emmer, Frank	3B	5	1	Rogan, Joe	P	5	2
Brucker, Earl	1B	4	1	Dixon, Rap	LF-CF	5	2
Christensen, Walt	LF	4	1	Mothel, Dink	LF-1B	5	1
Thompson,	C	2	1	Green,	RF	4	2
Wilkinson, Roy	P	2	0	Carr, Tank	1B	1	0
Hulvey, Hank	P	1	0	Stearnes, Turkey	CF	3	1
Brazill, Frank	PH	0	0				
Johnson,	C	0	0				
Totals		36	9			40	15

Shell Oil   0 0 3 1 1 0 0 0 0— 5—9—?
Cleveland Giants   0 0 0 1 1 1 0 7 0—10—15—?

Two base hits: Allen, Dixon
Home runs: Beckwith (2), Averill

	IP	H	SO	BB
Wilkinson, Roy (LP)			0	3
Hulvey, Hank			1	1
Rogan, Joe (WP)	9	9	4	5

Season Summaries 1925–1929

The 1928-29 winter season was definitely the year of the hitter. No less than five men broke into the magic .400 circle during the year, led by Earl Averill of the White Kings who won the batting championship with an average of .500. Not far behind the southpaw swinger were John Beckwith at .485, Biz Mackey at .459, Smead Jolley at .446, and Bullet Joe Rogan at .406. Other big bangers included Turkey Stearnes at .372, Newt Allen at .365, Rap Dixon at .360, Eddie Pick at .338, and Walt Golvin and Walt Christensen both at .333. Beckwith, the Cleveland Giants human hitting machine, led the league in home runs with 14. The leading pitcher was Chet Brewer with a record of 14-4, with Bullet Rogan close behind at 9-1.

Tall, lanky Chet Brewer was one of the top pitchers in California Winter League history, compiling a 42–13 record. (NoirTech Research)

1928-29 California Winter League
Final Standings—Incomplete

	Wins	Losses	Ties
Cleveland Giants	30	13	2
Shell Oil	8	9	2
Pirrone's All-Stars	10	20	1
White Kings	5	11	1

Cleveland Giants Batting Statistics 1928-29

Name	Pos	G	AB	H	D	T	HR	BA
Allen, Newt	SS	29	126*	46	14*	2	2	.365
Day, Connie	2B	29	119	31	6	1	1	.261
Mackey, Biz	1B	29	111	51*	10	1	5	.459
Beckwith, John	3B	27	101	49	9	0	14*	.485
Stearnes, Turkey	CF	30*	113	42	2	4*	7	.372
Dixon, Rap	LF	28	100	36	7	1	7	.360
Mothel, Dink	RF	27	100	28	2	1	0	.280
Pullen, Neal	C	6	19	7	0	0	0	.368
Rogan, Joe	P-CF	28	106	43	5	1	4	.406
Carr, Tank	1B	9	16	5	1	0	0	.313

Cleveland Giants Pitching Statistics 1928-29

Name	G	CG	W	L	IP	SO	BB	SH
Brewer, Chet	18*	13*	14*	4	146*	73*	64*	3*
Rogan, Joe	12	8	9	1	92	68	21	1

Cleveland Giants Pitching Statistics 1928-29

Name	G	CG	W	L	IP	SO	BB	SH
Gardner, Buzz	10	6	4	2	58	34	38	1
Glass, Carl	9	8	6	3	79	27	14	0

White Kings Batting Statistics 1928-29

Name	Pos	G	AB	H	D	T	HR	BA
Smith, Red	SS	4	19	4	0	0	0	.211
Kingdon, Wes	2B	12	52	11	0	0	0	.212
Brazill, Frank	3B	15	48	13	1	1	1	.271
Averill, Earl	CF	13	54	27	4	1	5	.500*
Vache, Tex	RF	12	51	14	2	0	0	.275
Golvin, Walt	1B	13	51	17	2	1	3	.333
Cox, Dick	LF	11	49	16	0	0	1	.327
Thompson,	C	8	31	5	1	0	0	.161
Rhyne, Hal	SS	12	42	14	4	0	1	.333

White Kings Pitching Statistics 1928-29

Name	G	Cg	W	L	IP	SO	BB	SH
Barnabe, Charlie	8	7	4	4	65	17	7	0
Hulvey, Hank	7	4	1	2	44	18	11	0
Barfoot, Clyde	3	3	0	3	24	8	12	0

Shell Oil Batting Statistics 1928-29

Name	Pos	G	AB	H	D	T	HR	BA
Swanson, Evar (?)	CF	5	18	5	1	0	0	.278
Kerr, John	2B	12	48	15	1	0	2	.313
Christensen, Walter	LF	15	54	18	1	2	0	.333
Emmer, Frank	3B	15	62	14	1	0	0	.226
Brucker, Earle	C	15	57	14	1	1	0	.246
Sweeney, Bill	RF	9	33	4	0	0	0	.121
Heath, Mickey	1B	12	41	11	2	0	1	.268
Lee, Dud	SS	13	52	11	4	1	1	.212
Lindimore, Howard	LF	9	21	5	0	0	0	.238
Jenkins, Joe	C	11	40	13	1	1	0	.325

Shell Oil Pitching Statistics 1928-29

Name	G	CG	W	L	IP	SO	BB	SH
Bell, Hi	6	0	1	0	30	16	9	0
Pillette, Herm	8	2	2	5	51	9	17	0
Wilkinson, Roy	7	3	3	1	42	6	6	0
Schupp, Ferdie	3	3	0	3	25	13	7	0

Pirrone's All-Stars Batting Statistics 1928-29

Name	Pos	G	AB	H	D	T	HR	BA
Moorehart, Ray	2B	18	73	18	0	2	0	.247
Haney, Fred	3B	15	55	14	1	1	0	.255
Meusel, Bob	CF	2	8	3	0	0	0	.375
Jolley, Smead	RF	19	74	33	8	0	6	.446
Pick, Eddie	SS	19	68	23	6	0	2	.338
Meusel, Irish	LF	17	63	17	1	0	3	.270

Pirrone's All-Stars Batting Statistics 1928-29

Name	Pos	G	AB	H	D	T	HR	BA
McMullen, Hugh	C	12	36	11	1	0	0	.306
Murray, Bobby	SS	11	36	7	0	0	0	.194
Sawyer, Carl	1B	7	20	5	1	0	0	.250
Cotter, Hooks	1B	12	38	11	0	0	2	.289
Gaston, Alex	C	7	27	7	1	0	0	.259
Pirrone, Joe	LF	11	35	8	0	3	0	.229

Pirrone's All-Stars Pitching Statistics 1928-29

Name	G	CG	W	L	IP	SO	BB	SH
Dumovich, Nick	8	4	0	6	39	26	10	0
Koupal, Lou	10	4	4	1	65	32	16	0
Thurston, Sloppy	6	6	2	4	52	21	17	0

Lou Koupal was the bellwether of Joe Pirrone's All-Star staff in 1928-29, pitching in 10 games, with a 4-1 record.

The 1929-30 Season

The 1929-30 California Winter League consisted of the Philadelphia Royal Giants, Pirrone's All-Stars, Shell Oil, and Kelley Kars. Although they had lost the heart of their batting order—Beckwith, Stearnes, and Dixon—the Giants still had Bullet Joe Rogan Biz Mackey, and Newt Allen, and they brought in Lee Livingston (who had just hit .300 with the Kansas City Monarchs), Leroy Taylor (who hit .355 for the same team), and Tom Young (another K.C. player), to help fill the void. As it turned out, Livingston had a phenomenal year with the bat, as did Leroy Taylor. And the club still had Chet Brewer and Rogan anchoring their world class pitching staff.

Joe Pirrone's All-Stars had pretty much the same team as the previous year. The Meusel brothers were back (Irish hit .327 for Sacramento, and Bob hit .261 for the Yankees), as was Smead Jolley (.387 for San Francisco), Fred Haney (.292 with L.A.), Ray Moorehart, and Carl Sawyer. Lefty Edleman and Archie Campbell handled most of the pitching chores. The Shell Oilers fielded a well balanced team led by Dud Lee (.262 with Hollywood), Frank Emmer (Led AA with 32 HRs in 1927), Mickey Heath (.349 for Hollywood), and Ray Jacobs (.332 for L.A.). Howard Craghead (21-12 with Oakland) assumed most of the pitching responsibilities. Kelley Kars was new to the league in 1929-30, but their roster was well known to area fans. Their pitching staff was headed by Charlie Barnabe (former Chicago White Sox pitcher), Earl "Pinches" Kunz (former Pittsburgh Pirate pitcher who won 18 games for San Francisco in 1927), and Wee Willie Ludolph (former Detroit Tiger pitcher who went 21-8 in Southern Association), and

Smead Jolley, one of the minor leagues' career batting leaders, hit .366 over a period of 20 years. (L. Robert Davids, SABR)

ingston, Mackey, Mothel, Joseph of the Giants, Suhr, Lazzeri, and Thurston of the All-Stars, hitting homers." Gus Suhr, on his way up to the Pittsburgh Pirates, was coming off a sensational season with the San Francisco Seals of the Pacific Coast League, where he hit .381 with 51 home runs and 177 RBIs in 202 games. "Poosh-em-up" Tony Lazzeri of the New York Yankees had led the mighty Bronx Bombers in batting in 1929 with an average of .354. He also drove in 106 runs. The game was a slugfest from start to finish, with the lead changing hands several times over the first six innings. The score was knotted at 8–8, until the Royal Giants pushed over two runs in both the seventh and eighth innings, to win 12–8.

the position players included Lou Almada (.305 with Seattle), Wes Kingdon (11 year veteran of AAA ball), Frank Brazill (lifetime .342 hitter in the PCL), Dick Cox (.314 for two years in the majors), and Joe Jenkins (.333 with Newark of the IL).

The winter league season opened on October 19 with a game between the Royal Giants and the All-Stars. Andy Cooper faced off against Sloppy Thurston at White Sox Park as a full house looked on. The *Chicago Defender* reported the game. "Manager Lonnie Goodwin of the Royal Giants presented the fans a great aggregation of ball players, a smart, fast-working bunch…. The Giants simply ate up the offerings of Hollis Thurston and Lefty Edleman. The two clubs set a Winter league record in hitting eight home runs in the game, Rogan, Liv-

Howard Craghead went 21–12 for the Oakland Oaks in the Pacific Coast League in 1929, then 1–1 for Shell Oil in the winter league. (Dick Dobbins)

Pirrone's All-Stars					Philadelphia Royal Giants			
Name	Pos	AB	H		Name	Pos	AB	H
Haney, Fred	3B	3	1		Mothel, Dink	2B	5	1
Lazzeri, Tony	2B	5	2		Allen, Newt	SS	5	3
Suhr, Gus	1B	5	1		Rogan, Joe	CF	4	1
Meusel, Bob	LF	4	1		Mackey, Biz	1B	5	1
Jolley, Smead	RF	5	1		Livingston, Lee	RF	5	3
Moorehart, Ray	SS	4	0		Joseph, Newt	3B	5	2
Wingo, Al	CF	4	1		Taylor, Leroy	LF	4	0
McMullen, Hugh	C	4	2		Young, Tom	C	4	1
Thurston, Sloppy	P	4	2		Cooper, Andy	P	4	3
Pirrone, Joe	PH	0	0					
Edleman, Lefty	P	0	0					
Meusel, Irish	PH	1	0					
Totals		39	11				41	15

```
Pirrone's All-Stars         1 0 3   0 0 4   0 0 0— 8—11—?
Philadelphia Royal Giants   2 0 2   0 3 1   2 2 x—12—15—?
```

Two base hits: Livingston, McMullen, Cooper
Home runs: Rogan, Joseph, Livingston, Mackey, Mothel, Thurston, Lazzeri, Suhr

	IP	SO	BB
Thurston, Sloppy (LP)	7	4	2
Edleman, Lefty	1	0	0
Cooper, Andy (WP)	9	7	2

Both teams kept their hitting shoes on for the Sunday finale, as noted in the *Defender*. "Chester Brewer of the Philadelphia Royal Giants pitching staff demonstrated today how a pitcher can walk eight batters and be credited with a victory. The Royal Giants won 8–7, for their second straight win over Joe Pirrone's All-Stars in the start of the Winter league season race. The win put the Royals at the top of the league. Livingston hit a homer in the third. Brewer fanned 10 of the Stars batters. Bullet Rogan saved the game in the fifth and sixth innings with two great catches in center field. Others who shared the glory were Newt Allen, who made some fine stops in short, and Mackey at first base. About 8000 fans turned out to see the Royals win." Gus Suhr did his best to arouse his team as he clubbed a double and a home run. Bob Meusel responded with a single and a double, and Al Wingo rapped two doubles, but it wasn't enough to beat the Giants.

As the young season progressed, it became apparent that Lonnie Goodwin's warriors would be hard to catch. The *California Eagle* noted the team's fast start. "Judging from the record of the last five games, the Giants are playing the greatest ball in the history of the park. The Giants have been to bat 187 times and made 62 hits and brought in a total of 47 runs, for a ... team batting average of .332.... They have won all five games, made ten home runs, stole fifteen bases including home plate and just about every record of the park for this early in the season."

Joe Pirrone, of course, would do anything he could to beat the Negro leaguers. And late in October he was presented with a golden opportunity. Al Simmons (.365 with 157 RBIs for the Philadelphia A's) and Jimmie Foxx (.354 with 118 RBIs for the same team), each had assembled an all-star team, and they were barnstorming the country, playing exhibition games against each other. On October 27, the Simmons All-Stars defeated the Foxx All-Stars 2–1 in

Los Angeles, with both "managers" hitting home runs. After a tour up the coast, the teams returned to L.A., and Pirrone quickly signed the two baseball legends to a one-game All-Star contract. The big game between Pirrone's "Simmons-Foxx" All-Stars and Lonnie Goodwin's Royal Giants took place on October 31. Once again the *Defender* was there. "Today was Jimmie Foxx and Al Simmons day and 5000 baseball fans packed White Sox Park to see Joe Pirrone's All-Stars play against the Philadelphia Royal Giants.

"The All-Stars were loaded up with Jimmie Foxx and Al Simmons of the world champion Philadelphia Athletics; (and) Archie Campbell and Bob Meusel of the Cincinnati Reds.

"Campbell started for the Stars and the Giants fell upon him in the second for five hits and six runs.

"Pudgy Gould was rushed in, but too late. Gould was driven from the mound in the fourth.

"Lefty Edleman and Jimmie Foxx finished the game.

"To pitcher Rogan went the credit for victory. The use of Rogan as the starting pitcher was a piece of manager Lonnie Goodwin's strategy, and the old master did everything possible to vindicate his manager. The All-Stars had to look at the blinding speed of Rogan and they melted before it. Rogan was never faster in his life and the Stars merely blinked at many of his offerings as they streaked across the plate.

"Rogan kept the Stars 10 hits well scattered and struck out eight men. Mackey and Joseph of the Giants hit homers, and Pick, pinch hitting in the ninth, hit a homer. Other features of the game were the all around fielding of shortstop Newt Allen with a double play unassisted, and the fielding of Joseph and Mackey and the catching of Young."

For the record, the Giants won the game 10–3, with Rogan throwing a shutout at Pirrone's troops over the first six innings, by which time the Giants had built a comfortable 10–0 lead. Jimmie Foxx earned his money, raking Rogan for three hits in three at-bats, including two doubles, but his A's teammate, Al Simmons, wasn't so lucky, drawing the collar in five attempts, with three strikeouts.

As good as the Giants played in the first half of the season, they were matched by the play of the Shell Oilers, who were undefeated. The Giants were finally felled by Pirrone's troops, 11–3 under a 19 hit barrage. Cooper and Brewer were the victims of the bludgeoning. Smead Jolley with four hits and Hooks Cotter with three, led the All-Stars. The *California Eagle* noted the Philadelphia Royal Giants' problem. "The Royal Giants play five games within the coming ten days and the loss of any two of those games will probably knock them out of the championship.... The championship is decided on the percentage column, which is not unusual. But it is unusual when you consider that the Giants play just twice as many games as Shell Oil and that, in order to win the championship, they must win more than twice as many games.... The Giants play Kelley Kars on Saturday and Sunday and Shell Oil on Monday (Armistice Day) at Shell Park, and then on Saturday and Sunday at White Sox Park ... the Giants ... must take four of those games to be in the running."

The Giants did their best. They beat the San Luis Giants 7–6, then split with Kelley Kars, winning the first game 9–2 behind Cooper, but dropping the second game 6–2. On Armistice Day, Chet Brewer rose to the occasion, outpitching the Oilers' Howard Craghead, 4–2. The two teams met again the following weekend at White Sox Park, and it was a lost weekend as far as the Giants were concerned. First, they lost their leading hitter, when Lee Livingston left the team to attend his mother's funeral in Dallas, Texas. Then, a strategic move on the part of manager Lonnie Goodwin backfired. Goodwin worked his pitchers hard during the week, to keep them in shape, but when the big series came, they seemed to be burned out.

The Oilers took the Saturday encounter 14–6, with Howard Craghead beating Chet Brewer. Both teams had 12 base hits, but the Oilers bunched theirs into the first three innings to score all their runs. Craghead had a 14–0 lead after 5½ innings, then was touched for five runs in the bottom of the sixth, but he quickly settled down and kept the Giants at bay over the last three innings. Christensen, Barbee, and Jacobs all chipped in with two hits apiece, including a double. In the Sunday game, both starters, Sweetland of the Oilers and Cooper of the Royal Giants, were punished early and often, as the Shell team again prevailed 16–14. Mickey Heath, coming off a .349 season with Hollywood, including 38 homers and 156 RBIs, launched two round trippers plus a single, in the rout. Dud Lee ripped four hits including two doubles, and four other players had two hits apiece.

The first half of the season ended on December 7. The *California Eagle* was there. "The season's first half of the Winter League baseball schedule ended with a thrill on Sunday, after the Royal Giants had beaten the Pirrone All-Stars 9 to 8 in a ten inning fray on Saturday and then 7 to 2 on Sunday to retain second place in the League standing, and with the tail-enders Kelley Kars, rejuvenated and giving the top spot Shell Oilers a second thrashing of 2 to 1. The results of the series left the clubs standing in their same positions with Shell Oil carrying off the championship of the first half on a percentage of regular League games." Of the box scores recovered, Shell

Newt Allen, one of the top second basemen in the Negro leagues, hit California Winter League pitchers for averages of .365 and .423 in 1928-29 and '29-'30. (Robert W. Peterson Collection, National Baseball Hall of Fame Library)

Oil compiled a record of 6–2, a percentage of .750, while the Royal Giants had a record of 16–7, a percentage of .696.

The second half of the race was even more closely contested than the first half, with the Giants, Shell Oil, and Pirrone's All-Stars jockeying for position. Shell Oil moved out front quickly by sweeping the All-Stars 6–1 and 1–0, but the Giants kept pace by taking Kelley Kars twice, both by 5–1 counts. In week two, the Oilers came up on the short end of both games, dropping a 7–1 decision to the San Luis Giants, and a 6–5 game to Lonnie Goodwin's warriors.

The final standings for the second half of the race show just how tightly the three contending teams were bunched. The Philadelphia Royal Giants won the second half with a record of 7–5–1. Pirrone's All-Stars finished second with a record of 8–6, followed by Shell Oil with a record of 5–4–1.

The playoff for the league championship began at Shell Park in Long Beach on February 1, with the Shell Oilers getting the jump on the Royal Giants to the tune of 5–2. No other results have been uncovered to date, so the final league champion is unknown.

The three contending teams all had some outstanding individual performances during the season. Lee Livingston, the Giants' powerful right fielder, won the batting championship with an average of .468. The Giants' third baseman Newt Joseph was the home run king with 8, teammate Newt Allen led in doubles with 13, and Perez, the backstop of the San Luis Giants, showed the way in triples with 3. Andy Cooper, the ace of the Philadelphia staff, had the most victories with 6, and also led in winning percentage with .857 on a 6–1 record.

It should be noted once again that it was difficult for players on teams other than the Negro league entry, to win individual honors, except for the batting championship and the pitching percentage leader, due to the fact that the Negro league teams usually played many more games than their white competitors.

Although Pirrone's All-Stars were shut out of the awards, they had some notable peformances. At the plate, Smead Jolley tattoed opposing pitching to the tune of .395, Hugh McMullen hit .382, and Irish Meusel hit .347. On the mound, Lefty Edleman went 5–1. Walt Christensen of Shell Oil sported a .391 batting average, and Roy Wilkinson was 3–0 on the mound.

1929-30 California Winter League
Final Standings—Incomplete

	Wins	Losses	Ties
Philadelphia Royal Giants	23	12	1
Shell Oil	11	6	1
Pirrone's All-Stars	11	12	0
San Luis Giants	9	15	0
Kelley Kars	4	10	0

Philadelphia Royal Giants Batting Statistics 1929-1930

Name	Pos	G	AB	H	D	T	HR	BA
Mothel, Dink	2B	27	113	37	5	1	3	.327
Allen, Newt	SS	28	111	47*	13*	2	0	.423
Rogan, Joe	P-1B	19	76	28	8	0	4	.368
Livingston, Lee	RF	24	94	44	11	0	5	.468*
Joseph, Newt	3B	26	92	31	10	1	8*	.337
Taylor, Leroy	LF	27	110	40	10	1	1	.364
Young, Tom	C	25	93	30	9	1	1	.323

Philadelphia Royal Giants Batting Statistics 1929-1930

Name	Pos	G	AB	H	D	T	HR	BA
Green, William	CF	15	49	14	1	1	2	.286
Mackey, Biz	1B	23	91	32	7	1	5	.352
Holloway, Crush	CF	15	54	20	6	2	0	.370

Philadelphia Royal Giants Pitching Statistics 1929-1930

Name	G	CG	W	L	IP	SO	BB	SH
Cooper, Andy	9	5	6*	1	59	42	14	0
Brewer, Chet	8	4	3	2	52	48	28*	0
Rogan, Joe	7	6	5	1	59	53*	21	0
Charleston, Porter	9	7*	5	3	75*	53*	17	0

Pirrone's All-Stars Batting Statistics 1929-1930

Name	Pos	G	AB	H	D	T	HR	BA
Haney, Fred	3B	17	69	22	2	2	0	.319
Cotter, Hooks	1B	14	62	13	1	0	0	.235
Pick, Eddie	SS	17	59	15	2	0	2	.254
Wingo, Al	CF	16	69	22	6	0	2	.319
Meusel, Bob	LF	3	13	4	1	0	0	.308
Moorehart, Ray	2B	12	46	10	0	0	0	.217
Sawyer, Carl	3B	11	37	5	0	0	0	.135
McMullen, Hugh	C	16	55	21	5	0	0	.382
Jolley, Smead	RF	8	38	15	1	0	3	.395
Meusel, Irish	RF	14	49	17	3	1	2	.347
Pirrone, Joe	CF	7	11	4	2	0	0	.364

Pirrone's All-Stars Pitching Statistics 1929-1930

Name	G	CG	W	L	IP	SO	BB	SH
Edleman, Joe "Lefty"	11*	3	5	1	50	—	—	0
Gould, Al	5	1	1	2	26	—	—	0
Campbell, Archie	6	2	3	3	39	—	—	0
Shanklin,	3	2	0	2	27	—	—	0

San Luis Giants Batting Statistics 1929-1930

Name	Pos	G	AB	H	D	T	HR	BA
Gamiz,	3B	19	81	19	3	1	0	.235
Gonzalez,	2B	18	55	12	2	0	0	.218
Santaella,	SS	19	73	24	6	1	0	.329
Perez,	C	19	72	24	4	3*	3	.333
Miranda,	1B	15	53	17	2	1	0	.321
Delgado,	CF	19	69	16	2	1	0	.232
Montufar, Felipe	3B	18	66	21	5	1	0	.318
Borges,	LF	19	67	16	1	0	1	.239
Vinas,	RF	11	36	6	3	0	0	.167

San Luis Giants Pitching Statistics 1929-1930

Name	G	CG	W	L	IP	SO	BB	SH
Martinez,	6	2	1	3	28	20	7	0
Shaw,	8	4	3	5	56	32	27	0
Vinas,	4	2	0	2	28	5	13	0
Ortiz,	6	4	3	1	42	18	20	0

Kelley Kars Batting Statistics 1929-1930

Name	Pos	G	AB	H	D	T	HR	BA
Almada, Lou	1B	13	52	10	1	0	3	.192
Kingdon, Wes	2B	12	39	8	0	0	1	.205
Brazill, Frank	3B	13	45	13	1	0	2	.289
Cox, Dick	LF	13	47	13	4	0	0	.277
Jahn, Art	1B	11	40	12	1	0	2	.300
Coleman, Ed	CF	13	49	10	2	0	0	.204
Falk, Bibb	SS	11	42	10	1	0	2	.238
Rego, Tony	C	7	15	3	0	0	0	.200
Jenkins, Joe	C	12	30	6	1	0	0	.200

Kelley Kars Pitching Statistics 1929-1930

Name	G	CG	W	L	IP	SO	BB	SH
Ludolph, Wee Willie	8	3	2	4	46	20	11	0
Barnabe, Charlie	6	3	0	4	31	—	—	0

Shell Oil Batting Statistics 1929-1930

Name	Pos	G	AB	H	D	T	HR	BA
Lee, Dud	SS	3	13	5	3	0	0	.385
Emmer, Frank	3B	6	27	3	1	0	0	.111
Heath, Mickey	1B	6	21	5	1	0	2	.238
Hurst, Don	RF	2	9	2	1	0	0	.222
Barbee, Dave	LF	6	23	7	2	0	0	.304
Christensen, Walter	CF	6	23	9	2	0	0	.391
Hoffman,	C	5	18	5	1	0	0	.278
Jacobs, Ray	2B	6	26	8	2	0	1	.308
Griffin, Ivy	RF	4	10	2	0	0	0	.200

Shell Oil Pitching Statistics 1929-1930

Name	G	CG	W	L	IP	SO	BB	SH
Craghead, Howard	4	3	1	1	31	19	17	0
Sweetland, Les	3	0	0	0	13	2	8	0
Wilkinson, Roy	3	2	3	0	18	15	6	0

6

Season Summaries 1930–1934

The 1930-31 Season

The 1930s produced some of the highest quality baseball ever seen on the west coast, particularly from the Negro league teams. The Negro leaguers fielded outstanding all-around teams year after year. They had spectacular defense with Newt Allen, Willie Wells, Sammy T. Hughes, Cool Papa Bell, and Biz Mackey; a powerful offense headed by Mule Suttles, Turkey Stearnes, Jud Wilson, and Wild Bill Wright; and overpowering pitching from such legends as Satchel Paige, Willie Foster, and Chet Brewer.

The 1930-31 California winter baseball season was particularly interesting because there were two competing integrated winter leagues, the "official" California Winter League, whose Negro league entry played out of White Sox Park, and whose primary competition was Pirrone's All-Stars, and the "other" Winter League, whose Negro league team played out of Wrigley Field. The new league had one major distinction. It marked the first time since 1916 that a Negro league team played in a Pacific Coast League park. The "official" winter league was called the Southern California Winter League in the newspapers of the day, both black and white. The "other" league was called simply the Winter League.

Although the Southern California Winter League was the "official" winter league, the "other" league seemed to have the stronger teams. The Royal Giants featured Mule Suttles, Jud Wilson, who might have been the greatest hitter in Negro league history, Newt Allen, Rap Dixon, Willie Wells, Biz Mackey, Willie Foster and Chet Brewer. Kelley Kars had Jigger Statz, the 1930 National League top rookie Wally Berger, Fred Haney, and Ferdie Schupp. Shell Oil had Ray Jacobs, Hal Rhyne, Hank Severeid, Ray French, and Herm Pillette. And the Commercial Club had Fuzzy Hufft, Wes Kingdon, George Burns, Archie Campbell, and Jim Turner.

They also had the most thrilling home run race in winter league history, matching "The Black Babe Ruth," Mule Suttles, against the sensational Boston Brave outfielder, Wally Berger, who set a rookie record in 1930 by blasting 38 home runs, to go along with a .310 batting average and 119 runs batted in. Suttles had led the Negro National League in home runs, with 20 in just 203 at-bats, in 1930, while stroking the ball at a .384 clip.

Joe Pirrone's "official" Winter League got off to a rousing start with the Nashville Elite Giants making a grand entrance into the city, as reported by the *California Eagle*. "Although at the end of a barnstorming automobile tour through the south from back east, they intended, like the Arabs, to

When the Royal Giants played in Wrigley Field in the fall of 1930, it marked the first time a Negro league team played in a Pacific Coast League park in 15 years. (Dick Dobbins)

quietly slip into town and steal away to rest, local fans, sportswriters, and baseball enthusiasts would not have it so, but learning what highway they were travelling, quite a delegation met their caravan of cars yesterday, and escorted them into the city where they will make baseball history this winter."

In an obvious reference to the outlaw league across town, the *Eagle* went on to say, "Of course there is a large percentage of whites, Mexicans and other nationalities among the fans who attend the winter league each season, but as naturally there is a large majority of colored fans, it is interesting to note why they will, as in years past, stick true to White Sox Park, regardless of any other park that attempts to use colored players in Winter League baseball. These are some of the reasons.

"Colored teams can play the year round in White Sox Park.

"Colored fans are extended special welcome and every comfort and convenience attended to, the year round.

"Colored men and boys form the large personnel of employees at the grounds. No other park in the city has year round colored employees.

"But most important of all is the fact that they will really get their moneys worth. Mr. Thos. Wilson, park owner, bus line owner, and leading businessman of Nashville, Tennessee, is one of the wealthiest Negroes in the United States, and it is his race pride more than anything else that has prompted him to leave his own field of business and come west in campaign to make the world realize the greatness of the Negro baseball players."

The "official" California Winter League had a strong nucleus of teams, with the Nashville Elite Giants, the Pirrone All-Stars, the Pasadena Merchants, who replaced Shell Oil in the league, and MGM Studio, who assumed the Kelley Kar franchise. A number of other teams were seen at White Sox Park during the winter, but these four constituted the main body of the league.

Tom Wilson came west with his usual

outstanding aggregation, anchored by the legendary Norman "Turkey" Stearnes, and ably supported by all-world first baseman Willie Bobo, Dewey Creacy, Bill Riggins, Jake Dunn, and Jack Ridley. The pitching chores were in the capable hands of Cherry Bell, "Cannonball" Jim Willis, Sam Ross, and Speedball Cannon.

Joe Pirrone's team featured old standbys Fred Haney (.312 with Los Angeles), Eddie Pick (.325 with the Kansas City Blues), Hugh McMullen, Carl Sawyer, and Al Wingo (.308 career average in the majors), along with pitchers Lou Koupal, John Walters, and Pirrone himself. MGM was led by Ernie Orsatti (St. Louis Cardinal outfielder and career .306 hitter), Irish Meusel, former New York Giant great, George Burns who hit .307 over a 16 year major league career, and Frank Sigafoos (.305 with L.A.), along with pitchers Hank Hulvey (11–10 with Hollywood) and Tex

Jud Wilson may have been the greatest hitter in baseball history — black or white. He led the Negro leagues with a career average of .355, and led the Cuban Winter League with an average of .372. He hit .469 in just 49 at-bats in California. (John B. Holway)

Carleton (13–13 with Rochester in the International League). The Merchants had Mule Haas, coming off a .299 year with the Philadelphia Athletics, and "Sunny Jim" Blakesley, plus pitchers Ferdie Schupp and Lefty Thomas.

In one of the early season games, the Nashville Elite Giants defeated Pirrone's

Ferdie Schupp, once the ace of John McGraw's New York Giant staff, ended his winter league career in 1930-31.

All-Stars 8–6 in one of the few games played by Babe Herman before he was forced to withdraw to meet Baseball Commissioner Landis' ruling. The game was close from start to finish with the All-Stars jumping out to a 1–0 lead in the first, the Giants taking the lead 2–1 in the second, the All-Stars tying it again in the third, then Tom Wilson's cohorts pulling out in front 4–2 in the bottom of the third, and nursing the lead the rest of the way.

Pirrone's All-Stars				Nashville Elite Giants			
Name	Pos	AB	H	Name	Pos	AB	H
LeBourveau, Bevo	RF	4	0	Ridley, Jack	RF	5	3
Orsatti, Ernie	3B	5	0	Riggins, Bill	2B	5	3
Herman, Babe	LF	5	2	Bobo, Willie	1B	5	2
Meusel, Irish	3B	5	2	Stearnes, Turkey	LF	4	3
Pick, Eddie	SS	5	1	Creacy, Dewey	3B	4	0
Wingo, Al	CF	5	2	Evans, Bill	CF	4	3
Baker,	2B	5	3	Williams, Poindexter	C	4	2
McMullen Hugh	C	5	1	Dunn, Jake	SS	5	1
Edleman, Joe	P	1	0	Willis, Jim	P	4	1
Walters, John	P	3	0				
Totals		40	11			40	18

Pirrone's All-Stars   1 0 1   0 0 3   0 0 1—6—11—?
Nashville Elite Giants   0 2 2   1 2 1   0 0 x—8—18—?

Two base hits: Pick, Stearnes, Riggins, Bobo, Williams, Willis
Home runs: Herman, Bobo

	IP	H	SO	BB
Edleman, Joe (LP)	3		0	1
Walters, John	5		2	2
Willis, Jim (WP)	9	11	4	1

The following week, MGM Studio defeated the Nashville Elite Giants 8–3 at White Sox Park. Hank Hulvey and Tex Carleton teamed up to limit the Giants to nine hits, while their teammates were ripping Sam Ross for 20 safeties, led by Ed Coleman (.301 with San Francisco) with a double and three singles, Irish Meusel with a homer and two singles, Cleo Carlisle (.326 with Hollywood) with a double and two singles, and Johnson with a triple and two singles. The game wasn't as easy as might appear however. In spite of all the offensive firepower, the MGM team trailed 3–2 in the bottom of the seventh, before they exploded for six runs, to win 8–3.

After the loss to MGM, the Elite Giants picked up the pace. They took Pirrone's All-Stars to task two out of three, whipping them 8–6 behind Cannonball Jim Willis and an 18 hit attack on October 29. Willie Bobo had a homer and a single, while Jack Ridley, Bill Riggins, Turkey Stearnes, and Bill Evans cracked out three hits each. Babe Herman had three hits including a home run for the losers. Baker collected three singles, while Irish Meusel and Al Wingo had two. The following weekend James Newton's Elite Giants split with the All-Stars, dropping the Saturday game 13–9, but bouncing back to take the finale 7–2. Willis was the winning pitcher Sunday, fanning four. Poindexter Williams launched a home run to go along with two singles. Dewey Creacy had three singles.

Nashville dropped a close one to MGM in mid–November by a score of 3–2, but took the nightcap 5–0 behind a tight

Babe Herman could always hit. He tortured major league pitchers to the tune of .324, batted .323 in the Pacific Coast League, and hit .357 in the winter league.

one-hitter by Speedball Cannon and two home runs by Turkey Stearnes.

The winter league was saddened by the news that the great black baseball pioneer, and founder of the Negro National League, Rube Foster, had died in a central Illinois hospital on Tuesday, December 9. The nation, black and white, mourned the passing of the legendary leader, as he was laid to rest in Chicago's Lincoln Cemetery at the stroke of noon on Monday. California fans were particularly heartbroken at the loss of the man who had brought integrated winter league baseball to the west coast way back in 1910.

Perhaps in tribute to their fallen leader, the Nashville Elite Giants went on a tear, winning 20 of the last 25 games of the season, against four losses and one tie. They finished the season with a doubleheader victory over Pirrone's All-Stars, winning 5–2 and 2–1. Cherry Bell tossed a five-hitter in the opener, and was backed by the slugging of Bobo, Stearnes, and Williams. In the nightcap, Cannonball Jim Willis limited the All-Stars to four hits.

Newton's Elite Giants finished the season with a record of 30–9–2, and faced the San Diego team in the playoffs. The *Chicago Defender* reported on game one. "Sam Ross and his spitball proved too slippery for Linn Platner's San Diegans and the white boys stumbled before Tom Wilson's Nashville Elite Giants 10–5 in the first of a three-game series for the Southern California Winter Baseball League championship. Ross struck out 11 men."

In game two, San Diego ripped Jim Willis for ten hits, to win going away, 7–5. The Giants jumped out to a 5–0 lead after five innings, but Willis couldn't hold it. Linn Platner's troops pushed across one run in the sixth, four in the seventh, and two more in the eighth. Jack Killeen fanned six and walked three in the victory.

In the finale, Cherry Bell shut down the San Diegans 5–2 on a six-hitter. He struck out four and issued just one free pass. Jake Dunn hit a home run for the winners, while Stearnes, Creacy, and Bobo punched out two hits apiece. The Giants drew first blood in the top of the first when Ridley ripped a double and scored on a two-out triple by Poindexter Williams. San Diego tied the game in the second, then took the lead in the fourth when Johnny Walters poled a home run into the left field bleachers. The Giants bounced back with two in the fifth to recapture the lead. Creacy tripled, Evans doubled, and Cherry Bell plated the tie breaking run with a single to center. Singles by Bobo and Stearnes and a sacrifice fly added to the lead in the eighth, and a home run by Jake Dunn to the top of the left field stands closed out the scoring in the ninth.

The Elite Giants championship celebration was quieted by the shocking news of the death of their all-star first baseman, as reported in the *Defender*. "Willie Bobo, 29 years old, known as the 'Black George Sisler,' of the Nashville Elite Giants baseball team, died Sunday at his hotel (in San Diego)," just hours after his team's momentous victory. Bobo had gone to Tijuana, Mexico to celebrate, "where it is alleged that he drank some cheap alcohol. Soon after returning to his hotel quarters he was found dead by manager James Newton and third baseman Dewey Creacy of the Giants. The deceased athlete was a great player and was the life of the club to which he belonged."

California Winter League accolades went to Turkey Stearnes and Cannonball Jim Willis. Stearnes led the league in batting with a mark of .373, and also showed the way with 50 base hits and 8 home runs. Willis led all pitchers with 14 complete games, 11 victories, and 3 shutouts.

1930-31 California Winter League
Final Standings—Incomplete

	Wins	Losses	Ties
Nashville Elite Giants	33	10	2
San Diego	10	9	2
Pirrone's All-Stars	5	13	0
MGM	2	1	0
El Paso Mexicans	2	8	0
Pasadena	1	2	1

Nashville Elite Giants Batting Statistics 1930-31

Name	Pos	G	AB	H	D	T	HR	BA
Ridley, Jack	RF	32	125	37	10*	3*	1	.296
Riggins, Bill	2B	33	119	43	10*	2	7	.361
Stearnes, Turkey	CF	33	130	49	9	2	8*	.377*
Williams, Poindexter	C	26	100	36	10*	1	4	.360
Creacy, Dewey	3B	32	107	33	5	2	0	.308
Dunn, Jake	SS	31	115	37	7	3*	5	.322
Evans, Bill	LF	34	116	40	5	2	0	.345
Bobo, Willie	1B	29	114	32	3	3*	1	.281
Carr, Tank	1B	8	21	8	1	2	2	.381

Nashville Elite Giants Pitching Statistics 1930-31

Name	G	CG	W	L	IP	SO	BB	SH
Bell, Cherry	9	9	6	2	81	43	25	1
Willis, Jim	14*	14*	11*	3	120	86	19	3*
Cannon, "Speedball"	8	6	6	0	63	42	34	1
Ross, Sam	6	5	6	0	48	29	9	0

San Diego Batting Statistics 1930-31

Name	Pos	G	AB	H	D	T	HR	BA
Rammage, Cy	SS	9	39	10	2	0	0	.256
Jones, Bobby	3B	14	58	15	1	0	0	.259
Ginglardi, Hank	RF	16	61	14	3	1	2	.230
Walters, Johnny	3B	14	51	19	2	0	5	.373
Lloyd, Elmer	2B	15	58	18	1	0	0	.310
Brucker, Earle	1B	13	52	13	4	0	0	.250
Rowe,	LF	9	28	2	0	1	0	.071
Warren Dallas	C	12	34	5	1	1	0	.147
Ingle, Shorty	RF	11	37	10	2	0	0	.270

San Diego Pitching Statistics 1930-31

Name	G	CG	W	L	IP	SO	BB	SH
Nielson, Gook	7	5	3	3	62	34	21	1
Killeen, Jack	9	8	5	2	78	50	24	1

Pirrone's All-Stars Batting Statistics 1930-31

Name	Pos	G	AB	H	D	T	HR	BA
Cotter, Hooks	1B	9	35	9	2	0	0	.257
Sawyer, Carl	2B	9	34	5	1	0	1	.147
Pick, Eddie	SS	11	41	11	3	0	1	.268
Wingo, Al	CF	10	39	11	2	0	1	.282
McMullen, Hugh	C	10	39	12	2	0	1	.308
Millican,	C	8	21	3	0	0	0	.143
LeBourveau, Bevo	RF	3	11	3	1	0	0	.273
Herman, Babe	LF	1	5	3	0	0	1	.600

Pirrone's All-Stars Pitching Statistics 1930-31

Name	G	CG	W	L	IP	SO	BB	SH
Edleman, Joe "Lefty"	5	5	1	4	42	10	4	0
Koupal, Lou	5	3	1	4	35	18	17	0
Walters, John	1	1	0	1	8	2	2	0

Miscellaneous Batting Statistics 1930-31

Name	Team	Pos	G	AB	H	D	T	HR	BA
Meusel, Irish	MGM	LF	3	14	6	1	0	1	.429
Haas, E.	Pasadena	RF	3	10	3	0	0	0	.300
Orosco,	El Paso	RF	4	13	2	1	0	0	.167
Lopez, B.	El Paso	3B	5	18	6	0	0	0	.333
Antista,	El Paso	LF	4	19	3	1	0	0	.158
Almada, Louis	El Paso	CF	5	22	6	2	0	1	.280
Galinda,	El Paso	2B	5	14	5	1	0	1	.377
Ocampo,	El Paso	1B	4	20	5	0	0	0	.250
Lima,	El Paso	SS	5	17	2	1	0	0	.118
Soto,	El Paso		4	14	2	0	0	0	.143

Miscellaneous Pitching Statistics 1930-31

Name	Team	G	CG	W	L	IP	SO	BB	SH
Hulvey, Hank	MGM	2	1	1	1	16	8	3	0
Salazer, Pete	El Paso	4	4	1	2	39	30	16	0

While the Nashville Elite Giants were thrilling the fans of east Los Angeles in the Southern California Winter League, Lonnie Goodwin's Royal Giants were running roughshod over their competition at the little ballpark on East 42nd Place and Avalon Boulevard, in the "other" Winter League. The season did not begin as Goodwin had hoped, as the Royal Giants were beaten by Kelley Kars by a score of 5–3, in the opener at Wrigley Field. It was a historic game however, in that it marked the first time a Negro league team had played in a Pacific Coast League park since PCL Commissioner Allen T. Baum's ban went into effect in the late teens.

A large crowd packed the stadium to see such major league talent as Wally Berger, Cedric Durst, Fred Haney, Jigger Statz, Johnny Rawlings, and Win Ballou,

Arnold "Jigger" Statz hit .285 in the major leagues, and .315 in the Pacific Coast League.

plus Negro league legends like Mule Suttles, Jud Wilson, Willie Wells, and Biz Mackey. The game lived up to its expectations, as both teams played superb baseball. The *Los Angeles Times* covered the game. "The Angel curve-ball hurler (Win Ballou) was in top shape, and for the most part kept the Giant sluggers baffled with his sharp-breaking curves. The colored club got only six hits off Ballou, who was at his best with men on bases. Only Slug Suttles, heavy hitting Giant first sacker could solve Ballou with any degree of success. Suttles didn't get any homers but hit the left field wall twice for two doubles that lacked only a few feet of clearing the barrier.

"Cedric Durst, Kelley Kar first sacker from the Boston Red Sox, Wally Berger, Boston Brave home run king, and skipper Haney, led the attack for the victors. Durst also fielded sensationally around the initial sack. Jigger Statz also sparkled in the outfield as well as on the bases, scoring the Kelley Kars first run on a double steal with Durst.

"(Porter) Charleston pitched good ball for the Giants but was the victim of bad breaks that came in the form of some lucky hits for the opposition."

Kelley Kars				Royal Giants			
Name	Pos	AB	H	Name	Pos	AB	H
Parker, Art	2B	5	1	Harris, Vic	LF	5	1
Statz, Jigger	CF	4	2	Allen, Newt	2B	4	0
Durst, Cedric	1B	4	1	Wilson, Jud	3B	3	0
Berger, Wally	LF	4	2	White, Chaney	CF	4	1
Schulmerich, Wes	RF	3	0	Suttles, Mule	1B	4	2
Haney, Fred	3B	3	2	Dixon, Rap	RF	4	1
Bassler, Johnny	C	4	1	Wells, Willie	SS	4	1
Rawlings, Johnny	SS	3	0	Mackey, Biz	C	3	2
Ballou, Win	P	4	1	Charleston, Porter	P	2	1
				Hunter, Bert	P	2	0
				Pullen, Neal	PH	1	0
Totals		34	10			36	9

Kelley Kars   0 1 1 0 0 1 2 0 0—5—10—2
Royal Giants   0 0 1 0 0 0 1 1 0—3— 9—1

Two base hits: Statz, Haney, Suttles (2)

	IP	H	SO	BB
Ballou (WP)	9	9	5	2
Charleston (LP)	6⅓	9	4	2
Hunter	2⅔	1	1	5

The following day, the Giants got their revenge. They battered Kelley Kars in both ends of a doubleheader, winning 3–2 and 9–1. The *Times* had the story. "The opener was a sizzling mound duel between Frank Shellenback, spitball ace of the Hollywood Stars, and George Britt, with the colored chucker gaining the verdict when the Giants shoved over the winning run after two were out in the ninth.... The game was a real thriller that gave the 3000 customers plenty of thrills right to the finish. It took some flashy and daring base-running on the part of Jud Wilson to bring over the winning tally. Wilson led off with a walk and stole second on Kelley Kars, who weren't used to playing baseball that way. Suttle's long sacrifice fly to Statz moved Wilson to third. Harris sent a short fly to Statz and Wilson dashed home just ahead of Jigger's throw to Bassler and the game was over."

The Giants scored two runs in the third on a single by Mackey, a double by Allen, and a two-run single by Rap Dixon. Kelley Kars scored one in the sixth on singles by Statz, Durst, and Schulmerich. They tied the game in the eighth when Britt balked with the bases loaded. Then Jud Wilson took matters into his own hands.

In the nightcap, Willie Foster rode a two-run homer by Suttles, and doubles by Dixon, Wells, and Wilson, to an easy victory.

As the season progressed, Mule Suttles and Wally Berger both unlimbered the big lumber and began pounding balls over the Wrigley Field fence in an exciting home run duel. By mid–November, both sluggers had hit for the circuit five times. The "Black Babe Ruth" caught Berger when he clubbed two against Kelley Kars, driving in seven runs, to spark the Giants to a close 11–10 victory. Suttles hit another four bagger on November 30 as the Giants romped over the Commercial Club 12–0 behind the five hit pitching of Andy Cooper. He led Wally Berger in the home run race, six homers to five, then.

By mid–December, the Royal Giants were far out in front of the pack, with a record of 11–2. The *L.A. Times* had nothing but praise for the talented Negro leaguers, who wouldn't lose another game the rest of the season. "Winter baseball followers acclaim the Giants as the greatest colored team to perform here in the last twelve years. The Giants have just about everything that goes to make a ball club. They have five good pitchers, a marvelous catcher in Mackey, a spectacular keystone combination in Wells and Allen, a wallop in their batting order, and a smart bunch of base runners. On top of that, they have plenty of pepper and are great crowd pleasers."

Wally Berger caught Suttles in the home run race, when he connected off Andy Cooper in a 6–3 loss to the Giants. The *Times* was there. "Walter Berger also homered in this game, his drive clearing the trees on the other side of Thirty-ninth Street and proving one of the hardest clouts ever made at Wrigley Field."

Berger was still on fire when the two teams met again on December 28, but once again his team was unable to capitalize on his heroics. In the opener of a twin bill, Lonnie Goodwin's cohorts eked out a ten inning, 9–8 victory over Kelley Kars, in spite of three home runs by their 6'2", 198 pound right-handed slugger. Berger's third and last homer tied the score in the eighth, but the Giants pulled it out in the tenth. Ferdie Schupp was a victim of his own wildness, as he walked ten men, hit four, and uncorked four wild pitches. In the nightcap, Willie Foster set Mr. Berger down twice without a hit, en route to a 3–0 whitewashing of the Kelley Kars team.

The season ground to its foregone conclusion on January 18, 1931, with Lonnie Goodwin's Royal Giants winning 28 games against just 2 losses and one tie. No one else came even close to playing .500 ball, and Wally Berger's Kelley Kars could manage only a single victory against 18 losses and one tie. Berger captured the home run crown with ten circuit blows to seven for Suttles. There was a mystery to the season however, that still has not been explained. Mule Suttles didn't play in any games after November 30, missing the final 12 games of the season. It had been noted in the *California Eagle* on November 28 that "Suttles has been hitting the ball murderously. Here's something about this boy Suttles that perhaps some of you fans don't know. Suttles is the sole support of his mother in the East and has been sending the major share of his winter league earnings back to her regularly. We say that a boy like that can't fail, he is bound to get some place. Suttles has forged ahead of Wally Berger for home run honors, and is leading with six." Whether the big first sacker was injured, or whether he was called home because of a family emergency is unknown. What is known is that he apparently lost the home run race to Berger. He did capture the batting title however, with an average of .474. Jud Wilson was second at .469, and Wally Berger came in third at .426. Ray Jacobs of Shell Oil hit a scorching .480 but didn't play the necessary ten games to qualify for the title. Willie Foster was the league's best pitcher, finishing with a mark of 9–0. He also showed the way in games pitched, complete games, innings pitched, strikeouts, and bases on balls.

The two-league competition apparently wreaked havoc on both leagues, as attendance was down significantly in both

Mule Suttles engaged in a torrid home run battle with Wally Berger in the 1930-31 winter league. He was leading the race when he inexplicably left the team. (Lawrence D. Hogan)

White Sox Park II and Wrigley Field. The damage may have been greater to the "other" League as noted by the *California Eagle*. "According to a statement by Joe Pirrone, the 'Father of Winter League baseball,' the action of an insurgent group in arranging with Wrigley Field to stage games there hurt baseball in general.... Winter league fans have been principally colored and as many as 6000 used to follow the colored teams to White Sox Park to see them play major and Coast League stars. With the crowd split and fans losing interest, neither team could succeed. The Wrigley Field promoters withdrew their permit and the team partly disbanded. Next season, Mr. Thos. Wilson owner of the Nashville Elite Giants will manage the ('official' winter) league and attempt to bring it back to the palmy days of three years ago, when Rogan, Carr, Duncan, and others packed White Sox Park."

1930-31 "Other" Winter League
Final Standings—Incomplete

	Wins	Losses	Ties
Philadelphia Royal Giants	28	2	1
Shell Oil	4	7	0

Commercial Club		3	10	0
Kelley Kars		1	18	1

Philadelphia Royal Giants Batting Statistics 1930-31

Name	Pos	G	AB	H	D	T	HR	BA
Harris, Vic	LF	14	50	13	1	1	1	.260
Allen, Newt	2B	15	63*	19	2	0	2	.302
Wilson, Jud	3B	15	49	23	9*	2*	3	.469
White, Chaney	CF	16*	61	20	1	0	4	.328
Suttles, Mule	1B	11	38	18	6	0	7	.474*
Dixon, Rap	RF	15	51	14	3	0	2	.275
Wells, Willie	SS	13	57	17	2	2*	2	.298
Mackey, Biz	C	14	43	18	4	1	0	.419

Philadelphia Royal Giants Pitching Statistics 1930-31

Name	G	CG	W	L	IP	SO	BB	SH
Foster, Willie	11*	7*	9*	0	68*	53*	20*	1*
Cooper, Andy	7	5	5	0	52	36	11	1*
Britton, George	5	2	4	1	38	20	16	0
Brewer, Chet	3	1	2	0	20	—	—	1*
Charleston, Porter	5	1	3	1	29	25	7	1*

Kelley Kars Batting Statistics 1930-31

Name	Pos	G	AB	H	D	T	HR	BA
Statz, Jigger	CF	8	34	10	2	0	0	.294
Parker, Art	2B	7	29	6	1	0	0	.207
Durst, Cedric	1B	10	40	10	1	0	2	.250
Berger, Wally	LF	12	45	20	2	0	10*	.426
Haney, Fred	3B	13	47	13	1	0	0	.277
Cox, Dick	C	5	10	2	1	0	0	.200
Bassler, Johnny	C	6	21	5	1	0	0	.238
Rawlings, Johnny	SS	9	32	12	1	0	0	.375
Schulmerich, Wes	RF	4	15	4	0	0	0	.267

Kelley Kars Pitching Statistics 1930-31

Name	G	CG	W	L	IP	SO	BB	SH
Schupp, Ferdie	2	2	0	2	17	—	—	0
Ballou, Win	4	2	1	2	25	15	12	0
Gabler, Glen	6	3	0	5	36	—	—	0

Shell Oil Batting Statistics 1930-31

Name	Pos	G	AB	H	D	T	HR	BA
Lee,	RF	5	19	4	1	0	0	.211
Jacobs, Ray	2B	6	25	12	1	2	0	.480
Griffin, W.	LF	6	24	9	1	0	2	.375
Severeid, Hank	C	4	15	4	0	1	0	.267
Hofman,	C	4	15	1	0	0	0	.067
Christensen, Walt	CF	4	14	5	1	0	0	.357
Rhyne, Hal	3B	5	19	4	1	0	0	.211
Kerr, John	SS	3	10	4	1	0	0	.400

Shell Oil Pitching Statistics 1930-31

Name	G	CG	W	L	IP	SO	BB	SH
Pillette, Ted	3	2	0	3	22	—	—	0
Pillette, Herm	4	0	0	2	12	—	—	0
French, Larry	3	0	1	1	19	—	—	0
McEvoy, Lou	5	2	3	0	36	18	9	0

Commercial Club Batting Statistics 1930-31

Name	Pos	G	AB	H	D	T	HR	BA
Hufft, Fuzzy	RF	12	44	12	1	0	3	.273
Moore, Johnny	CF	8	33	8	2	0	2	.242
Brazill, Frank	3B	10	37	10	3	0	0	.270
Danning, Ike	C	8	24	6	1	0	0	.250
Kingdon, Wes	SS	10	29	8	0	0	0	.278
Dorman, Red	LF	5	18	5	1	0	0	.278
Burns, George	1B	4	17	1	1	0	0	.059
Almada, Lou	LF	4	13	4	1	0	0	.308
Wright, Glenn (?)	2B	5	19	1	0	0	0	.053

Commercial Club Pitching Statistics 1930-31

Name	G	CG	W	L	IP	SO	BB	SH
Campbell, Archie	4	4	2	2	34	10	18	0
Turner, Jim	3	2	2	0	19	5	2	0
Thurston, Sloppy	1	0	0	1	3	4	0	0
Hollerson, George	3	3	0	3	23	11	12	0

The 1931-32 Season

Things returned to normal in the fall of 1931. There was just one winter league, with four teams, the Philadelphia Giants, Pirrone's All-Stars, the White Kings, and San Diego. There was also a new innovation in the league. The Pirrone brothers, Joe and John, outfitted White Sox Park with lights, permitting them to play night games during the week. Until this year, games could only be played during the day on weekends, and on holidays. The *Chicago Defender* reported, "The White Sox Park have put in lights for the coming season, and from indications, things look very bright. Joe and John Pirrone, owners of the park, have spent something like $7,000 improving the grounds. The schedule will call for five games (a week) this season instead of the regular three games."

The Negro league entry in the league, the Philadelphia Giants, combined rosters from the two competing teams of the previous year. Cherry Bell, Cannonball Jim Willis, and Dewey Creacy came over from the Nashville Elite Giants, while Mule Suttles, Willie Wells, Biz Mackey, Vic Harris, Chaney White, and Willie Foster came over from the Royal Giants. They also added one newcomer, a 25-year-old tall, skinny pitcher from the Pittsburgh Crawfords. His name was Satchel Paige.

Pirrone's All-Stars had their usual team, with Carl Sawyer, Eddie Pick (.318 with Kansas City of the AA), Hugh McMullen, Pirrone, Dud Lee (.275 with Hollywood), Lou Koupal, and Win Ballou (24–13 with Los Angeles). They also added a hard hitting outfielder from Columbus of the American Association, named Bevo LeBourveau. The 5'10", 175 pound left-handed hitter, a former member of the Philadelphia Phillies, had just completed an outstanding year in the Association, batting .375. He also won the AA batting title in

Willie Wells was a regular in the winter league from 1924 through 1944, leaving behind a career average of .301. (John B. Holway)

Carl Sawyer was the first "Clown Prince of Baseball." He played in the winter league for 18 years, and entertained the crowd with his comedy act before the game. (George E. Outland)

1930, with an average of .380, so he brought some badly needed offense to Pirrone's team.

The White Kings had many familiar faces, including Lou Almada (.289 with Seattle), Wes Kingdon (.277 with Chattanooga of the AA Sally League), Howard Lindimore (.331 with St. Joseph of the AA Western League), Cedric Durst, and Charlie Barnabe. San Diego had future major leaguers Earle Brucker and Pete (or Joe) Coscarart, former Detroit Tiger third baseman Bob Jones, and St. Louis Browns outfielder Earl McNeely.

Unfortunately, the newspapers did not leave much of a record of the season's performances. Only seven box scores have been recovered, along with two line scores. The opening game of the season was covered by the *Defender*, although no box score was published. "Playing under lights, Tom Wilson's Philadelphia Giants opened the California Winter League season tonight by defeating Joe Pirrone's Stars by a score of 8–1, with the redoubtable Satchel Paige on the mound. The Giants won an easy victory by hitting Sam Gibson, San Francisco Seal ace, for ten hits to score eight runs. Babe Herman of the Brooklyn Dodgers was in the All-Stars lineup and struck out four times in four trips to the plate. Satchel Paige, pitcher for the Giants, struck out eleven men and allowed but five hits."

In the fourth game of the season, the Giants were tripped up by the All-Stars 7–6, with the loss going to Willie Foster. It was Foster's only loss of the season. The crafty southpaw held a 4–1 lead after seven innings, but Pirrone's troops jumped on him for six runs in the eighth. Brooklyn Dodger second baseman Gordon Slade led the Star's attack with four hits. Billy Rhiel of the Detroit Tigers chipped in with three hits, and Homer Summa of the Philadelphia Athletics had two. Art "The Great" Shires played first base and went one for five. The Giants took the nightcap 9–1, behind Paige.

Apparently the Philadelphia Giants lost one other game during the first half of the season, but finished with a sparkling 18–2 record. One of the wins was a 1–0 shutout of the San Diegans, as reported by the Pittsburgh Courier. " Satchel Paige and Lefty Neilson hooked up in a pitching duel in the second game. Paige and Neilson allowed only one hit each, Paige striking out 13 and Neilson five. The Giants scored the only run of the game when catcher Warren missed the third strike on J. Bell, who reached first base by some fast running. He stole second and scored on Vic Harris' single. This was the greatest game ever played at White Sox Park."

Only four scores were recovered from the second half schedule, and the Giants won all four, giving them a 22–2 record for the season. The final game reported was another whitewash job by the Satchel man. He blanked Pirrone's All-Stars 3–0 on a three-hitter, fanning 15 batters along the way. Willie Wells, called "Pepper" by the *Defender*, punched out two of the Giants' six hits.

Mule Suttles led the league in batting with an average of .586, and tied for the lead in home runs, with catcher Larry Brown, with two each. Satchel Paige finished with a perfect 6–0 slate, while teammate Willie Foster won 9 games against a single loss. Ted Trent and Paige tossed two shutouts apiece.

1931-32 California Winter League
Final Standings—Incomplete

	Wins	Losses	Ties
Philadelphia Royal Giants	22	2	0
Pirrone's All-Stars	2	6	0
White Kings	0	6	0
San Diego	0	4	0

Philadelphia Royal Giants Batting Statistics 1931-32

Name	Pos	G	AB	H	D	T	HR	BA
Bell, Cool Papa	CF	9	41	17	1	0	0	.415
Harris, Vic	LF	7	35	15	0	0	1	.429
White, Chaney	RF	7	34	10	2	0	0	.294
Wells, Willie	SS	6	24	10	0	0	0	.417
Creacy, Dewey	3B	6	26	4	1	0	0	.154
Walker, Jess	2B	6	23	6	0	0	0	.261
Brown, Larry	C	6	23	8	0	0	2	.348
Suttles, Mule	1B	6	29	17	1	0	2	.586*

Philadelphia Royal Giants Pitching Statistics 1931-32

Name	G	CG	W	L	IP	SO	BB	SH
Paige, Satchel	7	6	6	0	58	70	—	2*
Trent, Ted	4	2	3	0	31	—	—	2*
Willis, Jim	3	1	3	0	—	—	—	0
Bell, Cherry	1	1	1	0	9	—	—	0
Foster, Willie			9	1				1

The 1932-33 Season

Newspaper coverage of the season was scant, with only three box scores having surfaced. Fortunately, the complete batting statistics for the Negro League entry, Wilson's Elite Giants, were published at the end of the season.

The league consisted of five teams; the Giants, Pirrone's All-Stars, the El Paso Mexicans, Firestone, and Redondo. The *California Eagle* was there for the opening of the season. "With Walter (Berger) of the Boston Braves, Jimmy Reese of the St. Louis Cardinals, Gordon Slade of Brooklyn, and Fay Thomas Brooklyn pitching ace as some of the World Series stars on Pirrone's All-Stars lineup, the Winter League opens at White Sox Park next Sunday (Oct. 16) at 2:00 0'clock.... Thomas Wilson's Royal Giants 1932 pennant winners meet the all-powerful white team in a duel destined to be jammed with thrills. The great Satchel Paige will pitch for the colored team, probably opposed by Win Ballou, Coast League star or Johnny 'Junk' Waters famous 'handy man' of the Coast League.... Beans Reardon, famous umpire of the National League, will officiate."

The *Eagle* commented on the game the next week. "With a fanfare of music, loud cheering, gaudy uniforms of legionaires, and gaily dressed femininity, the Winter League got going last Sunday with the first official Sunday game at White Sox Park. Of course fans were a little disappointed with the showing made by the Nashville Giants in the first game of the doubleheader, but the boys certainly made up for it in that second game.

"The boys are not exactly temperamental but a disputed decision made by the base umpire in the 4th inning got them mentally upset it seemed, and they all went haywire. Error after error was made and the Pirrone All-Stars romped home to a victory, that was only wiped out by the 4–0 shutout of the second game."

On October 23, the Giants whipped the El Paso Mexicans in a twin bill by scores of 7–1 and 9–2, behind Cannonball Jim Willis and Satchel Paige. Paige was making his first start of the season. Walter "Steel Arm" Davis and Tommy Dukes homered for Wilson's bombers.

Nashville continued its winning ways by knocking off the All-Stars in the first game of a doubleheader a week later, the second game ending in a 2–2 tie. Satchel Paige won the opener going away, 3–1. He held the All-Stars to just three hits, and sent 18 of them back to the dugout dragging their bats behind them. Third baseman Fern Bell homered for the only run off the rangy right-hander. The *Eagle* noted, "Airtight fielding on the part of Rhiel, Haney, Berkowitz, and Walters, kept the 13 hits nicked off pitcher French from stretching into more than three runs.... Pitcher Campbell held the Giants to four hits in the seven-inning finale. The hitting of Bell and Bodie for the All-Stars, and Radcliffe, 'Steel Arm' Davis, and Dunn, of the Giants, featured this contest."

The *California Eagle* was back at White Sox Park the next weekend. "While fans in the well filled stands applauded vociferously, and Alton Redd the 'Brown Paul Whiteman' led his classy band with an inspirational flood of musical and physical gyrations, Thos. Wilson's Royal Giants broke the deadlock of two previous tie games and won both games of a doubleheader last Sunday at White Sox Park. Pirrone's All-Stars were the opponents."

"These two ... Winter League (games) were closely fought (and) ended 8–1 and 11–2, with a lot of sensational plays on both sides ... the last two games between the two teams, one composed of the best major league and World Series stars, and the other of the pick of the Negro National League, were played on Armistice Day and the Sunday preceding. Both ended 3–3.

"Sunny skies and balmy air have made

Satchel Paige, the ultimate showman, and perhaps the world's greatest pitcher, mesmerized fans and hitters alike in the Negro leagues, the California Winter League, and the Puerto Rican Winter League.

Saturday and Sunday afternoons at the ballpark a popular diversion with the ladies, and now since the park management is admitting ladies free, the list of female fans is growing.

"Despite the hard hitting of Fred Haney who garnered four bingles out of six times at bat ... the Royal Giants took both games.... Satchel Paige allowed but seven safeties in the first contest. Haney captured three of them.... Larry French of Pittsburgh, who twirled for the All-Stars, allowed the Giants but four scattered hits until the eighth inning, when the colored boys landed on his slants and batted around, bringing in six runs to cinch the ball game." In game two, the Giants knocked Walters out of the box in the fourth inning, and won behind the pitching of Jim Willis, and home runs off the bats of Tommy Dukes, Sammy Bankhead, and Willis himself.

And the good times continued to roll for Tom Wilson's charges. Cannonball Jim Willis humbled the El Paso Mexicans 4–2, with a seven hit, four strikeout performance. "Steel Arm" Davis clocked one for the Giants, while Mel Almada of the Boston Red Sox homered for El Paso. After dropping one to Firestone, the Giants rebounded with victories over the All-Stars and El Paso by scores of 5–3 and 8–1 respectively. Paige was the winning pitcher against Pirrone's boys, with Dukes hitting another homer. "Steel Arm" Davis was on the mound against the Mexicans. There were no homers in the game, but Alex Radcliffe and Bankhead hit three-baggers for Nashville, and Bill Allington hit one for El Paso.

The deep economic depression in the United States during the early 1930s eventually caught up with baseball, not only on the west coast, but all across the country. Attendance in the major leagues dropped drastically during the '30s. The minor leagues struggled for their very existence. And in California, the winter league felt its effects in 1932-33, as noted in the *California Eagle*. "For the first time in the history of White Sox Park, Manager Joe Pirrone and the clubs of the Winter League have decided, after a lengthy conference, to cut the prices of admission. The drastic slashes were decided on after investigation revealed that it would be justice to former loyal patrons of the park who can not afford the regular admission as well as in former and more prosperous days.

Sam Bankhead was one of the top shortstops of his era. He could do it all, in the field, or at the plate.

"So bleachers have been cut to 25c which is within the reach of all, and grandstand seats are now down to 40c without the government tax. Ladies will be free as usual under the new policy adopted recently."

"Last Sunday with Willis facing Pina in the first, and Paige meeting "Buckshot" May in the second, the Giants took both games from El Paso 5–4 and 4–0."

The *Eagle* announced the end of the winter league season in its January 6th edition. "The season was cut short by a month in order to avoid the rainy season which seems just about due, and partly because Mr. Thos. Wilson, capitalist owner wants his boys back early enough for some extensive preparations," prior to the opening of the regular Negro league season in the east. "A doubleheader between three teams featured the pennant tilts Monday in the White Sox Park Winter League. The El Paso Mexicans took a trouncing from the Redondo Mexicans in the first, 9–4.

"In the second, the Royal Giants, playing their farewell game took on the winners, trimming them in a 4–0 shutout. Porter and Brown pitched for the Giants, allowing only four hits. Bill Smith hurling for Hermosa, allowed 7. On Sunday, the Giants beat Pirrone's 13–12, with 18 hits to 14."

The newspaper reports of winter league games included only three box scores, and a number of line scores and game descriptions. The total media coverage accounted for only 18 Nashville Elite Giants games. However, the published batting statistics for the team confirmed that as many as 33 games had been played.

Alex Radcliffe, brother of "Double Duty" Radcliffe, and an outstanding third baseman in the Negro leagues from 1932 to 1946, led the league in batting with an average of .381. The 27-year-old right-handed hitter also led the league in triples, with 6. Tommy Dukes, the Giants slugging backstop hit 7 home runs in 101 at-bats, to show the way in that category. Dukes was small by catcher's standards, packing a wispy 165 pounds on his 5'8" frame, but he did bat cleanup for Tom Wilson's Elite Giants in the Negro National League in 1933, so he must have had some pop in his bat. And being a left-handed hitter, he evidently had a knack for dropping fly balls over the short right field screen in White Sox Park. Satchel Paige won all five of his starts that were reported, fanning an estimated 65 batters in 45 innings.

1932-33 California Winter League
Final Standings—Incomplete

	Wins	Losses	Ties
Nashville Elite Giants	14	2	2
Pirrone's All-Stars	1	6	2
El Paso	0	8	0
Firestone	1	0	0
Redondo	1	1	0

Nashville Elite Giants Batting Statistics 1932-33

Name	Pos	G	AB	H	D	T	HR	BA
Radcliffe, Alex	3B	27	118	45	5	6*	4	.381*
Dunn, Jake	SS	31	108	41	4	3	5	.378
Bankhead, Sam	CF	33	116	43	6	6*	4	.371
Stratton, Leroy	LF	31	109	40	4	5	3	.366
Davis, Walt	RF-P	27	109	38	10*	4	5	.359
Dukes, Tommy	C	28	101	36	9	1	7*	.357
Walker, Jesse	SS	26	112	39	10*	4	3	.349
Lyons, Granville	1B	33	80	26	3	1	1	.325

Nashville Elite Giants Pitching Statistics 1932-33

Name	G	CG	W	L	IP	SO	BB	SH
Paige, Satchel	5	5	5	0	45	65	—	1
Davis, Walt "Steel Arm"	1	1	1	0	9	—	—	0
Willis, Jim	4	4	4	0	34	—	—	0
Porter, Andy "Pullman"	2	1	1	1	14	—	—	0

Miscellaneous Batting Statistics 1932-33

Name	Pos	G	AB	H	D	T	HR	BA
Haney, Fred	3B	2	6	4	0	0	0	.667
Bodie, Ping	LF	2	8	3	0	0	0	.375
Sawyer, Carl	2B	1	4	1	0	0	0	.250
McMullen Hugh	C	1	3	0	0	0	0	.000
Almada, Lou	LF	2	7	2	1	0	0	.287
Almada, Mel	RF	2	7	4	1	0	1	.571

Miscellaneous Pitching Statistics 1932-33

Name	G	CG	W	L	IP	SO	BB	SH
French, Larry	3	3	0	3	24	—	—	0
Campbell, Archie	2	2	1	1	15	—	—	0
Walters, Bucky	1	0	0	1	4	—	—	0

The 1933-34 Season

The three year period from 1933 through 1935 gave the Southern California baseball fans a look at some of the greatest black teams in California Winter League history. In the fall of 1933, Tom Wilson recruited a sensational lineup for his Elite Giants, with four future Hall of Famers, plus two potential HoFs. The team was anchored by pitching stars Satchel Paige and "Cannonball" Jim Willis. Position players Bell, Wells, Wright, Bankhead, Stearnes, Suttles, and Dukes gave the Giants air-tight defense, as well as explosive offense. The strength of the team was reflected in the fact that Turkey Stearnes, one of the greatest center fielders in Negro league history, had to move over to left field to make way for the brilliant speedster, "Cool Papa" Bell. The trio of Stearnes, Bell, and "Wild Bill" Wright, may have been the greatest outfield in the annals of baseball.

It was apparent to many Negro league experts that the other league clubs were greatly overmatched by the powerful black contingent. Pirrone's All-Stars had outstanding pitching when Koupal, French, Newsom, and Stine toed the rubber, but those four were not always available, and the team then had to rely on lesser talents. Also, the position players were out of their element when opposing Wilson's Wreckers. The White Kings had Sloppy Thurston, but little else. The rest of the pitching staff consisted of journeymen minor leaguers.

The opening game of the season pitted the Giants against Pirrone's All-Stars, with the Giants cruising to an easy 8–2 victory. Jim Willis, on the hill for Tom Wilson's troops, checked the Stars on six hits, three of them by Cleveland Indian shortstop, Bill Knickerbocker. Smead Jolley and Jim Oglesby both took the collar in four trips to the plate. The Giants were led by Mule Suttles who pounded out three doubles, Felton Snow who had two singles and a double, and Bell, Dukes, and Wright, with two hits each. The following day, Pirrone's boys eked out a split. After being humiliated by Satchel Paige, who blanked them 10–0 behind a 15 strikeout, three-hitter, in the

Cool Papa Bell, shown here leading off in the 1933 Negro League All-Star game, was inducted into the National Baseball Hall of Fame in 1974.

opener, they rebounded in game two, with Lee Stine edging the Giants Percy Miller 4–3 with a two run rally in the seventh.

The White Kings stormed into White Sox Park the next week and took the Giants' measure on Saturday 14–9, on the strength of a six run ninth, that broke open a tight 8–7 game. Once again, Percy Miller was the victim of the outburst. The Kings racked up 19 hits in the barrage, with Alan Strange of the St. Louis Browns, and Cliff Ograin hitting for the distance. Lou Almada, Ray Jacobs (former Chicago Cub outfielder), and Johnny Vusich had three hits apiece.

The Negro leaguers got their revenge on Sunday, taking both end of the twin bill by scores of 4–0 and 5–2. Paige tossed a one-hit shutout in the opener, liberally sprinkled with 17 strikeouts.

White Kings

Name	Pos	AB	H
Kingdon, Wes	2B	4	0
Gazella, Mike	3B	3	0
Almada, Lou	CF	4	0
Jacobs, Ray	1B	4	1
Vusich, Johnny	RF	3	0
Strange, Alan	SS	3	0
O'Grain, Cliff	LF	2	0
Mayer, T.	C	3	0
Thurston, Hollis	P	3	0
Totals		29	1

Elite Giants

Name	Pos	AB	H
Bell, "Cool Papa"	CF	4	2
Bankhead, Sam	2B	3	0
Wells, Willie	SS	3	2
Stearnes, Turkey	LF	2	1
Suttles, Mule	1B	4	0
Dukes, Tommy	C	4	1
Snow, Felton	3B	4	0
Wright, Bill	RF	4	1
Paige, Satchel	P	4	1
Totals		32	8

White Kings   0 0 0   0 0 0   0 0 0—0—1—0
Elite Giants 1 0 1   0 0 2   0 0 x—4—8—0

Two base hits: Dukes, Jacobs
Three base hits: Paige
Home runs: Wells

Pitching	IP	H	SO	BB
Thurston, Sloppy (LP)	8	9	3	3
Paige, Satchel (WP)	9	1	17	2

"Cannonball" Jim Willis captured the nightcap with a four-hitter.

Satchel Paige mesmerized the Los Angeles populace, fans and media alike, with his extraordinary pitching skills, his showmanship on the mound, and his charismatic personality off the field. His presence created tremendous publicity for the winter league, all over Southern California, and added an estimated 2,000 fans to the ballpark on days he was scheduled to pitch. In appreciation, the league sponsored a "Satchel Paige Day" at White Sox Park on Armistice Day, November 11.

The 6'3", 181 pound fireballer celebrated his "Day" by blanking the All-Stars 5–0. He tossed a three-hitter and fanned 14, in beating Pittsburgh Pirate southpaw Larry French. The game was a close 2–0 duel until the eighth when the Giants scored three runs on four base hits. Prior to that, the only runs were home runs by Bankhead and Suttles. Willie Wells led the hit parade with a perfect four for four, two doubles and two singles. Bankhead and Wright had two hits each. Pirrone's team kept the day from being a complete success by taking the measure of the Giants in game two, 4–1 behind Buck Newsom, who struck out 11 and walked only one. Cleo Carlyle and Gene Lillard homered in support of Newsom.

Paige finally tasted defeat for the first time on November 19 as reported in the *Chicago Defender*. "Hollis Thurston, veteran Brooklyn right hander ... halted the triumphant parade of Satchel Paige today at White Sox Park, when (he) handed the pitching ace of the Wilson Elite Giants his first defeat of the winter league season, 4–1.... Paige struck out 13 of the Kings, but he was wild, and the 10 walks he issued paved the way for his defeat. At that, only one of the Kings runs was earned, three scoring in the fifth inning after Bankhead had dropped Wells toss for a forceout that would have retired the side. ... Thurston was in rare form, limiting the Giants to seven hits, and pitching shutout ball until the ninth when Turkey Stearnes hit one over the right field wall for a homer.... One of the features of the game was a brilliant catch in the fourth inning by Stearnes which temporarily saved Paige, with two on and one out. The Giants came back strong to annex the nightcap by a 7–3 score.... Vusich and Snow hit home runs in the second game which saw the Giants hammer Buzz Wetzel for a four run lead in the opening inning."

One week later, Paige and Buck Newsom exchanged shutouts as the Giants split a doubleheader with the Portland Beavers. The Satchel-man, back in form, beat Brooklyn's Johnny Babich in the season's best pitching duel, 1–0. Paige threw a five-hitter, and struck out 13. Babich was even stingier, holding the Giants to two hits, while fanning 10. Willie Wells' long home run over the center field fence in the fourth inning was the only score of the game. In the nightcap, Newsom beat Percy Miller 5–0 in an abbreviated five inning game. The portly right-hander recorded ten of the fifteen outs via the strikeout route, in a masterful exhibition of pitching. Johnny Moore of the Cincinnati Reds ripped a single and a triple, while Reds teammate Alex Kampouris also contributed a three bagger to the cause. Former Boston Braves first baseman Earl Sheely, and former Pittsburgh Pirate shortstop Ben Sankey each had two singles.

As November ended, Wilson's Elite Giants stood atop the winter league with a record of 10–5. From that point on, they were almost invincible. Recovered scores credit the Giants with a 21–2–2 record from December through the end of the season on February 18. The only two losses suffered by Wilson's troops were an 11–7 beating at the hands of the All-Stars on December 3, and a 10–8 loss to Pirrone's boys on Christmas Day. Buck Newsom and Satchel Paige were both hit hard in the 10–8 battle, but the St. Louis Brown righty came away with the win. The Negro league ace was touched up for 11 hits including home runs by Ping Bodie and Gene Lillard, while Newsom yielded 14 safeties, including homers by Tommy Dukes and Cool Papa Bell. A three run rally in the eighth broke a 7-all tie and gave Newsom the victory. Bankhead, Stearnes, and Dukes each had three hits for the losers, while Fern Bell, Clement, Lillard and Bodie had two apiece for the All-Stars.

Satchel Paige and Buck Newsom faced each other at least six times during the season, and Newsom won only one time. Paige took the other five encounters by scores of 11–3, 7–2, 5–1, 3–2, and 6–0. The 3–2 game, their best battle, was reported by the *Los Angeles Times*. "'The Great' Newsom got a silver cup, a travelling bag, a lot of other nice presents, and an undeserved defeat out at White Sox Park yesterday, when 'Newsom Day' was celebrated in honor of the former Angel hurler, recently voted the Coast League's most valuable player. Newsom and Satchel Paige hooked up in a thrilling mound duel that saw the ... Royal Giants win a 3–2 decision over Joe Pirrone's All-Stars. Ragged support gave the Giants two of their three runs off Newsom who, like Paige, allowed but six hits.... Taking advantage of errors the Giants scored runs in the second and third innings, but the All-Stars tied it in the fourth frame when F. Bell singled, and Charlie Clements socked one of Paige's offerings over the right field screen.... (Cool Papa) Bell's infield hit and Mule Suttles smash off the right field screen gave the Giants their winning tally in the eighth.... Paige struck out 12 of the All-Stars."

The *Times* also noted the Giants' championship. "It will be flag-raising day for the Royal (Elite) Giants at White Sox Park today when the Winter League champions make their final appearance here by tackling the El Paso Mexican nine in a doubleheader. ... Satchel Paige, sensational colored right hander will take the mound for the

Buck Newsom, also known as Bobo, packed his suitcase 17 times during an eventful 20 year major league career.

Giants in the first game of the twin bill. Paige lost only two games all season, and will be out to wind up his sensational record in a blaze of glory.... Willie Wells, stellar Giant shortstop, will be out to end his winter season without an error to blemish his record. Wells is rated as one of the greatest shortstops in baseball." The Giants took both ends of the twin bill by scores of 4–3 and 10–4.

Tom Wilson's magnificent team maintained the practice of Negro league teams dominating the batting and pitching statistics for the season. That, of course, was to be expected since the Negro league teams routinely played many more games than their white counterparts, sometimes 2 or 3 times as many games.

In 1933-34, the Giants captured all the laurels. James "Cool Papa" Bell walked away with the batting championship, edging out his teammate Willie Wells, .362 to .355. "Wild Bill" Wright finished at .351. The California Winter League's all-time home run king, Mule Suttles, once again showed the way in that category, with 14 circuit blows in 157 at-bats, an average of 49 home runs for a full season of 550 at-bats. Catcher Tommy Dukes finished second in the league home run race with 7, while Bell and Wells had six each.

Wilson's team, who finished with an overall record of 34–8–2, also showed the way in the pitching department. Satchel Paige, the tall, angular pea-shooter of the Pittsburgh Crawfords, led the league in victories (16), games pitched (20), complete games (18), winning percentage (16–2, .888), innings pitched (171), strikeouts (244), shutouts (7), and total run average (1.63). Lost in the fantastic pitching performances of Paige was the tremendous contribution of his teammate Jim "Cannonball" Willis, whose impressive totals included 15 complete games, a 14–2 won-loss record, and 3 shutouts. In total, Giants pitchers tossed a record 12 shutouts in 44 games.

Unnoticed, but just as valuable as the team's offensive and pitching pyrotechnics, were their base running feats and their defensive acrobatics. In a typical Negro league performance, the flying feet of Cool Papa Bell (22 stolen bases), Willie Wells (16), Sam Bankhead (16), and Turkey Stearnes (14), drove opposing catchers to distraction, and sent shivers up the backs of enemy pitchers. All in all, Tom Wilson's jackrabbits swiped 82 bases during the season, an average of two bases a game.

Much of the defensive magic belonged to all-world shortstop Willie "Devil" Wells, whose brilliant infield play included going the entire 44 game schedule without making an error. Wells' nickname, was given to him in Mexico by adoring fans who constantly warned opposing batters, "Don't hit the ball to shortstop. The Devil plays out there." Bankhead, Stearnes, Wright, and Bell, also turned in spectacular plays on a routine basis.

1933-34 California Winter League
Final Standings—Incomplete

	Wins	Losses	Ties
Wilson's Elite Giants	34	8	2
White Kings	2	5	1
Pirrone's All-Stars	3	22	2
Portland	1	1	0
El Paso	0	2	0
May Co.	0	2	0

Wilson's Elite Giants Batting Statistics 1933-34

Name	Pos	G	AB	H	D	T	HR	BA
Bell, Cool Papa	CF	43*	163*	59*	15	4*	6	.362*
Wells, Willie	SS	41	158	58	19*	1	6	.355
Wright, Wild Bill	RF	41	151	53	12	2	3	.351
Bankhead, Sam	2B	43	157	54	10	2	4	.344
Dukes, Tommy	C	36	135	45	8	2	7	.334
Stearnes, Turkey	LF	39	121	40	10	2	5	.331
Suttles, Mule	1B	42	157	51	11	0	14*	.325
Snow, Felton	3B	43	149	48	6	0	6	.322

Wilson's Elite Giants Pitching Statistics 1933-34

Name	G	CG	W	L	IP	SO	BB	SH
Paige, Satchel	20*	18*	16*	2	171*	244*	47*	7*
Willis, Jim	19	15	14	2	116	93	34	2
Young, Slowtime	6	4	4	2	36	—	—	2
Miller, Percy "Lefty"	6	4	3	2	36	—	—	0

Pirrone's All-Stars Batting Statistics 1933-34

Name	Pos	G	H	AB	D	T	HR	BA
Knickerbocker, Bill	SS	6	21	5	2	0	0	.238
Carlisle, Cleo	CF	10	35	5	1	0	1	.143
Jolley, Smead	LF	3	10	2	0	0	0	.200
Lillard, Gene	3B	11	40	12	3	0	5	.300
McMullen, Hugh	C	12	33	6	1	0	0	.182
Berkowitz, Joe	2B	13	37	7	2	0	0	.189
Stainback, Tuck	RF	10	31	6	0	0	1	.194
Bell, Fern	LF	9	31	6	3	1	0	.194
Clements, Charlie	LF	10	30	8	0	0	3	.267
Sawyer, Carl	1B	6	16	0	0	0	0	.000

Pirrone's All-Stars Pitching Statistics 1933-34

Name	G	CG	W	L	IP	SO	BB	SH
Koupal, Lou	3	1	0	3	18	—	—	0
Walters, Johnny "Junk"	4	3	0	3	21	—	—	0
Newsom, Buck	8	7	3	5	58	53	21	1
French, Larry	1	1	0	1	8	3	3	0
Thurston, Sloppy	4	4	1	3	29	14	9	0
Stine, Lee	7	5	2	4	44	—	—	0

White Kings Batting Statistics 1933-34

Name	Pos	G	AB	H	D	T	HR	BA
Kingdon, Wes	2B	11	41	8	0	0	0	.195
Gazella, Mike	3B	6	21	7	0	0	1	.333
Almada, Lou	LF	3	12	4	0	0	0	.333
Jacobs, Ray	1B	7	27	5	3	0	0	.185
Vusich, Johnny	RF	7	25	4	1	0	0	.160
Strange, Alan	SS	6	17	5	1	0	1	.294
O'Grain, Cliff	LF	7	17	2	0	0	1	.118
Mayer, T.	C	7	23	4	2	0	0	.174
Allington, Bill	CF	4	13	2	0	0	0	.154

White Kings Pitching Statistics 1933-34

Name	G	CG	W	L	IP	SO	BB	SH
Thurston, Sloppy	See Pirrone's All-Stars							
Wetzel, Buzz	3	3	0	2	20	—	—	0
Weigel,	1	1	0	1	6	2	3	0
Jacobs, Art	2	2	1	1	17	13	2	0

The 1934-35 Season

The 1934-35 California Winter League looked like another mismatch. Tom Wilson was back in town with another dynamite squad. It was similar to the 1933-34 team that breezed through the schedule with a 34-8-2 record, with the exception of catcher, second base, and pitching. Larry Brown, a hard nosed defensive specialist replaced Tommy Dukes behind the plate, Sammy T. Hughes, maybe the Negro league's all-time greatest second baseman, took over for Sam Bankhead, and Andrew "Pullman" Porter joined Paige and Willis on the mound.

Joe Pirrone's All-Stars lost Buck Newsom from the '33 team, as well as Gene Lillard and Tuck Stainback. The addition of Red Frazier, Frank Demaree, and Fred Haney, helped offset those losses, but still left a huge gap between them and the proud Elite Giants. Demaree, in particular, was a valuable pickup. He was coming off a sensational year with the pennant winning Los Angeles of the PCL, hitting .383 with 45 home runs and 173 RBIs. The 1934 L.A. team has been called the greatest minor league team in history. The won 137 games against 50 losses, for a .733 winning percentage, and finished 37½ games ahead of second place Mission. The White Kings presented an interesting lineup with former Dodger Sloppy Thurston on the mound, slugger Les Powers of Sacramento of the PCL at first base, former Chicago White Sox infielder Ray French at second, and Steve Mesner of the Chicago Cubs at third, but they too did not seem to have enough all-around talent to make a serious run at Wilson's formidable charges. In fact, the Giants looked not only to be the class of the winter league, but also capable of challenging Frankie Frisch's World Series champion St. Louis Cardinals.

The Negro leaguers got off the mark quickly, as reported in the *Chicago Defender*. "Thomas Wilson's Elite Giants opened the winter league season at White Sox Park by defeating the Pirrone's All-Stars two out of three games played. A mammoth street parade formed at 12th and Central Avenue, marched south on Central to Vernon Avenue, then to the park. One hundred and fifty cars and three bands were in the line of march. This was the greatest winter league opening ever staged here. Supervisor Gordon L. McDonough pitched the first ball and Congressman William Treagur was the umpire. With Carter pitching, the Giants won the game Saturday by a score of 14–5." The game was never in doubt, as the Negro leaguers piled up three-run innings in the first, fourth, and sixth, and added a five spot in the seventh. Turkey Stearnes and Felton Snow each rapped out four singles in the 17 hit attack. Big George "Mule" Suttles had a single and a long home run, and Willie Wells contributed a single, double, and triple.

In the first game Sunday, Pullman Porter bested Larry French of the Pittsburgh Pirates, 7–4. The Giants got to French for four runs and five hits in the second inning to put the game on ice. Mule Suttles hit two home runs, giving him three for the series. Porter finished with a four-hitter, striking out eight. The All-Stars captured the abbreviated nightcap 6–3.

Suttles, the 6'3", 215 pound black

bomber, blasted two more homers against the White Kings on October 20–21, as the Giants again took two of three. In the opener, Carter bested Win Ballou 4–2 behind home runs by Suttles and Wells. The *Los Angeles Times* covered the Sunday games. "Hollis Thurston outlasted Pullman Porter and Cannonball Willis in the opener of yesterdays twin bill at White Sox Park, and the White Kings defeated the Royal Giants 8–6, after eleven hectic innings. The colored tossers came back strong in the night-cap, winning 3–0 behind the four-hit hurling of Porter.

"Five home runs featured the opener, Mule Suttles getting his fifth circuit clout in six games. Gene Lillard, Les Powers, Stearnes, and Hughes, also hit the ball out of the lot. Stearnes homer tied the score in the seventh. The second game was called after five inning because of darkness."

The Elite Giant express picked up speed in the third week of the season, sweeping the All-Stars three straight. Tom Wilson's bombers took a slugfest from Joe Pirrone's troops in the first game of the series, 9–8. Pitchers McDonald and Carter were both roughed up as the two teams unleashed their big bats. Hugh McMullen, Frank Demaree, and Mel Almada went long for the Stars, while Turkey Stearnes walloped two for the Giants, his second one being the game winner in the bottom of the eighth.

Pirrone's All-Stars

Name	Pos	AB	H
Haney	3B	5	0
Sawyer	1B	5	1
M. Almada	LF	5	2
Demaree	RF	5	2
Bell	CF	5	1
Knickerbocker	SS	5	1
Berkowitz	2B	4	0
McMullen	C	4	2
McDonald	P	2	1
Stine	P	2	1
Totals		42	11

Wilson's Elite Giants

Name	Pos	AB	H
J. Bell	CF	5	2
Hughes	1B	3	1
Wells	SS	4	2
Stearnes	LF	4	2
Suttles	RF	2	0
Williams	2B	4	2
Snow	3B	4	3
Brown	C	4	2
Carter	P	3	0
		33	14

Pirrone's All-Stars   2 0 1   0 0 0   4 1 0—8—11—2
Elite Giants   5 1 0   0 0 0   0 2 1—9—14—0

Two Base Hits: Stine, Snow
Home runs: Stearnes (2), M. Almada, Demaree, McMullen

	IP	H	SO	BB
McDonald			6	2
Stine (LP)			1	2
Carter (WP)	9	11	2	0

Sunday was "Frank Demaree Day" at White Sox Park, with the Pacific Coast League batting champion being honored between games of the doubleheader. A crowd of 4,500 fans, many of them from Demaree's home town of Santa Monica, showered him with gifts. The Giants also celebrated the day by raising the winter league pennant they won the previous year. The *Times* went on to say, "Hitting the ball hard and timely, the Royal Giants strengthened their hold on first place in the Winter League by defeating Joe Pirrone's All-Stars in both ends of yesterdays twin bill at White Sox Park. The scores were 6–4 and 10–4.

"Mule Suttles seventh homer in nine

games broke up a duel between Pullman Porter and Lou Garland in the eighth inning of the opener. The clout came with (Hughes on first base) and the scored tied. Frank Demaree, Garland, and Williams also hit home runs in the first game, while Wells and Stearnes cracked four baggers in the nightcap."

Tom Wilson's powerful club destroyed the White Kings in their rematch, winning by scores of 15–11, 13–2, and 8–2. The Giants scored 12 runs in the first two innings Saturday, and coasted home. Les Powers smashed two homers for the Kings, while Hughes and Snow hit for the circuit for the Giants. In the Sunday opener, the Black Bombers dazzled the fans, as well as the Kings, with their all-around play. Pullman Porter scattered nine hits, fanned five and didn't walk a man, in a masterful exhibition of pitching. The Giant sluggers flexed their muscles with an 18 hit attack that included homers by Stearnes and Dunn. And the rabbits were also in fine fettle, stealing seven bases — three by "Cool Papa" Bell, and one each by Wells, Suttles, Dunn, and Snow. In the nightcap, the Giants banged out 11 base hits in five innings, en route to an 8–2 victory, behind Cannonball Willis.

Satchel Paige arrived in town on October 23rd, but by that time Tom Wilson's troops already had the situation well in hand, with a commanding lead in the pennant race. Paige unlimbered his arm with a two inning stint against the White Kings on the 25th, then started his first game against the All-Stars the following week. Unfortunately for Pirrone's boys, he was the Satchel of old, tossing a five-hitter, and striking out 14 batters, in an easy 7–1 victory. Paige himself led the batting barrage with a single and a home run.

With Paige on board to support Porter and Willis, the league championship was no longer in doubt. The Giants continued to extend their lead week after week, as the "Big Three" were almost unbeatable, and Stearnes and Suttles averaged a homer a game between them. When Paige arrived on the scene, the Giants' record stood at 12–3. Over the last half of the season, they went 16–3, giving them an overall record of 28–6, with one tie. Their nearest competitor, Pirrone's All-Stars, had a record of just 5–16 in games that were recovered. The official published stats gave Tom Wilson's crew credit for 34 victories against 5 losses.

The most explosive game of the season was played on January 27, when the Giants hosted Pirrone's All-Stars in White Sox Park. It turned out to be Turkey Stearnes' day, as the 170 pound left-handed slugger crushed four home runs and a single, good for 17 total bases, and 12 runs batted in, in a 20–8 Giant victory. Hank McDonald was shelled from the mound in the first inning under an 11 run Giant outburst. Turkey Stearnes unloaded two home runs in the first inning, good for seven RBIs. He was held to a single in the third, but bounced back with a two-run homer in the fifth, and a three-run shot in the sixth, before finally being retired in the eighth. Stearnes set five records by hitting two home runs, and driving in seven runs in one inning, driving in a total of 12 runs in the game, hitting four home runs in one game, and punching out five straight base hits. Suttles contributed two doubles in the first inning, while Hughes and Wells each had two singles in the big frame. It was also pennant day, as the Giants were awarded the pennant for winning the championship of the Southern California League for the season of 1934 and 1935.

Satchel Paige, as usual, was the center of attention on the coast. The *Chicago Defender* had the following comments about the 29-year-old pitching sensation, after he racked up his eighth successive victory in late January. "The first time Satchel Paige loses a game for the Elite Giants in the winter league now in progress here, it will be his initial defeat since coming west. To be sure, the big fellow hasn't come even close to being defeated while facing some of the best pitchers the All-Stars have been able to borrow from the major leagues." Later, the *Defender* had this to say about Paige's Negro league salary demands. "Leroy Satchel Paige, the mighty right hander with the Pittsburgh Crawfords now, and likely to remain there, is the most sought after ball player in the land today, or he was until Gus announced the salary his star was receiving. Then down to brass tacks, they continue to want the star, but at least five owners have admitted they do not care for Leroy at his present rate of pay ... they point out thay cannot afford to pay such salaries and continue to operate."

When the final curtain came down on the 1934-35 California winter League season, Tom Wilson's Elite Giants were the proud possessors of a 34–5–1 record. The powerful Giants proved to be one of the most exciting all-around baseball teams ever to set foot on a diamond. They combined a powerful offense, with aggressive base running, a tight defense, and overpowering pitching. Wilson's charges, who averaged 6.7 runs per game, were explosive on offense. Burnis "Wild Bill" Wright ripped the ball at a torrid .481 pace, followed by Turkey Stearnes at .423. Les Powers, slugging first baseman of the White Kings and Pirrone All-Stars, swatted .414 in just eight recorded games. The Ruth and Gehrig of the California Winter League, Turkey Stearnes and Mule Suttles, clocked a fantastic 16 home runs each, in 97 and 96 at-bats respectively, a total that equates to 91 homers for every 550 at-bats. Once again, the smooth swinging Powers was penalized by a lack of available statistics. He hit 7 home runs in just 29 at-bats, a pace that would have rewarded him with the home run championship if he had been able to maintain it throughout the season. "Cool Papa" Bell spearheaded the Giants daring running game, by swiping 15 sacks. Sammy T. Hughes and Turkey Stearnes stole seven bases each. The Giants, whose skills on the bases demonstrated they were not a one dimensional ballclub, outran their opponents, 47 stolen bases to ten.

Andrew "Pullman" Porter, Cannonball Willis, and Satchel Paige gave the Giants outstanding pitching, game after game. Porter led the league in games pitched (19), complete games (16), victories (12), and innings pitched (122). Satchel Paige, the 28-year-old master, led in winning percentage (8–0, 1.000), and strikeouts (104 in 69 innings). Jim Willis chipped in with a 9–4 record and a league leading three shutouts.

The Negro league entry fielded one of the greatest defensive units in CWL history. They were spectacular up the middle, with Larry Brown behind the plate, Wells and Hughes protecting the keystone sack, and Bell patrolling the middle garden. Brown was an all-around defensive standout, who allowed only ten stolen bases all season. The "Devil" and Sammy T. thrilled the home fans with some of the flashiest twin killings ever seen on the coast. And Bell, who could run like a frightened fawn, nabbed everything hit in his direction, and kept base runners honest with his accurate throws. His outfield compatriots, Turkey Stearnes and "Wild Bill" Wright were just as dominating. The three of them gave opposing batters nightmares.

The 1934-35 Elite Giants, along with the 33–34 aggregation, may have been the greatest Negro league team ever to play in the California Winter League. It is impossible to differentiate between the two. The 1926-27 contingent of Rogan, Willie Foster, Stearnes, Allen, and company, also deserve consideration.

1934-35 California Winter League
Final Standings—Incomplete

	Wins	Losses	Ties
Wilson's Elite Giants	34	5	1
Pirrone's All-Stars	5	16	0
White Kings	2	10	0
May Co.	1	2	0

Wilson's Elite Giants Batting Statistics 1934-35

Name	Pos	G	AB	H	D	T	HR	BA
Bell, Cool Papa	CF	24	98	30	6	5*	1	.306
Hughes, Sammy T.	3B	30*	105*	39	8	1	3	.371
Wells, Willie	SS	27	94	30	9*	2	2	.319
Stearnes, Turkey	LF	26	97	41*	2	1	16*	.423
Suttles, Mule	1B	26	96	33	7	0	16*	.344
Williams, Chester	2B	7	29	14	3	1	1	.483
Snow, Felton	3B	21	77	27	6	0	1	.351
Brown, Larry	C	24	77	28	4	0	1	.364
Wright, Wild Bill	RF	17	54	26	7	0	3	.481*
Dunn, Jake	2B	3	11	4	2	0	1	.364

Wilson's Elite Giants Pitching Statistics 1934-35

Name	G	CG	W	L	IP	SO	BB	SH
Young, Slowtime	4	4	3	1	22	—	—	0
Porter, Pullman	19	16	12	3	122	66	21	1
Willis, Jim	15	12	9	4	118	72	26	3*
Paige, Satchel	10	7	8	0	69	104	20	2
Carter,	3	3	3	0	27	11	5	0
Griffin, Schoolboy	1	1	1	0	9	9	—	0

Pirrone's All-Stars Batting Statistics 1934-35

Name	Pos	G	AB	H	D	T	HR	BA
Haney, Fred	3B	5	20	6	1	0	0	.300
Demaree, Frank	RF	5	20	6	1	0	0	.300
Carlisle, Cleo	CF	9	30	8	0	0	3	.267
Berkowitz, Joe	SS	11	34	10	2	1	1	.294
McMullen, Hugh	C	8	22	4	1	0	1	.182
Colburn,	3B	8	28	9	0	0	0	.321
Sawyer, Carl	1B	8	26	3	0	0	0	.115
Bell, Fern	CF	10	35	6	2	0	2	.171
Ferraris, Angie	2B	9	25	3	1	0	0	.120

Pirrone's All-Stars Pitching Statistics 1934-35

Name	G	CG	W	L	IP	SO	BB	SH
French, Larry	3	2	0	2	19	10	5	0
McDonald, Hank	6	3	0	5	28	20	16	0
Stine, Lee	6	4	2	3	37	22	9	0
Frazier, Red	7	5	2	4	47	24	17	0

Miscellaneous Batting Statistics 1934-35

Name	Team	Pos	G	AB	H	D	T	HR	BA
Powers, Les	White Kings	1B	8	29	12	0	0	7	.414
Ograin, Cliff	White Kings	RF	5	16	3	1	0	0	.188

Miscellaneous Pitching Statistics 1934-35

Name	Team	G	CG	W	L	IP	SO	BB	SH
Thurston, Sloppy	White Kings	4	3	1	2	29	—	—	0
Ballou, Win	White Kings	2	2	0	2	16	8	6	0

7

Season Summaries 1935–1939

The 1935-36 Season

The saga of the Negro league domination of the California Winter League continued into the 1935-36 season, but with an almost imperceptible decrease in overall talent. "Cool Papa" Bell, Willie Wells, Pullman Porter, and Cannonball Jim Willis were not with the team, replaced by Zollie Wright, the brother of Wild Bill Wright, Jim West, Chet Brewer, and Schoolboy Griffin. The Royal Giants, however, still had the meat of their batting order intact, with Stearnes (Negro National League batting champion at .430), Suttles, Hughes, and Wright, terrorizing opposing pitchers. And the pitching load rested in the capable hands of Satchel Paige and Brewer.

The league consisted of four teams, the Giants, Pirrone's All-Stars, the White King Soapsters, and the Santa Monica Merchants. Joe Pirrone's team presented a strong challenge to the Giants' quest for another league title, with a talented mound staff headed by the Chicago Cubs' Larry French (17–10) and Brooklyn's Les Munns, and supported by World Series home run leader Frank Demaree, former Dodger shortstop Glenn Wright, National League batting champion Arky Vaughan (.385), and former Tiger third baseman Fred Haney. The White Kings headlined pitchers Herm "Old Folks" Pillette and Hollis "Sloppy" Thurston, but appeared to have limited firepower at the plate. Santa Monica was represented by Gene Lillard, the PCL's home run leader with 56, former Dodger Jigger Statz, Fern Bell, Dud Lee, and pitchers Ralph Buxton and Newt Kimball of the Los Angeles Angels.

The local press failed to give the winter league much coverage during the season, with just 12 box scores recovered, so batting and pitching statistics, particularly of the white teams, were severely limited. The *Los Angeles Times* did note a preseason party at Joe Pirrone's nightclub. "Baseball fans from all over the Southland will gather at Joe Pirrones Cafe at 623½ South Hill Street this evening to greet a host of World Series stars who will be on hand to celebrate the opening of the Winter League diamond season Saturday and Sunday at Wrigley Field.

"Among the World Series notables who will be on hand include Frank Demaree, Tuck Stainback and Larry French of the Chicago Cubs, and Joe Sullivan of the Tigers. Besides this quartet, such notable major leaguers as Melo Almada, Jesse Hill, Arky Vaughan, Billy Knickerbocker, and others, will be present to greet the crowd."

The opening weekend was covered by the *Times*. The Saturday edition noted ... "the lid will be pried off Winter League baseball season at Wrigley Field today at 2:15.

Gene Lillard had a long 23 year minor league career, 11 of which he spent in the Pacific Coast League. He hit .304 in the PCL, .303 overall. (Dick Dobbins)

Arky Vaughan won the National League batting title in 1935 with an average of .385, then went 5 for 10 for Pirrone's All-Stars in the winter league.

"Joe Pirrone, starting his fifteenth season of promoting winter ball had lined up a strong squad that includes no less than eight major league players.... Joe E. Brown and the Duncan sisters will be the guests of honor at both today's game and tomorrow's doubleheader which starts at 1:30."

Tom Wilson's Royal Giants rose to the occasion in the opener, according to the *Times*. "With big Mule Suttles leading their attack by hammering out two tremendous home runs, the Royal Giants won the Winter League opener at Wrigley Field yesterday when they defeated Pirrone's Cafe All-Stars, 8–3.

"Suttles smashed one over the left field fence with Snow on base in the first inning, and homered again in the sixth to knot the count after the big leaguers had bunched four hits off Griffin for three runs in the fourth.

"The Negro leaguers routed Red Frazier with a four run rally in the seventh and continued their attack on 'Big' Munns, Brooklyn right hander."

Manager "Candy Jim" Taylor of the Giants sent Tommy Thompson and Young to the mound in Sunday's doubleheader, opposed by Larry French and Big Munns. Once again, the *Times* covered the action. "Larry French, Chicago Cub southpaw, who lost the final game of the World Series to Detroit, dropped another decision in the last round yesterday at Wrigley Field. French, pitching for Joe Pirrone's Cafe All-Stars, was beaten by the Royal Giants, crack colored Winter League nine, 5–4, much to the delight and amazement of some 7,500 fans.

"After fanning a dozen of the Giants, and holding a 3–1 lead at the end of seven innings, French weakened with two away in the eighth, and the colored sluggers scored three times to go in front.

"The Pirrones tied it up in their half of the ninth, when Fred Haney singled, took second as Arky Vaughan walked, moved to third on a passed ball, and came in on Mel Almada's infield out.

"But the Giants came right back to win in the last of the ninth. Griffin, who replaced Thompson on the mound, and put down a Pirrone rally in the first half of the round, led off with a single. Stearnes bunted and Haney threw the ball to center, putting Giants on second and third with none away. French purposely walked Snow, but Zollie Wright drove a long fly to Jess Hill and Griffin trotted in after the catch with the winning run....

"Pirrone's crew gained some measure of revenge by copping the nightcap behind the four-hit hurling of Les Munns....

"Frank Demaree, the Cubs World Series home run king, drove out the deciding shot in the first inning of the finale, when he drove one over the left field wall to score Hill and Vaughan ahead of him."

First Game Box Score

Pirrone's All-Stars				**Royal Giants**			
Name	*Pos*	*AB*	*H*	*Name*	*Pos*	*AB*	*H*
Hill	CF	5	2	Stearnes	LF	4	2
Haney	3B	4	2	Snow	3B	4	0
Vaughan	SS	4	2	Wright	SS	4	0
Demaree	LF	4	1	Suttles	2B	4	1
Almada	1B	4	1	Mackey	C	3	2
G. Wright	2B	5	1	B. Wright	CF	3	0
Carlyle	RF	4	0	West	1B	4	3
Frankovich	C	4	0	Summers	RF	4	0
French	P	4	1	Thompson	P	3	1
				Griffin	P	1	1
Totals		38	10			34	10

Pirrone's All-Stars   3 0 0   0 0 0   0 0 1—4—10—1
Royal Giants   0 0 0   0 1 0   0 3 1—5—10—1

Two Base Hits: Stearnes
Three Base Hits: Vaughan
Home runs: Almada

	IP	H	SO	BB
French (LP)	8⅔	10	12	3
Thompson	8⅔	10	7	4

It should be noted that the Royal Giants pitcher known as Schoolboy Griffin was also called Griffith, and is usually identified as Griffith in Negro league records. He is listed as Griffith in the appendix.

The following week, the Giants beat French again, this time 3–2 in 11 innings. Griffin hurled eight-hit ball and shut down French's Santa Monica team after being touched up for a pair of runs in the second inning. Mule Suttles got the Giants even by putting a 475 foot shot into orbit over the right center field fence, with Snow on base in the top of the fourth. It was the first ball ever hit over that fence. Both pitchers settled down and pitched shutout ball through the tenth. Then, in the eleventh, "Candy Jim's" boys brought the crowd of 7,000 to their feet when Jim West cracked a double scoring Wild Bill Wright with the winning run.

The big news of the week was an announcement by Joe Pirrone that he had signed the inimitable Jerome Hannah "Dizzy" Dean to pitch for his All-Stars against the Royal Giants in a Thursday night game. Not one to miss a trick, Negro league legend Satchel Paige was assigned the duty of stopping the St. Louis Cardinal fireballer, who had once again led the National League in victories, with 28 in 1935. Dean's supporting cast included Jigger Statz, Tuck Stainback, Arky Vaughan, Wally Berger, Dolph Camilli, Frank Demaree, Fred Haney, and Gene Desautels.

As is often the case, the pregame hype exceeded the actual event, as noted by the *Los Angeles Times*. "The celebrated pitching duel between Paige and Dean failed to materialize when the Satchel retired after four innings and Dizzy left the game after the seventh. Dizzy was leading 3–2 at the time the cold weather forced him to drop the mound chores.

"Newt Kimball took up the hurling burden for the All-Stars and was promptly nicked for two runs as the Giants shot to the front 4–3.

"Demaree opened the ninth with a single. Lillard blasted out a single, sending Demaree to third. B. Wright, Giant center fielder, uncorked a wild throw, Demaree scoring and Lillard moving to third. Hannah then clicked out a single over third to count Lillard with the winning run.

"Wally Berger was the batting star, bagging a double and a triple. A crowd of 7000 saw the battle."

The following week, "Candy Jim" Taylor's ace was back in action against the White Kings, as reported in the *Times*. "Satchel Paige, baseball's Black Bullet made his winter league debut an auspicious one by striking out thirteen batters as he pitched the Royal Giants to a 7–0 victory over the White Kings in the opener of yesterday's doubleheader at Wrigley Field.

"Satchel allowed but four hits and only in the ninth inning did he lose control and issue a walk.

"The lanky Negro ace was never in trouble.

"The Wright brothers led the attack on Hollis Thurston. Zollie Wright clicked a homer and a double, while Bill Wright hit a single, double, and triple.

"The White Kings got revenge in the nightcap when Herman Pillette won a 1–0 pitching duel from Tommy Thompson, lean, lanky Giant right hander. Thompson lost his own game in the third when ... he balked to let Desautels in with the only run of the contest.

"Sensational fielding at second base by Hughes of the colored club featured the doubleheader, which lured a crowd of 2500 fans."

The Santa Monica Merchants, fielding one of the stronger teams in the league, shut out Joe Pirrone's sluggers on November 3, by a score of 5–0. Ralph Buxton tossed a four-hitter to defeat Les Munns. The *Times* noted, "Bill Brubaker's triple was the big swat of the game, while Dud Lee, playing short for the Pirrones, provided the fielding features, along with Jigger Statz, Santa Monica center fielder."

Chet Brewer made his debut for the Giants against the All-Stars, and almost didn't get out of the first inning. He was raked for five runs at the outset, but managed to survive the onslaught. He then settled down to blank Joe Pirrone's troops the rest of the way, while his mates fought back with a big eight run eighth inning to break open a 5–5 game. The *Chicago Defender* reported, "Home runs by Mule Suttles ... Bill Wright and ... Zollie Wright, a triple by Brewer, and three doubles by Turkey Stearnes featured Tom Wilson's (Royal) Giants attack.... The Giants gave Mallis a surprise party in the eighth inning when they scored eight runs on ten hits."

Satchel Paige had defeat staring him in the face in a game against the White Kings on November 24, but Lady Luck was with him, and he escaped unharmed, as reported by the *Times*. "Satchel Paige, great colored pitcher, who hasn't lost a Winter League game since 1933, had a narrow escape at Wrigley Field yesterday. Paige's team the Royal Giants, went into the ninth inning trailing the White Kings 3–2, but rallied to fill the bases with two out. Whereupon, Turkey Stearnes blasted a home run to give the Giants a 6–3 victory and save Satchel's record."

Manager Johnny Bassler's Santa Monica Merchants, now boasting Homer Summa, a career .302 hitter with the Cleveland Indians and Philadelphia Athletics, former Yankee shortstop Jimmie Reese, Pittsburgh Pirate infielder Bill Brubaker, and former Tiger backstop Larry Woodall, invaded Wrigley Field for a Thanksgiving Day doubleheader, with the express purpose of snatching first place from "Candy Jim" Taylor's embattled crew.

The Giants held a tenuous league lead on the basis of a shaky 8–5 start. But they always performed at their best when the chips were down, and this day was no exception. In the opener, Satchel Paige faced Merchant ace Ralph Buxton, with Buxton holding a slim 1–0 lead after six innings. In the seventh, after Chet Brewer relieved a fading Paige, the Giants came on to tie the game on the strength of a mighty home run by Mule Suttles. The game stayed deadlocked until the bottom of the ninth, when Turkey Stearnes drove a game winning homer over the right field screen. In game two, Tommy Thompson tossed a 1–0 shutout in a five inning abbreviated encounter.

From that point on, the powerful Negro league aggregation exploded, winning 15 games against a single loss and two ties. Paige went 5–0 down the stretch. One notable game was played on January 18, as reported in the *Times*. "...Santa Monica Merchants stopped the ten game winning streak of the Royal Giants yesterday when they defeated the crack colored nine 7–6 at Civic Stadium. It was the first loss for the Giants in a full length ball game, all their previous defeats having come in five and seven inning contests halted by darkness.

"Fern Bell was the hero of the Santa Monica win, the Newark outfielder smashing out four hits in five times at bat and driving home Dud Lee with the winning run in the eleventh when he singled to right....

"The Merchants drove the great Satchel Paige to the showers with a six run assault in four innings, but 'Slowtime' Young, after hurling six innings of shutout ball, was charged with the defeat in the eleventh.

"Hughes, Giant second-sacker, hit homers his first two times up, driving one over the left field wall and then making the second circuit on a drive inside the park.

"Dud Lee singled with one away in the eleventh for his third hit, took second on an out, and came home on Bell's single. Beck and Reese sparkled in the field for the victors."

January 31 was banner day for Tom Wilson's Royal Giants. They rang down the curtain on another successful winter league season by whipping Pirrone's All-Stars in a doubleheader, to capture the league championship. The *Los Angeles Times* headlined the day's events "Mule Kicks for Giants" with the following story. "Mule Suttles provided the kick that gave the Royal Giants a twin triumph over Joe Pirrone's All-Stars in yesterday's final Winter League club doubleheader. The scores were 5 to 2 and 2 to 1.

"Suttles hit two homers in the first game, one with the bases loaded, to drive in all five Giant runs as Griffith (or Griffin) won a hurling duel from Munns. In the nightcap, Suttles doubled and scored the winning run when Hughes singled him home. Hughes first inning homer accounted for the (first) Giant tally." Suttles' grand slam came in the sixth inning with the Giants down 1–0.

There are two pieces of information that need to be explained. The Giants referred to as the Royal Giants here, were called that by the local white newspapers. The black newspapers of the day referred to them as the Elite Giants since the owner of the team once owned the Nashville Elite Giants of the Negro National League. Also, the published league standings show all the league teams with a better than .500 winning percentage. That's because all the team's games, both league and non league, were counted in the standings.

The Royal Giants' convincing title march was no surprise to baseball experts or to the fans who packed Wrigley Field week after week. They were the class of the league, in all aspects of the game; batting, pitching, defense, and base running. Jim West, dubbed "One Wing" by west coast writers won the batting title with a scintillating .510 average. Wild Bill Wright pushed West throughout the season, before finishing at .426. Other offensive leaders were Turkey Stearnes and Zollie Wright with 7 doubles each, Felton Snow with 3 triples, and "Old Reliable" Mule Suttles with 11 home runs in just 57 at-bats, an average of one home run for every 5.2 at-bats (Barry Bonds averaged one home run for every 6.5 at-bats the year he hit 73). Suttles' pace would give him an unbelievable 106 homers for every 550 at-bats.

Satchel Paige once again captured the pitching accolades, going a perfect 13–0, with 113 strikeouts in 94 innings, with four shutouts.

Burnis "Wild Bill" Wright was called the most dangerous Negro league hitter by west coast baseball writers. (James A. Riley)

This was the last season the Negro league entry would field such an all-star aggregation. Never again would they offer as many as seven potential Hall of Fame players in one lineup. They would however go on to capture many more California Winter League pennants over the next thirteen years.

1935-36 California Winter League
Final Standings—Incomplete

	Wins	Losses	Ties
Wilson's Royal Giants	23	6	2
Pirrone's All-Stars	14	10	0
Santa Monica Merchants	13	10	1
White King Soapsters	12	11	1

Season Summaries 1935–1939

Wilson's Royal Giants Batting Statistics 1935-36

	Pos	G	AB	H	D	T	HR	BA
Sammy T. Hughes	2B	16	69	27	2	2	6	.391
Felton Snow	SS	14	58	13	0	3*	0	.224
Turkey Stearnes	LF	19	63	24	7*	2	5	.381
Mule Suttles	3B	19	57	17	1	0	11*	.298
Zollie Wright	RF	18	68	26	7*	0	5	.382
Biz Mackey	C	12	36	9	1	0	0	.250
Bill Wright	CF	17	61	26	3	2	2	.426
Jim West	1B	16	49	25	2	3	1	.510
John Hines	C	5	13	2	1	1	0	.154

Wilson's Royal Giants Pitching Statistics 1935-36

	G	CG	W	L	IP	SO	BB	SH
Bob "Schoolboy" Griffith a.k.a. Griffin	14	7	7	0	91	99	25	0
Tommy Thompson	8	7	4	2	47	—	—	1
Satchel Paige	16	6	13	0	94	113	28	4
Chet Brewer	9	5	3	1	49	—	—	1

Pirrone's All-Stars Batting Statistics 1935-36

	Pos	G	AB	H	D	T	HR	BA
Jess Hill	CF	3	12	3	1	0	0	.250
Fred Haney	3B	6	19	6	0	0	0	.316
Arky Vaughan	SS	3	10	5	1	1	0	.500
Frank Demaree	LF	4	11	4	1	0	1	.364
Mel Almada	1B	2	11	1	0	0	1	.091
Glenn Wright	2B	4	16	6	1	0	0	.375
Cleo Carlyle	RF	9	31	3	0	0	0	.097
Fern Bell	LF	10	32	7	0	0	0	.219
Dud Lee	SS	5	20	5	0	0	0	.250
Lin Storti	2B	4	10	2	0	0	0	.200
Larry Barton	LF	6	15	5	1	0	1	.333
George McDonald	1B	6	19	3	0	0	0	.158
Hugh McMullen	C	5	11	2	0	0	0	.182
Colburn	3B	4	10	2	0	0	0	.200

Pirrone's All-Stars Pitching Statistics 1935-36

	G	CG	W	L	IP	SO	BB	SH
Les Munns	8	6	1	6	52	—	—	0
Larry French	3	3	0	3	29	—	—	0
Cy Mallis	7	5	2	4	46	—	—	0

Miscellaneous Batting Statistics 1935-36

	Team	Pos	G	AB	H	D	T	HR	BA
Bill Allington	White Kings	CF	4	12	5	0	0	2	.417
Ray French	White Kings	SS	3	9	1	0	0	0	.111
Don Ross	White Kings	3B	4	13	4	0	0	1	.308
John Vusich	White Kings	RF	3	10	2	0	0	0	.200
Steve Mesner	May Co.	LF	3	12	6	1	0	1	.500

Miscellaneous Pitching Statistics 1935-36

	Team	G	CG	W	L	IP	SO	BB	SH
Herman Pillette	White Kings	6	5	4	2	48	—	—	2
Hollis Thurston	White Kings	2	2	0	2	12	—	—	0
Ralph Buxton	Santa Monica	6	2	2	1	35	—	—	2
Newt Kimball	Santa Monica	3	0	1	2	14	—	—	0

The 1936-37 Season

Media coverage of the 1936-37 California Winter League was minimal, as just one box score and 14 line scores were discovered in the newspapers of the day. The lone box score was reported in the *Chicago Defender* after Chet Brewer had recorded his fifth straight victory.

The winter league was once again anchored by two old reliables, the Royal Giants and Pirrone's All-Stars. The six team league also included the White Kings, May Co., San Diego Merchants, and Santa Monica Merchants. Tom Wilson brought another Negro league contingent to California for the season, but it was a far cry from the great black teams of the past. Bill Wright, Hughes, Bell, and Mackey, provided the Giants with a formidable offensive nucleus, but legendary performers like Mule Suttles and Turkey Stearnes were sorely missed. The pitching staff, with the exception of the veteran Chet Brewer, was average, making for a more competitive league.

Since newspaper coverage was lacking, very few player statistics were developed, although team rosters were published. Pirrone's All-Stars headlined George Caster (25–13 with the Portland Beavers of the PCL), and Jack Salveson (21–7 with the Los Angeles Angels), on the mound, supported by Frank Demaree, the Chicago Cubs' leading batsman with 16 homers, 96 RBIs and a .350 average, Fern Bell, who hit .313 with the Oakland Oaks, the Almada brothers, Lou and Melo, Dud Lee, former Boston Red Sox shortstop, and Johnny Kerr, former Washington Senator infielder. The White Kings featured Larry French (18–9 with the Chicago Cubs), Lou Koupal (23–11 with Seattle), Ray French of the Kansas City Blues of the American Association), Les Powers, and Jimmy Crandall, the son of former major league pitcher Doc Crandall. Santa Monica had Gene Lillard of the Chicago Cubs, Jigger Statz (.332 with the Los Angeles Angels), Johnny Bassler, Goldie Holt of the Portland Beavers, and Don Hurst, who hit .303 with 19 homers and 113 RBI's for the Angels. San Diego was led by pitcher Herm "Old Folks" Pillette, and the May Co. Had Berle Horne, former Chicago Cubs hurler, and outfielder Vince DiMaggio.

Prior to the opening of the winter league season, "Rowdy Dick" Bartell, the outspoken shortstop of the New York Giants, who was in the World Series against the Yankees, gave an interview regarding his experience against black players in the California Winter League. Bartell, who went on to hit .381 in a losing cause in the Series, claimed he had hit .400 against Satchel Paige and other Negro league pitchers on the coast, and said he wished he could face those same pitchers in the major leagues. Research by the *Chicago Defender* revealed the truth. Dick Bartell had played three games against Paige in California, batting about .091, with five strikeouts. Other major league players offered their opinions about Paige's ability. Several of them claimed his fastball was speedier than Lefty Grove's and his breaking ball was as good as Carl Hubbell's. Another big leaguer said Paige's biggest asset was his control. "That fellow can break an egg a block away and never touch the dish it is resting in."

The *Los Angeles Times*, in reviewing the

Royals team, said, "Heading the line-up will be Josh Gibson, sensational Negro hitting star, who will perform at catcher in the Royal array. Gibson will be behind the plate to catch the slants of pitcher Griffin (a.k.a. Griffith), whose hurling was a feature of the winter league last year." Unfortunately, for whatever reason, Gibson did not make the trip to California, and never did play in the winter league there.

The May Co. opened the winter league season with a non league game on October 11 and defeated Firestone Tire & Rubber by a count of 9–3, behind the pitching of Berle Horne, a 13 game winner with the Hollywood Stars in 1936. Vince DiMaggio, who had just hit .293 with 19 home runs and 102 RBIs with the San Diego Padres, smashed a home run. First baseman George McDonald (.317 with the Padres), rapped a triple and two doubles for the Mays. Winter League President Joe Pirrone announced a winter league opening day doubleheader at White Sox Park, between his own All-Stars, which he said, "will bristle with major and minor league stars," and the Royal Giants. The *L.A. Times* said, "The colored club will send 'Schoolboy' (Griffith) and 'Cannonball' Willis to the mound in the twin bill.' Another announcement claimed that Satchel Paige would pitch the opener—but, as usual in Paige's case, when opening day arrived, he was among the missing.

Larry French played major league baseball for 14 years, winning 197 games and losing 171.

The official opening day twin bill was played on Sunday, October 25. Schoolboy Griffith toyed with the All-Stars in the opener, winning 7–2 behind a 12 hit attack. The 6'5", 235 pound spitballer scattered seven hits and fanned 15 batters, in besting George Caster. Lin Storti homered for Pirrone's team. The second game, called on account of darkness after five innings, ended in a 3-all tie.

While Tom Wilson and the Giants team were pondering the whereabouts of the great Satchel Paige, a news story was breaking in Pittsburgh, as reported by the *Chicago Defender*. "It is highly probable that Leroy 'Satchel' Paige will not play winter baseball this season, but remain in Pittsburgh until the Crawfords open their spring training season.

"Paige is planning a series of articles to start November 7 and conclude late in January or early in February. These articles will cover his experiences and observations—hardest hitters he has faced, colored and white, outstanding pitchers and players at every position, new prospects, and the team he would select to work behind him against all forms of opposition." The *Defender* noted that the articles might be published in book form.

The Paige-less Giants took to the road as November got underway, and were defeated by the Santa Monica Merchants 4–3 at Santa Monica Municipal Stadium. Tommy Thompson took the loss in relief of Chet Brewer, as the Merchants scored the winning tally in the bottom of the ninth. Gene Lillard, former third baseman-turned pitcher, was on the mound for Santa Monica.

The Giants, back home in White Sox Park, made up for their loss to the Merchants by pounding the White Kings, 14–4 and 12–0, ripping 28 base hits in 13 innings. The *Times* was there. "Schoolboy Griffith, the colored ace for the Royal Giants, bested the Kings in the first game, allowing nine hits. French started for the Kings, but went out at the end of the fifth inning after getting nicked for twelve hits.

"Lou Koupal, who was one of the Coast League's leading pitchers last season, worked the last four innings for the Kings and allowed only four hits....

"Roy Morney, hard hitting Giant left fielder, was the batting star of the fray, getting five hits in five appearances at the plate, one of the bingles being a home run. Allington and Hughes also hit homers.

"In a five inning nightcap, the Giants hammered Red Frazier, Memphis right hander, for twelve hits and a resultant twelve runs. Pullman Porter, Giant twirler, allowed only three hits...."

Just when Tom Wilson thought his team was beginning to gel, they were brought back to earth with a thud on November 8. Joe Pirrone's troops came into White Sox Park and handed the Negro leaguers a rare double defeat, by scores of 8–5 and 5–1, taking over the league lead in the process. It was the first time in ten years that the Giants lost two games in the same day. George Caster, coming off a 3–0 shutout of San Diego, avenged his previous defeat at the hands of the Giants by outlasting Griffith and Porter. Cool Papa Bell was the only Giant to solve Caster's offerings, rapping a double, triple, and home run. Fern

James "Cool Papa" Bell played winter ball in California for more than a dozen years, hitting a "cool" .366.

Bell, Alan Strange, and Sloppy Thurston all took Griffith deep. The Giant right-hander, who only pitched four innings in the opener, started game two with similar results. The *Times* reported. "Four runs in the second inning of the second game sent the All-Stars off to a lead that the Giants could not overcome. Griffith, who worked all the second game for the colored nine, allowed seven hits during the five inning fray. Lou Koupal worked the second game for the All-Stars and was nicked for seven hits, but scattered them so that they did no harm. Fern Bell and J. (Cool Papa) Bell each hit a four-base blow in the second game. The All-Stars turned in a pretty double play, Strange to Kerr to Sawyer to Dedeaux (6-4-3-5), in the second contest to nip a Giant rally in the fourth frame." Third baseman Rod Dedeaux later became famous as the baseball coach at the University of Southern California. He sent many players on to major league stardom, including Fred Lynn and Mark McGwire.

The road remained bumpy for Wilson's embattled crew, as they were humbled by the White Kings 7-5, and by Santa Barbara 11-0. Red Frazier went the route in the ten inning lid-lifter, to beat Pullman Porter, who had relieved Chet Brewer in the fateful tenth. Home runs were hit by Allington, Bates, and Crandall of the Kings, and Morney and Griffith of the Giants. The winning run scored when Bates walked, went to second on a sacrifice by Moore, and came home on a single by Frazier.

Gene Lillard hurled the shutout over the Giants before a capacity crowd at Pershing Park in Santa Barbara. It was his third victory over the Royal Giants, running his record to 3-1.

A return doubleheader between the Royal Giants and Pirrone's All-Stars closed out the month of November. The event was vigorously hyped in all the local papers. The *California Eagle* said, "Promising a bitter contest for first place, Pirrone's new All-Stars will defend the top spot against Jim Taylor's Royal Giants next Sunday.

"Experts answering fans as to why the Giants have for the first time slipped back to second place, declare that the team is as good as ever but that the white teams of the league are stronger and have more big name major leaguers than ever before. This, they declare, is the kind of opposition that it takes to make winter league baseball tense and interest-holding."

The *Times* continued to beat the drum. "Joe Pirrone's Cafe All-Stars will defend their Winter League lead at White Sox Park...when they tackle the Royal Giants in a bargain bill starting at 1:30.

"Both teams have bolstered their line-ups for the doubleheader. The Giants can move into the lead if they take both games, and they've shifted their batting order to generate more punch, and signed Chet Brewer to strengthen their mound forces....

"Ladies will be admitted to the grandstand for 25 cents at today's bargain rates."

Candy Jim Taylor had his boys ready for the crucial encounters, and they gave the All-Stars a double dose of Louisville Slugger hardwood, by rapping 18 base hits in 14 innings, en route to a 2-1, 6-0 sweep. In the opener, Schoolboy Griffith tossed a six hitter in beating Bill Radonits, the Portland Beaver hurler. The game was hotly contested. Bob Boken, former Washington Senator slugger, hit one over the fence in the third to give the All-Stars a short-lived 1-0 lead. Cool Papa Bell tied the game with a round tripper of his own, leading to the Giants' winning rally in the sixth. Bill Wright carried over the winning tally after singling. Pullman Porter had an easier time in the nightcap, shackling Pirrone's troops on two hits over the five inning route. The Giants scored six runs on seven hits.

The Royal Giants now had a lead they would not relinquish. With Negro league great Chet Brewer on board for the remainder of the season, the Giants ran off seven wins in the last eight recorded games, to capture another California Winter League championship. The recorded games for the season credit the Royal Giants with a record of 10–6–1, with the surprising San Diego Merchants sneaking into second place with a 6–4 record, after whipping Santa Monica 13–1, Pirrone's All-Stars 3–2, and the White Kings 4–3. Additional information from newspaper articles, such as victories credited to Brewer and Porter, gave the Giants an additional eleven victories against one defeat, for a final record of 21–7–1.

1936-37 California Winter League Standings—Incomplete

	Wins	Losses	Ties
Royal Giants	21	7	1
San Diego Merchants	6	4	0
Pirrone's All-Stars	5	6	1
May Co.	2	1	0
White Kings	3	4	0
Santa Monica Merchants	3	5	0

Royal Giants Batting Statistics 1936-37

Name	Pos	G	AB	H	D	T	HR	BA
Bell, Cool Papa	CF	5	19	9	3	1	3	.474
Morney, Roy	SS	7	27	14	4*	0	5*	.519*
Hughes, Sammy T.	2B	3	12	6	0	0	2	.500
Mackey, Biz	C	3	10	3	0	0	1	.300
West, Jim	1B	3	11	3	0	0	1	.273
Snow, Felton	3B	2	8	4	1	1	0	.500
Wright, Bill	RF	2	9	2	0	0	1	.222

Royal Giants Pitching Statistics 1936-37

Name	G	CG	W	L	IP	SO	BB	SH
Griffith, Bob "Schoolboy"	12	12	10	2	95	101	—	0
Porter, Pullman	6	4	3	2	33	—	—	2
Brewer, Chet	6	6	6	0	—	—	—	0
Direaux, Jimmy	2	2	2	0	12	—	—	2

San Diego Batting Statistics 1936-37

Name	Pos	G	AB	H	D	T	HR	BA
Morehouse, Frank	SS	9	36	9	0	1	2	.250
Carson, Walter "Kit"	LF	7	28	6	0	1	0	.214
McNeely, Earl	CF	10	42	13	3	0	0	.250
Holman, Ernie	3B	8	33	12	0	1	0	.364
Brucker, Earle	1B	10	40	13	0	0	3	.325
Joerndt, Ash	RF	3	11	2	0	0	0	.182
Coscarart, Pete	2B	9	39	14	2	0	1	.359
Warren, Dallas	C	10	30	8	0	0	0	.267
Desautels, Gene	RF	7	22	6	0	0	0	.273
Luscomb, Rod	LF	4	13	1	0	0	0	.077

San Diego Pitching Statistics 1936-37

Name	G	CG	W	L	IP	SO	BB	SH
Pillette, Herm	8	3	3	2	62	22	11	0
Campbell, Archie	6	2	3	0	21	3	4	0

Miscellaneous Batting Statistics 1936-37

Name	Team	Pos	G	AB	H	D	T	HR	BA
Storti, Lin	Pirrone	2B	3	14	3	0	0	3	.214
Bell, Fern	Pirrone	LF	5	16	7	0	0	4	.438
Allington, Bill	White Kings	LF	5	17	7	2	0	3	.412

Miscellaneous Pitching Statistics 1936-37

Name	Team	G	CG	W	L	IP	SO	BB	SH
Caster, George	Pirrone	4	4	3	1	36	—	—	2
Koupal, Lou	Pirrone-WK	3	2	1	1	18	—	—	0
Radonits, Bill	Pirrone	2	2	0	2	18	—	—	0
French, Larry	White Kings	3	1	1	2	20	—	—	0
Frazier, Red	White Kings	5	3	2	2	30	—	—	0
Lillard, Gene	Santa Monica	4	4	3	1	33	—	—	0

The 1937-38 Season

The 1937-38 California Winter League season was unique in one respect. For the first time in 18 years, Pirrone's All-Stars were among the missing. Joe Pirrone, now the president of the winter league, was apparently too busy with other projects to enter a team. There were, however, two other old standbys who made the league recognizable: the Philadelphia Royal Giants, and the White Kings. Other members of the six team league consisted of another black team, the Detroit Stars, the San Diego Farleys, the San Diego Paris Inn, and the El Centro Mexicans.

Although the Royal Giants, under manager Biz Mackey, were not as strong as previous Negro league teams, they were slightly improved over the 1936-37 squad, with the return of home run king Mule Suttles, one of the most devastating sluggers ever to set foot on California soil. The addition of Leroy Matlock to a staff that already had Chet Brewer and Pullman Porter, gave the pitching effort a much needed boost. Suttles' supporting staff included Cool Papa Bell, Sammy T. Hughes, Wild Bill Wright, and Jim West.

The Detroit Stars boasted a lineup that included former California Winter League batting champion Alex Radcliffe, his brother, the legendary Ted "Double Duty" Radcliffe, Lonnie Summers, and Jake Dunn. Double Duty Radcliffe was one of the most versatile players ever to grace a professional baseball roster, not to mention one of its most intriguing and loquacious characters. Radcliffe was a two-position all-star in the Negro leagues, getting the call as both a pitcher and a catcher. He was given his nickname by Damon Runyon, after the New York sportswriter watched the stocky right-hander toss a shutout in the first game of a Yankee Stadium doubleheader, then catch Satchel Paige in the nightcap.

The White Kings were ably represented on the mound, with Dick Barrett (20–18 with Seattle), Lee Stine, and Vernon "Lefty" Gomez, a 21 game winner with the pennant winning New York Yankees. They were backed by Babe Herman (.348 with Toledo of the American Association), Max West (.330 with Mission of the PCL), Steve Mesner (.329 with L.A.), and Buster Adams (.299 with Sacramento). The San Diego Farley roster included Herm "Old

Sammy T. Hughes, a tall, rangy second baseman may have been the best ever in that position. (James A. Riley)

Nineteen-year-old Ted Williams played in the winter league in 1937-38 after batting .291 for San Diego in the PCL.

Folks" Pillette, Pete Coscarart (.253 with Portland), and Cedric Durst (.293 with San Diego). The San Diego Paris Inn disbanded midway through the season, and were replaced by the Gold Club with essentially the same roster, so the two teams were combined statistically. The Gold Club had only two players of note; Joe Orrell of the Detroit Tigers, and 19-year-old Ted Williams, on his way to major league stardom. On the surface, it did not appear as if any of the other teams had the pitching depth or the offensive firepower to challenge the Royal Giants. Mackey's crew went into the season as a prohibitive favorite to add another jewel to their championship belt.

The *California Eagle* reported the opening of the winter league season at White Sox Park. "With Chief of Police

Davis slated to pitch the first ball to be caught by Bill Robinson (Famous black dancer "Bojangles," who starred with Shirley Temple in several movies), while Clarence Muse (another movie actor) acts as umpire, the 1937-38 Winter League baseball season officially gets underway next Sunday at White Sox Park.

"According to the plans of the management, newly organized this summer, this years opening will not only be the most auspicious of the many past seasons, but will also have the largest number of clubs and the finest assortment of colored and white baseball stars.

"Impressive ceremonies are scheduled to precede the pitching of the first ball, featured by a parade to be participated in by Legion and Veterans of Foreign War Posts. LeBlanc's famous boy and girl band will lead the procession through the principal eastside streets to the park."

"...the white teams are composed of major leaguers who winter here on the coast after the World Series ends, and the Coast Leaguers, most of whom live here."

The *Times* reviewed the players for the visiting White Kings. "Casey Campbell, manager of the White Kings, has signed a galaxy of stars to perform for the Kings. Glenn Gabler, former Long Beach boy, who burned up the International League this year, will probably take the mound for the Kings, with D.C. Moore, former 'Iron Man' from Riis High, catching. Moore, who won All-Southern California halfback honors while at Riis, is now the property of the Cincinnati Reds, and considered one of the best young receivers in the game."

The *Eagle* covered the opening game. "Approximately 5,000 fans saw the Royal Giants down the White Kings Sunday afternoon at White Sox Park, 19-11, which opened the Winter League season.

"A barrage of base hits rattled off the Sox fence as powerful Giant hitters touched Gabler and Frazier, White King mound aces from Jersey City of the International League and Memphis of the Southern Association respectively, for (21) hits....

"Batting star of the game was Mule Suttles, long distance slugger, who secured two home runs, a double and a single in five times at bat."

The game was a slugfest from start to finish, with the Royal Giants jumping out to a big lead early, then holding off a late inning charge by the Kings. Mackey's troops raced to a 5-0 lead off Gabler out of the gate. Bell led off the pyrotechnics by slicing a triple down the left field line. Hughes singled over the pitcher's head for one run, Wright dropped a dying quail into short center, Suttles singled through third, plating Hughes, and West lofted a home run over the right field screen to score Suttles and Wright ahead of him. In the bottom of the second, it was more of the same. Hughes singled through the box with one out. Wright singled to center and continued around to third on Max West's error, with Hughes scoring. Red Frazier replaced Gabler on the hill for the Kings, but it didn't make any difference to the Negro leaguers. After Wright scored on a passed ball, Suttles boomed a long home run that disappeared over the center field fence at the 400 foot mark. Two more runs came across before the dust settled, and Mackey's team had a comfortable 10-0 lead.

They extended the lead to 12-1 in the third, on a triple by Hughes, a double by Wright, and a single by West, to more than offset Frazier's home run in the top of the inning. The Kings suddenly came to life in the fourth, and put up a four-spot on Max West's two-run homer, and a two-run double by Owens, the catcher. They added three more in the fifth. Les Powers singled and came around on a single by Buster Adams. Then, a two-out single by Bobby Allaire and a two base error by Bell brought in two more.

Chet Brewer took over the mound

chores in the top of the sixth with his team on top, 15–8. He coasted through the next three innings, holding the Kings scoreless. In the bottom of the eighth, after being shut down for two innings, Mackey's boys added insult to injury by tacking up another four-spot. All the scoring came with two out. According to the *California Eagle* "Suttles leaned on one of Frazier's slants for one of the longest homers of the day, the ball going over the wall in deep center." After West walked, Felton Snow put another ball over the center field fence. A walk to Jesse Walker and a double by Mackey closed out the Giant scoring for the day. But the White Kings were still not ready to pack it in. They raked Brewer for four runs in the ninth, on five singles, bringing the final total to 19–11.

White Kings				**Royal Giants**			
Name	*Pos*	*AB*	*H*	*Name*	*Pos*	*AB*	*H*
Almada, Lou	RF	3	1	Bell, Cool Papa	CF	4	1
Powers, Les	1B	4	1	Hughes, Sammy T.	2B	5	3
Mesner, Steve	SS	3	3	Wright, Bill	LF	5	3
West, Max	CF	3	2	Suttles, Mule	RF	5	4
Adams, Buster	LF	3	1	West, Jim	1B	4	3
Ross, Don	3B	3	2	Snow, Felton	3B	6	3
Allaire, Bobby	2B	4	3	Walker, Jesse	SS	4	1
Owens,	C	3	1	Mackey, Biz	C	4	2
Gabler, Glenn	P	0	0	Matlock, Leroy	P	2	1
Frazier, Red	P	2	1	Brewer, Chet	P	3	0
Totals		28	15			42	21

White Kings   0 0 1 4 3 0 0 0 3—11—15—?
Royal Giants   5 5 2 2 1 0 0 4 x—19—21—?

Two Base Hits: Hughes, Wright, Suttles, Snow, Walker, Mackey, Owens, Allaire, Mesner
Three Base Hits: Bell, Wright, Allaire
Home runs: Suttles (2), J. West, Snow, Matlock, Frazier, M. West

	IP	H	SO	BB
Gabler (LP)	1⅓	7	0	0
Frazier	6⅔	14	4	3
Matlock (WP)	5	8	7	0
Brewer	4	7	5	2

The Giants maintained their momentum for three weeks, running off six wins against one tie, before being brought back to earth. Their first recorded loss came at the hands of the Kings, by a score of 7–5. The Giants actually led 5–3 after seven innings, on a home run by Jesse Walker, a triple by Hughes, and timely hits by Wright and West. But, in the top of the eighth, the White Kings climbed all over the Giants' little lefty, Leroy Matlock, for six base hits, all singles, for a 7–5 lead. Powers, Ross, Mesner, Herman, Adams, and Allaire provided the firepower. Steve Mesner also contributed a two-run homer in the third. The Giants won game two, 3–2 behind Pullman Porter.

No other team could get untracked for any period of time. The Detroit Stars took the San Diego Paris Inn down, by a count of 9–5, then beat the White Kings 7–2 behind Submarine Moss, with Moss himself hitting a home run. They were tied by the Kings in the second game of the doubleheader, 2–2 in five innings, then fell to the Royal Giants twice, 11–3 and 5–4, with Brewer and Porter outdueling Tommy Thompson and Moss. In a late season game,

Farleys signed Babe Herman to play against the Stars, but that ploy was an abject failure. The former Dodger great struck out three times against Submarine Moss.

It was an easy run for Biz Mackey's long ball bombers, as they were never challenged. They walloped Paris Inn 18–1 in mid–November, as Porter chucked a four-hitter. Jim West hit two singles and a home run, Wild Bill Wright hit three singles, and Brewer, Walker, and Snow chipped in with two hits apiece. Later in the month, the Giants suffered their only other loss of the season, a 10–4 thumping at the hands of the San Diego Farleys. Mule Suttles was not in the lineup for the Farleys game, as he spent several weeks on the sick list. But he probably wouldn't have made any difference in this game. The Farley bats were hot, and so was "Old Folks" Pillette, on the mound.

The Royal Giants didn't lose another game. As predicted, they walked off with the California Winter League championship rather handily, compiling a 20–2–1 record. Down the stretch they defeated the White Kings 13–6, dropped the Detroit Stars three straight, swept a doubleheader from the Mexican All-Stars, and took the count of Pirrone's All-Stars 14–5 and 6–3. In the White Kings game, they ripped Red Barrett for 11 hits, including a three-run homer by Jimmy Direaux and a grand slam by Mule Suttles. The Mule also had two singles in four trips to the plate.

The most interesting story of the season was played out 50 miles south of L.A., in San Diego. The newly formed Gold Club met the Farleys in a four game series, for San Diego bragging rights, if nothing else. In game one, Joe Orrell tossed a three-hit shutout at Farleys, winning 3–0. Ted Williams contributed a double to a two-run, first inning uprising. The Farleys came back to take the second game of the series, 10–4, behind Herm Pillette, but Williams solved the old master for a double and a home run, described in the *San Diego*

Herm "Old Folks" Pillette played professional baseball for 29 years, including five in the major leagues. He compiled records of 34–32 in the majors, 264–264 in the minors, and 22–24 in the California Winter League. (Dick Dobbins)

Union. "...Williams poled a terrific homer far over the center field fence, one of the lustiest blows in the history of the park." The Farleys captured the third game 7–3 to win the city championship, but bowed in a final, fourth encounter, as Tex Reichert, a member of the U.S. Navy, pitched a no-hitter to beat Pillette 1–0. It was "Ted Williams Day" at Monroe Field, as the local fans poured out to honor their teenage hero. And fittingly, Williams scored the only run of the game after singling in the fourth inning. He went to second on a single by Junk Walters and came home on another single, by Joe Dobbins. Reichert struck out 7 and walked 3 in his masterpiece.

The big man, Mule Suttles, dominated the batting statistics, leading the league in home runs (7) and batting .429. Steve Mesner of the White Kings won the batting championship with an average of .476. Other .400 hitters included Suttles' teammates Jim West (.461), Sammy T. Hughes (.435), and Jesse Walker (.405), plus Red Davis of the Detroit Stars (.409), and Don Ross of the White Kings (.400). On the hill, Chet Brewer was the leading pitcher, with a 7–2 record. Andrew "Pullman" Porter finished with a perfect 5–0 slate.

Off the field, Cum Posey made news by selecting his all-time Negro league all-star team. Posey, who was associated with black baseball since 1911, as a player, manager, club owner (Homestead Grays), Negro National League official, and founder of the East-West League, was one of the foremost experts on black baseball. His team consisted of:

Catcher:	Josh Gibson, Biz Mackey
Pitcher:	Joe Williams, Dick Redding, Joe Rogan, Eustaqio "Bombin" Pedroso, Satchel Paige, Dave Brown, and Willie Foster
First Base:	Ben Taylor and Buck Leonard
Second Base:	Sammy T. Hughes
Shortstop:	John Henry Lloyd
Third Base:	Jud Wilson
Outfield:	Cristobal Torriente, Oscar Charleston, Pete Hill
Utility:	Dick Lundy, Chester Brooks

Of the 19 players selected by Posey for his all-star team, ten of them played in the California Winter League. Notably missing from his team were Mule Suttles, John Beckwith, Cool Papa Bell, and Turkey Stearnes.

1937-38 California Winter League
Final Standings—Incomplete

	Wins	Losses	Ties
Philadelphia Royal Giants	21	3	1
Paris Inn/ GoldClub	10	6	0
Farley Clothiers	6	9	0
Detroit Stars	5	10	0
White King Soapsters	4	10	1
El Centro	2	4	0

Philadelphia Royal Giants Batting Statistics 1937-38

Name	Pos	G	AB	H	D	T	HR	BA
Bell, Cool Papa	CF	10	41	14	0	2*	1	.341
Hughes, Sammy T.	2B	10	46	20	1	1	0	.435
Wright, Wild Bill	LF	10	45	17	2	2*	2	.378
West, Jim	1B	9	39	18	0	1	3	.461
Snow, Felton	3B	10	47	14	4	0	1	.298
Walker, Jesse	SS	10	37	15	2	0	3	.405
Mackey, Biz	C	9	37	12	3	0	0	.324
Suttles, Mule	RF	10	42	18	3	0	7*	.429

Philadelphia Royal Giants Pitching Statistics 1937-38

Name	G	CG	W	L	IP	SO	BB	SH
Matlock, Leroy	5	2	3	1	24	—	—	0
Brewer, Chet	10	6	7	2	73	54	11	0
Porter, Pullman	5	3	5	0	36	22	14	0

Detroit Stars Batting Statistics 1937-38

Name	Pos	G	AB	H	D	T	HR	BA
Eccles, Rud	CF	6	27	5	1	1	0	.185
Davis, Red	2B	5	22	9	3	0	0	.409
Dunn, Jake	SS	6	21	5	2	0	0	.238
Radcliffe, Alex	3B	3	12	4	0	0	0	.333
Radcliffe, "Double Duty"	C	4	18	6	0	0	1	.333
Brooks, Mossy	1B	2	8	2	0	1	0	.250
Summers, Lonnie	LF	6	23	7	1	0	2	.304
McGinnis, Bub	RF	5	15	4	1	0	1	.267
Perdy,	RF	5	18	4	0	0	0	.222

Detroit Stars Pitching Statistics 1937-38

Name	G	CG	W	L	IP	SO	BB	SH
Moss, Porter "Submarine"	9	5	2	3	63	—	—	0
Direaux, Jimmy	3	0	0	2	14	—	—	0

White Kings Batting Statistics 1937-38

Name	Pos	G	AB	H	D	T	HR	BA
Powers, Les	1B	2	9	2	0	0	0	.222
Ross, Don	3B	6	25	10	2	1	1	.400
Mesner, Steve	SS	6	21	10	1	0	3	.476*
Herman, Babe	1B	4	15	5	1	0	1	.333
Adams, Buster	CF	4	13	3	1	0	0	.231
Allaire, Bobby	2B	7	27	9	2	1	0	.333
Moore, D.C.		3	11	2	0	0	0	.181
Allington, Bill	LF	5	23	8	1	1	1	.348
West, Max	RF	7	25	10	1	0	2	.400

White Kings Pitching Statistics 1937-38

Name	G	CG	W	L	IP	SO	BB	SH
Gomez, Vernon "Lefty"	4	1	1	3	29	16	7	0
Stine, Lee	5	0	0	2	18	—	—	0
Barrett, Charles "Red"	1	0	0	1	4	—	—	0

San Diego Farleys Batting Statistics 1937-38

Name	Pos	G	AB	H	D	T	HR	BA
Johnson, Don	SS	6	30	7	1	0	0	.267
Coscarart, Pete	2B	9	39	10	1	0	2	.256
Durst, Cedric	CF	8	34	9	0	0	0	.265
Jacobs, Ray	1B	4	16	7	3	0	0	.438
Holman, Ernie	3B	13	48	12	6*	0	0	.250
Joerndt, Ashley	LF	13	46	10	0	1	0	.217
Doerr, Harold	C	13	36	10	1	0	2	.278
Sada, Sad Sam	RF	2	7	4	1	0	0	.571

San Diego Farleys Pitching Statistics 1937-38

Name	G	CG	W	L	IP	SO	BB	SH
Pillette, Herm "Old Folks"	12*	8*	4	8	93	50	15	0
Horne, Berle	3	1	1	1	17	—	—	0
Smith, Henry "Swede"	5	4	3	1	37	19	14	0

Paris Inn/Gold Club Batting statistics 1937-38

Name	Pos	G	AB	H	D	T	HR	BA
Morehouse, Frank	SS	9	36	7	2	0	0	.194
Smith, Chet	3B	4	15	2	0	0	0	.133
Williams, Ted	LF	4	14	4	2	0	1	.287
Walters, Johnny "Junk"	1B	9	37	15	5	0	0	.405
Warren, Dallas	C	8	32	12	0	0	1	.375
Luscomb, Rod	RF	7	22	4	0	0	0	.182
Robinson, Lory	2B	7	26	6	0	0	0	.231
Green Frank	1B	6	21	4	0	0	0	.190

Paris Inn/ Gold Club Pitching Statistics 1937-38

Name	G	CG	W	L	IP	SO	BB	SH
Orrell, Joe	2	2	1	1	17	15	8	1
Reichert, Tex	2	2	1	1	18	14	5	1

The 1938-39 Season

The gradual deterioration of the California Winter League continued into the 1938-39 season. The overall talent hovered around a low minor league level, and fan interest in the league, as reflected in the lack of press coverage, reached an all-time low. Newspapers reported only two box scores and a handful of line scores for the entire season that began on October 12 and ended on December 26.

Tom Wilson was back in California for the winter league season with another representative ballclub. Schoolboy Griffith and Pullman Porter once again anchored the pitching staff, while the position players were headed by Mule Suttles, Wild Bill Wright, Sammy T. Hughes, and Biz Mackey. The White Kings had Babe Herman, Johnny Lindell, Les Powers, and Steve Mesner, and the Detroit Stars were led by Pepper Bassett and Jake Dunn.

The Philadelphia Royal Giants were favored to run rampant over the rest of the six team league. The *California Eagle* had some interesting comments about the winter league, as well as the possible integration of organized baseball, in its October 6th edition. "The first game of the 1938-39 season will be a doubleheader between the Elite Giants and Casey Campbell's White Kings. The Royal Giants, pennant winners of last season, had a tough time every time they played the White Kings, which include some of the best Coast and major league players in the game. Of added importance this year will be the presence of Thos. Wilson, famous baseball magnate and owner of the Washington Elites.... He declared in a letter that indications point to the fact that the first draft of colored players into the major leagues may take place next year, hence he is anxious to see that his players show their mettle against big league players as never before.... Starting at Washington and Central Avenue at 12 o'clock next Sunday, a parade led by Prof. LeBlanc's and Alton Reed's band will proceed on Central to Vernon, then east to the park. A number of clubs and other organizations besides business firms plan to have cars or floats in the line. Chief of Police Davis will pitch the first ball."

The opening game proved to be an exciting contest, with the Giants pulling out a tough, ten inning 4–3 victory, as reported by the *Eagle*. "A crowd estimated at 5,500 that had rushed in to nearly fill White Sox Park following the colorful street parade, were not only impressed with the opening ceremonies, but were entertained as never before at the start of any previous Winter League season. Movie stars, celebrities and famous folks from all walks of life, joining in all the festivities.... Drafted from the major and minor leagues, the white players started off by copping two runs before the Giants got going. It was a pitchers duel with ... Schoolboy Griffith ... facing Lindell, one of the New York Yankees best hurlers. Griffith struck out ten men; Lindell six." The second game of the doubleheader ended with a King victory, with former U.S.C. and Coast League pitching ace Joe Gonzalez on the hill. Unfortunately, other details of the games were not covered in the published accounts, nor were box scores printed.

The Giants met the Detroit Stars in the second game of the season, after the Stars had shellacked the Santa Paula team on opening day. The clash matched Morris (Barney or Yellow Horse?) of the Giants against Jimmy "The Great" Derricks (Direaux?) of the Stars. A noisy throng of 6,000 fans jammed White Sox Park to watch the two black teams go at each other. It was a good match for Tom Wilson's charges, as they handed the Stars a 5–2 defeat, behind the pitching of Morris, and home run balls off the bats of Chester Williams and Jim West. Pepper Bassett hit one out for the Detroit team. The second game was called on account of darkness at the end of the fifth inning, with the score deadlocked at 1-all.

A rematch between the Philadelphia Royal Giants and the White Kings on November 23, resulted in a close victory for the Giants, by the score of 8–7. The game was a slugfest from start to finish, with 29 base hits rattling around White Sox Park. Mule Suttles put on an exciting slugging show for the packed house, by slamming two home runs into the California sky, then driving in the game winner with a single in the eighth inning. Chester Williams chipped in with a homer, triple, and double. Former Brooklyn Dodger favorite Babe Herman rapped three doubles for the losers.

The *Los Angeles Times* printed the account of the next game, between the Giants and the Detroit Stars. "Heavy hitting of Mule Suttles, colored 'Babe Ruth,' who hit a home run, featured the victory of Philadelphia Royal Giants over the Detroit Stars, 8 to 5, at White Sox Park in their Winter League game yesterday afternoon. A second contest was called at the end of the fifth inning because of darkness, with the Giants leading 3 to 2."

Winter League officials, in an attempt to generate more interest in the pennant race, announced that the league champion, in addition to receiving the championship trophy, would also receive a check for $1,000, to be divided among the players. The proprietors of White Sox Park, trying to renew interest in winter league games, continued their aggressive and successful marketing strategies. Prior to the game of November 4, the *Eagle* noted, "As a special treat from the Citizens Cooperative committee, free sandwiches and beer will be served to anyone who presents an I.D. at the 40 cents gate, paying only 25 cents for their entrance."

The White Kings and the Detroit Stars crossed bats on November 7, at White Sox Park, but no box score of the game, won by the Kings 24–15, has been found. Eight pitchers were used in the game, a rare occurrence in the winter league. Les Powers of the Kings hit two home runs, while Joe Berkowitz hit one. Miller, Lindell, and Macon all had triples. Wade, Dunn and Davis had doubles.

Joe Pirrone, the Father of Winter League baseball, who was noticeably absent when the season began, finally agreed to enter a team in the league in mid–November. Pirrone had not been out of baseball. He managed a semi-pro club that traveled around the state, playing independent games, winter and summer. But the lure of the fast paced professional game drew him into the fray one more time. The *L.A. Times* noted his return. "Rivalry of 18 years standing will flare anew today when Joe Pirrone, pioneer winter league baseball promoter, leads his All-Stars against the Philadelphia Royal Giants in a twin bill at White Sox Park, starting at 1:30.

"It was 18 years ago that Pirrone organized his first team of Coast and major leaguers and brought a colored team from the East to meet his tossers. Each year the Negroes, picked from the ranks of the National and American colored circuits of the East, have handed the Pirrone nine setbacks in a majority of games. In fact, the sepia tossers have beaten all opposition, Pirrone's team proving to be the toughest.

"This afternoon, Joe returns to the ball park he built, with a powerful line-up that includes Babe Herman, Fern Bell, Steve Mesner, and other stars.

"Mule Suttles, Submarine Moss, 'One Wing' West, Ace Jefferson, and Biz Mackey, are some of the high-powered Giants who, according to critics, would be worth a million dollars to any major league club were they permitted in organized baseball."

Details of the Giants-All-Stars games were not located other than one brief account. The Giants captured the opener of the doubleheader, 4–2, with Submarine Moss besting Dutch Lieber of the Philadelphia Athletics. In game two, the Giants won 6–3 in five innings.

Tom Wilson's well oiled machine continued to run roughshod over all opposition, on their way to another league championship. They destroyed the Standard Oil team three straight, taking the Sunday doubleheader by scores of 11–5 and 4–2. Mule Suttles continued his bombarding, blasting two homers in the twin bill. Sammy T. Hughes and Lonnie Summers also went deep.

The season wound down with the Giants entertaining Joe Pirrone's All-Stars in a Christmas doubleheader. The turkey didn't taste very good for the Stars, who once again suffered defeat at the hands of the Black Bombers, this time by a score of 3–1. Ace Jefferson, on the mound for the Giants, gained the decision over Kakevich. The score of the second game was not found.

In the final game of the year, the Giants outscored Walker's Roofers, 4–2. Submarine Moss was the winning pitcher, over Bejan. Felton Snow and Mule Suttles hit four-baggers for the winners.

Accurate statistics were unavailable due to the paucity of box scores and line scores in the newspapers of the day. What stats there were, showed Felton Snow to be the leading hitter with an average of .500 in four games. Mule Suttles cracked six home runs in five recorded games, to lead in that category. Submarine Moss was the leading pitcher with a perfect 3–0 record.

1938-39 California Winter League
Final Standings—Incomplete

	Wins	Losses	Ties
Philadelphia Royal Giants	11	2	1
White Kings	4	2	0
El Paso Mexicans	4	2	1
San Diego All-Stars	3	5	0
Detroit Stars	2	4	1
Santa Paula	0	3	0

Philadelphia Royal Giants Batting Statistics 1938-39

Name	Pos	G	AB	H	D	T	HR	BA
Suttles, Mule	RF	5	18	8	1	0	6*	.444

Philadelphia Royal Giants Batting Statistics 1938-39

Name	Pos	G	AB	H	D	T	HR	BA
Wright, Bill	CF	2	9	5	0	1	0	.555
Hughes, Sammy T.	2B	4	15	6	1	0	2	.400
Williams, Chester	SS	3	13	5	1	1	2	.385
West, Jim	1B	3	11	4	1	0	2	.364
Summers, Lonnie	LF	3	11	2	0	0	1	.182
Snow, Felton	3B	4	14	7	2	0	2	.500*
Mackey, Biz	C	2	7	2	1	0	0	.287

Philadelphia Royal Giants Pitching Statistics 1938-39

Name	G	CG	W	L	IP	SO	BB	SH
Moss, Porter "Submarine"	3	3	3	0	27	—	—	0
Jefferson, Bill	2	2	1	1	18	—	—	0
Griffith, Schoolboy	2	2	2	0	19	19	4	0

San Diego All-Stars Batting Statistics 1938-39

Name	Pos	G	AB	H	D	T	HR	BA
Myatt, George	3B	1	2	0	0	0	0	.000
Durst, Cedric	RF	2	4	0	0	0	0	.000
Harris, Spencer	LF	5	14	7	1	0	1	.500
Coscarart, Pete	2B	5	17	2	0	0	0	.118
Coscarart, Steve	2B	5	15	6	2	0	0	.400
Coscarart, Joe	RF	6	19	3	1	0	2	.158
Holman, Ernie	2B	5	15	1	0	0	0	.077
Starr, Bill	C	4	15	6	0	0	2	.400

San Diego All-Stars Pitching Statistics 1938-39

Name	G	CG	W	L	IP	SO	BB	SH
Pillette, Herm	5	1	2	2	31	16	6	0
Reichert, Tex	4	2	1	2	22	22	9	0
Craghead, Howard	3	1	0	1	17	9	1	0

Miscellaneous Batting Statistics 1938-39

	Name	Team	Pos	G	AB	H	D	T	HR	BA
Herman, Babe		Pirrone's, W.K.	RF	2	7	4	3	0	1	.571
Powers, Les		White Kings	1B	2	6	4	1	1	2	.667
Lindell, Johnny		White Kings	P	1	3	1	0	1	0	.333
Dunn, Jake		Detroit Stars	SS	3	11	2	2	0	0	.182
Davis, T.		Detroit Stars	2B	3	11	5	1	0	0	.455
Bassett, Pepper		Detroit Stars	C	2	8	3	0	0	1	.375

Miscellaneous Pitching Statistics 1938-39

Name	Team	G	CG	W	L	IP	SO	BB	SH
Lindell, Johnny	White Kings	3	1	0	1	18	—	—	0
Pillette, Herm	San Diego	1	1	1	0	9	—	—	0
Direaux, Jimmy	Detroit Stars	1	1	0	1	8	—	—	0

The 1939-40 Season

Thirty-eight-year-old George "Mule" Suttles led the Negro league aggregation into the new winter league season. And Joe Pirrone entered a team in the league, at the start of the season, for the first time in three years. The two anchor teams were joined by the White Kings, Walker Roofers, San Diego, and the Long Beach All-Stars.

Manager Bill Wright's Royal Giants no longer had Biz Mackey or Chet Brewer. Wright and Suttles were the last of the potential Hall of Fame players to grace the playing fields of sunny California. But the team did have some gifted talent with Jake Dunn, Jim West, Terris McDuffie, and Thomas "Lefty" Glover.

Pirrone's rejuvenated All-Stars headlined Ernie Orsatti (career .306 hitter with the St. Louis Cardinals), Frank Demaree (.304 with the Chicago Cubs), Lin Storti (.281 with Minneapolis of the A.A.), Lou Novikoff (.452 with Los Angeles), Larry French, Julio Bonetti (20–5 with Los Angeles), and Bob Feller. Novikoff, known as "The Mad Russian," would lead four different minor leagues in batting between 1938 and 1941, with averages of .367, .368, .363, and .370. The White Kings, behind manager Babe Herman (.317 with Hollywood), had Johnny Lindell (who would go 23–4 with Newark of the I.L. in 1941), Les Powers, Steve Mesner (Chicago Cub shortstop), and Cleo Carlyle (.271 with San Diego). Walker Roofers were led by sensational young second baseman Jerry Priddy (.333 with Kansas City of the A.A.), and shortstop Arky Vaughan (.306 with Pittsburgh). San Diego was represented by Pete Coscarart (.277 with the Brooklyn Dodgers), Cedric Durst, Hal Patchett (a .291 career hitter in the PCL), and Herm Pillette (24 year veteran of the PCL).

The winter league season got underway officially on Sunday, October 8, with a doubleheader between the Royal Giants and Pirrone's All-Stars. For just the second time in twenty years, the league games were not played in White Sox Park. They were played in Gilmore Stadium, the new home of the Pacific Coast League Hollywood Stars, as

Gilmore Stadium, home of the Hollywood Stars of the PCL, was the home field for the Philadelphia Royal Giants during the winter of 1939-40. (Ray Medeiros)

reported in the *California Eagle*. "During the Winter League season, it will serve as the home park of the Royal Giants.

"Joe Pirrone, organizer of the league, foresees the best season in the history of the loop. With the moving to larger quarters, better accommodations and parking facilities are to be had at the new park which was just completed....

"Heretofore the home park of the Winter League has been at White Sox Park on the Eastside. Larger seating space and better quarters prompted the move."

If the Giants thought the 1939-40 California Winter League would be another walk-over, they were rudely awakened on opening day. The *Times* covered. "Pirrone's All-Stars yesterday served notice on the Winter League in general, and the Philadelphia Royal Giants in particular, that they will be the team to beat. In the opening doubleheader at Gilmore Field, the All-Stars trounced the colored major leaguers, 5–3 and 3–2.

"Frank Demaree's timely home run in the ninth inning of the first game tied up the count at 3-all, when it appeared the All-Stars were unable to get at the tricky slants of Schoolboy McDuffie. The homer disconcerted the young colored star, who faltered, issuing the first walk of the game to Ernie Orsatti in the 10th with one away. Red Kress, Detroit star, flied out to center, but Fern Bell connected and landed on second, bringing Orsatti home.

"In the second seven-inning bobtailed feature, Jake Dunn's home run with Carter on first gave the Royal Giants a first inning lead. However, the old ball game was tied up in the fourth when the All-Stars reached pitcher Lefty Glover, colored speedball ace. A single and Larry Barton's home run over the right field wall did the trick.

"Kress' single in the fifth, plus a single by Fern Bell, and a wide throw to third by right fielder Mule Suttles, allowed Kress to slip home with the run that proved to be the winner."

First Game

Pirrone's All-Stars				Philadelphia Royal Giants			
Name	*Pos*	*AB*	*H*	*Name*	*Pos*	*AB*	*H*
Orsatti, Ernie	RF	4	2	Carter, Marlin	LF	5	1
Kress, Red	SS	5	1	Dunn, Jake	2B	5	0
Bell, Fern	CF	5	2	Wright, Bill	CF	5	1
Demaree, Frank	LF	3	1	Suttles, Mule	RF	5	2
Adams, Buster	3B	5	1	Hoskins, Bill	LF	4	2
Cissell, Bill	2B	5	1	West, Jim	1B	4	1
Barton, Larry	1B	4	0	Walker, Jesse	3B	4	2
Montgomery, Al	C	4	0	Bassett, Pepper	C	4	0
Bonetti, Julio	P	4	1	McDuffie, Terris	P	4	0
Totals		39	9			40	9

Pirone's All-Stars   0 0 0   0 0 0   1 1 1   2—5—9—3
Philadelphia Royal Giants   1 0 0   0 0 2   0 0 0   0—3—9—1

Two Base Hits: Bell (2), Dunn
Home Run: Demaree

	IP	H	SO	BB
Bonetti (WP)	9	9	1	0
McDuffie (LP)	9	9	3	2

As far as the season was concerned, that was the high point for the All-Stars. Their ship slowly disappeared beneath the waves as the season progressed. They did have one other shining moment however. On the Wednesday following opening day, Joe Pirrone signed American League pitching phenom, Bob Feller, to pitch for his team against the Royal Giants. The fuzzy cheeked 20-year-old flame-thrower out of Van Meter, Iowa, had just completed a sensational year in which he led the junior circuit in victories (24), and strikeouts (246). His appearance in the winter league generated considerable interest in Southern California, and helped pack the stadium. The big 6', 185 pound right-hander toyed with the Giants for seven innings, yielding just five hits, one of which was a triple by opposing pitcher Bill Harvey, and fanning 14 batters. He left with the game deadlocked at 2-apiece, but the Giants jumped on his replacement, Lee Stine, for three runs and a 5–3 victory.

The White Kings invaded Gilmore Stadium in week two, to challenge the powerful Philadelphia contingent. The game matched up-and-coming Johnny Lindell of the Oakland Acorns against Lefty Glover of the Baltimore Elite Giants. The Giants drew first blood when they countered three times in the bottom of the first, on an error by King second baseman Ralph Rhein, a triple by Wild Bill Wright, a single by Mule Suttles, and a single by Bill Hoskins. Suttles extended the Giants lead to 4–0 in the fifth when he drilled a Lindell knuckleball high over the left-center field wall. Glover was coasting until the seventh, when the wheels came off his wagon. Lindell singled with one out, and Bill Allington walked. Manager Babe Herman, leading by example, entered the game as a pinch-hitter and promptly lashed a two-run double to right-center field. Steve Mesner followed with a single over second to bring Herman in with the third run of the inning. The Kings took the lead with two runs in the top of the eighth on a Giant error, two walks, a single, and a double by third baseman Jewell, but the Giants came back to tie the count in the bottom of the inning on an error and singles by Walker and Bassett. The game remained tied into the tenth when the White Kings' pitcher, Johnny Lindell won his own game. He hit a two-out triple and carried over the game winner on a single by Allington.

The Philadelphia Giants record stood at a disappointing 1–3 after their loss to the Kings, but things would get worse before they'd get better. Walker Roofers came to town, looking for blood, and they got it. They swept a twin-bill from Bill Wright's charges, by scores of 7–4 and 2–1 in five innings. The opener was close for eight innings, with the Roofers scoring two in the first off Giant southpaw Bill Harvey, the Giants coming back to tie it with single runs in the second and third innings off J. Bittner, and the Roofers recapturing the lead with two runs in the top of the fifth. The score was still 4–2 when the Walker sluggers pummeled Harvey and McDuffie for a big three-spot in the top of the ninth. Singles by Hoskins and Bassett and a double by West narrowed the margin to 7–4, but that's where it ended. In the abbreviated nightcap, Arky Vaughan led off the game with a sharp single, and Jerry Priddy hit the ball over the left field fence, for a 2–0 Roofer lead. The Philadelphians scored one in the second on singles by Suttles and West and a sacrifice by Hoskins, but that was it. George "Lefty" Darrow made the two runs stand up for the win.

The Royal Giants pounded Pirrone's All-Stars 6–1 as October came to an end. Terris McDuffie shackled the Stars with six hits, striking out five. Jake Dunn with a single, double, and triple, led the Philadelphia attack. Wright and McDuffie had two hits apiece. That victory seemed to ignite Wild Bill Wright's boys. Over the final six weeks of the season, they were almost unbeatable, winning eight games against a single loss.

They started off November by sweeping the White Kings 4–0 and 3–1. The first game was a gem, as reported in the *Los Angeles Times*. "Lefty Glover, the tall, lean southpaw, bounced himself into baseball's winter annex of the Hall of Fame when he pitched a no-hit, no-run game as the Philadelphia Royal Giants blanked Babe Herman's White Kings, 4–0, ... at Gilmore Field.

"...Glover was the big noise of the day as he turned back the Soapsters by allowing only 30 White Kings to come to bat. The colored southpaw struck out only four, but allowed only three balls to be hit to the outfield as he kept the White Kings beating his curves into the dirt.

"The Giants scored off Lindell in the first inning when Carter walked, stole second, and scored on Dunn's single. That was enough, but they clinched it with three more in the sixth."

The following week, the Royal Giants got revenge for the two losses to Walker Roofers, by beating George McDonald's team twice, 5–3 and 2–1. "No-Hit" Glover bested Lefty Darrow in the opener, and Terris "The Great" McDuffie beat Degan in the nightcap. Dunn and Summers each had two hits in the opener. Dunn had two more hits in game two.

The long road back finally led to the promised land. When the Negro leaguers topped the All-Stars 8–6 on November 19, it gave them sole possession of first place, by ½ game over Pirrone's troops. The hero of the Giant victory was manager Wild Bill Wright whose long home run in the fourth inning got his team off and running. Summers and Hoskins followed Wright's example by driving balls over the fence in the same inning. The Giants added a two-spot in the fifth and a deuce in the sixth, and McDuffie made them hold up, but it was a struggle.

Joe Pirrone's battered warriors had one more chance to claim the winter league title when they met the Philadelphia Royal Giants in a season-ending doubleheader at Gilmore Stadium. The All-Stars had to win both game to take the flag. But Bill Wright's charges weren't about to let that happen. Terris McDuffie started on the hill for the Giants in game one, and Joe Pirrone countered with his ace, right-hander Johnny Lindell. Details of the game are few, but McDuffie tossed a four-hitter to clinch the championship 5–3. Triples by Lindell and Red Kress accounted for the All-Stars' scores. Bill Harvey blanked the Stars in the nightcap, 4–0, with Joe Pirrone taking the loss.

Jake Dunn, the Philadelphia Royal Giants outstanding second baseman, swatted the ball at a .350 clip to capture the batting championship. He also shared the home run crown with Bill Wright, each man hitting two. Terris "The Great" McDuffie showed the way in victories with five, and "No-Hit" Lefty Glover had the highest winning percentage at .750, on a 3–1 record. And, of course, Glover's sensational no-hitter was the highlight of the season.

1939-40 California Winter League
Final Standings—Incomplete

	Wins	Losses	Ties
Philadelphia Royal Giants	10	6	1
Long Beach All-Stars	1	0	0
Pirrone's All-Stars	3	5	1
Walker Roofers	2	3	0
White Kings	1	2	0
San Diego 7-Up	1	4	0

Philadelphia Royal Giants Batting Statistics 1939-40

Name	Pos	G	AB	H	D	T	HR	BA
Wright, Bill	CF	10	37	10	0	1	2*	.270
Suttles, Mule	RF	5	18	8	0	0	1	.444
Carter, Marlin	SS	7	30	4	0	0	0	.133
Dunn, Jake	2B	11	40	14	3	1	2*	.350*
Hoskins, Bill	LF	9	33	10	2	0	0	.303
West, Jim	1B	7	27	5	2	0	0	.185
Walker, Jesse	2B	7	25	4	0	0	0	.160
Bassett, Pepper	C	7	26	8	1	0	0	.308
Summers, Lonnie	RF	3	11	4	1	0	0	.364

Philadelphia Royal Giants Pitching Statistics 1939-40

Name	G	CG	W	L	IP	SO	BB	SH
McDuffie, Terris	9	6	5*	3	54	—	—	0
Harvey, Bill	4	2	2	1	28	—	—	1
Glover, Thomas "Lefty"	5	4	3	1	36	18	13	2

Miscellaneous Batting Statistics 1939-40

Name	Team	Pos	G	AB	H	D	T	HR	BA
Allington, Bill	White Kings	LF	2	6	2	0	0	0	.333
Mesner, Steve	White Kings	SS	3	13	3	0	0	1	.231
Powers, Les	White Kings	1B	2	8	1	0	0	0	.125
Herman, Babe	White Kings	RF	1	2	2	1	0	0	1.000
Orsatti, Ernie	Pirrone's A.S.	LF	4	16	5	0	0	0	.313
Kress, Red	Pirrone's A.S.	SS	6	23	9	0	1	0	.405
Cissell, Bill	Pirrone's A.S.	2B	4	17	6	0	0	0	.353
Barton, Larry	Pirrone's A.S.	1B	4	15	3	0	0	1	.200
Priddy, Jerry	Walker Roofers	2B	2	8	5	2	0	1	.625
Vaughan, Arky	Walker Roofers	SS	4	15	3	0	0	0	.200
Lindell, Johnny	Pirrone, W.K.	P	3	11	3	0	2	0	.273
Durst, Cedric	San Diego 7-UP	1B	4	15	5	1	0	0	.333
Holman, Ernie	San Diego 7-Up	3B	4	14	2	0	0	0	.143

Miscellaneous Pitching Statistics 1939-40

Name	Team	G	CG	W	L	IP	SO	BB	SH
Lindell, Johnny	Pirrones, W.K.	3	3	1	2	25	12	6	0
Feller, Bob	Pirrone's A.S.	1	0	0	0	7	14	—	0
Stine, Lee	Pirrone's A.S.	3	2	2	1	20	11	1	0
Darrow, Lefty	Walker Roofers	3	3	2	1	25	—	—	1
Tobin, Pat	San Diego 7-Up	3	0	1	2	19	13	7	0

8

Season Summaries 1940–1944

The 1940-41 Season

The decade of the 1940s witnessed the gradual demise of the California Winter League. After almost fifty years of providing entertainment and excitement for the fans on the west coast, the league slowly went the way of the horse-and-buggy and the Model-T. The reasons for its demise were many. In the late 1930s, opportunities for black players to practice their art exploded. In addition to the Cuban Winter League that provided integrated baseball as early as the 1880s, other leagues blossomed around the western hemisphere. A Dominican Republic summer league siphoned off some of the best talent in the Negro leagues in 1937. The Puerto Rican Winter League began in 1938, and is still active, more than sixty years later. A professional baseball league was formed in Mexico in 1937, and by 1940 such stars as Lonnie Summers, Wild Bill Wright, Frank Duncan, Sam Bankhead, Ted Radcliffe, and Hilton Smith were displaying their wares south of the border. They would be followed a year later by Josh Gibson, Cool Papa Bell, Ray Dandridge, Willie Wells, and Lefty Glover. A winter league was formed in Venezuela in 1946.

Another event that had a major impact on winter baseball in California was World War II. The global conflict decimated the baseball structure all over the country as thousands of able bodied men marched off to serve their country in the armed forces. The heavy loss of life during the war left professional baseball just a shell of its former self. The war also led indirectly to another momentous event that spelled finis to the California Winter League—the integration of organized baseball. The success of Jackie Robinson with the Brooklyn Dodgers opened up the floodgates, as one major league team after another scrambled to sign the great Negro league players to big league contracts.

In 1940, what with the talent drain from other countries in the western hemisphere, the level of play in the California Winter League decreased considerably, particularly from the Negro league side. Gone were the legendary players of the past, like Bullet Joe Rogan, Mule Suttles, and Turkey Stearnes. In their places were journeymen players like Henry Spearman, Red Moore, Bud Barbee, and Nate Moreland. Some of the veterans of previous winter league wars returned, including 43-year-old Biz Mackey and 35-year-old Felton Snow, but they were just playing out the string, long past their prime. Henry Kimbro was one new addition to the Baltimore Elite Giants who was a world class player. The 5'8", 175 pound left-handed hitting outfielder starred in the Negro leagues for 14 years, compiling a .316 batting average, and was, as Jim Riley noted, "a compact blend of speed and power ... he was an outstanding line-drive hitter for both average and power, and was a constant base stealing threat.... A good defensive center fielder with great range and a good arm, he was especially adept at going into the alleys on flys."

The Giants' lineup had Kimbro in left field, Snow at shortstop, Sammy T. Hughes at second, Spearman at third, Goose Curry, a 35-year-old outfielder, who would compile a .309 batting average over an 18 year Negro league career, in right, Red Moore on first, Charlie Biot in center, Biz Mackey behind the plate, and Barbee and Moreland on the mound. They were competitive, but not great.

Joe Pirrone countered with a solid major league and high minor league lineup that included Fern Bell, Jerry Priddy, Lou Novikoff, Babe Herman, Bill Cissell, Lou Stringer, Wally Berger, Jesse Flores, and Lee Stine. The White Kings had Les Powers, Steve Mesner, Babe Herman, Jerry Priddy, Bob Lemon, Bobby Sturgeon, Ralph Houk, Herschel Lyons, and Lou Tost. The fourth team in the league, the Mexican All-Stars, showcased such talents as Lonnie Summers, Jesse Flores, Francisco Castaneda, Jose Polomo, Manuel Arroyo, and Ramon Lagunas.

As noted previously, it was possible for the white players to play for more than one team, as was the case with Herman and Priddy, because the Negro league team played games every weekend, while the other teams usually played the Negro league entry on a rotating basis. Therefore, if Pirrone's All-Stars were scheduled to play, Herman and Priddy played for them. But if the All-Stars were off, and the White Kings were scheduled, Herman and Priddy donned White Kings uniforms.

The winter season opened on Sunday, October 13, with manager Felton Snow's Baltimore Elite Giants and Pirrone's All-Stars mixing it up in a twin bill. The game

Biz Mackey, the Negro leagues' finest receiver, was active in both the Negro leagues and the California Winter League from 1920 to 1945. (John B. Holway)

was played in White Sox Park, as reported by the *Pittsburgh Courier*. "Some 5,000 spectators, including many of Hollywood's Biggest names, were on hand for the festivities....

"Jerry Priddy, $50,000 New York Yankee purchase, ruined pitcher Barbee's league debut when he clouted a homer over the right field screen in the eighth with one aboard, icing the game for the Pirrones."

The game was a nail-biter to the end with the All-Stars winning 4–3. Lou Novikoff rapped four hits, including two doubles and a home run, while Priddy finished with three hits. Spearman and Barbee both had a single and a double for the losers. In the nightcap, the Giants bounced back behind the shutout pitching of 23-year-old southpaw Nate Moreland, to win

Babe Herman, out of the major leagues since 1937, went back to the Brooklyn Dodgers as a war-time replacement in 1945.

the inning to recapture the lead at 8–7. Then it was the Kings' turn. They tallied twice in the top of the ninth, but once again the Giants bounced back to tie it in the bottom half. In the tenth, winning pitcher Barbee, apparently tired of the way things were going, took matters into his own hands. He slammed a triple to left field and carried over the winning run on a single by Felton Snow.

After a 9–3 loss to Jesse Flores and the All-Stars, the Baltimore Elite Giants went on a roll. In quick succession, they beat the Chihuahua Mexicans 10–7, hammered the White Kings 17–12, beat the Mexicans again 5–3, and took the All-Stars into camp twice 11–4 and 6–2, to take a comfortable lead in the pennant race. In the Kings game, the powerful Negro leaguers unleashed an 18 hit attack, led by Snow, Spearman and Barbee with three hits apiece. Spearman and Bar-

the five inning affair 7–0. Henry Spearman belted a round tripper and two singles to pace the Giant attack.

Manager Snow kept his team running in high gear the entire eleven week season. They staged a stirring comeback to edge the White Kings in week two, 10–9. Bud Barbee of the Elites, and Lou Tost and Herschel Lyons of the Kings struggled throughout the game, with the lead changing hands several times. Barbee held a 3–1 lead after six innings, but the Kings fell on him for a big six spot in the top of the seventh, for a 7–3 lead. The Giants rallied in the bottom of

Lou Novikoff, called the Mad Russian, compiled a .337 batting average in the minor leagues, between 1937 and 1950. He also hit .282 with the Phillies and Cubs in the National League between 1942 and 1946. (Dick Dobbins)

bee each had a home run and Spearman chipped in with a triple. Red Moore, Felton Snow, and Sammy T. Hughes also hit for the circuit. The White Kings fielded a strong team against Baltimore, with such familiar names as Ralph Kiner, Bob Lemon, Bobby Sturgeon, Ralph Houk, and Peanuts Lowrey, but they were outclassed on this day.

White Kings

Name	Pos	AB	H
Leyrer,	CF	3	0
Powers, Les	1B	2	1
Mesner, Steve	2B	3	2
Kiner, Ralph	RF	4	1
Lemon, Bob	LF	3	1
Sturgeon, Bobby	SS	3	1
Lowrey, Peanuts	3B	2	1
Houk, Ralph	C	2	0
Tost, Lou	P	0	0
Gonzalez, Joe	P	2	2
Herman, Babe	PH	1	0
Crandall, Jimmy	PH	1	0
Totals		26	9

Baltimore Elite Giants

Name	Pos	AB	H
Kimbro, Henry	LF	5	1
Snow, Felton	SS	5	3
Hughes, Sammy T.	2B	4	2
Spearman, Henry	3B	4	3
Curry, Goose	RF	3	2
Moore, Red	1B	4	2
Biot, Charlie	CF	4	2
Mackey, Biz	C	4	0
Barbee, Bud	P	4	3
		37	18

White Kings   0 0 0   0 0 1   1— 2— 9—4
Baltimore Elite Giants   0 0 0   8 1 8   0—17—18—1

Two Base Hits: Spearman, Moore, Mesner, Gonzalez
Three Base Hits: Hughes
Home Runs: Spearman, Barbee, Moore, Hughes, Snow

	IP	H	SO	BB
Tost (LP)	3⅔	10	0	1
Gonzalez	2⅓	8	2	0
Barbee (WP)	7	9	3	6

As the season wound down, the All-Stars and White Kings fielded a combined team in an effort to derail the steamroller called the Baltimore Elite Giants. The combined team, which wasn't as strong as the Kings team that suffered through the 17-2 debacle, somehow managed to defeat Snow's charges, by a count of 10-6. Les Powers, the Kings left-handed hitting first baseman, pulled two balls over the short right field screen in White Sox Park. The Giants led 1-0 going into the eighth inning, but the White Kings put up a six spot in the eight and added four more in the ninth, for the victory. Powers homered in both innings. Winning pitcher Lou Tost also homered off Jesse Brown.

When the final curtain came down, the Baltimore Elite Giants were the California Winter League champions, with a record of 9-4. Henry Spearman took the batting crown with an average of .500. Sammy T. Hughes was the home run champion with four in ten games. Bud Barbee and Nate Moreland both finished with 3-1 records, and Barney Morris put up two victories without a loss.

1940-41 California Winter League
Final Standings—Incomplete

	Wins	Losses	Ties
Baltimore Elite Giants	9	4	0
Pirrone's All-Stars	4	3	0
White Kings	0	2	0
Chihuahua Mexicans	1	5	0

Baltimore Elite Giants Batting Statistics 1940-41

Name	Pos	G	AB	H	D	T	HR	BA
Kimbro, Henry	LF	9	38	13	1	0	0	.342
Snow, Felton	SS	10	42	13	3	0	2	.310
Hughes, Sammy T.	2B	10	38	12	2	1	4*	.316
Spearman, Henry	3B	9	36	18	4*	0	2	.500*
Moore, Red	1B	9	34	9	2	0	2	.276
Curry, Goose	RF	9	29	11	3	0	1	.379
Biot, Charlie	CF	9	28	5	1	0	0	.179
Mackey, Biz	C	13	23	4	1	0	0	.173
Wright, Bill	RF	2	7	3	0	0	2	.429

Baltimore Elite Giants Pitching Statistics 1940-41

Name	G	CG	W	L	IP	SO	BB	SH
Barbee, Bud	5	3	3	1	41	22	20	0
Moreland, Nate	5	3	3	1	25	20	5	1
Brown, Jesse	3	1	1	1	17	—	—	0
Morris, Barney	2	2	2	0	18	—	—	0

Pirrone's All-Stars Batting Statistics 1940-41

Name	Pos	G	AB	H	D	T	HR	BA
Bell, Fern	CF	4	13	2	0	0	0	.154
Novikoff, Lou	LF	3	11	6	1	0	2	.545
Cissell, Bill	2B	6	24	9	1	0	0	.375
Berger, Wally	RF	3	11	2	0	0	0	.188
Dapper, Cliff	C	5	14	5	2	1	0	.357
Barton, Larry	1B	3	13	2	0	0	0	.154

Pirrone's All-Stars Pitching Statistics 1940-41

Name	G	CG	W	L	IP	SO	BB	SH
Flores, Jesse (Incl. MEX.AS)	3	2	2	1	25	22	3	0
Gay, Fred	2	1	1	1	15	—	—	0

White Kings Batting Statistics 1940-41

Name	Pos	G	AB	H	D	T	HR	BA
Powers, Les (Incl. AS)	1B	3	13	4	0	0	3	.308
Mesner, Steve	3B	2	8	4	2	0	0	.500
Herman, Babe (Incl. AS)	RF	4	11	1	0	0	0	.082
Priddy, Jerry (Incl. AS)	2B	3	11	5	0	0	1	.455
Lemon, Bob	LF	2	8	2	0	0	0	.250
Sturgeon, Bobby (Incl. AS)	SS	3	11	5	0	0	0	.455
Houk, Ralph	C	2	6	2	1	0	0	.333

White Kings Batting Statistics 1940-41

Name	Pos	G	AB	H	D	T	HR	BA
Kiner, Ralph	RF	1	4	1	0	0	0	.250
Lowrey, Peanuts	3B	1	2	1	0	0	0	.500

White Kings Pitching Statistics 1940-41

Name	G	CG	W	L	IP	SO	BB	SH
Tost, Lou	2	0	0	1	9	—	5	0

The 1941-42 Season

War clouds loomed on the United States horizon as the 1941-42 California Winter League baseball season got underway. World War II had been raging in Europe since 1939, with Adolf Hitler's mighty German blitzkrieg rolling relentlessly over the European continent, from France in the west to Romania in the east, and from Norway in the north to the Greece in the south. Only the courageous British and Russian peoples stood between the Nazi war machine and complete domination of the hemisphere. Hitler's ally in the South, Benito Mussolini's Fascist Italy, was subjugating Libya and Sudan while, in the Far East, the Empire of Japan, the third member of the Axis coalition, was overrunning eastern China, French Indo-China, and the East Indies. It was almost certain that the United States would be dragged into the conflict sooner rather than later. In the fall of 1941, Uncle Sam stood on the brink of the great war.

The news media was more concerned with the political and military situation around the country and around the world in the fall of 1941 and, as a result, there was little coverage of the baseball activities on the west coast. What coverage there was indicated that the winter league consisted of just two teams, the Royal Giants and their perennial foes, Joe Pirrone's All-Stars. The first game of the season pitted the Royal Giants against the All-Stars, but it might have been a preseason exhibition game instead of an official winter league game. In any case,

Joe Pirrone had signed two of the greatest major league sluggers for the game, Ted Williams and Jimmie Foxx. Foxx was nearing the end of a glorious career, which saw him crack 534 career home runs (2nd to Babe Ruth), while batting .325 with 1,921 RBIs. Ted Williams, on the other hand, was just 23 years old, and was on the brink of greatness. In the American League season just completed, Boston's "Splendid Splinter" became the major league's last .400 hitter, finishing at .406. Williams' average stood at an even .400 on the last day of the season, and manager Joe Cronin offered to let him sit out the final doubleheader to preserve his average. But the brash Californian refused. Instead he went out and banged out six base hits in eight at-bats to pick up six points in his average. No one has approached .400 in the last sixty years.

The Major & Minor League All-Stars defeated the Royal Giants 9–6 in a thrilling matchup, under the lights in Wrigley Field. The All-Stars drew first blood when Peanuts Lowrey singled and came across on an infield hit by Williams. The Giants came back with two in their half of the first on a base hit off All-Star starter Jesse Flores, a walk, and a couple of errors. Biz Mackey's crew increased their lead to 3–1 in the third on a single by Hughes and a double by Flonnoy. That was the last lead the Giants would have. The Stars pushed over four runs in the bottom of the third. Ted Williams ignited the fireworks by slamming a two-run homer over the right field wall. Two more runs came over on a double by Novikoff and singles by Nanny Fernandez and Eddie Mayo. The teams traded runs in the sixth. Then, in the eighth, the major leaguers put the game away with another three spot. Ted Williams doubled with two on to drive in one, and Lou Novikoff slammed another double to drive in two more. Two runs in the ninth by the Giants made the final score 9–6.

The official winter league opener was played the following Sunday, October 12, but without Williams and Foxx. They were forbidden to play according to the rules laid down by Commissioner Kenesaw Landis. Pirrone's boys didn't need the two big American League sluggers however. They swept two from the Royal Giants by scores of 10–7 and 2–1, at Wrigley Field. The *Los Angeles Times* covered the opening day. "Joe Pirrone's all-star array of minor and major leaguers took both ends of a twin bill from the Eastern Colored Giants at Wrigley Field yesterday afternoon, winning 10–7 and 2–1, before about 3,000 fans who braved the drizzle and chilly weather.

"In the first, Jess Flores got credit for the victory although Lou Tost finished on the mound for the All-stars. Joe Fillmore was the losing pitcher. The score was knotted at 7-all going into the ninth and the All-Stars scored three runs in their half to gain the victory. 'Red' Kress, St. Paul manager, got four hits, two of them doubles, while Roy Partee drove in five runs with three hits to feature the slugging win of the All-Stars. Kimbro got three hits for the colored club." Chet Brewer started on the mound for the Giants, and left after six innings with a 5–4 lead, but Fillmore was knocked out of the box after surrendering three runs in ⅔ of an inning.

The last recorded game was played on October 26, with the same results. Jess Flores, the tough Mexican right-hander, shackled the Royal Giants 2–1 in 11 innings. Not only did Flores pitch a complete game, he also was the offensive star, scoring the tying run in the bottom of the ninth, then singling in the game winner in the 11th. Bill Jewell had three hits for the winners, while Fern Bell, Spencer Harris, Roy Partee, and Flores each had two. Jake Dunn and Joe Fillmore banged out two hits apiece for the Giants.

On December 7, 1941, aircraft belonging to the Empire of Japan suddenly and viciously attacked the United States fleet anchored in Pearl Harbor, in the Hawaiian Islands, plunging America into a long and bloody war. The winter baseball season came to an abrupt end, as the players, as well as the rest of the country, got down to more serious business.

1941-42 California Winter League
Final Standings—Incomplete

	Wins	Losses	Ties
Pirrone's All-Stars	4	0	0
Royal Giants	0	4	0

Miscellaneous Batting Statistics 1941-42

Name	Team	Pos	G	AB	H	D	T	HR	BA
Kimbro, Henry	Royal Giants	CF	2	10	4	0	0	0	.400
Hughes, Sammy T.	Royal Giants	2B	3	12	4	0	0	0	.333
Flonnoy,	Royal Giants	3B	2	10	2	0	0	0	.200
Dunn, Jake	Royal Giants	LF	2	8	3	0	0	0	.375
Mackey, Biz	Royal Giants	C	2	7	1	0	0	0	.143
Lowrey, Peanuts	Pirrone's AS	3B	3	11	3	0	0	0	.273
Fernandez, Nanny	Pirrone's AS	SS	2	10	1	0	0	0	.100
Novikoff, Lou	Pirrone's AS	LF	2	8	3	2	0	0	.375

Kress, Red	Pirrone's AS	2B	2	9	4	2	0	0	.444
Bell, Fern	Pirrone's AS	CF	2	8	5	0	0	0	.625
Partee, Roy	Pirrone's AS	C	2	8	5	0	0	0	.625
Williams, Ted	Pirrone's AS	LF	1	3	3	1	0	1	1.000
Foxx, Jimmie	Pirrone's AS	1B	1	3	1	0	0	0	.333

Miscellaneous Pitching Statistics 1941-42

Name	Team	G	CG	W	L	IP	SO	BB	SH
Brewer, Chet	Royal Giants	2	0	0	1	11	10	4	0
Flores, Jesse	Pirrone's AS	3	2	3	0	20	11	2	0

The 1942-43 Season

During 1942, America was in a state of turmoil as it struggled to convert its manufacturing facilities from consumer products to military arms and equipment. Able bodied men enlisted in the Army, Navy, and Marines in record numbers. A military draft was initiated, requiring all men between the ages of 21 and 35 to register for military duty. Around the world, the war exploded. The United States struck back at the Empire of Japan quickly and decisively. On April 18, 1942, Maj. Gen. James H. Doolittle led a squadron of B-25 bombers from the aircraft carrier *Hornet* on a bombing mission to the Japanese mainland, striking industrial plants and shipyards in Tokyo, Kobe, Yokohama, and Nagoya. Two months later, the Navy won a major sea victory at Midway Island. In the European theatre, American soldiers joined with their British allies in ending German aggression in Africa.

Although the entire world was at war, President Franklin D. Roosevelt urged the continuance of professional baseball as a morale booster on the home front. He felt the mothers and fathers of the fighting men, and the people working in the defense industries, needed some diversions to take their minds off the horrors of war. The game continued, but it struggled to survive during the war years. The minor league system, consisting of 40 leagues around the country in 1941, dropped to 31 leagues by the beginning of 1942, and to just 9 leagues by the end of 1943. The leagues that survived were made up of men who were either too young or too old for military service, or men who were deferred from service due to physical or emotional impairments, or because they held critical defense-related jobs at home. As noted in *The Encyclopedia of Minor League Baseball*, "The 1944 season saw one-armed Pete Gray hit .333 for Memphis, and The Sporting News Minor League Player of the Year was forty-year-old former major leaguer Rip Collins, who hit .389 for Albany ... wartime restrictions made the operation of minor league franchises difficult. Gasoline rationing affected teams that travelled by bus. Curtailed railroad transportation hurt other ballclubs."

The problems that affected organized baseball also affected winter baseball on the coast. Restrictions on travel limited the number of players available for the winter league. Negro league players were also affected in another way. The United States government had entered into an agreement with Mexico, allowing Negro leaguers to travel to Mexico to play baseball. In exchange, Mexico agreed to supply badly needed labor for the U.S. defense industry.

There were very few winter baseball games reported in California newspapers during the winter of 1942-43. The *Los Angeles Times* did report on one such encounter. "Loaded down with a number of stars from The Negro National League, the famed Elite Giants will clash with Chamberlain's Pasadena Athletics in a Winter

League doubleheader this afternoon at White Sox Park.

"Festivities will start at 1:15. Jess Cox, veteran baseball coach, will handle the Crown City club this afternoon with high hopes of knocking over the potent Giants." No details on the games were presented in subsequent editions of the paper, with the exception of the scores. Pasadena took the opener by a score of 4 to 2, and the Giants came back to take the nightcap, 2–1.

It appears there were two Negro league teams playing winter baseball in California in 1942-43, the Elite Giants and the Royal Giants. The Royal Giants may have been the same organization that had played in California since 1920. Their team included Wild Bill Wright, Chester Williams, Howard Easterling, and Nate Moreland. The Elite Giants players, Donald Troy, Andy Anderson, Bullett Hector, and a pitcher named Thomas, seemed to be war-time replacements of limited skills.

Only two games involving the Royal Giants were recovered. In an early November encounter, The Giants lost to the Major-Minor All-Stars, 11–5. George Caster of the St. Louis Browns (8–2 in 1942) was the winning pitcher, while Nate Moreland took the loss. Shortstop Vern Stephens, also of the Browns (.294 with 14 homers and 92 RBIs), was the batting star of the day with a single, a double, and two home runs, in five at-bats.

On December 27, at White Sox Park, the Los Alamitos Naval Air Base baseball team defeated the Royal Giants 5–3, behind the pitching of Vern Olson (6–9 with the Chicago Cubs in 1942). Cliff Dapper of the Brooklyn Dodgers was the catcher, while outfielder Jack Graham of the Dodgers slammed a two-run homer. Tommy Thompson absorbed the loss for the Giants.

During the war, the best professional baseball teams outside of organized baseball, were found in military installations, such as the Great Lakes Naval Training Station, Fort Riley, and Hickam Field. At one time, Hickam Field had three major league second basemen on its roster, Joe Gordon, Jerry Priddy, and Dario Lodigiani. To give some idea of the quality of the military teams, the Great Lakes Naval Training Station blasted the Cleveland Indians 17–4, while the Sampson Naval Training Station team pounded the Boston Red Sox 20–7. Some of the major league players who played on service teams included Ted Williams, Bob Feller, Pee Wee Reese, and Mickey Vernon.

The winter of 1942-43 was one of hope for Negro league baseball players, then one of despair. In December 1942, the *Chicago Defender* reported "The Los Angeles Coast League baseball team will abolish the color bar against Negro players and admit them to the club if any can qualify during the spring training season....

"The president of the club, Clarence 'Pants' Rowland ... has been observing Negro players this winter and is understood to have agreed to allow Nate Moreland, local righthand pitcher, to display his ability on the mound.

"Fans believe that should Moreland be given a try and make good, it will be only a matter of time when he will become a member of some major league club."

Two months later, Rowland was still verbalizing the possibility of integration in the *Courier*. "Negro baseball players, along with other nationalities ... will be given full opportunity to ... earn berths on the Los Angeles Coast League team this spring."

The *Courier* concluded, "Speculation is rife as to who among the several Negro pastimers wintering in the Southland will be on hand for the history making tryouts. Numbered among the players ... are Moreland ... Wild Bill Wright ... Biz Mackey ... and Chet Brewer."

With all the hype and promise to treat all men equally, when the chips were down, "Pants" Rowland and other baseball executives were found wanting, according to the Pittsburgh paper. "Coming as a last-minute disappointment, Clarence 'Pants' Rowland, president of the Los Angeles Pacific Coast Baseball league team, late last week, denied Negro ball players the promised opportunity of spring training trials.

"In a rather weak-kneed explanation, the Angels prexy and their manager Bill Sweeney gave as the sole reason for their sudden change in heart, the fact that a number of their farm clubs in leagues of lower brackets throughout the country had folded with the war and they therefore had an over-abundance of pastimers under contract."

Another opportunity had been missed by Negro league players, but there was a light at the end of the tunnel. Integration was less than three years away.

Another sad note to the winter season was the announcement by the *Pittsburgh Courier* "that Josh Gibson, $200,000 catcher of the Homestead Grays, has been confined to St. Francis Hospital following a nervous breakdown.

"According to reliable sources, the giant catcher has been ailing since the middle of the 1942 baseball season. Although his condition is not regarded as critical, it is serious enough to keep him in the hospital for a thorough examination and long needed rest."

1942-43 California Winter League
Final Standings — Incomplete

	Wins	Losses	Ties
Major-Minor League All-Stars	1	0	0
Los Alamitos Naval Air Station	1	0	0
Royal Giants	0	2	0

Miscellaneous Batting Statistics 1942-43

Name	Team	Pos	G	AB	H	D	T	HR	BA
Stephens, Vern	All-Stars	SS	1	5	4	1	0	2	.800
Wright, Bill	Royal Giants								
Williams, Chester	Royal Giants								
Mackey, Biz	Royal Giants								

Miscellaneous Pitching Statistics 1942-43

Name	Team	G	CG	W	L	IP	SO	BB	SH
Caster, George	All-Stars	1	1	1	0	9	—	—	0
Olson, Vern	Los Alamitos	1	-	1	0	—	—	—	0
Moreland, Nate	Royal Giants	2	1	0	1	—	—	—	0
Thompson, Tommy	Royal Giants	1	0	0	0	—	—	—	0
Brewer, Chet	Royal Giants	1	0	0	1	—	—	—	0

The 1943-44 Season

The *Pittsburgh Courier* announced the good news. "Latest advices indicate there will be a winter league after all. Hollywood Coast League Park, instead of Wrigley Field, will be the home club for the two local teams. San Diego, Long Branch, and service teams are entered as well from their respective locales. Season's opening date is Sunday, the 24th (October). Players expected to come west include Josh Gibson, Buck Leonard, Sammy Bankhead, Lefty Harvey, and Cool Papa Bell. Big Bill Wright is bringing a stellar aggregation of pastimers from the Mexican National loop."

West coast fans hoping to get a glimpse of the great Josh Gibson were disappointed once again. The big catcher stayed in Pittsburgh all winter. But Satchel Paige was on hand for the opening day doubleheader between the Baltimore Elite Giants and Pirrone's All-Stars. His supporting cast included Double Duty Radcliffe, Buck Leonard, Cool Papa Bell, Henry Kimbro, Spoon Carter, Clyde Spearman, Sammy Bankhead, and Howard Easterling. The All-Stars had Peanuts Lowrey (.292 with the Chicago Cubs), Babe Dahlgren (.287 with the Pittsburgh Pirates), Jesse Flores (12–14 with the Philadelphia A's), Carl Sawyer, Andy Pafko (.379 in 58 ABs with the Chicago Cubs), George "Catfish" Metkovich (.246 with the Boston Red Sox), Lou Novikoff (.279 with the Chicago Cubs), and Jerry Priddy (.271 with the Washington Senators).

The *L.A. Times* was on hand to record the opening doubleheader. "The box office magic of Leroy (Satchel) Paige, greatest of all Negro baseball players, was plainly demonstrated yesterday when 10,800 fans jammed Gilmore Field to see him pitch for the Baltimore Colored Giants against Joe Pirrone's all-star array of major and Coast leaguers.

"The teams broke even, the Stars capturing the opener, 8–2, and the Giants the finale, 4–1, but the games themselves were merely incidental.

"It was Paige whom the people came out to watch, and although he displayed his talents for only five innings of the opener before deciding to call it a day, he kept the crowd in an uproar with the wizardry of his slants.

"When he retired to rest his aging but still highly valuable bones, he held a 2–0 lead. He had permitted only two hits and he had whiffed five. And the opposition was nothing to be sneezed at either, for it included seven gents fresh out of big league competition.

Buck Leonard, called the Black Lou Gehrig, was the Negro league's greatest first baseman, hitting .335 with 15 home runs a year.

"Paige captivated the customers (and the opposing batsmen) by mixing up tantalizing slow balls with fast ones that literally smoked. He also favored a delayed delivery that invariably got the hitter 'out of tune.'"

After Paige's departure, the All-Stars pounded his successors for eight runs on ten hits, including doubles by Lowrey (2), Barton (2) and Metkovich. Booker McDaniel, who was raked for four of the runs, took the loss. McDaniel came back to take the abbreviated six inning nightcap, 4–1. Easterling's triple in the sixth inning with two men on base, broke open a 1–1 game.

The Giants and the All-Stars met again in week two, with Paige opposing Newt Kimball of the Philadelphia Phillies, in the lidlifter. Unlike the first game, Satchel Paige threw a complete game six-hitter, liberally sprinkled with 14 strikeouts but, for a time, the 7,000 fans at Gilmore Field thought he would be the losing pitcher as he trailed 3–0 entering the bottom of the ninth. But Paige is not only good. He is also lucky, and Lady Luck was with him again on this day. Six base hits rattled off the bats of Baltimore batters in the ninth, and the Satchel man walked away with a hard fought 4–3 victory. In game two, Bill Thomas and Submarine Moss battled to a 3–3 tie after six innings.

Pirrone's All-Stars

Name	Pos	AB	H
Lowrey, Peanuts	LF	3	0
English, Charlie	3B	4	1
Metkovich, George	RF	4	2
Pafko, Andy	CF	4	0
Calvey, Jack	SS	4	1
Priddy, Jerry	2B	4	1
Barton, Larry	1B	3	1
Partee, Roy	C	4	0
Kimball, Newt	P	4	0
Kress, Red	P	0	0
Totals		34	6

Baltimore Elite Giants

Name	Pos	AB	H
Hyde, Bubba	LF	5	2
Bell, Cool Papa	CF	3	1
Spearman, Clyde	RF	5	1
Leonard, Buck	1B	5	2
Easterling, Howard	3B	4	3
Sampson, Sam	2B	4	1
Radcliffe, Ted	C	4	1
Walker, Jesse	SS	4	2
Paige, Satchel	P	4	0
		38	13

Pirrone's All-Stars   0 0 0   0 0 2   0 0 1—3— 6—2
Baltimore Elite Giants   0 0 0   0 0 0   0 0 4—4—13—2

Two Base Hits: Metkovich, Easterling, Hyde
Three Base Hits; Metkovich, Sampson

	IP	H	SO	BB
Kimball, Newt	8	10	2	1
Kress, Red (LP)	⅓	3	0	1
Paige, Satchel (WP)	9	6	14	2

The All-Stars evened things with the Baltimore club in their next meeting, defeating Jack Matchett 4–2. Jerry Priddy's bases-loaded triple in the fifth inning was the game winner. The next day, November 6, the two teams crossed swords for a sixth time, with Satchel Paige meeting Buck Newsom, who was coming off a combined 13–13 year with the Dodgers, Browns, and Senators. The game lacked the artistry of previous Paige performances, but he pitched well enough to win. Things looked grim for the Baltimore ace at the outset, when Peanuts Lowrey and Charlie English both hit Paige's first pitch for doubles. Before the crowd had settled in their seats, the lanky right-handed fireballer was down 2–0, but the great Newsom couldn't stand prosperity. The Giants nibbled away, scoring single runs in the first and second innings, and a brace of runs in the third, to give Paige a 4–2 lead. The 37-year-old Negro league ace retired to the comfort of the clubhouse after five innings, with a 6–3 lead. The All-Stars narrowed the gap to 6–5 with two runs in the seventh inning, but the Giants came back with three of their own in the eighth, to give themselves a comfortable 11–5 lead entering the ninth. Then, they almost let the game slip away. Submarine Moss pitched into the ninth, but hit a stone wall before he could retire the side. Two base hits and three bases on balls brought two runs across the plate to narrow the margin to 11–7, with two men out. Booker McDaniels came on, only to walk in another run. Finally, John Markham came to the rescue to retire the last man, giving Satchel Paige an 11–8 victory. Buck Newsom pitched six innings, giving up six runs on eight hits, to take the loss. Markham lost the five inning nightcap to Bill Thomas, 4–3.

As in 1941-42, the league appeared to be a two-team league, the Giants and All-Stars playing each other every week. There was other action on the coast, with two other black teams playing, but they seemed to be on an independent schedule, rather than in a league. The Negro league All-Stars had several familiar faces, including Biz Mackey, Chet Brewer, and Nate Moreland, but they also had some new men, like Lou Dials, Kenny Washington, and Lorenzo "Piper" Davis. Their opponents were Alan Lane's Major League All-Stars, with six of Pirrone's players—Lowrey, Priddy, Partee, Metkovich, Kress, and Kimball—plus Johnny Lindell of the New York Yankees, Al Zarilla of the St. Louis Browns, Vern Stephens of the Browns, and George Caster. The major leaguers romped over the Negro league All-Stars, 9–0, with Lindell, Caster, and Kimball, all tossing three shutout innings. Losing pitcher Louie Bell and Nate Moreland were raked for 14 base hits by the big leaguers. Lane's bombers jumped on Bell for four runs in the first inning, on a single by Priddy, a double by Zarilla, a triple by Lowrey, and a homer by Rip Russell. Al Zarilla led the hit parade with four hits in five trips to the plate, adding a second double to his production later in the game. Jerry Priddy went two for four.

The other black team in Los Angeles was the Kansas City Royals, with Howard Easterling, Willard Brown, Quincy Trouppe, Buck Leonard, Wild Bill Wright, Bonnie Serrell, Henry Spearman, and Terris "The Great" McDuffie. Their opponents in what also appeared to be a non-league affiliated game were the Western Pipe & Steel Boilermakers, with a bevy of major league players—Skeeter Newsome, shortstop of the Boston Red Sox, Al Zarilla of the Browns, Lou Novikoff of the Cubs, Johnny Lindell of the Yanks, Vern Stephens of the Browns, former Dodger Gilly Campbell, Jesse Flores of the Philadelphia A's, Steve Mesner of the Cincinnati Reds, plus W. Quinn of the Los Angeles Angels, Bill Seinsoth of the St. Louis Browns, and catcher Millican.

The game, played under the lights at Wrigley Field, drew 4,000 fans, to see Flores battle "The Great" McDuffie. The game was tight for 4½ innings, with the Boilermakers holding a 1–0 lead, on a second

Willard Brown was considered by many baseball experts to be the greatest Negro league hitter of the 1940s. He was idolized in Puerto Rico, where he compiled the highest career batting average, .350, and was called "Ese Hombre" (That Man). (Yuyo Ruiz)

inning run, the result of a single by Lindell and a double into left center field by Quinn. But, in the bottom of the fifth, the roof fell in on Philadelphia's 12 game winner. Before you could blink an eye, the Royals pushed over three runs on singles by McDuffie and Easterling, a ringing double by Wild Bill Wright, and a booming triple by Willard "Home Run" Brown. Bill Seinsoth relieved Flores with two men out and surrendered another run on a two base hit by Trouppe. That was all McDuffie needed, as he set the Western team down with five hits, fanning three and walking one. Easterling and Brown had two hits each for Kansas City.

The Kansas City Royals next faced Bill Feistner's Major All-Stars, also called the San Diego Bombers, in a doubleheader at Wrigley Field. Attendance was approximately 5,500. In the opener, Walter Olson of the Dodgers, outpitched right-hander Jack Matchett, 6–2. A four run rally by Feistner's boys broke open a 1–1 game in the top of the fifth. In the nightcap, Bill Seinsoth and Chet Brewer engaged in a good old fashioned pitchers' duel, with Seinsoth coming out on top, 1–0. Both pitchers yielded three safeties in seven innings.

Just when the season was getting into high gear, the Negro leaguers' old enemy, Kenesaw Mountain Landis, tossed another monkey wrench into the gears. He ordered all major leaguers to stop playing winter baseball in California. The *Pittsburgh Courier* covered the story. "...Landis ... is now conducting an investigation of the California Winter League, in which 19 major league players have been playing. Most of the games ... have been against Negro teams. Landis insists on enforcing the major league rule, which prohibits participation in exhibition games 10 days after the major league season closes.

"The big leaguers have played most of their games against Satchel Paige and his Kansas City Giants, which includes players from the Negro National and American Leagues.

"If Landis cracks down, ... he will wipe out the sole means of measuring the abilities of Negro players with major leaguers.

"In 10 games played out here in the last five weeks, Paige and his mates won four games, the big leaguers won five, and one was tied.

"The big leaguers under investigation are: Peanuts Lowrey and Lou Novikoff of the Chicago Cubs, Babe Dahlgren and Newell Kimball of the Philadelphia Phillies, George Metkovich, Skeeter Newsome, and Roy Partee of the Boston Red Sox, Jerry Priddy and Bobo Newsome of the Washington Senators, ... Jesse Flores of the Philadelphia Athletics, Johnny Lindell, New York Yankees, ... Al Zarilla, St. Louis Browns.

With the ban on major leaguer players in effect, Joe Pirrone had to rely on all Coast Leaguers for his next game against Satchel Paige and the Baltimore Elite Giants, but the Coast boys rewarded their boss with a 3–2 victory. Catcher Harry Land drove a Paige fastball over center fielder Bell's head for a two-run triple in the top of the sixth, giving his team a 3–2 lead. Booker McDaniel took over the mound chores for the Baltimore team in the seventh, and held the Coast Leaguers scoreless over the last three innings, but the Giants were unable to score against hard throwing right-hander Dick Conger of the Phillies, in relief of winning pitcher Jodie Phipps (17–5 with the Los Angeles Angels). Land and Larry Barton each had two hits for the winners, while Cool Papa Bell and Easterling punched out two hits for the losers.

Commissioner Landis' investigation resulted in a few eye-opening revelations, as reported in the *Times*. "...Johnny Lindell of the worlds championship New York Yankees, whose cut of the World's Series pie amounted to $6139, reported to Commissioner Landis that he got only $3 a game.

"Pafko, purchased by the Cubs from Los Angeles ... is reported to have earned $400 playing winter baseball."

The Kansas City Royals were back in action on November 29, once again taking on Bill Feistner's All-Stars, before 1,500 fans in Wrigley Field. Chet Brewer and the Royal bats stopped Walter Olson and the Stars, 7–2. The second game ended in a 2-all deadlock, called at the end of the seventh inning, on account of darkness. No details of either game were available.

In the final Winter League doubleheader of the season, the Baltimore Elite Giants and Joe Pirrone's All-Stars went at it in Gilmore Field before 2,000 fans. This time the Coast Leaguers were no match for the fired-up Negro league stars, who swept the twin bill by scores of 4–1 and 4–0. In the lidlifter, Terris "The Great" McDuffie crossed swords with Happy Hansman, and Terris got the best of it, limiting the Stars to just five hits, and fanning six. Sammy Sampson was the batting star of the game, going three for four, and stealing two bases. In game two, Submarine Moss chucked a three-hit shutout over seven innings, to beat Dick Conger, 4–0. Six different Giant players had one hit apiece, with Easterling hitting a triple, and Moss and Bell chipping in with doubles.

Herman Hill, the sportswriter for the *Pittsburgh Courier* selected the following Winter League All-Star team:

Catcher:	Double Duty Radcliffe
	Roy Partee
Pitcher:	Satchel Paige
	Newt Kimball
	Terris McDuffie
	Buck Newsom
First Base:	Buck Leonard
Second base:	Sam Sampson
Shortstop:	Bob Sturgeon
Third Base:	Jerry Priddy
Outfield:	Willard Brown
	Bill Wright
	Harry Lowrey
Utility:	Howard Easterling
	Charlie English
	George Metkovitch
	Bubba Hyde

The 1943-44 Winter League batting champion was Sammy Sampson with an average of .433, in nine games. There were no home runs recorded in any of the reported games. Satchel Paige was once again the top pitcher with a 3–1 record.

1943-44 California Winter League
Final Standings—Incomplete

	Wins	Losses	Ties
Baltimore Elite Giants	7	5	1
Pirrone's All-Stars	5	7	1

Baltimore Elite Giants Batting Statistics 1943-44

Name	Pos	G	AB	H	D	T	HR	BA
Hyde, Bubba	RF	9	34	12	3	1	0	.353
Bell, Cool Papa	CF	10	31	10	3	0	0	.323
Spearman, Clyde	LF	9	30	6	1	0	0	.200
Leonard, Buck	1B	10	31	11	0	2*	0	.355
Easterling, Howard	3B	9	29	7	1	2*	0	.241
Sampson, Sammy	2B	9	30	13	2	1	0	.433*
Radcliffe, Double Duty	C	7	22	4	0	0	0	.182
Walker, Jesse	SS	9	26	7	0	0	0	.269

Baltimore Elite Giants Pitching Statistics 1943-44

Name	G	CG	W	L	IP	SO	BB	SH
Paige, Satchel	5	1	3	1	30	35	10	0
Moss, Submarine	3	2	1	0	17	—	—	1
Markham, John	2	1	0	1	7	—	—	0
McDuffie, Terris	3	2	2	0	21	11	3	0
McDaniel, Booker	3	1	1	1	11	4	6	0

Pirrone's All-Stars Batting Statistics 1943-44

Name	Pos	G	AB	H	D	T	HR	BA
Lowrey, Peanuts	LF	8	29	8	3	2*	0	.276
English, Charlie	3B	8	31	8	1	0	0	.258
Metkovich, Catfish	RF	8	27	8	4*	1	0	.296
Pafko, Andy	CF	6	21	6	2	0	0	.287
Priddy, Jerry	2B	6	20	8	2	1	0	.400
Barton, Larry	1B	8	23	7	2	0	0	.304
Partee, Roy	C	4	13	2	0	0	0	.154
Novikoff, Lou	LF	3	10	1	1	0	0	.100
Zarilla, Al	RF	3	11	6	2	0	0	.545
Russell, Rip	1B	2	8	3	0	0	1*	.375

Pirrone's All-Stars Pitching Statistics 1943-44

Name	G	CG	W	L	IP	SO	BB	SH
Kimball, Newt	3	0	1	0	17	—	—	0
Kress, Red	3	1	0	2	9	—	—	0
Newsom, Buck	2	0	0	1	7	6	5	0
Olson, Walter	3	3	1	2	25	—	—	0
Seinsoth, Bill	2	1	1	0	7	—	—	0

1943-44 Independent Schedules

	Wins	Losses	Ties
Lane's Major Leaguers	1	0	0
Feistner's Major All-Stars	2	1	1
Kansas City Royals	3	2	1
Negro All-Stars	0	1	0
Western Pipe & Steel Boilermakers	0	1	0
Long Beach All-Stars	0	1	0

Kansas City Royals Batting Statistics 1943-44

Name	Pos	G	AB	H	D	T	HR	BA
Simms, Willie	LF	2	9	2	0	0	0	.222
Easterling, Howard	SS	2	9	3	0	0	0	.333
Wright, Bill	RF	2	7	2	2	0	0	.287
Brown, Willard	CF	3	11	5	1	1	0	.455
Trouppe, Quincy	C	3	7	1	1	0	0	.143
Leonard, Buck	1B	See Baltimore Elite Giants						
Serrell, Bonnie	2B	2	6	1	0	0	0	.167
Spearman, Henry (?)	3B	2	6	1	0	0	0	.167

Kansas City Royals Pitching Statistics 1943-44

Name	G	CG	W	L	IP	SO	BB	SH
McDuffie, Terris	See Baltimore Elite Giants							
Matchett, Jack	3	2	0	2	18	—	—	0
Brewer, Chet	3	2	1	1	20	—	—	0

The 1944-45 Season

In spite of the war, the California Winter League was back in action again. The season was scheduled to run from October 15 until December 17, a period of nine weeks, a long way from the winter leagues of the old days, which ran from October through February. During the 1920s and early '30s, the season ran for about 17 weeks, for a total of 40–42 games. Then in the late '30s the season was gradually reduced to 13 weeks and finally, in the '40s to 8 or 9 weeks.

The 1944-45 winter league consisted of four teams, the Birmingham Black Barons, the Kansas City Royals, the Service All-Stars, and the Naval Dry Dock. The Black Barons lineup included Cool Papa Bell, Artie Wilson, Sam Bankhead, Piper Davis, Booker McDaniel, and John Markham. The Kansas City Royals, under manager Chet Brewer, fielded a team consisting of Wild Bill Wright, Bonnie Serrell, Ray Dandridge, Len Pearson, Hilton Smith, Willie Wells, Theolic Smith, Sam Jethroe, Parnell Woods, Nate Moreland and, of course, Brewer himself. It was an impressive aggregation, with five Hall of Fame candidates in Hilton Smith, Brewer, Wells, Dandridge, and Wright.

The Service All-Stars, considerably strengthened by World War II inductees, could count on Red Ruffing (14–7 with the Yankees in 1942 before entering the U.S. Army), Harry Danning of the New York Giants, Nanny Fernandez (Boston Braves), Jerry Priddy (.271 with the Washington Senators in 1943), Catfish Metkovich (.277 with the Boston Red Sox), Babe Dahlgren (.289 with Pittsburgh), Vince DiMaggio (.240 with Pittsburgh), Peanuts Lowrey (.292 with the Cubs), Roy Partee (.243 with the Red Sox), and Red Barrett (9–16 with the Boston Braves). Irish Meusel's Naval Dry Dock team had six-year major leaguer Rip Russell, Jack Rothrock (a .276 career hitter primarily with the Boston Red Sox), Cecil Garriott, and Ray Prim (22–10 with

Hilton Smith, called "Satchel's Relief Man" because he usually followed Paige to the mound after the great one had completed his mandatory four or five innings, was elected to the National Baseball Hall of Fame in 2001. (John B. Holway)

the Los Angeles Angels). Prim would go 13–8 with the Chicago Cubs in 1945, and start and lose Game Four of the World Series against the Detroit Tigers), Jack Calvey (San Diego Padres), and Ken Richardson (Hollywood Stars).

The *Pittsburgh Courier* announced the opening of the league. "Sponsors of the winter loop, which for the first time in several seasons, promises to be more than a mere series of barnstorming games, are Marshall G. Armstrong, Chet Brewer, and Bill Feistner. The trio has received the complete cooperation of both Wrigley Field and Hollywood Park managements, and have succeeded in blocking several promoters who were interested mainly in a short-sighted, money-making proposition.

"A schedule of regular winter league games will ... be played on the 22nd and 29th and each Wednesday night at Wrigley Field.

"Because of pro football, Wrigley Field is not available for Sunday contests.

"Henry Armstrong, Lionel Hampton, George Raft, and Sheriff Eugene Biscauluz, are expected to act as the honorary battery for the winter league's opening day doubleheader between the Kansas City Royals and the Service All-Stars at Hollywood coast league park. Red Ruffing, ex–New York Yankee ace, will hurl for the servicemen."

The first game of the season was an exhibition game played on October 11, four days before the official opening. It matched the Royals against the Major All-Stars. It was an exciting beginning, according to the *Chicago Defender*. "A group of cool-headed Negro and white baseball players averted a riot at Wrigley Field here on Wednesday ... when umpire Connie Conrad ruled Vince DiMaggio safe at home plate in the ninth inning, thereby giving his all-major league team a 5–4 victory over the Kansas City Royal Giants.

"After Conrad's decision, a number of irate fans quit the stands to congregate about the umpire and render loud protests. However, he was finally escorted through an emergency exit without serious incident after police squad cars arrived."

Theolic Smith's team held a comfortable 4–1 lead over Red Barrett and the All-Stars after seven innings of play, but Vince DiMaggio's boys exploded for three runs in the eighth to knot the count at 4-all. Chet Brewer came on the scene in the ninth, and was victimized by poor defensive play. Third baseman Jesse Williams let DiMaggio's ball go through his legs and roll down into the left field corner, for a two-base error. Then Bonnie Serrell misplayed Peanuts Lowrey's grounder, throwing to first base too late to catch the runner, and first baseman Bill Simms' throw home to catcher Biz Mackey was too late to catch the flying DiMaggio. Lowrey led the All-Star attack with three hits, while Jesse Williams led the Royals, also with three hits.

The results of the official California Winter League opening day doubleheader between the Royals and Feistner's All-Stars have not been located. The games may have been rained out. In any event, the following week, Bill Wright's formidable forces met and defeated Bill Feistner's Service All-Stars in a three game series. In the Friday night opener at Wrigley Field, Nate Mooreland, fresh from a two year stint with Tampico in the Mexican League, blanked the army boys, 3–0. Willie Wells got the show on the road in the fourth inning, when he walked, stole second, and scored on Jesse Williams' single to center. Two innings later, the Royals extended their lead to 2–0 when Wild Bill Wright blasted a triple to left center field and scored on Theolic Smith's three bagger. The final run came across in the seventh on singles by Serrell, Dandridge, and Wright.

In the Sunday twin bill, played at Hollywood Park, the Kansas City team was victorious, 3–1 and 2–0. Hilton Smith tossed a three-hitter at the soldiers in game one.

Fiestners team grabbed a 1–0 lead in the fourth when Eddie Bockman singled and later scored, but the Royals came back to take the lead in the sixth on a double by Bonnie Serrell, an infield hit by Ray Dandridge, an error by Bobby Adams, and a sacrifice fly by Theolic Smith. They scored the final run in the eighth on hits by Dandridge and Wells. In the seven inning nightcap, Pepper Bassett, a catcher by trade, took the hill, and shut down the All-Star sluggers with two hits. Johnny Burns of the Stars yielded only seven hits, but the Royals bunched two of them to score both their runs in the sixth.

On October 25, the two talented black teams met on the field of battle for the first time. More than 5,000 fans crowded into Wrigley Field to watch Booker McDaniels of the Barons match pitches with the Royals' curveball artist, Hilton Smith, who was elected to the National Baseball Hall Of Fame in 2001. In this game, McDaniels had all the better of it. After a slow start in which Bill Wright's two base hit accounted for two first inning runs for the Kansas City crew, the 6'2", 195 pound fastball pitcher settled down and blanked Chet Brewer's team the rest of the game. In the meantime, Birmingham jumped on Smith for a run in the first, then knocked him out of the box with a three run deluge in the third. Brewer and Moreland followed Smith to the mound and kept the Black Barons under control the rest of the game, but it was a case of too little, too late, with Birmingham winning by a count of 6–2. Cool Papa Bell led the winners with four hits in five times at bat. Artie Wilson and Piper Davis both contributed two hits.

The *Pittsburgh Courier* posted the following story after the game. "Still plagued by weak hitting, the Royals management has sent out an SOS for two outfielders and a catcher.

"Roy Campanella, Baltimore Elites backstop, had wired his acceptance, and transportation expenses amounting to $100 were sent him, but his subsequent failure to put in an appearance has resulted in Federal charges being levied against him by Royal owners for accepting money under false pretenses." The full story was never made known, but apparently the charges were subsequently dropped. Campanella did not play in California that year.

The Black Barons played a doubleheader against Irish Meusel's Naval Drydock team on October 29, winning the first game 6–1 behind the five-hit pitching of Schoolboy Howard. The big, hard throwing right-hander was never in trouble after his teammates pushed over four runs in the top of the first. The second game ended in a 3–3 tie after nine innings. Tom Baker pitched for the Dry Dock team while Bubber Huber and Johnny Taylor shared the mound duties for Birmingham.

The next week, Birmingham and Kansas City met in a rematch, with both teams out for blood. This time, it was the Royals' turn to gloat. In a tense pitcher's duel, Theolic Smith and Booker McDaniels exchanged goose-eggs for six innings. Chet Brewer relieved Smith in the top of the seventh after the Black Barons had scored the first run of the game. They added another run off Brewer in the eighth and entered the bottom of the ninth with a 2–0 lead. The *Courier* carried the story. "Trailing 2–0 with two away in the ninth, and having nicked Baron hurler Booker McDaniels for but two measly bingles, the Royals appeared doomed until Simms and Dandridge both singled. Bill Wrights smash to left scored Simms. Willie Wells line single knotted the count when he drove Dandridge across the plate.

"Jesse Williams broke up the story book ball game when he slammed a one-baser to tally Wright."

Chet Brewer had the Royals in high gear as they met the Navy Dry Dockers in a doubleheader. They began the day with a four game winning streak, and made it five in a row with a 7–1 win in the opener. Nate Moreland handcuffed Emil Meusel's team with a tight four-hitter, shutting them out after Jack Calvey's home run in the first inning. Kansas City put up a big six spot in the second, and that was the game. Jesse Williams paced the Kansas City attack with two doubles. The game was called after 5½ innings, and game two was cancelled completely, because of rain.

The next matchup between Birmingham and Kansas City showed how evenly matched the two teams were. In a hard fought battle, the game ended in a 3–3, 11 inning tie. Neither team could claim a victory, but both teams could point to their performance with pride. There were many heroes in the game, including Chet Brewer and Al Saylor. The Kansas City manager relieved Theolic Smith in the third, after the Black Barons had scored three runs, and he shut them down over the last ten plus innings, fanning ten men along the way. Booker McDaniels held the Royals to one hit over the first five innings, but in the sixth, Theolic Smith's double with two on, and Bill Simms' single, knotted the count. Saylor took the hill for Birmingham in the ninth and fanned the side on ten pitches. The *Courier* noted, "(Piper) Davis, lanky Baron first sacker, clouted a 345 foot homer in the second frame. Both teams played heads-up ball with infielders Sam Bankhead, Willie Wells, and Ray Dandridge turning in fielding gems."

The Black Barons and the Royals met for the last time on November 15. It was another hard fought pitchers' duel, and this time Winfield Welch's Barons came out on top, 3–2, with Johnny Markham on the mound. The game was decided in the top of the sixth, when Sammy Bankhead blasted a triple to right field, and carried across the game-winner on a single by Harry Williams. Wild Bill Wright had three hits for the losers. The game was marked by a spirited debate in the ninth inning when Royal manager Chet Brewer, who should know, accused Black Baron pitcher Johnny Markham of cutting the ball. Markham, in a fit of pique, threw the ball over the grandstand.

Unfortunately for Brewer's crew, time was running out for them to overtake Birmingham, whose manager and players had returned to the east after their last encounter. Manager Winfied Welch left to coach the Harlem Globetrotters basketball team, and the players went home to rest before going to spring training for the upcoming Negro league season. The Royals kept plugging away, but they suffered a severe setback when they were beaten by the Service All-Stars, 3–2 in ten innings. Walter Olson shackled the Royals on seven hits. The Royals came back to take the All-Stars in the next game, 7–1, behind Nate Moreland, and swept a pair from the Navy Dry Dock team, 3–1 and 2–0, but they came up short at the end, finishing in second place behind the Birmingham Black Barons. In the final doubleheader, Moreland won his sixth straight game on a five hitter, and Chet Brewer blanked Emil Meusel's team, tossing a one-hitter in the seven inning finale.

Wild Bill Wright won the batting title with an average of .421 in just five recorded games. Three players hit one home run apiece to tie for the lead in that department. And Nate Moreland was the top pitcher in the league with a perfect 6–0 mark, including two shutouts.

News out of Chicago informed the baseball world of the death of Kenesaw Mountain Landis, the Commissioner of Baseball for 24 years, who succumbed to a heart attack on November 25. Fans nationwide mourned the man who had ruled baseball with an iron fist for more than two decades, but the news of his passing was received with mixed emotions by many in the black community, and even by some in the white community. It is always sad when someone dies, but many people felt that Landis had hindered the progress of baseball

Judge Kenesaw Mountain Landis, the Commissioner of Baseball from 1920 to 1945, probably set integration back at least 20 years with his policies.

through his sometimes questionable and tyrannical actions. As early as 1920, when he barred the eight Black Sox defendants from organized baseball for life, many people felt that Buck Weaver and Joe Jackson were treated unfairly. And over the years, the man from Illinois opposed integration, preventing many Negro league stars like Bullet Joe Rogan, Smokey Joe Williams, Turkey Stearnes, Mule Suttles, and Biz Mackey from realizing their dreams.

1944-45 California Winter League
Final Standings—Incomplete

	Wins	Losses	Ties
Birmingham Black Barons	4	1	2
Kansas City Royals	11	6	1

Service All-Stars		3	3	0
Naval Dry Dock		0	4	1

Kansas City Royals Batting Statistics 1944-45

Name	Pos	G	AB	H	D	T	HR	BA
Simms, Bill	RF	5	16	4	0	0	0	.250
Serrell, Bonnie	1B	6	20	5	1	0	0	.300
Wells, Willie	SS	3	9	2	0	0	0	.222
Dandridge, Ray	3B	6	20	7	0	0	0	.350
Wright, Bill	CF	5	19	8	1	2*	0	.421*
Williams, Jesse	3B	5	19	8	3*	0	0	.421*
Smith, Theolic	P-LF	5	15	2	1	1	0	.133
Bassett, Pepper	C	2	4	1	1	0	0	.250
Mackey, Biz	C	4	7	3	0	0	0	.429

Kansas City Royals Pitching Statistics 1944-45

Name	G	CG	W	L	IP	SO	BB	SH
Smith, Hilton	3	1	1	1	17	—	—	0
Brewer, Chet	6	1	2	2	29	—	—	1
Moreland, Nate	7	5	6	0	52	—	—	2

Birmingham Black Barons Batting Statistics 1944-45

Name	Pos	G	AB	H	D	T	HR	BA
Bell, Cool Papa	LF	3	13	8	1	0	0	.615
Williams, Harry	3B	3	10	2	0	0	0	.200
Davis, Piper	1B	3	10	5	1	0	1	.500
Wilson, Artie	SS	2	7	2	0	0	0	.287
Bankhead, Sammy	2B	2	5	1	0	1	0	.200

Birmingham Black Barons Pitching Statistics 1944-45

Name	G	CG	W	L	IP	SO	BB	SH
McDaniels, Booker	3	2	1	1	23	—	—	0
Markham, John	2	1	1	0	12	—	—	0
Howard, Schoolboy	1	1	1	0	9	—	—	0

Service All-Stars Batting Statistics 1944-45

Name	Pos	G	AB	H	D	T	HR	BA
Coscarart, Pete	2B	2	7	3	0	0	0	.429
Metkovich, Catfish	RF	2	7	2	0	2	0	.287
Elliott, Bob	3B	2	7	2	0	0	0	.287
Lowrey, Peanuts	LF	2	6	3	0	0	0	.500
Stevens, Chuck	1B	2	6	4	0	0	1	.667

Service All-Stars Pitching Statistics 1944-45

Name	G	CG	W	L	IP	SO	BB	SH
Olson, Al	3	3	3	0	28	—	—	0
Barrett, Red	2	1	1	0	10	—	—	0

9

Season Summaries 1945–1947

The 1945 Season

The last few months of 1945 were a historic time in the United States, but it was not because of anything that happened in the California Winter League. In fact, the winter league had to take a back seat to the momentous events that unfolded across the continent, in Brooklyn, New York. Jackie Robinson, one of the west coast's greatest all-around athletes at Pasadena Junior College and UCLA in the late 1930s, and the shortstop for the Kansas City Monarchs of the Negro American League during the summer of 1945, visited the Dodgers' executive offices in early September to meet with Dodger prexy Branch Rickey. Rumors were rife about the reason for the meeting. One rumor had Rickey forming a new Negro league club to be called the Brooklyn Brown Dodgers. Another rumor said that the devout Methodist baseball executive was about to break the color barrier, by signing Robinson to a Brooklyn Dodger contract.

At the same time Robinson and Rickey were meeting, California Winter League baseball promoters were busily planning their strategy for upcoming season, and hopes were high that the postwar baseball fever would be as high as it had been in the mid–1930s, when some of the best professional baseball in the country was played on the west coast. The announcement that Wrigley Field, the summer home of the Los Angeles Angels of the Pacific Coast League, had been leased by the Kansas City Royals of the winter league, was good news for the fans, who could enjoy outstanding professional baseball games in the comfort of a modern, well maintained, stadium.

There was additional excitement around Los Angeles in the early fall, with the announcement by the new baseball commissioner, Happy Chandler, that major league players would be permitted to play exhibition games for thirty days after the close of the baseball season, instead of the usual 15 days. With the World Series ending on October 10, that meant that major league players could compete in the winter league until November 9. The promoters of the winter league moved quickly to take advantage of the commissioner's ruling. Opening day was set for Sunday September 22, with the Negro league entrant, the Kansas City Royals, meeting Butch Moran's Coast League All-Stars. The rest of the seven week season was scheduled at a fast and furious pace, with two or three night games to be played during the week, in addition to the usual Sunday doubleheaders.

The winter league consisted of six teams, Kansas City, the Birmingham Black Barons, the San Diego All-Stars, the Coast League All-Stars, the Major League All-Stars, and the Saltillo Mexicans. Chet

Members of the Kansas City Royals in the mid–1940s. *Left to right:* Archie Ware, Jesse Williams, Ray Neil, Bonnie Serrell. (NoirTech Research)

Brewer's Royals fielded a lineup that included Jackie Robinson, who hit .387 with the Kansas City Monarchs, Jesse Williams, Wild Bill Wright, John Williams, ace of the Indianapolis Clowns' pitching staff, Theolic "Fireball" Smith, and Brewer himself. Birmingham had Piper Davis, Ed Steele, a powerful line drive hitter who played with the Barons in the Negro American League during the summer, Jim West, Double Duty Radcliffe, and pitchers John Markham and Frank "Groundhog" Thompson. The Major League All-Stars boasted of a strong team headed by Vern Stephens, the American League home run champion with 24, Jerry Priddy (Washington Senator shortstop), Lou Stringer (Chicago Cubs shortstop), Jackie Tobin (Boston Red Sox third baseman), George "Catfish" Metkovich (.260 with the Boston Braves), Bob Elliott (.290 with 108 RBIs for Pittsburgh), Eddie Miller (Cincinnati shortstop), Bill Salkeld (.311 with the Pittsburgh Pirates), Red Barrett (23 game winner in the National League), Ed Heusser (11–16 with Cincinnati), and Buster Adams (.292 with 20 homers and 101 RBIs for the Cardinals). The Coast League All-Stars lineup showcased such talents as Les Powers, Red Steiner (Hollywood Stars), Spencer Harris (a career .318 minor league hitter with 3,617 base hits), Rosie Cantrell (a career .315 minor league hitter with 2,163 base hits), Ken Richardson (a career .282 minor league hitter with 2,168 base hits), and pitchers Bob Williams (7–11 with Hollywood), and R. Mishasek (16–16 with Hollywood).

The attention of baseball fans, particularly the black fans, on the west coast, was divided between the winter league and the continuing news reports circulating about Robinson and the Dodgers. And, since Robinson was playing for the Kansas City Royals in California, the league quickly resembled a Jackie Robinson traveling baseball show. The media documented, and embellished, his every move, as evidenced by the opening day coverage in the Pittsburgh courier. "Paced by the peerless all-around play of shortstop Jackie Robinson, the Kansas City Royals opened the annual winter league exhibition series Sunday with a 4–2 victory over the Service All-Stars at Recreation Park in Long Beach. An overflow crowd attended.

"Robinson hit a homer inside the park, and was riot on the paths and fielded brilliantly."

Tuesday night, the Royals won again, beating the Coast League All-Stars 3–1 behind John Williams, a rugged 6'2", 208 pound, right-hander. San Diego finally slowed down the Kansas City express by dealing Chet Brewer's crew a 6–2 thumping in the border city. But KC got back on track by taking the measure of the Coast Leaguers 10–5, with John Williams once again gaining the victory. The *Courier* was there. "Big Bill Wright, centerfielder, drove in four tallies with a homer and a rousing single.

"Robinson doubled twice, scored four times, and ran the opposition daffy on the bases.

"In the seventh he walked, pilfered second, went to third on a fly out, and streaked for home to score, as Herb Souell dropped a perfect bunt in front of the plate."

On Friday, the Royals were blanked by San Diego, 1–0, but they bounced back the following night, behind the hard throwing Williams, to beat the Coast League All-Stars, 8–0. Two days later, Kansas City tangled with the Coast Leaguers in a twin bill, and the bright sunny day brought out more than 9,000 enthusiastic Angelinos, to cheer for their heroes. Both games were closely contested, with the Royals eking out a 6 to 5 victory in the ten inning opener, and the Coast Leaguers coming back to take game two, 5–4. John Williams, in relief of Nate Moreland, gained his third victory of the young season. Jackie Robinson carried the winning run across the plate in game one, when he doubled, went to third on a sacrifice, and scored on an infield grounder. Clyde Nelson, Chicago American Giants infielder, was the hero of game two, rapping two singles, a double, and home run. Nelson batted .311 in the Negro American League from 1945 through 1948.

Vince DiMaggio brought his Major League All-Stars to town on October 7 for a big four game series. Brewer's bombers got off the mark first, stopping Red Barrett of the Boston Braves 1–0. John Williams dazzled the big leaguers, tossing a one-hitter, striking out two and walking four. Jackie Tobin of the Red Sox had the only hit off Williams, a single in the fifth inning. Barrett was nearly as good as Big John, except for one inning. Jackie Robinson legged out a bunt, went to second on a fielder's choice, and scampered home on a single to left by Clyde Nelson, for the only run of the game.

Barrett got his revenge in the nightcap, when he came on in relief in the sixth inning with the bases loaded and one out. He retired both Wild Bill Wright and Bill Hoskins with no runs scoring, to save the 4–3 win for Ed Heusser. Buster Adams of the St. Louis Cardinals led the Major League attack with three hits. Again, the *Courier* zeroed in on Jackie Robinson. "Robinson provided the enthusiastic crowd of 8,000 with thrills aplenty in the fifth inning of the nightcap when he got on after being hit with a pitched ball. When pitcher O'Neil attempted to keep him on the bag to prevent him from stealing, he threw wild, and the fleet-footed Robinson made two bases on the misplay.

"Prancing up and down the third base line and making fake dashes for home,

Jackie upset the pitcher's poise, and he finally cut loose with a wild heave over the Pittsburgh Pirate's catcher, Billy Salkeld's head, on which Robinson scored standing up."

The big leaguers kept their momentum going two days later, when they pounded Pullman Porter and John Williams of the Royals 9–5 before 2,000 fans in Wrigley Field. They made it three in a row the next night, when Vern Stephens, power hitting shortstop for the St. Louis Browns, sent two balls into orbit during a 13 run first inning explosion off Ronnie Smith, igniting his team to a 22–7 rout of the famed Kansas City club.

Chet Brewer finally got his team focused on the task at hand by sweeping a twin bill from the Saltillo Mexican All-Stars four days later, by scores of 4–2 and 2–1. John Williams tossed a five hitter in the lid lifter, and Pullman Porter did likewise in the nightcap. More than 7,500 fans crammed into Wrigley Field to witness the festivities.

October 23, 1945, was a day that will forever be engraved in the history of our proud nation. For, on that day, a black man signed a contract to play professional baseball for a previously all-white team in organized baseball. Jackie Robinson, after several intense sessions with Brooklyn Dodger president, Branch Rickey, signed a contract to play ball with the Dodger farm team in Montreal, Canada. Suddenly the California Winter League was all but forgotten, as

Jackie Robinson integrated organized baseball in 1946. He was a true pioneer and a hero, who had to undergo the most vicious physical threats by bigots in the game.

baseball fans across the country, of both races, discussed the merits of the move by the Dodgers, as well as the myriad of problems associated with it.

In spite of all the furor over the Robinson signing, baseball went on as usual. And, in a major sporting event, just three days later, 15,000 fans pushed their way into Wrigley Field to see two legendary mound artists go at it—Satchel Paige of the Kansas City Royals and Bob Feller of the Major League All-Stars. The fans more than got their money's worth as the world's two fastest pitchers fed off each other, and simply overpowered the opposing batters. Feller held the Royals to one run and four hits in seven innings, fanning 13. Paige yielded a single run on five hits and struck out eight. The Major League Stars won the game in the tenth inning when Ed Bockman singled off losing pitcher Williams, Joe Woods tripled, and Jack Graham singled. The Royals fought back in their half of the tenth, scoring one run on singles by John Smith, Jesse Williams, and Bill Hoskins, but came up short at 3–2.

A minor brouhaha erupted during Feller's visit to the City of Angels, but it was a tempest in a teapot, blown out of proportion in typical fashion by the press. When asked about Jackie Robinson's prospects in the major leagues during an interview, Feller gave an honest answer. "(I can't) foresee any future for Robinson in big league baseball. (He is) tied up in the shoulders and couldn't hit an inside pitch to save his life." Robinson responded in the *Pittsburgh Courier*. "I value what Feller says because I have faced him a couple of times and he is a very good pitcher. However, if it is left to my hitting ability, I think I will do all right. The few times I have faced Feller has made me confident that the pitching I have hit in the Negro American League was as tough as any I will have to face if I make it at Montreal."

The Kansas City Royals finished off October in grand style, by sweeping a doubleheader against the Major League All-Stars, 4–3 and 1–0, then edging the Birmingham Black Barons 4–3. Theolic Smith and Chet Brewer pitched in the first game of the All-Star series, with Pullman Porter tossing a four-hit shutout in game two. Chet Brewer was the winning pitcher against the Barons.

During the last week of the season, Chet Brewer's Royals met the Black Barons three more times. Pullman Porter cruised in the Thursday night game, 12–3, when the Royals pushed over four runs in the first inning off Gready McKinnis of the Chicago American Giants, then put up a big eight spot in the second. But the resilient Birmingham team came right back on Friday night, edging the Royals 4–3. John Huber, who tossed a shutout in the 1944 Negro World Series, was the winning pitcher, with relief help from McKinnis. The Black Barons also took the final game of the series, winning 6–1, with tiny 5'2" southpaw, Groundhog Thompson, throwing a complete game five-hitter. Satchel Paige took the loss.

The *Pittsburgh Courier* once again selected an all-star team for the season.

Catcher:	Buster Haywood, Jim Steiner
Pitcher:	Satchel Paige, Bob Feller, Red Barrett, Groundhog Thompson, John Williams
First Base:	Jerry Priddy
Second Base:	Piper Davis
Shortstop:	Jackie Robinson
Third Base:	Jackie Tobin
Outfield:	Buster Adams, Vern Stephens, Art Pennington
Utility:	Lou Stringer, Jesse Williams, Bob Elliott, Bill Wright
Manager:	W.S. Welch (Baltimore)

Statistics were minimal for the season, as only one complete box score was uncovered. A few additional stats were recovered from game accounts. The Kansas City Royals appeared to be the California Winter League champions for 1945, winning 14 games against 10 losses. The San Diego All-Stars finished at 3–1. There was no batting champion selected bacause of insufficient data. Vern Stephens led the league in home runs with two. John Williams was the leading pitcher with a record of 5–2.

1945 California Winter League

	Wins	Losses	Ties
Kansas City Royals	14	10	0
San Diego All-Stars	3	1	0

	Wins	Losses	Ties
Major League All-Stars	4	4	0
Birmingham Black Barons	2	2	0
Coast League All-Stars	1	5	0
Saltillo Mexican All-Stars	0	2	0

Kansas City Royals Batting Statistics 1945

Name	Pos	G	AB	H	D	T	HR	BA
Robinson, Jackie	SS	4	14	6	3	0	1	.429
Souell, Herb	3B	2	6	3	0	0	0	.500
Nelson, Clyde	1B	3	12	6	1	0	1	.500
Smith, Johnny	RF	4	15	5	0	1	0	.333
Williams, Jesse	2B	3	11	5	0	1	0	.455
Wright, Bill	CF	3	8	2	0	0	1	.250
Hoskins, Bill	LF	4	14	2	0	0	1	.143
Haywood, Buster	C	1	3	1	0	0	0	.333

Kansas City Royals Pitching Statistics 1945

Name	G	CG	W	L	IP	SO	BB	SH
Moreland, Nate	2	1	0	1	15	—	—	0
Williams, John	8	3	5	2	37	—	—	1
Paige, Satchel	4	1	1	1	27	27	12	0
Brewer, Chet	3	1	2	1	16	—	—	0
Porter, Pullman	3	2	2	0	19	—	—	1

The 1946 Season

Once again the California Winter League schedule was tailored to meet the rules set down by the baseball commissioner, to the effect that major league players could participate in exhibition games for thirty days after the close of the major league season. In fact, the winter league season seemed to be much shorter than that, based on recovered newspaper articles. The winter league opened on October 6, nine days before the World Series ended, and no games were found after October 27, a period of just three weeks.

Fall baseball on the Coast in 1946 often resembled a barnstorming tour rather than an organized league. The announced winter league consisted of four teams, the Kansas City Royals, the Hollywood Stars, the Major-Minor All-Stars, and the Major League All-Stars (sometimes called Feller's All-Stars). The Royals had a lineup composed of Bubba Hyde, Ed Steele, Bill Hoskins, Clyde Nelson, Lee Moody, Sam Hairston, Booker McDaniels, and Satchel Paige. Butch Moran's Hollywood Stars fielded a team that included Ken Richardson, Bud Sheely, Al Unser, Frankie Kelleher, Frank Kalin, Bud Stewart, Gabby Stewart, and Ed Erautt. The Major League All-Stars were loaded, with players like the Yankees' Phil Rizzuto, Johnny Berardino of the St. Louis Browns, Mickey Vernon of the Washington Senators, Charlie Keller of the Yankees, Jeff Heath, slugging outfielder of the Cleveland Indians, Ken Keltner of the Indians, Sam Chapman of the Philadelphia A's, and Frankie Hayes, Bob Lemon and Bob Feller of the Indians. The Major-Minor All-Stars had Chuck Stevens, Ken Richardson, Eddie Bockman, Bud Stewart, Cliff Dapper, Don Lang, and pitchers Manny Perez and Ronnie Smith of the Hollywood Stars.

While the winter league was preparing for the season, the Jackie Robinson saga was playing out in Canada. Robinson burst upon the organized baseball scene with a spectacular opening day exhibition. He sparked the Montreal Royals to a 14–1 rout of the Jersey City Giants, with four hits in five at-bats, four runs scored, four runs batted in, a home run, and two stolen bases. And he never let up all season. The Royals ran away with the International League pennant, outdistancing their nearest rival by 18½ games. Robinson led the league in batting (.349), runs scored (113) and fielding percentage (.985), and was voted the league's Most Valuable Player as a result. The Little World Series against the American Association champion, Louisville Colonels, was another personal triumph for the black superstar. He was barraged with racial slurs and threats during the three games in Louisville, and was deeply affected by it, hitting just .091 and watching his team go down to defeat twice in three games. Returning to the cozy confines of Montreal's Hector Racine Stadium, he found his batting stroke, and led his team to victory. He knocked in the winning run in game four, then belted a double and a triple in game five, as the Royals won 5–3 to take a 3–2 edge in games. In the finale, before a packed house of 19,171 screaming Canadians, he made several defensive gems to snuff out Louisville rallies, and scored the winning run as former Brooklyn Dodger star, Curt Davis tossed a nine-hit, 2–0 victory, giving Montreal the coveted Little World Series crown, four games to two. At the conclusion of the game, the joyous fans carried manager Clay Hopper, Curt Davis, and Jackie Robinson, to the clubhouse on their shoulders. Robinson went 7 for 9 at home to finish with an average of .400.

The curtain went up on the California Winter League in Wrigley Field two days after the Little World Series ended, with a doubleheader between the Kansas City Royals and Butch Moran's Hollywood Stars. Five thousand fans saw very little offense during the twin bill, but the Royals put together enough to escape with a 2–1 win in the opener, and a seven inning 0–0 tie in the afterpiece. Booker McDaniels, Jimmy Newbury, and Verdell Mathis combined on a two-hit shutout in game one, with Mathis getting the win over Manny Perez. Chet Brewer's boys scored two runs in the bottom of the sixth, to overcome a 1–0 Hollywood lead. In game two, Paul Gregory and John Williams shut down the offenses, with Gregory allowing a single hit, and Williams yielding two.

Game three of the five game series was played under the Wrigley Field lights the following Wednesday, with John Williams facing off against Newt Kimball (19–21 with Hollywood in 1945). The Royals made it two straight over Butch Moran's club, winning 4–3. A crowd of 3,521 saw Bill Hoskins bang a homer run in the sixth inning to give Brewer's boys a 3–1 lead at the time. Then, after the Stars came back to knot the count at 3-all in the top of the seventh, Kansas City pulled it out in the ninth, when Clyde Nelson's one-out single plated Ray Neil with the winning run.

The last two games of the series were played on Sunday afternoon, starting at 1:30. Hollywood's hopes to even the series were dashed in game one. For a time, it looked like the Royals might have an easy time, but the Hollywood boys wouldn't quit. In the top of the eighth, trailing 7–1, the Stars pushed across four runs, three of them on Gabby Stewart's triple with the bases loaded, to narrow the margin to 7–5. But that was all they would get. Johnny Williams, who struggled throughout the game, had enough left to blank the Stars in the ninth, and claim the victory. In game two, an abbreviated seven inning affair, Verdell Mathis, the ace of the Memphis Red Sox, beat Paul Gregory (9–5 with Hollywood), 3–1 on a three-hitter.

The most exciting part of the winter league season was about to begin. Bob Feller's Major League All-Stars entered

Bob Feller, one of the greatest pitchers ever, played more than two dozen exhibition games against Satchel Paige. It was a magnificent rivalry.

Wrigley Field to do battle with the Kansas City Royals. And, in the wings, two legendary pitchers stood waiting—Satchel Paige, perhaps the greatest pitcher in Negro league history, and Bob Feller, who might have been the greatest major league pitcher of all time. The *Los Angeles Times* previewed the first game. "The fastest pitch ever officially clocked—145 feet per second—and a new major league strikeout record for one season (348) which broke Rube Waddell's 42-year-old mark by five! That's the phenomenal record 27-year-old Bob Feller of Cleveland, with his 16 flying major league stars, brings to Wrigley Field tomorrow night for a duel with Satchel Paige, greatest of Negro pitchers, who won 24 and lost two games, while pitching the Kansas City Monarchs to both halves of the American Negro League pennant."

Bob Feller fielded a team that included all the players noted above—Rizzuto, Keller, Keltner, etc. And Paige was backed up by the powerful Royals lineup of Bubba Hyde, Bill Hoskins, and Ed Steele. The Major Leaguers and Bob Feller drew first blood in the series, nipping the Royals 4–3. The Cleveland ace and the Monarch fireballer each pitched five innings, with Feller getting the best of it. Hits were few and far between for both teams, with the Royals clipping the pride of Iowa for five singles, and the Stars getting to Paige for just three. But the Stars made their hits count. Johnny Berardino rapped a home run over the left field wall in the third, and Frankie Hayes hit a two-run single in the fourth.

Traveling south to San Diego, the two teams tangled again the next night, with the same result, Feller winning 2–0. Both pitchers went five innings again, with "Rapid Robert" tossing a shutout, and the Negro league ace yielding two runs.

Taking a "timeout" from the series, Kansas City met the Major-Minor All-Stars in a doubleheader in L.A. while Bob Feller's boys traveled north to Sacramento, to meet the Coast All-Stars. The Royals had better luck with the M & M club, sweeping the twin bill, 11–2 and 3–1, before 4,102 fans in Wrigley Field. Jimmy Newbury pitched a four-hitter in the opener, backed by a 13 hit attack. In the nightcap, Bill Hoskins hit a three-run homer in the fifth inning, to give southpaw Walter McCoy a 3–1 victory. Up north, Feller worked two innings, giving up two runs, and fanning four. He was followed to the mound by Johnny Sain and winning pitcher Dutch Leonard, as the major leaguers scored a run in the seventh and two in the eighth, to win 4–3.

Jackie Robinson, back home after a sensational debut season in organized baseball, formed an all-star team of his own, and played several exhibition games against Bob Feller's major leaguers. In the first meeting, Robinson's Negro leaguers were blanked by the big-leaguers 6–0 in San Francisco. The *Pittsburgh Courier* followed the action. "...the Robinson nine battled the Feller

Stars to 4–0 and 4–3 thrillers at San Diego and Los Angeles on Thursday and Friday nights respectively.

"On Thursday night, Jackie's valiants led the game 2–1 up to two out in the eighth inning when Stan Musial singled, Charlie Keller doubled off the right field wall, and both scored on Jeff Heath's single to center.... Friday nights game was a thriller and left the fans literally hanging from the rafters when the Robinsons came from behind to score three runs and go down swinging in the ninth with two men on." More than 12,000 screaming fans attended the Friday game in Wrigley Field, to see Rapid Robert square off against Nate Moreland, just back from a tour of duty in the Mexican League. Feller was on top of his game, as he no-hit the Robbies during his five inning stint, fanning ten of the 15 men he faced, and coming away with the victory.

The Cleveland ace was back at it the next night, pitching four innings against the Major-Minor All-Stars in Recreation Park in Long Beach. A crowd of 3,500 spectators saw the Iowan farmboy nicked for a long home run off the bat of Jack Graham of the New York Giants in the second inning. The M & M club made the 1–0 lead stand up for six innings. Then, the big leaguers tied it up in the seventh, and won it in the eighth when Cleveland's Bob Lemon jerked a home run over the left field wall with Rollie Hemsley on base.

The last recorded game of the fall pitted the Major League All-Stars against the Kansas City Royals in a Wrigley Field doubleheader on Sunday October 27. In the opener, before 3,142 fans, Bob Lemon tossed a complete game two-hitter to shackle Chet Brewer's boys 5–0. The nightcap was tied at 2–2 when darkness ended the struggle at the end of the fifth inning.

The Kansas City Royals were the California Winter League champions with a record of 6–3–1, but Feller's All-Stars, a traveling team, had the best record on the coast, winning all eight games that were recovered. Bill Hoskins was the top batter and home run hitter, with an average of .444 with two home runs, in three recorded games. Bob Feller led the pitchers with a 3–0 record.

Sometime after the close of the winter league season, two well known Negro league baseball players passed from the scene. Walter Ball, a famous old time Negro league pitcher, died in Cook County Hospital in Chicago, Illinois, on December 15, at the age of 69. Ball, who pitched professionally for 23 years, was regarded as one of the best pitchers of his time. He was best remembered for pitching an exhibition game against Mordecai "Three-Fingered" Brown and the Chicago Cubs in 1909, losing 4–2.

Another heartbreaking loss was the sudden death of Negro league legend, Josh Gibson, the greatest home run hitter in Negro league history. The happy-go-lucky Gibson succumbed to a stroke at his home in Pittsburgh on January 20, 1947. He was just 35 years old. His loss was particularly painful in view of Jackie Robinson's recent integration of organized baseball. In another time, it might have been the legendary Homestead Grays' backstop who was the pioneer. But, fate dealt him another hand, one that was painful and self-destructive and, in the end, fatal. Josh Gibson will always be remembered as a big, overgrown kid who enjoyed playing the game, and who hit prodigious home runs all over the western hemisphere, not only in the Negro leagues, but in exhibition games against major league opposition, as well as in leagues in Mexico, Puerto Rico, the Dominican Republic, and Cuba. Josh Gibson, in the prime of his career, before his decline, was one of the greatest baseball players ever to set foot on a diamond.

1946 California Winter League

	Wins	Losses	Ties
Kansas City Royals	6	3	1
Major League All-Stars	1	0	1
Major-Minor All-Stars	0	3	0
Hollywood Stars	0	4	0

Independent Teams

	Wins	Losses	Ties
Feller's All-Stars	8	0	0
Jackie Robinson's All-Stars	0	4	0

Miscellaneous Batting Statistics 1946

Name	Team	Pos	G	AB	H	D	T	HR	BA
Hoskins, Bill	Kansas City Royals	LF	3	9	4	0	0	2	.444
Robinson, J.	Robinson's All-Stars	SS	2	5	1	1	0	0	.200
Musial, Stan	Feller's All-Stars	CF	3	9	2	0	0	0	.222
Keller, Charlie	Feller's All-Stars	LF	2	6	1	1	0	0	.167
Keltner, Ken	Feller's All-Stars	3B	2	7	1	1	0	0	.143
Heath, Jeff	Feller's All-Stars	RF	2	4	1	0	0	1	.250
Lemon, Bob	Feller's All-Stars	P	2	5	1	0	0	1	.200

Miscellaneous Pitching Statistics 1946

Name	Team	G	CG	W	L	IP	SO	BB	SH
Paige, Satchel	Kansas City Royals	3	0	0	2	15	21	12	0
Newbury, J.	Kansas City Royals	3	2	1	0	16	—	—	0
Feller, Bob	Feller's All-Stars	6	0	3	0	26	25	10	0
Lemon, Bob	Feller AS, MLAS	3	1	2	0	15	—	—	1

The 1947 Season

THERE IS NO WINTER LEAGUE THIS YEAR. That might well have been the sign outside Wrigley Field in 1947. The integration of organized baseball had written the final chapter to an American classic, the thirty-seven-year-old integrated California Winter League. It had its day, and its day had passed.

But baseball was not quite dead on the coast. There remained one last shot to be fired, a dazzling pitching exhibition that could only be delivered by two of baseball's immortal flamethrowers, Satchel Paige and Bob Feller. The two hurlers faced off three times between October 15 and November 9, and each game was a masterpiece. In addition, Paige also matched weapons with the Cincinnati Reds' lanky fireballer, Ewell "The Whip" Blackwell, a 6'6" right-hander, whose buggywhip motion sent the ball plateward from the vicinity of third base. Almost 50,000 fans crammed Wrigley Field to witness the five games, marking the end of the celebrated annual legendary pitching matchups. In 1948, Satchel Paige did return to Los Angeles one more time, but he didn't face off against Bob Feller. His Kansas City Royals lost to Bob Lemon's All-Stars, 8–4.

The first game of the winter series took place in Wrigley Field on Wednesday evening, October 15. Bob Feller came out on top in the first encounter between the two baseball giants. Both Paige and Feller pitched four innings, with the Cleveland ace hurling shutout ball, while striking out two, and the Monarch ace being touched for a single run, while fanning seven. Jeff Heath's sacrifice fly in the fourth inning scored Ken

Keltner with the first run of the game. Both teams scored in the seventh to bring the final tally to 2–1.

Game two was played four days later, with 12,160 fans raising the rafters in Wrigley Field, cheering for their favorite. Satchel Paige outpitched his major league opponent, leaving with a 1–0 lead after five innings. The Satchel man's blazing fastball set eight batters down on strikes. Feller who was touched up for a single run, fanned five and walked none. The All-Stars picked on Satchel's reliever, John Williams, for the two winning runs, a homer by Andy Pafko in the sixth, and the game winning blast by Jerry Priddy in the seventh.

Ewell Blackwell, the National League's leading pitcher, brought an all-star team to town as soon as Feller's team left. Games were scheduled for Thursday night and Sunday afternoon. The *Times* previewed the matchup. "In outpitching Bob Feller twice last week, although the team lost each game by a 2–1 margin, Paige tonight goes against the best the other league has to offer. Blackwell pitched a no-hitter, won 16 consecutive games, and wound up with not only a 22 and 8 won and lost record, but also led the National League in strikeouts with 191. Feller led the American loop with 196."

The game was another Wrigley Field thriller. The Kansas City Bombers nicked Blackwell for single runs in both the first and second innings, and the score was still 2–0 when the two starting pitchers departed after four innings. The great Satchel Paige held the major leaguers to two hits and sent nine of them back to the bench dragging their bats behind them. Blackwell was less impressive, yielding two runs, fanning four and walking four. The All-Stars tied the game in the top of the ninth, then took the lead 3–2 in the 13th when Peanuts Lowrey's sacrifice fly scored Roy Partee. Jesse Flores of the Philadelphia A's, working into his ninth inning, filled the bases with two gone, then Goose Tatum of Harlem Globetrotter fame singled to drive in both Ed Steele and Piper Davis with the winning runs.

On Sunday, the Blackwells, thirsting for revenge, took a 2–1 lead against Paige when Al Zarilla took the lanky black hurler deep in the fourth inning. Kansas City came right back with a run in the bottom of the fifth off Blackwell, knotting the count at 2–2. The score stayed the same until the last of the eighth when Chet Brewer's boys pushed over the winning run. Piper Davis led the Kansas City attack with a single and a double. Paige gave up two runs in four innings, fanning five. Ewell Blackwell was touched for two runs in five innings, but struck out eight of the fifteen men he retired.

A review of the pitching performances of the three pitchers, showed Satchel Paige to have all the best of it, in spite of an 0–1 record. The 6'4" Negro league legend pitched seventeen innings, with only one earned run being scored against him. He fanned 29 major leaguers including Ralph Kiner and Johnny Berardino three times, and Andy Pafko, Bob Lemon, Peanuts Lowrey, and Catfish Metkovich, twice each.

The fans around Los Angeles awaited the last encounter between the two pitching goliaths, Feller and Paige, a Wrigley Field extravaganza set for Sunday, November 2. Both pitchers were anxious to wrap up their west coast exhibitions in grand style, and both vowed to pitch the entire game. As it turned out, both pitchers did go the route, but only one lived up to his reputation. Satchel Paige, the timeless 41-year-old master craftsman, mesmerized the big leaguers, tossing a tight four-hit shutout, and striking out 15 of the "pros." The *Los Angeles Times* reported. "If he wasn't striking the opposition out, his mates were backing him up in great style, something that Feller didn't have, to aid him.

"The Cleveland fireballer had much to overcome. His infield bogged down in the third and four runs, three of them unearned, crossed over. At other times balls went for hits that might just as easily have been fielded.

However, two of them were resounding wallops by Joe Greene and Piper Davis for home runs, each with the bases empty."

The final score was 8–0 in favor of the Kansas City Royals.

Feller's All-Stars

Name	Pos	AB	H
Lowrey, Peanuts	CF	4	0
Bockman, Eddie	3B	4	0
Stevens, Chuck	1B	3	0
Graham, Jack	RF	4	0
Lemon, bob	LF	3	1
Priddy, Jerry	2B	3	1
Sturgeon, Bob	SS	4	2
Partee, Roy	C	2	0
Feller, Bob	P	3	0
Mapes, Cliff	PH	1	0
Totals		31	4

Kansas City Royals

Name	Pos	AB	H
Williams, Jesse	SS	5	2
Neil, Ray	2B	5	1
Steele, Ed	RF	4	1
Davis, Piper	1B	3	2
Hoskins, Bill	LF	3	1
Renfro, Othello	3B	4	1
Abernathy, George	CF	4	1
Greene, Joe	C	2	1
Paige, Satchel	P	3	0
Haywood, Buster	C	1	1
		34	11

```
Feller's All-Stars    0 0 0   0 0 0   0 0 0— 0— 4–3
Kansas City Royals    1 1 4   0 0 0   1 1 x— 8—11–0
```

Two Base Hits: Sturgeon, Neil, Lemon
Home Runs: Greene, Davis

	IP	R	H	SO	BB
Feller, Bob (LP)	8	8	11	5	1
Paige, Satchel (WP)	9	0	4	15	4

Kansas City finished their schedule by whipping a minor league all-star team, 5–2 in Wrigley Field. Paige closed out his storied California winter baseball career, by blanking the minor leaguers for four innings, and striking out four. As usual, he didn't get a victory. The minor leaguers scored five runs in the eighth off one of Satchel's relievers, either Richardson or Newbury, en route to a 5–2 win.

1947 Winter Baseball Exhibitions

	Wins	Losses	Ties
Feller's All-Stars	4	2	0
Kansas City Royals	4	5	0
Minor League Stars	1	0	0
Major-Minor League All-Stars	0	1	0
Blackwell's All-Stars	0	2	0

Kansas City Royals Batting Statistics 1947

Name	Pos	G	AB	H	D	T	HR	BA
Williams, Jesse	SS	6	25	9	2	1	0	.360
Neil, Ray	2B	5	21	3	1	0	0	.143
Steele, Ed	RF	6	19	5	2	0	1	.263
Davis, Piper	3B	5	21	6	1	0	2	.287
Hoskins, Bill	LF	5	19	4	1	0	0	.211
Tatum, Goose	1B	3	11	2	0	0	0	.182
Greene, Joe	C	4	8	1	0	0	1	.125

Kansas City Royals Batting Statistics 1947

Name	Pos	G	AB	H	D	T	HR	BA
Paige, Satchel	P	5	9	2	0	0	0	.222
Haywood, Buster	C	4	9	1	0	0	0	.111
Renfro, Othello	3B	4	14	3	0	0	0	.214

Kansas City Royals Pitching Statistics 1947

Name	G	CG	W	L	IP	SO	BB	SH
Paige, Satchel	7	1	2	1	35	60	14	1
Williams, John	3	0	0	1	14	0	3	0
Newbury, Jimmy	3	0	2	1	16	4	4	0

Miscellaneous Batting Statistics 1947

Name	Team	Pos	G	AB	H	D	T	HR	BA
Metkovich, G.	Blackwell's A.S.	1B	2	10	1	0	0	0	.100
Lindell, John	Blackwell's A.S.	P	2	10	0	0	0	0	.000
Zarilla, Al	Blackwell's A.S.	RF	2	8	4	0	0	1	.500
Partee, Roy	Blackwell's A.S.	C	2	8	4	1	0	0	.500
Sturgeon, Bob	Blackwell's A.S.	SS	2	7	3	0	0	0	.429
Pafko, Andy	Feller's All-Sstars	CF	2	8	2	0	0	1	.250
Kiner, Ralph	Feller's All-Stars	LF	2	8	2	1	0	0	.250
Priddy, Jerry	Feller's All-Stars	2B	3	10	4	0	0	1	.400

Miscellaneous Pitching Statistics 1947

Name	Team	G	CG	W	L	IP	SO	BB	SH
Blackwell, E.	Blackwell's A.S.	2	0	0	0	9	12	7	0
Feller, Bob	Feller's All-Stars	6	1	3	1	32	22	2	1

10

A Final Look Back

America lost a historical institution in 1947 when the California Winter League faded from the scene. For a period of 38 years the integrated winter circuit had provided the baseball fans of Southern California with some of the best, if not THE BEST, professional baseball played in the United States. The baseball audience around Los Angeles, more than 1,500 miles distant from the westernmost major league city of St. Louis, were fortunate to be able to watch such major league standouts as Bob Meusel, Babe Herman, Charlie Root, Hollis "Sloppy" Thurston, Tony Lazzeri, and Bob Feller. They were also blessed to see some of the best players from the Negro leagues; superb pitchers, fielders, and hitters, like Bullet Joe Rogan, Cyclone Joe Williams, John Henry Lloyd, Turkey Stearnes, Mule Suttles, and Satchel Paige.

The California Winter League, the first integrated professional baseball league within the continental limits of the United States, was the most important professional league in the country during the first half of the twentieth century, surpassing both the Negro leagues and the major leagues, because it pitted the best players in the majors against the greatest players in Negro league history, prior to the Jackie Robinson era, in head to head competition. It was, in fact, the only true major league between 1920 and 1947.

When the league was reorganized in 1920 under the direction of Doc Anderson and Joe Pirrone, it was established as an integrated league because previous experience showed that mixed-race games attracted two or three times as many fans as other games. Since the league was usually a four team league with one Negro league team and three white teams, the Negro league team played a three-game series every weekend, while the white teams only played every third week unless they could schedule a series with another white club, which was infrequent.

Most of the legendary Negro league players of the first four decades of the century spent some winters playing baseball on the west coast. Spot Poles, Pete Hill, Dobie Moore, Oscar Charleston, Biz Mackey, Cool Papa Bell, and Willie Wells all competed there, in addition to the players noted above. They were opposed by major leaguers like Earl Averill, Smead Jolley, Ping Bodie, Jigger Statz, Specs Meadows, Ferdie Schupp, Buck Newsom, Heinie Manush, and Larry French. Some detractors of the California Winter League insisted that the league was not truly a competitive league because the major league players did not play hard, and did not give an honest effort. Nothing could be further from the truth. The games were spirited and competitive, and with good reason. In the first place, the salaries of major league players, during the '20s, '30s, and '40s, were only slightly

Ray Neil and Cool Papa Bell played for the Royal Giants in the mid-1940s as the winter league was gearing down. (NoirTech Research)

higher than the wages of the average blue collar worker in the United States. Given the fact that the gate receipts were split 60–40 (and occasionally 75–25), with the winning team's players dividing 60 percent of the gate and the losing teams players 40 percent, there was a big incentive to win, to players of both races. Also, many major leaguers, like South Carolinian Buck Newsom, were prejudiced against blacks, and they were humiliated any time they lost to a black team. Newsom was once quoted as saying "I'll never go up to the big leagues until I can beat these niggers." Supposedly, Cool Papa Bell, on hearing the comment, just smiled and said, "Let's make him stay out here about two years."

Negro league entries in the California Winter League more than held their own against the big leaguers, winning well over 60 percent of all the games played. They also dominated the championship trophy chase, at one point between 1924 and 1939 capturing 13 of 16 flags. The individual performances of the Negro league players participating in the California Winter League made it very clear that the integration of organized baseball came at least twenty years too late. If the majors had been open to men of all races in the 1920s, the names of Chet Brewer, Mule Suttles, Biz Mackey, Dobie Moore, Jud Wilson, Wild Bill Wright, John Beckwith, and Sammy T. Hughes would be household names in baseball America. And there's a good chance that all of them would have their plaques permanently mounted on the wall of the National Baseball Hall of Fame in Cooperstown, New York.

Satchel Paige proved his greatness in his encounters with Bob Feller. He held Feller to a draw in their meetings, even though he was over 40 years of age at the time.

Major league players like Irish Meusel, Bob Meusel, Babe Herman, and Smead Jolley all performed well on the west coast, but their achievements were overshadowed by their Negro league counterparts. Satchel Paige stood astride the California Winter League like the celebrated Colossus of Rhodes. His extraordinary repertoire of pitches like his bee-ball, his bat-dodger, his hurry-up ball, and his hesitation pitch, brought oohs and aahs from the fans, and groans from opposing batsmen. The great Satchel devastated enemy lineups, fanning an average of 12 batters a game during his long west coast career, and throwing 17 shutouts in 77 games. His won-lost record of 56–7 seemed other-worldly. In fact, his entire California Winter League career seemed like one long fairy tale. The lanky right-hander, who fired smoke, did not lose a California Winter League game for more than two years, from the early fall of 1931 to December of 1933. In his prime, during the 1930s, the native of Mobile, Alabama, strung together an unbelievable record of 50–2. He was 16–2, with 7 shutouts, in 1933–34, with a spectacular 1.63 Total Run Average, and 13 strikeouts a game. And Paige didn't build his record against second-rate pitchers. He was usually matched up against the ace of the opposing staff, like Larry French (197–171 major league won-loss record), Buck Newsom, (211–222), and Sloppy Thurston (89–86), and he dominated them all. He was 8–2 against those three pitchers. Even in his later years, as a senior citizen, he matched fast balls with the great Bob Feller, and came away with a draw.

Other Negro league pitchers, like Bullet Joe Rogan (42–14), Chet Brewer (43–13), and Cannonball Jim Willis (41–9), also shone brightly in the California sun.

Two of the more devastating hitters in the California Winter League, Mule Suttles and Turkey Stearnes, were products of the Negro leagues. George "Mule" Suttles, the 6'3", 215 pound, right-handed bomber from Louisiana, toyed with major league pitching. During a magnificent nine year career on the coast, the big first baseman tattooed opposing pitchers for an amazing 64 home runs in 450 at-bats, a figure that averages out to be 79 home runs for every 550 at-bats, an all-world record. That number is all the more impressive when you realize that the "Sultan of Swat," Babe Ruth, averaged 50 home runs per 550 at-bats during his long major league career, while his eventual heir, Mark McGwire, also averaged 50. Josh Gibson, the Negro leagues' mighty bomber, averaged 48 home runs for every 550 at-bats. And Sadaharu Oh, Japan's home run king, pounded out 52. Mule Suttles was not only a slugger, however. He also hit for average, as evidenced by his lifetime .378 mark, #3 on the all-time California Winter League hit parade. Even when facing some of the "name" pitchers, the Mule never slowed down. He hit Larry French for a .389 average, with 5 home runs in just 18 at-bats, and he punished Hollis "Sloppy" Thurston for 4 home runs in 23 at-bats.

Norman "Turkey" Stearnes was almost as destructive as his teammate. He played winter ball in California for ten years, compiling a career average of .373 in 754 at-bats, with 56 home runs (41 per 550 at-bats), second in the league to Suttles. Included in Stearnes' home run totals was a sensational four-homer game against Pirrone's All-Stars. The slender left-handed slugger took Hank McDonald, former St. Louis Browns hurler, deep twice in the opening frame, then homered off both Syl Johnson and Larry French later in the game. Over his career, he batted .378 against Sloppy Thurston with 5 homers in 37 at-bats, and throttled Buck Newsom for a .448 average in 29 at-bats.

The major leaguers also had some big clubbers. Smead Jolley, Buzz Arlett, and Babe Herman were three of the more explosive hitters in the league. Jolley banged Negro league pitchers for a .402 average in 127 at-bats. His victims included Chet Brewer (.500) and Andy Cooper (.500). Buzz Arlett hit .368 for the White Kings in 95 at-bats, going 3 for 9 against Plunk Drake, and 5 for 8 against Rube Currie. Babe Herman, a home town boy, played in the winter league for 14 years, hitting .351 in 268 at-bats. Like Stearnes and Suttles, Brooklyn's all-time leading hitter, played no favorites. He hit Rube Currie for a .441 average in 34 at-bats, hit Jess Hubbard for a .400 average, and was .429 (3 for 7) against William "Plunk" Drake.

Other torrid hitters in California were Earl Averill, the Meusel brothers—Bob and Irish—Wally Berger, and Dick Cox. Averill, a career .318 hitter over a 13 year period in the major leagues, smoked the ball at a .500 clip one year on the coast. Bob Meusel compiled a .310 batting average over an 11 year major league career, Irish hit .309 in 11 years, Wally Berger hit .300 in 11 years, and Dick Cox hit .314 in two years. In California they produced averages of .324, .313, .431, and .313 respectively, basically the same as their big league stats. Berger's winter league stats are somewhat misleading, because he had only 51 at-bats, however he blasted 10 home runs in those at-bats, enough to capture the 1930-31 home run title, and to give him a glossy average of 108 homers for every 550 at-bats.

A review of the batting and pitching statistics in the league make the Negro league players look like supermen, when compared to their major league counterparts. But looks can be deceiving. You can't compare Turkey Stearnes' .373 average directly with Irish Meusel's .313. Nor Mule Suttles' .377 average with Babe Herman's .351. The same is true with the pitchers. Satchel Paige's won-loss record cannot be compared to the won-loss record of Larry French. That's like comparing apples to oranges.

Unfortunately for the white teams, the California Winter League did not present a level playing field to all competitors. For one thing, the players did not compile their averages against the same teams. Unlike players in the major leagues, who played 86 percent of their games against common opponents, the Negro league players competed primarily against white teams, while the white players usually competed against Negro league teams. Since Negro league rosters were stable throughout the season, the white batters faced the same high quality pitchers, like Paige, Rogan, Brewer, and Foster, week in and week out. Negro leaguers, on the other hand, had an advantage. They might face major league and AAA minor league pitchers on occasion, but because the white teams were always in a state of flux, they often faced lower level pitchers, with a few local amateurs (like Joe Pirrone himself) thrown in.

Also, black teams often came to the coast as a unit, directly after completing their summer Negro league schedules. And since most of them played baseball twelve months a year, they stayed in reasonably good playing condition. Not so with the the major-minor leaguers. Most players from the major leagues and the Coast League resided in California, and had other interests in addition to baseball, so their participation in the league was sporadic at best. Some of the white pitchers might only pitch once or twice a month. The same was true for the position players. Others were more or less on call, and only played in an emergency. Occasionally a big name star like Jimmie Foxx or Al Simmons would visit Los Angeles just long enough to play a game or two, then move on to another town, and another paycheck. And then there was Commissioner Landis, whose directives limited major league players to playing exhibition games for just 30 days after the completion of the major league schedule. A few players circumvented the Commissioner's directives by playing under assumed names, while others just ignored the edict.

Fortunately, the relative differences between the major leagues, the AAA leagues, and the Negro leagues, were part of another study, published in *Baseball's Other All-Stars*, so the skill level of the California Winter League can be estimated fairly accurately (see the tables in the appendix). Black players, with at least 400 at-bats in both the Negro leagues and the California Winter League (Allen, Bell, Carr, Dixon, Holloway, Mackey, Rogan, Stearnes, Suttles, Wells), hit 21 points above their Negro league averages in California, indicating the overall pitching faced by Negro leaguers on the west coast was probably no better than a AA level. While many of the pitchers on Pirrone's All-Stars, the White Kings, and Shell Oil were major league stars, pitchers on some of the other teams were merely journeymen minor leaguers.

The white players averaged .260 in the major leagues, .284 in AAA ball, and .273 in California. The top ten major league players in the California Winter League, with more than 1000 at-bats in both the majors and AAA ball (Jolley, Herman, B. Meusel, I. Meusel, Bodie, Haney, J.C. Smith, Griggs, Rhyne, and Statz), hit 25 points above their major league averages on the coast, indicating the Negro league pitching was about a AAA level or slightly higher. Some Negro league pitchers, like Paige, Rogan, Brewer, and Willie Foster, were major leaguers in fact, if not in name. Others were not.

The Negro league teams at times appeared to be AAA quality, and may occasionally have been major league quality. At other times, their roster was closer to a AA level. Some of the white teams, like Pirrone's All-Stars, the White Kings, and Shell Oil, occasionally fielded teams of at AAA caliber or higher. But other teams like the Mexican All-Stars, El Paso, and some of the San Diego teams, were frequently low level minor league teams.

Although there was a significant difference between the Negro league teams and their white opponents in the California Winter League, the individual contests between top-notch major leaguers and their Negro league counterparts, still provided a legitimate measurement of the relative skills of the two groups. Bob and Irish Meusel, Babe Herman, Dick Cox, Smead Jolley, Chicken Hawks, and Babe Twombly, were all career .300 hitters in the major leagues. Others like Fuzzy Hufft (.346), Frank Brazill (.342), Pete Schneider (.333), Smead Jolley (.372), Eddie Pick (.319), Buzz Arlett (.342), Cleo Carlyle (.316), Art Griggs (.315), and Jigger Statz (.316), raised havoc in the AAA coast league. On the mound, Larry French won 197 games in the big time, Buck Newsom won 211, Specs Meadows won 188, Doc Crandall won 102, and Bob Feller won 266 despite losing almost four years to military service in World War II. In the Pacific Coast League, Win Ballou won 154 games, Clyde Barfoot won 104, Doc Crandall 230, Wheezer Dell 138, Willie Ludolph 156, Herm Pillette 226, and Sloppy Thurston 106.

In the one-on-one encounters between the best of the Negro leagues and the best of the major-minor leagues, the two groups came out about equal. The appendix has a breakdown of how the top Negro league batters fared against individual major league pitchers, and how the best major league batters fared against individual Negro league pitchers. The overall results are what you might expect. The good hitters, both black and white, could hit any pitcher, but not necessarily all pitchers. Every batter had one or more pitchers who had their number. And the right-left factor often came into play. For instance, Turkey Stearnes hit righties hard—.378 against Sloppy Thurston and .448 against Buck Newsom, but was held pretty well in check—by southpaws—.267 against Ferdie Schupp and .273 against Larry French. Mule Suttles battered the southpaws, Win Ballou (.583), and Larry French (.389 with 5 home runs in 18 at-bats), but Buck Newsom held him to just 8 hits in 29 at-bats (.276), with two home runs. Earl Averill, a southpaw swinger, treated right-handers Chet Brewer and Bullet Rogan like long lost cousins, hitting .467 against Brewer and .571 against Rogan. Most other big league hitters had a lot of trouble with Rogan. Smead Jolley hit him at a .333 clip, but the best Babe Herman could do was .276. Rogan held Bob Meusel to a .278 average, Irish Meusel to .239, Jigger Statz to .143, and Casey Stengel to .286. Southpaw swingers fared much better against Bullet Joe than their right-handed hitting teammates. The lefties batted .270 against the Negro league ace, while the righties could do no better than .220.

The California Winter League was probably between a AA and AAA level overall, but the one-on-one matchups between Turkey Stearnes and Buck Newsom, Biz Mackey and Hollis Thurston, Babe Herman and Bullet Joe Rogan, and Earl Averill and Chet Brewer, were major league all the way, and definitely made the league the most significant professional baseball league in the United States during the first half of the twentieth century. It gave the country a rare look at high level integrated professional baseball more than 25 years before organized baseball got the message.

Appendix A

League Champions, Season by Season

YEAR	TEAM	RECORD	
1906-07			
1907-08	Santa Ana Yellow Sox	13-3-2	Official League Champion
1908-09	San Diego Bears	3-1	Official League Champion
1909-10	Santa Barbara	7-0	Probable League Champion
1910-11	San Diego Griefers	7-4	Official League Champion
1911-12			Insufficient data
1912-13	San Diego Bears	7-4	Probable League Champion
1913-14	San Bernardino	4-1	Possible League Champion
1914-15	El Centro	14-8	Valley League Champion
1915-16	Chicago American Giants	10-6	Official League Champion
	El Centro	8-2	Valley League Champion
1916-17	San Pedro	19-1	Probable League Champion
1917-18			Insufficient data
1918-19	Hollywood	4-0	Possible League Champion
1919-20			No league in operation
1920-21	Los Angeles White Sox	24-15-2	Probable League Champion
	Lincoln Giants	20-2	Independent
1921-22	Colored All-Stars	25-15-1	Probable League Champion
1922-23	Los Angeles White Sox	9-11-2	Official League Champion
1923-24	St. Louis Stars	6-3	Best Records Recovered
	San Diego	3-1	Best Records Recovered
1924-25	White Kings	20-9	Official League Champions
	St. Louis Giants	27-13-1	So. Calif. W.L. Champions
1925-26	Philadelphia Royal Giants	26-15-3	Official League Champion
1926-27	Philadelphia Royal Giants	26-11-1	Co-Champion, won 2nd half
	Shell Oil	19-15-1	Co-Champion, won 1st half
1927-28	Philadelphia Royal Giants	19-11-2	Official League Champion
1928-29	Cleveland Giants	30-13-2	Official League Champion
1929-30	Philadelphia Royal Giants	23-12-1	Probable Co-Champions
	Shell Oil	11-6-1	Probable Co-Champions
1930-31	Philadelphia Royal Giants	28-2-1	"Other" W.L. Champion
	Nashville Elite Giants	33-10-2	Official League Champion
1931-32	Philadelphia Giants	21-2	Official League Champion
1932-33	Wilson's Elite Giants	18-3-4	Official League Champions
1933-34	Wilson's Elite Giants	34-8-2	Official League Champion
1934-35	Wilson's Elite Giants	34-5-1	Official League Champion
1935-36	Wilson's Royal Giants	23-6-2	Official League Champion

YEAR	TEAM	RECORD	
1936–37	Wilson's Royal Giants	21–6–1	Probable League Champion
1937–38	Philadelphia Royal Giants	21–3–1	Official League Champion
1938–39	Philadelphia Royal Giants	11–2–1	Probable League Champion
1939–40	Philadelphia Royal Giants	10–6–1	Official League Champion
1940–41	Baltimore Elite Giants	9–4	Official League Champion
1941–42	Pirrone's All–Stars	4–0	
1942–43	Major–Minor All–Stars	1–0	
	Los Alamitos Naval Air Base	1–0	
	Elite Giants	7–1	Two leagues
1943–44	Baltimore Elite Giants	7–5–1	Probable League Champion
1944–45	Birmingham Black Barons	4–1–2	Probable League Champion
1945	Kansas City Royals	14–10	Probable League Champion
1946	Kansas City Royals	6–3–2	
	Feller's All–Stars	8–0	
1947	Feller's All–Stars	4–2	

Appendix B
Individual Career Leaders

Batting

Batting (minimum 300 at-bats)

Walter "Dobie" Moore	.385 (377 AB)
George "Mule" Suttles	.378 (450 AB)
Burnis "Wild Bill" Wright	.375 (416 AB)
Norman "Turkey" Stearnes	.373 (754 AB)
James "Cool Papa" Bell	.368 (596 AB)
Raleigh "Biz" Mackey	.366 (957 AB)
Wilbur "Bullet Joe" Rogan	.362 (434 AB)
Jake Dunn	.335 (328 AB)
George "Tank" Carr	.336 (715 AB)
Herbert "Rap" Dixon	.326 (479 AB)
Dick Cox	.326 (322 AB)
Emil "Irish" Meusel	.319 (399 AB)

Batting average (minimum 70 at-bats)

John Beckwith	.413 (172 AB)
Jim West	.404 (137 AB)
Smead Jolley	.397 (131 AB)
Jess "Mountain" Hubbard	.390 (208 AB)
Sammy T. Hughes	.384 (294 AB)
Alec Radcliffe	.380 (130 AB)
Oscar Charleston	.375 (88 AB)
Art Griggs	.373 (118 AB)
Russell "Buzz" Arlett	.368 (95 AB)
Spot Poles	.365 (74 AB)
Babe Herman	.351 (268 AB)

Doubles

Raleigh "Biz" Mackey	62
George "Tank" Carr	52
Willie Wells	40
Norman "Turkey" Stearnes	39
Newt Allen	35
Rap Dixon	33
James "Cool Papa" Bell	31
George "Mule" Suttles	29
Walter "Dobie" Moore	28
"Wild Bill" Wright	26
Wilbur "Bullet Joe" Rogan	25

Triples

Raleigh "Biz" Mackey	17
George "Tank" Carr	17
Norman "Turkey" Stearnes	16
Walter "Dobie" Moore	13
James "Cool Papa" Bell	12
Hurley McNair	12
Emil "Irish" Meusel	12
Burnis "Wild Bill" Wright	11

Home Runs

George "Mule" Suttles	64
Norman "Turkey" Stearnes	56
Raleigh "Biz" Mackey	28
George "Tank" Carr	27
John Beckwith	19
Herbert "Rap" Dixon	18
Sammy T. Hughes	17
James "Cool Papa" Bell	16
Wilbur "Bullet Joe" Rogan	15
Burnis "Wild Bill" Wright	15
Tommy Dukes	14
Joseph "Jake" Dunn	13

Pitching

Games Pitched

Satchel Paige	80
Chet Brewer	72
James "Cannonball" Willis	68
Wilbur "Bullet Joe" Rogan	64
Rube Currie	61
Herm "Old Folks" Pillette	54
Andy Cooper	43
Lou Koupal	38
Roy Wilkinson	35

Appendix B

Andrew "Pullman" Porter	35
George Payne	30

Complete Games

Wilbur "Bullet Joe" Rogan	52
Satchel Paige	47
James "Cannonball" Willis	47
Chet Brewer	42
Rube Currie	35
Herm "Old Folks" Pillette	26
Andrew "Pullman" Porter	25
Walter Johnson	24
Hollis "Sloppy" Thurston	23
George Payne	22
Andy Cooper	22
Robert "Schoolboy" Griffith	22
Ferdie Schupp	19
Cherry Bell	18
Jack Killeen	18
William "Plunk" Drake	17
Archie Campbell	17

Innings Pitched

Satchel Paige	572
Wilbur "Bullet Joe" Rogan	516
Chet Brewer	445
Rube Currie	402
James "Cannonball" Willis	397
Herm "Old Folks" Pillette	358
Andy Cooper	260
George Payne	230
Andrew "Pullman" Porter	224
Hollis "Sloppy" Thurston	223
Lou Koupal	219
Walter Johnson	219

Victories

Leroy "Satchel" Paige	56
Chester "Chet" Brewer	43
Wilbur "Bullet Joe" Rogan	42
James "Cannonball" Willis	41
Rube Currie	26
William "Willie" Foster	24
Andrew "Pullman" Porter	23
Andy Cooper	22
Herman "Old Folks" Pillette	21
George Payne	21
Robert "Schoolboy" Griffith	20
Walter Johnson	18
Archie Campbell	13
Ferdie Schupp	12
Jack Killeen	10
Robert "Schoolboy" Griffith	9
Clifford "Cherry" Bell	7

Winning Percentage

William "Willie" Foster	24–1	.960
Robert "Schoolboy" Griffith	20–2	.909
Leroy "Satchel" Paige	56–7	.889
Walter Johnson	18–3	.857
George Payne	21–4	.840
James "Cannonball" Willis	41–10	.804
Erv Kantlehner	12–3	.800
Andrew "Pullman" Porter	23–6	.793
Andy Cooper	22–6	.786
Curly Brown	7–2	.777
Chet Brewer	42–13	.764
Wilbur "Bullet Joe" Rogan	42–14	.750
Bob Feller	6–2	.750

Strikeouts

Satchel Paige	766
Bullet Joe Rogan	351
Walter Johnson	321
Jim Willis	257
Robert "Schoolboy" Griffith	223
Chet Brewer	211
Rube Currie	162
Cherry Bell	127
Erv Kantlehner	117
Ferdie Schupp	108
Sloppy Thurston	108

Shutouts

Leroy "Satchel" Paige	17
Walter Johnson	12
James "Cannonball" Willis	8
Chester "Chet" Brewer	6
Wilbur "Bullet Joe" Rogan	5
Andrew "Pullman" Porter	4
William "Willie" Foster	4
Rube Currie	4
Andy Cooper	4
Curly Brown	3
Cherry Bell	3
Jess "Mountain" Hubbard	3

No–Hitters

* Walter Johnson of Santa Ana tossed a no-hitter against the Los Angeles Hoegees on January 19, 1908, winning 1-0.

* Walter Johnson pitched a no-hitter for Santa Ana against Salt Lake City on December 26, 1909.

* Tex Reichert pitched a no-hitter for the San Diego Farleys against the San Diego Gold Club on January 16, 1938, winning 1-0.

* Thomas "Lefty" Glover pitched a no-hitter for the Philadelphia Royal Giants against the White Kings on November 5, 1939, winning 4-0. He struck out 4 and walked 2 in his masterpiece.

Appendix C
Individual Season Leaders

Year	Batting Leader		Home Run Leader		Most Wins, Pitcher		Best Percentage	
1906								
1907					W. Johnson	7	W. Johnson	7-2
1908					C. Hall	5	C. Hall	5-0
1909					W. Johnson	9	W. Johnson	9-0
1910	W. Carlisle	.412	Five tied with	1	T. Seaton	5	T. Seaton	5-0
1911								
1912	T. Downey	.435	W. Monroe	2	B. Lindsay	3	T. Johnson	3-0
			B. Pierce	2	T. Johnson	3		
					E. Hamilton	3		
1913								
1914	H. Maggert	.385	I. Meusel	2	E. Kantlehner	11	E. Kantlehner	11-3
			G. Downs	2				
1915	J.H. Lloyd	.409	Three tied with	2	F. Wickware	6	F. Wickware	6-1
1916	G. Carr	.458	P. Schneider	1	Mooney	4	P. Schneider	2-0
			Field	1				
1917	I. Meusel	.438	None recorded		C. Brown	3	C. Brown	3-0
1918	C. Chadbourne	.429	F. Haney	1	Tally	4	Tally	4-0
1919	Ins. AB's		B. Ruth	1	Three tied at	1	Three tied at	1-0
1920	J. Rogan	.368	J. Rogan	5	R. Currie	12	R. Currie	12-4
1921	I. Meusel	.425	B. Mackey	4	J. Jeffries	9	H. McNair	4-0
1922	O. Johnson	.340	W. Kingdon	2	Four tied at	3	Four tied at	3-1
1923	H. Blackman	.341	Four tied with	2	Four tied with	2	A, Cooper	2-0
							Doyle	2-0
1924	D. Moore	.487	D. Moore	12	W. Drake	11	G. Payne	10-3
1925	J. Jenkins	.544	T. Carr	8	J. Rogan	12	J. Rogan	12-2
1926	D. Murphy	.419	T. Stearnes	6	H. Pillette	8	W. Foster	6-0
			B. Mackey	6				
1927	J. Hubbard	.442	T. Stearnes	7	B. Holland	7	G. Payne	5-0
1928	E. Averill	.500	J. Beckwith	14	C. Brewer	14	J. Rogan	9-1
1929	L. Livingston	.468	N. Joseph	8	A. Cooper	6	A. Cooper	6-1
1930	T. Stearnes	.387	T. Stearnes	5	J. Willis	11	R. Cannon	6-0
			B. Riggins	5				
			J. Walters	5				
	M. Suttles	.474	W. Berger	10	W. Foster	9	W. Foster	9-0
1931	M. Suttles	.586	M. Suttles	2	W. Foster	9	S. Paige	6-0
1932	A. Radcliffe	.381	T. Dukes	7	S. Paige	7	S. Paige	7-0
1933	J. Bell	.362	M. Suttles	14	S. Paige	16	S. Paige	16-2
1934	B. Wright	.481	T. Stearnes	16	A. Porter	12	S. Paige	8-0
			M. Suttles	16				
1935	J. West	.510	M. Suttles	11	S. Paige	13	S. Paige	13-0
1936	L. Morney	.519	L. Morney	5	B. Griffin	10	C. Brewer	6-0
1937	S. Mesner	.476	M. Suttles	7	C. Brewer	8	A. Porter	5-0

Appendix C

Year	Batting Leader		Home Run Leader		Most Wins, Pitcher		Best Percentage	
1938	F. Snow	.500	M. Suttles	6	P. Moss	3	P. Moss	3-0
1939	J. Dunn	.350	Wright, Dunn	2	T. McDuffie	5	T. Glover	3-1
1940	C. Spearman	.500	S.T. Hughes	4	B. Barbee	3	B. Morris	2-0
					N. Moreland	3		
1941	F. Bell	.625	None		J. Flores	2	J. Flores	2-0
	R. Partee	.625						
1942								
1943	S. Sampson	.433	R. Russell	1	S. Paige	3	S. Paige	3-1
1944	B. Wright	.421	Three tied w/	1	N. Moreland	6	N. Moreland	6-0
	J. Williams	.421						
1945	insuff. Data		V. Stephens	2	J. Williams	5	A. Porter	2-0
1946	B. Hoskins	.444	B. Hoskins	2	B. Feller	3	B. Feller	3-0
1947	J. Williams	.360	P. Davis	2	B. Feller	3	B. Feller	3-1

Appendix D

Who's Who in the California Winter League

Players from the Negro Leagues
Batting Statistics

ALLEN, NEWTON "NEWT"

Year	Team	G	AB	H	D	T	HR	BA
1925-26	Philadelphia Royal Giants	29	118	31	4	1	0	.254
1926-27	Philadelphia Royal Giants	21	78	22	1	0	0	.282
1927-28	Cleveland Stars	13	56	14	1	1	0	.250
1928-29	Cleveland Giants	29	126	46	14*	2	2	.365
1929-30	Philadelphia Royal Giants	28*	111	47*	13*	2*	0	.423
1930-31	Philadelphia Royal Giants	15	63*	19	2	0	2	.302
Totals		135	552	179	35	6	4	.324

Newt Allen starred in the Negro leagues for 23 years. A master of the double play, he was generally regarded as one of the top second basemen in league history. He also contributed on offense, hitting .302 and running the bases aggressively.

BANKHEAD, SAMUEL "SAM"

Year	Team	G	AB	H	D	T	HR	BA
1932-33	Wilson's Elite Giants	33*	114	42	6	6*	4	.371
1933-34	Wilson's Elite Giants	45	157	54	10	2	4	.344
1937-38		PLAYED IN CUBA—BATTED .366						
1938-39		PLAYED IN CUBA—BATTED .229						
1939-40		PLAYED IN CUBA—BATTED .321						
1940-41		PLAYED IN CUBA—BATTED .244						
1944-45	Birmingham Black Barons	2	5	1	0	1	0	.200
Totals		80	276	96	16	9	8	.351

Sam Bankhead was an outstanding all-around shortstop. He is best remembered for hitting the pennant winning home run in the infamous Dominican Summer League in 1937. In addition to his 21 year Negro league career (.285), Sam also starred in Cuba (.297), Puerto Rico (.311), and Mexico (.335).

BARBOUR, JESS

Year	Team	G	AB	H	D	T	HR	BA
1912-13	Chicago American Giants	6	22	5	1	0	0	.227

Year	Team	G	AB	H	D	T	HR	BA
1915-16	Chicago American Giants	12	51*	12	0	0	2*	.235
Totals		18	73	17	1	0	2	.233

Jess Barbour was an outfielder in the Negro leagues for 17 years, primarily with the Chicago American Giants. He was an excellent base stealer and defensive player, but hit only .270. He batted .233 in Cuba and .207 in Florida.

BECKWITH, JOHN

Year	Team	G	AB	H	D	T	HR	BA
1927-28	Philadelphia Royal Giants	19	71	22	4	1	5	.310
1928-29	Cleveland Giants	27	101	49	9	0	14*	.485
Totals		46	172	71	13	1	19	.413

John Beckwith had the second highest career batting average in the Negro leagues, tormenting opposing pitchers to the tune of .352, with 30 home runs a year.

BELL, JAMES "COOL PAPA"

Year	Team	G	AB	H	D	T	HR	BA
1922-23	St. Louis All-Stars	3	6	4	0	0	1	.667
1923-24	St. Louis Stars	7	17	3	0	0	2	.176
1924-25	St. Louis Giants	30	120	48	2	0	1	.400*
1928-29	PLAYED IN CUBA—BATTED .325							
1929-30	PLAYED IN CUBA—BATTED .285							
1930-31	PLAYED IN CUBA—BATTED .315							
1930-31	Nashville Elite Giants	11	31	8	0	0	1	.258
1931-32	Philadelphia Giants	9	41	17	1	0	0	.415
1933-34	Wilson's Elite Giants	43*	163*	59*	15	4*	6	.362*
1934-35	Nashville Elite Giants	24	98	30	6	5*	1	.306
1936-37	Wilson's Elite Giants	5	19	9	3	1	3	.474
1937-38	Philadelphia Royal Giants	10	41	14	0	2*	1	.341
1940-41	PLAYED IN CUBA—BATTED .297							
1940-41	Birmingham Black Barons	2	9	6	0	0	0	.666
1943-44	Baltimore Elite Giants	12	38	13	3	0	0	.323
1944-45	Black Barons, K.C. Royals	3	13	8	1	0	0	.615
Totals		159	596	219	31	12	16	.368

"Cool Papa" Bell was reportedly the fastest man in Negro league baseball. His 12 triples in California testify to his blazing speed. He pounded out 1,561 base hits in the Negro leagues, good for a .328 average. He also hit .292 in Cuba, and a sizzling .398 in Mexico.

BLACKMAN, HENRY

Year	Team	G	AB	H	D	T	HR	BA
1920-21	Lincoln Giants	19	49	15	1	3	0	.306
1921-22	L.A. Wh.Sox—Col. A.S	22	77	31	4	3	3	.403
1922-23	St. Louis All-Stars	9	37	11	0	1	1	.297
1923-24	St. Louis All-Stars	12	44	15	1	1	2	.341
Totals		62	207	72	6	8	6	.348

Henry Blackman was an outstanding third baseman in the Negro leagues from 1920 to 1924. His untimely death from an illness in 1924 ended a potential Hall of Fame career.

BOBO, WILLIE

Year	Team	G	AB	H	D	T	HR	BA
1924-25	St. Louis Giants	36*	129*	42	6	5	5*	.326

Who's Who in the California Winter League

Year	Team	G	AB	H	D	T	HR	BA
1930-31	Nashville Elite Giants	31	123	36	3	3*	1	.293
Totals		67	252	78	9	8	6	.310

Willie Bobo was an outstanding all-around first baseman between 1923 and 1930. He died suddenly from alcohol poisoning in 1931. He batted .314 with 10 home runs a year in the Negro leagues.

BROWN, LARRY

Year	Team	G	AB	H	D	T	HR	BA
1931-32	Philadelphia Royal Giants	6	23	8	0	0	2	.348
1934-35	Wilson's Elite Giants	24	77	28	4	0	1	.364
Totals		30	100	36	4	0	3	.360

Larry Brown was another in the long line of superior defensive Negro league receivers. He played in the Negro leagues for 31 years, hitting .259 according to Jim Riley. He also averaged .252 for six years in Cuba.

BURNETT, TEX

Year	Team	G	AB	H	D	T	HR	BA
1922-23	St. Louis All-Stars	7	28	9	2	1	0	.321
1923-24	St. Louis All-Stars	7	22	10	1	1	0	.455
1927-28	Philadelphia Royal Giants	9	31	8	0	0	0	.258
Totals		23	81	27	2	2	0	.333

Tex Burnett played in the Negro leagues for 25 years. He batted about .263, but was slow and had little power.

BUTCHER, SPENCER

Year	Team	G	AB	H	D	T	HR	BA
1920-21	Los Angeles White Sox	4	16	0	0	0	0	.000
1920-21	Alexander's Giants	79	314	87	10	5	3	.277
1923-24	Los Angeles White Sox	7	28	2	1	0	0	.071
1924-25	LAWS., St. L., Col. AS	35	130	32	4	1	0	.246
1926-27	Philadelphia Royal Giants	2	0	0	0	0	0	.000
1927-28	Philadelphia Royal Giants	1	3	1	0	0	0	.333
Totals		128	491	122	15	6	3	.248

No record of Butcher has been located in Negro league journals. He may have been a local player who usually played with teams like Alexander's Giants, and who was picked up by Negro league teams during the winter to fill out the roster.

CARR, GEORGE "TANK"

Year	Team	G	AB	H	D	T	HR	BA
1915-16	Los Angeles White Sox	1	5	2	—	—	—	.400
1916-17	Los Angeles White Sox	7	24	11	2	1	0	.458*
1917-18	Los Angeles White Sox							
1918-19	Los Angeles White Sox							
1919-20	Los Angeles White Sox	Player-Manager						
1920-21	Los Angeles White Sox	31	123	34	7	2	1	.276
1921-22	Colored All-Stars	35*	141*	48	9	5	3	.340
1922-23	Los Angeles White Sox	16	56	12	0	2	0	.214
1924-25	L.A. W.S., Colored A.S.	32	115	44	12	3	11	.383
1925-26	Philadelphia Royal Giants	3	146	50	16*	1	8*	.342
1926-27		PLAYED IN CUBA—BATTED .416						
1927-28	Philadelphia Royal Giants	19	69	26	4	1	2	.377

Year	Team	G	AB	H	D	T	HR	BA
1928-29	Cleveland Giants	9	16	5	1	0	0	.313
1930-31	Nashville Royal Giants	8	21	8	1	2	2	.381
Totals		197	715	240	52	17	27	.336

Tank Carr was a 6'2", 230 pound switch hitter who batted .309 with 10 home runs a year in the Negro leagues. He also hit .416 during his one year tour of duty in Cuba.

CHARLESTON, OSCAR

Year	Team	G	AB	H	D	T	HR	BA
1921-22	Colored All-Stars	23	88	33	8	6*	0	.375

Oscar Charleston may have been the greatest all-around player in Negro baseball history. He could do it all—sensational center fielder, aggressive baserunner, and a great hitter. His .340 batting average was the 6th highest in Negro league history, and his 26 home runs a year was #8.

CREACY, A.D. "DEWEY"

Year	Team	G	AB	H	D	T	HR	BA
1924-25	St. Louis Giants	34	127	43	7*	8*	1	.339
1930-31	Nashville Elite Giants	34	115	36	5	2	0	.313
1931-32	Philadelphia Giants	6	26	4	1	0	0	.154
Totals		74	268	83	13	10	1	.310

Dewey Creacy was a hard hitting third baseman in the Negro leagues for 17 years. He was a .300 hitter with home run power from 1924 to 1928, but tailed off late in his career, finishing with a career average of .278.

DANDRIDGE, RAYMOND "RAY"

Year	Team	G	AB	H	D	T	HR	BA
1944-45	Kansas City Royals	6	20	7	0	0	0	.350

Ray Dandridge was arguably the greatest third baseman in Negro league history. He was a stalwart on defense as well as a lifetime .350 hitter. He also sported a .282 average for 12 years in the Cuban Winter League, .347 in the Mexican League, and .316 late in his career, in the American AAA minor leagues.

DAVIS, WALTER "STEEL ARM"

Year	Team	G	AB	H	D	T	HR	BA
1932-33	Nashville Elite Giants	27	109	38	10*	4	5	.359

Steel Arm Davis played the outfield and pitched in the Negro leagues for 13 years. He was an all-star third baseman, who hit for a .332 average with good power.

DAY, WILSON C. "CONNIE"

Year	Team	G	AB	H	D	T	HR	BA
1922-23	St. Louis All-Stars	9	38	4	0	0	0	.105
1923-24	St. Louis Stars	13	52	11	1	0	1	.212
1924-25	Los Angeles White Sox	39	147	47	5	4*	8	.320
1925-26	Royal Giants	34	132	37	10	0	3	.280
1927-28	Cleveland Stars	12	44	9	2	1	0	.205
1928-29	Cleveland Giants	29	119	31	6	1	1	.261
Totals		136	532	139	24	6	13	.261

Connie Day was a sensational defensive second baseman in the Negro leagues for 13 years, but just an average hitter.

DIXON, HERBERT "RAP"

Year	Team	G	AB	H	D	T	HR	BA
1925-26	Philadelphia Royal Giants	41	140	38	8	2	4	.271
1926-27	Philadelphia Royal Giants	35	109	38	9	1	0	.349
1927-28	Philadelphia Royal Giants	20	79	30	6*	3*	5	.380
1928-29	Cleveland Giants	28	100	36	7	1	7	.360
1930-31	Royal Giants	15	51	14	3	0	2	.275
Totals		139	479	156	33	7	18	.326

Rap Dixon was an outstanding all-around player in the Negro leagues from 1922 through 1937. He could do it all—hit (.309), hit with power (12 home runs a year), run, field, and throw. He has been selected on many all-time Negro league all-star teams.

DOWNS, BUNNY

Year	Team	G	AB	H	D	T	HR	BA
1920-21	Lincoln Giants	19	72	23	6	4	0	.319

Bunny Downs was a second baseman in the Negro leagues for 13 years. He was a good defensive player, and a good bat handler, hitting around .280.

DUKES, TOMMY "DIXIE"

Year	Team	G	AB	H	D	T	HR	BA
1932-33	Wilson's Elite Giants	28	101	36	9	1	7*	.357
1933-34	Wilson's Elite Giants	36	135	45	8	2	7	.334
Totals		64	236	81	17	3	14	.343

Tommy Dukes played in the Negro leagues from 1928 through 1945. He was a small (5'8", 165 pound) catcher, who frequently batted cleanup for his team. His career average was .286.

DUNCAN, FRANK "PETE"

Year	Team	G	AB	H	D	T	HR	BA
1912-13	Chicago American Giants	7	27*	6	0	1*	1	.222
1915-16	Chicago American Giants	13	50	14	3*	3	0	.280
Totals		20	77	20	3	4	1	.260

Pete Duncan was an outstanding defensive outfielder from 1909 through 1928. But hit only about .260 in the Negro leagues. However, he batted .345 one year in Cuba, and had the highest career batting average in the Florida Hotel League, at .320, outhitting such notables as John Henry Lloyd, Pete Hill, and Spot Poles.

DUNCAN, FRANK, JR.

Year	Team	G	AB	H	D	T	HR	BA
1926-27	Philadelphia Royal Giants	24	58	16	3	0	0	.276
1927-28	Cleveland Stars	8	21	8	2	0	0	.381
Totals		32	79	24	5	0	0	.304

Frank Duncan, Jr. was one of the top catchers in Negro league baseball between 1920 and 1948, playing mostly with the Kansas City Monarchs. He was just an average hitter with a career average in the .268 range. He hit slightly higher in Cuba, .272 over a seven year period.

DUNN, JOSEPH "JAKE"

Year	Team	G	AB	H	D	T	HR	BA
1930-31	Nashville Elite Giants	33	123	39	7	3*	5	.317
1932-33	Wilson's Elite Giants	31	108	41	4	3	5	.378
1934-35	Wilson's Elite Giants	3	11	4	2	0	1	.364
1937-38	Detroit Stars	6	21	5	2	0	0	.238

Year	Team	G	AB	H	D	T	HR	BA
1938-39	Philadelphia Royal Giants	3	11	2	2	0	0	.273
1939-40	Philadelphia Royal Giants	11	40	14	3	1	2	.350
1940-41	Baltimore Elite Giants	1	4	2	0	0	0	.500
1941-42	Royal Giants	2	8	3	0	0	0	.375
1943-44	Baltimore Elite Giants	1	2	0	0	0	0	.000
Totals		91	328	110	20	7	13	.335

Jake Dunn was a shortstop with a powerful throwing arm. He played in the Negro leagues for twelve years, from 1930 to 1941, with a respectable .273 career batting average. He played both shortstop and second base in California.

EVANS, BILL

Year	Team	G	AB	H	D	T	HR	BA
1930-31	Nashville Elite Giants	33	112	39	5	2	0	.348

Bill Evans, known as the Gray Ghost, was an exceptional defensive second baseman in the Negro leagues, but a weak hitter, averaging around .250.

FAGAN, ROBERT W. "BOB"

Year	Team	G	AB	H	D	T	HR	BA
1920-21	Los Angeles White Sox	27	96	29	4	0	0	.302
1921-22	Colored All-Stars	32	121	33	3	1	2	.280
1922-23	St. Louis Stars, L.A.W.S.	20	66	17	1	0	0	.258
1923-24	St. Louis Stars	14	44	12	0	1	0	.273
1924-25	L. A., Colored A.S.	41	146	35	8	1	0	.240
1925-26	L.A. White Sox	2	7	2	0	0	0	.333
Totals		136	480	129	16	3	2	.269

Bob Fagan had a short four year career in the Negro leagues. The second baseman was one of the members of the famed 24th infantry division of the U.S. Army, along with Joe Rogan and Dobie Moore, who joined the Kansas City Monarchs in 1920.

FOREMAN, F.S. "HOOKS"

Year	Team	G	AB	H	D	T	HR	BA
1924-25	Los Angeles White Sox	36	129	39	12	0	1	.302

Hooks Foreman played in the Negro leagues from 1921 to 1933, as a journeyman catcher and outfielder.

HARRIS, VIC

Year	Team	G	AB	H	D	T	HR	BA
1930-31	Philadelphia Royal Giants	14	50	13	1	1	1	.260
1931-32	Philadelphia Royal Giants	7	35	15	0	0	1	.429
Totals		21	85	28	1	1	2	.329

Vic Harris enjoyed a 28 year career in the Negro leagues with an estimated .328 batting average. He hit .417 for two years in Florida and .259 one year in Cuba.

HAWKINS, LEMUEL "LEM"

Year	Team	G	AB	H	D	T	HR	BA
1908-09	Los Angeles Giants	11	41	12	1	0	0	.293
1909-10	Occidentals	4	17	1	1	0	0	.059
-20	U.S. Army—25th Infantry Division							
1919-20	Los Angeles White Sox							
1920-21	Los Angeles White Sox	29	107	27	1	0	0	.252

1921-22	Colored All-Stars	32	126	42	10*	3	0	.333
1922-23	Los Angeles White Sox	16	63*	14	2	0	0	.222
1924-25	Los Angeles White Sox	44*	175*	58	9	4*	0	.331
Totals		136	529	154	24	7	0	.291

Lem Hawkins was a smooth fielding infielder, but just an average hitter. He played in the Negro leagues for eight years, from 1921 through 1928, averaging .257 between 1924 and 1927 according to James Riley.

HILL, JOHNSON "JOHN"

Year	Team	G	AB	H	D	T	HR	BA
1920-21	Lincoln, Alexanders	25*	92*	28	6	4	0	.304

John Hill was a good all around third baseman in the Negro leagues from 1920 to 1927. Prior to joining the Negro National League, Hill spent most of his career in Texas.

HILL, PRESTON "PETE"

Year	Team	G	AB	H	D	T	HR	BA
1912-13	Chicago American Giants	10	34	8	5*	0	0	.235
1915-16	Chicago American Giants	13*	51*	19*	1	3*	1	.373
Totals		23	85	27	6	3	1	.318

Pete Hill was the Negro league's first superstar, a five point player. He was a centerfielder with outstanding speed, wide range, and a great throwing arm. He hit for average, hit with power, and ran the bases like Joe DiMaggio. He hit for a .307 average during six years in the Cuban Winter League, leading the league in triples three times. He was an all-time great.

HOLLOWAY, CHRISTOPHER "CRUSH"

Year	Team	G	AB	H	D	T	HR	BA
1922-23	St. Louis All-Stars	8	37	10	2	0	0	.270
1923-24	St. Louis Stars	12	48	12	2	1	0	.250
1924-25	PLAYED IN CUBA—BATTED .311							
1925-26	Royal Giants	41*	159*	59*	7	1	4	.371
1926-27	Royal Giants	33	122	30	4	1	1	.246
1927-28	Cleveland Stars	14	56	14	0	0	2	.250
1928-29	PLAYED IN CUBA—BATTED .265							
1929-30	Royal Giants	15	54	20	6	2*	0	.383
Totals		123	476	144	21	5	7	.303

Crush Holloway was an aggressive ballplayer who ran the bases with abandon. He was a good hitter who normally hit in the leadoff spot. He had a career average of about .296 for 19 years. He also batted .290 for two years in Cuba.

HUBBARD, JESS "MOUNTAIN"

Year	Team	G	AB	H	D	T	HR	BA
1920-21	Lincoln Giants	11	30	11	3	3	0	.367
1925-26	Philadelphia Royal Giants	31	101	35	6	3*	2	.347
1927-28	Philadelphia Royal Giants	20	77	34*	1	1	2	.442*
Totals		62	208	80	10	7	4	.390

Jess Hubbard was a big, rugged right-handed pitcher, standing 6'2" tall and weighing 200 pounds. He played 18 years in the Negro leagues, mostly as a pitcher, but also played the outfield where he enjoyed great success. He had a lifetime batting average of .316 in the Negro leagues.

Hughes, Sammy T.

Year	Team	G	AB	H	D	T	HR	BA
1934-35	Nashville Elite Giants	30*	105*	39	8	1	3	.371
1935-36	Wilson's Elite Giants	17	69	27	3	2	6	.391
1936-37	Wilson's Elite Giants	3	12	6	0	0	2	.500
1937-38	Philadelphia Royal Giants	10	46	20	3	1	0	.435
1938-39	Philadelphia Royal Giants	4	15	6	1	0	2	.400
1939-40	PLAYED IN CUBA—BATTED .246							
1940-41	Elite Giants	10	38	12	2	1	4*	.316
1941-42	Royal Giants	2	9	3	0	0	0	.333
Totals		76	294	113	17	5	17	.384

Sammy T. Hughes is generally regarded as the greatest second baseman in Negro league history. A lifetime .300 hitter, the 6'3" Hughes was a magnificent fielder who had no weaknesses. He hit .324 his one year in Mexico but just .246 in 146 at-bats in Cuba.

Johnson, Oscar "Heavy"

Year	Team	G	AB	H	D	T	HR	BA
1922-23	Los Angeles White Sox	11	46	16	2	1	1	.340*
1923-24	PLAYED IN CUBA—BATTED .345							

Heavy Johnson was one of the most devastating hitters in Negro league history. John Holway's research indicated that the 6" tall, 250 pound bomber had a career batting average of .350 with 16 home runs a year. He played from 1922 to 1933.

Joseph, Walter Newton "Newt"

Year	Team	G	AB	H	D	T	HR	BA
1926-27	Royal Giants	31*	101	24	7	0	1	.238
1928-29	PLAYED IN CUBA—BATTED .273							
1929-30	Royal Giants	26	92	31	10	1	8*	.337
Totals		57	193	55	17	1	9	.285

Newt Joseph was a stocky little third baseman who hit for a .281 average over an 18 year Negro league career. He showed a .273 average for one year in Cuba.

Leonard, Walter Fenner "Buck"

Year	Team	G	AB	H	D	T	HR	BA
1943-44	Balt. E.G., K.C. Royals	10	31	11	0	2	0	.355

Buck Leonard is known as the greatest first baseman ever produced in the Negro leagues. He pounded the ball at a .335 clip in the Negro leagues between 1933 and 1950, with 21 home runs a year. He also .325 with 20 home runs in Mexico, .284 in Cuba, and .390 in Puerto Rico.

Livingston, L.D. "Lee"

Year	Team	G	AB	H	D	T	HR	BA
1929-30	Philadelphia Royal Giants	24	94	44	11	0	5	.468*

Lee Livingston had a short career in the Negro leagues, lasting only five years—1928 to 1932. Not much is known about him other than he was a decent hitter, averaging about .300.

Lloyd, John Henry

Year	Team	G	AB	H	D	T	HR	BA
1915-16	Chicago American Giants	13*	44	18	3*	2	1	.409*

John Henry Lloyd is compared favorably with Honus Wagner as one of the two greatest shortstops in baseball history, black or white. He hit .337 in the Negro leagues between 1906 and 1932, and .329 in Cuba from 1908 to 1930. He is often called the greatest player in Negro league history.

MACKEY, RALEIGH "BIZ"

Year	Team	G	AB	H	D	T	HR	BA
1920-21	Lincoln, Alexander Giants	25*	81	40*	8*	5	0	.494*
1921-22	Colored All-Stars	33	130	51*	8	6*	4*	.392
1922-23	Los Angeles White Sox	13	50	17	3	1	0	.340
1924-25	PLAYED IN CUBA—BATTED .309							
1925-26	Philadelphia Royal Giants	38*	146	48	9	2	6*	.329
1926-27	Philadelphia Royal Giants	28	95	30	4	0	5	.316
1927-28	Philadelphia Royal Giants	18	65	25	5	0	3	.385
1928-29	Cleveland Giants	29	111	51*	10	1	5	.459
1929-30	Philadelphia Royal Giants	23	91	32	7	1	5	.352
1930-31	Philadelphia Royal Giants	14	43	18	4	1	0	.419
1935-36	Wilson's Elite Giants	12	37	9	1	0	0	.243
1936-37	Wilson's Elite Giants	3	10	3	0	0	1	.300
1937-38	Philadelphia Royal Giants	9	37	12	3	0	0	.324
1938-39	Philadelphia Royal Giants	2	7	2	1	0	0	.286
1940-41	Elite Giants	13	23	4	1	0	0	.173
1941-42	Royal Giants	3	7	1	0	0	0	.143
1942-43	Royal Giants							
1943-44	Baltimore Giants	5	17	4	0	0	0	.235
1944-45	Kansas City Royals	4	7	3	0	0	0	.429
Totals		272	957	350	62	17	28	.366

Biz Mackey is arguably the greatest all-around catcher in Negro league history. A lifetime .322 hitter with 11 home runs a year, Mackey had no equals on defense. Roy Campanella, one of the greatest backstops in major league history, was groomed by Mackey. If you saw Campanella play, you saw Mackey.

MCNAIR, HURLEY

Year	Team	G	AB	H	D	T	HR	BA
1920-21	Los Angeles White Sox	32	131	41	11*	6*	2	.313
1921-22	Colored All-Stars	32	124	36	6	6	2	.290
1922-23	Los Angeles White Sox							
1923-24								
1924-25	L.A. W.S., St. L. Giants	15	59	24	4	0	1	.407
Totals		79	314	101	21	12	5	.322

Hurley McNair was a .321 hitter (#15 all-time) in the Negro leagues from 1911 to 1937. Standing only 5'6" tall and weighing a wispy 150 pounds, McNair was a consistent contact hitter and a good base runner.

MENDEZ, JOSE

Year	Team	G	AB	H	D	T	HR	BA
1917-18	Los Angeles White Sox							
1921-22	Colored All-Stars	26	90	23	3	3	2	.256
1922-23	Los Angeles White Sox	14	50	12	1	0	0	.240
Totals		40	140	35	4	3	2	.250

Jose Mendez was one of Cuba's greatest pitchers. He played in the Negro leagues for 19 years, managing for seven of them. He was 3-1 as a pitcher for the L.A. White Sox in 1922-23, but was primarily a shortstop.

MOORE, WALTER "DOBIE"

Year	Team	G	AB	H	D	T	HR	BA
1920-21	Los Angeles White Sox	34*	139*	46*	7	6*	1	.331
1921-22	Colored All-Stars	22	80	22	4	3	0	.275
1922-23	DIDN'T PLAY							
1923-24	PLAYED IN CUBA—BATTED .356							
1924-25	Los Angeles White Sox	40	158	77*	17*	4*	12*	.487*
Totals		96	377	145	28	13	13	.385*

Dobie Moore may have been the greatest shortstop in Negro league history, although his brief seven year career eliminated him from consideration by most experts. Moore was a superior defensive infielder with great range and a deadly throwing arm. He was also one of the greatest hitters ever produced by the Negro leagues, hitting a torrid .355, which was the highest average ever attained by a player with more than 1,500 at-bats. What set him apart from his competition was his outstanding power. He averaged 35 doubles, 15 triples, and 16 home runs for every 550 at-bats. He also tortured Cuban Winter League pitchers to the tune of .356 during the 1923-24 season.

MOTHEL, CARROLL "DINK"

Year	Team	G	AB	H	D	T	HR	BA
1926-27	Philadelphia Royal Giants	32	114	30	2	0	0	.263
1927-28	Cleveland Stars	14	54	19	3	0	1	.352
1928-29	Cleveland Giants	27	100	28	2	1	0	.280
1929-30	Philadelphia Royal Giants	27	113*	37	5	1	3	.327
Totals		100	381	114	12	2	4	.299

Dink Mothel could play any position in the infield or outfield. He was an average hitter who enjoyed a 15 year career in the Negro leagues.

PETTUS, BILL

Year	Team	G	AB	H	D	T	HR	BA
1909-10	Occidental	3	14	5	0	0	0	.357
1910-11	Leland Giants	14	54	13	4	2*	1*	.241
1912	PLAYED IN CUBA—BATTED .272							
1920-21	Lincoln, Alexanders	23	81	33	4	7*	2*	.404
Totals		40	149	51	8	9	3	.342

Bill Pettus, also known as Zack, was a big, strong, left-handed hitting first baseman, whose Negro league career ran from 1909 through 1923. Incomplete statistics published by Jim Riley credit Pettus with a .404 average for four years. Riley considered him to be one of the most underrated players of his era.

PETWAY, BRUCE

Year	Team	G	AB	H	D	T	HR	BA
1912-13	Chicago American Giants	6	20	7	1	0	0	.350
1915-16	Chicago American Giants	9	33	3	0	0	0	.111
Totals		15	53	10	1	0	0	.189

Bruce was one of the greatest defensive catchers in baseball history, with a rifle arm. But he was a mediocre hitter, averaging about .274 in the Negro leagues, .210 for four years in Cuba, and .160 in Florida.

POLES, SPOTTSWOOD "SPOT"

Year	Team	G	AB	H	D	T	HR	BA
1920-21	Lincoln Giants	19	74	27	3	5	1	.365

Spot Poles was one of the great all-around baseball players of the second decade of the twentieth century. He was compared to Ty Cobb for his speed and all around ability.

PULLEN, O'NEAL "NEAL"

Year	Team	G	AB	H	D	T	HR	BA
1920-21	Lincoln Alexander Giants	17	51	17	1	2	0	.333
1921-22	Colored All-Stars	12	46	15	1	1	1	.326
1922-23	L.A. W.S., St. L. A.S.	4	13	3	0	0	0	.155
1923-24	L.A. W.S., St. L. A.S.	11	45	20	2	1	2	.444
1924-25	L.A. W.S., St. L. Giants	15	59	20	3	1	2	.339
1925-26	Philadelphia Royal Giants	36	130	33	9	0	6	.254
1926-27	Philadelphia Royal Giants	15	35	12	4	0	0	.343
1927-28	Cleveland Stars, Phil. R.G.	9	34	7	0	0	0	.206
1928-29	Cleveland Giants	6	19	7	0	0	0	.368
1930-31	Royal Giants	2	5	3	0	0	0	.600
Totals		127	437	137	21	5	11	.314

Neal Pullen played in the Negro leagues for eight years. His career was two years late in starting because of his military service in World War I. He was a good defensive catcher and a fair hitter, but he had a weight problem that curtailed his development.

RADCLIFFE, ALEXANDER "ALEC"

Year	Team	G	AB	H	D	T	HR	BA
1932-33	Nashville Elite Giants	27	118*	45*	5	6*	4	.381*
1937-38	Detroit Stars	3	12	4	0	0	0	.333
Totals		30	130	49	5	6	4	.380

Alec Radcliffe was one of the best third baseman in the Negro leagues from 1932 to 1946. He was a solid defensive player and a decent, although not great, hitter. He had above average power, and was noted as an excellent clutch hitter.

RADCLIFFE, TED "DOUBLE DUTY"

Year	Team	G	AB	H	D	T	HR	BA
1937-38	Detroit Stars	4	18	6	0	0	1	.333
1943-44	Baltimore Elite Gianst	7	22	4	0	0	0	.182
Totals		11	40	10	0	0	1	.250

Double Duty Radcliffe was one of the legends of Negro league baseball. He was an all-star at two positions—pitcher and catcher.

RAY, OTTO

Year	Team	G	AB	H	D	T	HR	BA
1920-21	Los Angeles White Sox	18	64	13	3	2	0	.203
1923-24	St. Louis Stars	9	32	5	0	0	0	.156
Totals		27	96	23	3	2	0	.240

Otto "Jaybird" Ray had a five year career in the Negro leagues. He was a good defensive catcher, but a weak hitter.

REESE, JOHN

Year	Team	G	AB	H	D	T	HR	BA
1924-25	Los Angeles White Sox	32	103	26	7*	1	0	.252

John Reese was an outfielder in the Negro leagues from 1918 to 1931. He was an excellent defensive player and had great speed, which made him dangerous both in the field and on the bases. But he was just an average hitter.

Ridley, Jack

Year	Team	G	AB	H	D	T	HR	BA
1930-31	Nashville Elite Giants	34	131	38	10*	3*	1	.290

Jack Ridley played in the Negro leagues from 1924 until 1934. A tragic automobile accident cost him his arm, ending his baseball career.

Riggins, Orville "Bill"

Year	Team	G	AB	H	D	T	HR	BA
1922-23	St. Louis All-Stars	9	38	9	1	0	0	.236
1923-24	St. Louis Stars	13	49	17	1	1	0	.347
1924-25	St. Louis Giants	16	62	17	3	1	1	.274
1930-31	Nashville Elite Giants	34	122	44	9	2	5*	.361
Totals		72	271	87	14	4	6	.321

Bill Riggins enjoyed a 17 year career in the Negro leagues. He was an outstanding shortstop, and compiled a lifetime batting average of .304.

Robinson, Jack Roosevelt "Jackie"

Year	Team	G	AB	H	D	T	HR	BA
1945	Kansas City Royals	4	14	6	3	0	1	.429
1946	Jackie Robinson All-Stars	2	5	1	1	0	0	.200
Totals		6	19	7	4	0	1	.368

Jackie Robinson was the first black player in organized baseball in the 20th century. He compiled a .311 batting average with the Brooklyn Dodgers between 1947 and 1956. His Negro league average was .387 for one year.

Rogan, Wilbur "Bullet Joe"

Year	Team	G	AB	H	D	T	HR	BA
1917-18	Los Angeles White Sox							
1920-21	Los Angeles White Sox	30	106	39	3	4	5*	.368*
1924-25	PLAYED IN CUBA							
1925-26	Philadelphia Royal Giants	30	89	30	8	0	2	.326
1926-27	Philadelphia Royal Giants	23	57	17	2	0	0	.298
1928-29	Cleveland Giants	28	106	43	5	1	4	.406
1929-30	Philadelphia Royal Giants	19	76	28	8	0	4	.368
Totals		130	434	157	25	5	15	.362

"Bullet Joe" Rogan was one of the greatest all-around players in Negro league history. He is generally regarded as one of the top three pitchers of all time—along with Paige and Williams. He had the most recorded victories in Negro league history with 151, and his .699 winning percentage is #5 all-time. He was also considered to be the best fielding pitcher in the league, and one of its best hitters. Playing on the powerful Kansas City Monarchs, Rogan hit out of the cleanup slot, to take advantage of his .348 lifetime average and power (30 doubles, 15 triples and 16 home runs a year).

Snow, Felton

Year	Team	G	AB	H	D	T	HR	BA
1933-34	Wilson's Elite Giants	43	149	48	6	0	6	.322
1934-35	Wilson's Elite Giants	21	77	27	6	0	1	.351
1935-36	Wilson's Royal Giants	14	58	13	0	3	0	.224
1936-37	Wilson's Royal Giants	2	8	4	1	1	0	.500
1937-38	Wilson's Royal Giants	10	47	14	4	0	1	.298
1938-39	Wilson's Royal Giants	4	14	7	2	0	2	.500*
1939-40	PLAYED IN CUBA—BATTED .223							

Year	Team	G	AB	H	D	T	HR	BA
1940-41	Wilson's Royal Giants	10	42	13	2	1	4	.316
Totals		101	395	126	21	5	14	.319

Felton Snow was a solid third baseman in the Negro leagues from 1931 to 1947. He could make all the plays defensively, and was an above average hitter with above average power.

Spearman, Henry

Year	Team	G	AB	H	D	T	HR	BA
1940-41	Baltimore Elite Giants	9	36	18	4*	0	2	.500*

Henry Spearman was an outstanding third baseman in the Negro leagues from 1936 to 1946, batting .323. He hit .276 one year in Cuba.

Stearnes, Norman "Turkey"

Year	Team	G	AB	H	D	T	HR	BA
1922-23	St. Louis All-Stars	9	37	12	2	1	3	.324
1923-24	St. Louis Stars	8	32	11	0	1	2	.344
1924-25	PLAYED IN CUBA—BATTED .224							
1926-27	Philadelphia Royal Giants	27	101	38	4	2	6*	.376
1927-28	Cleveland Stars	12	53	20	3	0	7*	.377
1928-29	Cleveland Giants	30*	113	42	2	4*	7	.372
1930-31	Nashville Elite Giants	37	137	53*	9	3	5*	.387*
1933-34	Wilson's Elite Giants	39	121	40	10	2	5	.331
1934-35	Wilson's Elite Giants	26	97	41*	2	1	16*	.423
1935-36	Wilson's Elite Giants	19	63	24	7	2	5	.381
Totals		207	754	281	39	16	56	.373

Turkey Stearnes played in the Negro leagues from 1923 through 1942. He was a superstar—a great outfielder and a dangerous hitter. He compiled a batting average of .352 with 33 doubles, 18 triples, and 30 home runs a year (550 at-bats).

Stratton, Leroy

Year	Team	G	AB	H	D	T	HR	BA
1932-22	Nashville Elite Giants	31	109	40	4	5	3	.366

Leroy Stratton played in the Negro leagues from 1920 to 1933. He was a good defensive third baseman but a weak hitter, averaging about .216.

Suttles, George "Mule"

Year	Team	G	AB	H	D	T	HR	BA
1930-31	Philadelphia Royal Giants	11	38	18	6	0	7	.474*
1931-32	Philadelphia Royal Giants	8	29	17	1	0	2*	.586*
1933-34	Wilson's Elite Giants	42	157	51	11	0	14*	.325
1934-35	Wilson's Elite Giants	26	96	33	7	0	16*	.344
1935-36	Wilson's Elite Giants	19	57	17	1	0	11*	.298
1936-37	DNP							
1937-38	Philadelphia Royal Giants	10	37	18	2	0	7*	.429
1938-39	Philadelphia Royal Giants	5	18	8	1	0	6*	.444
1939-40	Philadelphia Royal Giants	5	18	8	0	0	1	.444
Totals		126	450	170	29	0	64*	.378

Mule Suttles was a terrifying longball hitter in the Negro leagues from 1918 through 1944. He hit the ball farther than any other batter. His career batting average was .329 with 34 home runs a year.

Taylor, Leroy

Year	Team	G	AB	H	D	T	HR	BA
1929-30	Philadelphia Royal Giants	27	110	40	10	1	1	.364

Leroy Taylor was a speedy outfielder and a good bat handler. He played in the Negro leagues for 12 years, hitting .290.

Thomas, Clint

Year	Team	G	AB	H	D	T	HR	BA
1927-28	Philadelphia Royal Giants	21	85	18	3	1	1	.212

Clint Thomas was an outstanding all-around player in the Negro leagues for 19 years, averaging around .312 with good power and blazing speed. He batted .310 for six years in Cuba.

Thomas, Jules "Home Run"

Year	Team	G	AB	H	D	T	HR	BA
1920-21	Lincoln Giants	19	74	19	1	1	1*	.257

Jules Thomas was an excellent outfielder and a powerful hitter in the Negro leagues, averaging .371 for the five years uncovered by Jim Riley. He played in the Florida Hotel League for ten years, hitting .206 in a pitchers league.

Walker, Jesse "Hoss"

Year	Team	G	AB	H	D	T	HR	BA
1931-32	Philadelphia Giants	6	23	6	0	0	0	.261
1932-33	Wilson's Elite Giants	32	112	39	10	4	2	.349
1936-37	Wilson's Royal Giants	2	5	2	0	0	0	.400
1937-38	Philadelphia Royal Giants	10	37	15	2	0	3	.405
1939-40	Philadelphia Royal Giants	7	25	4	0	0	0	.160
1943-44	Baltimore Elite Giants	9	26	7	0	0	0	.269
1944-45	Kansas City Royals	4	15	5	2	0	0	.333
1945	Kansas City Royals	3	11	5	0	1	0	.455
1947	Kansas City Royals							
Totals		73	254	83	14	5	5	.328

Jesse Walker enjoyed a 22 year career in the Negro leagues, from 1929 to 1950. He was an average shortstop but a mediocre hitter. His .205 career average pales in comparison to his lofty average in California.

Ward, C. "Pinky"

Year	Team	G	AB	H	D	T	HR	BA
1920-21	Los Angeles White Sox	13	49	10	0	0	0	.204
1921-22	Colored All-Stars	10	37	8	1	0	1	.216
1922-23	Los Angeles White Sox	2	6	0	0	0	0	.000
1923-24	Los Angeles White Sox	8	31	7	0	0	0	.226
1924-25	St. L. Giants, L.A. W.S.	48	185	61	3	5	0	.330
Totals		81	308	86	4	5	1	.279

Pinky Ward played 12 years in the Negro leagues. He was a good hitter, but had an unsavory reputation as a thief.

Warfield, Frank

Year	Team	G	AB	H	D	T	HR	BA
1923-25	PLAYED IN CUBA—BATTED .300							
1927-28	Philadelphia Royal Giants	22*	88*	25	2	0	1	.284
1929-30	PLAYED IN CUBA—BATTED .313							

Frank Warfield played in the Negro leagues from 1915 to 1932. He was regarded as an outstanding defensive second baseman, and a good bat-handler. He batted over .300 at least five times during his career, with a high of .342 in 1924. During a fight with Oliver Marcelle in Cuba in 1930, he bit off a piece of Marcelle's nose, effectively ending the great third baseman's career.

WELLS, WILLIE

Year	Team	G	AB	H	D	T	HR	BA
1924-25	St. Louis Giants	9	32	10	1	0	1	.313
1926-27	Philadelphia Royal Giants	33	105	19	6	1	0	.181
1927-28	Philadelphia Royal Giants	14	48	15	3	0	0	.313
1928-29	PLAYED IN CUBA—BATTED .336							
1929-30	PLAYED IN CUBA—BATTED .322							
1930-31	Philadelphia Royal Giants	13	57	17	2	2*	2	.275
1931-32	Philadelphia Royal Giants	6	24	10	0	0	0	.417
1933-34	Wilson's Royal Giants	41	158	56	19*	1	6	.355
1934-35	Nashville Elite Giants	27	94	28	9*	2	2	.319
1935-1940	PLAYED IN CUBA—BATTED .317							
1941-42	PLAYED IN PUERTO RICO							
1944-45	Kansas City Royals	3	9	2	0	0	0	.222
Totals		146	528	159	40	6	11	.301

Willie Wells was one of the greatest shortstops in Negro league history. He was outstanding on defense, and could hit for both average and power. His .328 career average is #13 all time, and his 20 home runs a year is #9. Wells also hit .320 in Cuba and .330 in Mexico.

WEST, JAMES "JIM"

Year	Team	G	AB	H	D	T	HR	BA
1935-36	Wilson's Royal Giants	16	49	25	2	3	1	.510*
1936-37	Wilson's Royal Giants	3	11	3	0	0	1	.273
1937-38	Wilson's Royal Giants	9	39	18	0	1	3	.461
1938-39	Wilson's Royal Giants	3	11	4	1	0	2	.364
1939-40	Wilson's Royal Giants	7	27	5	2	0	0	.185
Totals		38	137	55	5	4	7	.404

Jim West was a fancy fielding first baseman who could hit and hit with power. He compiled a lifetime .308 average in the Negro leagues between 1930 and 1947.

WHITE, CHANEY

Year	Team	G	AB	H	D	T	HR	BA
1930-31	Philadelphia Royal Giants	16*	61	20	1	0	4	.328
1931-32	Philadelphia Royal Giants	7	34	10	2	0	0	.294
Totals		23	95	30	3	0	4	.316

Chaney White was one of the best players in the Negro leagues between 1919 and 1936. He was an aggressive player in all phases of the game. He had a .302 lifetime average in the Negro Leagues, and a .347 average for four years in Cuba.

WILLIAMS, POINDEXTER

Year	Team	G	AB	H	D	T	HR	BA
1930-31	Nashville Elite Giants	25	95	34	9	1	4	.358

Poindexter Williams was a catcher in the Negro leagues from 1921 to 1933. Partial statistics for four years, credit him with a .347 batting average.

WILSON, ERNEST "JUD" OR "BOOJUM"

Year	Team	G	AB	H	D	T	HR	BA
1925-30	PLAYED IN CUBA—BATTED .372							
1930-31	Philadelphia Royal Giants	15	49	23*	9*	2*	3	.469

Jud Wilson was one of the greatest hitters in Negro league history, with a .354 career average. He was also the career leader in the Cuban Winter League with a sizzling .372 average, and two batting titles, over a six year period.

WRIGHT, BURNIS "WILD BILL"

Year	Team	G	AB	H	D	T	HR	BA
1933-34	Nashville Elite Giants	41	151	53	12	2	3	.351
1934-35	Nashville Elite Giants	17	54	26	7	0	3	.481*
1935-36	Wilson's Elite Giants	17	61	26	3	2	2	.426
1936-37	Wilson's Elite Giants	2	9	2	0	0	1	.222
1937-38	Philadelphia Royal Giants	10	45	17	2	2*	1	.378
1938-39	Philadelphia Royal Giants	2	9	5	0	1	0	.555
1939-40	Philadelphia Royal Giants	10	37	10	0	1	2	.270
1940-41	Elite Giants	2	7	3	0	0	2	.429
1942-43	Royal Giants							
1943-44	Kansas City Royals	4	16	4	1	1	0	.250
1944-45	Kansas City Royals	5	19	8	1	2	0	.421
1945	Kansas City Royals	3	8	2	0	0	1	.250
Totals		112	416	156	26	11	15	.375

"Wild Bill" Wright was an outstanding all-around player from 1932 to 1956. He spent his first eight years in the Negro leagues, but most of the next 15 years in Mexico where he was a hero. Wright hit .341 in the U.S. and .335 south of the border. He averaged 28 doubles, 14 triples, and 14 home runs a year.

WRIGHT, ZOLLIE

Year	Team	G	AB	H	D	T	HR	BA
1935-36	Wilson's Royal Giants	18	68	26	7*	0	5	.382

Zollie Wright, a stocky 5'9", 190 pound outfielder, was a strong defensive player, and a .300 hitter until late in his career.

YOUNG, TOM

Year	Team	G	AB	H	D	T	HR	BA
1929-30	Philadelphia Royal Giants	25	93	30	9	1	1	.323

Tom Young caught in the Negro leagues for 17 years, primarily with the Kansas City Monarchs. He was a good journeyman player, who was noted for his hustle.

Pitching Statistics

BELL, CLIFFORD "CHERRY"

Year	Team	G	CG	W	L	IP	SO	BB	SH
1924-25	Los Angeles White Sox	18	8	7	6	111	84*	44	2*
1927-28	PITCHED IN CUBA								
1928-29	PITCHED IN CUBA								
1929-30	PITCHED IN CUBA								
1930-31	PITCHED IN CUBA								
1930-31	Nashville Elite Giants	9	9	6	2	81	43	25*	1
1931-32	Philadelphia Royal Giants	1	1	1	0	9	—	—	0
Totals		28	18	14	8	201	127	69	3

"Cherry" Bell was brother of Fred and "Cool Papa" Bell. He pitched in the Negro leagues for 11 years, 1921–1931. He also pitched in Cuba four years, winning 25 and losing 17.

BELL, FRED "LEFTY"

Year	Team	G	CG	W	L	IP	SO	BB	SH
1923-24	St. Louis Stars	7	1	1	4	40	26	18	0
1924-25	St. Louis Giants	11	7	8*	3	81	34	36	0
Totals		18	8	9	7	121	60	54	0

Fred Bell, "Cool Papa"'s brother, pitched in the Negro leagues for eight years, with mediocre results.

BREWER, CHESTER "CHET"

Year	Team	G	CG	W	L	IP	SO	BB	SH
1926-27	Philadelphia Royal Giants	1	1	1	0	9	9	5	0
1928-29	Cleveland Giants	18*	14*	14*	4	146*	73*	64	3
1929-30	Philadelphia Royal Giants	8	4	3	2	52	48	28	0
1930-31	Philadelphia Royal Giants	3	1	2	0	20	—	—	1
1930-31	PLAYED IN CUBA								
1935-36	Wilson's Elite Giants	9	5	3	1	52	17	3	1
1936-37	Wilson's Elite Giants	6	6	6	0	—	—	—	—
1937-38	Philadelphia Royal Giants	10	6	8	1	73	54	11	0
1941-42	Royal Giants	2	0	0	1	11	10	4	0
1942-43	Royal Giants	1	0	0	1	5	—	—	—
1943-44	Kansas City Royals	5	3	2	1	32	—	—	—
1944-45	Kansas City Royals	6	1	2	1	29	—	—	1
1945	Kansas City Royals	3	1	2	1	16	—	—	—
1946	Kansas City Royals								
Totals		72	42	43	13	445	211+	—	6

Chet Brewer was a tall, lanky finesse pitcher, who starred in the Negro leagues from 1925 to 1948. His 104-69 won-loss record included 12-1 in 1926, 17-3 in 1929, 10-3 in 1943, and 12-6 in 1947. He also pitched in Mexico for three years, going 17-5 in 1938, en route to a career 32-24 record.

BRITTON, GEORGE (A.K.A. GEORGE BRITT)

Year	Team	G	CG	W	L	IP	SO	BB	SH
1925-26	Philadelphia Royal Giants	17	7	6	6	105	74	28	2

George Britton enjoyed a successful 25 year career in the Negro leagues, from 1920 to 1944. The stocky 170 pound right-handed hurler had a back breaking curve ball. The versatile Britton also played catcher, infield and outfield, batting over .300 in several seasons.

CANNON, RICHARD "SPEEDBALL"

Year	Team	G	CG	W	L	IP	SO	BB	SH
1930-31	Nashville Elite Giants	8	6	6	0	63	42	34	1

Speedball Cannon was a power pitcher who pitched in the Negro leagues between 1928 and 1934.

CHARLESTON, PORTER

Year	Team	G	CG	W	L	IP	SO	BB	SH
1929-30	Philadelphia Royal Giants	9	7*	5	3	75*	53*	17	0
1930-31	Philadelphia Royal Giants	5	1	3	1	29	25	7	1*
Totals		14	8	8	4	104	78	24	1

Porter Charleston pitched in the Negro leagues from 1927 through 1935. He went 16-4 for Hilldale in 1934.

COOPER, ANDY "LEFTY"

Year	Team	GC	CG	W	L	IP	SO	BB	SH
1922-23	St. Louis All-Stars	6							
1923-24	St. Louis Stars	9	5	4	2	59	—	—	1
1923-24	PLAYED IN CUBA								
1924-25	PLAYED IN CUBA								
1926-27	Royal Giants	10	5	5	2	71	—	—	1
1927-28	Cleveland Stars	6	5	5	1	51	25	17*	1
1928-29	PLAYED IN CUBA								
1929-30	Royal Giants	9	5	6*	1	59	42	14	1
1930-31	Philadelphia Royal Giants	3	2	2	0	20	—	—	—
Totals		43	22	22	6	260	—	—	4

Andy Cooper pitched in the Negro leagues from 1920 to 1941, compiling a record of 121-54, for a winning percentage of .691, #7 all-time. The big 6'2", 220 pound southpaw strung together seasons of 14-5, 15-8, 12-5, 12-1, 12-8, 7-3, 13-7, and 13-3 from 1922 to 1929. His Cuban experience produced an 11-17 record.

CURRIE, REUBEN "RUBE"

Year	Team	G	CG	W	L	IP	SO	BB	SH
1920-21	Los Angeles White Sox	18*	17*	12*	4	154*	43	20	1*
1922-23	Los Angeles White Sox	6	6	2	3	52	26	18	1
1923-24	PITCHED IN CUBA—WENT 10-5								
1924-25	Los Angeles White Sox	23*	8	7	8	123	60	39	2*
1925-26	Philadelphia Royal Giants	14	4	5	4	73	33	17	0
Totals		61	35	26	19	402	162	94	4

Rube Currie was a 6'4", 195 pound curveball artist, with outstanding control, as witnessed by his 20 bases on balls in 154 innings pitched in 1920-21. Currie pitched in the Negro leagues for 13 years, from 1920 through 1932. He was at his best in the World Series, pitching Hilldale to the World Championship in 1925.

DRAKE, WILLIAM "PLUNK"

Year	Team	G	CG	W	L	IP	SO	BB	SH
1924-25	Los Angeles White Sox	20	17*	11*	5	155*	70	54*	1

Plunk Drake was one of the top pitchers in the Negro leagues between 1915 and 1930. As Jim Riley noted, "Drake was a tough competitor who earned his nickname "Plunk" because he kept batters loose in the batters box." John Holway credits Drake with a 99–61 record in the Negro leagues

FLOURNOY, JESSE "PUD"

Year	Team	G	CG	W	L	IP	SO	BB	SH
1927-28	Philadelphia Royal Giants	12*	7	6	3	92*	31	8	0
1930-31	Nashville Elite Giants	1	1	1	0	9	2	3	0
Totals		13	8	7	3	101	33	11	0

Pud Flournoy was an outstanding pitcher in the Negro leagues from 1919 to 1933. He was a chubby southpaw with good control, an excellent fastball and a variety of curveballs.

FOSTER, WILLIAM "WILLIE"

Year	Team	G	CG	W	L	IP	SO	BB	SH
1926-27	Philadelphia Royal Giants	7	5	6*	0	55	49*	17	2*
1927-28	PLAYED IN CUBA								

Year	Team	G	CG	W	L	IP	SO	BB	SH
1930-31	Philadelphia Royal Giants	11	7	9	0	68	53	20	1
1931-32	Philadelphia Giants	—	—	9	1	—	—	—	1
Totals		18	12	24	1	—	—	—	4

Willie Foster is generally regarded as the greatest left-handed pitcher in Negro league history. Foster won 146 games (#3 all-time) between 1923 and 1938, with a winning percentage of .689 (#9). He had a full repertoire of pitches, and was considered to be one of the greatest money pitchers of all time.

GARDNER, KENNETH "PING"

Year	Team	G	CG	W	L	IP	SO	BB	SH
1920-21	Lincoln Giants	9	7	8	1	73	39	23	1
1928-29	Cleveland Giants	10	6	4	2	58	34	38	1
Totals		19	13	12	3	131	73	61	2

Ping Gardner was a small left-handed submarine pitcher, who toiled in the Negro leagues from 1918 through 1932.

GLASS, CARL "LEFTY"

Year	Team	G	CG	W	L	IP	SO	BB	SH
1928-29	Cleveland Giants	9	8	6	3	79	27	14	0

Carl Glass enjoyed a 14 year career in the Negro leagues, primarily with the Memphis Red Sox.

GRIFFITH, ROBERT "SCHOOLBOY" (A.K.A. GRIFFIN)

Year		G	CG	W	L	IP	SO	BB	SH
1934-35	Wilson's Elite Giants	1	1	1	0	9	9	—	0
1935-36	Wilson's Royal Giants	14	7	7	0	91	99	25	0
1936-37	Wilson's Royal Giants	12	12	10	2	95	101	—	0
1937-38	PITCHED IN CUBA—LED LEAGUE WITH 12–6 RECORD								
1938-39	PITCHED IN CUBA—WENT 4-5								
1938-39	Philadelphia Royal Giants	2	2	2	0	19	19	4	0
Totals		29	22	20	2	214	228	29+	0

Bob "Schoolboy" Griffith pitched in the Negro leagues from 1933 to 1949. He also pitched in the Dominican Republic (2-1), Cuba (16-11), and Mexico (24-18). He compiled as record of 6-5 for Granby of the Provincial League in 1951 at the age of 38, after the integration of organized baseball

GURLEY, JAMES

Year	Team	G	CG	W	L	IP	SO	BB	SH
1924-25	St.L.Giants, L.A.W.S.	14	8	7	3	94	52	48	1

James Gurley pitched in the Negro leagues from 1922 to 1933. He pitched, and played first base and the outfield, but no details are available on his career.

HARNEY, GEORGE

Year	Team	G	CG	W	L	IP	SO	BB	SH
1926-27	Philadelphia Royal Giants	16	9	7	5	116*	—	—	2
1927-28	Cleveland Stars	5	4	1	3	39	—	—	—
Totals		21	13	8	8	155	—	—	—

George Harney was an outstanding spitball pitcher for the Chicago American Giants from 1923 to 1930. He helped pitch the Giants to two consecutive Negro National League pennants.

Holland, Elvis "Bill"

Year	Team	G	CG	W	L	IP	SO	BB	SH
1922-24	PITCHED IN CUBA—WENT 27–22								
1927-28	Philadelphia Royal Giants	11	10*	7*	3	90	36	10	4*

Bill Holland pitched in the Negro leagues from 1920 to 1941. Incomplete statistics credit him with a record of 127–99, for a fine .562 winning percentage. In 1930, he became the first black pitcher to pitch in Yankee Stadium.

Hubbard, Jess "Mountain"

Year	Team	G	CG	W	L	IP	SO	BB	SH
1920-21	Lincoln Giants	10	9	9	1	87	60	33	3
1925-26	Philadelphia Royal Giants	4	1	1	3	16	—	—	0
1927-28	Philadelphia Royal Giants	1	1	1	0	9	—	—	0
Totals		15	11	11	4	112	—	—	3

Jess Hubbard was a big, rugged right-handed pitcher who spent 18 years in the Negro leagues, 1917 to 1937. He was not only an outstanding pitcher, he was a good hitter with a lifetime .316 batting average.

Jeffries, James "Jim"

Year	Team	G	CG	W	L	IP	SO	BB	SH
1921-22	Colored All-Stars	14	11	9*	5	98	46	28	1*

Jim Jeffries had a long, successful career in the Negro leagues, from 1914 to 1931. He pitched and played the outfield. He batted .254 in California in 1924.

McDuffie, Terris "The Great"

Year	Team	G	CG	W	L	IP	SO	BB	SH
1939-40	Philadelphia Royal Giants	9	6	5*	3	54	—	—	0
1943-44	Baltimore Elite Giants	3	2	2	0	21	11	3	0
Totals		12	8	7	3	75	11+	3+	0

Terris McDuffie was a big hard throwing right-hander in the 1930s and '40s. He pitched all over the western hemisphere, going 43–27 in the Negro leagues, 37–43 in Cuba, 21–33 in Mexico, 5–5 in Puerto Rico, 21–9 in the Dominican Republic, and 3–4 in the Texas League.

Mooney,

Year	Team	G	CG	W	L	IP	SO	BB	SH
1909-10	Trilbys	1	1	0	1	12	9	3	0
1910-11	Leland Giants	4	4	2	1	29	12	6	1
1916-17	Los Angeles White Sox	6*	3*	4*	1	39*	31*	5	0
1920-21	Alexander's Giants	3	2	1	2	22	8	8	0
Totals		14	10	7	5	102	60	22	1

Nothing is known of Mooney, not even his first name. He was a left-handed submarine pitcher, and he was the ace of the White Sox staff in 1916-17.

Moreland, Nate

Year	Team	G	CG	W	L	IP	SH	BB	SH
1940-41	Baltimore Elite Giants	5	3	3	1	25	20	5	1
1942-43	Royal Giants	2	1	0	1	—	—	—	0
1944-45	Kansas City Royals	7	5	6	0	52	—	—	2
1945	Kansas City Royals	2	1	0	1	15	—	—	0
Totals		16	10	9	3	92+	—	—	3

Nate Moreland played in the Negro leagues from 1940 to 1945, then spent ten years in the minor leagues, mostly in lower level leagues.

PAIGE, ROBERT LEROY "SATCHEL"

Year	Team	G	CG	W	L	IP	SO	BB	SH
1931-32	Philadelphia Giants	7	6	6	0	58	70	—	2
1932-33	Tom Wilson's Elite Giants	7	7	7	0	63	91	—	1
1933-34	Tom Wilson's Elite Giants	20*	18*	16*	2	172*	245*	47	7*
1934-35	Tom Wilson's Elite Giants	10	7	8	0	69	104	20	2
1935-36	Tom Wilson's Elite Giants	16	6	13*	0	94	113	28	4
1943-44	Baltimore Elite Giants	6	1	3	1	36	39	10	0
1945	Kansas City Royals	4	1	1	1	27	27	12	0
1946	Kansas City Royals	3	0	0	2	15	21	7	0
1947	Kansas City Royals	7	1	2	1	35	60	14	1
Totals		80*	47	56*	7	572*	770*	138+	17*

Satchel Paige is one of the three greatest pitchers in Negro baseball history, along with "Smokey Joe" Williams and "Bullet Joe" Rogan. Paige was a true showman who drew spectators to the games in droves. But he was more than that. He was an overpowering strikeout pitcher with pinpoint control. His 147–92 career Negro league record is misleading because, as the major drawing card, he pitched frequently, and usually left the game after four innings. As a result, he couldn't be the winning pitcher, but he could be the losing pitcher.

PORTER, ANDREW "PULLMAN"

Year	Team	G	CG	W	L	IP	SO	BB	SH
1932-33	Nashville Elite Giants	2	1	1	1	14	—	—	0
1934-35	Wilson's Elite Giants	19	16	12	3	122	66	21	1
1936-37	Wilson's Elite Giants	6	4	3	2	33	—	—	2
1937-38	Philadelphia Royal Giants	5	3	5	0	36	22	14	0
1938-39	Philadelphia Royal Giants	1	0	1	0	7	—	—	0
1939-40	PITCHED IN CUBA								
1940-41	PITCHED IN CUBA								
1941-42	Royal Giants	1	0	0	0	5	3	2	0
1945	Kansas City Royals	1	1	1	0	7	—	—	1
Totals		35	25	23	6	224	—	—	4

"Pullman" Porter was a tall, strong, right-handed pitcher with a blazing fast ball. He starred in the Negro leagues and Mexico for 19 years, from 1932 to 1950. Fragmentary records credit him with an excellent 37–16 record in the Negro leagues. In Mexico, he went 49–47 over six years, including a 21–14 slate in 1940, with 232 strikeouts in 296 innings.

ROGAN, WILBUR "BULLET JOE"

Year	Team	G	CG	W	L	IP	SO	BB	SH
1917-18	Los Angeles White Sox								
1920-21	Los Angeles White Sox	16	16	8	8	144	110*	74*	1*
1924-25	PLAYED IN CUBA								
1925-26	Philadelphia Royal Giants	18*	16*	14*	2	153*	82*	52*	1
1926-27	Philadelphia Royal Giants	11*	6	6	2	68	38	21*	2*
1928-29	Cleveland Giants	12	8	9	1	92	68	21	1
1929-30	Philadelphia Royal Giants	7	6	5	1	59	53*	21	0
Totals		64	52*	42	14	516	351	189	5

"Bullet Rogan," as noted earlier, was one of the greatest pitchers in the annals of Negro baseball.

Ross, William

Year	Team	G	CG	W	L	IP	SO	BB	SH
1924-25	St. Louis Giants	15*	12*	7	5	118*	67*	38	1
1930-31	Nashville Elite Giants	6	5	6	0	48	29	9	0
Totals		21	17	13	5	166	96	47	1

William Ross played in the Negro leagues from 1923 to 1930. He pitched for the St. Louis Stars for four years, and won 9 games against 6 losses in 1926.

Taylor, Jonathon "John"

Year	Team	G	CG	W	L	IP	SO	BB	SH
1921-22	Colored All-Stars	15*	12*	7	6	118*	67*	38*	1*

John Taylor, one of the five famous Taylor brothers, was an outstanding pitcher in the Negro leagues from 1903 to 1925. The 5'10", 170 pound right-hander was dubbed "Steel Arm" because of his blazing speed.

Wickware, Frank "The Red Ant"

Year	Team	G	CG	W	L	IP	SO	BB	SH
1910-11	Leland Giants	4	3	2	2	30	27	7	1
1915-16	American Giants	7*	4*	6*	1*	46*	27	24	2*
Totals		11	7	8	3	76	54	31	3

Frank Wickware was another of the great fastball pitchers in the Negro leagues. His career lasted from 1910 to 1925, including nine years with Rube Foster's Chicago American Giants. Partial statistics credit him with a 30–16 record. He led the Cuban Winter League in pitching in 1912, finishing with a 10–4 mark.

Williams, Joe "Cyclone"

Year	Team	G	CG	W	L	IP	SO	BB	SH
1909-10	Trilby's	1	1	0	1	9	5	4	0
1910-11	Leland Giants	7*	6*	4	1	60*	78*	16*	2*
1915-16	Chicago American Giants	7*	3	2	3	42	27	20	0
Totals		15	10	6	5	111	110	40	2

Cyclone Joe Williams was arguably the greatest pitcher in Negro league history. He was elected to the National Baseball Hall of Fame in 1999.

Willis, James "Cannnonball"

Year	Team	G	CG	W	L	IP	SO	BB	SH
1930-31	Nashville Elite Giants	14*	14*	11*	3	120*	92*	21	3*
1931-32	Philadelphia Giants	3	1	3	0	—	—	—	—
1932-33	Nashville Elite Giants	17	5	4	1	43	—	—	0
1933-34	Nashville Elite Giants	19	15	14	2	116	93	34	2
1934-35	Nashville Elite Giants	15	12	9	4	118	72	26	3
Totals		68	47	41	10	397	257+	81+	8

"Cannonball" Willis pitched in the Negro leagues for 13 years, from 1927 to 1939. His Negro league statistics are still unavailable, but his California Winter League stats speak for themselves.

Young, "Slowtime"

Year	Team	G	CG	W	L	IP	SO	BB	SH
1933-34	Wilson's Elite Giants	6	4	4	2	36	—	—	2
1934-35	Wilson's Elite Giants	4	4	3	1	22	—	—	0
Totals		10	8	7	3	58	—	—	2

Players from the Major Leagues and High Minor Leagues
Batting Statistics

ALLINGTON, WILLIAM "BILL"

Year	Team	G	AB	H	D	T	HR	BA
1932-33	Pirone's All-Stars	1	3	1	0	1	0	.333
1933-34	White Kings	4	13	2	0	0	0	.077
1934-35	All-Stars, White Kings	7	24	6	0	0	0	.250
1935-36	White Kings	4	12	4	0	0	2	.333
1936-37	All-Stars, White Kings	2	6	2	0	0	2	.333
1937-38	White Kings	3	13	4	0	1	1	.308
1939-40	White Kings	2	6	2	0	0	0	.333
Totals		23	77	21	0	2	5	.273

Bill Allington played one year with Seattle in the PCL, batting .312 in 202 at-bats. He is better known as the manager of the Rockford Peaches in the All-American Girls Professional Baseball League.

ALMADA, LOU

Year	Team	G	AB	H	D	T	HR	BA
1929-30	Kelley Kars	13	52	10	1	0	3	.192
1930-31	Commercial Club	4	13	4	1	0	0	.308
1931-32	White Kings	1	4	0	0	0	0	.000
1932-33	El Paso	2	7	2	1	0	0	.287
1933-34	White Kings	3	12	4	0	0	0	.250
1934-35	Pirone's All-Stars	2	8	3	1	1	1	.375
1936-37	Pirone's All-Stars	1	4	2	1	0	0	.500
1937-38	White Kings	1	3	1	0	0	0	.333
Totals		27	103	26	5	1	4	.255

Lou Almada, a native of Mexico, was the brother of Mel Almada. Lou played in the Pacific Coast League between 1929 and 1937, batting .300.

ALMADA, MEL

Year	Team	G	AB	H	D	T	HR	BA
1932-33	El Paso	2	7	4	1	0	1	.571
1934-35	Pirone's All-Stars	2	7	1	0	0	1	.143
1935-36	Pirone's All-Stars	3	11	1	0	0	1	.091
1936-37	Pirone's All-Stars							
Totals		7	25	6	1	0	3	.240

Mel Almada was one of Mexico's greatest ballplayers, and is a member of the Mexican Baseball Hall of Fame. He played major league baseball for seven years, batting .284 in 2483 at-bats.

ARLETT, RUSSELL "BUZZ"

Year	Team	G	AB	H	D	T	HR	BA
1924-25	White Kings	25	95	35	6	2	4	.368

Buzz Arlett was one of the greatest minor league hitters. Over a 20 year career, he accumulated 2726 base hits, including 432 home runs, and batted .341. He hit .313 in 121 major league games, but his defensive deficiencies prevented him from enjoying a long major league career.

AVERILL, EARL

Year	Team	G	AB	H	D	T	HR	BA
1928-29	White Kings, Shell Oil	13	54	27	4	1	5	.500*

Earl Averill was one of the best hitters in major league history. His 13 year career included 2,019 base hits in 6,353 at-bats, for an average of .318, #48 all time. He averaged 35 doubles, 11 triples and 21 home runs a year.

BANCROFT, DAVE "BEAUTY"

Year	Team	G	AB	H	D	T	HR	BA
1912-13	Tufts-Lyons	5	18	8	4	0	0	.444
1914-15	El Centro	11	43	14	4	0	1	.326
Totals		16	61	22	8	0	1	.361

Dave "Beauty" Bancroft was one of the top major league shortstops of his era. He played in the National League for 16 years, with the Phillies, Giants, Braves, and Dodgers. During his career he garnered 2,004 base hits, and batted .279. He was elected to the National Baseball Hall of Fame in 1971.

BASSLER, JOHNNY

Year	Team	G	AB	H	D	T	HR	BA
1919-20	Dyas All-Stars	1	2	1	1	0	0	.500
1920-21	Pirrone's All-Stars	5	17	2	0	0	0	.118
1925-26	Pirrone's All-Stars	4	15	4	0	0	0	.267
1926-27	Pirrone's All-Stars	1	3	1	0	0	0	.333
1930-31	Kelley Kars	6	21	5	1	0	0	.238
1936-37	Santa Monica	1	3	1	1	0	0	.333
Totals		18	61	14	3	0	0	.230

Johnny Bassler played in the major leagues for nine years, batting .304 in 2,319 at-bats. He played in the Pacific Coast League for 15 years, batting .321 with 1,353 base hits in 4,215 at-bats.

BELL, FERN

Year	Team	G	AB	H	D	T	HR	BA
1932-33	Pirrone's All-Stars	3	11	4	0	0	1	.364
1933-34	Pirrone's All-Stars	9	31	6	3	1	0	.194
1934-35	Pirrone's All-Stars	10	35	6	2	0	2	.171
1935-36	All-Stars, White Kings	10	32	7	0	0	0	.219
1936-37	Pirrone's All-Stars	5	16	7	0	0	4	.438
1939-40	Pirrone's All-Stars	2	8	3	2	0	0	.375
Totals		39	133	33	7	1	7	.248

Fern Bell played in the major leagues for two years with the Pittsburgh Pirates. He batted .283 in 83 games.

BERGER, WALTER "WALLY"

Year	Team	G	AB	H	D	T	HR	BA
1930-31	Kelley Kars	13	47	20	2	0	10*	.426
1935-36	Dean's All-Stars	1	4	2	1	1	0	.500
Totals		14	51	22	3	1	10	.431

Wally Berger set a major league rookie record by hitting 38 home runs for the Boston Braves in 1930. He batted .300 and hit 242 home runs during an 11 year big league career.

BERKOWITZ, JOSEPH "JOE"

Year	Team	G	AB	H	D	T	HR	BA
1930-31	Pirrone's All-Stars	2	6	3	1	0	0	.500
1931-32	Pirrone's All-Stars	3	14	2	0	0	0	.143
1933-34	Pirrone's All-Stars	13	37	7	2	0	0	.189
1934-35	Pirrone's All-Stars	11	34	10	2	1	1	.294
1938-39	White Kings	1	3	1	0	0	1	.333
1939-40	White Kings	1	4	0	0	0	0	.000
Totals		31	98	23	5	1	2	.235

Joe Berkowitz played in the Pacific Coast League during the mid to late 1930s. He hit .297 for San Diego in 1938.

BLAKESLEY, JAMES "SUNNY JIM"

Year	Team	G	AB	H	D	T	HR	BA
1925-26	Shell Oil	10	37	13	0	1	0	.351
1926-27	Shell Oil	29	112	30	2	1	1	.268
1930-31								
Totals		39	149	43	2	2	1	.289

Jim Blakesley played minor league baseball for 14 years, compiling a career batting average of .333. He played for Vernon in the Pacific Coast League in 1925 and 26, batting .304.

BLUE, LUZERNE "LU"

Year	Team	G	AB	H	D	T	HR	BA
1920-21	Pirrone's, Dyas, Blue's AS	10	33	8	1	0	0	.242
1921-22	Pirr., Meusel, Sawyer AS	17	58	16	3	2	2	.276
Totals		27	91	24	4	2	2	.264

Lu Blue had a productive 13 year major league career, primarily with the Detroit Tigers. He batted .287 with 1,696 base hits.

BODIE, FRANK "PING"

Year	Team	G	AB	H	D	T	HR	BA
1922-23	Pirrone, Bodie A.S.	5	19	7	2	1	0	.368
1923-24	Harlow All-Stars	1	4	1	0	0	0	.250
1924-25	White Kings, AllStars	22	87	29	7	2	4	.333
1926-27	Pirrone's All-Stars	25	81	23	2	0	2	.284
1927-28	Pirrone's All-Stars	10	40	11	0	0	1	.275
1932-33	Pirrone's All-Stars	2	8	3	0	0	0	.375
Totals		65	239	74	11	3	7	.310

Ping Bodie played in the major leagues for nine years, batting .275. He also hit .308 over a 15 year minor league career, six of them in the Pacific Coast League.

BOECKEL, NORMAN "TONY"

Year	Team	G	AB	H	D	T	HR	BA
1916-17	Anheuser-Busch, Western	2	8	1	0	0	0	.125
1917-18	Navy, Std-Murphy	5	19	5	1	0	0	.263
1918-19	Dyas All-Stars	2	8	5	0	1	0	.625
1920-21	Pirrone's All-Stars	13	55	15	1	0	0	.273
1921-22	Meusel, Pirrone, Fisher AS	17	64	22	3	3	0	.344
Totals		34	136	41	6	3	0	.301

Tony Boeckel enjoyed a six year career as a major league third baseman. He batted .282 in 777 games with the Pittsburgh Pirates and the Boston Braves between 1917 and 1923. He died in an automobile crash in February 1924.

Brazill, Frank

Year	Team	G	AB	H	D	T	HR	BA
1925-26	White Kings, All-Stars	23	93	30	1	0	5	.301
1926-27	White Kings, All-Stars	16	42	7	0	0	0	.167
1928-29	White Kings, Shell Oil	15	48	13	1	1	1	.271
1929-30	Kelley Kars	13	45	13	1	0	2	.277
1930-31	Commercial Club	10	37	10	3	0	0	.270
Totals		77	265	73	6	1	8	.275

Frank Brazill batted .258 in 72 games in the major leagues. He pounded minor league pitching for 2,873 base hits over a 20 year career, good for a .331 batting average.

Brucker, Earle

Year	Team	G	AB	H	D	T	HR	BA
1928-29	Shell Oil	15	57	14	1	1	0	.246
1930-31	San Diego	13	52	13	4	0	0	.250
1936-37	San Diego Merchants	10	40	13	0	0	3	.325
1938-39	San Diego Farleys	1	3	0	0	0	0	.000
Totals		39	152	40	5	1	3	.263

Earle Brucker played with the Philadelphia Athletics from 1937 to 1943, batting .290.

Carey, Max

Year	Team	G	AB	H	D	T	HR	BA
1920-21	Pirrone's All-Stars	12	44	12	0	0	0	.273

Max Carey played in the major leagues from 1910 to 1929, batting .285 with 2,665 base hits in 9,363 at-bats.

Carlyle, Hiram Cleo

Year	Team	G	AB	H	D	T	HR	BA
1924-25	Gilmore Oil	13	49	13	2	1	1	.265
1930-31	MGM	2	9	4	1	0	0	.444
1933-34	Pirrone's All-Stars	10	35	5	1	0	1	.143
1934-35	Pirrone's All-Stars	9	30	8	0	0	3	.267
1935-36	Pirrone's All-Stars	9	31	3	1	0	0	.097
1939-40	White Kings	2	6	0	0	0	0	.000
Totals		45	160	33	5	1	5	.206

Cleo Carlyle played in the major leagues in 1927, batting .234 in 278 at-bats He batted .316 in an eleven year Pacific Coast League career, and had over 2,500 base hits in the minor leagues.

Chadbourne, Chet

Year	Team	G	AB	H	D	T	HR	BA
1912-13	McCormicks	2	9	3	1	0	0	.333
1917-18	Vernon	4	16	2	0	0	0	.125
1918-19	Hollywood, Dyas A.S.	7	28	12	3	0	0	.429
1919-20	Weaver's All-Stars	2	9	2	0	0	0	.222
1920-21	Fisher's A.S., Dyas A.S.	14	54	10	1	0	0	.185
1923-24	Pirrone's All-Stars	6	20	6	3	0	0	.300
1924-25	Vernon	15	63	21	4	0	0	.333
Totals		50	199	56	12	0	0	.281

Chet Chadbourne played in the major leagues for five years between 1906 and 1918. He batted .255 in 1,353 at-bats.

CHRISTENSEN, WALTER "CUCKOO"

Year	Team	G	AB	H	D	T	HR	BA
1928-29	Shell Oil	15	54	18	1	2	0	.333
1929-30	Shell Oil	6	23	9	2	0	0	.391
1930-31	Shell Oil	4	14	5	1	0	0	.357
Totals		25	91	32	4	2	0	.352

Walter Christensen played in the major leagues for two years, batting .315 in 514 at-bats for the Cincinnati Reds.

COSCARART, PETE

Year	Team	G	AB	H	D	T	HR	BA
1936-37	San Diego	9	39	14	2	0	1	.359
1937-38	San Diego Farleys	9	39	10	1	0	2	.256
1938-39	San Diego Farleys	5	17	2	0	0	0	.118
1939-40	San Diego 7-Up	1	3	0	0	0	0	.000
1944-45	Service All-Stars	2	7	3	0	0	0	.429
Totals		26	105	29	3	0	3	.276

Pete Coscarart played in the major leagues for nine years, from 1938 to 1946, with the Brooklyn Dodgers and Pittsburgh Pirates, batting .243 in 2,992 at-bats.

COX, ELMER "DICK"

Year	Team	G	AB	H	D	T	HR	BA
1922-23	Pasadena Eagles	1	4	2	0	0	1	.500
1923-24	Pasadena	2	8	5	1	2	1	.625
1924-25	White Kings, Glendale	21	81	30	7	1	1	.370
1925-26	All-Stars	14	61	20	1	0	2	.328
1926-27	Shell, White Kings	17	57	17	1	0	1	.298
1927-28	All-Stars	3	13	4	0	0	0	.308
1928-29	White Kings	11	49	16	0	0	1	.327
1929-30	Kelley Kars	13	47	13	4	0	0	.277
1930-31	Kelley Kars	5	10	2	1	0	0	.200
Totals		85	322	105	15	3	7	.326

Dick Cox played outfield for the Brooklyn Dodgers in 1925-26, batting .314 in 832 at-bats, with 40 doubles, 14 triples, and 8 home runs.

CUTSHAW, GEORGE

Year	Team	G	AB	H	D	T	HR	BA
1914-15	Brawley	2	7	1	0	0	0	.143
1917-18	San Pedro	2	8	2	0	0	0	.250
1918-19	Pasadena	3	12	2	0	0	0	.167
1926-27	Marion Co.	4	17	3	0	0	0	.176
Totals		11	44	8	0	0	0	.182

George Cutshaw was a mainstay in the Brooklyn Dodgers' 1916 National League championship team. The second baseman played in the major leagues for 12 years, with 1,487 base hits and a .265 batting average.

DEMAGGIO, "NICK"

Year	Team	G	AB	H	D	T	HR	BA
1911-12	Jeffries	1	4	0	0	0	0	.000
1914-15	San Pedro	3	12	3	0	0	0	.250
1917-18	Submarine Base	3	12	5	1	0	0	.417

Year	Team	G	AB	H	D	T	HR	BA
1918-19	Rall's A.S., Los Angeles	2	10	3	0	0	0	.300
1921-22	Pirrone's A.S., Calpaco	7	27	8	1	1	1	.296
1922-23	Pirrone's All-Stars	16	61	13	1	0	0	.213
1923-24	Pirrone, Union Pacific	8	30	5	0	0	0	.167
1925-26	Blue Diamond	1	4	0	0	0	0	.000
1926-27	Julian, Maywood	6	22	7	0	0	0	.318
1927-28	Pirrone's A.S., Palms	8	30	5	0	1	0	.167
Totals		55	212	49	3	2	1	.231

No record of Nick DeMaggio has been located in organized baseball.

DURST, CEDRIC

Year	Team	G	AB	H	D	T	HR	BA
1925-26	White Kings	16	72	20	2	1	0	.278
1930-31	Kelley Kars	10	40	10	1	0	2	.250
1931-32	White Kings	1	4	1	0	0	0	.250
1934-35	May Co.	2	7	1	1	0	0	.143
1936-37	May Co.	1	4	1	0	0	0	.250
1937-38	San Diego Farleys	8	34	9	1	0	2	.265
1938-39	San Diego Farleys	2	4	0	0	0	0	.000
1939-40	San Diego 7-Up	4	15	5	1	0	0	.333
Totals		42	176	47	6	1	4	.267

Cedric Durst enjoyed a seven year major league career with the St. Louis Browns and the New York Yankees between 1922 and 1930. He batted .244 in 481 games.

EMMER, FRANK

Year	Team	G	AB	H	D	T	HR	BA
1926-27	Shell Oil	28	88	24	5	5*	0	.273
1928-29	Shell Oil	15	62	14	1	0	0	.226
1929-30	Shell Oil	6	27	3	1	0	0	.111
Totals		49	177	41	7	5	0	.232

Frank Emmer played in the major leagues two years, hitting .182 in 122 games. He led the American Association in home runs with 32 in 1927.

FALK, BIBB

Year	Team	G	AB	H	D	T	HR	BA
1923-24	Hammond	2	8	2	0	1	0	.250
1924-25	White Kings	12	41	11	0	0	0	.268
1926-27	Pan Gas	1	4	1	0	0	0	.250
1929-30	Kelley Kars	11	42	10	1	0	2	.238
Totals		26	95	24	1	1	2	.253

Bibb Falk played in the major leagues from 1920 to 1931. He batted .314 in 4,652 at-bats.

FONSECA, LEW

Year	Team	G	AB	H	D	T	HR	BA
1926-27	Pirrone's All-Stars	16	51	14	5	0	0	.275

Lew Fonseca played in the major leagues for 12 years. He batted .316 in 3404 at-bats. He led the American League in batting in 1929 with an average of .369.

FOXX, JAMES EMORY "JIMMIE"

Year	Team	G	AB	H	D	T	HR	BA
1929-30	Pirrone's All-Stars	1	3	3	2	0	0	1.000

Jimmie Foxx was one of the greatest sluggers in baseball history. He banged out 534 home runs over an historic 20 year major league career. He also hit 458 doubles and 125 triples, to go along with a .325 batting average. His RBI total was an impressive 1,922 (#6 all-time).

FRENCH, RAY

Year	Team	G	AB	H	D	T	HR	BA
1921-22	Meusel's All-Stars	3	14	5	1	0	0	.357
1924-25	Glendale	2	4	3	0	0	0	.750
1926-27	White Kings	17	51	16	3	1	0	.314
1934-35	White Kings, Pirrone's	6	15	4	1	0	0	.267
1935-36	White Kings	3	9	1	0	0	0	.111
Totals		31	93	29	5	1	0	.312

Ray French played in the major leagues for three years, between 1920 and 1924, batting .193 in 82 games. He was an outstanding shortstop in the Pacific Coast League from 1915 to 1934. He holds several PCL career records for shortstops, including most games played, most at-bats, most fielding chances, most putouts, and most assists. He led the league in fielding twice, and left a career batting average of .269 in 8,145 at-bats, with 407 doubles.

GOLVIN, WALT

Year	Team	G	AB	H	D	T	HR	BA
1924-25	White Kings	27	92	30	1	0	0	.326
1926-27	White Kings	11	25	3	0	0	0	.120
1928-29	White Kings	13	51	17	2	1	3	.333
Totals		51	168	50	3	1	3	.298

Walt Golvin played for the Chicago Cubs in 1922, going 0 for 2.

GRIGGS, ARTHUR "ART"

Year	Team	G	AB	H	D	T	HR	BA
1915-16	San Bernardino	2	6	2	0	0	2	.333
1919-20	Killefer's All-Stsrs	1	4	2	0	0	0	.500
1920-21	Pirrone's, Love's A.S.	6	20	7	1	2	0	.350
1923-24	Universal Studios	4	7	5	1	0	0	.714
1925-26	White Kings	12	49	16	1	0	0	.327
1926-27	White Kings	11	32	12	0	0	0	.375
Totals		36	118	44	3	2	2	.373

Art Griggs played in the major leagues for seven years, batting .277 in 1,370 at-bats. He hit the ball at a .315 clip in nine years in the Pacific Coast League, from 1933 to 1942.

HANEY, FRED

Year	Team	G	AB	H	D	T	HR	BA
1918-19	Los Angeles	2	5	1	0	0	1	.200
1920-21	San Pedro, Love's A.S.	5	13	3	0	0	0	.231
1921-22	Kruger's All-Stars	1	5	1	0	0	0	.200
1925-26	Pirrone's All-Stars	5	13	2	1	0	0	.154
1926-27	Pirrone's All-Stars	2	8	2	0	0	0	.250
1927-28	Pirrone's All-Stars	14	55	20	2	2	0	.364
1928-29	Pirrone's All-Stars	15	55	14	1	1	0	.255
1929-30	Pirrone's All-Stars	17	69	22	2	2	0	.319
1930-31	Kelley Kars, All-Stars	13	47	13	1	0	0	.277
1931-32	Pirrone's All-Stars	3	13	3	0	0	0	.231
1932-33	Pirrone's All-Stars	2	6	4	0	0	0	.667
1934-35	Pirrone's All-Stars	5	20	6	1	0	0	.300
1935-36	Pirrone's All-Stars	6	19	6	0	0	0	.316
Totals		90	328	97	8	5	1	.296

Fred Haney played in the major leagues for seven years, compiling a career batting average of .275. He averaged 18 doubles, 6 triples, and 2 home runs a year.

HANNAH, JAMES "TRUCK"

Year	Team	G	AB	H	D	T	HR	BA
1917-18	Standard-Murphy	1	4	1	0	0	0	.250
1919-20	Killefer's All-Stars	1	4	0	0	0	0	.000
1920-21	Pirrone, Blue, Fisher A.S.	17	60	16	1	2	0	.267
1921-22	Sawyer's All-Stars	2	6	2	1	0	0	.333
1922-23	Pirrone A.S., Vernon	6	22	9	1	0	0	.409*
1924-25	Vernon Tigers	8	22	5	0	0	0	.227
1925-26	White Kings	1	4	3	2	0	0	.750
1926-27	White Kings	13	40	8	1	0	0	.200
1935-36	Dean's All-Stars	1	3	1	0	0	0	.333
Totals		50	165	45	6	2	0	.273

Truck Hannah was a legendary minor league catcher. He played the game for 32 years, including a 12 year stint with the Los Angeles Angels. He batted .277 in 2,267 games.

HAWKS, NELSON "CHICKEN"

Year	Team	G	AB	H	D	T	HR	BA
1923-24	Universal Studios	5	15	5	0	0	2	.333
1924-25	Chadbourne, Vernon	2	9	4	1	0	0	.444
1925-26	Pirrone's All-Stars	30	108	31	7	0	0	.287
1926-27	Pirrone's All-Stars	13	49	16	5	0	0	.327
Totals		50	181	56	13	0	2	.309

Chicken Hawks played in the major leagues in 1921 and 1925, batting .316 in 146 games.

HEATH, MINOR "MICKEY"

Year	Team	G	AB	H	D	T	HR	BA
1928-29	Shell Oil	12	41	11	2	0	1	.268
1929-30	Shell Oil	6	21	5	1	0	2	.238
1930-31	Shell Oil	3	8	6	1	0	1	.750
Totals		21	70	22	4	0	4	.314

Mickey Heath played 46 games with the Cincinnati Reds in 1931 and '32, batting .213. He had a long successful minor league career, primarily in AAA ball, batting .298 with 285 home runs in 7,654 at-bats. In 1929, he hit .349 with 38 homers for Hollywood in the PCL. The next year he hit .324 with 37 homers.

HERMAN, FLOYD CAVES "BABE"

Year	Team	G	AB	H	D	T	HR	BA
1921-22	Pirr. A.S., Meusel's A.S.	2	8	3	1	0	0	.375
1922-23	Pirrone's All-Stars	6	24	9	4*	1	0	.375
1923-24	Buick, Un. Pac., Pirr. Glen.	9	38	10	4	1	1	.290
1924-25	Pirrone's All-Stars	17	66	26	6	1	2	.394
1925-26	Pirrone's All-Stars	15	61	21	1	0	0	.344
1926-27	Pirrone's All-Stars	1	4	3	0	1	1	.750
1927-28	Pirrone's All-Stars	5	19	7	1	0	2	.368
1928-29	Pirrone's All-Stars	1	4	0	0	0	0	.000
1930-31	Pirrone's All-Stars	1	5	3	0	0	0	.600
1931-32	Pirrone's All-Stars	1	4	0	0	0	0	.000
1937-38	White Kings	4	15	5	1	0	1	.333
1938-39	White Kings, All-Stars	2	7	4	3	0	1	.571

Year	Team	G	AB	H	D	T	HR	BA
1939-40	White Kings	1	2	2	1	0	0	1.000
1940-41	White Kings, All-Stars	4	11	1	0	0	0	.091
Totals		69	268	94	22	4	8	.351

Babe Herman was the greatest hitter ever to play for the Brooklyn Dodgers. In 1930, he hit .393 with 48 doubles, 11 triples and 35 home runs. He compiled a .324 average over a 13 year major league career. After leaving the majors, Herman batted .325 in six years with Hollywood in the Pacific Coast League, finally retiring in 1945.

HOLMAN, ERNIE

Year	Team	G	AB	H	D	T	HR	BA
1936-37	San Diego Merchants	8	33	12	0	1	0	.364
1937-38	San Diego Farleys	13	48	12	6*	0	0	.250
1938-39	San Diego Farleys	5	15	1	0	0	0	.067
1939-40	San Diego 7-Up	4	14	2	0	0	0	.143
Totals		30	110	27	6	0	0	.245

Ernie Holman never played in the major leagues, but he hit .314 for San Diego in the PCL in 1936, and led the league in fielding at third base with an average of .954.

HOOD, WALLACE "WALLY"

Year	Team	G	AB	H	D	T	HR	BA
1922-23	Pirrone's All-Stars	2	6	3	0	0	1	.500
1924-25	White Kings	27	110	28	8	2	0	.255
1925-26	White Kings	17	72	19	2	0	1	.264
1926-27	Shell Oil, Santa Monica	15	60	17	1	2	1	.283
Totals		61	248	67	11	4	3	.270

Wally Hood played parts of three seasons in the major leagues, batting .237 in 80 at-bats.

HUFFT, IRWIN "FUZZY"

Year	Team	G	AB	H	D	T	HR	BA
1926-27	Pirrone's A.S., Shell Oil	26	95	27	1	0	0	.284
1927-28	Pirrone's A.S	6	22	6	0	0	0	.273
1930-31	Commercial Club	12	44	12	1	0	3	.273
Totals		44	161	45	2	0	3	.280

Fuzzy Hufft was a career minor leaguer. His 13 year career included seven years in the Pacific Coast League where he hit a sizzling .346 with 294 doubles, 46 triples, and 166 home runs in 4,176 at-bats.

JACOBS, RAYMOND "RAY"

Year	Team	G	AB	H	D	T	HR	BA
1926-27	Shell Oil, White Kings	26	90	21	1	1	0	.233
1929-30	Shell Oil	6	26	8	2	0	1	.308
1930-31	Shell Oil	6	25	12	1	2	0	.480
1933-34	White Kings	6	21	2	2	0	0	.095
1934-35	May Co.	1	4	0	0	0	0	.000
1935-36	White Kings	3	9	2	0	0	0	.222
1937-38	San Diego	4	16	7	3	0	0	.438
Totals		52	191	52	9	3	1	.272

Ray Jacobs played two games for the Chicago Cubs in 1928. His long minor league career included 14 years in the Pacific Coast League where he hit .294, with 198 home runs, in 5,882 at-bats.

Jenkins, Joseph "Joe"

Year	Team	G	AB	H	D	T	HR	BA
1920-21	Dyas All-Stars	2	7	2	0	0	0	.287
1924-25	White Kings, Pirrone's AS	22	66	16	2	0	0	.242
1925-26	W.K., Pirrone's, Shell	16	57	31	0	0	2	.544*
1926-27	W.K., Pirrone's, LaGuna	21	57	16	1	0	1	.281
1927-28	Pirrone's All-Stars	6	13	2	0	0	0	.154
1928-29	Shell Oil	11	40	13	1	1	0	.325
1929-30	Kelley Kars	12	30	6	1	0	0	.200
Totals		90	270	86	5	1	3	.319

Joe Jenkins played 60 games in the major leagues between 1914 and 1919, batting .133. His minor league career, which spanned 19 years, was more successful. He played in the Pacific Coast League for seven years, batting .303.

Jolley, Smead

Year	Team	G	AB	H	D	T	HR	BA
1926-27	No. Long Beach	1	5	1	0	0	0	.200
1928-29	Shell Oil, All-Stars	19	74	33	8	0	6	.446
1929-30	Shell Oil, All-Stars	8	38	15	1	0	3	.382
1933-34	Pirrone's All-Stars	3	10	2	0	0	0	.200
1936-37	San Diego	1	4	1	0	0	0	.250
Totals		32	131	52	9	0	9	.397

Smead Jolley was a born hitter, batting .305 during a four year major league career. In the minor leagues, over a 20 year period, he tattooed opposing pitchers to the tune of .366, with 3,037 base hits and 334 home runs.

Jones, Robert "Bob"

Year	Team	G	AB	H	D	T	HR	BA
1926-27	Shell Oil	26	97	35	3	0	0	.361
1930-31	San Diego	14	58	15	1	0	0	.259
Totals		40	155	50	4	0	0	.323

Bob Jones enjoyed a nine year major league career, from 1917 to 1925. He batted .265 in 2,990 at-bats.

Kenna, Edward "Eddie"

Year	Team	G	AB	H	D	T	HR	BA
1925-26	Shell Oil	8	30	6	0	0	0	.200
1926-27	Shell Oil	24	73	19	3	0	0	.260
Totals		32	103	25	3	0	0	.243

Eddie Kenna was a catcher for the Washington Senators in 1928. He hit .297 in 118 at-bats.

Kerr, Johnny

Year	Team	G	AB	H	D	T	HR	BA
1926-27	Shell Oil	26	98	27	4	1	2	.276
1928-29	Shell Oil	12	48	15	1	0	2	.313
1930-31	Shell Oil	3	10	4	1	0	0	.400
Totals		41	156	46	6	1	4	.295

Johnny Kerr played in the major leagues for eight years, batting .266 in 1,457 at-bats.

KINGDON, WESCOTT "WES"

Year	Team	G	AB	H	D	T	HR	BA
1918-19	Hollywood	3	4	0	0	0	0	.000
1919-20	Weaver's All-Stars	1	3	1	0	0	0	.333
1920-21	Dyas All-Stars	3	10	1	0	0	0	.100
1921-22	Sawyer's All-Stars	2	8	0	0	0	0	.000
1922-23	Pirrone's All-Stars	16	58	19*	3*	2*	2	.328
1923-24	Buick's All-Stars	6	21	3	1	0	0	.143
1924-25	White Kings	26	75	24	5	0	0	.320
1925-26	W.K., Saugus, Commercial	8	12	5	1	0	1	.417
1926-27	All-Stars, Commercial	14	56	19	1	0	0	.339
1927-28	Commercial Club	2	8	2	0	0	0	.250
1928-29	White Kings	12	52	11	0	0	0	.212
1929-30	Kelley Kars	12	39	8	0	0	1	.205
1930-31	Commercial Club	10	29	8	0	0	0	.276
1931-32	White Kings	1	4	0	0	0	0	.000
1933-34	All-Stars, White Kings	11	41	8	0	0	0	.195
Totals		127	420	109	11	2	4	.260

Wes Kingdon played 18 games with the Washington Senators in 1932, batting .324. The little shortstop played 22 years of minor league ball, including seven years in the International League. He collected 2,081 base hits in the minors, batting .275.

LAZZERI, ANTHONY "TONY"

Year	Team	G	AB	H	D	T	HR	BA
1927-28	Pirrone's All-Stars	1	4	0	0	0	0	.000
1928-29	Pirrone's All-Stars	1	3	0	0	0	0	.000
1929-30	Pirrone's All-Stars	2	10	3	0	0	1	.300
Totals		4	17	3	0	0	1	.176

Tony Lazzeri was a key player in the New York Yankee dynasty from 1926 through 1939. He played on eight American League pennant winners and Seven World Championship teams. He hit .292 in 1,740 games with 334 doubles, 115 triples and 178 home runs.

LEE, ERNEST "DUD"

Year	Team	G	AB	H	D	T	HR	BA
1928-29	Shell Oil	13	52	11	4	1	1	.212
1929-30	Shell Oil	3	13	5	3	0	0	.385
1930-31	Shell Oil	5	19	4	1	0	0	.210
1931-32	Pirrone's All-Stars	2	7	1	0	0	0	.143
1935-36	Pirrone's All-Stars	5	20	5	0	0	0	.250
1936-37	Santa Monica	2	8	1	0	0	0	.125
Totals		30	119	27	8	1	1	.227

Dud Lee played shortstop for the St. Louis Browns and Boston Red Sox from 1920 to 1926. He batted .311 in 732 at-bats. He also enjoyed a ten year career in the PCL, batting .257 in 6,347 at-bats.

LINDIMORE, HOWARD

Year	Team	G	AB	H	D	T	HR	BA
1924-25	White Kings, Pasadena	18	75	26	2	0	2	.347
1925-26	White Kings	16	64	17	2	0	1	.266
1926-27	White Kings, All-Stars	13	47	14	2	0	0	.298
1928-29	Shell Oil	9	21	5	0	0	0	.238
1929-30	Kelley Kars	1	2	0	0	0	0	.000
Totals		57	209	62	6	0	3	.297

Howard Lindimore played minor league baseball from 1916 to 1933. He played in the Pacific Coast League from 1921 to 1926, batting .303. In 1924 he led the Coast League in runs scored with 183.

LOWREY, HARRY "PEANUTS"

Year	Team	G	AB	H	D	T	HR	BA
1940-41	White Kings	1	2	1	0	0	0	.500
1941-42	Pirrone's All-Stars	2	8	2	0	0	0	.250
1943-44	Pirrone's All-Stars	9	33	8	3	2*	0	.242
1944-45	Major League All-Stars	1	5	3	0	0	0	.600
1947	Feller, Blackwell All-Stars	2	13	0	0	0	0	.000
Totals		15	61	14	3	2	0	.233

Peanuts Lowrey played in the major leagues for 13 years, seven of them with the Chicago Cubs. He batted .273 in 1,401 games.

MANUSH, HENRY "HEINIE"

Year	Team	G	AB	H	D	T	HR	BA
1922-23	Pirrone's All-Stars	6	23	7	3	0	0	.304
1923-24	Glendale	5	18	5	3	0	0	.278
1924-25	Vernon	2	7	2	0	0	0	.287
Totals		13	48	14	6	0	0	.292

Heinie Manush played in the major leagues from 1923 through 1939, compiling a .330 batting average with 2,524 base hits in 7,654 at-bats. He is a member of baseball's Hall of Fame.

McMULLIN, FRED

Year	Team	G	AB	H	D	T	HR	BA
1914-15	El Centro	11	40	7	1	0	0	.175
1915-16	El Centro	5	21	3	0	0	0	.143
1916-17	Los Angeles	1	4	2	0	0	0	.500
1917-18	All-Majors	1	4	0	0	0	0	.000
1918-19	Pasadena, Rall's A.S.	4	16	4	1	0	0	.250
1919-20	Killefer's All-Stars	1	4	2	0	0	0	.500
Totals		23	89	18	2	0	0	.202

Fred McMullin was one of the Black Sox conspirators. He was banned from organized baseball for life in 1920.

McMULLEN, HUGH

Year	Team	G	AB	H	D	T	HR	BA
1925-26	All-Stars	14	53	16	1	0	1	.302
1926-27	All-Stars	27	82	26	2	0	2	.317
1927-28	All-Stars	4	13	4	2	0	0	.308
1928-29	All-Stars	12	36	11	1	0	0	.306
1929-30	All-Stars	16	55	21	5	0	0	.382
1930-31	All-Stars	10	39	12	2	0	1	.308
1931-32	All-Stars	1	3	0	0	0	0	.000
1932-33	All-Stars	1	3	0	0	0	0	.000
1933-34	All-Stars	12	33	6	1	0	0	.182
1934-35	All-Stars	8	22	4	1	0	1	.182
1935-36	All-Stars	1	3	1	0	0	0	.333
1936-37	All-Stars	5						
1937-38	White Kings	1	4	0	0	0	0	.000
Totals		112	346	101	15	0	5	.292

Hugh McMullen played in the major leagues for four years, batting .176 in 64 games.

MESNER, STEPHEN "STEVE"

Year	Team	G	AB	H	D	T	HR	BA
1934-35	White Kings	3	7	1	0	0	0	.143
1935-36	May Co.	3	12	6	1	0	1	.500
1936-37	Pirrone's All-Stars	1	4	3	0	0	0	.750
1937-38	Pirrone's All-Stars	6	21	10	1	0	3	.476*
1939-40	Pirrone's All-Stars	3	13	3	0	0	1	.231
1940-41	Pirrone's All-Stars	2	8	4	2	0	0	.500
1943-44	Pirrone's All-Stars	1	3	1	0	0	0	.333
Totals		19	68	28	4	0	5	.412

Steve Mesner played in the major leagues for six years, three of them with the Cincinnati Reds. The third baseman batted .252 in 451 games. Over a 21 year minor league career, 11 of them in the Pacific Coast League, he blistered the ball at a .311 clip.

METKOVICH, GEORGE "CATFISH"

Year	Team	G	AB	H	D	T	HR	BA
1943-44	Pirrone's All-Stars	9	31	9	4	1	0	.290
1944-45	Major League All-Stars	1	4	2	0	2	0	.500
1945	Major League All-Stars							
1947	Blackwell's All-Stars	2	10	1	0	0	0	.100
Totals		12	45	12	4	3	0	.273

Catfish Metkovich played in the major leagues for ten years, with a .261 batting average in 3,585 at-bats.

MEUSEL, EMIL "IRISH"

Year	Team	G	AB	H	D	T	HR	BA
1913-14	Los Angeles Hoegees	1	5	4	2	0	1	.800
1914-15	El Centro	10	39	13	2	4*	2*	.333
1915-16	El Centro	5	20	6	2	0	0	.300
1916-17	Western Pool Hall	1	5	1	0	0	0	.200
1917-18	San Pedro, Sub Base	4	16	7	1	0	0	.438*
1918-19	Pasadena	4	20	3	0	1	0	.150
1919-20	Dyas A.S., Ruth All-Stars	2	5	2	1	0	0	.400
1920-21	Pirrone's All-Stars	8	34	8	1	4	0	.235
1921-22	Meusel's All-Stars	10	40	17	1	1	1	.425*
1926-27	Pirrone's All-Stars	15	52	10	4	1	0	.192
1927-28	Pirrone's All-Stars	9	37	14	3	0	2	.378
1928-29	Pirrone's All-Stars	17	63	17	1	0	3	.270
1929-30	Pirrone's All-Stars	14	49	17	3	1	2	.347
1930-31	MGM	3	14	6	1	0	1	.375
Totals		103	399	125	22	12	12	.313

Irish Meusel played in the major leagues for 11 years, mostly with the New York Giants, and played in four World Series. He had a lifetime batting average of .310, with 30 doubles, 10 triples, and 12 home runs a year. He also played in the "outlaw" California Baseball League in 1913, hitting .306, and in the Pacific Coast League for five years, hitting an even .300.

MEUSEL, ROBERT "BOB"

Year	Team	G	AB	H	D	T	HR	BA
1916-17	Western Pool Hall	1	3	0	0	0	0	.000
1917-18	Submarine Base	2	8	2	1	1	0	.250
1918-19	Dyas A.S., Ralls A.S.	2	10	5	1	0	0	.500
1919-20	Weaver's A.S., Ruth's A.S.	3	11	6	1	1	0	.545

Year	Team	G	AB	H	D	T	HR	BA
1920-21	Pirrone's, Ralls All-Stars	12	49	14	1	2	0	.286
1921-22	Meusel's All-Stars	9	39	12	2	2	2	.308
1923-24	Pirrone's All-Stars	1	4	2	0	1	0	.500
1926-27	Pirrone's All-Stars	2	8	2	0	0	0	.250
1927-28	Pirrone's All-Stars	5	20	6	1	0	1	.300
1928-29	All-Stars, White Kings	2	8	3	0	0	0	.375
1929-30	All-Stars	3	13	4	1	0	0	.308
1930-31	MGM	2	10	3	1	0	0	.300
1935-36	Pirrone's All-Stars	1	0	0	0	0	0	.000
Totals		45	182	59	9	7	3	.324

Bob Meusel played in the major leagues for 11 years, primarily with the New York Yankees. He was a teammate of Babe Ruth's, and played in six World Series. He compiled a lifetime batting average of .309, averaging 37 doubles, 10 triples, and 16 home runs a year. He led the American League in home runs in 1925 with 33.

MONTUFAR, FELIPE

Year	Team	G	AB	H	D	T	HR	BA
1929-30	San Luis	18	66	21	5	1	0	.318

Felipe Montufar was a Mexican Hall of Fame baseball player. He starred in Mexico for 15 years during the 1920s and 1930s.

MOREHOUSE, FRANK

Year	Team	G	AB	H	D	T	HR	BA
1936-37	San Diego Merchants	9	36	9	0	1	2	.250
1937-38	S.D. Paris Inn, Gold Club	9	36	7	2	0	0	.194
1938-39	San Diego Farleys	1	3	2	0	0	2	.667
1939-40	San Diego 7-Up	1	1	1	0	0	0	1.000
Totals		20	76	19	2	1	4	.250

Frank Morehouse played for Sacramento and Hollywood in the Pacific Coast League between 1936 and 1939, averaging .262

MURRAY, BOBBY

Year	Team	G	AB	H	D	T	HR	BA
1925-26	Pirrone's All-Stars	20	86	26	3	0	0	.302
1926-27	Pirrone's All-Stars	27	95	25	3	0	0	.263
1927-28	Pirrone's All-Stars	13	54	12	0	0	0	.222
1928-29	Pirrone's All-Stars	11	36	7	0	0	0	.194
1929-30	Pirrone's All-Stars	6	24	4	0	0	0	.167
Totals		76	295	74	6	0	0	.251

Bobby Murray batted .189 in ten games for the Washington Senators in 1923.

NIEHOFF, JOHN "BERT"

Year	Team	G	AB	H	D	T	HR	BA
1920-21	Pirrone's All-Stars	14	57	14	4	2	0	.246
1922-23	Pirrone's All-Stars	7	27	8	4*	0	0	.296
1923-24	Universal Studios	5	19	6	1	0	0	.316
1925-26	Pirrone's All-Stars	5	16	4	0	0	0	.250
Totals		31	119	32	9	2	0	.269

Bert Niehoff enjoyed a six year major league career as a second baseman. He batted .240 in 2,037 at-bats.

PAFKO, ANDREW "ANDY"

Year	Team	G	AB	H	D	T	HR	BA
1943-44	Pirrone's All-Stars	6	21	6	2	0	0	.287
1947	Feller's All-Stars	2	8	2	0	0	1	.250
Totals		8	29	8	2	0	1	.276

Andy Pafko was an outstanding slugging outfielder in the major leagues for 17 years. He batted .285 with 1,796 base hits and 213 home runs.

PICK, EDGAR "EDDIE"

Year	Team	G	AB	H	D	T	HR	BA
1926-27	Pirrone's All-Stars	28	101	30	7	1	0	.297
1928-29	Pirrone's All-Stars	19	68	23	6	0	2	.338
1929-30	Pirrone's All-Stars	17	59	15	2	0	2	.254
1930-31	Pirrone's All-Stars	11	41	11	3	0	1	.268
1931-32	Pirrone's All-Stars	4	18	2	0	0	0	.111
Totals		79	287	81	18	1	5	.282

Eddie Pick played in the major leagues for three years, batting .178 in 66 games. In the minor leagues, he hit at a solid .317 clip over a 12 year period, including ten years in AAA ball.

PIRRONE, JOSEPH "JOE"

Year	Team	G	AB	H	D	T	HR	BA
1916-17	Western Pool Hall	2	6	2	0	0	0	.333
1919-20	Ruth's All-Stars	1	0	0	0	0	0	.000
1920-21	Pirrone's All-Stars	17	69	12	3	0	0	.174
1921-22	Pirrone, Meusels A.S.	14	54	10	1	1	1	.185
1922-23	Pirrone's All-Stars	13	48	8	1	0	0	.167
1923-24	Pirrone's All-Stars	10	25	7	0	0	0	.280
1924-25	Pirrone's All-Stars	19	71	16	0	0	0	.225
1925-26	Pirrone's All-Stars	13	27	5	0	0	1	.211
1926-27	Pirrone's All-Stars	16	44	10	1	0	0	.227
1927-28	Pirrone's All-Stars	6	23	6	0	0	0	.261
1928-29	Pirrone's All-Stars	11	35	8	0	3	0	.229
1929-30	Pirrone's All-Stars	7	11	4	2	0	0	.364
1930-31	Pirrone's All-Stars	5	5	1	0	0	0	.200
1931-32	Pirrone's All-Stars	1	3	1	0	0	1	.333
1932-33	Pirrone's All-Stars							
1933-34	Pirrone's All-Stars	1	1	0	0	0	0	.000
1935-36	Pirrone's All-Stars							
Totals		136	422	90	8	5	3	.213

Joe Pirrone, a native of Southern California, was one of the area's top amateur and semi-professional pitchers in the late teens. His professional record is unknown, but he reportedly played with Yakima in the Pacific Coast International League in 1921. He sponsored the first major league-minor league all-star team to play in the California Winter League, in 1920. In 1924 he built White Sox Park II to host the winter league games. His dedication to the California Winter League earned him the title of "Father of the Winter League."

POWERS, LES

Year	Team	G	AB	H	D	T	HR	BA
1934-35	White Kings	8	29	12	0	0	7	.414
1936-37	White Kings	2	10	4	0	0	1	.400
1937-38	White Kings	2	9	2	0	0	0	.222
1938-39	White Kings	2	6	4	1	1	2	.667

Year	Team	G	AB	H	D	T	HR	BA
1939-40	White Kings	2	8	1	0	0	0	.125
1940-41	White Kings	2	7	2	0	0	0	.287
1945	Service All-Stars	1	2	0	0	0	0	.000
Totals		19	71	25	1	1	10	.352

Les Powers played in the major leagues for two years, compiling a .327 batting average in 55 at-bats. The left-handed hitting first baseman played in the Pacific Coast League several years, batting .308 for San Francisco in 1935.

PRIDDY, JERRY

Year	Team	G	AB	H	D	T	HR	BA
1939-40	Walker's Roofers	2	8	5	2	0	1	.625
1940-41	All-Stars, White Kings	3	11	5	0	0	1	.455
1943-44	All-Stars	6	20	6	2	1	2	.300
1945	Major League All-Stars							
1947	Feller's All-Stars	3	10	4	0	0	1	.400
Totals		14	49	20	4	1	5	.408

Jerry Priddy played major league baseball for 11 years, from 1941 to 1953. The second baseman had 1,252 base hits during his career, for a batting average of .265. He averaged 27 doubles, 5 triples and 7 home runs a year.

RAWLINGS, JOHN "JOHNNY"

Year	Team	G	AB	H	D	T	HR	BA
1911-12	Pomona	1	4	1	0	0	0	.250
1921-22	Meusel's All-Stars	9	35	11	1	2	0	.314
1926-27	Pirrone's All-Stars	20	66	16	2	0	0	.242
1930-31	Kelley Kars	9	32	12	1	0	0	.375
Totals		39	137	40	4	2	0	.292

Johnny Rawlings was a 12 year major league veteran. The little second baseman batted .250 in 3,719 at-bats.

REESE, JAMES "JIMMIE"

Year	Team	G	AB	H	D	T	HR	BA
1925-26	Pacific Electric	4	18	6	0	0	0	.333
1926-27	White Kings	12	44	12	2	1	0	.273
Totals		16	62	18	2	1	0	.290

Jimmie Reese had a three year major league career from 1930 to 1932. He hit .278 in 742 at-bats. He also enjoyed a 14 year career in the Pacific Coast League where he hit .289 in 6,256 at-bats.

RHYNE, HAL

Year	Team	G	AB	H	D	T	HR	BA
1926-27	Shell Oil	12	47	12	2	1	0	.255
1928-29	Shell Oil, White Kings	12	42	14	4	0	1	.333
1929-30	Shell Oil	3	12	4	0	0	0	.333
Totals		27	101	30	6	1	1	.297

Hal Rhyne played in the major leagues from 1926 to 1933, batting .250 in 2,031 at-bats. He also enjoyed a ten year career in the Pacific Coast League where he hit .288 in 5,610 at-bats.

RUTH, BABE

Year	Team	G	AB	H	D	T	HR	BA
1919-20	Weaver's, Ruth's A.S.	3	9	2	1	0	1	.222

The Sultan of Swat hit 714 career home runs and batted .342 during a 22 year major league career. He also went 94–46 as a pitcher, with two 20 victory seasons.

SAWYER, CARL

Year	Team	G	AB	H	D	T	HR	BA
1916-17	San Pedro	2	7	1	0	0	0	.143
1917-18	San Pedro	2	12	6	0	0	0	.500
1918-19	Pasadena	4	19	6	0	0	1	.316
1920-21	Pasadena	4	14	2	0	0	0	.143
1921-22	Sawyers AS, Meusels AS	13	51	15	5	2	0	.294
1922-23	Sawtelle	1	5	3	0	0	0	.600
1924-25	Pirrone's All-Stars	19	67	16	3	0	0	.239
1925-26	Pirrone's All-Stars	9	31	11	0	0	0	.348
1926-27	Pirrone's All-Stars	15	33	8	1	0	0	.242
1927-28	Pirrone's All-Stars	12	44	11	3	0	0	.250
1928-29	Pirrone's All-Stars	7	20	5	1	0	0	.250
1929-30	Pirrone's All-Stars	11	37	5	0	0	0	.135
1930-31	Pirrone's All-Stars	6	21	3	0	0	0	.143
1931-32	Pirrone's All-Stars	4	9	1	0	0	0	.111
1932-33	Pirrone's All-Stars	1	4	1	0	0	0	.250
1933-34	Pirrone's All-Stars	6	16	0	0	0	0	.000
1934-35	Pirrone's All-Stars	8	26	3	1	0	0	.174
1936-37	Pirrone's All-Stars							
Totals		118	399	90	14	2	1	.226

Carl Sawyer, a career minor leaguer, played with the Washington Senators in 1915 and '16, hitting .222 in 26 games. He led the American Association in doubles, with 50, in 1920 at the age of 30.

SCHNEIDER, PETE

Year	Team	G	AB	H	D	T	HR	BA
1911-12	Santa Monica							
1913-14	Long Beach							
1914-15	El Centro	2	6	2	0	0	2	.333
1915-16	San Diego	1	3	0	0	0	0	.000
1916-17	San Pedro	1	4	2	1	0	1	.500
1917-18	Vernon, All-Majors	5	14	4	1	0	0	.287
1918-19	Dyas	3	6	2	0	0	0	.333
1920-21	Fisher's All-Stars	12	44	12	1	1	1	.273
1921-22	Meusel's All-Stars	2	9	1	0	1	0	.111
1922-23	Bodie's All-Stars							
1923-24	Pirrone's All-Stars	4	14	4	0	0	1	.287
1924-25	Vernon Tigers	7	28	4	1	0	1	.143
1925-26	Shell Oil	1	4	0	0	0	0	.000
Totals		38	132	31	4	2	6	.235

Pete Schneider pitched in the major leagues for six years, winning 59 games and losing 86. In 1917 he went 20–19 for the Cincinnati Reds. He was later converted to an outfielder and enjoyed a seven year career in the Pacific Coast League where he batted .333 with 66 home runs in 1,627 at-bats.

SIMMONS, ALOYSIUS "AL"

Year	Team	G	AB	H	D	T	HR	BA
1929-30	Pirrone's All-Stars	1	5	0	0	0	0	.000

Al Simmons played in the major leagues for 20 years, primarily with the Philadelphia Athletics. He compiled a lofty .334 batting average (#20 all-time) along with 2,927 base hits, 539 doubles, 149 triples, and 307 home runs. He knocked in 1,827 runs.

SMITH, JAMES CARLISLE "RED"

Year	Team	G	AB	H	D	T	HR	BA
1920-21	Fisher's All-Stars	14	50	10	0	1	0	.200
1921-22	Pac. Natl, Sawyer, Pirrone	9	37	9	1	0	1	.243
1922-23	Pirrone's All-Stars	16	58	15	3	0	0	.259
1924-25	Pirrone's All-Stars	12	49	15	0	0	1	.306
Totals		51	194	49	4	1	2	.253

Red Smith was an excellent defensive third baseman for the Brooklyn Dodgers and Boston Braves from 1911 to 1919, and he batted .278 in 3,907 at-bats. He also had a long minor league career, compiling a .327 batting average in 5,833 at-bats. He played with Vernon in the Pacific Coast League from 1920 to 1923, hitting .323.

STATZ, ARNOLD "JIGGER"

Year	Team	G	AB	H	D	T	HR	BA
1924-25	Sawyer's A.S.	2	9	1	1	0	0	.111
1925-26	Pirrone's All-Stars	9	41	7	5	0	0	.175
1926-27	White Kings	6	25	7	0	0	0	.280
1927-28	Pirrone's All-Stars	1	4	0	0	0	0	.000
1930-31	Kelleys Kars	8	34	10	2	0	0	.294
1932-33	Pirrone's All-Stars	1	4	0	0	0	0	.000
1936-37	Pirrone's All-Stars	1	5	2	0	0	0	.400
Totals		28	122	27	8	0	0	.221

Jigger Statz batted .285 over an eight year major league career. And he hit .315 in 18 years with the Los Angeles Angels in the Pacific Coast League. He is the PCL career leader in games played (2,790), runs scored (1,996), base hits (3,356), doubles (595), and triples (137).

SWEENEY, WILLIAM "BILL"

Year	Team	G	AB	H	D	T	HR	BA
1924-25	Shell Oil	4	14	4	0	1	0	.287
1925-26	Shell Oil	9	33	6	0	0	0	.182
1926-27	Shell Oil	18	64	21	2	0	0	.328
1928-29	Shell Oil	9	33	4	0	0	0	.121
Totals		40	144	35	2	1	0	.243

Bill Sweeney had a short three year career in the major leagues, batting .286 in 1,050 at-bats.

TWOMBLY, CLARENCE "BABE"

Year	Team	G	AB	H	D	T	HR	BA
1924-25	Long Beach	5	19	6	2	0	1	.316
1925-26	White Kings	17	77	20	3	0	1	.260
1926-27	White Kings, Shell Oil	19	70	23	1	1	1	.329
Totals		41	166	49	6	1	3	.295

Babe Twombly played with the Chicago Cubs in 1920 and 1921, batting .304 in 165 games.

WARREN, DALLAS

Year	Team	G	AB	H	D	T	HR	BA
1936-37	San Diego Merchants	10	30	8	0	0	2	.267
1937-38	San Diego Gold Club	8	32	12	0	0	1	.375
1939-40	San Diego 7-Up	4	14	4	1	0	0	.287
Totals		22	76	24	1	0	3	.316

Dallas Warren was a catcher, but nothing is known of his professional career. He did not play in the major leagues.

WEAVER, "BUCK"

Year	Team	G	AB	H	D	T	HR	BA
1919-20	Weaver's All-Stars	2	7	2	0	1	0	.287
1926-27	Sherman							
1927-28	Sherman, Merchants Natl.	6	22	6	1	1	0	.273
Totals		8	29	8	1	2	0	.276

Buck Weaver was one of the best third basemen in baseball history. Unfortunately, he was banned from baseball for life in 1920 for having knowledge of the Black Sox conspiracy, and not notifying anyone about it.

WILLIAMS, TED

Year	Team	G	AB	H	D	T	HR	BA
1937-38	San Diego Gold Club	4	14	4	2	0	1	.287
1938-39	San Diego Farleys	1	4	0	0	0	0	.000
1941-42	Pirrone's All-Stars	1	3	3	1	0	1	1.000
Totals		6	21	7	3	0	2	.333

Ted Williams was the greatest major league hitter since Ty Cobb retired in 1928. Many people consider him to be the best ever.

Pitching Statistics

BARFOOT, CLYDE

Year	Team	G	CG	W	L	IP	SO	BB	SH
1925-26	White Kings	10	5	4	3	52	—	—	1
1926-27	White Kings	7	2	2	3	42	3	17	0
1928-29	White Kings	3	3	0	3	24	8	12	0
Totals		20	10	6	9	118	—	—	1

Clyde Barfoot pitched in the major leagues for three years, appearing in 86 games, mostly as a relief pitcher. He compiled a record of 8–10. His 25 year minor league career was very successful, as he won 314 games against only 243 losses. In 1925 he went 26–15 for the Vernon team in the Pacific Coast League.

BLAEHOLDER, GEORGE

Year	Team	G	CG	W	L	IP	SO	BB	SH
1926-27	Shell Oil	8	5	4	2	54	28	7	1

George Blaeholder pitched in the major leagues from 1925 to 136, winning 104 games and losing 125.

BROWN, CHARLES "CURLY"

Year	Team	G	CG	W	L	IP	SO	BB	SH
1913-14	Santa Barbara	8	7	4	2	74	—	—	2
1917-18	San Pedro	4	4	3	0	36	31	4	1
Totals		12	11	7	2	110	—	—	3

Curly Brown pitched in the major leagues four years between 1911 and 1915, winning three games while losing eight. He pitched for Los Angeles in the Pacific Coast League from 1917 to 1920, compiling a 62–42 record. In 1919 he went 25–8 in 314 innings, with a 2.03 ERA. He led the Southern Association in pitching in 1914 with a record of 21–7.

CAMPBELL, ARCHIBALD, "ARCHIE"

Year	Team	G	CG	W	L	IP	SO	BB	SH
1923-24	Buick's All-Stars	1	1	0	1	8	4	1	0

Year	Team	G	CG	W	L	IP	SO	BB	SH
1926-27	Santa Monica, White Myst.	6	6	3	3	54	—	—	1
1929-30	Pirrone's All-Stars	6	2	3	3	39	—	—	0
1930-31	Commercial Club	4	4	2	2	34	10	18	0
1932-33	Pirrone's All-Stars	2	2	1	1	16	—	—	0
1935-36	Santa Monica	1	0	1	0	3	—	—	0
1936-37	San Diego	6	2	3	0	21	3	4	0
Totals		26	17	13	10	195	—	—	1

Archie Campbell pitched parts of three seasons in the major leagues, compiling a 2–6 mark in 86 innings. He pitched for Hollywood and San Diego in the Pacific Coast League from 1934 to 36, winning 30 games and losing 39.

CAVET, TILLER "PUG"

Year	Team	G	CG	W	L	IP	SO	BB	SH
1924-25	Pirrone's All-Stars	10	7	4	3	71	28	12	0
1925-26	White Kings, Shell Oil	11	3	1	3	47	—	—	0
1926-27	Bell Merchants	1	1	0	1	8	—	—	0
Totals		22	11	5	7	126	—	—	0

Pug Cavet pitched in the American League between 1911 and 1915. He compiled a record of 11–9 with a 2.99 ERA. Pitching in the minor leagues between 1908 and 1930, Cavet won 291 games against 243 losses.

CHECH, CHARLIE

Year	Team	G	CG	W	L	IP	SO	BB	SH
1912-13	McCormicks	2	2	0	2	17	2	5	0
1913-14	Oxnard, Los Angeles	3	3	2	1	27	—	—	0
1914-15	El Centro	1	1	0	1	9	—	—	0
1915-16	San Diego, San Bernardino	4	4	2	2	36	—	—	0
1917-18	Vernon Tigers	1	1	0	1	9	5	3	0
Totals		11	11	4	7	98	—	—	0

Charlie Chech pitched in the major leagues from 1906 through 1909, with a record of 33–30.

CRANDALL, JAMES "DOC"

Year	Team	G	CG	W	L	IP	SO	BB	SH
1920-21	San Pedro, Ralls, Dyas	6	5	0	5	46	15	8	0
1924-25	White Kings	10	5	3	2	61	22	11	0
1926-27	White Kings	1	0	0	1	1	0	0	0
Totals		17	10	3	8	117	37	19	0

Doc Crandall pitched in the major leagues for ten years between 1908 and 1918, winning 102 games while losing only 62. In 1915 he went 21–15 for the St. Louis Terriers.

DELL, WILLIAM "WHEEZER"

Year	Team	G	CG	W	L	IP	SO	BB	SH
1918-19	Vernon	2	0	1	0	9	—	—	0
1920-21	Fisher's All-Stars	6	3	0	5	39	29	9	0
1925-26	Pirrone's All-Stars	8	4	0	4	44	—	—	0
1926-27	Arcadia	8	8	4	4	71	—	—	1
Totals		24	15	5	13	163	—	—	1

Wheezer Dell pitched four years in the major leagues, mostly with the Brooklyn Dodgers. His career slate showed a 19–23 record. He was a star pitcher in the Pacific Coast League from 1919 through 1922, winning more than 20 games each of the four years. He led the PCL with 28 victories in 1921.

EHMKE, HOWARD

Year	Team	G	CG	W	L	IP	SO	BB	SH
1914-15	Coast League A.S.	1	1	1	0	9	—	—	0
1917-18	Submarine Base	3	3	2	1	26	17	6	1
1918-19	Pasadena	2	1	1	0	16	12	2	0
Totals		6	5	4	1	51	—	—	1

Howard Ehmke had a successful 15 year major league career (1916–30), winning 166 games agaisnt 166 losses. In 1923 he went 20–17 for the Philadelphia Athletics.

FELLER, ROBERT "BOB"

Year	Team	G	CG	W	L	IP	SO	BB	SH
1939-40	Pirrone's All-Stars	1	0	0	0	7	14	—	0
1945	Major League All-Stars	3	0	0	1	18	33	3	0
1946	Feller's All-Stars	5	0	3	0	26	25	10	0
1947	Feller's All-Stars	6	1	3	1	32	22	2	1
Totals		15	1	6	2	83	92	—	1

Bob Feller is one of the four or five greatest pitchers in baseball history. He won a total of 266 games against just 162 losses over an 18 year career, while missing almost four years due to military service. He pitched three no-hitters, eleven one-hitters, and led the American League in strikeouts seven times.

FLORES, JESSE

Year	Team	G	CG	W	L	IP	SO	BB	SH
1940-41	Pirrone's A.S., Mex.AS	3	2	2	1	25	22	3	0
1941-42	Pirrone's A.S.	3	2	3	0	20	11	2	0
1943-44	Pirrone's A.S.	1	0	0	1	5	2	1	0
Totals		7	4	5	2	50	35	6	0

Jesse Flores pitched in the major leagues for seven years between 1942 and 1950. He compiled a record of 44–59 with the Chicago Cubs, Philadelphia Athletics, and Cleveland Indians.

FRENCH, LAWRENCE "LARRY"

Year	Team	G	CG	W	L	IP	SO	BB	SH
1930-31	White Kings	1	0	0	0	7	—	—	0
1932-33	Pirrone's All-Stars	4	4	0	4	32	—	—	0
1933-34	Pirrone's All-Stars	1	1	0	1	8	3	3	0
1934-35	Pirrone's All-Stars	3	2	0	2	19	10	5	0
1935-36	White Kings, Santa Monica	3	2	0	2	29	—	—	0
1936-37	White Kings	2	1	1	2	20	—	—	0
Totals		14	10	1	11	115	—	—	0

Larry French was a quality major league pitcher for 14 years, from 1929 to 1942. He won 18 games three times, on his way to a career record of 197–171.

HITT, ROY

Year	Team	G	CG	W	L	IP	SO	BB	SH
1911-12	Pomona								
1912-13	Tufts-Lyons	1	1	0	1	8	4	3	0
1914-15	Calexico, San Pedro	3	2	3	0	24	14	9	1
1915-16	San Diego	4	4	1	3	36	28	8	0
Totals		8	7	4	4	68	46	20	1

Roy Hitt pitched for the Cincinnati Reds in 1907, winning 6 games against 10 losses. He had a record of 209–156 in the minor leagues, mostly in the Pacific Coast League. Hitt won more than 20 games in a season seven times in the PCL, including 31–12 in 1906 and 25–18 in 1914.

Johnson, Walter

Year	Team	G	CG	W	L	IP	SO	BB	SH
1907-08	Santa Ana	11	11	7	2	102	152	5	5
1908-09	Santa Ana	4	4	2	1	36	52	4	3
1909-10	Santa Ana	9	9	9	0	81	117	3	4
Totals		24	24	18	3	219	321	12	12

Walter Johnson may have been the greatest pitcher in major league baseball history. His career record shows 416 victories against 279 losses, with a fantastic 110 shutouts, 20 more than the next highest man.

Kantlehner, Ervin "Erv"

Year	Team	G	CG	W	L	IP	SO	BB	SH
1914-15	El Centro	14	12	11	3	124	105	25	2
1915-16	El Centro	2	1	1	0	12	12	7	0
Totals		16	13	12	3	136	117	32	2

Erv Kantlehner pitched in the major leagues for three years, with a record of 13–29.

Keating, Raymond "Ray"

Year	Team	G	CG	W	L	IP	SO	BB	SH
1920-21	Pirrone, Ralls, A.S.	8	8	4	2	68	20	18	0
1926-27	White Kings	12	4	4	5	81	18	30	0
Totals		20	12	8	7	149	38	48	0

Ray Keating pitched in the major leagues from 1912 to 1919, mostly with the New York Yankees. He won 30 games against 51 defeats for teams that generally finished in the second division.

Killeen, Jack

Year	Team	G	CG	W	L	IP	SO	BB	SH
1914-15	San Diego	1	0	0	1	6	0	0	0
1915-16	San Diego Pantages	4	4	1	3	36	18	28	0
1916-17	San Diego Pantages	2	1	1	0	12	—	—	0
1922-23	San Diego, Balboa Park	3	3	1	2	26	19	10	0
1923-24	San Diego, Balboa Park	3	2	2	1	26	5	5	0
1930-31	San Diego	9	8	5	2	78	50	24	1
Totals		22	18	10	9	184	92+	67+	1

No details of Killeen's professional baseball career are known. A Jack Killeen led the South Atlantic League with 27 victories in 1925.

Koupal, Louis "Lou"

Year	Team	G	CG	W	L	IP	SO	BB	SH
1926-27	Pirrone's All-Stars	10	4	2	4	50	—	—	1
1927-28	Pirrone's All-Stars	4	1	0	2	30	14	5	0
1928-29	Pirrone's All-Stars	10	4	4	1	65	32	16	0
1930-31	Pirrone, Commercial Club	5	3	1	4	35	18	17	0
1931-32	Pirrone's All-Stars	1	0	0	0	3	—	—	0
1933-34	Pirrone's All-Stars	3	1	0	3	18	6	9	0
1934-35	May Co.	2	0	0	0	6	2	1	0
1936-37	Pirrone's All-Stars	3	2	1	1	18	—	—	0
Totals		38	15	8	15	225	—	—	1

Lou Koupal pitched in the major leagues for six years between 1925 and 1937, appearing in 101 games, with a 10–21 record.

LEMON, ROBERT "BOB"

Year	Team	G	CG	W	L	IP	SO	BB	SH
1946	Major League All-Stars	3	1	2	0	15	—	—	1

Bob Lemon was the mainstay of the Cleveland Indian pitching staff from 1948 to 1956, winning 20 or more games seven times, enroute to a career 207–128 record. He pitched in two World Series, with a 2–2 record. His two victories in the 1948 Classic propelled Lou Boudreau's Indians to the World Championship.

LEWIS, "SAM"

Year	Team	G	CG	W	L	IP	SO	BB	SH
1921-22	Meusel, Sawyer's A-S	7	6	5	2	56	41	12	0

Details on the organized baseball career of Sam Lewis have not been found.

LOVE, EDWARD "SLIM"

Year	Team	G	CG	W	L	IP	SO	BB	SH
1914-15	El Centro	1	1	0	1	9	4	4	0
1919-20	Killefer's All-Stars	1	0	1	0	8	2	1	0
1920-21	Fisher's, Love's A.S.	2	1	0	1	10	10	2	0
1921-22	Kruger's, Edington's A.S.	4	1	0	3	20	—	—	0
1924-25	Vernon	1	0	0	0	7	—	—	0
Totals		9	3	1	5	54	—	—	0

Slim Love pitched in the majors for six years, between 1913 and 1920, with a record of 28–21. His best year was 1918 when he went 13–12 for the New York Yankees. He was 23–15 for Los Angeles in the PCL in 1915.

LUDOLPH, WILLIAM "WEE WILLIE"

Year	Team	G	CG	W	L	IP	SO	BB	SH
1924-25	Vernon	4	3	3	1	37	11	8	0
1925-26	Pirrone's All-Stars	1	1	1	0	9	3	2	0
1926-27	Pirrone's All-Stars	8	3	1	2	50	19	21	0
1927-28	Pirrone's All-Stars	2	1	1	1	15	7	3	0
1929-30	Kelley Kars	8	3	2	4	46	20	11	0
Totals		23	11	8	8	157	60	45	0

Wee Willie Ludolph actually stood 6'1½" tall and weighed a solid 170 pounds. His major league career consisted of just three games with no record. His 17 year minor league career was more successful. He won a total of 243 games against 171 losses, including back to back twenty win seasons with Oakland of the PCL in 1935 and '36.

MUNNS, LESLIE "BIG ED"

Year	Team	G	CG	W	L	IP	SO	BB	SH
1935-36	Pirrone's All-Stars	8	6	1	6	52	26	21	0

Les Munns pitched in the major leagues for three years, compiling a record of 4–13.

NEWSOM, LOUIS "BUCK" OR "BOBO"

Year	Team	G	CG	W	L	IP	SO	BB	SH
1933-34	All-Stars, Portland	8	7	3	5	58	53	21	1
1943-44	All-Stars, San Diego	5	1	0	4	31	16	9	0
Totals		13	8	3	9	89	69	30	1

Buck Newsom was a well travelled pitcher who played for 17 teams in a 20 year major league career. He was a tireless workhorse who pitched more than 200 innings in a season thirteen times. He won a total of 211 major league games against 222 losses.

OLDHAM, JOHN "RED"

Year	Team	G	CG	W	L	IP	SO	BB	SH
1920-21	Pirrone, Blue's A.S.	4	2	2	2	25	22	4	0
1921-22	Pirrone's A.S., Calpaco	2	2	2	0	18	—	—	0
1922-23	Pirrone's All-Stars	1	1	0	1	8	1	1	0
1925-26	Pirrone's All-Stars	3	2	1	1	19	—	—	0
1926-27	Pirrone's All-Stars	5	0	0	3	19	8	3	0
Totals		15	7	5	7	89	—	—	0

Red Oldham had a seven year major league career, winning 39 games against 48 losses. Pitching for Detroit, Oldham went 11–14 in 1921 and 10–13 the following year.

PAYNE, GEORGE

Year	Team	G	CG	W	L	IP	SO	BB	SH
1924-25	White Kings	14	10	10	3	113	75	21	1
1925-26	White Kings	7	3	3	0	37	—	—	0
1926-27	Pasadena, Palos Verde	4	4	3	1	35	—	—	1
1927-28	Radiant	5	5	5	0	45	44	10	0
Totals		30	22	21	4	230	—	—	1

George Payne pitched for the Chicago White Sox in 1920, with a 1–1 won-loss record. In the minor leagues he won 348 games against 262 losses between 1913 and 1940. He pitched 155 games in the Pacific Coast League from 1924 to 1926, with a 52–51 record. In 1924, Payne had a 21–13 record for Los Angeles, giving him a total record, summer and winter, of 31–16.

PERTICA, WILLIAM "BILL"

Year	Team	G	CG	W	L	IP	SO	BB	SH
1917-18	Los Angeles	1	0	1	0	7	5	3	0
1918-19	Pasadena, L.A.,	3	0	0	2	6	7	4	0
1919-20	Killefer's All-Stars	1	1	1	0	9	1	3	0
1920-21	Pirrone's, A.S., Pasadena	2	2	1	1	17	6	2	0
1921-22	Pirrone AS, Meusel AS	3	3	2	1	27	12	7	0
1924-25	White Kings, Pasadena	7	4	3	2	45	24	7	0
Totals		17	10	8	6	111	55	26	0

Bill Pertica pitched in the major leagues for four years, compiling a record of 22–18 with the Boston Red Sox and the St. Louis Cardinals. He was 14–10 with the Cards in 1921.

PIERCY, WILLIAM "BILL"

Year	Team	G	CG	W	L	IP	SO	BB	SH
1915-16	El Centro	2	1	1	1	14	11	4	0
1918-19	Pasadena	1	0	0	0	2	2	4	0
1919-20	Killefer's All-Stars	1	1	1	0	9	1	3	0
1920-21	Fisher's All-Stars	2	0	0	0	5	4	2	0
1925-26	Pirrone's All-Stars	6	2	0	3	37	21	22	0
1927-28	Pirrone's All-Stars	1	0	0	1	6	0	0	0
1929-30	Kelley Kars	1	0	0	1	4	5	4	0
Totals		14	4	2	6	77	44	39	0

Bill Piercy had a six year career in the major leagues between 1917 and 1926, winning 27 games against 43 losses.

PILLETTE, HERMAN "OLD FOLKS"

Year	Team	G	CG	W	L	IP	SO	BB	SH
1926-27	Shell Oil	17	8	8*	6	100	—	—	0
1928-29	Shell Oil	8	2	2	5	51	9	17	0
1930-31	Shell Oil	4	0	0	2	12	—	—	—
1935-36	White Kings	5	5	3	2	40	—	—	2
1936-37	San Diego	8	3	3	2	62	22	11	—
1937-38	San Diego	11*	7*	4	6	84	45	14	0
1938-39	San Diego	1	1	1	0	9	—	—	—
Totals		54	26	21	23	358	—	—	—

Herman Pillette was a legend in organized baseball, pitching for 29 years, 23 of them in the Pacific Coast League. His four year American League career showed 34 victories against 32 losses. He went 19–12 for the Detroit Tigers in 1922. His minor league slate showed 264 victories against the same number of losses. Overall, he won more than ten games in a season seventeen times. He holds the PCL career record for most games pitched, 704.

ROOT, CHARLES "CHARLIE"

Year	Team	G	CG	W	L	IP	SO	BB	SH
1925-26	White Kings	6	2	2	2	24	—	—	0

Charlie Root pitched in the major leagues for 17 years, amassing 201 victories against 160 losses. He pitched in four World Series and, in 1932, yielded Babe Ruth's famous "called shot" home run.

RUETHER, WALTER "DUTCH"

Year	Team	G	CG	W	L	IP	SO	BB	SH
1915-16	Calexico	2	0	0	0	6	6	4	0

Dutch Ruether pitched in the major leagues for eleven years, from 1917 to 1927, winning 137 games against 95 losses. In 1922 he went 21–12 for the Brooklyn Dodgers.

RYAN, JACK

Year	Team	G	CG	W	L	IP	SO	BB	SH
1913-14	Imperial	2	1	1	1	15	—	—	0
1914-15	Imperial	9	8	2	6	64	50	27	1
1915-16	Imperial	3	2	1	2	23	21	9	0
Totals		14	11	4	9	102	—	—	1

Jack Ryan pitched in the major leagues for three years, compiling a 5–5 won-loss record. Pitching for Los Angeles between 1914 and 1916, he went 24–11 in 342 innings pitched, 26–21 in 373 innings, and 29–10 in 350 innings respectively.

SCHNEIDER, PETE

Year	Team	G	CG	W	L	IP	SO	BB	SH
1911-12	Santa Monica	1	1	1	0	9	8	—	0
1913-14	Long Beach	1	1	1	0	9	—	—	0
1915-16	San Diego	1	1	0	1	9	3	3	0
1916-17	San Pedro	2	2	2	0	18	—	—	1
1917-18	Vernon	5	4	2	3	40	16	9	0
1918-19	Dyas, Pasadena	4	1	2	0	39	15	20	0
1923-24	Union Pacific	1	1	0	1	9	7	2	0
1924-25	Vernon	1	0	0	1	1	—	—	0
Totals		16	11	8	6	134	—	—	1

Pete Schneider pitched for the Cincinnati Reds from 1914 through 1919, winning 59 games while losing 86. In 1917 he was 20–19.

SCHUPP, FERDINAND "FERDIE"

Year	Team	G	CG	W	L	IP	SO	BB	SH
1924-25	Gilmore Oil, White Kings	11	10	8*	3	91	62	21	0
1925-26	Shell Oil	6	3	3	2	46	22	26	0
1926-27	Shell Oil	3	1	1	0	14	11	7	0
1928-29	Shell Oil	3	3	0	3	25	13	7	0
1930-31	Kelley Kars	2	2	0	2	17	—	—	0
Totals		25	19	12	10	193	108	61	0

Ferdie Schupp pitched ten years in the major leagues, most of it with the New York Giants. He compiled a career record of 61 wins against only 39 losses. In 1917 he led the National League in winning percentage with .750 on the basis of a 21–7 record.

STINE, LEE

Year	Team	G	CG	W	L	IP	SO	BB	SH
1933-34	Pirrone's All-Stars	7	5	2	4	44	32	20	0
1934-35	Pirrone's All-Stars	6	4	2	3	37	20	5	0
1935-36	Pirrone's All-Stars	3	2	1	1	15	6	3	0
1937-38	White Kings	5	0	0	2	18	9	7	0
1939-40	Pirrone's All-Stars	1	1	1	0	9	2	0	0
Totals		22	12	6	10	123	69	35	0

Lee Stine pitched in the major leagues during parts of four seasons, compiling a record of 3–8. He pitched in the Pacific Coast League for a number of years and, in 1940, went 18–10 for the Los Angeles Angels.

THOMAS, CLAUDE "LEFTY"

Year	Team	G	CG	W	L	IP	SO	BB	SH
1920-21	San Pedro	3	3	0	3	25	13	5	0
1921-22	Pirrone, Fisher All-Stars	9	8	2	6	71	35	18	0
1924-25	Vernon Tigers	1	0	0	0	1	0	0	0
Totals		13	11	2	9	97	48	23	0

Lefty Thomas pitched in the major leagues in 1916, with a 1–2 record. His minor league career, covering 17 years, saw him go 223–216, including 80–79 in the Pacific Coast League between 1920 and 1924.

THURSTON, HOLLIS "SLOPPY"

Year	Team	G	CG	W	L	IP	SO	BB	SH
1920-21	Pirrone's All-Stars	4	3	2	1	34	12	6	0
1922-23	Pirrone, Bodie A.S.	4	4	2	2	35	9	4	0
1924-25	Pirrone's All-Stars	1	1	1	0	9	5	0	0
1928-29	Pirrone's All-Stars	6	6	2	4	65	32	16	0
1929-30	Pirrone's All-Stars	1	0	0	1	7	4	2	0
1930-31	Commercial Club	1	0	0	1	3	4	0	0
1933-34	White Kings, All-Stars	4	4	1	3	29	14	9	0
1934-35	White Kings	4	3	1	2	29	19	6	0
1935-36	White Kings	2	2	0	2	12	9	2	0
Totals		27	23	9	16	223	108	45	0

Sloppy Thurston compiled an 89–86 record during a nine year major league career. He also went 106–96 in the Pacific Coast League between 1920 and 1938, including 22–11 in 1929.

VANCE, CLARENCE "DAZZY"

Year	Team	G	CG	W	L	IP	SO	BB	SH
1909-10	El Centro	1	1	1	0	9	—	—	0
1915-16	El Centro	3	1	2	0	19	22	9	1
1923-24	Montebello	1	1	0	1	9	4	5	0
Totals		5	3	3	1	37	26	14	1

Dazzy Vance pitched in the major leagues from 1915 through 1935. He won 197 games against 140 losses. He led the National League in strikeouts his first seven years in the league. In 1924 he won 28 games against only 6 losses.

WILKINSON, ROY

Year	Team	G	CG	W	L	IP	SO	BB	SH
1926-27	Pirrone's AS, Shell Oil	18*	7	4	7	85	—	—	0
1927-28	Pirrone's All-Stars	7	2	1	1	26	—	—	0
1928-29	White Kings, Shell Oil	7	3	3	1	42	6	6	0
1929-30	Pirrone's All-Stars, Shell	3	2	3	0	18	15	6	0
Totals		35	14	11	9	171	—	—	0

Roy Wilkinson had a five year major league career, with a record of 12–31.

WILLIAMS, CLAUDE "LEFTY"

Year	Team	G	CG	W	L	IP	SO	BB	SH
1914-15	Calexico	2	2	2	0	18	8	4	0
1915-16	Calexico	2	1	1	1	16	17	4	0
1923-24	So. Calif. Gas	6	6	6	0	54	27	14	1
1925-26	Montebello, Redondo, Downey	4	4	2	1	36	—	—	0
1927-28	Pacific Electric	5	4	3	0	41	21	15	1
Totals		19	17	14	2	165	73+	37+	2

Lefty Williams was a major contributor to the famous Black Sox scandal of 1919. When he was barred from major league baseball, he had won 82 games against just 48 losses, for a lofty .631 winning percentage.

Appendix E
Batters vs. Pitchers

How Negro League Hitters Fared Against Major League Pitchers

NEWT ALLEN

Pitcher	ML Record	G	AB	H	D	T	HR	BA
Charlie Root	201–160	3	13	5	1	0	0	.385
Ferdie Schupp	61–39	5	20	7	2	1	0	.350
Lou Koupal	10–21	2	9	4	1	0	0	.444
Sloppy Thurston	89–86	4	19	10	1	0	0	.526
Herm Pillette	34–32	3	14	4	1	0	0	.287
Clyde Barfoot	8–10	2	9	2	1	0	0	.222
Wheezer Dell	19–23	1	4	1	0	0	0	.250
Frank Shellenback	10–15	1	4	2	1	0	0	.500
Jim Turner	69–60	2	8	3	0	0	0	.375
Win Ballou	19–20	3	14	4	1	0	1	.287
Totals	520–466	26	113	42	9	1	0	.372

JOHN BECKWITH

Pitcher	ML Record	G	AB	H	D	T	HR	BA
Bill Piercy	27–43	1	4	0	0	0	0	.000
Lou Koupal	10–21	4	18	7	0	0	2	.389
Herm Pillette	34–32	3	12	7	2	0	3	.583
Ferdie Schupp	61–39	2	8	5	0	0	0	.625
Roy Wilkinson	12–31	2	8	5	0	0	2	.625
Clyde Barfoot	8–10	2	7	7	2	0	0	1.000
Sloppy Thurston	89–86	4	17	6	3	0	1	.353
Totals	241–261	18	74	37	7	0	8	.500

COOL PAPA BELL

Pitcher	ML Record	G	AB	H	D	T	HR	BA
Ferdie Schupp	61–39	4	15	4	0	0	0	.267
Bill Pertica	22–18	2	9	3	0	0	0	.333
Lou Koupal	10–21	4	13	4	0	0	1	.308
Bucky Walters	198–160	2	4	1	0	0	0	.250
Buck Newsom	211–222	8	23	7	1	0	1	.304
Larry French	197–171	1	5	0	0	0	0	.000
Sloppy Thurston	89–86	4	14	6	3	0	0	.429
Win Ballou	19–20	1	5	0	0	0	0	.000
Al Gould	9–11	1	4	1	0	0	0	.250
Totals	916–748	27	92	26	4	0	2	.283

Henry Blackman

Pitcher	ML Record	G	AB	H	D	T	HR	BA
Bill Pertica	22–18	2	8	2	0	0	0	.250
Red Oldham	39–48	3	12	2	0	0	0	.167
Slim Love	28–21	2	7	4	1	1	0	.571
Totals	89–87	7	27	8	1	1	0	.296

George "Tank" Carr

Pitcher	ML Record	G	AB	H	D	T	HR	BA
Bill Pertica	22–18	6	19	6	2	1	1	.316
Bill Piercy	27–43	7	27	10	0	0	0	.370
Red Oldham	39–48	7	32	7	1	0	1	.219
Slim Love	28–21	3	13	7	1	2	0	.538
Pug Cavet	11–9	3	11	4	1	1	0	.364
Ferdie Schupp	61–39	5	18	5	0	1	2	.278
Charlie Root	201–160	4	18	7	2	0	2	.389
Clyde Barfoot	8–10	3	14	4	1	0	2	.287
Wheezer Dell	19–23	2	8	4	1	0	0	.500
Lou Koupal	10–21	1	3	0	0	0	0	.000
Sloppy Thurston	89–86	5	20	5	0	0	0	.250
Roy Wilkinson	12–31	2	2	0	0	0	0	.000
Win Ballou	19–20	1	4	1	0	0	0	.250
Totals	546–529	49	189	60	9	5	8	.317

Oscar Charleston

Pitcher	ML Record	G	AB	H	D	T	HR	BA
Bill Pertica	22–18	2	7	4	2	1	0	.571
Red Oldham	39–48	3	12	2	0	0	0	.167
Slim Love	28–21	3	12	4	0	0	0	.333
Totals	89–87	7	31	10	2	1	0	.323

Rap Dixon

Pitcher	ML Record	G	AB	H	D	T	HR	BA
Clyde Barfoot	8–10	3	10	3	0	1	1	.300
Charlie Root	201–160	3	10	3	0	0	0	.300
Ferdie Schupp	61–39	7	24	8	2	0	1	.333
Lou Koupal	10–21	4	16	7	1	0	1	.438
Sloppy Thurston	89–86	3	11	2	1	0	1	.181
Herm Pillette	34–32	6	20	6	2	0	0	.300
Win Ballou	19–20	3	11	2	0	0	0	.181
Frank Shellenback	10–15	1	4	1	0	0	0	.250
Jim Turner	69–60	2	8	4	2	0	1	.500
Totals	501–443	32	114	36	8	1	5	.316

Sammy T. Hughes

Pitcher	ML Record	G	AB	H	D	T	HR	BA
Larry French	197–171	2	6	1	0	0	1	.167
Sloppy Thurston	89–86	2	9	4	1	0	1	.444
Totals	286–257	4	15	5	1	0	2	.333

Biz Mackey

Pitcher	ML Record	G	AB	H	D	T	HR	BA
Bill Pertica	22–18	3	11	5	1	2	0	.455
Red Oldham	39–48	7	27	9	1	0	0	.333
Slim Love	28–21	2	8	2	1	0	0	.250
Sloppy Thurston	89–86	11	44	20	2	0	2	.455
Wheezer Dell	19–23	3	13	6	0	0	1	.462
Bill Piercy	27–43	4	16	5	0	0	0	.313
Charlie Root	201–160	4	15	4	0	0	0	.267
Ferdie Schupp	61–39	9	34	13	4	1	1	.382
Pug Cavet	11–9	2	9	5	0	1	0	.555
Clyde Barfoot	8–10	6	22	4	0	0	0	.182
Ray Keating	30–51	2	9	2	0	0	0	.222
Lou Koupal	10–21	7	27	12	4	0	1	.444
Herm Pillette	34–32	8	27	10	4	0	0	.370
Roy Wilkinson	12–31	5	20	7	0	0	1	.350
Win Ballou	19–20	4	10	7	0	0	0	.700
Frank Shellenback	10–15	1	3	1	0	0	0	.333
Jim Turner	69–60	2	6	4	1	0	0	.667
Totals	689–687	80	301	116	18	4	6	.385

Hurley McNair

Pitcher	ML Record	G	AB	H	D	T	HR	BA
Duster Mails	32–25	2	8	3	0	1	0	.375
Ray Keating	30–51	7	32	8	3	0	1	.250
Red Oldham	39–48	3	13	4	2	0	0	.308
Sloppy Thurston	89–86	4	17	4	2	1	0	.235
Bill Pertica	22–18	1	5	2	1	0	0	.400
Frank Shellenback	10–15	1	4	1	0	0	0	.250
Speed Martin	29–42	1	5	1	0	0	0	.200
Wheezer Dell	19–23	3	12	5	1	1	0	.416
Doc Crandall	102–62	1	3	2	0	0	0	.667
Totals	372–370	23	99	30	9	3	1	.303

Dobie Moore

Pitcher	ML Record	G	AB	H	D	T	HR	BA
Bill Pertica	22–18	5	19	7	0	0	1	.368
Red Oldham	39–48	4	15	3	0	1	0	.200
Slim Love	28–21	2	8	3	2	0	0	.375
Pug Cavet	11–9	3	10	4	2	0	2	.400
Ferdie Schupp	61–39	2	9	6	0	0	0	.666
Duster Mails	32–25	2	7	2	0	1	0	.287
Ray Keating	30–51	7	33	11	2	1	1	.333
Sloppy Thurston	89–86	4	16	4	0	2	0	.250
Frank Shellenback	10–15	1	4	2	1	0	0	.500
Specs Meadows	188–180	1	4	2	1	0	0	.500
Speed Martin	29–42	1	4	2	0	0	0	.500
Wheezer Dell	19–23	3	11	3	0	0	0	.273
Doc Crandall	102–62	1	4	1	0	0	0	.250
Totals	660–617	36	144	50	8	5	4	.347

Bullet Joe Rogan

Pitcher	ML Record	G	AB	H	D	T	HR	BA
Wheezer Dell	19–23	5	17	8	1	0	1	.471
Bill Piercy	27–43	5	18	4	0	0	0	.222
Charlie Root	201–160	3	9	5	1	0	1	.555
Ferdie Schupp	61–39	6	18	4	0	0	0	.222
Pug Cavet	11–9	2	5	1	0	0	1	.200
Clyde Barfoot	8–10	5	18	6	2	0	0	.333
Ray Keating	30–51	7	28	10	1	1	0	.357
Herm Pillette	34–32	8	24	8	0	0	1	.333
Roy Wilkinson	12–31	7	27	9	6	0	0	.333
Duster Mails	32–25	2	8	1	0	0	0	.125
Red Oldham	39–48	3	12	4	1	1	0	.333
Sloppy Thurston	89–86	9	35	11	1	0	2	.314
Bill Pertica	22–18	1	4	0	0	0	0	.000
Frank Shellenback	10–15	1	3	0	0	0	0	.000
Specs Meadows	188–180	1	4	2	0	0	0	.500
Speed Martin	29–42	1	3	1	0	0	0	.333
Wheezer Dell	19–23	3	10	6	0	0	1	.600
Totals	831–835	76	274	87	13	2	9	.318

Turkey Stearnes

Pitcher	ML Record	G	AB	H	D	T	HR	BA
Ray Keating	30–51	3	8	3	0	0	0	.375
Lou Koupal	10–21	7	27	11	2	1	1	.407
Clyde Barfoot	8–10	3	13	5	0	0	2	.385
Herm Pillette	34–32	8	33	12	0	1	1	.364
Roy Wilkinson	12–31	6	19	9	0	0	3	.474
Ferdie Schupp	61–39	4	15	4	1	0	0	.267
Larry French	197–171	3	11	3	0	0	0	.273
Sloppy Thurston	89–86	10	37	14	0	0	5	.378
Bucky Walters	198–160	2	6	3	1	0	0	.500
Buck Newsom	211–222	8	29	13	3	0	1	.448
Totals	850–823	54	198	77	7	2	13	.389

George "Mule" Suttles

Pitcher	ML Record	G	AB	H	D	T	HR	BA
Larry French	197–171	5	18	7	0	0	5	.389
Buck Newsom	211–222	8	29	8	3	0	2	.276
Bucky Walters	198–160	1	4	3	0	0	1	.750
Herm Pillette	34–32	3	11	4	0	0	2	.384
Sloppy Thurston	89–86	7	23	8	1	0	4	.348
Lou Koupal	10–21	3	10	7	3	0	2	.700
Wheezer Dell	19–23	2	8	5	0	0	1	.625
Win Ballou	19–20	3	12	7	3	0	0	.583
Frank Shellenback	10–15	1	3	3	0	0	0	.333
Jim Turner	69–60	2	6	3	1	0	1	.500
Totals	856–810	35	124	55	11	0	18	.444

Willie Wells

Pitcher	ML Record	G	AB	H	D	T	HR	BA
Ray Keating	30–51	3	12	0	0	0	0	.000
Lou Koupal	10–21	6	19	9	3	0	0	.474

Pitcher	ML Record	G	AB	H	D	T	HR	BA
Clyde Barfoot	8–10	1	4	2	1	0	0	.500
Herm Pillette	34–32	5	15	3	0	0	0	.200
Roy Wilkinson	12–31	5	17	5	2	0	0	.294
Bucky Walters	198–160	1	2	0	0	0	0	.000
Sloppy Thurston	89–86	7	27	10	3	0	3	.370
Buck Newsom	211–222	8	29	10	5	0	0	.345
Larry French	197–171	3	12	6	4	0	0	.500
Win Ballou	19–20	4	13	1	0	0	0	.077
Frank Shellenback	10–15	1	4	0	0	0	0	.000
Jim Turner	69–60	2	7	1	0	0	0	.143
Ferdie Schupp	61–39	1	4	3	0	1	0	.750
Totals	948–918	47	165	50	18	1	3	.303

JUD WILSON

Pitcher	ML Record	G	AB	H	D	T	HR	BA
Ferdie Schupp	61–39	1	5	2	0	2	0	.400
Win Ballou	19–20	3	8	4	3	0	0	.500
Frank Shellenback	10–15	1	2	0	0	0	0	.000
Jim Turner	69–60	2	6	2	2	0	0	.333
Sloppy Thurston	89–86	1	5	2	1	0	0	.400
Totals	248–220	8	26	10	6	2	0	.385

WILD BILL WRIGHT

Pitcher	ML Record	G	AB	H	D	T	HR	BA
Larry French	197–171	3	11	4	0	0	0	.364
Buck Newsom	211–222	4	15	2	0	0	0	.133
Bucky Walters	198–160	2	7	3	1	0	1	.429
Lou Koupal	10–21	2	8	3	1	0	1	.375
Sloppy Thurston	89–86	6	21	10	1	1	2	.476
Herm Pillette	34–32	3	12	4	0	1	1	.333
Totals	739–692	20	74	26	3	2	5	.351

How Major League Hitters Fared Against Negro League Pitchers

EARL AVERILL

Pitcher	NL Record	G	AB	H	D	T	HR	BA
Chet Brewer	87–63	4	15	7	2	0	0	.467
Bullet Rogan	151–65	3	14	8	1	0	3	.571
Totals	238–128	7	29	15	3	0	3	.517

BUZZ ARLETT

Pitcher	NL Record	G	AB	H	D	T	HR	BA
Plunk Drake	99–61	3	9	3	0	0	0	.333
Rube Currie	70–44	2	8	5	0	1	2	.625
Cherry Bell	Inc.	2	5	3	0	0	2	.600
Jim Gurley	Inc.	1	5	2	0	0	0	.400
Totals	169–105	8	27	13	0	1	4	.481

Ping Bodie

Pitcher	NL Record	G	AB	H	D	T	HR	BA
Plunk Drake	99–61	4	15	6	1	0	2	.400
Rube Currie	70–44	1	5	3	1	0	1	.600
Satchel Paige	147–92	1	5	2	0	0	1	.400
Totals	169–105	6	25	11	2	0	4	.440

Fred Haney

Pitcher	NL Record	G	AB	H	D	T	HR	BA
Satchel Paige	147–92	2	8	5	1	0	0	.625
Willie Foster	146–66	3	12	5	1	0	0	.416
Andy Cooper	121–54	4	13	5	0	1	0	.385
Ted Trent	109–56	1	5	2	1	0	0	.400
Jess Hubbard		4	14	3	1	0	0	.143
Rube Currie	70–44	2	7	2	1	0	0	.287
Bill Holland	127–99	5	20	5	0	1	0	.250
Chet Brewer	87–63	7	27	8	0	0	0	.296
Joe Rogan	151–65	8	35	9	0	0	0	.257
Totals	523–268	36	141	44	5	1	0	.312

Babe Herman

Pitcher	NL Record	G	AB	H	D	T	HR	BA
Bill Holland	127–99	3	12	3	0	0	0	.250
Joe Rogan	151–65	8	29	8	0	0	0	.276
Rube Currie	70–44	9	34	15	3	1	0	.441
Jose Mendez		1	3	0	0	0	0	.000
Plunk Drake	99–61	2	7	3	2	0	0	.429
Jess Hubbard		3	15	6	1	0	0	.400
Totals	457–269	26	100	35	6	1	0	.350

Smead Jolley

Pitcher	NL Record	G	AB	H	D	T	HR	BA
Chet Brewer	89–63	7	30	15	1	0	3	.500
Joe Rogan	151–65	9	36	12	4	0	2	.333
Andy Cooper	121–54	2	10	5	0	0	0	.500
Totals	361–182	18	76	32	5	0	5	.421

Bob Meusel

Pitcher	NL Record	G	AB	H	D	T	HR	BA
Bill Holland	127–99	3	11	1	0	0	0	.091
Joe Rogan	151–65	9	36	10	1	2	0	.278
Andy Cooper	121–54	1	4	1	0	0	0	.250
Chet Brewer	89–63	1	5	2	1	0	0	.400
Rube Currie	70–44	6	25	8	0	0	0	.320
Totals	558–325	20	81	22	2	2	0	.272

Irish Meusel

Pitcher	NL Record	G	AB	H	D	T	HR	BA
Rube Currie	70–44	4	15	3	0	2	0	.200
Joe Rogan	151–65	12	46	11	1	1	3	.239
Chet Brewer	89–63	5	15	4	0	0	0	.269

Pitcher	NL Record	G	AB	H	D	T	HR	BA
Bill Holland	127–99	4	15	9	3	0	2	.600
Andy Cooper	121–54	2	5	2	1	0	0	.400
Jim Jeffries	35–28	5	17	5	1	1	0	.294
Totals	593–353	32	113	34	6	4	5	.301

JIGGER STATZ

Pitcher	NL Record	G	AB	H	D	T	HR	BA
Jess Hubbard		3	15	5	3	0	0	.333
Rube Currie	70–44	2	7	0	0	0	0	.000
Joe Rogan	151–65	2	7	1	0	0	0	.143
Bill Holland	127–99	1	4	0	0	0	0	.000
George Harney	37–20	2	9	2	0	0	0	.222
Totals	395–228	10	42	8	3	0	0	.190

CASEY STENGEL

Pitcher	NL Record	G	AB	H	D	T	HR	BA
Bullet Joe Rogan	151–65	5	21	6	1	0	0	.286

Appendix F

Batting Statistics, League to League

Name	Major Leagues AB	HR	BA	AAA Leagues AB	HR	BA	California Winter League AB	HR	BA
C. Twombly	358	5	.304				166	10	.295
E. Pick	191	6	.178	5418	10	.319	276	8	.282
S. Jolley	1710	15	.305	8298	10	.319	127	39	.402
B. Herman	5603	18	.324	2145	15	.323	248	13	.357
B. Meusel	5475	16	.309	1242	9	.332	182	9	.324
I. Meusel	4900	12	.310	1560	8	.300	399	17	.313
P. Bodie	3670	6	.275	4590	15	.295	231	17	.307
N. Boeckel	2880	5	.282				136	0	.301
F. Brazill	190	0	.258	3860	21	.342	265	17	.275
C. Carlyle	278	2	.234				160	17	.206
R. Cox	832	5	.314				322	12	.326
F. Haney	1977	2	.275	3825	6	.279	313	2	.296
W. Hood				4996	14	.314	248	7	.270
J. Jenkins				2260	14	.303	270	6	.319
W. Kingdon				4078	7	.268	420	5	.260
H. Lindimore				2907	5	.303	209	18	.297
H. McMullen	108	0	.176				333	7	.292
F. Bell	265	4	.283				111	30	.216
J.C. Smith	3907	4	.278	2493	3	.323	194	6	.253
T. Hannah				5506	6	.279	162	0	.273
B. Niehoff	2037	3	.240				119	0	.269
F. Emmer	313	0	.182				177	0	.232
A. Griggs	1370	2	.277	4378	12	.315	118	9	.373
N. Hawks	393	10	.316				181	6	.309
W. Sweeney	1050	3	.286				144	0	.243
J. Blakesley				1112	12	.304	149	4	.289
C. Durst	1103	7	.244				123	9	.260
F. Hufft				4176	22	.346	161	10	.280
R. Jacobs				5882	19	.294	180	3	.267
E. Kenna	118	5	.297				103	0	.243
J. Kerr	1457	2	.266				156	14	.295
J. Rawlings	3719	2	.250				137	0	.292
H. Rhyne	2031	1	.250	5610	2	.288	101	5	.297
P. Schneider				1627	22	.333	132	25	.235
J. Statz	2585	4	.285	10657	3	.315	122	0	.221

Appendix F

The averages are based on—1000 at-bats (major league)—1000 at-bats (AAA leagues)—100 at-bats California Winter League

All averages have been adjusted to the major league base point of 19 home runs and a .260 batting average.

	19	.260	22	.281		
	19	.260			24	.284
			20	.287	18	.261
average	19	.260	21	.284	21	.273

This table indicates that the Negro league pitching faced by the major league and AAA league batters in the California Winter League was at a AAA level or slightly higher.

KEY:
AB—At-bats   HR—Home runs per 550 at-bats   BA—Batting average

Negro League vs. California Winter League

	Negro League		California Winter League		
Name	HR	BA	AB	HR	BA
N. Allen	3	.302	552	4	.324
S. Bankhead	6	.285	271	16	.351
J. Beckwith	30	.352	172	61	.413
J. Bell	9	.328	571	14	.366
W. Bobo	10	.314	247	15	.310
G. Carr	10	.309	712	21	.336
D. Creacy	13	.291	263	2	.310
H. Dixon	12	.309	479	21	.326
C. Holloway	5	.296	473	8	.303
S. Hughes	9	.300	268	29	.384
N. Joseph	10	.281	193	26	.285
B. Mackey	11	.322	935	16	.366
H. McNair	5	.322	314	9	.322
D. Moore	16	.355	377	19	.385
A. Radcliffe	9	.291	125	18	.368
O. Riggins	11	.304	249	18	.321
W. Rogan	16	.348	434	19	.362
N. Stearnes	30	.352	754	44	.373
G. Suttles	34	.329	450	79	.377
W. Wells	20	.328	528	11	.301
B. Wright	13	.341	392	20	.380
Average	13	.317		22	.345

Adjusted to Negro league base point of 15 home runs and a .308 batting average.

	15	.308		25	.336

The averages for the top ten batters, having more than 400 at-bats in the California Winter League are:

	15	.308		23	.329

These statistics indicate that the quality of pitching faced by the Negro league batters in the California Winter League was at a AA level or below.

League to League Comparisons
Summary

Major Leagues		AAA Leagues		Negro Leagues		California Winter League	
HR	BA	HR	BA	HR	BA	HR	BA
				15	.308	23	.329 (top10 >400 AB)
		20	.287			18	.261 (top 22> 100 AB)
19	.260 (top 16 > 1000 AB)					24	.284
19	.260	21	.281 (top 9 > 1000 AB)				

Averages—Adjusted to ML base point::

Major Leagues		AAA Leagues		Negro Leagues		California Winter League	
19	.260	21	.284			21	.273
				15	.308	25	.336

Appendix G

Satchel Paige's Spectacular 1933–34 Winter League Record

Date	Opponent	Pitchers	Score	CG	W–L	IP	SO	BB	SHO
11/3/33	Pirrone's A.S.	B. Walters	10–0	1	W	9	15	2	1
11/9/33	Pirrone's A.S.	B. Newsom	11–3	1	W	9	13	3	0
11/17/33	White Kings	S. Thurston	4–0	1	W	9	17	2	1
11/24/33	Pirrone's A.S.	L. French	5–0	1	W	9	14	2	1
11/30/33	Pirrone's A.S.	B. Newsom	7–2	1	W	9	10	2	0
12/1/33	White Kings	S. Thurston	1–4	1	L	9	13	10	0
12/3/33	Pirrone's A.S.	B. Newsom	5–1	1	W	9	9	1	0
12/8/33	Portland	J. Babich	1–0	1	W	9	13	3	1
12/22/33	White Kings	S. Thurston	7–1	1	W	9	13	2	0
12/29/33	Pirrone's A.S.	B. Newsom	3–2	1	W	9	12	3	0
1/5/34	Pirrone's A.S.	B. Newsom	8–10	1	L	9	9	3	0
1/19/34	Pirrone's A.S.	Newsom/Stine	6–0	1	W	9	14	1	1
1/26/34	Pirrone's A.S.	L. Stine	7–3	1	W	9	14	1	0
1/28/34	Pirrone's A.S.	L. Stine	7–5	0	ND	4			0
2/2/34	Pirrone's A.S.	L. Stine	2–0	1	W	9	12	1	1
2/8/34	Pirrone's A.S.	L. Stine		0	ND	6			0
2/11/34	Pirrone's A.S.	L. Koupal	3–1	1	W	9			0
2/16/34	May Co.	A. Jacobs	8–0	1	W	9	13	1	1
Totals	18 games				14–2	154	191	37	7

The following reconstructed record assumes two additional, complete game victories, based on his published record of 16–2. Strikeouts and bases on balls have been adjusted for the total number of innings pitched. Paige averaged 13 strikeouts and two bases on balls for every nine innings pitched. The TRA is based on his 16 complete games in the record.

G	CG	W	L	IP	SO	BB	SH	TRA
20	18	16	2	172	245	47	7	1.69

Paige allowed a total of 27 runs in 16 games, and 10 of those runs came in one game. His TRA for the other 15 games was a minuscule 1.13.

Appendix H
Satchel Paige vs. Bob Feller

A Sampling

Date	Location	Winner	Paige Summary IP	W	L	SO	BB	ER	Feller Summary IP	W	L	SO	BB	ER
10-05-41	Sportsman's Pk, SL	Feller's All-Stars, 4–1	4	0	1			4	4	1	0			1
10-02-45	Wrigley Field, L.A.	Feller's All-Stars, 4–2	5	0	0	8		0	5	0	0	6		1
10-06-45	San Diego	Kansas City Royals, 6–0	5	1	0			0		0	1			
10-27-45	Wrigley Field, L.A.	Feller's All-Stars 3–2 in 10	7	0	0	8	—	1	7	0	0	13	—	1
09-29-46	Forbes Field, Pitt.	Feller's All-Stars, 3–0		0	1					1	0			
10/05/46	Yankee Stad., N.Y.	Paige's All-Stars 4–0	5	1	0	4	1	0	5	0	1	0	4	2
10-07-46	Columbus, OH.	Paige's All-Stars, 4–3		0	0				3	0	0	5		0
10-08-46	Dayton, OH.	Feller's All-Stars, 7–6	3	0	0			5	3	0	0			1
10/09/46	Comiskey Pk., Chc.	Feller's All-Stars 6–5	3	0	0	3	0	0	3	0	0	1	2	0
10/12/46	Kansas City, MO	Paige's All-Stars 3–2	5	0	0	—	—	0	5	0	0	—	—	0
10-13-46	Wichita, KS.	Feller's All-Stars, 5–3												
10/16/46	Wrigley Field, L.A.	Feller's All-Stars 4–3	5	0	1	7	4	4	5	1	0	7	2	3
10/17/46	San Diego, CA.	Feller's All-Stars 2–0	5	0	1	—	—	2	5	1	0	2	—	0
10/18/47	Wrigley Field, L.A.	Feller's All-stars 2–1	5	0	0	8	1	0	5	0	0	5	1	1
10/24/47	Wrigley Field, L.A.	Feller's All-Stars 2–1	4	0	1	7	1	1	4	1	0	2	1	0
11/03/47	Wrigley Field, L.A.	Royal Giants 8–0	9	1	0	15	4	0	8	0	1	5	1	5
Totals			65	3	5	60	17	17	62	5	3	46	15	15

The pitching matchups are summarized below, on a per-game basis, using the above statistics

Name	IP	SO	BB	ERA
Satchel Paige	9	13	3	2.35
Bob Feller	9	8	3	2.18

Bob Feller said he and Satchel Paige faced each other more than twenty times over the years. The games played in Wrigley Field, L.A. and in San Diego were part of the California Winter League

Legend:

IP	Innings Pitched	SO	Strikeouts	CG	Complete Games
W	Win	BB	Bases on Balls	ERA	Earned Run Average
L	Loss	ER	Earned Runs		

Bibliography

Books

Beck, Warren, and David A. Williams. *California, A History of the Golden State*. New York: Doubleday & Company, 1972.

Carter, Craig, ed. *Daguerreotypes, 8th* Edition. St. Louis: The Sporting News Publishing Company, 1990.

Cisneros, Pedro Treto, ed. *Encliclopedia Del Beisbol* Mexicano. Mexico, 1996.

Clark, Dick, and Larry Lester, eds. *The Negro Leagues Book*. Cleveland: Society for American Baseball Research, 1994.

Encyclopaedia Brittanica. *The New Encyclopaedia Brittanica, Vol. 23.* Chicago: 1994.

Hoie, Bob, and Carlos Bauer. *The Historical Register*. San Diego: Baseball Press Books, 1998.

Holway, John B. *Blackball Stars*. Westport, CT.: Meckler Books, 1998.

Holway, John B. *The Complete Book of Baseball's Negro Leagues*. Fern Park, FL.: Hastings House, 2001.

Holway, John B. *Josh and Satch*. New York: Carroll & Graf, 1991.

Holway, John B. *Voices from the Great Black Baseball League*. New York: Da Capo Press, 1992.

Johnson, Lloyd, and Miles Wolff, eds. *The Encyclopedia of Minor League Baseball*. Durham, N.C.: Baseball America, Inc., 1993.

Lavender, David. *California: A Bicentennial History*. New York: W. W. Norton & Company, 1976.

Riley, James A. *The Biographical Encyclopedia of the Negro Baseball Leagues*. New York: Carroll & Graf, 1994.

Rogosin, Donn. *Invisible Men*. New York: Macmillan Publishing Company, 1983.

Shatzkin, Mike, ed. *The Ballplayers*. New York: William Morrow & Company, 1990.

Snelling, Dennis. *The Pacific Coast League: A Statistical History, 1903-1957*. Jefferson, N.C.: McFarland & Company, 1995.

Society for American Baseball Research. *Minor League Baseball Stars, Vol. I, II, III*. Cleveland: 1978, 1985, 1992.

Spalding, John E. *Always on Sunday: The California Baseball League, 1886 to 1915*. Manhattan, KS.: Ag Press, 1992.

Thorn, John, and Pete Palmer, eds. *Total Baseball*, New York: Viking Penguin, 1997.

Correspondence

Figueredo, Jorge. Cuban Winter League statistics.

Holway, John B. Negro League statistics.

Newspapers

California Eagle, Los Angeles, CA., 1900–1948
Chicago Defender, Chicago, IL., 1900–1948
Los Angeles Examiner, Los Angeles, CA., 1900–1947
Los Angeles Times, Los Angeles, CA., 1900–1948
Pittsburgh Courier, Pittsburgh, PA., 1921–1948
San Diego Union, San Diego, CA., 1912–1946

Index

Aaron, Hank 2
Abernathy, George 234
Ables, Harry 58
Adams, Bert 89, 91
Adams, Bobby 219
Adams, "Buster" 185, 187, 188, 191, 197, 224, 225, 227
Ainsmith, Eddie 69, 75
Alcock, Scotty 63, 75
Alexander, Walt 47–49, 56
Alexander's Giants 70, 74, 77, 78, 251, 255, 257, 258, 268
Allaire, Bobby 187, 188, 191
All-American Girls Professional Baseball League 271
Allen, Newt 14, 18, 22, 104, 107, 108, 110–112, 114, 117, 118, 121, 126–128, 130–133, 135, 137–140, 143, 150, 151, 153, 170, 240, 245, 249, 298, 306
Allington, Bill 159, 166, 179, 182, 183, 185, 191, 198, 200, 271
All-Majors 282, 287
All-National (Baseball team) 31
All-Nations 57
All-Professional League *see* California Winter League
All-Stars 33–35, 271, 272, 274, 275, 278–82, 284, 286, 287, 293
Almada, Lou 136, 142, 149, 154, 155, 159, 161, 162, 166, 180, 188, 271
Almada, Mel 161, 168, 173, 175, 179, 180, 271
Altrock, Nick 76
American Association 12, 95, 105, 114, 154, 180, 185, 196, 207, 229, 276, 287
American League 12, 15, 16, 18, 20, 25, 28, 31, 45, 71, 93, 198, 206, 207, 224, 233, 276, 281, 284, 290, 291, 295
American Negro League 194
Anaheim (Baseball team) 24, 123
Anderson, Andy 209
Anderson, Doc 14, 47, 66–72, 84, 86, 87, 89, 108, 236

Anderson Park 67, 80, 81, 93
Anheuser-Busch (Baseball team) 57–59, 273
Antista 149
Arbogast, Charlie 50
Arcadia (Baseball team) 290
Arlett, Buzz 18, 97, 98, 101, 239, 240, 245, 271, 302
Armstrong, Henry 218
Armstrong, Marshall G. 218
Army (Baseball team) 61
Arroyo, Manuel 202
Athletic Park (Los Angeles) 11
Athletic Park (San Diego) 51, 53
Athletics (Baseball team) 62
Athletics (San Francisco) 10,11
Atlanta (Baseball team) 105, 112
Atlantics (San Francisco) 10
Austin, Jimmy 64, 65, 119, 120
Autry, Chick 13, 25, 30, 39, 51, 53–55
Averill, Earl 3, 22, 23, 129, 131–134, 236, 239, 241, 247, 272, 302
Azusa (Baseball team) 30, 92

Babich, Johnny 163, 308
Bachant 96
Bacharach Giants 128
Bader (or Baeder) 47, 50
Baerwald 48, 49
Bailey, Bill 90, 91
Baker 58, 60, 71, 74, 146
Baker, Tom 219
Baker Bowl 68
Ball, Neal 3, 12, 35, 39
Ball, Walter 35, 37, 38, 231
Ballou, Win 149, 150, 153, 154, 157, 168, 172, 240, 241, 298–302
Baltimore Colored (Elite) Giants 198, 201, 203–205, 208, 209, 211–217, 219, 244, 250, 254, 256, 257, 259, 261, 262, 264, 268, 269
Bancroft, Dave 13, 40, 43, 47, 49, 272
Bankhead, Sam 111, 159–167, 201,
210, 211, 217, 220, 222, 249, 306
Banks 33
Banks, Ernie 2, 15
Barbee, Dave 139, 142
Barbee, Lamb "Bud" 201–205, 248
Barbour, Jess 41, 42, 52–55, 249, 250
Barfoot, Clyde 105, 107, 108, 113, 115, 123, 129, 134, 241, 289, 298–302
Barnabe, Charlie 99, 129, 134, 135, 142, 155
Baro, Bernardo 2
Barrett, Charles "Red" 189, 191, 217, 218, 222, 224, 225, 227
Barrett, Dick 185
Bartell, "Rowdy Dick" 180
Bartlett(s) 29, 30
Barton, Larry 179, 197, 200, 205, 211, 212, 214, 216
Bass (Editor) 124
Bassett, "Pepper" 192, 193, 195, 197, 198, 200, 219, 222
Bassler, Johnny 47, 49, 75, 93, 150, 153, 177, 180, 272
Bates, Hubert "Bud" (?) 183
Battles 30
Bauchman, Harry 52–55
Baugh, Johnny "Wizard" 77, 78
Baum, Allen T. 13, 46, 59, 67, 149
Bayless, Dick 50–52, 54, 55
Beck, Clyde 177
Beck (Umpire) 118
Becker, Beals 48, 50
Beckley, Jake 25
Beckwith, John 3, 21–23, 124, 125, 127, 130–133, 135, 190, 237, 245, 247, 250, 298, 306
Bejan 194
Bell, Clifford "Cherry" 95, 96, 99, 100, 102, 145, 147, 148, 154, 156, 246, 264, 265, 302
Bell, Fern 157, 164, 166, 168, 171, 173, 177, 179, 180, 182, 183, 185, 194, 197, 202, 205, 207, 208, 272, 305

314   Index

Bell, Fred 88–92, 102, 103, 265
Bell, Hi 105, 109, 110, 113, 114, 134
Bell, Jay "Cool Papa" 3, 87–92, 102, 103, 111, 143, 156, 161, 162, 164–166, 168, 170, 171, 173, 180, 182–185, 187, 188, 190, 201, 210–212, 214, 215, 217, 219, 222, 236, 237, 240, 245, 247 248, 250, 298, 306
Bell, Louie 213
Bell Merchants (Baseball team) 290
Bennett, Justin "Pug" 13, 43, 51, 53–55
Berardino, Johnny 228, 230, 233
Berger, Heinie 32
Berger, Joe 13, 43, 51, 55
Berger, Wally 143, 149–153, 157, 176, 202, 205, 239, 247, 272
Berkowitz, Joe 157, 166, 168, 171, 193, 273
Bernard, Curt 33, 38
Bieloper 54, 55
Billings, Josh 75
Biot, Charlie 202, 204, 205
Birmingham Black Barons 217, 219–224, 227, 228, 244, 249, 250
Biscauluz, Eugene 218
Bittner, J. 198
Black 33
Blackman, Henry 76–78, 81, 83, 88–91, 247, 250, 299
Blackwell, Ewell "The Whip" 232, 233, 235
Blackwell's All-Stars 234, 235, 282, 283
Blaeholder, George 114, 120, 122, 289
Blakesley, "Sunny Jim" 105, 114, 117, 119, 121, 145, 273, 305
Bliss 55
Blue, Lu 69, 70, 71, 74–76, 79–81, 83, 87, 273
Blue Diamond (Baseball team) 276
Blue's All-Stars 70, 74, 273, 278, 294
Bobo, Willie 102, 103, 145–148, 250, 251, 306
Bockman, Eddie 219, 227, 228, 234
Bodie, Ping 3, 15–17, 84, 87, 89, 92, 93, 95–97, 99, 100, 114, 118, 119, 121, 123, 128, 157, 161, 164, 236, 240, 273, 303, 305
Bodie All-Stars 273, 287, 296
Boeckel, Tony 57, 61, 63, 69, 72, 74, 75, 79, 81, 83, 91, 273, 305
Bogart 75
Boggs 28, 30
Bohne, Sam 56
Boken, Bob 183
Bonds, Barry 178
Bonetti, Julio 196, 197

Booker, Pete 12, 35
Borges 141
Boston Braves 40, 47, 52, 56, 57, 84, 91, 143, 150, 157, 163, 217, 224, 225, 272, 273, 288
Boston Red Sox 16, 24, 40, 52, 56, 90, 150, 159, 180, 206, 209, 211, 213, 214, 217, 224, 225, 281
Boudreau, Lou 293
Boynton Beavers 45
Bradshaw 78
Brainard, Asa 10
Branson 33
Brashear, Kitty 32, 35, 40
Brawley (Baseball team) 32, 35, 47–51, 56, 275
Brazill, Frank 18, 22, 105, 108, 110, 113, 115, 116, 123, 129, 132, 134, 136, 142, 154, 240, 274, 305
Brazleton, Clarkson 55
Breakers Hotel 40
Breen, R. 38
Brett, Herb 114, 122
Brewer, Chet 3, 18, 22, 128, 130, 131, 133, 135, 137–139, 141, 143, 153, 173, 176, 177, 179, 180, 182–185, 187–190, 196, 207–210, 213–215, 217–220, 222–229, 231, 233, 237–241, 245, 246, 247, 265, 302, 303
Bridwell, Al 40
Britton, George (aka Britt) 104, 107, 108, 110, 111, 113, 151, 153, 265
Brock 28, 30
Bronson 29
Brooklyn Brown Dodgers 223
Brooklyn Dodgers 15, 18, 47, 48, 57, 71, 84, 95, 104, 105, 155, 157, 163, 167, 173, 174, 189, 193, 196, 201, 203, 209, 212, 213, 223, 225, 226, 229, 239, 260, 272, 275, 279, 288, 290, 295
Brooklyn Royal Giants 41
Brooklyn Superbas 25
Brooks 50
Brooks, Chester 190
Brooks, Mossy 191
Brown 160
Brown, Curly 45, 61, 246, 247, 289
Brown, Dave 190
Brown, Drummond 12, 35
Brown, Eddie "Glass Arm" 2, 95
Brown, Jesse 204, 205
Brown, Joe E. 174
Brown, Larry 156, 167, 168, 170, 171, 251
Brown, Mordecai "Three-Fingered" 231
Brown, Willard "Home Run" 213–216
Browning, Frank 31
Brubaker, Bill 22, 176, 177

Brucker, Earle 22, 132, 134, 148, 155, 184, 274
Buffalo Bisons 97, 105
Buffalo Buffeds 47, 51
Buick Auto (Baseball team) 92, 278, 281, 289
Burnett, Fred "Tex" 89, 92, 125, 127, 251
Burnett, Peter H. 12
Burns 33
Burns, George 143, 145, 154
Burns, Johnny 219
Burns, "Sleepy Bill" 25
Burrell, L. 37, 39
Bush 29
Butcher, Spencer 78, 95, 100, 251
Butler 49, 50
Butler, Frank "Kid" 58
Butler, Johnny 114
Buxton, Ralph 173, 176, 177, 180
Byler, C. 81

Cabrillo, Juan Rodriguez 5
Calexico (Baseball team) 46–50, 56, 57, 291, 295, 297
California Eagle 23, 63, 66, 68, 79, 80, 93, 98, 99, 106, 110, 118, 123, 129, 130, 137–139, 143, 144, 152, 157, 159, 160, 183, 186–188, 192, 193, 197
California League 11, 12, 91, 283
Californias (The) 10, 11
Calpaco (Baseball team) 78, 81, 83, 84, 276, 294
Calvey, Jack 212, 218, 220
Camilli, Dolph 176
Campanella, Roy 2, 15, 19, 219, 257
Campbell 33, 92
Campbell, Archie (?) 99, 135, 138, 141, 143, 154, 157, 161, 185, 246, 289, 290
Campbell, Casey 187, 192
Campbell, Gilly 213
Camp Kearny (Baseball team) 61
Cannon, Richard "Speedball" 145, 147, 148, 247, 265
Cantrell, Rosie 224
Carey, Max 68, 69, 74, 75, 274
Carleton, Tex 145, 146
Carlisle, Cleo 101, 102, 146, 163, 166, 171, 175, 179, 196, 240, 274, 305
Carlisle, Walter "Rosy" 3, 25, 36–38, 247
Carpenter 29
Carr, George "Tank" 3, 14, 19, 52, 57–60, 64, 68, 70–74, 78, 79, 81, 83, 84, 86, 88, 96, 98–100, 102, 104, 106–108, 110–112, 124–128, 132, 133, 148, 152, 240, 245, 247, 251, 252, 299, 306
Carroll 30
Carroll Park 76
Carroll, William 76

Index

Carson, Alex 36, 39
Carson, Walter "Kit" 184
Carter 167, 168, 171
Carter, Marlin 197, 199, 200
Carter, "Spoon" 211
Castaneda, Francisco 202
Caster, George 180–182, 185, 209, 210, 213
Castleman, Roy 43
Castro, Fidel 1
Cates, Eli 33
Cavet, Tiller "Pug" 3, 95–97, 99, 101, 105, 110, 113, 114, 290, 299–301
Chadbourne, Chet 43–45, 61–63, 65, 75, 76, 89, 90, 92, 95, 101, 247, 274
Chadbourne's All-Stars 278
Chamberlain 208
Chance, Frank 25
Chandler, Albert "Happy" 223
Chapman, John 6
Chapman, Sam 228
Charleston, Oscar 2, 3, 14, 79–81, 83, 111, 190, 236, 245, 252, 299
Charleston, Porter 141, 150, 153, 265, 266
Chase, Hal 24, 25
Chattanooga (Sally League) 155
Chech, Charlie 13, 43, 45, 47, 49, 51, 52, 54–56, 61, 290
Chicago American Giants 13, 39–43, 46, 47, 51–55, 57, 225, 227, 243, 249, 250, 253, 255, 256, 258, 267, 270
Chicago Black Sox 47, 56, 64, 127, 221, 282, 289, 297
Chicago Cubs 16, 47, 108, 114, 162, 167, 173–175, 180, 196, 203, 209, 211, 213–215, 217, 218, 224, 231, 277, 279, 282, 288, 291
Chicago Defender 13, 23, 42, 46, 47, 54, 58, 80, 106, 107, 117, 119, 120, 131, 132, 136, 137, 147, 148, 154–156, 163, 167, 169, 170, 176, 180, 182, 209, 218
Chicago Leland Giants 2, 12, 29, 35–38, 258, 268, 270
Chicago White Sox 3, 16, 18, 20, 47, 51, 64, 129, 131, 167, 294
Chihuahua Mexicans 202, 203, 205
Christensen, Walter 22, 129, 131–134, 139, 140, 142, 153, 275
Christopher-Levys (Baseball team) 25, 26, 28
Chutes Park 11, 24, 33
Cicotte, Eddie 64
Cincinnati Reds (Red Stockings) 1, 10, 13, 25, 31, 33, 36, 41, 47, 48, 51–54, 56, 64, 138, 163, 187, 213, 224, 232, 275, 278, 283, 287, 291, 295
Cissell, Bill 197, 200, 202, 205
Civic Stadium (Santa Monica) 177

Civil War 1
Clark, Bill (?) 34
Clark, Buddy 26, 29–31
Clark, Dick 1, 69
Clements, Charlie 164, 166
Cleveland Giants 22, 23, 123, 128–134, 243, 249, 252, 253, 257–261, 265, 267, 269
Cleveland Indians 3, 12, 15, 20, 25, 33, 35, 40, 52, 57, 71, 129, 161, 177, 209, 228, 230–233, 291, 293
Cleveland Stars 123–128, 249, 252, 253, 255, 258, 259, 261, 266, 267
Cline-Cline (Baseball team) 51, 52, 55, 56
Clonson 55
Clynes 39
Coast League 45
Coast League All-Stars 51, 223–225, 228, 230, 291
Cobb, Lorenzo S.N. 89, 102, 123, 125, 126
Cobb, Ty 76, 77, 259, 289
Colburn 171, 179
Cole, Leonard "King" 47, 49, 51
Coleman, Ed 142, 146
Collins 28
Collins, Rip 208
Colored All-Stars 78–83, 103, 123, 243, 250–252, 254, 255, 257–259, 262, 268, 270
Columbus (AA) 154
Comiskey Park 309
Commercial Club 143, 151, 153, 154, 271, 274, 279, 281, 290, 292, 296
Concannon 45
Conger, Dick 214, 215
Conrad, Connie 218
Cook 45, 101, 113
Coombs, Jack 31
Cooney, Jimmie 2
Cooney, Johnny 102
Cooper 60, 78
Cooper, Andy 89–92, 114, 119–121, 125, 127, 136–141, 151, 153, 239, 245–247, 266, 303, 304
Cooper, Sam 127
Corhan, Roy 47, 48, 50
Cortes, Hernando 5
Coscarart, Joe 23, 155, 195
Coscarart, Pete 23, 155, 184, 186, 191, 195, 196, 222, 275
Coscarart, Steve 23, 195
Cotter, Harvey "Hooks" 135, 138, 141, 149
Cox, Dick 92, 97, 101, 104–106, 113, 119, 123, 129, 134, 136, 142, 153, 239, 240, 245, 275, 305
Cox, Jess 209
Craghead, Howard 135, 136, 138, 139, 142, 195
Crandall, Doc 18, 61–63, 69, 76,

96–99, 101, 107, 114, 180, 240, 241, 290, 300
Crandall, Jimmy 180, 183, 204
Cravath, Gavvy 12, 25, 33, 64, 65
Crawford, Sam 61, 64, 65
Creacy, Dewey 102, 103, 145–148, 154, 156, 252, 306
Crespi, Father Junipero 6
Cronin, Joe 206
Cryor, George 93
Cuban Winter League 1, 2, 19, 35, 39, 40, 52, 58, 73, 85, 87, 88, 104, 145, 201, 231, 249–251, 253–258, 260–270
Cullop, Nick 123
Currie, Rube 19, 68, 69, 71–75, 79, 84, 86–88, 95, 96, 98, 100, 102, 104, 106, 107, 110, 111, 113, 239, 245–247, 266, 302–304
Curry, "Goose" 202, 204, 205
Curtis 78
Cutshaw, George 47, 50, 61, 63, 76, 79, 83, 275
Cuyler, Kiki 15, 76

Dahlgren, Babe 211, 214, 217
Daley, Tom 37
Dandridge, Ray 201, 217–220, 222, 252
Daniels, Bert 48, 50
Danning, Harry 217
Danning, Ike 125, 154
Dapper, Cliff 205, 209, 228
Darrow, George "Lefty" 198–200
Davids, L. Robert 136
Davis 78
Davis (Chief of Police) 187, 192
Davis, Curt 229
Davis, Lorenzo "Piper" 213, 217, 219, 220, 222, 224, 227, 233, 234, 248
Davis, Red 190, 191, 193
Davis, T. 195
Davis, Walter "Steel Arm" 157, 159–161, 252
Day, Connie 22, 89, 90, 91, 95, 99, 100, 106–108, 110–112, 127–133, 252
Deal, Charlie 101
Dean, Dizzy 15, 176
Dean's All-Stars 272, 278
Dedeaux, Rod 183
Degan 199
Delgado 141
Delhi, Flame 36, 39
Dell, Wheezer 18, 61, 63, 69, 70, 75, 76, 80, 113, 241, 290, 298–301
DeMaggio, Nick 51, 61, 63, 83, 84, 86–89, 92, 125, 128, 275, 276
Demaree, Frank 167–169, 171, 173, 175, 176, 179, 180, 196, 197
Dempsey, Jack 72
Desautels, Gene 176, 184

Detroit Stars 89, 185, 188–195, 253, 259
Detroit Tigers 18, 28, 47, 52, 70, 104, 114, 135, 155, 156, 173, 174, 177, 186, 197, 218, 273, 294, 295
Dials, Lou 213
Dihigo, Martin 1
Dillon, Frank "Pop" 25, 33
DiMaggio, Joe 2, 255
DiMaggio, Vince 180, 181, 217, 218, 225
Direaux, Jimmy 184, 189, 191, 193, 195
Dismukes, Dizzy 51, 53, 55
Disney, Walt 8
Dixon, Rap 14, 22, 104, 106, 110, 112, 114, 116–121, 124–128, 130–133, 135, 143, 150, 151, 153, 240, 245, 253, 299, 306
Dobbins, Dick 48, 70, 87, 98, 118, 136, 144, 174, 189, 203
Dobbins, Joe 189
Doby, Larry 15
Doerr, Harold 191
Dolgeville (Baseball team) 25, 26, 28
Dominican League 18, 20, 201, 231, 249, 267, 268
Donaldson, John 14, 19, 57–61
Doolittle, Maj.Gen. James H. 208
Dorman, Red 154
Dougherty, Pat 41, 43
Downey (Baseball team) 64, 297
Downey Playgrounds 64
Downey, Tom 3, 36, 39, 43, 47, 50, 51, 53–55, 247
Downs, Jerry "Red" 47, 48, 50, 247
Downs, McKinley "Bunny" 77, 253
Doyle, Jess 89, 90, 92, 247
Doyle, Larry 92
Doyles (Baseball team) 35–39
Drake, William "Plunk" 95, 98–100, 239, 246, 247, 266, 302, 303
Dreke, Valentin 1
Dressen, Chuck 2
Driscoll 43
Duck, Donald 8
Duffy Florals (Baseball team) 127
Dukes, Tommy 157, 159–162, 164–167, 245, 247, 253
Dumovich, Nick 84, 130, 135
Duncan, Frank "Pete" 13, 14, 40–42, 51–55, 253
Duncan, Frank, Jr. 95, 116, 120, 121, 127, 152, 201, 253
Duncan sisters 174
Dunn, Jake 145–148, 157, 160, 169, 171, 185, 191–193, 195–200, 207, 245, 248, 253, 254
Durst, Cedric 105, 107, 108, 110, 113, 149–151, 153, 186, 191, 195, 196, 200, 276, 305
Dyas All-Stars 62, 63, 70, 76–78, 83, 272–274, 280, 281, 283, 287, 290, 295

Eagan, Truck 33, 34
Easterling, Howard 209, 211–216
Easterly, Ted 12, 30, 32, 35, 52
Eastern Colored Giants 95, 207
Eastern Colored League 76
Ebbets Field 68
Eccles, Rud 191
Echonda 29
Edington, Jacob "Stump" 70–72
Edington's All-Stars 70, 74, 81, 83, 84, 293
Edison, Thomas A. 26
Edisons (Baseball team) 25, 28, 30
Edleman, "Lefty" 135–138, 140, 141, 146, 149
Edmonds 46
Ehmke, Howard 47, 51, 61, 63, 291
El Centro (Imperial Valley League) 243, 287, 290, 292–294, 297
El Centro Mexicans 32, 35, 47–49, 56, 57, 185, 189, 272, 282, 283
Eldred, Brick 115, 122
Elite Giants *see* Baltimore Elite Giants
Elliott, Bob 222, 224, 227
Elliott, Carter 52, 61, 71, 72, 75
Ellis, Rube 3, 12, 25, 30, 39, 40, 43
El Paso Mexicans 148, 149, 157, 159, 160, 164, 165, 194, 240, 271
Elysian Field 1, 9
Emmer, Frank 22, 117, 120, 122, 132, 134, 135, 142, 276, 305
English, Charlie 212, 215, 216
Erautt, Ed 228
Evans, Bill 95, 146–148, 254

Fabrique, "Bunny" 74, 76
Faeth, Tony 84, 86, 89
Fagan, Bob 71, 73, 74, 79, 81, 83, 84, 86–89, 91, 92, 95, 99, 100, 254
Falk, Bib 92, 101, 142, 276
Fanning, Skeeter 47, 48, 50
Faulk 98
Federal League 12
Feistner, Bill 214, 218, 219
Feistner's Major League All-Stars 214–216, 218, 219
Feller, Bob 3, 15, 16, 196, 198, 200, 209, 226–236, 238, 240, 246, 248, 291, 309
Feller's All-Stars 228–230, 232–235, 244, 282, 285, 286, 291, 309
Felsch, Happy 64
Fernandez, Nanny 206, 207, 217

Ferraris, Angie 171
Ferraris, Sam 40, 51
Fiesta Park 11, 24
Fillmore (Baseball team) 40
Fillmore, Joe 207
Firestone Tire and Rubber (Baseball team) 157, 159, 160, 181
Fisher 65
Fisher, Bobby 75, 80
Fisher, Thomas 9
Fisher's All-Stars 70, 74–78, 81, 83, 84, 273, 274, 278, 287, 288, 290, 293, 294, 296
Fitchner 52
Fittery 65
Fitzgerald 51
Flick, Elmer 12, 25, 30, 31, 35, 61
Flonnoy 206, 207
Flores, Jesse 202, 203, 205–208, 211, 213, 214, 233, 248, 291
Florida Hotel League 14, 40, 59, 250, 253, 254, 258, 262
Flournoy, Jesse "Pud" 124, 127, 266
Fonseca, Lou 121, 276
Foote, Bill 74, 75, 78, 83, 96, 102
Forbes Field (Pittsburgh) 309
Ford, Russ 26, 30
Foreman, Sylvester "Hooks" 96, 100, 102, 254
Foreman, Zack 19
Fort Riley (Baseball team) 209
Fort Worth (Texas League) 115
Foster, Eddie 47, 50
Foster, Rube 2, 3, 12, 29, 35, 38, 40–43, 46, 52–54, 57, 59, 111, 114, 119, 147
Foster, Willie 3, 21, 119, 121, 122, 143, 151–156, 170, 190, 239, 240, 246, 247, 266, 267, 303
Fournier, Jack 61, 64, 65
Fowler, John "Bud" 1
Foxx, Jimmie 3, 15, 137, 138, 206–208, 240, 276, 277
Foxx's All-Stars 137
Frankovich 175
Frazier, Red 167, 171, 174, 182, 183, 185, 187, 188
Freidlander, Mr. 65
French, Charlie 52
French, Larry 3, 15, 18, 154, 159, 161, 163, 166, 171, 173–175, 179–182, 185, 196, 236, 238–241, 291, 298, 299, 301–303, 308
French, Ray 102, 123, 143, 167, 179, 180, 277
Frisch, Frankie 167
Fullerton-Anaheim (Baseball team) 61, 123

Gabler, Glenn 153, 187, 188
Galinda 149
Gamiz 141
Gandil, Chick 64
Gans, Jude 53–55, 62

Index

Gardner, Buzz 134
Gardner, Ping 76–78, 128, 130, 267
Gardner, Rube 48, 49
Garland, Lou 169
Garriott, Cecil 217
Gaston, Alex 135
Gatewood, Bill 35, 38, 43
Gay, Fred 92, 205
Gazella, Mike 162, 166
Gehrig, Lou 130, 170, 211
Getz, Gus 48, 50
Gibson, Josh 181, 201, 210, 231, 238
Gibson, Sam 155
Giddings, Joshua 1
Gilmore Oil (Baseball team) 101, 102, 274, 296
Gilmore Stadium (Field) 196–199, 211, 212, 215
Ginglardi, Hank 148
Gipes, Alvah 48, 49
Glass, Carl "Lefty" 128, 130, 131, 134, 267
Gleichman, Gus 48–50
Glendale White Sox 103, 275, 277, 278, 282
Glenn 59
Glover, Thomas "Lefty" 196–201, 246, 248
Golvin, Walt 97, 99, 101, 123, 129, 133, 134, 277
Gomez, "Lefty" 185, 191
Gonzalez 141
Gonzalez, Joe 193, 204
Goodrich, Joe 103
Goodwin 60
Goodwin, Alonzo Alfred "Lonnie" 79, 80, 93, 95, 96, 98, 99, 102, 104, 107, 108, 110, 111, 114, 116, 117, 119, 120, 136–140, 151
Gordon, Joe 209
Gorman 101
Goslin, Leon "Goose" 92, 102
Gould, Al 138, 141, 298
Graham, Charlie 48, 50
Graham, George "Peaches" 31, 37
Graham, Jack B. 209, 227, 231, 234
Graham, J.H. 79
Granby (Provincial League) 267
Gray, Dolly 30
Gray, Pete 208
Greater Southern California Baseball Association 93
Great Lakes Naval Training Station (Baseball team) 209
Green 22, 120, 132
Green, Frank 192
Green, William 141
Greene, Joe 234
Greenlee, Gus 170
Gregg 48, 50
Gregory, Paul 229

Griffin, Ivy 101, 105, 114, 119, 122, 142
Griffin, W. 153
Griffin, "Schoolboy" *see* Griffith, Robert
Griffith, Robert "Schoolboy" (aka Griffin) 171, 173–175, 177, 179, 181–184, 192, 193, 195, 246, 247, 267
Griggs, Art 52, 65, 74, 75, 90, 92, 105, 108, 110, 113, 120, 123, 240, 245, 277, 305
Grindle 39
Grove, "Lefty" 180
Gurley, Jim 99, 102, 103, 267, 302

Haas, George "Mule" 63, 76, 101, 102, 145, 149
Haid, Hal 104, 113
Hairston, Sam 228
Hale, Sammy 70, 71
Hall, Charlie 24, 30, 40, 247
Hamburgers (Baseball team) 24
Hamilton, Earl 40, 43
Hammond (Baseball team) 92, 276
Hamock 60
Hampton, Lionel 218
Haney, Fred 3, 63, 74, 76, 79, 104, 113, 114, 123, 125, 128, 134, 135, 137, 141, 143, 145, 149, 150, 153, 157, 158, 161, 167, 168, 171, 173, 175, 176, 179, 240, 247, 277, 278, 303, 305
Hanford, Charlie 52
Hannah, Truck 61, 65, 70, 71, 75, 76, 80, 83, 84, 87, 89, 101, 110, 123, 278, 305
Hansman, "Happy" 215
Harkness, Fred 30
Harlem Globetrotters 220, 233
Harlow All-Stars (Baseball team) 92, 273
Harney, George 114, 119, 121, 127, 267, 304
Harris and Frank (Baseball team) 40
Harris, Nate 37, 38
Harrison 33, 34
Harris, Spencer 195, 207, 224
Harris, Vic 150, 151, 153, 154, 156, 254
Hartman, Charlie 24
Harvey, Bill 198–200, 210
Hasty, Bob 37, 39, 115, 123
Hawkins, Lem 30, 32–34, 62, 64, 68, 72, 74, 79, 81, 83, 84, 86, 88, 95, 96, 99, 100, 102, 111, 254, 255
Hawks, Nelson "Chicken" 89, 91, 92, 102, 113, 114, 121, 240, 278, 305
Hayes, Frankie 228, 230
Haywood, "Buster" 227, 228, 234, 235

Hazard (Baseball team) 63
Hazard Playgrounds 63
Heath, Jeff 228, 231, 232
Heath, Mickey 134, 135, 139, 142, 278
Hector, Bullett 209
Hector Racine Stadium (Montreal) 229
Heilmann, Harry 80
Hemsley, Rollie 231
Hendricks, H. 29.
Hendricks, W. 29
Henley, Weldon 31
Henry and Cornett (Baseball team) 40
Herman, Babe 3, 14, 15, 18, 83, 84, 86–89, 92, 93, 95, 96, 100, 104, 106, 113, 116, 124, 125, 128, 146, 147, 149, 155, 185, 188, 189, 191–195, 198–200, 202–205, 236, 238–241, 245, 278, 279, 303, 305
Hermosa (Baseball team) 160
Hetling, Gus 47, 48, 50
Heusser, Ed 224, 225
Hickam Field (Baseball team) 209
Higginbotham, Irv 43
Hill, Herman 215
Hill, Jesse 173, 175, 179
Hill, John 77, 78, 255
Hill, Pete 13, 35, 39–42, 51–55, 190, 236, 253, 255
Hillman 101
Hillsdale *see* Philadelphia Royal Giants
Hines, John 179
Hinkle 31, 33
Hitler, Adolph 206
Hitt, Roy 13, 24, 25, 41, 43, 47, 48, 50, 51, 53, 55, 56, 291, 292
Hoegee Flags (Baseball team) 24–26, 28–30, 45, 246, 283
Hoffman (or Hofman) 45, 142, 153
Hogan, Happy 30
Hogan, Lawrence D. 152
Holland, Bill 124–127, 268, 303, 304
Hollerson, George 154
Holloway, Christopher "Crush" 14, 88–91, 104, 106, 110–112, 116, 117, 121, 127, 141, 240, 255, 306
Hollywood (Baseball team) 243, 274, 281
Hollywood Coast League Park 210, 218
Hollywood Merchants 103
Hollywood Stars 62, 63, 129, 135, 139, 145, 146, 151, 154, 181, 196, 218, 224, 228, 229, 232, 278, 284, 290
Holman, Ernie 184, 191, 195, 200, 279
Holt, Goldie 180

Index

Holtville (Baseball team) 32, 34, 35, 46
Holway, John 1, 19, 23, 36, 38, 60, 68, 69, 77, 111, 122, 145, 155, 201, 217, 266
Homestead Grays 190, 210, 231
Hood, Wally 87, 97, 101, 105, 107, 108, 110, 113, 114, 122, 279, 305
Hooper, Harry 13
Hopper, Clay 229
Horne, Berle 180, 181, 191
Hoskins, Bill 197–200, 225, 227–232, 234, 248
Hosp, Franz 39, 50, 52, 54, 55, 63
Houck, Byron 69, 75
Houck, Ralph 202, 204, 205
Howard, Frank 79
Howard, Ivan 38
Howard, Carranza "Schoolboy" 219, 222
Hubbard, Jess "Mountain" 76–78, 104, 106, 108, 110, 112, 113, 124–127, 239, 245–247, 255, 268, 303, 304
Hubbell, Carl 180
Huber, John "Bubber" 219, 227
Hubert 29, 30, 33
Hudspeth, Bob 112
Hufft, Fuzzy 18, 114, 116, 121, 123, 125, 128, 143, 154, 240, 279, 305
Huggins, Miller 80
Hughes, Sammy T. 21, 143, 167–171, 173, 176, 177, 179, 180, 182, 184–188, 190, 192, 194, 195, 202, 204–207, 237, 245, 248, 256, 299, 306
Hulvey, Hank 22, 23, 131, 132, 134, 145, 146, 149
Hunt, J. 29–31, 33
Hunter, Bert 150
Hurst, Don 142, 180
Hutchinson, Fred 41, 43
Hyde, "Bubba" 212, 215, 228, 230

Imperial (Baseball team) 32, 35, 46, 47, 49, 50, 56, 295
Imperial Valley League 32, 35, 46–51, 56, 60
Indianapolis ABC's 79
Indianapolis Clowns 224
Ingle, Shorty 148
International Association 1
International League 97, 105, 136, 145, 187, 196, 226, 227, 281
Iron and Oil League 1
Irvin, Monte 15

Jackie Robinson's All-Stars 232
Jackson, "Shoeless Joe" 64, 221
Jacobs, Art 167, 308
Jacobs, Ray 123, 135, 139, 142, 152, 153, 162, 166, 191, 279, 305
Jahn, Art 115, 123, 142

Japanese All-Stars 34
Jefferson, Bill "Ace" 194, 195
Jeffries (Baseball team) 40, 275
Jeffries, Jim 79, 81, 83, 247, 268, 304
Jenkins, Horace 55
Jenkins, Joe 22, 76, 97, 99, 101, 105, 111–113, 123, 128, 134, 135, 142, 247, 280, 305
Jersey City Giants 187, 229
Jethroe, Sam 217
Jewell, Bill 207
Joerndt, Ashley 184, 191
Johnson 65, 132
Johnson, Chappie 3, 12, 35, 37, 38
Johnson, Dicta 43, 247
Johnson, Don 191
Johnson, Oscar "Heavy" 84–88, 247, 256
Johnson, Syl 239
Johnson, Walter 12, 16, 24–32, 34, 52, 69, 84, 246, 247, 292
Johnston, Jimmy 57
Jolley, Smead 3, 15, 16, 22, 128, 130–137, 140, 141, 161, 166, 236, 239–241, 245, 280, 303, 305
Jones, Bob 114, 117, 120, 121, 148, 155, 280
Jones, Oscar 25, 32, 35, 39
Jones, Percy 98, 101
Joseph, Newt 116, 121, 136–138, 140, 247, 256, 306
Julian (Baseball team) 276

Kakevich 194
Kalin, Frank 228
Kampouris, Alex 163
Kansas City Blues 114, 145, 154, 180, 196
Kansas City Feds 52
Kansas City Giants see Baltimore Elite Giants
Kansas City Monarchs 18, 19, 32, 52, 57, 73, 95 104, 135, 223, 224, 230, 232, 253, 254, 260, 264
Kansas City Packers 12
Kansas City Royals 213, 215–230, 232–235, 244, 250, 252, 256, 257, 262–265, 268, 269, 309
Kansas State League 1
Kantlehner, Erv 47–49, 57, 62, 246, 247, 292
Kaylor, Tom 47, 50
Keating, Ray 69, 72, 73, 75, 115, 123, 292, 300, 301
Kelleher, Frankie 228
Keller, Charlie 228, 230–232
Keller, Don Mateo 7
Kelley Kars 104, 135, 138–140, 142–144, 149–151, 153, 271, 272, 274–277, 280, 281, 286, 288, 293, 294, 296
Kelly, George 58

Keltner, Ken 228, 230, 232
Kenilworth 100
Kenna, Eddie 114, 117, 119, 122, 280, 305
Kerr, Johnny 22, 114, 117, 119, 121, 129, 131, 134, 153, 180, 183, 280, 305
Killefer, Bill 65
Killefer's All-Stars 64, 65, 277, 278, 282, 293, 294
Killefer, Wade "Red" 43
Killeen, Jack (?) 51, 55–57, 92, 147, 149, 246, 292
Killilay, Jack 36, 39
Kimball, Newt 173, 176, 180, 212–216, 229
Kimbro, Henry 201, 202, 204, 205, 207, 211
Kimshi Productions, Inc. 111, 128
Kiner, Ralph 204, 206, 233, 235
King 58, 60
Kingdon, Wes 63, 76, 83, 84, 86–88, 92, 97–99, 101, 105, 115, 121, 134, 136, 142, 143, 154, 155, 166, 247, 281, 305
Klipper 45
Knickerbocker, Bill 161, 166, 168, 173
Konetchy, Ed 31
Koupal, Lou 120, 121, 124, 128, 129, 135, 145, 149, 154, 161, 166, 180, 182, 183, 185, 245, 246, 292, 293, 298–302, 308
Kress, Red 197, 199, 200, 207, 208, 212, 213, 216
Kruger, Art 63, 76, 83
Kruger's All-Stars 83, 84, 277, 293
Kunz, Earl "Pinches" 90, 92, 135
Kyle 60
Kyle, Andy 71, 72, 74
Kyle, W. 71

Lafferty 36, 39
LaGuna (Baseball team) 280
Lagunas, Ramon 202
LaLonge 38, 50
Lamar (Advertising Manager) 124
Land, Harry 214
Landis, Kennesaw Mountain 14, 15, 64, 123, 146, 207, 214, 220, 221, 240
Lane 29–31
Lane, Alan 213
Lane, Isaac 37, 38
Lane's Major Leaguers 213, 216
Lang, Don 228
Langford, Ad 32–35
Lanley 33
Lapan, Pete 76, 84, 89, 90, 92, 95, 96, 100
Lavette (Sports Editor) 124
Lazzeri, Tony 3, 123, 129, 130, 136, 137, 236, 281
Leake 63

Leathers, Hal 61, 63
LeBlanc (Professor) 187, 192
LeBourveau, Bevo 146, 149, 154
Le Brandt 25
Lee, Dud 129, 131, 134, 135, 139, 142, 153, 154, 173, 176, 177, 179, 180, 281
Leifield, Albert "Lefty" 25
Leland Giants *see* Chicago Leland Giants
Lemon, Bob 202, 204, 205, 228, 231, 232, 234, 293
Lemon's All-Stars 232
Leonard, Buck 190, 210–213, 215, 216, 230, 256
Lester, Larry 69
Leverenz, Walter 43
Lewis, Sam 81, 84, 293
Leyrer 204
Lieber, Dutch 194
Lillard, Gene 163, 164, 166–168, 173, 174, 176, 180, 182, 185
Lima 149
Lincoln Giants *see* New York Lincoln Giants
Lincoln Stars 34
Lindell, Johnny 192, 193, 195, 196, 198–200, 213, 214, 235
Linder (aka Lightner) 88
Lindimore, Howard 97–99, 101, 102, 105, 110, 113, 115, 122, 129, 132, 134, 155, 281, 282, 305
Lindsay, Bill 13, 38, 41, 43, 247
Litschi, Louis 45, 50, 53–55
Little Rock (Baseball team) 95
Little World Series 229
Livingston, Lee 135, 137, 138, 140, 247, 256
Lloyd, Elmer 148
Lloyd, John Henry 2, 3, 13, 14, 35, 39, 46, 51–55, 62, 190, 236, 247, 253, 256, 257
Locker 31
Lodigiani, Dario 209
Long Beach All-Stars 45, 101, 196, 199, 216, 287, 288, 295
Long Branch (Baseball team) 210
Lopez, B. 149
Los Alamitos Naval Air Station (Baseball team) 209, 210, 244
Los Angeles (Baseball team) 60, 62, 63, 80, 282, 290, 294, 295
Los Angeles Angels 11, 13, 16, 18, 25, 28, 29, 31, 33, 36, 47, 95, 96, 97, 104, 105, 108, 115, 135, 145, 154, 164, 167, 173, 180, 185, 196, 209, 210, 213–215, 218, 223, 278, 288, 289, 293, 294, 296
Los Angeles Brewery 45
Los Angeles Colored Giants 40, 43, 45
Los Angeles Examiner 23
Los Angeles Giants 24, 26, 28–30, 32–34, 243

Los Angeles Herald 28, 29
Los Angeles Hoegees *see* Hoegees
Los Angeles Morans 24, 26
Los Angeles Pacifics 24
Los Angeles Times 23, 26, 30, 32, 33, 36, 37, 41, 43, 45, 48, 49, 52, 57, 62, 64, 65, 70–72, 80, 84, 86, 87, 90, 93, 95–98, 150, 151, 164, 168, 173, 174, 176, 177, 180, 181, 183, 187, 193, 197, 199, 207, 208, 211, 214, 230, 233
Los Angeles White Sox 14, 46, 52, 57–60, 63, 64, 67–74, 76, 78–81, 84, 86–90, 93, 95–100, 102, 106, 108, 243, 250–252, 254–260, 262, 264, 266–269, 276, 277
Louisville Colonels 229
Love, Slim 47, 48, 65, 69, 76, 79, 84, 293, 299, 300
Love's All-Stars 76, 77, 277, 293
Lowrey, Peanuts 204, 206, 207, 211–215, 217, 218, 222, 233, 234, 282
Ludolph, William "Wee Willie" 99, 101, 104, 113, 116, 120, 121, 135, 142, 241, 293
Lundy, Dick 190
Lunetti 130
Luscomb, Rod 184, 192
Lynn, Fred 183
Lynn Live Oaks 1
Lyons, Granville 160
Lyons, Hershel 202, 203

Mack, Connie 31, 90
Mackey, Biz 3, 14, 19, 22, 76–81, 83, 84, 86–88, 104, 106–108, 110–112, 114, 117–121, 124, 125, 127, 128, 130–133, 136–138, 141, 143, 150, 151, 153, 175, 179, 180, 184–190, 192, 194–196, 201, 202, 204–207, 209, 210, 213, 218, 221, 222, 236, 237, 240, 241, 245, 247, 257, 300, 306
Macon 193
Macy Park 32
Madeiros, Ray 196
Maggert, Harl 47, 50, 51, 247
Maier Joy Riders 29, 31, 40
Maier Park 37, 40, 46, 58, 59, 61, 62
Mails, Duster 69, 71–73, 75, 80, 300, 301
Major League All-Stars *see* Pirrone's All-Stars
Major-Minor League All-Stars 206, 209–211, 228, 230–232, 234, 244
Malarcher, Dave 60
Mallis, Cy 176
Manes 38
Manush, Heinie 84, 86, 88, 236, 282
Mapes, Cliff 234

Maples 65
Marcelle, Oliver 263
Marion County (Baseball team) 275
Markham, John 213, 216, 217, 220, 222, 224
Marshall, James 6
Martin, Eddie 51
Martin, Elwood "Speed" 69, 72, 75, 300, 301
Martinez 141
Matchett, Jack 212, 214, 217
Mathis, Verdel 229
Matlock, Leroy 185, 188, 190
May, "Buckshot" 159
May County (Baseball team) 165, 171, 179–181, 184, 276, 279, 283, 292, 308
Mayer, T. 162, 166
Mayo, Eddie 207
Mays, Willie 2, 15
Maywood (Baseball team) 276
McAdoo, Tully 52–55
McArdle, H. 39
McAuley, Ike 97, 99, 101, 110, 113
McCarthy 48, 50
McClain 29–31, 33
McClellan, Dan 34
McClelland 25, 36, 37, 39
McClure, Bob 89, 91, 92
McCormick Shamrocks 25, 26, 28, 30, 31, 33–43, 274, 290
McCoy, Bernie 35
McCoy, Walter 230
McCredie, Walter 46, 59
McDaniels, Booker 211, 213, 214, 216, 217, 219, 220, 222, 228, 229
McDonald, George 179, 181, 199
McDonald, Hank 168, 169, 171, 239
McDonough, Ed 330
McDonough, Gordon L. 167
McDowell 92
McDuffie, Terris "The Great" 196–200, 213–217, 248, 268
McEvoy, Lou 154
McGinnis, Bub 191
McGraw, Bob 96, 97, 106, 113
McGraw, John 15, 16, 41, 145
McGwire, Mark 183, 238
McIntyre, Harry 25
McKay, Bernie 38
McKechnie, Bill 80
McKinnis, Gready 227
McKune, Terry 35
McLain *see* McClain
McMillan 45
McMullen, Hugh 106, 113, 116, 120, 121, 124, 128, 135, 137, 140, 141, 145, 146, 149, 154, 161, 166, 168, 171, 179, 182, 305
McMullin, Fred 47, 49, 56, 63–65, 282
McNair, Hurley 19, 67, 68,

70–72, 74, 75, 79, 81, 83, 84, 95, 100, 245, 247, 257, 300, 306
McNeely, Earl 155, 184
Meadows, Specs 69, 71, 75, 236, 240, 300, 301
Meats 28
Meeks (Baseball team) 25, 26, 28
Memphis Red Sox 128, 229, 267
Memphis (Southern Association) 182, 187
Mendenhall, Jack 63, 64
Mendez, Jose 1, 3, 19, 60, 79, 83–88, 257, 303
Mensor, Ed 52
Merchants National Bank (Baseball team) 127, 289
Merkle, Fred 40
Mesner, Steve 167, 179, 185, 188, 189, 191, 192, 194, 196, 198, 200, 202, 204, 205, 213, 247, 283
Metkovich, George "Catfish" 211–213, 215–217, 222, 224, 233, 235, 283
Metz, Frank 114
Meusel, Bob 3, 14–16, 23, 61, 63–65, 68, 69, 71, 72, 74, 75, 79–83, 114, 121, 123–125, 128, 129, 134, 135, 137, 141, 236, 238–241, 283, 284, 303, 305
Meusel, Emil "Irish" 3, 15, 16, 23, 45, 47–49, 56, 61–65, 68, 69, 71, 72, 74, 75, 79–81, 83, 114, 116, 120, 121, 124, 125, 128, 129, 131, 134, 135, 137, 140, 141, 145, 146, 149, 217, 219, 220, 238–241, 245, 247, 283, 303, 305
Meusel's All-Stars 78–81, 83, 84, 273, 277, 278, 283–285, 287, 291, 293, 294
Mexican All-Stars *see* El Centro Mexicans, Chihuahua Mexicans
Mexican Baseball Hall of Fame 271, 284
Mexican League 18, 165, 201, 208, 210, 218, 231, 249, 256, 263–265, 267–269
Meyers, Chief 13, 31, 40, 43
MGM Studio (Baseball team) 144–146, 148, 149, 274, 283, 284
Middleton, Roxy 33, 47, 50
Miller 63, 193
Miller, Eddie 224
Miller, Frank 37
Miller, Hack 80
Miller, Percy 89–91, 162, 163, 166
Millican 149, 213
Milwaukee (AA) 105
Minneapolis Millers 12, 95, 196
Minor League Stars 234
Miranda 141
Mishasek, R. 224
Mission (Baseball team) 80, 120, 129, 167, 185

Mitchell, Johnny 51, 75
Mohawk Giants (Schenectady) 34
Mohler, Kid 3, 33, 36, 39
Moncado, Fernando Rivera Y, Captain 6
Monroe, Bill 13, 41, 43, 247
Monroe Field 189
Montebello (Baseball team) 92, 297
Montgomery, Al 197
Montreal Royals 226, 227, 229
Montufar, Felipe 141
Moody, Lee 228
Moon, Leo 119
Mooney 34, 36, 58–60, 78, 247, 268
Moore 33
Moore, D.C. 183, 187, 191
Moore, Dobie 2, 18, 19, 21, 68, 71–74, 79, 80, 83, 84, 96, 98–100, 102, 104, 236, 237, 245, 247, 254, 258, 300, 306
Moore, James "Red" 201, 202, 204, 205
Moore, Johnny 154, 163
Moore, Mike 35, 37, 38
Moorehart, Ray 130, 134, 135, 137, 141
Moran, "Butch" 228
Morans *see* Los Angeles Morans
Morehouse, Frank 184, 192
Moreland, Nate 201, 202, 204, 205, 209, 210, 213, 217–220, 222, 225, 228, 231, 248, 268, 269
Morney, Ray 182–184, 247
Morris, Barney 193, 204, 205, 248
Morris, Harold "Yellowhorse" 127, 193
Morse 75
Moss, "Submarine" 188, 189, 191, 194, 195, 212, 215, 216, 248
Mothell, Dink 22, 95, 116–119, 121, 127, 131–133, 136, 137, 140, 258
Moudy, Dick 123, 124
Mouse, Mickey 8
Munion 96, 98, 100, 102
Munoz, Luis 90
Munns, Les 173–175, 177, 179, 293
Murphy, Danny 101, 117, 120, 122, 247
Murphy, Dod (Rod)? 93, 101
Murray, Bobby 113, 114, 121, 124, 128, 130, 135
Murray, Mitch 103
Muse, Clarence 187
Musial, Stan 15, 231, 232
Mussolini, Benito 206
Myatt, George 195
Myers 39

Nagle, Walter 41
Nashville Elite Giants 15, 143–149,

152, 154, 157, 159–164, 178, 243, 250–254, 256, 259–261, 263–266, 269, 270
National Baseball Hall of Fame 2, 3, 19–21, 35, 73, 85, 89, 104, 114, 139, 161, 162, 178, 196, 199, 217, 219, 237, 250, 270, 272, 282
National League 1, 12, 18, 31, 91, 143, 157, 173, 174, 176, 203, 224, 233, 272, 275, 296, 297
Naval Dry Dock (Baseball team) 217, 219, 220, 222
Navy (Baseball team) 61
Negro All-Stars 216
Negro American League 214, 223–225, 227, 230
Negro Eastern League 93
Negro Leagues 1, 3, 12–15, 18–23, 29, 32, 36, 39–41, 52, 54, 57–59, 62, 63, 66–69, 73, 77, 79, 82, 84, 85, 90, 93, 104–106, 108, 111, 112, 115, 119, 128, 130, 137, 139, 140, 143–145, 149–151, 154, 157, 158, 160–162, 164, 165, 167, 170, 173–178, 180, 182, 183, 185, 187, 190, 195, 199, 201–203, 208–215, 221, 223, 230, 231, 233, 236–241, 249–270, 306, 307
Negro National League 18, 35, 52, 79, 89, 93, 100, 128, 143, 147, 157, 160, 173, 178, 190, 194, 208, 214, 267
Neil, Ray 224, 229, 237
Neilson, Lefty 156
Nelson, Clyde 225, 228, 229
Neve, Felipe de, Governor 6
Newark Bears (IL) 136, 177, 196
Newbury, Jimmy 229, 230, 232, 234, 235
New Orleans (Baseball team) 91, 95
Newsome, Buck (Bobo) 3, 15, 16, 161, 163, 164, 166, 212–214, 216, 236–241, 293, 294, 298, 301, 302, 308
Newsome, Skeeter 213
Newton All-Stars 45
Newton, E.J. "Doc" 30
Newton, James 146, 148
New York Fire Department (Baseball team) 34
New York Giants 16, 25, 26, 40, 56, 76, 80, 105, 145, 180, 217, 231, 272, 283, 296
New York Highlanders 26
New York Lincoln Giants 34, 70, 76–79, 243, 250, 253, 255, 258, 259, 262, 267, 268
New York State League 58
New York Yankees 15–17, 36, 47, 56, 71, 80, 82, 118, 129, 135, 136, 177, 180, 185, 193, 202, 213, 214,

Index

217, 218, 228, 276, 281, 284, 292, 293
Niehoff, Bert 75, 88, 90, 92, 305
Nielson, Gook 149
NoirTech Research 32, 133, 224, 237
Northern California Winter League 11
North Long Beach (Baseball team) 280
Northwestern League 26
Novikoff, Lou 196, 202, 203, 205–207, 211, 213, 214, 216

Oakland Oaks (Acorns) 11, 36, 46, 47, 135, 136, 180, 198, 293
Oakland Wide Awakes 9
Ocampo 149
Occidentals (Baseball team) 24, 32–34, 254, 258
Oeschger, Joe 57
Oglesby, Jim 161
O'Grain, Cliff 162, 166, 172
Oh, Sadaharu 238
Oldham, John "Red" 69, 70, 73, 75, 79, 84, 86, 88, 104, 106, 120, 121, 294, 299–301
Olindas, Fullerton (Baseball team) 24
Olives (Baseball team) 28, 29
Olson, Al 222
Olson, Ivy 13, 40, 41, 43
Olson, Vern 209, 210
Olson, Walter 214–216, 220
Omaha (Baseball team) 90, 105
Oms, Alejandro 2
O'Neil, Emmett(?) 225
Orange County Club (Baseball team) 31, 123, 124, 127
Orange County Park 125
Orosco 149
Orr, Billy 105, 114
Orrell, Joe 186, 189, 192
Orsatti, Ernie 145, 146, 196, 197, 200
Ortiz 141
Ossie Vitt's All-Stars 57
Outland, George E. 17, 45, 97, 105, 112, 115, 116, 118, 126, 155
Otto, Ray 91
Owens 188
Oxnard (Baseball team) 40, 45, 51, 290

Pacific Base Ball League 10
Pacific Coast International League 68, 285
Pacific Coast League 3, 11–16, 18, 24–26, 28, 29, 33, 35–38, 41, 45–48, 59, 61, 66–68, 89, 95–97, 104, 105, 108, 114–116, 120, 123, 128, 129, 136, 143, 144, 147, 149, 150, 152, 154, 157, 164, 167, 168, 173, 174, 180, 182, 186, 187, 193, 196, 210, 214, 215, 223, 240, 271–274, 277–281, 283, 284, 286–296
Pacific Electric (Baseball team) 57–59, 61, 286, 297
Pacific League 10, 11
Pacific National (Baseball team) 83, 288
Pacific Redi-Cuts 76
Pacifics (San Francisco) 10
Pafko, Andy 211, 212, 215, 216, 233, 235, 285
Page 50
Paige, Satchel 3, 12, 15, 16, 18–20, 143, 154–166, 169–171, 173, 176–182, 185, 190, 211–217, 226–228, 230, 232–236, 238–240, 245–248, 269, 303, 308, 309
Paige's All-Stars 309
Palmer, Bill 53, 54
Palms (Baseball team) 276
Palos Verde (Baseball team) 294
Pan Gas (Baseball team) 276
Parker, Art 150, 153
Partee, Roy 207, 208, 212–217, 233–235, 248
Pasadena (Baseball team) 59, 60, 62, 63, 76, 88, 92, 275, 281–283, 287, 294, 295
Pasadena Athletics 208, 209
Pasadena Eagles (Baseball team) 24, 25, 28, 29, 31, 96, 275
Pasadena Junior College 223
Pasadena Merchants 101–103, 144, 145, 148, 149, 291
Patchett, Hal 196
Payne, George 18, 96–101, 104, 110, 113, 246, 247, 294
Pearson, Len 217
Peckham, Frank 86, 88
Pedroso, Eustaqio "Bombin" 190
Penner, Ken 63
Pennington, Art 227
Perdy 191
Perez 140, 141
Perez, Manny 228
Perris (Baseball team) 45
Perritt, Pol 52, 56
Perry, Carl 57, 58, 60, 74, 77, 78
Pershing Park (Santa Barbara) 183
Pertica, Bill 61, 63, 69, 73, 75, 84, 99, 101, 102, 294, 298–301
Peterson, Robert W. 21, 73, 85, 95, 139
Pettus, Bill (Zack) 3, 33–35, 37–39, 76–78, 258
Petway, Bruce 13, 35, 39–42, 46, 51, 52, 54, 55, 258
Pfeffer, Jeff 47, 50
Pfirrman 39
Philadelphia Athletics 31, 102, 137, 138, 145, 156, 177, 194, 211, 213, 214, 228, 233, 274, 287 291
Philadelphia Phillies 48, 57, 62, 71, 90, 97, 114, 154, 203, 212, 214, 272
Philadelphia Royal Giants 13, 14, 47, 104, 106–127, 129, 135–141, 144, 149–159, 185, 186, 188, 190, 192–200, 202, 206–210, 237, 243, 244, 246, 249–270, 309
Phipps, Jodie 214
Phoenix (Baseball team) 45
Pick, Charlie 56
Pick, Eddie 114, 121, 130, 133, 134, 138, 141, 145, 146, 149, 154, 240, 285, 305
Pierce, Bill 41, 42, 247
Piercy, Bill 56, 57, 62, 63–65, 75, 76, 84, 104, 106, 113, 294, 298–301
Pike 55
Pillette, Herm 3, 18, 22, 114, 117, 119, 120, 122, 129, 131, 134, 143, 154, 173, 176, 180, 185, 186, 189, 191, 195, 196, 241, 245, 246, 295, 298–302
Pillette, Ted 154
Pina 159
Pioneers (Baseball team) 24
Pirrone, Joe 14, 22, 59, 66–73, 75, 81, 83, 84, 86–90, 92, 93, 95–98, 100, 104, 106, 108, 113, 114, 118, 121, 123–125, 128, 129, 131, 135, 137, 138, 141, 143, 145, 152, 154, 159, 163, 168, 173, 174, 176, 177, 181–183, 185, 193–199, 202, 206, 207, 211, 214, 236, 239, 285
Pirrone, John 93, 129, 154
Pirrone Park 68, 95
Pirrone's All-Stars 14, 21, 68–75, 78, 80–82, 84, 86–93, 95–98, 100, 101, 104, 106, 108, 112–121, 123–131, 133–135, 137, 138, 140, 141, 144–149, 154–157, 159–161, 163–166, 168–171, 173–185, 189, 194–200, 202–208, 212–216, 218, 223–228, 240, 244, 271–274, 276–294, 296, 297, 308
Pitman 37
Pitts 40
Pittsburgh Courier 23, 116, 117, 120, 123, 125, 130, 156, 202, 209, 210, 214, 215, 218–220, 225, 227, 230
Pittsburgh Crawfords 154, 170, 182
Pittsburgh Pirates 47, 57, 62, 104, 159, 163, 167, 177, 196, 211, 217, 224, 272, 273, 275
Platner, Linn 147
Poles, Bertha 77
Poles, Spot 14, 62, 76–78, 236, 245, 253, 258, 259
Polomo, Jose 202
Pomona (Baseball team) 40, 286, 291
Pope 101
Porter, Andy "Pullman" 160, 161,

167–171, 182, 184, 185, 188–190, 192, 226–228, 246–248, 269
Portland (Baseball team) 293, 308
Portland Beavers 36, 97, 129, 163, 165, 180, 183, 186
Posey, Cum 190
Powers, Les 167–170, 172, 180, 187, 188, 191–193, 195, 196, 200, 202, 204, 205, 224, 285, 286
Praul 124, 125, 128
Priddy, Jerry 196, 198, 200, 202, 205, 209, 211–217, 224, 227, 233–235, 286
Prim, Ray 217
Provincial League 267
Pryor, Wes 30, 32–34, 39
Public National (Baseball team) 78
Public Service (Baseball team) 78, 83
Puerto Rican Winter League 19, 20, 158, 201, 212, 231, 249, 256, 263, 268
Pullen, Neal 77, 78, 81, 83, 89, 92, 95, 100, 102, 108, 110–112, 117, 118, 120, 121, 127, 133, 150, 259
Purdue 121
Purse, Edward 12

Quinn, W. 213, 214

Radcliffe, Alex (Alec) 21, 157, 159, 160, 185, 191, 245, 247, 259, 306
Radcliffe, Ted "Double Duty" 160, 185, 191, 201, 211, 212, 215, 224, 259
Rader, Don 56, 63, 113
Radiant (Baseball team) 294
Radonits, Bill 183, 185
Raft, George 218
Ralls All-Stars 62, 63, 70, 74, 76, 276, 282–284, 292
Rammage, Cy 148
Rathskellers (Baseball team) 61
Rawlings, Johnny 52, 64, 65, 79, 81, 83, 114, 121, 149, 150, 153, 286, 305
Ray, Otto 19, 71, 72, 74, 259
Reardon, "Beans" 72, 157
Recreation Grounds 9
Recreation Park 11, 225
Red Rovers 9
Redd, (or Reed) Alton 157, 192
Redding, Dick 190
Redondo Mexicans 157, 160, 297
Reed, Alton see Redd
Reese, Jimmy 157, 177, 286
Reese, John 102, 103, 259
Reese, Pee Wee 209
Rego, Tony 142
Reichert, "Tex" 189, 192, 195, 246
Renfro, Othello 234, 235
R.H. Dyas see Dyas All-Stars

Rhiel, Billy 156, 157
Rhein, Ralph 198
Rhyne, Hal 22, 117, 119, 120, 122, 132, 134, 143, 153, 240, 286, 305
Richardson, Ken 218, 224, 228, 234
Rickey, Branch 15, 223, 226
Riddle 74, 120
Ridley, Jack 145, 146, 148, 260
Rieger, Elmer 26, 30, 33, 34, 36, 37, 39, 43, 84, 87, 101
Riggins, Bill 89–91, 103, 145, 146, 148, 247, 260, 306
Riley, Jim 41, 57, 69, 76, 77, 178, 186, 201, 251, 255, 258, 262, 266
Risberg, Swede 64
Rizzuto, Phil 228, 230
Robinson 33
Robinson, Bill "Bojangles" 187
Robinson, Jackie 2, 15, 201, 224–228, 231, 236, 260
Robinson, Lory 192
Robinson, Wilbert 95
Roche, Jack 43, 54, 55, 57
Rochester Redwings 145
Rockford Peaches (AAGPBL) 271
Rogan, "Bullet Joe" 3, 12, 14, 18, 19, 22, 23, 60, 67–75, 79, 84, 104, 105, 107–109, 111–114, 116, 117, 119, 121, 129–133, 135–138, 140, 141, 170, 190, 201, 221, 236, 238–241, 245–247, 260, 269, 301–304, 306
Roosevelt, Franklin Delano 15, 208
Root, Charlie 15, 16, 105, 106, 109, 113, 236, 295, 298–301
Rose, Midget 71, 81, 83
Ross 65, 78
Ross, Don 179, 188, 190, 191
Ross, Sam 102, 145–148
Ross, William 102, 103, 270
Rothrock, Jack 217
Rowe 148
Rowland, Clarence "Pants" 209, 210
Royal Giants see Philadelphia Royal Giants
Royal Poinciana Hotel 40
Ruether, Dutch 56, 57, 80, 295
Ruffing, "Red" 217, 218
Ruiz, Yoyo 212
Runyon, Damon 185
Russell, John Henry 103
Russell, Rip 213, 216, 217, 248
Ruth, Babe 2, 15, 16, 20, 64, 65, 93, 130, 143, 151, 170, 193, 206, 238, 247, 286, 287, 295
Ruth's All-Stars 65, 283, 285, 286
Ryan, Jack 46, 47, 50, 57, 295

SABR 37, 136
Sacramento (PCL Baseball team) 135, 185, 284

Sacramento Gilt Edge 11
Sada, "Sad Sam" 191
Sain, Johnny 230
St. Louis All-Stars 250–252, 255, 259–261, 266
St. Louis Browns 40, 58, 93, 105, 155, 162, 164, 209, 212–214, 226, 228, 239, 276, 281
St. Joseph (Western League) 155
St. Louis Cardinals 16, 25, 31, 36, 40, 47, 51, 53, 56, 58, 105, 109, 145, 167, 176, 196, 224, 225
St. Louis Giants 93, 102, 103, 243, 250, 252, 260, 262, 265, 270
St. Louis Stars 87, 89–92, 243, 250, 252, 254, 255, 259–261, 265, 266, 270
St. Paul (AA) 207
Salazar, Lazaro 61
Salazar, Pete 149
Salkeld, Bill 224, 226
Sally League 155
Saltillo Mexicans 223, 226, 228
Salt Lake City (Baseball team) 29–31, 35, 89, 104, 105, 246
Salveson, Jack 180
Samis 71
Sampson Naval Training Station (Baseball team) 209
Sampson, Sam 212, 215, 248
Sanberg, Gus 107, 108
San Bernardino (Baseball team) 24, 25, 31, 35, 40, 51, 52, 55, 56, 243, 277, 290
San Diego All-Stars 194, 195, 223, 225, 227
San Diego Balboa Park 292
San Diego (Baseball team) 12, 24, 31, 36–39, 77, 88, 91, 92, 147–149, 154, 156, 186, 210, 243, 274, 275, 280, 287, 291–294
San Diego Bears 42, 43, 243
San Diego Bombers see Feistner's Major All-Stars
San Diego Farleys 185, 189–191, 246, 274–276, 279, 284, 289
San Diego Gold Club 186, 189, 190, 192, 246, 284, 288, 289
San Diego Griefers 35, 243
San Diego Hulls 57–59
San Diego Merchants 180, 182, 184, 274, 279, 284, 288
San Diego Padres 181, 218, 273, 279, 290
San Diego Pantages 13, 51–56, 292
San Diego Paris Inn 185, 186, 188, 189, 192, 284
San Diego Pickwicks 28, 29
San Diego 7-Ups 196, 199, 200, 275, 276, 279, 284, 288
San Diego Union 42, 189
San Francisco (Baseball team) 80, 129
San Francisco Eagles 9, 10

San Franciscos 9
San Francisco Seals 31, 46, 47, 135, 146, 155, 286
Sankey, Ben 163
San Jose (Baseball team) 11, 25
San Luis Giants 138, 140, 141, 284
San Pedro Merchants 25, 26, 28–30, 51, 57–61, 70, 74, 76, 77, 243, 275, 277, 283, 287, 289–291, 295, 296
Santa Ana Yellow Sox 25, 26, 28–31, 34, 123, 243, 246, 292
Santa Barbara (Baseball team) 183, 289
Santa Barbara Eagles 24–26, 28, 31, 35, 45, 51, 59
Santa Clara University (Baseball team) 62
Santa Cruz (Baseball team) 12
Santaella 141
Santa Maria (Baseball team) 45
Santa Monica Beach Combers 40
Santa Monica Merchants 25, 28, 173, 175–177, 180, 182, 184, 185, 272, 279, 281, 287, 290, 291, 295
Santa Monica Municipal Stadium 182
Santa Paula 193, 194
Saugus (Baseball team) 281
Savage 95
Sawtelle (Baseball team) 287
Sawyer, Carl 58, 61, 63, 76, 81, 83, 93, 95, 121, 124, 128, 135, 141, 145, 149, 154, 155, 161, 166, 168, 171, 183, 211, 287
Sawyer's All-Stars 78, 82–84, 93, 273, 278, 281, 287, 288
Saylor, Alfred "Al" 220
Schmidt, Walter 47, 50
Schneider, Pete 13, 40, 45, 51, 55, 56, 61–63, 75, 76, 80, 89, 92, 240, 247, 287, 295, 305
Schulmerich, Wes 150, 151, 153
Schultz 65
Schultz, Mickey 51
Schupp, Ferdie 3, 15, 16, 99, 102, 105, 107, 114, 115, 119, 120, 122, 129, 134, 143, 145, 151, 153, 236, 241, 246, 296, 298–302
Scott 65
Scott, Pete 99, 101, 107, 113
Scott, Robert 77
Scott, "Death Valley" Jim 32, 35, 47, 50
Seaton, Tom 3, 12, 33, 36, 38, 39, 247
Seattle Seals (PCL) 97, 115, 155, 180, 271
Seinsoth, Bill 213, 214, 216
Serrell, Bonnie 213, 216–219, 222, 224
Service All-Stars 217, 218, 220, 222, 225, 275, 286
Severeid, Hank 143, 153

Shafer, Tillie 40
Shanklin 92, 141
Shatzkin, Mike 84
Shaw 141
Shaw, Ted 124, 127
Sheely, Bud 163, 228
Shellenback, Frank 61, 69–71, 75, 92, 150, 298–302
Shell Oilers 22, 23, 105, 107, 108, 112, 114–122, 128–136, 138–140, 142–144, 152–154, 240, 243, 272–276, 278–281, 286–290, 295–297
Shell Park (Long Beach) 132, 138, 140
Sherlock, Jack "Monk" 124, 125, 128
Sherman Athletic Association (Baseball team) 127, 289
Shires, Art "The Great" 156
Shorrs 71
Sigafoos, Frank 145
Signal Hill 115, 119, 131
Simmons, Al 3, 15, 137, 138, 240, 287
Simmon's All-Stars 137
Simms, Willie (Bill) 216, 218–220, 222
Sisler, George 80, 148
Slaback, Lester 25
Slade, Gordon 101, 156, 157
Slagle, Walt 43, 58
Slater 29, 30, 33
Smith 58
Smith, Bill 160
Smith, Chet 192
Smith, Clarence 47, 51
Smith, Henry "Swede" 191
Smith, Hilton 201, 217, 219, 222
Smith, James C. "Red" 75, 83, 84, 86, 88, 89, 91, 95, 100, 134, 240, 288, 305
Smith, Jedediah 6
Smith, Johnny 227, 228
Smith, Jud 33
Smith, Lyman 97, 100
Smith, Marvin 100
Smith, Ronnie 226, 228
Smith, Theolic 218–220, 222, 224, 227
Snodgrass, Fred 13, 24–25, 30, 31, 40
Snow, Felton 161–163, 166–169, 171, 174, 175, 178, 179, 184, 188–190, 194, 195, 201–205, 248, 260, 261
Snyder 114
Soto 149
Souell, Herb 225, 228
South Atlantic League 292
Southern Association 91, 95, 105, 112, 135, 187, 289
Southern California Gas 297
Southern California Winter League 102, 103, 123, 143, 149, 161

Southside Park 11
Spalding, John E. 9–11
Spearman, Clyde 211, 212, 215, 248
Spearman, Henry 201–205, 213, 216, 261
Sportsman's Park (St. Louis) 309
Stainback, Tuck 166, 167, 173, 176
Standard-Murphy (Baseball team) 61, 273, 278
Standard Oil (Baseball team) 194
Stark, Dolly 47, 50
Starr, Bill 195
Statz, Jigger 3, 18, 93, 102, 104, 106, 113, 115, 116, 122, 143, 149, 150, 153, 173, 176, 236, 240, 241, 288, 304, 305
Stearnes, Norman "Turkey" 3, 12, 18, 20–22, 88, 89, 91, 111, 114, 117, 119–121, 125–127, 130–133, 135, 143, 145–148, 161–171, 173, 175–180, 190, 201, 221, 236, 238–241, 245, 247, 301, 306
Steele, Ed 224, 228, 230, 234, 261
Steen, Bill 57
Steiner, Jim "Red" 224, 227
Stengel, Casey 71, 108, 113, 241, 304
Stengel's All-Stars 70, 71
Stephens, Jake 124, 125, 127
Stephens, Vern 209, 210, 213, 224, 226, 227, 248
Stevens, Chuck 222, 228, 234
Stewart, Edward "Bud" 228
Stewart, Glen "Gabby" 228, 229
Stewart, Harry 36, 39
Stine, Lee 162, 166, 168, 171, 185, 191, 198, 200, 202, 296, 308
Stockton (Baseball team) 25, 45, 91
Storti, Lin 179, 181, 185, 196
Stovall, George 12, 30, 31, 33, 35, 40
Strange, Alan 162, 166, 183
Stratton, Leroy 160, 261
Stringer, Lou 202, 224, 227
Sturdy, Guy 114, 117, 118, 120, 121
Sturgeon, Bobby 202, 204, 205, 215, 234, 235
Submarine Base (Baseball team) 61, 275, 283, 291
Suhr, Gus 136, 137
Sullivan, Bruce 1,
Sullivan, Joe 173
Sulphur Dell Stadium (Nashville) 93
Summa, Homer 156, 177
Summers, Lonnie 175, 185, 191, 194, 195, 199–202
Sutter, John 6
Suttles, Mule 3, 12, 18, 20, 21, 143, 150–154, 156, 161, 163–171, 173–180, 185, 187–190, 192–198, 200, 201, 221, 236–241, 245, 247, 248, 261, 301, 306

Swanson, Evar (?) 134
Sweeney, Bill 114, 117, 120, 121, 134, 210, 288, 305
Sweetland, Les 139, 142

Tacoma (Baseball team) 26
Tally 62
Tampico (Mexican League) 218
Tatum, "Goose" 233, 234
Taylor, Ben 79, 190
Taylor, "Candy Jim" 41, 43, 79, 174–177, 183
Taylor, John 79, 80, 83, 219, 270
Taylor, Leroy 135, 137, 140, 262
Temple, Shirley 187
Tennant, Tom 36, 37, 39
Terry, Bill 18
Texas League 115, 268
Thomas 125, 209
Thomas, Bill 212, 213
Thomas, Chet 75
Thomas, Claude "Lefty" 76, 79, 84, 145, 296
Thomas, Clint 72, 125, 127, 262
Thomas, Fay 157
Thomas, Henry W. 25, 28
Thomas, Jules "Home Run" 76, 77, 262
Thomas, Pinch 43, 63, 65
Thompson 132, 134
Thompson, Fred "Groundhog" 224, 227
Thompson, "Gunboat" 34
Thompson, Pete 97, 99, 101
Thompson, Tommy 174, 175, 177, 179, 182, 188, 209, 210
Thorpe, Jim 46
Thurston, Hollis "Sloppy" 3, 72, 73, 75, 84, 86, 89, 93, 101, 129–131, 135, 136, 154, 161–163, 166–168, 172, 173, 176, 180, 183, 236, 238, 239, 241, 246, 296, 298–302, 308
Tobey, Dan 93
Tobin, Frank 86
Tobin, Jack 224, 225, 227
Tobin, Pat 200
Toledo (American Association) 185
Toldeo Club (Union Association) 1
Tonneson 33, 39
Torriente, Cristobal 2, 190
Tost, Lou 202–204, 206, 207
Tozer, Bill 33, 34, 36, 39, 45
Treagur, William 167
Trent, Ted 156, 303
Trilbys (Baseball team) 12, 24, 32, 34, 268
Trotting Park Race Track 10, 11
Trouppe, Quincy 213, 214, 216
Troy, Donald 209
Trujillo, Rafael, General 20
Tufts-Lyons 24, 25, 41–43, 45, 61, 272, 291

Turner, Jim 154, 298–302
Twombly, Babe 101, 102, 107, 110, 113, 240, 288, 305

UCLA 223
Union Association 1
Union Pacific (Baseball team) 92, 276, 278, 295
United States Army 25th Infantry Division 18, 73, 84, 254
United States Navy (Baseball team) 189, 273
Universal Studio (Baseball team) 89–92, 277, 278
University of Southern California 183
Unser, Al 228
Urbita Stars (San Bernardino) 45

Vache, Ernest "Tex" 90, 91, 102, 134
Valencia 29
Vance, Dazzy 32, 35, 56, 57, 62, 92, 297
Vaughan, Arky 173–176, 179, 196, 198, 200
Venezuelan Winter League 201
Venice (Baseball team) 48
Ventura (Baseball team) 40
Vernon (Baseball team) 80, 104, 273, 274, 282, 287, 288, 293, 295
Vernon, Mickey 209, 228
Vernon Park (Grounds) 11, 24, 37, 46, 58, 59
Vernon Tigers 36, 37, 61–63, 88, 89, 93, 95, 98, 100, 101, 278, 289, 290, 296
Vickers, Rube 24
Vinas 141
Vizcaino, Sebastian 5
Vusich, Johnny 162, 163, 166, 179

Waddell, Rube 230
Wade 193
Wagner, Honus 257
Wagner, Joe 52
Walker, Jesse 156, 160, 188–190, 197, 198, 200, 212, 215, 262
Walker, Moses Fleetwood 1
Walker, Tillie 40
Walker, Welday 1
Walker Roofers 194, 196, 198–200, 286
Walters, Bucky 161, 298, 301, 302, 308
Walters, Johnny "Junk" 145–149, 157, 159, 166, 189, 192, 247
Walton, J.E. 79
Ward 74
Ward, C. "Pinky" 88, 103, 262
Ward, Tom 83, 86
Ware, Archie 224
Warfield, Frank 124, 127, 128, 262, 263

Warren, Dallas 148, 156, 184, 192, 288
Warrender 36, 37, 39
Washington, Kenny 213
Washington, Namon (?) 57, 60, 74, 78
Washington Elites 192
Washington Gardens 11
Washington Park 11, 24, 61, 93, 95, 97
Washington Senators 25, 26, 28, 40, 47, 56, 58, 180, 183, 211, 212, 214, 217, 224, 228, 280, 281, 284, 287
Weaver, Buck 64, 65, 126, 127, 221, 289
Weaver's All-Stars 64, 65, 274, 281, 283, 286, 289
Webster, Spec 39
Weed 25
Weigel 167
Weinreich, GSCBA President 93
Welch, Winfield 220, 227
Wells, Willie 3, 67, 102, 111, 114, 117, 121, 127, 143, 150, 151, 153–156, 161–163, 165–171, 173, 201, 218–220, 222, 236, 240, 245, 263, 301, 306
Western Association 105
Western League 90, 105, 155
Western Pipe & Steel Boilermakers 213, 214, 216
Western Pool Hall (Baseball team) 59, 68, 273, 283, 285
Western Stars 77
Westhall 71
West, Hi 52, 57, 58
West, Jim 173, 175, 178, 179, 184, 185, 188–190, 193–198, 200, 224, 245, 247, 263
West, Max 185, 187, 188, 191
Wetzel, Buzz 163, 167
Whaley, Bill 101
Whaling, Bert 12, 30, 31, 35, 40, 43, 51, 52, 57, 100
Whitaker, Bill 91, 99, 101
White, Chaney 150, 153, 154, 156, 263
White, James, P. 79, 1203–125
White, Sol 32–34
White Base Ball and Amusement Association 79
White King Soapsters 3, 14, 92, 93, 95, 97, 98–102, 104, 106–117, 119, 120, 122, 123, 128, 130, 131, 133, 134, 154–156, 161–163, 165–173, 176–180, 182–185, 187–196, 198–200, 202–206, 239, 240, 243, 246, 271–286, 288–292, 294–297, 308
White Mystery (Baseball team) 290
White Sox Park 14, 20–22, 67, 72, 80, 84, 90, 93, 98, 106, 108, 115, 117–119, 123–126, 129, 131, 136,

138, 143, 144, 146, 149, 152, 153, 156, 157, 159, 160, 162–164, 167–169, 181–183, 186, 187, 192–194, 196, 197, 202, 204, 209, 285
Whiteman, Paul 157
Whitworth, Richard 55
Wickware, Frank 2, 3, 12, 14, 34–36, 38, 39, 51–53, 55, 62, 247, 270
Wiggs, Jim 32, 35
Wilhoit, Joe 47, 50, 56
Wilkinson, Roy 120–122, 125, 128, 131, 132, 134, 140, 142, 297, 298–302
Williams 86, 88
Williams, Alva 50
Williams, Bob 224
Williams, Chester 169, 171, 193, 195, 209, 210
Williams, Claude "Lefty" 47, 50, 56, 57, 64, 126, 297
Williams, Gerard (?) 78
Williams, Harry A. 64, 220, 222
Williams, "Honolulu Johnny" 52
Williams, Jesse 218–220, 222, 224, 227, 228, 234, 248
Williams, Joe "Cyclone" (Smokey Joe) 2, 3, 12–14, 34–38, 46, 51–55, 221, 236, 270
Williams, John 224–229, 233, 235, 248

Williams, Ken 93
Williams, Poindexter 146–148, 263
Williams, Ted 15, 186, 189, 192, 206–209, 289
Willis, Jim "Cannonball" 145–148, 154, 156, 157, 159, 161, 163, 165–171, 173, 181, 238, 245–247, 270
Willis, R. 47, 51
Wilson 33
Wilson, Artie 217, 219, 222
Wilson, Jud 2, 21, 143, 145, 150–153, 237, 264, 302
Wilson, Lyle K. 40, 43
Wilson, Thomas 15, 144, 146, 147, 152, 155, 157, 159–161, 163, 165, 167, 169, 170, 174, 177, 178, 180–183, 192–194
Wilson's Royal Giants (Elite Giants) 157, 160, 163–171, 173–184, 243, 244, 249–251, 253, 256, 257, 260–265, 267, 269, 270
Wingo, Al 137, 145, 146, 149
Winston, Bobby 37, 38
Woodall, Larry 177
Woods, Joe 227
Woods, Parnell 217
Woods, William 57, 58, 60, 71, 74, 78
World War I 61, 259
World War II 15, 16, 201, 206, 217, 240

Wright, Burnis "Wild Bill" 18, 20, 143, 161–163, 165, 166, 170, 171, 173, 175, 176, 178–180, 183–185, 188–190, 192, 195–201, 205, 209, 210, 213–220, 222, 224, 225, 227, 237, 245, 248, 264, 302, 306
Wright, George 10, 37, 38
Wright, Glenn (?) 154, 173, 175, 179
Wright, Harry 10
Wright, Zollie 173, 175, 176, 178, 179, 264
Wrigley Field 13, 47, 143, 144, 149, 151, 152, 173, 174, 176–178, 206, 207, 210, 213, 214, 218, 219, 223, 226, 229, 230, 232–234, 309

Yakima (Baseball team) 68, 285
Yankee Stadium (New York) 309
Young, Cy 2, 16
Young, "Slowtime" 166, 171, 177, 270
Young, Tom 135, 137, 140, 264
Yuma (Baseball team) 32, 35

Zarilla, Al 213, 214, 216, 233, 235
Zuckerman, Larry 11

www.ingramcontent.com/pod-product-compliance
Lightning Source LLC
Chambersburg PA
CBHW081157230426
43666CB00016B/2846